THE HEXATEUCH

ACCORDING TO THE REVISED VERSION

THE HEXATEUCH

ACCORDING TO THE REVISED VERSION

ARRANGED IN ITS CONSTITUENT DOCUMENTS
BY MEMBERS OF THE

SOCIETY OF HISTORICAL THEOLOGY, OXFORD

EDITED

*WITH INTRODUCTION, NOTES, MARGINAL REFERENCES
AND SYNOPTICAL TABLES*

BY

J. ESTLIN CARPENTER, M.A. LOND.

AND

G. HARFORD-BATTERSBY, M.A. OXON.

IN TWO VOLUMES

VOL. I: INTRODUCTION AND TABULAR APPENDICES

WIPF & STOCK · Eugene, Oregon

Wipf and Stock Publishers
199 W 8th Ave, Suite 3
Eugene, OR 97401

The Hexateuch According to the Revised Version, Volume 1 Introduction
and Tabular Appendices Arranged in its Constituent Documents by
Members of the Society of Historical Theology, Oxford: Edited with
Introduction, Notes, Marginal References, and Synoptical Tables
By Carpenter, J. Estlin and Harford-Battersby, G.
Copyright © 1900 by Carpenter, J. Estlin All rights reserved.
Softcover ISBN-13: 979-8-3852-4053-1
Hardcover ISBN-13: 979-8-3852-4054-8
eBook ISBN-13: 979-8-3852-4055-5
Publication date 12/3/2024
Previously published by Longmans, Green and Co., 1900

This edition is a scanned facsimile of the original edition published in 1900.

PREFACE

THESE volumes are intended to place before English readers the principal results of modern inquiry into the composition of the first six books of the Old Testament

The work was first executed by a small Committee appointed by the Society of Historical Theology, Oxford, 1891[a]. The original members were G Harford-Battersby, MA[b], J E Carpenter, MA[c], E I Fripp, BA[d], C G Montefiore, MA[e], and W B Selbie, MA[f], with the Rev Prof T K Cheyne for consultative reference in special matters. On the removal of Mr Selbie from Oxford, his place was taken by G Buchanan Gray, MA[g], and the Committee was further reinforced by the co-operation of Prof W H Bennett, MA[h].

The preparation of the Analysis occupied about three years, the results were very carefully revised during another year, and Messrs Carpenter and Harford-Battersby were then requested to prepare the work for the press This task was again and again set aside (sometimes for long periods) in consequence of other more urgent duties, and further delay was caused by the endeavour to keep pace with the advance of critical literature, and to utilize its results

In the final product it was found necessary to divide the labour For the arrangement of the text and the substance of the notes the Editors share a joint responsibility. In a few cases they have departed from the results previously registered[i], further study having led to modifications of view. The probability that such changes might be made to a limited extent was of course anticipated

---

[a] A Committee of the Taylerian Society had already sketched out the plan during the previous year, and made some experiments towards a suitable form for displaying the materials when analyzed.

[b] Author of the articles 'Exodus' 'Leviticus' and 'Numbers' in Hastings' *Dictionary of the Bible*

[c] Editor of Ewald's *History of Israel*, vols iii–v; joint editor with Prof T W Rhys Davids of the *Dīgha Nikāya* and *Sumangala Vilāsinī*; author of *The First Three Gospels*.

[d] Author of *The Composition of the Book of Genesis*, 1892.

[e] Joint editor of *The Jewish Quarterly Review*, and author of the Hibbert Lectures on *The Religion of the Ancient Hebrews*, 1892.

[f] Then Tutor in Mansfield College, Oxford.

[g] Author of *Studies in Hebrew Proper Names*, 1896, and of the forthcoming volume on 'Numbers' in the *International Critical Commentary*.

[h] Author of the volumes on 'Jeremiah' (ii) and 'Chronicles' in the *Expositor's Bible*, *A Primer of the Bible*, 1897, editor of 'Joshua' in Haupt's *Sacred Books of the Old Testament*, and joint-author of *A Biblical Introduction*, 1899.

[i] This remark affects especially some portions of the distribution of J and E in the Joseph-cycle Gen 40-45, and in the Joshua narratives Josh 2-10.

by the Committee. The Introduction in vol i, with the exception of chap xv most kindly contributed by Prof Cheyne, was written by Mr Carpenter, on the basis of a detailed abstract first approved by the rest of the Analysts. The special Introduction to Joshua (vol ii pp 303–319) takes up some of the editorial and other problems which it was not convenient to discuss in the main work. The notes[a], word-lists, and marginal references[b] have been prepared by the same hand, Mr Harford-Battersby having kindly placed at his colleague's disposal his first drafts of lists for J and E, and of notes on Leviticus and the early chapters of Numbers. Mr Harford-Battersby has compiled the Tables of Laws and Institutions and the Synopsis of Narratives. The whole has been read either in MS or in proof by Mr G Buchanan Gray, to whom the Editors are indebted for many useful suggestions.

This recital renders it unnecessary further to point out that the responsibility of the Society in which the work took its rise is limited to the appointment of the original Committee, while the Committee in its turn must be understood rather to sanction the method of presentation and the general distribution than to guarantee the allotment of each separate half-verse.

The text employed is that of the Revised Version. For the permission to use this the Committee express their sincerest gratitude to the Delegates of the University Press. The Editors have occasionally availed themselves of the liberty further conceded to them of introducing marginal renderings into the text, or reducing different renderings of the same Hebrew to uniformity, in cases bearing on the documentary partition[c]. One important instance, however, is better mentioned here. It is part of the case for the composite origin of the Pentateuch that the divine name rendered 'the LORD' is used freely in one document from the beginning of human history, while in two others it is supposed to have been first revealed to Moses. It is well known, however, that the title 'the LORD' is derived from a substitute for the four sacred letters of the ancient Hebrew text YHWH. This name, according to the best modern scholarship[d], should be pronounced Yahweh or Yahwé, with the accent on the second syllable. The use of this name has been kindly sanctioned

---

[a] These are intended to set forth the grounds of the analysis, and questions of interpretation are only discussed in this connexion.

[b] These are designed for various illustrative purposes. Sometimes they supply parallel occurrences in the same document which were not sufficiently numerous to find a place in the word-list. Sometimes they indicate the similar use by J and E or by J and P &c of the same turns of phrase, thus displaying not the divergence but the common stock of linguistic expression. They sometimes point to parallels in the language of prophecy, disclosing a harmony of thought or speech with Jeremiah or Ezekiel (for instance) which cannot be discovered with Amos or Isaiah. They are also intended in the case of rare words to show how far the language is characteristic rather of poetry than of prose, and what is the scope of a writer's vocabulary; J, for instance, using a number of words which occur nowhere else.

[c] In most instances, such as 'present' and 'offer,' 'come near' and 'draw nigh,' 'depart' and 'go,' the uniformity of the original Hebrew in parallel passages is indicated by ֍ in the left-hand margin. An important group of cases arises out of the treatment of the Hebrew particle of connexion *Waw* (Vav) 'and,' which is used in a very large variety of senses, and is often rendered by 'so,' 'then,' 'therefore,' &c. The logical dependence thus implied in a narrative combined from different sources is sometimes unsuitable when the composite matter is distributed into its constituent parts. In such instances the Editors have substituted the simpler conjunction, placing the text-word ᵀ (see Table of Abbreviations 2) in the note, e g Gen 3²³.

[d] It is enough here to refer to the article 'Jehovah' in the *Encycl Brit*; to the article entitled 'Recent Theories on the Origin and Nature of the Tetragrammaton' by Prof Driver in *Studia Biblica* 1 1885, or to the earlier essay by the late Mr R Martineau appended to the second volume of the English edition of Ewald's *History of Israel*.

for this edition by the guardians of the Revised Version. The same authorities further allowed the occasional transposition of phrases which there was reason to think had become detached from their true context in the processes of editorial compilation

The Editors have of course reared their own structure on the labours of their predecessors in this field. It would have been easy to have loaded the notes with additional references, from the pioneer work of Colenso and Kalisch more than thirty years ago to the latest monographs of critical research. The standard treatises of Kuenen [a], Wellhausen [b], and Dillmann [c], have been freely used. To the elaborate *Einleitung in den Hexateuch*, published in 1893 by Dr H Holzinger, both the Committee at large, and the Editors especially, have been greatly indebted. His copious collections of critical opinions, and his admirable summaries of the characteristics of the several documents, have been of especial aid to the writer of the Introduction in this volume. The masterly expositions of the distinguished American scholar, the Rev (now Prof) B W Bacon, in the two books entitled *The Genesis of Genesis* (1892) and *The Triple Tradition of the Exodus* (1894), proved highly stimulating, and the Editors gladly express their appreciation of his clearness and penetration. They have also had the advantage of comparing their results with those of the Rev W E Addis, whose work [d] was planned about the same time as their own on entirely independent lines, and with those of Ball [e] and Holzinger [f] on Genesis, of Driver and White on Leviticus [g], of Staerk and Steuernagel on Deuteronomy [h], and of Bennett [i] and Steuernagel [j] on Joshua. They regret that it has been impossible for them to use some important contributions to Hexateuch criticism issued since this work was first sent to press in the autumn of 1898; such are the treatise of Prof van Hoonacker, *Le Sacerdoce Lévitique dans la Loi et dans l'Histoire des Hébreux*, the essay of Steuernagel entitled 'Der Jehovistische Bericht uber den Bundesschluss am Sinai' in *Studien und Kritiken*, 1899, iii, and the valuable summary of the results of archaeology for the Old Testament with which Prof Driver opens the recently published volume, *Authority and Archaeology, Sacred and Profane* [k].

It remains only for the Editors to offer to their colleagues of the Committee their heartfelt appreciation of much indulgence and consideration in the long delayed execution of their common project; to acknowledge with sincere and respectful thanks the liberal aid of the Hibbert Trustees in the publication of the book, and to express to the Controller of the University Press and his

---

[a] *The Religion of Israel* (Dutch 1869-70, English 1874); *The Hexateuch* (vol 1 of the second edition of the *Historisch-critisch Onderzoek*, English translation by Rev P H Wicksteed, 1886)

[b] *Composition des Hexateuch* (in *Skizzen* ii second edition *Comp²* 1889); *Prolegomena to the History of Israel*, 1885; *Israelitische und Judische Geschichte*, 1894.

[c] In the *Kurzgefasstes Handbuch*, based on the prior commentary of Knobel. *Genesis* is cited in the English translation, *Ex-Lev* in the later edition of Ryssel.

[d] *The Documents of the Hexateuch*, vol i 'The Oldest Book of Hebrew History' 1892, vol ii comprising Deuteronomy and the Priestly Code, 1898.

[e] *Genesis* in Haupt's *Sacred Books of the Old Testament*, 1896.

[f] *Genesis* in the *Kurzer Hand-Commentar*, 1898

[g] *Leviticus* in Haupt's *Sacred Books of the Old Testament*, 1898

[h] See vol ii p 246 Bertholet's *Deuteronomium* in the *Kurzer Hand-Commentar* came too late for use

[i] *Joshua* in Haupt's *Sacred Books of the Old Testament*, 1895.

[j] *Joshua* in the *Handkommentar*, 1899.

[k] Edited by David G Hogarth, 1899. Compare Nicoll, *Recent Archaeology and the Bible*, and Ball, *Light from the East*.

assistants their grateful recognition of the patience, courtesy, and skill with which numerous typographic difficulties were successively overcome.

In conclusion it is hoped that this work may show that co-operation in Biblical research is not only possible but advantageous among students of different religious communions. The one indispensable condition is a common trust that no truth can be established in any field of historical theology which does not ultimately minister *ad majorem Dei gloriam*.

J ESTLIN CARPENTER.
G HARFORD-BATTERSBY.

OXFORD, *October 26,* 1899

ADDITIONAL NOTE

PAGE 64 (δ) With the extract from the 'Archaeological Commentary on Genesis,' contributed by Professor Sayce to the *Expository Times*, the reader may compare the more guarded language of *The Early History of the Hebrews*, 57–61, where stress is laid on the word 'shekel,' and the phrase 'weighed the silver' Gen 23[16], in proof of the affinity of Gen 23 with Babylonian usage

THE HEXATEUCH

CONTENTS OF VOLUME I

THE COMPOSITION OF THE HEXATEUCH

CHAPTER I. CRITICISM AND THE OLD TESTAMENT

	PAGE
1 The Criticism of the Hexateuch part of a wider inquiry into the literature of Israel	1
α The books of *Psalms, Proverbs, Isaiah, Daniel*	1
β Application of general methods of literary investigation	2
2 Differences in earlier treatment of historical records	4
α Asser's *Life of Alfred* the *Saxon Chronicle*	4
β Early English Laws	5
γ Buddhist and Brahmanical sacred literatures	6
δ The *Diatessaron* of Tatian	8
ε The *Books of Chronicles*	11
3 Degrees of probability in critical results	13
α In the field of art	14
β Various grounds for determining literary dates	14
4 The Pentateuch a composite work	16
α The course of the inquiry	16
β Analogy with the growth of a cathedral	16

CHAPTER II. THE CLAIM TO CONTEMPORARY AUTHORSHIP

1 Allusions to the record of events or laws	17
α Exodus	17
β Numbers	18
γ Deuteronomy	18
δ Joshua	18
ε References to poetical collections	18
ζ Resulting inference	19
2 Growth of the conception of Mosaic legislation	19
α Indications in prophetic literature	19
β Allusions in *Kings* and *Chronicles*	20
γ The Synagogue and the Church	21

CHAPTER III. SIGNS OF POST-MOSAIC DATE

1 Early speculations concerning Moses and Ezra	21
2 The Spanish Rabbis	22
3 Catholics and Reformers in the sixteenth century	22

CHAPTER IV. SIGNS OF DIVERSITY OF DOCUMENTS

1 Criticism in the Seventeenth Century	23
α Hobbes	23
β de la Peyrère	24
γ Spinoza	24
δ Simon	25
ε Le Clerc	26
2 The search for a clue	27
α Incongruities of dates	28
β Duplicate narratives	29
γ Repetitions of Laws	30
δ Inconsistencies within the same narrative	31

CHAPTER V. THE CLUE TO THE DOCUMENTS

1 Astruc's *Conjectures*	33
2 Evidence of Ex 6^{2-8}	33
3 The Revelations of El Shaddai and the use of the name Yahweh	34
α Other links between Ex 6^{2-8} Gen 17 and 35^{9-15}	34
β Antecedents of Gen 17	35
γ Discovery of a *tol^{e}dhoth* narrative in Genesis employing the name Elohim	36
4 Inferences concerning the contents of this document	36

CHAPTER VI. THE COMPOSITION OF GENESIS–NUMBERS

1 Significance of duplicates when the *tol^{e}dhoth* sections are removed	37
α Discovery of a second narrative in Genesis employing the name Elohim	37
β Resemblances between this narrative and the Yahwist	38
2 Application of analytical methods to Ex-Num	39
α Continuation of the *tol^{e}dhoth* document in the Priestly Code	39
β The Yahwist and Elohist as national historians	40
γ Deuteronomy	41

CHAPTER VII. THE DOCUMENTARY THEORIES

1 Eichhorn and 'the higher criticism'	42
2 Ilgen distinguishes between E^1 and E^2 in Genesis	43
3 Impossibility of separating Genesis and the middle books	44
α Geddes ascribes the Pentateuch and Joshua to Solomon's reign	44
β The 'fragment-hypothesis,' J S Vater	44
4 De Wette's *Contributions to the Introduction to the Old Testament*	45
α Distinction between the literary and the historical problem	45
β Deuteronomy the product of the seventh century	46
5 The composition of the Pentateuch according to Ewald	47

CHAPTER VIII. THE JUSTIFICATION OF THE PARTITION

The different criteria available	48
I *The Argument from Religious Institutions*	49
1 Sacrifice	49
α The pre-Mosaic usage: the persons	50
β The place	50
γ Classes of sacrifice	51
2 Representations of the Mosaic Sanctuary	51
3 The Ten Words and the Ark	52
4 The Ministry at the Sanctuary	53
5 The Calendar of Feasts	53
6 Arrangements for the relief of the poor	54
7 Manumission of slaves	55
II *The Argument from Religious Ideas*	56
1 Conceptions of religious history and the Mosaic age	56
2 Presentations of Divine manifestation	57
α To the patriarchs	57
β To Moses and Israel	58
3 Different aspects of the Divine being	59
III *The Argument from Language and Style*	61
1 Contrasts of matter and terminology suggest inquiry	61
2 Resulting indications of diversity of source	62
α Different terms employed for the same thing	62
β Differences in grammatical forms and constructions	62
γ Variations in religious phraseology	63
δ Is Gen 23 a translation from a Babylonian document?	64
ε Promises of posterity to the patriarchs	64
ζ Two lists of the feasts in Moses' last year	65
η Parallel laws for asylum in case of accidental homicide	66
IV *The Development Hypothesis*	67
1 The literary and the historic chronology of the documents	67
2 Relation of Deuteronomy and the Priestly Code	68
3 Progress of the modern view since 1833	68

CONTENTS OF VOLUME I

CHAPTER IX. THE ORDER OF THE DOCUMENTS

i *The Antecedents of Deuteronomy* 70
  1 Dependence on JE's narrative 70
    α The Horeb Scenes 70
    β The wanderings and the Trans-jordanic conquest . 71
    γ No clear proof of D's acquaintance with P . . 72
  2 D's legislative scheme excludes the Sinaitic code . . 72
    α Parallels to Deuteronomic laws 73
    β Modifications of laws in Ex 21-23 75
    γ The principle of the unity of the sanctuary . . 75
  3 Priority of D compared with the Levitical arrangements 76
    α The Priesthood 76
    β The Priestly dues 77
    γ The Calendar of Feasts the Jubile . . . 78
ii *The Testimony of History* 79
  1 Religious usage of Israel after the settlement in Canaan 79
    α Plurality of sacred places 79
    β No trace of Levitical institutions 80
  2 The Erection of the Temple 82
    α Continuation of the local sanctuaries . . . 82
    β Indications in J E, Amos and Hosea . . . 83
    γ Isaiah and Micah reforms ascribed to Hezekiah . 83

CHAPTER X. DEUTERONOMY

1 Indications connecting Deuteronomy with the seventh century 85
2 Parallels with the language of Jeremiah 87
3 The first definite recognition of Deuteronomy . . 91
  α The discovery of a 'law-book' in Josiah's eighteenth year 91
  β The consequent reformation founded upon Deuteronomic demands 91
4 Was Josiah's law-book identical with D? . . . 92
  α Variety of its constituent elements 92
  β Probability that even the Code in 12-26 is a growth 93
  γ Peculiarities of distribution and amalgamation . 93
5 The original book of Deuteronomy 95
  α Possible limits of Josiah's law-book . . . 95
  β Reasons for placing its composition not long before 621 96

CHAPTER XI. THE ORIGINS OF J

1 General summary of its contents 97
2 Modes of historic and religious representation . . 98
  α Revelation and attributes of Yahweh . . . 98
  β Motives and conceptions of early prophecy . . 99
  γ Interest in the patriarchs, their localities and worship 100
  δ Significance of the Mosaic age 100
3 Method and spirit of J's narration 102
  α Sources in oral tradition, varied characteristics of reflection and poetry 102
  β Places, names, sacred objects and usages . . 103
  γ Large view of human affairs 103
4 Place of its composition 104
  α Rise of stories at local sanctuaries 104
  β Connexion of J with Judah 105
5 Diversity of its contents 106
  α The systematization of tribal traditions . . . 106
  β Reduction to writing between 850 and 750 B C . 107
6 J represents a school rather than a single author . . 108
  α Additions to the early history of mankind . . 108
  β A secondary story in Abram's life 108
  γ Hortatory expansions 109
  δ Extensions in the style of J begotten by the union of J and E 109
  ε Enlargements of brief collections of law . . . 109

CHAPTER XII. CHARACTERISTICS AND ORIGINS OF E

1 Comparison with the scope and contents of J . . 110
2 Divergences amid general resemblance . . . 112
  α View of the progress of Revelation . . . 112
  β Methods of Divine communication . . . 112
  γ The great personalities of the national story . . 113
  δ The patriarchal cultus 113
  ε The Mosaic institutions 114
3 Characteristics of narration 115
4 Ascription of E to Ephraim 116
5 Growth of E 117
  α General indications of date under the monarchy 117
  β Opposite views of the priority of J or E . . 117
  γ Probable reduction to writing before 750 B C . 118
  δ Elements of various date 119

CHAPTER XIII. THE PRIESTLY CODE

1 Its significance as the groundwork of the Pentateuch . 121
2 Stages of its history and legislation 122
  α View of primeval history compared with J . . 122
  β The patriarchal age 123
  γ Theory of religious progression 124
  δ The adoption of Israel by Yahweh to be his people 124
  ε P's definite literary method 125
3 Advanced ritual and hierarchical organization compared with D 126
  α Ezekiel's view of the cultus of regenerated Israel . 126
  β Future division of the Levite priests into two orders 127
  γ Other indications that Ezekiel did not know the Priestly Law 128
  δ Ezekiel's Temple and the Levitical Dwelling . 129
  ε Conceptions of the Ideal Future realized in P . 130
4 Signs of the late date of the Priestly Code . . . 131
  α Unrecognized in *Kings*, but employed by *Chronicles* 131
  β Parallels to the theological ideas of P in Ezekiel . 132
  γ Literary affinities of P with Ezekiel and his successors 133
  δ The argument from proper names 134
  ε Possible dependence on cuneiform data . . . 134
5 First Traces of the Levitical Law 135
  α Unacknowledged by Haggai, Zechariah, or Malachi 135
  β Parallels of phraseology amid divergences of practice 136
6 The age of Ezra and Nehemiah 137
  α The Promulgation of the Law 137
  β The celebration of Booths according to P . . 138
  γ Was Ezra's Law-book limited to P? . . . 138
  δ Did the Covenant of Neh 10³⁰⁻³⁹ precede or follow the promulgation of the Law? 140
7 Was Ezra's Law-book complete? 141
  α The Priestly Code contains various smaller collections 141
  β Its groundwork, P^g 142
  γ Successive groups inserted into it 142
8 The Holiness-legislation, P^h 143
  α Characteristics of Lev 17-26 143
  β Its composite character 144
  γ Traces of the Holiness-legislation elsewhere . 145
  δ Elements of various age 145
  ε Parallels with Ezekiel 147
  ζ Lev 26³⁻⁴⁵ probably later than Ezekiel . . 149
9 Priestly Teaching, P^t 152
  α Groups of *torah* independent of the wanderings . 152
  β Anterior to the Dwelling and the Aaronic Priesthood 152
10 Secondary additions, P^s 153
  α Supplemental narratives and laws . . . 153
  β Grounds for recognition in greater freedom of style 155
11 Place and Time of the compilation of P . . . 155
  α Probability that P^h and P^t were united with P^g before Ezra's mission 155
  β Post-Ezran additions 156

CHAPTER XIV. UNCLASSIFIED DOCUMENTS

1 Gen 14 157
  α Belongs neither to J nor P 157
  β Peculiarities of style pointing to late date . . 158
  γ Significance of cuneiform evidence . . . 158
2 The Blessing of Jacob, Gen 49²⁻²⁷ 159
3 The Song of Moses, Ex 15²⁻¹⁸ 160
4 The Song of Moses, Deut 32¹⁻⁴³ 161
  α Relation to prophecies of the captivity . . . 161
  β Parallels of language 162
5 The Blessing of Moses, Deut 33²⁻²⁹ 163

CONTENTS AND ABBREVIATIONS

CHAPTER XV. CRITICISM AND ARCHAEOLOGY (contributed by Rev. Prof T K Cheyne DD)

	PAGE		PAGE
1 Need of more carefully tested Assyriological evidence	164	6 Gen 14	167
2 Narratives of the Creation of the world and man	165	α Controversy and criticism	167
α Babylonian culture in Palestine	165	β The Babylonian Inscriptions	168
β The narrative in Gen 1–2⁴ᵃ	165	γ The name Chedorlaomer	169
3 The Story of the Deluge	166	7 The Exodus	169
4 Periods of Israelitish interest in Babylonian myths	166	8 Modifications of older traditions	170
5 Personal names in P	167		

CHAPTER XVI. THE UNION OF THE DOCUMENTS

	PAGE		PAGE
1 The fusion of J and E	171	3 Combination of JED with P	176
α Editorial activity in the patriarchal narratives	171	α The Scribes at Jerusalem	176
β Traditions and laws of the Mosaic age	172	β Illustrations of the conservative method of Rᴾ	176
γ Employment of JE by D	173	γ Transpositions and efforts at harmonizing	177
2 Incorporation of D in JE	174	δ Different process in the compilation of Joshua	178
α Traces of Rᵈ in Gen-Ex	174	ε Amalgamation of JEDP probably completed by 400 B C	179
β Elements of E preserved in D	175		
γ Wide range of time-limit	175		

TABULAR APPENDICES

A. SELECT LISTS OF WORDS AND PHRASES

Introductory Note	183	II The Deuteronomic School, D	200
I. The Prophetic Narrators, JE	185	III The Priestly Law and History Book, P	208
J¹⁻⁹³ E⁹⁴⁻¹¹⁹ JE¹²⁰⁻²³⁷		Pᵍᵗˢ1–191 Pʰ192–220	

B. LAWS AND INSTITUTIONS L1–16

Introductory Note	222	6a–n Clean and Unclean	231	12a–m The Sanctuary in P	255
1a–o The Family	223	7a–z Sacrifices	234	13a–g Conspectus of Codes	256
2a–k Persons and Animals	224	8a–l Sacred Dues	240	14a–l The Codes compared	266
3a–l Property	225	9a–k Sacred Seasons	243	15a–g Statistics of usage	268
4a–w Judgement and Rule	227	10a–e Sacred Places	247	16a–b Contents and Index	270
5a–k Idolatry and Superstition	229	11a–q Sacred Persons	250		

C. ANALYSIS AND SYNOPSIS OF THE HEXATEUCH

Genesis	272	Leviticus	277	Deuteronomy	278
Exodus	275	Numbers	277	Joshua	279

CONTENTS OF VOLUME II

GENESIS–DEUTERONOMY	1–302
Introduction to Joshua	303

Indications of diversity of authorship	304	3 Supplemental character of Rᵈ's work	313
1 Duplicate accounts of the same events	304	α Deuteronomic additions not all of the same age	313
2 Incompatibilities within the same narrative	304	β They imply the historic and hortatory settings of D	314
2 Continuation of previous documents	304	γ Phraseological indications	314
3 The Conquest of Canaan according to JE	305	δ Approximations to the language of P	314
1 Can J and E be distinguished?	305	5 Character and Place of P	315
α Signs of the general scope of J	306	1 Not adopted as the literary groundwork of Joshua	315
β Probability that the J sections are of various dates	306	2 Secondary character of much of its materials	316
2 Characteristics of E	308	3 Relation to other documents priority of JE	316
3 The union of J and E	309	α Is P earlier or later than Rᵈ?	316
4 The Deuteronomic revision of JE	310	β Indications of Rᴾ's revision of Rᵈ	317
1 Addition of homiletic and other passages	310	γ Supposed signs of Rᵈ on Rᴾ	317
2 Expansion of the earlier narratives	311	6 Continuous process of redaction	319
JOSHUA			320

ABBREVIATIONS

1 ABBREVIATED TITLES OF BOOKS OFTEN CITED

COT, Schrader's *Cuneiform Inscriptions and the Old Testament*.
DB, Hastings' *Dictionary of the Bible*
DB², Smith's *Dictionary of the Bible*, vol 1, 2nd ed
ICC, *International Critical Commentary*.
JQR, *Jewish Quarterly Review*.
LOT⁶, Driver's Introduction to the Literature of the OT, 6th ed.
NDJ, Dillmann on *Num–Deut–Josh* in *Kurzgef Hdbuch* (1886)
NKZ, *Neue Kirchliche Zeitschrift*
OTJC², W. Robertson Smith, *The Old Testament in the Jewish Church*, 2nd ed
PSBA, *Proceedings of the Society for Biblical Archaeology*
RHR, *Revue de l'Histoire des Religions*
RS, Budde, *Die Bucher Richter und Samuel* (1890).
RV, *Revised Version*.
SBOT, *Sacred Books of the Old Testament*, edited by Prof Paul Haupt
ZATW, *Zeitschrift für Alttestamentliche Wissenschaft*.
ZDMG, *Zeitschrift der Deutschen Morgenländischen Gesellschaft*.

It has not been thought necessary to supply any complete list of the modern literature upon the Hexateuch. The references in the following work will, it is hoped, enable the reader to identify the authorities cited without difficulty. In a few cases the views of scholars have been mentioned without direct quotation. A short list of the least obvious of these is here appended.

Baudissin, *Die Geschichte des Alttest Priestertums* (1889)
Giesebrecht, *Jeremia*, in the *Handkommentar* (1894).
Kautzsch, *Die Heilige Schrift des Alten Testamentes* (1894)
Kautzsch and Socin, *Die Genesis mit ausserer Unterscheidung der Quellenschriften* (2nd ed 1891)
Meisner, *Der Dekalog*, Teil 1 (1893).
Montet (F), *Le Deuteronome et la Question de l'Hexateuque* (1891)
Oettli, *Deut and Josh* in the *Kurzgefasster Kommentar* (1893).
Strack, *Gen–Num* in the *Kurzgefasster Kommentar* (1894).
Wildeboer, *Die Litteratur des Alten Testaments* [German Translation] (1895).

KEY TO THE ANALYSIS

The text is printed consecutively in one or other of two columns divided by a vertical line, JE being on the left and P on the right. Wherever JE and P are much interwoven (cp Ex 14 Num 13–16) the columns are both of the same width. Elsewhere the occupied column is widened to save space. Thus it is only the relative position, and not the width, of a column or section of a column that is significant. See also footnote on D.

Left-hand margin	J E	JE	J E	P^h or ^{t}	P^g	P^s	Right-hand margin

a b c in the text point to references given here to parallel or contrasted passages

L in the text points to a reference given here to the Tables of Laws and Institutions in vol 1, the verses covered by the reference being specified

See below for * † 𝔥 &c

Large roman type on the left is used for the main thread of **J**; *large italic type for supplements by writers of the same school* (J^s cp Gen 12^{9N}); small roman type for harmonizing additions, &c by R^{je} (cp 15^{12N}) or R^d (cp 1^{1N}); *small italics for ditto by* R^p (cp 7^{7N})
Small roman type in separate paragraphs denotes longer and later J^s supplements (cp 12^{10N}).

Large roman type on the right is used for the main thread of **E** from Gen 15 ‡ ; *large italics for supplements by writers of the same school* (E^s cp 30^{26N}); small roman type for harmonizing additions, &c by R^{je} (cp 31^{10N}) or R^d (cp Josh 3^{3N}); *small italic type for similar additions by* R^p (cp 35^{5N})
Small roman type in separate paragraphs denotes longer and later E^s supplements (cp Num 12)

Large italic type in the centre is used for longer harmonizing additions and expansions by R^{je} *(cp Gen* 22^{15N}*).*
Small roman type in separate paragraphs in the centre marks longer supplements by R^d (cp Josh 1^3); still smaller type distinguishes later R^d additions (cp 7^N), *small italics being kept as above for* R^p (cp 11^{20dN})

Large roman type in the centre (or up to Ex 29 across the whole column) is used for the main stock or priestly groundwork (P^g); *small italics for editorial additions by* R^p (cp Gen 48^7)
Small roman type in separate paragraphs denotes longer supplements (P^s) up to Ex 29 (cp Gen 34)
Large roman type on the left is used after Ex 29 for the main stock of P^h and P^t; *large italic type for supplements by writers of the same school*; *small italic type for editorial and other additions by* R^p
Small roman and *italic* types are used in separate paragraphs for later strata of P^t

Large roman type on the right denotes material in harmony with P^g but written later (P^s); *large italic type is used for supplements of the same school, and small italic type for later editorial additions*
Small roman type is used in separate paragraphs for supplements of a later school, *small italic type sometimes distinguishing the latest strata.*

a b c in the text point to references given here to the appropriate Word List in vol 1, Appendix A, where three Lists are given, for JE, D, and P respectively

‡ Up to Gen 15 large roman type on the right is used for early and substantial J^s supplements to J^g.

Footnotes.

^{N} in the text points to a footnote given below
^{M} in the text indicates that an alternative marginal rendering of the *RV* will be found below.
^{T} in the text indicates that the margin of the *RV*, or a rendering used elsewhere for the same Hebrew word or phrase, has been adopted, and that the rejected rendering will be found below. In all cases notes are given in order under the number of the verse in which the ^{N} ^{M} or ^{T} occurs. Where more than one note refers to a single verse, the verse number is repeated with ^{a} ^{b} ^{c} affixed.

D The arrangement of the text of Deut is on a similar plan. The main stock (D^g) is on the left in an additional central column, later supplements (D^s) are on the right, a few passages distinct from D^g but not clearly later being placed in the centre. Distinctions of type mark minor insertions or alterations.

ABBREVIATIONS (*continued*)
2 General Abbreviations and Signs

J, the Yahwist document (*Introd* 1 41)
E, the Elohist document (*Introd* 1 41).
JE, the combined document formed from these two sources
D, the main Deuteronomic documents (*Introd* 1 41)
J^s E^s D^s, secondary elements in J E D (*Introd* 1 108 119 92).
P, the Priestly Law and History (*Introd* 1 40)
P^g, the 'Grundschrift' or groundwork of **P** (*Introd* 1 141)
P^h, the Holiness-legislation incorporated in P^g (*Introd* 1 143, § 8)
P^t, earlier and independent groups of Priestly Teaching incorporated in P^g (*Introd* 1 152, § 9)
P^s, secondary extensions of P^g (*Introd* 1 153, § 10).
R^{je}, the editorial hands which united and revised J and E
R^d, the editorial hands which united and revised JE and D.
R^p, the editorial hands which united and revised JED and P.
$^{JE\ D\ P}$ before thick figures (as $^{JE}27$) refer to the documentary word-lists
T, *RV* text. **M**, *RV* margin. Additions to the words of *RV* **M** are separated by —.
· before or after a passage in the text denotes that its original context has not been preserved by the compiler
[ ] enclose words printed in italics by the Revisers
* after references, indicates all occurrences in the Hexateuch
† all occurrences in the Old Testament.

∥ introduces a parallel from another context
§ means 'in part, for details see analysis or full text.'
· (or ·) after a verse numeral e g 2^4 (or ^{8}) means 'and following verse (*or* verses)'
→ indicates the connexion of passages believed to have been transposed.
— — mark passages transposed from their context and now replaced
^{a} ^{b} ^{c} &c after numerals (e g 2^a ^{4b}) mark successive portions of verses (without reference to the Hebrew punctuation).
al = *alibi*   Cp = compare.   Ct = contrast.
( ) enclosing a figure after the name of a book show the number of occurrences in that book, e g Ezek (17), seventeen times in Ezekiel.
𝔥, the Massoretic Hebrew text.
𝔊, the Greek text (edited by H B Swete) · $𝔊^{AB}$ &c, the codices $𝔊^L$ is occasionally employed to denote the Lucian recension edited by Lagarde.
𝔏, the Latin version of Jerome   𝔏, the Old Latin.
𝔖, the Syriac text of the Peshitta
Sam, the Samaritan Pentateuch.
𝔗, the Targum of Onkelos.

THE COMPOSITION OF THE HEXATEUCH

INTRODUCTION

CHAPTER I

CRITICISM AND THE OLD TESTAMENT

THE five 'books of Moses' which stand at the beginning of the Old Testament were known in the early Church as the Pentateuch[a]. In the belief that the book of Joshua can be proved to be their literary sequel, the name Hexateuch has been extended by analogy to the entire collection. The justification of this belief is one of the objects of this Introduction. It depends on the application of critical methods to a group of documents which were formerly accepted on the basis of a great ecclesiastical tradition as the work of Moses.

1. The criticism of the Hexateuch is only, however, a part of a wider inquiry into the literature of ancient Israel.

(a) Beside the books of sacred law stand others associated in like manner with illustrious names which, when carefully examined, reveal manifold indications of composition under other circumstances and at different dates. Thus the majority of the Psalms are ascribed by their traditional titles to David, as the splendid representative of lyrical devotion. But there are many reasons for regarding these titles as of much later origin than the poems to which they are attached. Some of these poems, again, refer to circumstances which did not exist in David's day; the temple stands upon the holy hill; the ruined walls of Jerusalem are to be rebuilt; the prisoners in captivity shall be restored. Moreover the poet sometimes uses words or grammatical forms inconsistent with residence in Judah a thousand years B C; or he betrays acquaintance with religious ideas of later prophecy psychologically incongruous with those historically attributed to the successor of Saul[b]. As David is the heroic centre of song, so is Solomon the picturesque exponent of wisdom. But the Book of Proverbs no less than the Psalter is found to be composed out of separate collections; the same sayings are sometimes repeated in different groups; many show an advanced stage of literary art and even of philosophical reflexion; while others are obviously unsuitable to the position and habits of the magnificent but self-indulgent king. The satirical comments on royal misgovernment in Ecclesiastes are still less appropriate to him; nor can it be understood how he

---

[a] In Greek, ἡ Πεντάτευχος, sc βίβλος (Orig in Ioann xiii 26); Latin, Pentateuchus, sc liber (Tert adv Marc i 10).

[b] Cp the implications of 1 Sam 26¹⁹ 2 Sam 21⁸. with the advanced conceptions of Pss 51 and 139.

should have used an occasional Persian word or a Greek phrase, or have habitually employed a vocabulary full of expressions unknown to Biblical Hebrew but familiar in the later Aramaic and the language of the Jewish Mishnah (in the second century of our era). Again, the prophecies grouped under the name of Isaiah are soon perceived to stand in no regular chronological succession. Some of them can be connected with contemporary events attested by the witness of the Assyrian monuments. Some of them bear the stamp of the prophet's exalted spirit, though the year of their composition may still be uncertain. But others are conceived in another scene—the plains of Babylonia—and respond to another religious atmosphere—the deep depression produced by the fall of Jerusalem and the decay of hope till the conquests of Cyrus re-quickened the expectation of return. And yet others seem to belong neither to the eighth century nor to the sixth: they hint at the dangers and difficulties of a period later still, as Jerusalem struggles against the enemies which jealously watch its revival, or the dim clash of forces is heard when mighty empires totter and fall, and judgement goes forth over all the earth. Within the book of Isaiah, if some modern scholars read it aright, are gathered the voices of prophecy from the age of Tiglath Pileser and Sennacherib to the vast enterprises of Alexander the Great[a]. Or yet once more, the story of Daniel can no longer be regarded as written by an eye-witness of its scenes. Its representations of the court of Belshazzar, of the fall of Babylon, of the reign of Darius the Mede, cannot be reconciled with the evidence of contemporary inscriptions[b]. Its language is in parts the Aramaic of Palestine; in other cases it freely employs Persian words before Cyrus and his troops have appeared upon the field; and it names Greek musical instruments in Nebuchadrezzar's orchestra. One of these Greek terms, *symphonia*, is used by Polybius in special connexion with the festivities of Antiochus Epiphanes[c]; and if words like *census, centurion, legion*, in the New Testament bear testimony to the presence of the Romans in Palestine, the book of Daniel by similar reasoning must be placed in the Greek age. Moreover, the author is well acquainted with the events of the reign of Antiochus Epiphanes (176-164 B C); he describes his campaigns against Egypt and his persecution of the Jews; he has in view the desecration of the Temple and its purification three years later (December, 165 B C). The analogy of interpretation thus renders it in the highest degree probable that the book was closely connected with the terrible national suffering which called forth the heroic efforts of the Maccabean leaders.

(β) The method by which such results as these have been obtained is not peculiar to the study of the Old Testament. It simply consists in applying to the literature of Israel the principles of criticism which have long since been acknowledged as valid in other fields. When the Renaissance awoke the slumbering mind of Europe to the knowledge of the treasures of the classic past, the efforts of scholars were at first chiefly concerned with the form rather than with the matter of ancient literature. Then came the laborious endeavours, the minute and massive learning, of Joseph Scaliger and Isaac Casaubon, who sought to reconstruct the chronological framework of antiquity and fill its picture of life with familiar detail. But it was only two hundred years ago that Bentley's famous *Dissertation on the Epistles of Phalaris*[d] laid the real foundation of a new criticism, which tested the claims of traditional authorship

---

[a] The date of Isaiah 24-27 is still under discussion Dr Driver, *LOT*⁶, places it in the Persian age; Kuenen, Smend, and recently Prof Cheyne, *Introd to Isaiah*, and Haupt's *SBOT*, assign the group to the fourth century B C; and Duhm (*Handkommentar*, 1892) finds elements later still.
[b] Cp Sayce, *Higher Criticism and the Monuments* 526
[c] Cp Driver, *LOT*⁶ 502.
[d] First sketched in 1697, and appended to the second edition of Wotton's *Reflections on Ancient and Modern Learning*, revised and enlarged in 1698, and published separately, 1699

by strict reasoning, and supplied the first illustrious example of learning and insight concentrated on literary and historical research[a]. By that time the seventeenth-century criticism of the Pentateuch had already made important advances; but the contrast between the guesses of Spinoza or the gropings of Father Simon and the science of Bentley is obvious (cp chap IV 1β). Bentley's contemporary, Le Clerc, approached much nearer to the English scholar's conception both of the aim and the method of inquiry (cp chap IV 1ε); he did not, however, possess the same large grasp of his subject-matter, and his attempt failed permanently to persuade even himself[b]. Yet another century passed before Wolf proposed (in 1795) to break up the unity of the Iliad into a cycle of lays collected under Pisistratus, almost immediately after a Scotch Roman Catholic, Dr Geddes, had resolved the Pentateuch and Joshua (1792) into a compilation out of written documents and oral traditions effected under the monarchy between Solomon and Hezekiah (cp chap VII 3a). The labours of Wolf prepared the way for Niebuhr, just as the investigations of Niebuhr on early Roman history sent Ewald to reconstruct the patriarchal age of Israel. The whole field of literature has thus been opened up by the toil of successive generations of scholars; and no branch of it can escape from critical inquiry, though diversity of materials and opportunity may prevent the results from attaining more than varying degrees of certainty. If it be desired to arrange the dialogues of Plato or the plays of Shakespeare in the chronological order of their production, the result must depend on the skilful combination of a variety of different lines of evidence: where indications of a positive historical character are lacking, considerations of style or rhythm, of the internal development of ideas, or the suitability of particular conceptions to successive phases of thought and experience, may be legitimately advanced. And if these compositions may be thus compared and examined, if the genuine may be sifted from the spurious, if tests of authorship may be formulated and canons of judgement established, it is plain that the methods which are valid for the writings of Plato may be no less applicable to those of Paul. The Revised Version still retains (in spite of the Manuscripts) the superscription of the Textus Receptus 'The Epistle of Paul the Apostle to the Hebrews.' Yet already the Alexandrian fathers perceived the peculiarities which led Luther to ascribe it to Apollos. The difficulties of investigating the composition of a series of books like those attributed to Moses may be greater, but they must be approached and overcome—if they can be overcome at all—along similar lines. On the modern hypothesis that the Pentateuch is a collection of documents representing successive periods in the national life of Israel, the critic who attempts to disentangle them, and reconstruct their contents and sequence, must proceed with the same caution as the geologist who would explain the phenomena of a particular district. The student of the earth's crust discovers that its rocks may be sorted into groups. He examines the arrangement of the strata; he measures their incline; he learns to interpret peculiarities of position, when he finds them broken or contorted; he traces the extent of a 'fault'; he collects the characteristic fossils; he can even identify the wandering blocks carried by icebergs through ocean-currents, and deposited hundreds of miles away from the parent rock. He thus arrives at a provisional reconstruction of the history of the area which he has examined. Particular incidents such as volcanic intrusion, or submergence beneath the sea, or the extension of the great ice sheet, are all referred to their proper places in the geologic series, though none of them can be assigned to given dates in absolute time within tens of thousands of years. Not dissimilar is the aim of the historical

[a] Cp Jebb, *Bentley* ('English Men of Letters') 83
[b] A closer parallel to Bentley's work might be found in De Wette's masterly *Beiträge* (1806-7) cp chap VII 4.

student. He, too, must classify his materials; he must examine their indications of mutual dependence or the reverse; he must study their forms and discover, if possible, the causes which have impressed their special character on different parts of the record. If external indications seem deficient, he must seek for the clue to their internal sequence, until, having established their true succession, he can adjust them appropriately to the historical development to which they belong. It may, indeed, happen (witness the case of India) that there is little other clue to that historical development but the documents themselves under investigation. The embarrassments of the student are multiplied, but neither his object nor his procedure is substantially changed. His primary duty must always be to collect and compare the facts; and the most satisfactory hypothesis will be that which most fully and clearly accounts first for the most important, and secondly for the largest number.

2. In such an inquiry the student is confronted at once with very different conceptions of the significance of documents and the value and treatment of historical records.

(a) When Archbishop Parker edited Asser's Life of Alfred (1574), he did not hesitate to incorporate into it passages from the so-called Annals of Asser. These annals were no doubt believed to have proceeded from the same author; Parker's amalgamation of materials thus seemingly enabled the original writer to enrich his story out of his own collections. But a little examination discloses the fact that the Annals were only compiled towards the end of the twelfth century[a], and contained extracts from many sources, including a life of St Edmund by Abbo, who wrote at least fourscore years after Asser's death. In republishing Parker's text in 1603, Camden took a further step. Without the faintest hint that he was making any addition, with no attempt to justify himself by manuscript authority, he inserted into the work for the first time the celebrated passage ascribing to Alfred the foundation of the University of Oxford. If such was the practice of the scholars of three hundred years ago in the light of the revival of letters, it is not surprising that earlier documents should show continuous signs of growth by similar processes of accretion. The Saxon Chronicle first emerges into light under Alfred's direction. It is founded originally on the Bishops' Roll in Winchester[b], a series of meagre and irregular annals in the Latin tongue, concerned chiefly with local events from the days of the preaching of Birinus. It is enlarged under the influence of Swithun; it receives fresh entries describing the coming of the fathers; it is brought into relation with the national history. Then Alfred takes it up; he resolves that it shall be made accessible to the unlearned, and written in the English tongue; with the translation fresh materials are grouped, drawn from the narrative of Bede; the story is carried back to the Incarnation; and the growth of the English people is thus brought into relation with the central event of history. It is at once the product, and also in its turn the promoter, of the growing national consciousness. Copies are deposited in different monasteries, and there the work of continuation proceeds. Some are interested in the work; in some it is neglected. Various hands carry on the story; special events are noted here in Kent, and there in Mercia or Northumbria; there are local peculiarities of orthography, or differences in chronological arrangement; one copy possesses additions distinctive of Canterbury, another of Abingdon, a third of Peterborough[c]. Florence of Worcester in his turn founds himself on the Chronicle together with the work of Irish Marian, whose history began with the creation of the world, and fuses the two together into a compound narrative, in which it is difficult to say how much is really his own. The results of this

---

[a] Hardy, *Descriptive Catalogue of Materials* 1 557.   [b] Cp Green, *Conquest of England* 165.
[c] Cp Hardy, *Descriptive Catalogue* 1 650–660.

method of composition are thus expounded by Sir Thomas Hardy (*Descriptive Catalogue* iii p xl):—

> Monastic chronicles were seldom the production of a single hand, as in the case of Malmesbury and of Beda. They grew up from period to period; each age added fresh material, and every house in which they were copied supplied fresh local information, until the tributary streams often grew more important than the original current. The motives and objects of the mediaeval chronicler were different from those of the modern historian. He did not consider himself tied by those restrictions to which the latter implicitly submits. The monastic annalist was at one time a transcriber, at another time an abridger, at another an original author.... He epitomized or curtailed or adopted the works of his predecessors in the same path without alteration and without acknowledgement just as best suited his own purpose or that of his monastery. He did not work for himself but at the command of others. His own profit and his own vanity were not concerned in the result. It was enough if he pleased his superior. So with no feeling of individual aggrandizement or responsibility, he adopted what he thought good or worth preserving, at the same time adding or interpolating according to his individual knowledge, taste, or opportunities. And as he acted towards others, so others in succession acted towards him. Thus it was that a monastery chronicle grew like a monastic house, by the labour of different hands and different times. But of the head that planned it, of the hands that executed it, or of the exact proportion contributed by each, no satisfactory record was preserved. The individual was lost in the community.

Not dissimilar, it may be conjectured, with due allowance for different religious and political conditions, was the progress of historiography in Israel, out of which emerged the anonymous books of Judges, Samuel, and Kings. And not dissimilar, it will be argued hereafter, was the growth of the original narratives which were the earliest to assume written form in recounting the ancient traditions from the immigration of Abraham to the conquest under Joshua, and (in one case at least) connected the vicissitudes of the Twelve Tribes with the general course of human history from the day when earth and sky were made.

(β) The collections of early English laws are also not without some interesting instances of processes which will be hereafter traced more fully in connexion with the formation of the Pentateuchal codes. That the 'dooms' or 'judgements' sanctioned by the kings of Kent or Wessex should show marked affinities with each other, is of course to be expected. They spring out of the same social conditions; they are directed against the same offences; they employ a common terminology for the redress of wrong; they aim at enforcing the same standard of right, and seek to impress parallel if not identical moral conceptions. The mode in which a new group was founded upon its predecessors may be illustrated by the language of Alfred[a]:—

> In many synod-books they wrote, at one place one doom, at another another. I, then, Alfred, king, gathered these together, and commanded many of those to be written which our forefathers held, those which to me seemed good; and many of those which seemed to me not good I rejected them, by the counsel of my 'witan,' and in otherwise commanded them to be holden; for I durst not venture to set down in writing much of my own, for it was unknown to me what of it would please those who should come after us. But those things which I met with, either of the days of Ine my kinsman, or of Offa king of the Mercians, or of Æthelbryght, who first among the English race received baptism, those which seemed to me the rightest, those I have here gathered together, and rejected the others.

The curious reader may trace through these laws an increasing complexity, as the simpler rules of an older day are applied with various modifications to fresh cases. 'Alfred's Dooms,' however, begin with a recital of the Ten Commandments, followed by the substance of the First Legislation in Exodus 20–23. The freedom with which these are treated is highly significant. Thus the first commandment appears in the form 'Love thou not other strange gods above me.' The second is ignored altogether, until a corresponding utterance enters at the close, in the tenth place, 'Make thou not to thyself golden or silver gods[b].' If this rearrangement was permissible in dealing with the Ten Commandments, it is easily intelligible that the succeeding

---

[a] Thorpe, *Ancient Laws and Institutes of England* i 59
[b] Cp Ex 20^{23} 'gods of silver, or gods of gold, ye shall not make unto you.'

laws should be reproduced in a form more suitable to English society in the tenth century. A single passage will suffice for illustration:—

Ex 22²⁵–23⁷	Alfred's Dooms
²⁸ Thou shalt not revile God, nor curse a ruler of thy people. ²⁹ Thou shalt not delay to offer of the abundance of thy fruits, and of thy liquors. The firstborn of thy sons shalt thou give unto me. ³⁰ Likewise shalt thou do with thine oxen, *and* with thy sheep seven days it shall be with its dam; on the eighth day thou shalt give it me. ³¹ And ye shall be holy men unto me therefore ye shall not eat any flesh that is torn of beasts in the field, ye shall cast it to the dogs. ²³¹ Thou shalt not take up a false report put not thine hand with the wicked to be an unrighteous witness. ² Thou shalt not follow a multitude to do evil; neither shalt thou speak in a cause to turn aside after a multitude to wrest *judgement*. ³ neither shalt thou favour a poor man in his cause.	Revile thou not thy Lord God nor curse thou the Lord of the people Thy tithes, and thy first fruits of moving and growing things, render thou to God. All the flesh that wild beasts leave, eat ye not that, but give it to the dogs. To the word of a lying man reck thou not to hearken, nor allow thou of his judgements; nor say thou any witness after him. Turn thou not thyself to the foolish counsel and unjust desire of the people, in their speech and cry, against thine own reason, and according to the teaching of the most unwise; neither allow thou of them.
⁴ If thou meet thine enemy's ox or his ass going astray, thou shalt surely bring it back to him again. ⁵ If thou see the ass of him that hateth thee lying under his burden, and wouldest forbear to help him, thou shalt surely help with him	If the stray cattle of another man come to thy hand, though it be thy foe, make it known to him.
⁶ Thou shalt not wrest the judgement of thy poor in his cause ⁷ Keep thee far from a false matter, and the innocent and righteous slay thou not: for I will not justify the wicked	Judge thou very evenly · judge thou not one doom to the rich, another to the poor; nor one to thy friend, another to thy foe, judge thou. Shun thou ever leasings. A just and innocent man, him slay thou never.

'These are the dooms,' continues the king, 'which the Almighty God himself spake unto Moses and commanded him to keep' He then briefly narrates the founding of Christianity, and cites the apostolic letter Acts 15²³⁻²⁹, with an interesting addition of his own:—

It seemed good to the Holy Ghost and to us that we should set no burthen upon you above that which it was needful for you to bear: now that is that ye forbear from worshipping idols, and from tasting blood or things strangled, and from fornications · *and that which ye will that other men do not unto you, do ye not that to other men From this one doom a man may remember that he judge every one righteously he need heed no other doom-book. Let him remember that he adjudge to no man that which he would not that he should adjudge to him, if he sought judgement against him.*

So natural was it for new law-giving to combine and supplement the old; so easily did hortatory expansion add a comment to the text.

(γ) A glance into the history of India, mother of so many religions and home of such colossal literary products, reveals many interesting analogies to the processes which have been already illustrated from our own country. The great aggregations of the sacred books of Buddhism in India, China, or Tibet, are full of curious instances of the treatment of a common tradition under different influences of religious conception. But their textual relations are at present too little known to furnish any secure parallels on the ground of the sacred law. The story of the Buddha's early life may, however, be followed through a series of compositions by unknown authors, in which the later have obviously used the materials of their predecessors, expanding and transforming the original elements so as to exalt the person and deeds of the Teacher. Thus the Mahā-Vagga of the Vinaya-Piṭaka, or rules for the Order, according to the Southern (and oldest) Canon, opens with a description of the events immediately following the attainment of Buddhahood by Gotama, after the great crisis which secured for him supreme enlightenment. It doubtless embodies very ancient tradition, and it forms the basis of a similar narrative embodied in one of the discourses of the Long Collection in the Sutta-Pi*t*aka[a], where it is preceded by an ideal biography beginning with the miraculous Birth. Much of this is in its turn reproduced in the post-canonical Introduction to the Jātaka-book[b], a comparison of the texts showing how the older story has been worked up by a later hand. And so the sacred legend is propagated, and Burma, China, Tibet, must each re-tell the wondrous tale, often incorporating the forms of antique speech in the midst of materials of much later type. The Brahmanical literature, also, exhibits signs of filiation in another field, and the researches of a century of scholars have overthrown many a cherished tradition of authorship. It is now known that the ancient Vedic lore was propagated in various centres throughout India, where groups of students attached themselves to a particular Veda, and began the long labours—carried on with so much passionate persistence—on which the immense structures of later Brahmanical science were based. In these schools the text was recited and transmitted from generation to generation; around it gathered the needful instruction in grammar, in ritual, and the other great divisions of learning; and here were formulated the early codes of moral duties, and the rules for the administration of justice and the conduct of kings. Some of these codes still survive, designated by famous names in the past, the oldest, by general consent, being that of Gautama, connected with the Sāma Veda[c]. Among these two may be specially noticed here. In the 'Institutes of Vish*n*u[d]' tradition sees a book of sacred law (chaps 2–97) revealed by Vish*n*u to the goddess of the earth (chap 1). But a careful examination brings other facts to light. The laws, when compared with parallel texts of undoubted antiquity, bear the stamp of ancient composition in one of the schools of the Black Yajur Veda. But they have been recast by an adherent of Vish*n*u, who has added an opening and a final discourse, and inserted groups of verses—perhaps whole chapters—in different parts of the book. Such additions may be distinguished by various criteria, by peculiarities of metre, by their partial recurrence in other works, by references to philosophical systems known to be of late growth, and in one case by the introduction of the week of the Greeks and Romans, which can hardly (it is believed) have been recognized in India before the third or fourth century A D. Most famous of all, perhaps, in Hindu literature, is the great law-book of Manu. The native orthodoxy ascribed to it an enormous antiquity and a supernatural authority. For it professed to be derived from Manu, the first man, eponymous ancestor of the human race, who had himself been instructed in sacred truth by the Creator. He begins to impart his knowledge to the great sages, until the task is handed on to one of his ten sons, who transmits the revelation which he has received from his sire. Such a work (it was supposed) must at least have emerged from the most distant past, and at the outset of modern Sanskrit study Sir Wm Jones believed himself able to fix its date about the year 1280 B C. But recent investigation has destroyed the confident conviction of its early origin. Its metrical form, and other peculiarities, long ago suggested to Prof Max Muller the probability that it was the successor of a prior work in prose, which had been recast and versified. In the general revision of traditional views effected by European scholarship, the period of Manu has changed by leaps and bounds. Sir M Monier-Williams thought it possible at one time to detain it at about 500 B C[e]. Prof Cowell and Mr Wheeler carried it down to the centuries immediately preceding or following our era; Prof Buhler argues that it certainly existed before 200 A D[f], while Dr Burnell proposes the fourth century, and

---

[a] The *Mahā-Padhāna Sutta*, in the *Dīgha-Nikāya*.
[b] Cp the translation by Prof T W Rhys Davids, *Buddhist Birth-Stories* 53. .; for the events after the attainment of Buddhahood, cp *Vinaya-Pitaka* (ed Oldenberg) 1 p 3.., with *Jātaka* (ed Fausböll) i p 80...
[c] Cp Buhler, SBE 11 p liv.   [d] SBE vii, with Prof Jolly's introduction.
[e] *Indian Wisdom*³ 215, and the more guarded language of *Religious Thought and Life in India* 51.
[f] SBE xxv p cxvii   Cp Jolly, *Recht und Sitte* 16 (in Buhler's *Grundriss der I A Philologie*).

Prof Max Müller is prepared to see it assigned to a date even later still. The change is of much significance for the social history of India. The supposition that the complicated system of caste divisions, the elaborate philosophy, the highly developed ritual, implied in this code, existed in a remote antiquity, and belonged to an era not far removed from that of the Exodus, made it difficult to bring them within historic view at all. Long before there was anything that could be properly called historical evidence of the actual condition of India, it was supposed to have reached advanced heights of speculative thought, of ceremonial religion, or of class organization. If Manu had been contemporary with Moses, no coherent picture of the evolution of Indian faiths would have been possible.

(δ) The instances just cited are concerned rather with the general use of ancient consecrated material in new and later forms than with the actual welding of two or more sources into a single whole. But this process also may be traced in a remarkable instance in the early Christian Church [a]. The Diatessaron of Tatian, the pupil of Justin the Martyr in Rome in the middle of the second century, was long conjectured to be a harmony of the Gospels. It was known that after Justin's death Tatian left Rome and returned to the East. The Diatessaron which bore his name speedily became popular in the Syrian Churches, and was even regarded in the fourth century as the standard form in which the Church at Edessa had preserved the Gospel [b]. In the fifth century it was publicly used in more than two hundred churches, and was known by the name of the 'Composite' Gospel, in contrast with the 'Separate' or 'Distinct.' For purposes of church service it was ultimately replaced by the canonical Gospels, but it was still copied for centuries; commentaries were written upon it; and an Arabic reproduction appeared soon after 1000 A D, which continued in circulation for another 300 years. The publication in 1876 of a Latin translation of a commentary by Ephraem the Syrian preserved in Armenian awoke the interest of Western scholars: twelve years later Father Ciasca issued the text of an Arabic version (Rome, 1888) founded on two MSS, one of which had been brought to the Vatican about 1719, while the other only reached Rome from Egypt in 1886. The materials of the Harmony obviously fall asunder into two groups, the First Three Gospels, and the Fourth. Of the latter nearly the whole has been preserved [c]; of the rest, about one-third has been sacrificed. The omissions are due partly to the existence of a large amount of common matter, though in any incident related by all the Evangelists the significant details are carefully collected from each, partly to doctrinal or other reasons (as in the case of the genealogies of Matthew and Luke) which cannot be precisely determined. While the causes are for the present purpose immaterial, the fact is significant. The purpose of combining the whole was not inconsistent with the rejection of some of the parts. As the Diatessaron opens and closes with passages from the Fourth Gospel, and the succession of the Johannine feasts is fairly maintained [d], John may be said in a general sense to constitute its literary base. But this is not inconsistent with the most startling transpositions. That the cleansing of the temple should be transferred to the final visit to Jerusalem is due to the desire to bring the narrative into accordance with the Synoptic testimony; but that the conversation with the Samaritan woman John 4^{4-15a} should be detached from its connexion (chap 6) and inserted after the return from Phenicia Mark 7^{31-37} (chap 21) is a singular instance of violent dislocation. In the non-Johannine sections each Gospel in turn seems to take the temporary lead, in

[a] Prof G F Moore first called attention to this parallel in his article entitled 'Tatian's Diatessaron and the analysis of the Pentateuch,' *Journal of Biblical Literature* (1890) 201–215
[b] *Doctrine of Addai*, transl Phillips, p 34; *Dict of Christian Biogr* iv 796[b].
[c] Prof Moore reckons 847 verses out of 880, or over 96 per cent, to Matthew he assigns 821 out of 1071, or 76 5 per cent; to Mark 340 out of 678, or a fraction over 50 per cent; to Luke 761 out of 1151, or 66 2 per cent. *Journ of Bibl Lit* (1890) 203
[d] John 2^{23a} is omitted, and 2^{3b-25} is placed between Luke 7^{36-50} and 10^{1-12}, chap 15.

accordance with the apparent fullness of detail characteristic of special passages[a]. Thus the method of the Harmonist is constantly varying, and he perpetually adapts his materials to fresh combinations. Sometimes parallel passages are reproduced in sequence, by simple aggregation; thus the Sermon on the Mount Mt 5–7 receives into itself not only corresponding passages from Luke's version of the great discourse (e g Mt 5^{43-48} Lk 6^{32b-36} Mt 5^{47}.), but also numerous cognate sayings gathered elsewhere from Mark and Luke. The junctions are sometimes effected by a Gospel phrase (eg Jn 4^{46-54} Lk 4^{44} Mt 4^{13-16} in chap 6^{26-39}), or by some slight modification in which a subject is omitted or supplied, or by fresh particles of connexion which occasionally only emphasize the incompatibility of the sequence. Thus the narrative of the arrival of the Magi at Bethlehem Mt $2^{1..}$, the flight into Egypt, and the massacre of the Innocents, is introduced by the harmless-looking words 'and after that[b]' in place of the date 'Now when Jesus was born in Bethlehem' &c. The reason is plain: the passage follows Luke 2^{1-39}, which concludes with the return of Joseph and Mary with the babe 'to Galilee, to Nazareth their city.' The Harmonist thus satisfied himself with an arrangement that was obviously incongruous[c]. It is a singular instance (as Prof Moore remarks) of the conscientiousness with which the sources were reproduced, that the extract from Luke 2^{1-39} was not terminated at ^{38}, so as to avoid the contradiction involved in the sequence of ^{39} and Mt $2^{1..}$[d]. The general aspect of the product resulting from these methods may be realized by a couple of instances, one representing the treatment of narrative, the other the amalgamation of discourse[e]:—

Matthew	Mark	Luke	John
3^{13} Then came Jesus from Galilee to the Jordan to John, to be baptized of him.			
		3^{23a} And Jesus was about thirty years old, and it was supposed that he was the son of Joseph.	
			1^{29} And John saw Jesus coming unto him, and said, This is the Lamb of God, that taketh on itself the burden of the sins of the world. ^{30} This is he concerning whom I said, There cometh after me a man who was before me, because he was before me ^{31} And I knew him not; but that he should be made manifest to Israel, for this cause came I to baptize with water.
^{14} And John was hindering him and saying, I have need of being baptized by thee, and			

[a] Eg Matthew with Luke and Mark woven in, chap 11; Mk with Mt and Lk inserted, chap 7^{1-24}, Lk with incorporation of Mt and Mk, chap 6^{40-54}. So in the compound narrative of JE in the Hexateuch, now J and now E seems to provide the base. cp the predominance of J in the Abraham story Gen 12–25, and of E in the Egyptian scenes of Joseph's life Gen 40...

[b] Cp in Genesis the expression 'after these things' ^{JE}95.

[c] Similar incongruities may be found in the Pentateuch, cp notes on Gen 25^{21} Ex 16^2 18^{12}.

[d] Cp notes on Ex $34^{1..}$ and Deut $10^{1..}$.

[e] The translation is that of the Rev Hope W Hogg, BD (*Ante-Nicene Christian Library*, 1897); cp J Hamlyn Hill, BD, *The Earliest Life of Christ*, &c, 1894

Matthew	Mark	Luke	John
comest thou to me? ¹⁵ Jesus answered him and said, Suffer this now thus it is our duty to fulfil all righteousness. Then he suffered him.			
		²¹ᵃ And when all the people were baptized, Jesus also was baptized.	
¹⁶ᵃ And immediately he went up out of the water and heaven opened to him,			
		²²ᵃ And the Holy Spirit descended upon him in the similitude of the body of a dove	
¹⁷ And lo, a voice from heaven, saying, This is my beloved Son, in whom I am well pleased.			
			1³² And John bare witness and said, I beheld the Spirit descend from heaven like a dove; and it abode upon him. ³³ But I knew him not; but he that sent me to baptize with water, he said unto me, Upon whomsoever thou shalt behold the Spirit descending and lighting upon him, the same is he that baptizeth with the Holy Spirit ³⁴ And I have seen and borne witness that this is the Son of God.
		4¹ᵃ And Jesus returned from the Jordan, filled with the Holy Spirit.	
	1¹² And immediately the Spirit took him out into the wilderness,		
4¹ᵇ to be tried of the devil;			
	¹³ᵇ and he was with the beasts.		
²ᵃ And he fasted forty days and forty nights.			
		²ᵇ And he ate nothing in those days, and at the end of them he hungered	
7¹ Judge not, that ye be not judged			
		6³⁷ᵇ Condemn not, that ye be not condemned forgive, and it shall be forgiven you release, and ye shall be released · ³⁸ give, that ye may be given *unto* with good measure, abundant, full, shall they thrust into your bosoms	

Matthew	Mark	Luke	John
	4²⁴ᵇ See *to it* what ye hear: with what measure ye measure it shall be measured to you; and ye shall be given more. ²⁵ I say unto those that hear, He that hath shall be given *unto*, and he that hath not, that which he regards as his shall be taken from him.	With what measure ye measure it shall be measured to you.	
		³⁹ And he spake unto them a parable, can a blind man, &c	
⁶ Give not that which is holy unto the dogs, neither cast your pearls before the swine, lest they trample them with their feet, and return and wound you			
		11⁵ And he saith unto them, Who of you that hath a friend, &c.	

In such a product the problem of discovering and reconstructing the materials would be much harder than that presented by the Pentateuch. The sections from the Fourth Gospel could indeed be eliminated without difficulty. But the resolution of the remainder could only for the most part be tentative^a, though it might be certain that the narratives of the infancy, for example, were from different sources, or that the aggregation of parallel clauses in the Sermon on the Mount, chap 9¹⁵⁻²¹, pointed to a 'conflation' of independent texts. The evidence for the composition of the Pentateuch may be unhesitatingly pronounced to be far more decisive, though it must of course vary in clearness from passage to passage. The Pentateuch, which modern criticism resolves into four principal documents, is in fact the Diatessaron of the Old Testament.

(ε) Finally it may be pointed out that the Old Testament itself contains a conspicuous instance of the free treatment of earlier sources. The Books of Chronicles are generally recognized as the product of the Greek age [b]. They relate the story of the Davidic monarchy under the influence of the religious faith and usage of a later time. Advanced Levitical piety is here reflected back over the events of preceding centuries, and the conduct of princes is conformed to the standards of a period long subsequent to their own. The proof of this is found in the comparison of the representations of the Chronicler with the Books of Samuel and Kings. These books formed his chief source for the history of Judah [c], and his method of dealing with them is highly significant. From the death of Saul onward his narrative is based upon his predecessors, though these documents are not always treated in the same manner. Sometimes the statements of the older books are simply transferred to his own pages, and entire passages are reproduced *verbatim*. In other cases important modifications or additions indicate the presence of wholly fresh material. Whether this was derived from

---

[a] As is also the case with single Gospels like Matthew or Luke, which have the character of compilations from antecedent materials

[b] Driver, *LOT*⁶ 518 (in favour of a date subsequent to BC 300 rather than before) : W Robertson Smith, *OTJC*² 140 : Cheyne, *Jewish Religious Life after the Exile* xvi, about 250 BC, cp 213 W H Bennett, *Expositor's Bible* (Chronicles) 4, 'between BC 300 and BC 250.'

[c] Cp Driver, *LOT*⁶ 527, where a list of other works cited by the Chronicler will be found.

other works, or was supplied by the Chronicler himself, need not be now investigated; the characteristics of the process remain unaffected. Among the most remarkable incidents of David's reign is the description of the removal of the ark to Zion under Levitical protection, which is followed by the institution of a musical service of praise. The account of the ceremonial will be more fittingly considered elsewhere[a]; the festival closed with a solemn psalm 1 Chron. 16$^{7-36}$ to which the people joyously responded Amen. Even if this be regarded with Reuss as a later insertion[b], its composition is not less significant; it is compiled from Pss 105$^{1-15}$ 96 106$^{1-47}$. The correspondence between Solomon and Hiram is largely expanded, cp 2 Chron 2$^{3-16}$ with 1 Kings 5$^{3-9}$. In Solomon's prayer at the dedication of the Temple a different close is substituted, derived from Ps 132^8. The mode in which the old and the new are woven together may be illustrated from the reign of Amaziah, thus:—

2 Kings 14	2 Chron 25
^{2} He was twenty and five years old when he began to reign, and he reigned twenty and nine years in Jerusalem: and his mother's name was Jehoaddin of Jerusalem. ^{3} And he did that which was right in the eyes of Yahweh, yet not like David his father · he did according to all that Joash his father had done . . . ^{5} And it came to pass, as soon as the kingdom was established in his hand, that he slew his servants which had slain the king his father. ^{6} but the children of the murderers he put not to death according to that which is written in the book of the law of Moses, as Yahweh commanded, saying, The fathers shall not be put to death for the children, nor the children be put to death for the fathers; but every man shall die for his own sin ^{7} He slew of Edom in the Valley of Salt ten thousand, and took Sela by war, and called the name of it Joktheel, unto this day. ^{8} Then Amaziah sent messengers to Jehoash, the son of Jehoahaz son of Jehu, king of Israel, saying, Come, let us look one another in the face. ^{9} And Jehoash the king of Israel sent to Amaziah king of Judah, saying, The thistle that was in Lebanon sent to the cedar that was in Lebanon, saying, Give thy daughter to my son to wife: and there passed by a wild beast that was in Lebanon, and trode down the thistle. ^{10} Thou hast indeed smitten Edom, and thine heart hath lifted thee up glory thereof, and abide at home; for why shouldest thou meddle to *thy* hurt, that thou shouldest fall, even thou, and Judah with thee? ^{11} But Amaziah would not hear. So Jehoash king of Israel went up; and he and Amaziah king of Judah looked one another in the face at Beth-shemesh, which belongeth to Judah ^{12} And Judah was put to the worse before Israel; and they fled every man to his tent.	^{1} Amaziah was twenty and five years old when he began to reign; and he reigned twenty and nine years in Jerusalem · and his mother's name was Jehoaddan of Jerusalem. ^{2} And he did that which was right in the eyes of Yahweh, but not with a perfect heart. ^{3} Now it came to pass, when the kingdom was established unto him, that he slew his servants which had killed the king his father. ^{4} But he put not their children to death, but did according to that which is written in the law in the book of Moses, as Yahweh commanded, saying, The fathers shall not die for the children, neither shall the children die for the fathers; but every man shall die for his own sin. . . . ^{11} And Amaziah took courage, and led forth his people, and went to the Valley of Salt, and smote of the children of Seir ten thousand. ^{17} Then Amaziah king of Judah took advice, and sent to Joash, the son of Jehoahaz the son of Jehu, king of Israel, saying, Come, let us look one another in the face ^{18} And Joash king of Israel sent to Amaziah king of Judah, saying, The thistle that was in Lebanon sent to the cedar that was in Lebanon, saying, Give thy daughter to my son to wife: and there passed by a wild beast that was in Lebanon, and trode down the thistle. ^{19} Thou sayest, Lo, thou hast smitten Edom; and thine heart lifteth thee up to boast abide now at home; why shouldest thou meddle to *thy* hurt, that thou shouldest fall, even thou, and Judah with thee? ^{20a} But Amaziah would not hear; . . . ^{21} So Joash king of Israel went up; and he and Amaziah king of Judah looked one another in the face at Beth-shemesh, which belongeth to Judah ^{22} And Judah was put to the worse before Israel; and they fled every man to his tent.

Here 2 Kings 14^4 is omitted by the Chronicler as altogether incongruous with his view of Judah's religion; new materials are inserted $^{14-16}$ designed to prepare the way for the explanation of the victorious Amaziah's subsequent defeat, the secret of which is thus revealed:—

2 Kings 14	2 Chron 25
^{11} But Amaziah would not hear. So Jehoash king of Israel went up, &c.	^{20} But Amaziah would not hear; for it was of God, that he might deliver them into the hand *of their enemies*, because they had sought after the gods of Edom. ^{21} So Joash king of Israel went up, &c.

[a] Cp chap IX ii 1.   [b] *Gesch der Heil Schr des A Ts* 588.

The source of the statement concerning Amaziah's Edomite idolatries 2 Chron 25$^{14-16}$ is unknown; but in other instances it can hardly be doubted that the Chronicler simply ascribes to a king of noted piety the conduct which the situation seems to him to demand. Thus he reproduces in 2 Chron 29$^{1\cdot}$ the opening of the account of Hezekiah's reign in 2 Kings 18$^{2\cdot}$. But immediately after, stimulated by the reference to his reforming zeal in the older narrative, he starts on a highly independent course, and describes a solemn purification of the temple $^{3-36}$, according to the developed ritual of his own time. The proceedings extend through the first month of the first year, beyond the date assigned in the Levitical law for the celebration of the Passover. This is accordingly postponed to the second month 30^2, and proclamation is made from Beer-sheba to Dan summoning all Israel to Jerusalem ^{5}. The king's message $^{6-9}$ implies that the Assyrian deportation is already past, and his authority in the northern districts is uncontested, though Samaria was not captured till Hezekiah's sixth year 2 Kings 18^9, and Hoshea was still on the throne. The feast is kept with great joy, in a style unknown since the days of Solomon ^{26}. Concerning this celebration the older authority is entirely silent. The author of Kings has his own view of the first proper observance of the Passover; it did not occur till more than a hundred years later in connexion with the reforms in the eighteenth year of Josiah 2 Kings 23$^{21-23}$:—

^{21} And the king commanded all the people, saying, Keep the passover unto Yahweh your God, as it is written in this book of the covenant ^{22} Surely there was not kept such a passover from the days of the judges that judged Israel, nor in all the days of the kings of Israel, nor of the kings of Judah; ^{23} but in the eighteenth year of king Josiah was this passover kept to Yahweh in Jerusalem.

Of this ceremony, also, the Chronicler has his own account 2 Chron 35$^{1-19}$, in curious disproportion to the narrative which immediately precedes. A king so devout as Josiah could hardly have waited till his eighteenth year to purge his realm of its idolatries. According to 2 Chron 34$^{3-7}$, therefore, the reformation is placed in the twelfth year, the narrative in $^{3-5}$ being founded (with considerable modifications) on 2 Kings 23$^{4\ 6\ 14\ 20}$. The discovery of the book of the law is then related 2 Chron 34$^{8\cdot\cdot}$, on the basis of the account in 2 Kings 22$^{3\cdot\cdot}$ with numerous additions; the king's distress, the deputation to Huldah, the prophetess's reply, the great convocation in the temple, and the national covenant, all follow in due course. But these important events lead to nothing. The extract in 2 Chron 34$^{15-32}$ which reproduces 2 Kings 22^8-23^3 suddenly comes to a close, and a vague general statement ^{33} replaces the detail of Josiah's measures 2 Kings 23$^{4-20}$, which the Chronicler has already anticipated. That these exercises of pious imagination were not inconsistent with the deepest moral feeling, is plain from the entire tenor of the book. Rather were they the vehicle through which his faith expressed itself. Like the painter who depicted the penitent thief on the way to Calvary receiving from a monk the last consolations of the Church, he uttered in the only symbols which he knew the depth of his attachment to the established institutions of religion, and the strength of his trust in the righteousness of his God.

3. The processes by which ancient documents have assumed their present form are necessarily matters of inference. The earlier materials are superseded when they have been embodied in completer works; they are discarded and survive no more. In the endeavour to trace the growth of any great collection of poetry, history, or law, the student must be content to advance step by step. The methods of experimental demonstration are not at his command. His results depend on a number of considerations, the value of which will be differently estimated by different minds. Such arguments may suffice to establish certain negative conclusions: but the effort to attain positive results is continually baffled by the circumstance that this kind of reasoning can only reach varying degrees of certainty. Yet, on the other hand,

when a number of probabilities converge on a common conclusion, their strength in combination is much greater than would at first sight appear from the simple enumeration of them side by side[a].

(α) The judgements of the art-student, for example, are continually based upon this cumulative effect. By what criteria can a statue or picture be correctly referred to a particular sculptor or painter? External evidence may be altogether deficient, or only partially secure. The trained critic, who is conversant with the works of the founders and principal masters of each school, has learned to discriminate between their genuine productions and those of their pupils and imitators. He may, perhaps, seem to the unlearned to rely on a general impression; but he has himself arrived at this result by a number of different considerations which a practised judgement can sum up rapidly. He examines the choice of a subject, whether it be classical, sacred, or romantic. He contemplates the general design, the motives of the composition. He compares the peculiarities of form and expression, the pose of a figure, the shape of a face, the treatment of a hand or of an ear, the folds of a drapery, till he can perhaps assign them to successive periods in the career of a specific artist, under the varying influences of different great masters. Fresh evidence may be drawn from the scale and harmonies of colour, from the values of light and shade, from the adjustment of the perspective, or from the characteristics of the landscape with its arrangements of mountains, or trees, or sky. Beneath the surface-work of the unskilful restorer, he will try to frame some estimate of underlying peculiarities of method or technique. And he may sometimes become convinced that the hand of more than one artist is to be traced in the same picture through inequalities of execution or incongruities of style. It may be difficult, or indeed impossible, to say precisely where the touch of the master ceases and that of the pupil begins, yet there may be a practical certainty of judgement that the work is composite and must be assigned to a special school.

(β) The inquiry into the age and constituents of documents of unknown authorship reaches its conclusions, in like manner, along many different lines of evidence; and the strength of the result depends on the number of independent circumstances which point in the same direction. (i) The most satisfactory kind of external testimony is to be found in quotations in works of known date. But even this must be received with caution, for (1) the quotation or allusion may itself be suspected as an addition[b], while (2) in the case of a work which there is reason to regard as composite, the citation of an earlier portion does not guarantee the existence of the whole. Because Deut 24^{16} is quoted in 2 Kings 14^6 as an extract from the 'law of Moses,' it is not safe to infer that that title then included the entire Pentateuch. Again (ii) a document may contain a reference to the institutions of a particular age, or may employ a name whose origin is otherwise known. Thus it was early seen that the reference to the monarchy in Gen 36^{31} was incompatible with Mosaic authorship (cp chap III 3): while the statement that Abram pursued the invading kings as far as Dan Gen 14^{14}, at once places the existing form of the narrative (whatever may have been its antecedents) after the Danite migration Judg 18^{29}, unless the desperate hypothesis be invoked that there was an earlier and independent place of the same name. How far ancient sayings in prophetic form can be employed as witnesses to the events which they foretell, must depend largely on the general estimate which may be formed concerning the narrative in which they occur. The modern scholar finds in the well-known prophecy that the

---

[a] This is easily shown mathematically. If on each of several (say 3) independent grounds, it is only slightly probable (say 4 chances to 3) that a particular statement is true, the total chances in its favour will be 64 to 27: while high probability on one ground will overbalance lesser degrees of improbability on the other two.

[b] On 1 Sam 2^{22b} and its omission by 𝔊, cp Driver, *Notes on Sam* 26, and below chap XIII 4a.

descendants of Aeneas are to rule over the Trojans [a], a probable indication of interpolation due to local interests, and pointing to the existence of an Aenead dynasty in the Troad [b]. When Isaac announces on the one hand the lordship of Israel over Edom, and on the other Edom's successful revolt Gen $27^{29\,40}$, may it not be affirmed on similar literary grounds that the character of the language has been determined by later political events?   Another line of argument (iii) may be founded on incongruities within the same narrative. Are its representations of fact consistent with each other? Does it offer throughout the same view of religious history, of the progress of revelation? Or is it marked by differences of general conception and varieties of leading idea? Again, does it portray the events and institutions of a given period harmoniously, and, if not, what is the cause of the discrepancy? It will be seen from the following exposition that the modern theory of the Pentateuch has been slowly forced on successive generations of scholars by the diversity of its statements on the one hand concerning the divine dealings with the ancestors of Israel and the progenitors of the human race, and on the other concerning the regulations for worship established through the agency of Moses. If such diversity can be proved to exist, the several elements cannot all be of one date, and it may be possible to establish some order of succession among them.   But (iv) it may reasonably be expected that materials of different ages, drawn from separate sources, will be marked by their own characteristics of style or expression. Peculiar turns of phrase, due to the vivacity of oral narrative, or significant of legal precision, or repeated by the impassioned earnestness of the preacher, may be found to coincide with different groups of narrative or law already distinguished from each other by incompatibilities of content. The recurrence of these peculiarities becomes in its turn a warning; and each additional instance, in accordance with the general law of probabilities, brings far more than its own individual weight. Moreover their effect is again heightened if there is reason to believe that they can be in any way connected with other forces of thought and life. The journalist who should lightly talk of 'the tendency not ourselves' or of 'sweetness and light' might safely be placed with Matthew Arnold in the second half of the Victorian age. The teacher who dwelt on 'the silences' and 'the eternities' could not have taught before Carlyle. A cause must be found for the different philosophical vocabulary of Coleridge compared with that of Hume. The devotional utterance of Watts and Doddridge is couched in a different idiom from that of Newman and Faber. In the same way if one group of chapters which there is independent reason to assign to the seventh century, shows marked affinities of expression with Jeremiah, and another group with Ezekiel, it may be possible to explain the resemblances on the hypothesis of the indebtedness of the prophets, but the student must also consider the probability that they may be due to the influences of separate religious schools [c].   Lastly (v) the combination of independent documents will give rise, it may be anticipated, to occasional irregularities of junction, to editorial attempts at harmonizing conflicting statements, to the suppression of material from one source in favour of the account of another. Sometimes the preservation of a passage at a later stage in the story may enable the critic to conjecture the contents of an earlier and missing section, and even to assign a reason for its removal. The value of such suggestions must be greater or less according to the number and concurrence of the several lines of evidence which lead to them. The attempt to reconstruct the original contents of the different documents now traceable in a single whole, must necessarily be beset by manifold degrees of uncertainty. It may, however, be affirmed that though the close intermingling of various materials in some parts of the Hexateuch makes the task of criticism more difficult, yet the practical

---

[a] *Il* xx 307-8. [b] Cp Munro, *Encycl Brit* xii 119ᵃ.
[c] Cp chap X 2b and chap XIII 8ζ.

efficacy of the available criteria reduces the area of passages about which grave doubt remains within narrow limits, and confines them to details which are relatively unimportant. And the nature of the subject-matter compared with that of isolated Psalms or Prophecies is usually more favourable to definiteness of critical decision.

4. In the following pages it is sought to present to the English reader a general view of the grounds for believing that the Pentateuch is a composite work, compiled from materials of very various ages.

(a) The investigation starts from the statements which the books themselves present concerning the origin of the materials which they contain (chap II). The mode in which the existence of elements of post-Mosaic date was early recognized is briefly indicated (chap III), and the progress of inquiry into the signs of plurality of authorship is traced through the criticism of the seventeenth century (chap IV). On the clue supplied by Astruc's famous *Conjectures* (1753) the usage of the divine names between Gen 1 and Ex 6^2 is then examined (chap V); and evidence of diversity of source is obtained from the conflicting statements of the narrative itself. The recognition of this fact leads to the provisional determination of the number of the constituent documents (chap VI), and a sketch of the principal critical theories concerning their relations (chap VII). At this point the inquiry is widened to embrace a larger range of circumstances, such as the evidences of diversity in the representations of the institutions of the Mosaic age, of contrast in religious ideas, or of peculiarities in modes of expression; and it is shown that the laws and narratives tend to sort themselves into groups marked by similarity of historic view and by internal coherence of thought and language (chap VIII). The hypothesis which best seems to suit the facts is that the Pentateuch has been compiled out of three main sources, (1) a book of priestly law preceded by a short narrative introduction cast chiefly into genealogical form, **P**, (2) a book of national history, itself composite, deeply marked by prophetic ideas, wrought out of two strands respectively designated **J** and **E**, and (3) the Deuteronomic code **D**. On a consideration of their order of succession, it becomes highly probable that **D** holds the middle place between **JE** and **P** (chap IX). An examination of the laws and discourses of Deuteronomy establishes a connexion between them and the seventh century; the reformation of Josiah, 621 B.C., being the immediate result of the discovery and publication of the 'book of the law' (chap X). For **J** and **E** the origins are sought in the preceding period under the monarchies of Judah and Ephraim (chaps XI, XII); while the steps which led to the promulgation of the priestly legislation under Ezra and Nehemiah are traced in chap XIII, and the principal groups of material now aggregated in **P** are compared and distinguished. These general results are then set side by side with the facts established by archaeological research (chap XV, contributed by Prof Cheyne); and a sketch is finally offered (chap XVI) of the processes by which the Pentateuch may be supposed to have reached its present form.

(β) In this attempt to discriminate the constituents of the Five Books, as in the analysis which follows, the main results depend on the convergence of numerous lines of evidence. It appears no longer possible to resist the conclusion that different documents have been used. But though there may be practical certainty that a particular narrative may not be throughout homogeneous, the attempt to assign its different parts to specific sources can often only reach results of shifting probability, according to the variety and the value of the available criteria. It is inevitable that the indications should not always be equally numerous, or possess equal strength. But that does not disprove the legitimacy of the method, or cast doubts upon the general conclusion. The structure of the Pentateuch may be compared to the fabric of a great cathedral, whose external history is only imperfectly recorded. The origins of the church which first stood upon its site may be irrecoverably lost, though fragments of its stones may still be lodged in the foundation walls. The plan of the building may have been again and again enlarged; the transepts may now stand where once the west front was erected; the nave may have been converted from Norman to Perpendicular or may be a wholly fresh construction. Under successive bishops portions may have been pulled down and rebuilt; the style changed with the century; yet here a Norman arch remains contiguous with a piece of Early English, or the ancient vaulting has been preserved unharmed. Chapels have been added, windows enlarged, chantries inserted, and by perpetual small adaptations the new has been combined (though not always harmonized) with the old. It may happen that the cathedral archives or the chronicles of the adjacent abbey have preserved some mention of the completion of a tower, or the dedication of an altar. Yet the real story is inscribed upon the venerable walls. By the comparison of the parts among themselves, and with other edifices of known date, it becomes possible first to relate them to each other, and then to establish their probable order in time within tolerably exact limits. The mind that planned and the hands that executed the chief features of the design may have passed away, to remain for ever obscure; but we may still know who were their contemporaries, and under what influences they wrought the soaring arch or lifted pinnacle and spire towards heaven. Not dissimilar in method is the process which seeks to trace in the growth of the Pentateuch through succeeding centuries the rise of the sanctuary of Israel's faith and life. And just as the devotion of many generations remains unaffected by the discovery that the history of the church-fabric may have been misread in a less discerning age, so if the venerable work here considered be now seen to embrace the main courses of the development of the religion of Israel, it still stands with unimpaired grandeur as the stately introduction to the great series of sacred writings which find their climax in the New Testament.

CHAPTER II

THE CLAIM TO CONTEMPORARY AUTHORSHIP

THE investigation into the origins of the books of Moses and Joshua naturally begins with the inquiry whether they raise any claim themselves to have been composed by the authors whose names have been attached to them. This question can only be settled by a brief review of the evidence.

1. The books of Genesis and Leviticus make no allusion to the reduction of their narratives or laws to writing. But in other parts of the Hexateuch occasional references may be observed.

(*a*) Thus in Ex 17^{14} Moses is instructed to record the divine intention to efface Amalek :—

> And Yahweh said unto Moses, Write this for a memorial in a book, and rehearse it in the ears of Joshua that I will utterly blot out the remembrance of Amalek from under heaven [a]

According to 24^4 'Moses wrote all the words of Yahweh,' and the document was the foundation of a solemn covenant of obedience. What was 'this book of the covenant'? Ewald (*Hist* i 74^1) identified the words with the Decalogue. But the majority of recent critics, in view of the fact that in ³ the 'words of Yahweh' are combined with 'the judgements,' identify the Covenant-book (according to the present

---

[a] Interpreters differ as to the scope of the record. If the marginal rendering 'for' be adopted (in place of 'that'), the command 'write this' will not refer to the subsequent declaration of Yahweh's purpose, but to the Amalekite attack ⁸, with its savage cruelty to the weak and weary in the rear Deut 25^{17-19}, which is assigned as the reason why Amalek's remembrance should be erased.

arrangement of the text) with the entire section 20^{22}-23^{33}, the 'judgements' entering at 21^1. The problem is complicated (as will be seen by the notes on the passage) by a reference to a second set of covenant 'words' in 34^{27}:—

> And Yahweh said unto Moses, Write thou these words: for after the tenor of these words I have made a covenant with thee and with Israel.

The statement in the sequel ^{28} is, however, obscure: 'And he wrote upon the tables the words of the covenant, the ten words.' Who was the actual writer, Moses, or Yahweh, who in 34^1 had himself promised to reinscribe on the new tables the words which he had engraven on the first? The probable answer to this question will be found in the analysis: at present it need only be noted that if the writer be identified with Moses, the narrative does not claim more for him than the record of the sacred 'words.'

(β) The book of Numbers only attributes to Moses a list of the stages of the Israelite march 33^2. It is doubtful whether the actual survey of the wanderings $^{3-49}$ is to be identified with this list. Apart from peculiarities in its form, the context suggests that the supposed Mosaic document was employed by the author, who used it as his source, but did not profess to reproduce it *verbatim*.

(γ) The affirmations of Deuteronomy are more explicit. Two accounts are given in 31^{9-13} and $^{24-26}$ of the writing of 'this law,' which is then committed to the custody of the Levites:—

31	31
^{9} And Moses wrote this law, and delivered it unto the priests the sons of Levi, which bare the ark of the covenant of Yahweh, and unto all the elders of Israel	^{24} And it came to pass, when Moses had made an end of writing the words of this law in a book, until they were finished, ^{25} that Moses commanded the Levites, which bare the ark of the covenant of Yahweh, saying, ^{26} Take this book of the law, &c.

What, then, is included in the expressions 'this law,' 'this book of the law'? It is plain from other passages, such as 1^5 4^8, that it is limited to the law communicated in the land of Moab. The law is described as consisting of 'statutes and judgements' 5^1, and appears formally to begin in 12^1:—

> These are the statutes and the judgements, which ye shall observe to do in the land which Yahweh, the God of thy fathers, hath given thee to possess it, all the days that ye live upon the earth.

We are not concerned now with the fact that the law appears to have existed as a book before it was written 28^{58} ^{61} 29^{20} ^{27} 30^{10}: it is sufficient to observe that its announcement is still in the future in 4^8, and it cannot therefore include more than the discourses and commands comprised in 5–30 [a]. In addition to 'this law,' 31^{22} further attributes to Moses the composition of the Song in 32^{1-43}. The Blessing recorded in 33 is not said to have been *written* by him.

(δ) Finally in Josh 24^{26} it is said that 'Joshua wrote these words in the book of the law of God.' There is some difficulty in determining the precise application of this statement. It is commonly limited to the discourse in 24^{1-23} (so Briggs, *Higher Criticism* 11; Dillmann proposes also to include 23). But Kuenen points out that the reference is rather to the terms of the covenant ^{25}. The record in the law-book was concerned with the contents of the 'statute and ordinance' then first imposed [b]. In no case, however, is there any warrant for extending the phrase to cover the existing book of Joshua.

(ϵ) Apart, however, from the allusions to Mosaic writing, there are occasional indications of other sources. The antique poetic fragments in the early stories of

---

[a] Whether it even contained so much is discussed elsewhere. See notes to Deut 1^1 5^1 12^1 27^1.
[b] For further detail see notes *in loc.*

Genesis are not expressly derived from any lyric collection. But in Num 21^{14} a few lines of verse are preserved which are attributed in our present text to 'the book of the wars of Yahweh.' No other citation from this book occurs in the Old Testament. The passage is undoubtedly obscure ^{a}, but it is a reasonable supposition that the poem was derived from a book bearing the name of 'The Wars of Yahweh.' The analogy of other works suggests that this was a collection of poems of various ages celebrating the heroic enterprises of Israel in fighting the battles of Yahweh Judges 4^{14} 5$^{4\ 11\ 23}$ &c 1 Sam 18^{17} 25^{28}: and the view of the Davidic campaigns in this light 2 Sam 8$^{6\ 14}$ 7^1 renders the early monarchy a probable date for such an anthology ^{b}. A similar work is cited in Josh 10$^{12.}$ under the name of the Book of Jashar. To this book also belongs the lament of David over Saul and Jonathan 2 Sam 1$^{18..}$, and perhaps the ancient version of Solomon's words at the dedication of the Temple ^{c} 1 Kings 8$^{12..}$. A corresponding period is thus reached for the two quotations.

(ζ) So far, then, as written sources are specified for the Hexateuch, it would seem that they were of various dates. No doubt, as the tradition of the Synagogue shows in a later age, a presumption arose in after generations that laws which were said to have been revealed to Moses were also put in writing by him. On the other hand, the implications in the passages which expressly refer to Mosaic composition are unfavourable to the view that the Five Books were reduced to their present form by him.

2. The indications of subsequent literature suggest that Moses was only gradually connected by tradition with the production of a continuous body of legislation.

(a) To Hosea he was the prophet by whom Yahweh brought Israel up out of Egypt 12^{13}. Micah groups him with Aaron and Miriam 6^4; Jeremiah associates him with Samuel 15^1. Even to the author of Is 63$^{11..}$ Moses is the heroic leader under divine guidance to whom Israel owed its liberty rather than its laws. Malachi is the first of the prophets to refer to a Mosaic code 4^4. For the pre-exilian seers there was no fixed and definite 'law,' recorded in precise and authoritative form. The term denoted originally a 'teaching' or pronouncement. This 'teaching' was in ancient times in the charge of the priestly tribe of Levi Deut 33^{10}; and their deliverances at the sanctuary constituted a body of instruction which might have many different themes, and rest on varying antecedents. Thus it had a judicial significance, when appeals were heard and decisions were given 17^{11}; in this aspect *torah* bore the character of a 'judgement.' Or it might be concerned with ritual or ceremonial practice, as was contemplated by Ezekiel 44^{23}; while Haggai (2^{11} 'ask the priests for a *torah*') shows that even after the exile this duty still remained with the priests But it might also have purely moral and religious aspects, as when Isaiah equates the term with the prophetic word 1^{10} 5^{24}, and employs it to denote the substance of his teaching. That written *torah* existed in the eighth century is certainly implied in the language of Hosea 8^{12}:—

Though I write for him my law in ten thousand *precepts*, they are counted as a strange thing.

But the 'teaching' which Yahweh thus continues to indite, is plainly no fixed or completed 'law': it is the sum of revelation which is perpetually receiving fresh additions ^{d}.

---

^{a} In the *Academy* for Oct 22, 1892, Prof Sayce proposed to correct the text thus, 'Wherefore it is said in a book, The wars of Yahweh were at Zahabh in Suphah.'
^{b} Meyer and Stade propose to place it in the ninth century.
^{c} So first Wellhausen. The suggestion is adopted with confidence by W Robertson Smith, *OTJC*^{2} 124, 435 Cp Cheyne, *Origin of Psalter* 212; Driver, *LOT*^{6} 192.
^{d} It has been argued from Jer 7$^{21..}$ that Jeremiah, though himself a priest, was unacquainted with any recognized body of ritual *torah* claiming Mosaic origin or authority. On the prophetic use of the term, cp Driver, *Joel and Amos* 230.

(β) The books of Judges and Samuel contain no references to Mosaic 'teaching'; but the editors of Kings undoubtedly have a definite standard of religious law which plainly includes the Deuteronomic code. When the dying David conveys his final counsels to his successor, his political advice is introduced by a brief exhortation 1 Kings 2³ :—

> Keep the charge of Yahweh thy God, to walk in his ways, to keep his statutes, and his commandments, and his judgements, and his testimonies, according to that which is written in the law of Moses, that thou mayest prosper in all that thou doest.

The colouring of the language at once points to the book of Deuteronomy^a, and this identification is strengthened by 2 Kings 14⁶ :—

> But the children of the murderers he put not to death according to that which is written in the book of the law of Moses, as Yahweh commanded, saying, The fathers shall not be put to death for the children, nor the children be put to death for the fathers, but every man shall die for his own sin.

where the writer obviously cites Deut 24¹⁶ :—

> The fathers shall not be put to death for the children, neither shall the children be put to death for the fathers every man shall be put to death for his own sin.

Further evidence might easily be accumulated^b, but the proof that the 'book of the law' to which the compilers refer elsewhere 2 Kings 22⁸ really consisted of Deuteronomy^c, will be best exhibited at a future stage of the argument (cp chap X 3β). The second version of the history of the monarchy, however, in Chronicles, with its continuation in the books of Ezra and Nehemiah, rests apparently upon a different basis. They contain repeated allusions to the 'law of Yahweh,' the 'law of God,' but also to 'the law (or book) of Moses' 2 Chron 23¹³ 30¹⁶ 35¹² Ezr 3² 6¹⁸ 7⁶ Neh 8¹. These passages imply an acquaintance not only with Deuteronomy (as in 2 Chron 25⁴ Neh 13¹) but also with the main requirements of the Levitical ritual. Delitzsch has, indeed, expressed his belief^d that 'nowhere in the canonical literature of the Old Testament do the terms "the law," "the book of the law," "the law of Moses," cover the Pentateuch in its present form.' Reasons will be offered hereafter for believing that to be true of Ezr 6¹⁸ 7⁶ Neh 8¹ (cp chap XIII 6). But in view of the use which the Chronicler makes not only of the Levitical institutions but also of the genealogical forms of Genesis, it can hardly be doubted that the 'book of the law of Moses' which served for him as the norm of Israel's worship, comprised the united documents much as we have them now^e. In the Greek age, then, to which the Chronicles must be assigned^f, the Mosaic tradition may be regarded as fully formed. But it must be borne in mind that the earliest testimony to Moses as the author of the Pentateuch is thus found to date a thousand years after the Exodus^g.

(γ) The Jewish people naturally maintained and propagated this view. In Moses it found the teacher of a divine lore which could only have been derived from the wisdom of God himself; and in his priority before the later civilization of Greece the champions of Judaism delighted to discover proof that their nation had thus supplied the most brilliant of the Mediterranean races with the primary truths of religion. The learning of Palestine and the philosophy of Egypt were in this matter entirely

---

^a Cp ² 'be strong' Deut 31⁷ Josh 1⁶ ⁹ ¹¹ ᴰ106 ³ 'walk in his ways' ᴰ115, 'keep' &c ᴰ82⁰, 'statutes, commandments' &c ᴰ104ᵃ, 'prosper' Deut 29⁹ Josh 1⁷. . ⁴ 'with all their heart and with all their soul' ᴰ59.
^b Cp Ryle, *Canon of the Old Testament* 53.
^c In its earliest and simplest form, cp chap X 4.   ^d *Genesis* 13
^e The possibility of subsequent editorial additions is of course not excluded
^f Cp Driver, *LOT*⁶ 518.   ^g Adopting the common figure, about 1320 B C.

at one. The Rabbis in the schools, Josephus addressing the cultivated minds of the Empire, Philo wrestling at Alexandria with the problem of combining the highest forms of Hellenic thought with the ripest fruits of Hebrew faith, all started from the same fundamental assumption. It passed by natural sequence into the Christian teaching. It is ascribed by the Evangelists to Jesus Christ. It appears in the records of apostolic preaching, as it also underlies the epistolary arguments of St Paul. It is the common theme of the Talmud and the Christian apologist; and became the accepted basis of the entire conception of historical revelation alike for the Synagogue and for the Church.

CHAPTER III

SIGNS OF POST-MOSAIC DATE

The byways of both Jewish and Christian literature are not without traces of occasional departure from the customary view. In the absence of critical method the reasons for divergence might at first have no other basis than legend or doctrinal dislike; until the attention of scholars was slowly and hesitatingly called to facts which appeared inconsistent with the received tradition, and the search was at length fairly begun for the true principles of literary and historical inquiry [a].

1. Before the first century of our era ran out, the apocryphal work known as the Fourth Book of Ezra [b] related a strange story which showed how deep an impression had been made by the tradition of Ezra's literary labours. The law had been burned, and Ezra prayed for the gift of holy spirit that he might write anew all that had happened in the world since the beginning 2 Esdr 14^{21}... He was directed to take with him five men, and they went forth into the field. There on the next day he heard a voice bidding him open his mouth, and drink what was given him. It was a draught like fire, so that his heart poured forth understanding and for forty days he dictated to his companions, who needed food only at night, till ninety-four books were complete. These were divided into twenty-four, the former number of the Hebrew scriptures, with seventy new ones; and Ezra was thus represented as the great restorer of a lost literature. The tale was not without its influence on later writers. Irenaeus represents a moderate form of it in ascribing to Ezra the inspired rearrangement of the words of earlier prophets and the re-establishment of the Mosaic legislation [c]. Clement of Alexandria affirms that by the exercise of prophecy Ezra restored again the whole of the ancient Scriptures [d]. Tertullian, arguing that Noah preserved through the deluge the memory of the book of Enoch his great-grandfather, asserts that even if it had been destroyed by the violence of the flood he could have renewed it by the inspiration of the spirit, as Ezra was generally admitted to have done in the case of the entire Jewish literature [e]. After two centuries more Jerome was equally willing to speak of Moses as the author of the Pentateuch or Ezra as its renewer [f]. This view did not of course affect the question of a Mosaic origin. But this was early called in question both within and without the Church. The Jewish sect of Nasareans were said by John of Damascus in the eighth century to have asserted that the Pentateuch was not by Moses [g]. The author of the Clementine homilies assumed that Moses had promulgated

---

[a] See the catena in Holzinger's *Einleitung* 1 § 6 p 25; Westphal, *Sources du Pentateuque* 1.
[b] Commonly ascribed to the reign of Domitian.
[c] *Adv Haer* iii 21.   [d] *Strom* i 22   [e] *De Cult Fem* 3.
[f] 'Sive Moysen dicere volueris auctorem Pentateuchi, sive Esdram eiusdem instauratorem operis non recuso.' *Adv Helvid* (de Perpetua Virginitate B Mariae) 7.
[g] *De Haer* 19. Cp Epiphan *Adv Haer* 1 18, and *Dict of Christ Biography*, 'Nasaraei.'

his teaching orally, and communicated the law to seventy elders. They in their turn departed from the founder's intention by reducing it to writing, but even their work had undergone so many vicissitudes of destruction and renewal, that the form in which the Church received it stood at many removes from the original injunctions of its first author[a]. These casual speculations were plainly founded on grounds of doctrine or usage, and had no genuine critical base. The only contribution towards a real historic criticism which this age affords, is to be found in Jerome's identification of the law-book of Josiah with Deuteronomy[b].

2. The first beginnings of criticism came from the Spanish Rabbis. The Mosaic convention was so deeply impressed on the life and thought of Israel, that it could only be questioned under a veil of the most cautious reserve. Nevertheless a certain Isaac, sometimes identified with Isaac ben Jasos (otherwise known as Jischaki) of Toledo, A D 982-1057, pointed out that Gen 36^{31} must be later than the foundation of the Hebrew monarchy, and proposed to assign the chapter in its present form to the age of Jehoshaphat. Ibn Ezra (1088-1167) through whom alone Isaac's criticism reaches us, was himself prepared to proceed much further. To the words 'beyond Jordan' in Deut 1^1 he attached this mysterious commentary: 'and if thou understandest the mystery of the twelve; and Moses wrote; and the Canaanite was then in the land; in the mount of Yahweh it shall be provided; also behold his bed was a bedstead of iron,—thou shalt discern the truth.' The riddles are most of them plain for all to read. Of the first, however, more than one solution is possible. The mystery or 'secret of the twelve' seems most appropriately explained of the twelve verses of Deut 34 which describe the death of Moses. It has also been identified with the twelve curses which the Levites were to recite on Gerizim 27^{15-26}, or the twelve stones of which (said the rabbis) the altar on Ebal was built 27^4. Josh 8^{30}. As the whole law was to be written on these stones, it must have been far less copious than the present Pentateuch. The citation 'and Moses wrote,' derived from Deut 31^9, is apparently the statement of another person. The allusion to the Canaanite Gen 12^6 is only intelligible when the Canaanites had ceased (as in Solomon's reign) to be a distinctive portion of the population. The proverb in 22^{14} was understood to refer to the 'mount of Yahweh' or temple-mountain (cp Moriah ^{2}), and again pointed to the age of Solomon at the earliest. Lastly the 'bedstead' of Og Deut 3^{11} is specified as an interesting relic of a vanished race; but how is such a description consistent with the view that Moses is relating the victory of a few months (or weeks) before? These passages, therefore, clearly proved the existence of post-Mosaic additions or expansions in the Five Books.

3. The hints of Ibn Ezra remained long unfruitful. No teacher of the synagogue was found to venture further along his perilous path[c]. But with the advent of the sixteenth century the new learning began to work upon men's minds. Already in 1520 Carlstadt published at Wittenberg an essay concerning the canonical scriptures, in which he observed that as the style of narration after the death of Moses remained unchanged, it was a defensible view that Moses was not the author of the Five Books. On the other hand the definite ascription of writing to Moses and Joshua Deut 31^9 · · Josh 24^{26}, and the story of the discovery of the law-book under Josiah 2 Kings 22,

---

[a] *Clem Hom* III 47   [b] *Comm in Ezek* 1^1
[c] A word should perhaps be said of the learned Isaac Abravanel (Abarbanel) who died at Venice in 1509, after a life of romantic vicissitude which proved not inconsistent with copious literary production. He expounded the Pentateuch, but his most distinguished work was a commentary on the 'Prophetae Priores,' the books of Joshua, Judges, Samuel, and Kings. In the preface to Joshua he advocated a theory of the composition of the books out of collections of documents in which public scribes from time to time recorded important events. The theory of archivists was destined to gain some prominence afterwards, at the hands of Du Maes; and is expressly cited by Father Simon (*Critical History of the OT*, 1682) chap II. Cp chap IV 18.

rendered it impossible to attribute them to Ezra. Their real author, therefore, remained obscure. Luther, who maintained a highly independent position towards the ecclesiastical tradition about scripture, asked what it mattered if Moses had not himself written the Pentateuch, and pointed, like R Isaac, to the allusion to the monarchy in Gen 36^{31}. Catholic scholars, also, began to call attention to neglected facts. Andrew du Maes, a Flemish priest, published a commentary on Joshua in 1570 at Antwerp. He boldly regarded the book as part of a series of records extending through Judges, Samuel, and Kings, which were arranged out of previous materials by some man of piety and learning like Ezra or one of his contemporaries, under the guidance of the Holy Spirit. He cited the reference to the Book of Jashar Josh 10^{13} as the mark of a later writer producing ancient testimony in confirmation of what had been lost in dim antiquity. He pointed to the use of the name Dan in 19^{47} and Gen 14^{14} as evidence of composition long after the days of Moses and Joshua; and drew a similar conclusion with respect to the Pentateuch from Josh 14^{15}. If Caleb's family gave the name Hebron to a city which was formerly called Kiriath-arba, then the references to Hebron in the previous books (eg Gen 13^{18} $23^{2\,19}$ 35^{27} 37^{14} Num 13^{22}) must be all post-Mosaic. The Jesuit theologians followed along the same lines. The Spanish Bento Pereira^{a} ranged himself with Du Maes, quoting his words though not his name. A quarter of a century later another Fleming, Jacques Bonfrère, argued that if Joshua made additions to the sacred law Josh 24^{26}, there could be no objection to the view that the Pentateuch had received insertions from a later hand. Such passages, like the reference to the Danite conquest in Josh 19^{47}, might have been appended by Samuel or Ezra. Nor were the Reformers of Holland less willing to acknowledge post-Mosaic material than the members of the Society of Jesus. The learned Episcopius, who died at Leyden in 1643, expressed his belief^{b} that not only had the last six verses of Deuteronomy been added by Joshua or Eleazar, but a good many others also had been inserted here and there by Ezra (ie in Deut), as well as throughout the other books, examples being found in Num 12^3 Gen 35^{19} 48^7 *aliaque complura*.

CHAPTER IV

SIGNS OF DIVERSITY OF DOCUMENTS

THE theory of Du Maes, in assimilating the composition of the Pentateuch to that of the historical books which follow it in the Hebrew Canon, assumed its compilation out of numerous antecedent documents. Nearly two centuries, however, were to elapse before the key to their separation was supplied by another student from the Low Countries.

1. In the latter half of this period the problem was attacked by numerous writers, representing widely different schools both in religion and philosophy. A brief sketch of their arguments will show what it was possible to accomplish while criticism was still feeling after a method, and had not yet discovered the right clue.

(*a*) In the third part of the *Leviathan* xxxii (1651), Hobbes put aside the title 'five books of Moses' as of no weight in deciding the question of authorship. Who supposed that the Judges, or Ruth, or the kings of Israel and Judah, had written the books bearing their names? 'In titles of books the subject is marked as often as the writer.' The evidences of post-Mosaic additions were ready to hand; the familiar passages were

---

[a] In commentaries published at Lyons, 1594-1600
[b] *Institut Theol* III v 1, Amsterdam, 1650.

quoted with incisive little comments: Gen 12^6 'must needs be the words of one that wrote when the Canaanite was not in the land, and consequently not of Moses who died before he came into it': Num 21^{14} 'the writer citeth another more ancient book.' Still it might be concluded that 'Moses wrote all that he is said to have written^a, as for example, the volume of the Law which is contained as it seemeth in the eleventh of Deuteronomy and following chapters to the twenty-seventh.' Hobbes here anticipates an important modern view in thus isolating the Deuteronomic code from its envelope of historic recital and homiletic exhortation; and he took another step in identifying it with the law 'which, having been lost, was long after found again by Hilkiah and sent to King Josiah 2 Kings 22^8.'

(β) Five years after the publication of the *Leviathan* a little book appeared anonymously in London under the strange title *Men before Adam*. It was a translation of a Latin treatise called *Prae-adamitae*, founded on Rom 5$^{12-14}$, which had been published in Paris in 1654, with a *Systema Theologicum ex prae-adamitarum hypothesi*. The author, Isaac de la Peyrère, was a Calvinist, who had formed the view that the Pentateuch described the origin only of the Jewish people, the greater part of humanity being descended neither from Adam, nor from Noah. He was thus led into a literary inquiry concerning its compilation; it was no autograph of Moses, it consisted of extracts and copies arranged by another. Fresh examples (beside those already so often cited) appear upon his pages^b. Thus, the allusions to Jair Deut 3^{14} and to Og 3^{11} belonged to later days. In Deut 2 he thought that he detected a reference to the Davidic conquest of Edom, celebrated in Ps 108. For proof that the materials of the narratives were composite, he pointed to the abruptness of the introduction of Lamech's song in Gen 4^{23} without any previous explanation, and to the fragmentary character of the story of circumcision in Ex 4$^{24-26}$. The episode of Gen 20 was placed too late, for Sarah, when past ninety years of age, could hardly have been sought as a wife by Abimelech. A similar difficulty beset the similar incident in 26$^{7..}$, where Rebekah is represented as still beautiful and a possible object of desire, long after her sons were grown up. Other displacements occurred in Ex 18 (where an additional perplexity was noted in the appearance of Jethro with the wife and sons whom Moses had taken to Egypt 4^{20}), and in Deut 10, where the separation of Levi and the death of Aaron were attached to wrong dates and localities. In this obscurity and confusion, as if hot conflicted with cold and moist with dry, the only possible conclusion was that the different statements were derived from different documents.

(γ) The same result was reached by Spinoza in the *Tractatus Theologico-politicus* (1671^c, viii-ix), who devoted special attention to the chronological embarrassments. Starting from the passages already discerned by Ibn Ezra, he pointed out further that the writer of the Mosaic story not only continually spoke of Moses in the third person, but even testified to his exalted eminence, e.g. Num 12^3 14^{14} Deut 33^1 (Moses was a 'divine man'). The stress laid on Mosaic writing^d showed that he had composed a book containing commentaries on the law, but the book as it issued from the hand of Moses was no longer extant. Spinoza was largely under the influence of the Ezra legend, and he identified the book promulgated by Ezra Neh 8^9 with Deuteronomy, 'written fairly out, annotated, illustrated, and explained' by him. His general view is thus expounded:—

> I am, moreover, disposed to conclude that this was the first book written by Ezra of all that came from his hand, and for this reason, that it contains the law of the country which is the most

---

^{a} Pereira had already called attention to the passages in Ex 17 24 and Deut 31.
^{b} Book IV chap 1.
^{c} The passages here cited are derived from the English translation published in 1862.
^{d} Spinoza identified the words and judgements Ex 24$^{4\ 7}$ with 20$^{22-23}$.

requisite to be known to the people; and also because this book is not connected with the one which precedes it by any conjunction, as all the others are with their antecedents. . . . Having achieved this first work, the purpose of which was to make the knowledge of the laws accessible to the people, I believe that Ezra then set about the task of narrating the entire history of the Hebrew nation, from the creation of the world to the destruction of Jerusalem, in which large undertaking he inserted this book of Deuteronomy in its proper place.

Ezra, indeed, did little but gather materials from earlier writers: 'but,' continues Spinoza,—

these ancient documents having all perished, we have no resource but critically to study the histories that have come down to us, to scrutinize their order and connexion, the various repetitions in their course, and finally the discrepancies in the reckonings of the years, in order that we may form a judgement of what remains.

Of these chronological difficulties Spinoza discusses two conspicuous examples. The first is that of the descendants of Judah and Tamar Gen 38, his conclusion being that Ezra reproduced it 'as he found it, without examining the matter very particularly, or making sure that it accurately fitted in with the other circumstances with which it was connected[a].' The second is founded on the narrative of Jacob, his marriages, and his children Gen 29-34[b]. The case is taken as a sample of the whole:—

Dinah could scarcely have been seven when she was violated by Shechem; and Simeon and Levi, again, scarcely twelve and eleven when they ravaged a city and put all the inhabitants thereof to the sword. But there is here no occasion to pass the whole of the Pentateuch under review; any one who observes that in these five books precept and narrative are jumbled together without order, that there is no regard to time, and that one and the same story is often met with again and again, and occasionally with very important differences in the incidents,—whoever observes these things, I say, will certainly say that in the Pentateuch we have merely notes and collections to be examined at leisure, materials for history, rather than the digested history itself.

(δ) The drastic criticisms of Spinoza were not left without reply in the brilliant age of the great French Catholics. The task of vindicating the authority of Scripture against speculative philosophy, and the principle of ecclesiastical tradition against exclusive reliance on an imperfect documentary record, was attempted by Father Simon, of the Congregation of the Oratory, whose *Critical History of the Old Testament* was published in an English translation[c] immediately after its appearance on the Continent[d]. Simon worked on the basis of his Catholic predecessors, Du Maes, Pereira, and Bonfrère. Much after the manner of Du Maes he framed a theory of the composition of the Pentateuch out of documents drawn up from time to time by recorders or keepers of public archives under the direction of Moses. He distinguished between the commandments divinely imparted to Moses himself, and the narratives in which they were set:—

As to what passed every day in his own presence, it was not necessary that God should dictate it to him; he had under him persons who put in writing all the considerable actions

---

[a] The position of Gen 38 places its events after Joseph had been sold into Egypt, when he cannot have been younger than seventeen 37^2. According to 41^{46} he was thirty when he stood before Pharaoh. The seven plenteous years follow immediately ^{47}, and two famine years have passed when he sends for Jacob 45^6. Between Joseph's arrival in Egypt and the descent of Jacob and his family, there is thus an interval of about twenty-two years. Now in 38^1 Judah marries Shua, and her children are Er, Onan, and Shelah. Er grows up and marries Tamar ^{6}. On his death Onan marries her; but when he also dies, she is not given to the surviving brother Shelah ^{11}. The result is that she conceives by her father-in-law ^{18}; her children are Perez and Zerah; and the sons of Perez, Hezron and Hamul, in the third generation from Judah, go down with Jacob 46^{12}. All this is crushed into the period of twenty-two years between 37^2 and 45-46.

[b] Spinoza's results seem to have been reached thus:—Jacob remained with Laban twenty years 31^{41}. His children were all born after his marriages, which took place after the first seven years of service 30^{20}., i e during the last thirteen years 29^{32-34}. Simeon and Levi, then, were scarcely twelve and eleven respectively at the Gilead interview 31^{23}.., and the events of 33-34 are regarded as following continuously without a break.

[c] London, 1682.

[d] Nothing is here said of the importance of this book for general Old Testament study, e g its discussion of the text and the versions. It is considered only in connexion with the history of Pentateuchal investigation.

and had the care of preserving them to posterity. We need but cast our eyes upon the method that the Pentateuch is composed in, to be persuaded of this truth, and to see that some other than Moses has corrected the historical parts.

This method could be carried back from the events of Moses' own time to the book of Genesis, which contained no reference to composition under supernatural dictation or by aid of the spirit of prophecy. The manner of the histories and genealogies was simple, 'as if Moses had taken them from some authentic books, or else had had a constant tradition.' Behind the books, as they have been received and propagated by the Church, there lay, therefore, a variety of documents which differed from each other in style and contents, even when they appeared to deal with the same subject or event. Hence arose confusions of order, so that after the creation of man and woman in Gen 1^{27}, 'the woman is supposed not to be made, and in the following chapter the manner how she was taken from Adam's side is described.' These confusions were especially manifest in the conflicting statements in the Deluge narrative concerning the length of the time that the waters remained upon the earth. Of 7^{17-24} Simon shrewdly observed, 'It is probable that if only one author had composed this work, he would have explained himself in fewer words, especially in a history.' The difficulties involved in the dates[a] were further hypothetically relieved by an ingenious conjecture of the misplacement of the 'leaves or scrolls on which the books were writ.' But this could not account for the 'variety of the style.' Here Simon recognized 'a convincing argument that one and the same man was not the author. Sometimes we find a very curt style, and sometimes a very copious one, although the variety of the matter does not require it.' It is perhaps surprising that Simon should have seen so far, yet not seen further. One step more, however, was possible before the true clue was discovered. That step was taken by one of Simon's critics, the Dutch Le Clerc.

(ε) Three years after Simon's treatise appealed to the English public, a small volume of letters was issued at Amsterdam, bearing the elaborate title *Sentimens de quelques Théologiens de Hollande sur l'Histoire critique du Vieux Testament composée par le P. Richard Simon*[b]. The real author, Jean Le Clerc, revealed at the outset a new conception of the scope and aim of Old Testament study. He placed it in line with all historic inquiry, and demanded that the conditions under which any given work was produced, should be carefully examined. The investigator should seek to discover what was the author's purpose, what led him to write at all, to what opinions or events he might allude[c]. This was the method which Eichhorn a hundred years later was to designate for the first time as 'the higher criticism.' Le Clerc accordingly set to work to ascertain what inferences might be drawn from the Pentateuch concerning the circumstances of its origin and authorship. From passages like Gen 2^{11}. 10^3..11^{1-9} he concluded that the writer had himself been in the countries which he described: 'God,' said he, 'was not concerned to reveal to Moses that the gold of that land was good.' Nineveh he connected with Ninus, whom he placed by the aid of secular history in the age of Deborah. The use of the

---

[a] The death of Isaac, Simon pointed out, was put too soon in Gen 35^{29}: Joseph had been sold into Egypt long before, yet that transaction was not related till 37. Jethro's visit, narrated in Ex 18, 'seems not to be placed in the time wherein it was, forasmuch as Jethro seems not to have come till the second year after the finishing of the Tabernacle, as may be proved out of Deuteronomy.'
[b] Amsterdam, 1685
[c] 'Faire l'Histoire d'un Livre n'est pas simplement dire quand et par qui il a été fait, quels Copistes l'ont transcrit, et quelles fautes ils ont commises en le transcrivant Il ne suffit pas de nous dire qui l'a traduit, et de nous faire remarquer les défauts de sa Version ; ni même de nous apprendre qui l'a commenté, et ce qu'il y a de défectueux dans ces Commentaires Il faut encore nous découvrir, si cela se peut, dans quel dessein l'Auteur l'a composé, quelle occasion lui a fait prendre la plume, et à quelles opinions, ou à quels évènemens, il peut faire allusion dans cet Ouvrage, surtout lorsqu'il ne s agit pas d'un livre qui contienne des réflexions générales ou des véritez éternelles, qui sont les mêmes dans tous les Siècles, et parmi tous les peuples du monde,' p 6.

term 'Ur of the Chaldees^a' $11^{28\ 31}$ was founded by anticipation upon Chesed 22^{22}, the same country being otherwise called Paddan-aram: now none but writers who lived when the Israelites had some intercourse with the Chaldeans, or who had been in Chaldea, called it the land of the Chaldeans, e g Ezek 1^3 11^{24}. To the usual passages indicating a post-Mosaic date Gen 12^8 13^{17} 14^{14} 35^{21} [cp Mic 4^8 Neh 3^1] 37^{14} 40^{15} Ex 6^{26} 16^{35} [cp Josh 5^{11}.] Deut 1^1 he added the important observation that the term *nabî* 'prophet' Gen 20^7 was not in use till the time of Samuel, as was stated in 1 Sam 9^9. The composition of the Pentateuch, therefore, must be carried down at least to the period of the monarchy. It was compiled from documents some of which might have been originally written before Moses, but fragments only had been preserved. These ancient books were not the work of public recorders. The discovery of the law under Josiah proved that such official registers could not have existed, for they would not have been suffered to fall into such decay. They were of private origin, and various date. To whom, then, did they owe their union? The conditions to be satisfied were that the author should have flourished after Samuel, and should have lived in Chaldea. Spinoza's resort to Ezra was out of the question, for the Samaritans would not have copied a law-book introduced by him. Le Clerc accordingly turned, at the close of his sixth letter^b, to the narrative 2 Kings 17^{28} of the priest who was dispatched from the captivity of the Ten Tribes to persuade the new settlers in their ancient land to abandon the false worship of many gods. The mission of this instructor culminated in the production of 'a history of the creation of the world by the One Only God.' This was not, indeed, written till after the eighteenth year of Josiah, for the law-book then discovered was adopted as an essential part of the work. Its incorporation apparently procured for the whole the sanction of the temple officers at Jerusalem; and the letter concludes with a triumphant demonstration that this hypothesis fulfils all reasonable demands.

2 The criticism of the seventeenth century had thus made considerable advances. It had formulated the real aim of historical investigation in the field of literature, viz the determination of the circumstances, the purpose, the spirit, of any given document, and its relation to the time and the place in which the writer lived. But before it could really proceed to this task, a preliminary labour was required in the case of the Pentateuch, viz the determination of the actual contents, the literary limits and characteristics, of the constituent documents themselves. Some brilliant guesses had been made. Particular legislative groups had been isolated from their surrounding narratives, and pronounced Mosaic, in contrast with the adjacent histories or discourses. The covenant-book in Ex 20^{22}–23, the covenant words in 34, the law code which stands at the core of Deuteronomy, in 12–26, had been selected from the mass of adjacent material, which was referred in general terms to other writers. But no true critical method had yet been devised. Inquirers had been feeling after a clue, but had failed to find one. It was generally recognized that the Pentateuch contained numerous statements inconsistent in various ways with composition in the Mosaic age; but many of these might be very plausibly regarded as supplemental, they might be assigned to later editorial revision, yet leave the substantial integrity of the books unimpaired. There was, further, a general disposition to admit the compilation of the Pentateuch out of a number of documents, which were written by different hands, and under varying conditions. No one, however, appeared to have the least idea how to distinguish them. It was admitted that some were prior to Moses; but by what marks these were to be recognized, there was no attempt to determine. This hypothesis was adopted (among other reasons) to explain the incompatibilities presented by the chronology: it had yet to be ascertained how far the schemes of numbers presented definite affinities, and could be correlated together. It was further urged that this view alone could explain the phenomena of duplicate

^{a} ℌ *Chasdim*, as if plural of Chesed $\qquad$ ^{b} p 129 narratives, whether side by side, as in the contiguous accounts of the Creation Gen 1 and 2, or in combination, as in the story of the Flood. Criticism, so far, was negative. All that it could do was to prove that Moses did not write the Pentateuch as we have it. Along this line it may be said to have effectively prepared the way for completer demonstration. To the proofs already cited, a few more illustrative examples may be added, before the attention of the reader is invited to the next step towards positive results—the discovery by Astruc of a criterion for the partition of the documents in Genesis.

(a) One of the strongest arguments in the hands of Spinoza and Simon alike was founded on the incongruities of the dates with the circumstances which they professed to set in proper time order. A characteristic instance is here presented in the words of Prof Driver[a]:—

> We all remember the scene Gen 27 in which Isaac in extreme old age blesses his sons, we picture him as lying on his death-bed. Do we, however, all realize that according to the chronology of the book of Genesis he must have been thus lying on his death-bed for eighty years (cp 25^{26} 26^{34} 35^{28})? Yet we can only diminish this period by extending proportionately the interval between Esau marrying his Hittite wives 26^{34} and Rebekah's suggestion to Isaac to send Jacob away, lest he should follow his brother's example 27^{46}, which, from the nature of the case, will not admit of any but a slight extension. Keil, however, does so extend it, reducing the period of Isaac's final illness by forty-three years, and is conscious of no incongruity in supposing that Rebekah, thirty-seven years after Esau had taken his Hittite wives, should express her fear that Jacob, then aged seventy-seven, will do the same.

The instances which roused the attention of the critics of the seventeenth century were all derived from the book of Genesis. But the narratives of the Mosaic age also exhibit perplexing chronological phenomena, though not quite of the same kind. For while some episodes are related with great fullness, such as the dealings of Moses with Pharaoh Ex 5–11, or the visit of Balaam to Balak Num 22–24, and the Midianite war 31, in other cases gaps occur at critical points in a manner incompatible with contemporary or nearly contemporary authorship. Thus in Ex 1^{6-8} the narrative passes without warning from the generation which witnessed the death of Joseph to that which saw the birth of Moses. A combination of the dates proves that this involves a silent leap over 280 years[b]. A second and more significant instance occurs in Num 20. The Israelites arrive at Kadesh in the first month[1], apparently of the third year, reckoning from the Exodus, the last previous date marking the departure from Sinai in the second month of the second year 10^{11}. In 20^{22} the march is resumed, and in consequence of the refusal of Edom to allow a passage through its territory, a long circuit is necessary. The first stage brings them to Mount Hor, where Aaron dies upon the summit. In the list of the encampments in 33^{37} this incident is fixed in the fortieth year of the wanderings. Between 20^1 and ^{22} there is thus an interval of at least thirty-seven years (cp Deut 2^{14}, from Kadesh to the brook Zered thirty-eight years). Is it credible that the 'journals' of Moses found nothing worthy of record in this long period beyond a solitary instance of popular discontent, and a fruitless embassy to the king of Edom? Did an entire generation pass away, without any further trace than the bones of its 'fighting men' upon the wilderness? Only at a later day could imaginative tradition have rounded off the whole into a fixed form of forty years, and been content to leave the greater part a blank[c].

[a] *Contemporary Review* lvii 221

[b] According to the well-known statement in Ex 12^{40} the sojourn of Israel in Egypt lasted 430 years (𝔊 and Sam, however, include in this figure the whole period from Abraham's migration) Moses was eighty at the Exodus Ex 7^7, and Joseph about forty on the arrival of Jacob (cp Gen 41^{46}, thirty when he predicted the seven years of plenty which seem to have begun immediately, thirty-nine when he sent for his father 45^{11}). Joseph died at the age of 110 Deducting seventy years for Joseph in Egypt, and eighty years for Moses, there remains an interval of 280 years. How the genealogical lists can be adapted to this scheme, it is not necessary at present to inquire

[c] For another solution of this difficulty cp Analysis Num 20^{lx}. 'It is a commonplace of Biblical students,' says Prof Sayce, *Early History of the Hebrews* 142, 'that numbers are peculiarly liable to

(β) The foregoing difficulties are unfavourable to the hypothesis of contemporary authorship, but they throw no light on the composition of the narrative. The critics of the seventeenth century, however, pointed to another order of phenomena, which plainly involved the plurality of the sources, whether oral or documentary, from which the narrative had been compiled. Repeated reference was made, for example, to the resemblance of the incidents in Gen 12^{10-20} 20 and 26^{6-11}. In like manner a son is thrice promised to Abraham, in 15 17 18; and three allusions to laughter connect themselves with the name Isaac (literally, 'he laughs') 17^{17-19} 18^{12}. 21^6. Twice is Hagar expelled from Abraham's tent 16^{4-14} 21^{9-21}. The same cause is assigned on each occasion in the jealousy of Sarah. The crisis of suffering arrives in the same scene, near a well in the wilderness on the south. Deliverance follows by the intervention of an angel: and the heavenly promises contain similar announcements of greatness for Hagar's posterity, and similar references to the name of her son Ishmael:—

Gen 16	Gen 21
[10] And the angel of Yahweh said unto her, I will greatly multiply thy seed, that it shall not be numbered for multitude [11] And the angel of Yahweh said unto her, Behold, thou art with child, and shalt bear a son, and thou shalt call his name Ishmael [God heareth], because Yahweh hath heard thy affliction	[17] And God heard the voice of the lad; and the angel of God called to Hagar out of heaven, and said unto her, What aileth thee, Hagar? fear not, for God hath heard the voice of the lad where he is. [1b] Arise, lift up the lad, and hold him in thine hand; for I will make him a great nation.

Different accounts are given both of local and personal names. Twice is Beer-sheba derived from a covenant, in the one case between Abraham and Abimelech Gen 21^{22-32}, in the other between Isaac and the same king at Gerar some seventy years later 26^{26-33}. Jacob bestows the designation Bethel [God's house] upon the ancient Luz on his flight to Haran 28^{19}, and again on his return to Canaan 35^{15}. Even his own name Israel is twice divinely conferred, first on the banks of the Jabbok, and again at Bethel:—

Gen 32	Gen 35
[27] And he said unto him, What is thy name? And he said, Jacob. [28] And he said, Thy name shall be called no more Jacob, but Israel: for thou hast striven with God and *with* men, and hast prevailed	[10] And God said unto him, Thy name is Jacob: thy name shall not be called any more Jacob, but Israel shall be thy name: and he called his name Israel.

Such instances might be easily explained prima facie on the assumption that Moses combined in Genesis different documents or traditions which had descended from the patriarchal age; and the first attempts to discover the composition of the book in the last century by Astruc and Eichhorn rested on that basis. But the assumption becomes insecure when it is observed that the narratives of the Mosaic age contain analogous duplicates. Thus the revelation of the divine name Yahweh to Moses is recorded twice Ex 3^{14} and 6^2. It is accompanied in each case by a promise to deliver the afflicted people 3^{7-9} and 6^{5-8}. Moses is twice solemnly charged to demand their liberation from Pharaoh 3^{10-18} 6^{11}, he twice hesitates, and Aaron is twice appointed as his spokesman 4^{10-16} and 6^{12} $30-7^2$. Only the sequels differ: on the first occasion

---

corruption, and that consequently little dependence can be placed on the numbers given in the text of the Old Testament But the conclusion does not follow from the premiss The later dates of Israelitish history are for the most part reliable, and it would be strange if the causes of corruption were fatal only to the dates of an earlier period' 'The period of forty years,' he observes subsequently, p 146, 'which meets us again and again in the book of Judges, is simply the equivalent of an unknown length of time; it denotes the want of materials, and the consequent ignorance of the writer.' Does this statement cease to be true when for 'Judges' we read 'Numbers'? And if not, what becomes of the theory of contemporary authorship, especially in view of such a passage as Num 14^{33}? The evidence accumulated in Colenso's examination of the statistics of the Pentateuch (*Pent* part I), will be found to have a special bearing on the character of one of its constituent documents, and will be more conveniently considered at a later stage (cp chap XIII 2ε).

the people believe, they bow their heads and worship 4^{31}: on the second, they hearken not for anguish of spirit and for cruel bondage 6^9. It might be argued, indeed, that these corresponding series were still successive; that Moses on the first shock of disappointment at his fruitless attempts to befriend his people needed the encouragement of fresh assurance. But it is at least strange that the second colloquies with Deity should run precisely parallel with the first and should contain no reference to them, so that the same fraternal aid is promised to Moses in his despondency without any consciousness that it has been already tried and found wanting. There is, however, no actual discrepancy in the record, such as may be observed elsewhere. The father-in-law of Moses is called Reuel in Ex $2^{18\ 21}$ 10^{29}; but he is named Jethro in 3^1 4^{18} 18^1. Twice do quails appear in connexion with the daily manna Num $11^{4-6\ 31\cdot\cdot}$ and Ex 16^{13}. Twice does Moses draw water from the rock, when the strife of Israel begets the name Meribah [strife] Ex 17^{1-7} and Num 20^{1-13}. The inconsistent locations of Aaron's death Num 33^{38} Deut 10^{6b} were noticed by Peyrère (*ante* p 24) who also remarked the divergence between the accounts of the separation of Levi in Deut 10^8 and Num 3 and 8. It is somewhat curious that two of the most conspicuous instances of conflicting statements of fact in the record of the Mosaic institutions should have excited no comment in the seventeenth century—the construction of the ark and the place of the sanctuary. In Ex $25^{10\cdot\cdot}$ Moses, who is then upon the sacred mount, receives directions to prepare the ark. These are ultimately carried out by Bezaleel, after Moses has received the new tables during his second sojourn on the mount $37^{1\cdot\cdot}$, and the tables are solemnly placed in it 40^{20}. But in the recital of the great apostasy in Deut 9· Moses describes himself as commanded to make an ark before ascending for the renewal of the Ten Words 10^1. He makes the ark himself ^{3}, which is thus ready to shelter the reinscribed tables on his return from the interview with Yahweh: they are accordingly deposited in it at once, and there ^{5} they remain[a]. Where, however, was the ark preserved? In Ex 25-29 the ark is placed in the inner sanctuary of the sacred tent which is entitled Yahweh's Dwelling, though it is also known as the Tent of Meeting. This Dwelling is pitched in the middle of the camp. Immediately around it, west, south, and north, are the Levites; on the east are Moses, Aaron, and his sons Num 3^{38}; and the members of the sacred order are further guarded by the twelve tribes, three on a side 2. A corresponding arrangement on the march divides the host into two groups of six tribes each; between them is carried the whole fabric of the Dwelling and its furniture, the ark being specially assigned to the Kohathites 2^{17} $3^{30\cdot\cdot}$. But before the preparations for the Dwelling have begun Ex $35^{4\cdot\cdot}$, the Tent of Meeting has been instituted $33^{7\cdot\cdot}$. It is pitched outside the camp at a distance, and every one who wishes to inquire there is obliged to quit the camp and go out to it. This is described as the usage of Moses already at the foot of the sacred mount. And the usage does not cease when the Dwelling is reared. The Tent of Meeting is still outside long after the camp order has been established Num 11^{24-30} 12^4. It is in harmony with this representation of the isolation of the sanctuary that the ark does not travel in the midst of the tribes, but in front of them 10^{33}. What further differences these conceptions involve, will be seen hereafter. It is sufficient to affirm at present that they cannot both have proceeded from the same writer. If either is Mosaic, then the other is not.

(γ) Hardly less striking, at least when its historic significance is fully understood, is the evidence presented by the laws. A cursory examination is sufficient to show that the same theme is treated again and again in different forms. Apart from the

---

[a] The words '*and there they be*, as Yahweh commanded me' render the hypothesis of a temporary ark afterwards superseded by that of Bezaleel absolutely impossible. The writer of Deut 10^5 could not also have written Ex 37^1· and 40^{20}.

regulations affecting the altar or the priesthood, which will require more careful examination hereafter, it may be observed that the legislation of the Pentateuch tends to fall into groups of laws, sometimes longer and sometimes shorter, bound together by certain harmonies of conception and language. Such groups sometimes occur in tolerably close proximity, e g Ex 23 and 34; sometimes they are aggregated together into larger collections, as in the books of Leviticus and Deuteronomy. But the result is not favourable to the hypothesis of unity of authorship. Why, for example, should Moses only once lay on Israel the solemn command 'Thou shalt love Yahweh thy God with all thy heart and with all thy soul and with all thy might,' and repeat three times over the prohibition 'Thou shalt not seethe a kid in its mother's milk' Ex 23^{19} 34^{26} Deut 14^{21}? A reference to the table of Laws on such subjects as the worship of other gods (¶ 5 a), idolatry (¶ 5 b), magic (¶ 5 j), the sabbath (¶ 9 b), the stranger (¶ 2 a), will bring to light, firstly, the singular manner in which they are scattered through the whole complex mass of narrative and legislation, and, secondly, the important fact that they are not all homogeneous either in character, contents, or expression. A comparison of the brief festival cycle as instituted in Ex 23^{14}.. (and its parallel in 34^{18}..) with the elaborate order in Lev 23 will at once raise doubts whether the two series were actually instituted in successive years: and these doubts will be confirmed when it is observed that the Deuteronomic list Deut 16 reverts to the first type and ignores the second. A parallel phenomenon may be observed in the laws affecting the slavery of Israelites. The first code Ex 21^{1-6} permits a Hebrew after six years' service to contract for life-long servitude, and places the ceremony of formal enslavement under religious sanction. Before Israel has left Sinai, however, in the next year, this arrangement is tacitly abrogated. In Lev 25^{39-42} it is laid down that no Israelite shall sell himself to another; temporary slavery may, indeed, last till the jubile; but the poor 'brother' is entitled then to liberty for himself and his family ^{41} (in Ex 21^4 the wife and children remain in the possession of the master), on the express ground that their freedom was a divine gift and could not be alienated by slavery for life. That is the exalted view of the second year after the Exodus. But at the end of the wanderings, thirty-eight years later, Moses returns to his earlier scheme. In Deut 15^{12}.. the theory that every Israelite is Yahweh's bondman is quietly abandoned, and the process of voluntary enslavement in the seventh year is again legitimated. It cannot be said that the intervening law had been tried without success, for it was expressly designed Lev 25^2 for the settlement in Canaan. Yet it is wholly ignored when Moses makes his final address, and an arrangement entirely inconsistent with it is re-enforced. The conflict of principle is here as clear as the conflict of fact in the case of the position of the sacred tent or the construction of the ark. It will hereafter be suggested that the three laws belong to three different stages of religious and social order. At present it must suffice to observe that if the law of Exodus or Deuteronomy is Mosaic, then that of Leviticus is not, and vice versa.

(δ) There is a further class of cases which is perhaps the most suggestive of all. It has been shown that in the narratives whether of the patriarchal or the Mosaic ages there are duplicate statements of fact which cannot be reconciled. It has also been argued that in the laws ascribed to Moses there are provisions which are founded on incompatible ideas and which lead to incongruous results. But it is further possible to prove that the same narrative contains dual items inconsistent with each other[a]. A familiar instance had already attracted the notice of Simon. In the narrative of the deluge Gen 7^{12} it is stated that 'the rain was upon the earth forty

---

[a] A similar thesis might be also offered concerning certain passages of legislation, but the proof would be at present too complicated

days and forty nights': but in ^{24} it is affirmed that 'the waters prevailed upon the earth an hundred and fifty days.' What was the real duration before the flood began to abate? Another well-known difficulty arises in the same story. According to 6^{19}. Noah is required by Elohim to take into the ark one pair of each kind of animal, irrespective of any differences in their size, class, or ceremonial value. But in 7^2. Yahweh directs him to divide the beasts into clean and unclean, taking seven pair of the former to one of the latter, the birds being treated in like manner. Which of these commands was he to obey? Two versions of Joseph's enslavement lie side by side in Gen 37. In $^{27\ 28b}$ his brothers sell him to a caravan of Ishmaelites, who carry him to Egypt and sell him to Potiphar an officer of Pharaoh 39^1, by whom he is afterwards imprisoned 39^{20}. But in 37^{28a} Joseph is not sold at all; he is kidnapped: 'and there passed by Midianites, merchantmen, and they drew and lifted up Joseph out of the pit.' They, too, were on the way to Egypt, where they disposed of their prize to the captain of the guard ^{36}. In his service it falls to Joseph's duty to minister to the prisoners under his care 40^4; and to them the young slave bewails his hapless lot ^{15}, 'for indeed I was stolen away out of the land of the Hebrews.' These divergences are certainly not irreconcilable with a theory of Mosaic compilation of the book of Genesis. They point, indeed, to diversities of source or tradition: but there is nothing in them which renders it impossible that the writer who amalgamated them might have been Moses. The argument, however, receives a new complexion when it is noticed that the same phenomenon recurs in the accounts of transactions in which Moses played the leading part. Thus in the narrative of the plagues it will be found that one set of stories places the Israelites in Goshen, where the wonders that are wrought in Egypt do not affect them Ex $8^{22}\ 9^{26}$; while another locates them among the Egyptians and secures them miraculous exemption 10^{21-23} cp 7^{8N}. When the twelve spies are sent into Canaan Num 13 they explore the extreme length of the country ^{21}, reaching the northern pass known as 'the entering in of Hamath.' But the next verse ^{22} represents them as starting afresh, they arrive at Hebron, and enter the valley of Eshcol, where they cut down a cluster of grapes which they then carry back to Moses at Kadesh in fulfilment of his previous instructions ^{20}. The impressions with which they return are equally far apart. In ^{27} they report that the land flows with milk and honey: but in ^{32} it is accused of devouring instead of sustaining its inhabitants. Finally, Caleb, according to one version, endeavours to persuade the people to make an immediate advance 13^{30}, and receives the promise that he and his seed shall possess the land which he had traversed 14^{24}: while another version associates with him Joshua the son of Nun $14^{6\ 30\ 38}$ promising exemption to both from the doom pronounced upon the murmurers^a. Once more, the rebellion of Korah, Dathan, and Abiram, in Num 16, issues in the strange result that their two hundred and fifty followers ^{2} are first engulfed in the midst of all their possessions ^{32}, and then devoured by fire at the entrance of the tent of meeting ^{35}. The process by which this singular consequence has become possible is set forth in detail in the Analysis: its explanation, like the explanation of many similar difficulties, is found in the attempt to combine two independent stories. But could such a combination be the work of an eye-witness, himself the agent of a double fate?

---

^{a} In this passage 13^6 Caleb is stated to belong to the tribe of Judah. But in 32^{12} and Josh 14^6 Caleb is not an Israelite at all, he is a descendant of the desert tribe of Kenaz, cp Gen $15^{19}\ 36^{11\ 15\ 42}$ Josh 15^7.

CHAPTER V

THE CLUE TO THE DOCUMENTS

The examples which have been offered in the last chapter appear sufficient to prove the main thesis of the seventeenth-century criticism, viz the composition of the Pentateuch out of different documents. But they throw no light on the mode by which these documents may be distinguished; still less do they enable us to conjecture their number, their character, their extent, or their mutual relations. For this end criticism has to take a further step. It is not a little significant that the original clue was discovered in the field of Genesis alone by an investigator who firmly believed that the Five Books were the work of Moses.

1. In 1753 Jean Astruc of Montpelier, physician by profession and Catholic by religion (his father had been a Huguenot pastor), published anonymously at Brussels the little book which contained the key to the whole position. It was modestly entitled *Conjectures sur les mémoires originaux dont il paroît que Moyse s'est servi pour composer le livre de la Genèse*. Observing that some portions of the book were distinguished by the use of the name Elohim, and others by that of Yahweh, he suggested that these were really drawn from different sources. They were in fact extracts from separate documents which he supposed Moses to have arranged in four parallel columns. These were subsequently amalgamated into one, the present confusion of the text being largely due to the negligence of the copyists. The main distribution fell under two heads, an Elohim narrative, A, and a Yahweh story, B, which ran through the entire book. The Elohim source consisted of $1-2^3$ 5 6^{9-22} 7^{6-10} 19 22 24 8^{1-19} 9^{1-10} 12 $16.$ $28.$ 11^{10-26} 17^{3-27} 20^{1-17} 21^{2-32} 22^{1-10} 23 25^{1-11} 30^{1-23} 31^{4-47} $51-54$ 32^{1-3} $25-33$ 33^{1-16} 35^{1-27} 37 $40-48$ 49^{29-33} 50 Ex $1-2$. To the Yahweh document he assigned 2^{4-4} 6^{1-8} 7^{1-5} $11-18$ 21 24 8^{20-22} 9^{11} $13-15$ $18-29$ 10 11^{1-9} $27-32$ $12-13$ $15-16$ 17^{1-2} $18-19^{28}$ 20^{18} 21^{1} $33.$ 22^{11-19} 24 25^{19-34} 26^{1-33} $27-28^5$ $10-22$ 29 30^{24-43} 31^{1-3} $48-50$ 32^{4-24} 33^{17-20} 38 39 49^{1-28}. There remained a small number of passages which did not seem homogeneous with either of the two main narratives, or with each other. According to the letters which he employed for their designation (pp. 308-315), they stood thus: C $7^{20\ 23\cdot}$, D $35^{28\cdot}$, E 14, F 19^{29-38}, G 22^{20-24}, H 25^{12-18}, I 34, K $26^{34\cdot}$, 28^{6-9}, L 36^{1-21} $31-43$, M 36^{20-30}. Most of these are concerned with events or tribes outside the main current of the patriarchal history. They were derived in Astruc's view from the Midianites among whom Moses sojourned, or the nomads of the desert whom he encountered in the wanderings. The modern analysis differs in many respects from Astruc's, which especially suffers from the limitations which he imposed upon it. He did not carry it beyond the first two chapters of Exodus, in which he found the continuation of his document A. As this passage related the early life of Moses, he ascribed it (together with the group to which it belonged) to Amram, Moses' father. Had he studied the composition of the succeeding books, he might have been able greatly to strengthen his fundamental hypothesis. But it is rather surprising that he should have effected so much, than that his instruments of partition should have been imperfect, and his results consequently incomplete. If Eichhorn afterwards covered a wider field of learning and became the true founder of Old Testament criticism in its broadest sense, the study of the Pentateuch owes most to Astruc.

2. The real key to the composition of the Pentateuch may be said to lie in Ex 6^{2-8}. The passages which are gradually found to be allied with it confront us in turn with all the complicated questions concerning the constituents of the Five Books. It opens with the solemn declaration of Elohim to Moses :—

^{2b} I am Yahweh ³ and I appeared unto Abraham, unto Isaac, and unto Jacob, as God Almighty [ה *El Shaddai*], but by my name Yahweh I was not known to them. ⁴ And I have also established

my covenant with them, to give them the land of Canaan, the land of their sojournings, wherein they sojourned. ⁵ And moreover I have heard the groaning of the children of Israel, whom the Egyptians keep in bondage; and I have remembered my covenant.

Two facts of the utmost importance are here definitely asserted. In revealing himself as Yahweh, God affirms that he had not been known by that name to the forefathers of Israel; but he had appeared to them as El Shaddai. On the basis of these words it would be reasonable to look for traces in Genesis of divine manifestations to the patriarchs under the title El Shaddai, and their discovery would afford a presumption that they belonged to the same document. On the other hand the occurrence of similar manifestations in the character of Yahweh would directly contradict the express words of the text, and could not be ascribed to the same author. The distinction which Astruc adopted has thus the direct sanction of the Pentateuch itself, and its immediate application is simple and easy. Does the book of Genesis contain revelations of God to Abraham, Isaac, and Jacob as El Shaddai? To Abraham and Jacob, certainly: 'I am El Shaddai' Gen 17¹ and 35¹¹; but the corresponding announcement to Isaac is missing. Mingled with these, however, are other passages of a different nature, such as the divine utterance to Abram 15⁷ 'I am Yahweh that brought thee out of Ur of the Chaldees'; or to Jacob 28¹³ 'I am Yahweh, the God of Abraham thy father, and the God of Isaac.' Side by side with these stand many others describing the recognition of Yahweh by the patriarchs and their contemporaries. Between Bethel and Ai Abram 'built an altar unto Yahweh, and called upon the name of Yahweh' 12⁸ cp 13⁴ ¹⁸ 21³³. To the king of Sodom Abram declared that he had sworn 'to Yahweh' to take none of the 'goods' recovered from the Mesopotamian invaders 14²². Sarai complained to her husband, 'Yahweh hath restrained me from bearing' 16². When the mysterious visitor rebukes her for her incredulity, he asks 'Is anything too hard for Yahweh?' 18¹⁴. Lot is warned by the men whom he has entertained, 'Yahweh hath sent us to destroy' this place 19¹³. But it is not needful to accumulate further instances. The name is known beyond the confines of Canaan. The 'man' in search of a bride for his master's son is welcomed with it at the city of Nahor by Laban, 'Come in, thou blessed of Yahweh' 24³¹. And it is of such ancient use that it can be said of the family of Adam, 'then began men to call upon the name of Yahweh' 4²⁶. But unless the writer of Ex 6² contradicts himself, not one of these passages can have issued from his hand[a].

3. An examination of the passages containing the three revelations to Abraham, Jacob, and Moses, at once reveals a number of other important links connecting them together.

(a) The record in Ex 6⁴ refers to the 'establishment' of a covenant with them, the purpose of which is to give them the land of Canaan, further described as the 'land of their sojournings.' This covenant is first announced to Abraham :—

Gen 17⁷ And I will establish my covenant between me and thee and thy seed after thee throughout their generations for an everlasting covenant, to be a God unto thee and to thy seed after thee ⁸ And I will give unto thee, and to thy seed after thee, the land of thy sojournings, all the land of Canaan, for an everlasting possession; and I will be their God.

The promise is then repeated to Jacob :—

35¹² The land which I gave unto Abraham and Isaac, to thee I will give it, and to thy seed after thee will I give the land.

Around this main declaration cluster others, displaying marked resemblances. The revelation is in each case accompanied by a change in the patriarch's name; Abram

---

[a] It does not, however, follow that he would never have employed the name in narrative.

becomes Abraham 17^5, and Jacob Israel 35^{10}. Each is addressed as the sire of a race of kings:—

17^{5b} The father of a multitude of nations have I made thee.... ^{6b} and I will make nations of thee, and kings shall come out of thee.	35^{11b} A nation and a company of nations shall be of thee, and kings shall come out of thy loins.

Abraham is further assured that El Shaddai will 'multiply' him, and make him 'exceeding fruitful' $17^{2\ 6}$, a similar destiny being also in store for Ishmael 17^{20}; while Jacob receives the command 'be fruitful and multiply' 35^{11}. The 'appearing' ends in each case with the divine ascension, 'and God went up' 17^{22} 35^{13}.

(β) The community of thought and language between these three passages is unmistakable; and 17 35^{9-15} Ex 6^{2-4} may be confidently assigned to a common source. This at once makes it probable that they are not isolated fragments. It is true that the document to which they belong has not been incorporated entire, for the promise to Isaac mentioned in both Gen 35^{12} and Ex 6^3 is not to be found. But the presumption is strong that these great scenes were linked by narratives which related the history of the patriarchs, and this is clearly established by the sequel in 6^5 which affirms that God has 'heard the groaning of the children of Israel, whom the Egyptians keep in bondage.' Between the bestowal of the name Israel and the announcement of the deliverance of his posterity from servitude must lie some account of the patriarch's progeny, and of their migration from Canaan into Egypt. Similarly the relation of Gen 35^{9-15} to 17 implies that the descent of Jacob from Abraham formed part of the same story; and the allusions to Sarah and Ishmael in 17 indicate that a family history lies behind. The immediate antecedents, indeed, are not far to seek. Abraham was then ninety-nine years old and Ishmael thirteen $17^{1\ 24\cdot\cdot}$. These dates cohere with the record of Ishmael's birth 16^{15} when Abram was 'fourscore and six years old.' There, a new person is introduced upon the scene, Ishmael's mother Hagar. She is the heroine of the previous story 16^{4-14}, where the use of the name Yahweh $^{5\ 11}$ in actual speech forbids the ascription to the writer of 17 and Ex 6^2. But Gen 16^3 supplies another date 'after Abram had dwelt ten years in the land of Canaan' (cp 'land of Canaan' 17^8), and ^{3} obviously carries ^{1} with it, though ^{2} is inadmissible in consequence of Sarai's reference to Yahweh. When Abram received Hagar at Sarai's hand, he must have been eighty-five years old. Ten years before he had entered Canaan. Was his arrival chronicled by this writer? The covenant in 15 is plainly not his record: it is made by Yahweh ^{18}, and it announces a gift far wider in extent than the 'land of Canaan' promised in 17. The acts of worship specified in $13^{4\ 18}$ and $12^{7\cdot}$ cannot likewise proceed from him. But in $12^{4b\ 5}$ there is a description which tallies exactly with 16^3:—

^{4b} And Abram was seventy and five years old when he departed out of Haran ^{5} And Abram took Sarai his wife, and Lot his brother's son, and all their substance that they had gathered, and the souls that they had gotten in Haran; and they went forth to go into the land of Canaan; and into the land of Canaan they came.

Ten years, therefore, before Abram took Hagar to wife he had brought Sarai into the land of Canaan from Haran. By a similar method we learn from 11^{31} that Abram was the son of Terah, who had himself started the great removal but had died upon the way, the 'generations (*tol^edhoth*^a) of Terah' being traced in $11^{27\cdot\cdot}$. Terah's pedigree is set forth, in its turn, in 'the generations of Shem' 11^{10-26}. At this point the inquiry takes a wider range. The 'generations of Shem' are connected with 'the generations of the sons of Noah, Shem, Ham, and Japheth' 10^1: these point back to a similar heading for their father, 6^9 'these are the generations of Noah.' The descent of

---

^a For this peculiar formula cp ^{p}77; another word appears in $6^9\ 9^{12}\ 17^{7\ 9\ 12}$, cp ^{p}76.

Noah from Adam is exhibited in 5, entitled 'the book of the generations of Adam.' This opens with a plain reference to the creation of man in the likeness of Elohim 1^{27}, male and female together: and the narrative of the creative process concludes in 2^{4a} with the corresponding formula 'these are the generations of the heaven and of the earth.'

(γ) A probability is thus created that there runs through the book of Genesis a document in which the name Yahweh was excluded from recognition by the patriarchs, while the name Elohim was employed freely (in Gen $1-2^{4a}$ it occurs thirty-five times). The document was further divided into sections, entitled 'these are the generations of . . .' As the revelation of El Shaddai to Isaac has been dropped in amalgamation with other documents, so (it would seem likely) the 'generations of Abraham' have been put aside; but the titles for Ishmael 25^{12}, Isaac 25^{19}, and Jacob 37^{2a}, have all been preserved. The task that next confronts the investigator is to determine, if he can, the contents of these sections. To the three leading passages already considered, in 17 35^{9-15} Ex 6^{2-5}, the narrative of the creation in Gen $1-2^{4a}$ may with some confidence be added. These serve as a standard of inquiry, and supply us with numerous harmonies of thought and language. For example, when Isaac sends Jacob to find a wife in Paddan-aram, and invokes on him the blessing with which El Shaddai had blessed Abraham, it is plain that $28^{3 \cdot}$ depends on $17^{5-8\,a}$. Similarly, when Jacob recites to Joseph $48^{3 \cdot}$ the 'appearing' of El Shaddai to him at Luz, his words are a free reproduction of the declaration in $35^{11 \cdot\,b}$. Such instances of quotation are necessarily rare. But in other passages practical certitude is attained by the recurrence of characteristic phrases in such definite groups as to render it in the highest degree improbable that they are of diverse origin. Thus when Elohim announces the impending flood to Noah Gen 6^{13} he promises ^{18} to 'establish his covenant' with him. The phrase is identical with that in $17^{7\ 21}$, but differs from the making of the covenant by Yahweh 15^{18}. In preparation for the catastrophe Noah is commanded to take into the ark one pair of each species of living thing, male and female 6^{19} (cp 1^{27}). The classification 6^{20} runs side by side with $1^{21\ 24-26\ 30}$, as is indicated by the peculiar formula 'after its kind.' When the terrible year of destruction has passed, Elohim's blessing and covenant in 9^{1-17} combine the terminology of both 1 and 17. The command to Noah and his sons ^{1} 'be fruitful and multiply and replenish the earth' is that addressed to the original humanity 1^{28}: the 'moving things' that are given for food as the green herb ^{3}, recall the gift of 1^{29}: as the waters had 'swarmed' at the original creative word $1^{20 \cdot}$, so let the race of men which should start from Noah and his sons 9^{7}. The covenant is then 'established' ^{9} in fulfilment of the divine promise 6^{18}: it is established with Noah and his seed after him (cp 17^{7}) 'for perpetual generations' ^{12} (cp 17^{7} 'throughout their generations'): like that with Abraham it is marked by a 'token' $9^{12-17}\ 17^{11}$, and each is further described as 'everlasting' $9^{16}\ 17^{7\ 13}$. It thus becomes practically certain that $1-2^{4a}$ 5 6^{9-22} 9^{1-17} are blocks of a common narrative, to which the El Shaddai revelations also belonged.

4. It is perhaps unnecessary to carry further the general exposition of the analytical method thus founded upon the statement of Ex 6^{2-5}. The passages which have been already extracted show us a document which opened with the creation. In a stately order heaven and earth are wrought out of the darkness and the waters of the deep; the earth is clothed with verdure; sun, moon, and stars are set in the sky; sea, air, and land receive their appropriate inhabitants, and man appears, the crown and glory of the

---

[a] Cp 'bless, make fruitful, and multiply' $17^{2\ 6\ 16\ 20}$; 'thee and thy seed after thee' 17^{7}, 'land of thy sojournings' 17^{8}

[b] It is curious that 28^{3} and 48^{4} are further linked together by the unique phrase 'company of peoples'

whole. The lives of ten patriarchs carry the story on to Noah, when it is discovered that the earth is full of wickedness, and Elohim announces that he will destroy all flesh. Noah and his family only are saved; they become the progenitors of a new race, and in the table of nations in Gen 10 the author sketches the distribution of the peoples within his ken, arranging them in three groups derived respectively from Shem, Ham, and Japheth. The scope of his narrative is then contracted to a particular line of the posterity of Shem, through which is derived the family of Terah. Of the three sons of Terah the family of Abram is then selected. The scene shifts to the land of Canaan. There Abraham is depicted as the father of nations, and receives the promise of the land for the posterity of a son yet to be born to him. The burial of Sarah in the cave of Machpelah 23 secures for Abraham an actual possession in the soil; and there in due time he himself is interred by his sons Isaac and Ishmael $25^{9..}$. From these two the younger is chosen; with a brief enumeration of Ishmael's 'generations' 25^{12-17} the writer passes to Isaac's family 25^{19}. Once more a double line opens in the persons of Esau and Jacob; but when Isaac has been duly laid to his rest 35^{27-29}, the migration of Esau to Edom $36^{6.}$ clears the ground for the sole occupancy of Jacob $37^{1\ 2a}$. At this point the narrative breaks off abruptly, to be resumed only in fragments describing the removal of Jacob to join Joseph in Egypt $46^{8..}$, his reception by Pharaoh $47^{7..}$, and his death after seventeen years' residence beside the Nile. His last act was to charge his sons to bury him in the family sepulchre in the field of Machpelah 49^{29-33}, and they duly fulfilled his command $50^{12..}$. In a few brief sentences the author indicates the enslavement which reduced a subsequent generation beneath the Egyptian tyranny, and affirms that 'Elohim remembered his covenant with Abraham, with Isaac, and with Jacob' Ex $1^{1-5\ 7\ 13\ 14b}\ 2^{23b-25}$. The way is thus open for the declaration to Moses $6^{2..}$. As this has behind it a long past, stretching back to the creation of the world, so it also opens up an immediate future. In $^{6-8}$ Moses is commanded to announce to his countrymen the redemption which Yahweh purposes to accomplish. The deliverance will be marked by 'great judgements,' and it will be followed by a solemn act of divine adoption when Yahweh will take Israel for a people and will be to them a God (cp Gen 17^8 ⌘). In the sequel Israel shall enter the country where Abraham, Isaac, and Jacob had sojourned, and it shall be given them for an heritage. The document thus sketches out its own contents; it may be expected to carry on the narrative through the manifestation of Yahweh's outstretched arm against Pharaoh, through the perils of the Red Sea and the wilderness, through the foundation of the religious institutions which would demonstrate God's presence in their midst, till the children of Israel are settled safely in the promised land.

CHAPTER VI

THE COMPOSITION OF GENESIS—NUMBERS

When the *tol^edhoth* sections are removed from the book of Genesis, what remains?

1. It is soon apparent that their elimination has not solved all the problems. A number of duplicates still remain, neither of which can be satisfactorily assigned to the *tol^edhoth* document.

(*a*) For example, it has been already pointed out that the story of Hagar in Gen 16^{4-14} does not belong to the *tol^edhoth* account of Abram $16^{1\ 3\ 15.\ 17}$. Not only does the indignant Sarai appeal for vindication to Yahweh ^{5}, but Yahweh's angel himself addresses Hagar with the promise that Yahweh has heard her affliction ^{11}. But this incident has its counterpart in 21 where the angel of Elohim calls to Hagar out of heaven with the assurance that Elohim has heard the voice of her dying boy. Yet this narrative $^{12-20}$, which employs the name Elohim exclusively, shows no affinities with the *tol^edhoth* book. The play on the name Ishmael (God hears) in ^{17} has been already introduced in 17^{20} ('as for Ishmael I have heard thee'), but the promise of future greatness for Ishmael which this passage contains finds but a faint echo in the restrained language of 21^{13}. The angelic message out of the sky has no parallel in the *tol^edhoth* stories, while these heavenly agencies reappear elsewhere in fresh connexions. They ascend and descend on the ladder of Jacob's dream 28^{12}, so that when he awakes he exclaims 'this is none other but the house of God' (Bethel) $^{17\ 22}$. This passage cannot be assigned to the writer of 17 and 35^{9-15}, for 35^{15} affirms that the name Bethel was conferred by Jacob, not on his flight to Haran, but on his return to Canaan from Paddan-aram. Similar phenomena are presented elsewhere. The angel of Elohim again appears to Jacob in a dream in $31^{11\ 13}$, and Elohim himself visits Laban in the same manner a few nights afterwards 31^{24}. This is but the parallel to a visit to Abimelech of Gerar 20^3 on behalf of Abraham's wife whom he had innocently taken for himself. But it is altogether unlikely that the author of 17 who puts Sarah at ninety ^{17}, should describe her afterwards (when she is miraculously with child) as sought in marriage by Abimelech. It would seem then that the remaining narratives of Genesis when the *tol^edhoth* sections are withdrawn fall again into two groups. Of these, one is marked by the recognition of the name Yahweh from the earliest times 4^{26}. The other avoids it, and in story after story employs the name Elohim alone. Now it has been already shown (*ante* p 29) that the revelation of Yahweh in Ex 6^2, the commission to Moses, and the appointment of Aaron as his spokesman, have their counterpart in a previous narrative 3–4. A second clue is thus afforded to the separation of the materials which still exhibit conflicting phenomena. The *tol^edhoth* document was not alone in its view of the progress of revelation. Another narrative of the patriarchal history was constructed on the same assumption that the name Elohim only was in the possession of Abraham and his descendants, the name Yahweh being first revealed to Moses. It is true that 3^{13-15} does not explicitly affirm like 6^3 that the name Yahweh had not been previously in use. Yet the passage can hardly bear any other interpretation. When Moses inquires of Elohim what answer he shall give if his people ask for the name of the God by whose authority he speaks, it is apparent that the reply 'Thus shalt thou say unto the children of Israel, Yahweh the God of your fathers . . . hath sent me unto you' *contains a new name*. Though it is not asserted, it is assuredly implied that the designation by which the ancestral Deity will from that time be known, had not been known up to that time.

(β) The document which thus runs a parallel course with the *tol^edhoth* book, really resembles it only in this single conception. Its scope is far more limited. It makes its first appearance at any length in Gen 20. Whether it originally contained a view of the origins of the Hebrew people before Abraham, cannot be ascertained. But it is hardly probable that it traversed the entire course of human affairs from creation, or some definite traces of it would surely have been preserved. When, however, it is compared with the Yahwist narratives on the one hand and the *tol^edhoth* sections on the other, it is clear that in spite of the difference concerning the divine name, its whole spirit and method, its thought, its style, and its diction, assimilate it to the first group rather than to the second. The Elohist story of Abraham and Sarah 20 has its parallels in the Yahwist stories of Abram in 12^{10-20} and Isaac 26^{6-11}. The Elohist covenant between Abraham and Abimelech 21^{22} is matched by the Yahwist between Isaac and Abimelech 26^{26} · (cp 21^{22} 'Elohim is with thee in all that thou doest,' 26^{28} 'we saw plainly that Yahweh was with thee'). The two accounts of the Bethel revelation are actually interwoven 28^{10-22}, and both differ essentially from the *tol^edhoth* version 35^{9-15}. The return of Jacob from Mesopotamia is related by the *tol^edhoth* writer in his brief migration formula 31^{18b} (cp 12^5 36^6), while the Yahwist and Elohist invest it with a multiplicity of romantic detail. The characteristics of the three sources, however, will be better apprehended at a further stage in the inquiry. Assuming at present that they can be discriminated, at least as regards their main contents, between Gen 1 and Ex 6, the question immediately arises whether they are continued beyond that limit.

2. The analysis of Astruc was confined to the book of Genesis. Even Eichhorn, while indicating in masterly style the method by which it might be established on a sound literary basis, did not attempt to carry it further. But as criticism advanced and acquired a securer grasp of its material, it was inevitable that the measure which Astruc had meted out to the first book should be applied to its successors.

(a) It has been already observed that the revelation in Ex 6^8 points forward to the settlement of Israel in Canaan. Its counterpart in 3$^{10-15}$ lays on Moses the duty of leading forth Elohim's people out of Egypt, and declares that the proof of his divine commission will be realized when they serve Elohim upon mount Horeb. The parallel in the Yahwist narrative cannot of course contain the first announcement of a new name for Deity. But it also charges Moses to report the divine purpose of deliverance 3^{16}·, and inform his countrymen that Yahweh has come down to their aid 3^8, and will bring them up out of Egypt into a good land and a large, flowing with milk and honey. All three documents, therefore, presumably related the Exodus, and two at least, if not the third, continued the narrative till the Israelites were safely planted in the country where Abraham, Isaac, and Jacob had once sojourned. Does the rest of the Pentateuch justify this expectation? The composition of the book of Exodus undoubtedly presents phenomena analogous to those of Genesis. There are similar indications of the amalgamation of independent narratives. There are similar diversities of view, and conflicts of fact, implying the combination of two or more sources. But the problems are in many cases more intricate and perplexing. There are passages where the tests which were available for the partition in Genesis seem to fade away; and the results of the analysis are reduced to various degrees of probability. Yet when all deductions are made, the composition of Exodus out of the triple strand constituting the narratives of Genesis is practically certain. The continuation of the book to which the *tol^edhoth* sections in the pre-Mosaic story formed the introduction, admits of no doubt whatever. It is true that in comparison with the Yahwist source, the exclusive adherence to the divine name Elohim (or El Shaddai on occasions of great solemnity) is maintained no longer. But this hardly adds to the difficulty of distribution. There are now two narratives freely using the divine name Yahweh, just as there were two sources in Genesis which regularly employed the name Elohim[a]. On the other hand a very important element of comparison is introduced here for the first time, supplying a significant series of fresh criteria. This is the element of sacred law, of the institutions of worship, and the usages of religion. As will be seen hereafter, the Yahwist and Elohist narratives in Genesis resemble each other in sharing a common conception of the patriarchal cultus. The Yahwist recognizes prayer and sacrifice as among the earliest of human acts 4$^{3.\ 26}$. The Elohistic Abraham has scarcely made his appearance before he is summoned to offer up his son Isaac 22. But in the *tol^edhoth* sections Noah provides no sweet savour for his divine deliverer (ct 8^{21}); no altars are built, no hallowed name is invoked. In imposing a law of abstinence from flesh with the blood in it 9^4 Elohim is not laying down a rule for Israel only: the command is addressed to humanity at large. Even the rite of circumcision demanded from Abraham is performed on Ishmael, and passes out of the limits of Canaan and the sacred line. But the continuation of the *tol^edhoth* document proves

---

[a] The case of the third narrative of Genesis is peculiar, inasmuch as there are passages in Exodus and Numbers where it still seems to prefer the name Elohim.

beyond doubt that its main object is to portray the religious institutions of Israel, its sanctuary, its sacrifices, its solemn festivals, and its sacerdotal order. To this source (the proof will be found in the analysis) belongs not only a story of the 'judgements' by which Yahweh secured Israel's deliverance and brought the people in safety out of Egypt, but also a vast code of priestly law, in which the Dwelling or Abode of Yahweh in the midst of the tribes is described with the most minute precision, and the arrangements for the consecration of its officers are ordained Ex 25-30 35-40. The theme is resumed with a manual of sacrifice at the opening of the book of Leviticus, the whole of which has been incorporated into this great work. It is further elaborated in the picture of the camp life of Israel in Num 1-10; and it reappears from time to time in the incidents of the march from Sinai until Israel is on the eve of crossing the Jordan and the death of Moses is announced 26-36. Nor does it terminate even there. The expectation generated by the language of Ex 6^{2-9} is fulfilled by an account of the distribution of the land of Canaan among the tribes who have crossed the Jordan in the book of Joshua. This comprehensive treatise has received the name of the Priestly Code, and is indicated by the letter **P**.

(β) The characteristics of **P** are so clear and well marked, that there can only occasionally be any doubt concerning the passages to be assigned to it. Its definite ideas and its firmly knit institutions supply an invaluable standard of comparison. Whatever doubts may yet remain about its origin and date, the diversity of opinion about its actual constituent parts is confined within very narrow limits. The case is otherwise with the Yahwist and Elohist narratives. The criterion supplied by the different divine names in Genesis was there of great importance, owing to the general similarity of the religious atmosphere of the two sources. After Ex 3 that criterion tends to decline in frequency and value, though it does not wholly disappear. Happily it is by no means the sole instrument of discrimination. There are indeed cases in Exodus as in Genesis where there is palpable evidence that the narrative is composite, yet its actual elements can only be separated with differing degrees of probability. Yet there seems no substantial reason for doubting that when the portions due to **P** have been removed from Exodus, the remainder belongs to the Yahwist and Elohist of Genesis. Neither of these writers is, like **P**, primarily concerned with religious institutions. Yet each has included a brief collection of ancient law Ex 21-23 and 34, whose correspondences with each other and variations from **P** are of the utmost interest and significance. By one the sacred mountain is called Horeb, by the other Sinai; but both agree in making it the scene of a covenant between Yahweh and Israel, in which the conduct required from the people in their future home is laid down. Each has its tale of incidents upon the march; each relates the beginnings of the conquest north of Moab; each carries the Israelites across the Jordan after the death of Moses, and describes their settlement under Joshua in the land of their forefathers. Nor indeed do they seem, like **P**, to have stopped there. As their chief interest was historical, it was not limited to the religious foundations of the Mosaic age. The books which follow Joshua display many of the peculiarities already observed in Genesis and its successors. Judges and Samuel, likewise, contain abundant traces of compilation. Duplicate narratives lie side by side, or are even woven together. The same methods which lead to the decomposition of Genesis can be applied to them with corresponding results. It is natural, therefore, to ask in what relation their constituent elements stand to the documents of the Hexateuch. No clear traces can be discerned of **P**, though there is at least one episode showing occasional curious parallels of phrase (Judg 20-21). Two other groups, however, range themselves by natural affinity with the Yahwist and Elohist of the Hexateuch: and it seems a probable conjecture that these narratives constituted two great collections of the national traditions down to the establishment of the monarchy. Not till after the conquests of

David were the ideal limits of Israel's dominion set at the Egyptian frontier on the south west and the Euphrates in the north east Gen 15^{18}. It is not impossible that the document which related the promise also described its fulfilment. For purposes of convenience it is usual to denote the Yahwist narrative which employs the sacred name JHVH from the beginning by **J**; while the Elohist is naturally represented by **E**. The obvious fact that Genesis opens with a passage from the priestly code **P**, and that the *tol^{e}dhoth* sections form the literary groundwork of the whole structure of the patriarchal stories, justifies the provisional view that whatever may be the respective dates of the documents, **P** forms the actual basis of the present amalgamation. As **J** is the next to enter 2^{4b}, while **E** makes its appearance last, the composition of the first four books, Genesis—Numbers, may be summarized by the formula **PJE**. These elements, moreover, can all be recognized again in Joshua. But in the meantime a new item of the highest importance has been introduced.

(γ) The Book of Deuteronomy occupies a peculiar position in the Hexateuch. It is formed out of a series of discourses delivered by Moses to Israel immediately before his death. These discourses are partly historic, in the shape of a recital of the events at Horeb or during the wanderings since; they are partly hortatory; and partly concerned with the promulgation of statutes and judgements, some of which correspond with earlier issues, while some are wholly new. The question at once arises as to the connexion of Deuteronomy with what precedes. On the traditional hypothesis of unity of authorship a very singular phenomenon presents itself. Chronologically the book belongs to the same year as the concluding chapters of Numbers 26-36^a. In that group of narrative and law the organization of the people is regularly described by certain terms, 'congregation,' 'tribe' (מטה), 'princes of the congregation;' the Levites are formally endowed with forty-eight cities 35$^{1-8}$; Joshua receives a final charge from Moses (since his end is near) 27^{18}·· and is solemnly set before Eleazar the priest and all the congregation. But in the book of Deuteronomy all this is changed. The 'congregation' disappears, and an 'assembly' takes its place. The tribes are always designated by another term (שבט); the 'princes' are converted into 'heads of tribes' and 'elders.' The Levites are declared to have no inheritance; they live scattered among the homesteads of the people; and in consequence they are constantly commended to public charity along with the widow and the orphan. Finally, on the approach of Moses' death 31^{14}·· he gives Joshua a solemn charge. No mention, however, is made of Eleazar the priest or of the congregation. Yahweh himself is at once its witness and its sanction, standing in the pillar of cloud by the entrance of the sacred tent. These are but a few of the obvious differences which divide Deuteronomy (which will in future be indicated by **D**) from the supposed contemporary passage Num 26-36. The basis of comparison is sufficiently large to prove that the same writer could not have written both. Three lines of evidence lead to a common conclusion. In the first place, the vocabulary changes completely at the opening of **D**, and the change is consistently maintained (save for a few verses) throughout the book. Secondly, in its historic allusions **D** takes again and again a different view of the actual facts. And thirdly, it ignores the legal and religious institutions assumed or enacted in Num 26-36, and produces fresh ones of its own. Why, for example, after an elaborate law has been ordained in 35$^{9-34}$ for the provision of cities of refuge for accidental homicide, should it be necessary to repeat it within a few months with different arrangements and a fresh set of formulae in Deut 19$^{1-13}$? The evidence under these three heads will be more fully presented at a future stage (cp chap VIII iii 2ζη). It will perhaps be admitted that a prima facie case has been established for the view that among the Five Books **D** may

---

^{a} Cp Num 20^{2v}· 33^{38} Deut 1^3.

be tentatively regarded as a separate literary whole. Further inquiry will reveal that large portions of the book of Joshua exhibit the same significant marks. The whole structure of the Hexateuch, therefore, may be comprised under the symbol **PJED**.

CHAPTER VII

THE DOCUMENTARY THEORIES

IN the foregoing sketch the results of more than a century of criticism have been provisionally expounded. Their fuller justification, and the inquiry into some of the many problems which they suggest, will perhaps best be introduced by an indication of the mode in which the distribution just described has been forced by the facts upon successive schools and generations of investigators. Astruc's work reached much further than he knew. The questions that immediately arose out of it concerned (1) the number, the scope, and the characteristics of the constituent documents; and (2) the determination of their mutual age and relations.

1. The first great step was taken by Johann Gottfried Eichhorn, of Gottingen [a]. In the first volume of his *Introduction to the Old Testament* (published in 1780) he adopted the general results of Astruc, on the basis of his own independent investigation. It is even possible to doubt whether he had ever seen the *Conjectures*; there is some reason to believe that he knew the work of his predecessor only by the comments which it evoked [b]. Seven years later, however, in the preface to the second edition of his Introduction, he formulated in brief the aim of what he was the first to designate 'the Higher Criticism':—

I have been obliged to bestow the greatest amount of labour on a hitherto entirely unworked field, the investigation of the inner constitution (*Beschaffenheit*) of the separate books of the Old Testament by the aid of the Higher Criticism (a new name to no Humanist).

He endeavoured accordingly, after giving a full account of the external resources of criticism in a history of the text and its versions, to ascertain the characteristics and composition of each work in the Hebrew Canon. From his justification of his treatment of Genesis, the compilation of which he ascribed to Moses, some sentences may still be quoted (ii 295 § 424):—

For the discovery of the inner constitution (*Beschaffenheit*) of the first book of Moses, party spirit will perhaps for a couple of decades snort at the Higher Criticism, instead of rewarding it with the thanks which are really due to it. For, first, the credibility of the book obviously gains by it. Did ever a historical inquirer go more religiously to work with his sources than the arranger of these? He is so certain of the genuineness and truth of his documents that he gives them as they are . . The gain which history, interpretation, and criticism derive from this discovery is exceptionally great The historian is no longer obliged to rely on one reporter in the history of the most distant past; and in the duplicated narratives of the same event he is not obliged to force into harmony the unessential differences in accessory circumstances by artificial devices. He sees in such divergences the marks of independent origin, and finds in their agreement in the main important mutual confirmation . . The interpreter, when the Higher Criticism has separated his documents for him, need no longer wrestle with difficulties which before were insoluble. He will no longer explain the second chapter of Genesis by the first, or the first by the second, and the world will cease to lay on Moses the burden of the sins of his younger expositors Finally, when the Higher Criticism has distinguished between the writers, and characterized each of them by his general method, his diction, his favourite expressions and other peculiarities, her lower sister who occupies herself only with words and spies out false readings, lays down her own rules and principles for determining the text, discovering glosses, and detecting interpolations and transpositions.

[a] Cp Cheyne, *Founders of Old Testament Criticism* 13.
[b] So Westphal, *Les Sources du Pentateuque* 1 119 Eichhorn himself says (*Einleit* [2] ii 247) that he worked independently of Astruc that his own point of view might not be *verruckt* (deranged). After referring to J F W Jerusalem and J J Schultens, he adds, 'none of them all penetrated so deep into the matter as Astruc'

The general result at which Eichhorn arrived was similar to that of Astruc. Both recognized an Elohist and a Yahwist document running through Genesis. Both also recognized the presence of occasional independent pieces which could not be assigned to either leading source. Such was the blessing of Jacob Gen 49$^{1-27}$, and such also the narrative of the invasion of the four kings 14, of which Eichhorn observed that its peculiar character, its glosses and explanations, and its unique divine names, all pointed to its separate origin at the hand of a writer who must have lived near the time of the occurrence (ii 262-3)^a. By a careful analysis of the story of the Flood Eichhorn endeavoured to arrive at a clearer conception of the literary marks of each source. He drew up tables of their characteristic words and classified their expressions, so that he might have the means of recognizing them elsewhere. He rightly described his Elohist (in the Noah tol^edhoth the modern P) as following a chronological method; to J with less reason he attributed a special interest in cosmography. The 'higher criticism' was thus fairly started; but when applied to Exodus and Leviticus it did not get beyond the suggestion (ii 356) that they had in part grown out of a collection of separate documents, many of them incomplete and fragmentary, yet all belonging to the Mosaic age. These pieces he made no attempt to connect with each other, or with the sources of Genesis. It was to become apparent later on that either (1) the books from Exodus to Numbers must be regarded as continuous with Genesis, or (2) Genesis itself must be reduced to a similar collection of fragments.

2. The stimulating work of Eichhorn soon called fresh students into the field. Before passing to the fuller development of Eichhorn's 'fragment-hypothesis,' it is due to the almost forgotten name of Karl David Ilgen^b to call attention to his important contribution to the analysis of Genesis. The title of his book *The Original Documents of the Temple Archives at Jerusalem in their Primitive Form* (Halle, 1798) indicates the point of view from which he started. The history of Israel could not be properly studied till its sources had been rescued from the confusion, disorder, and mutilation which had befallen them. In the first volume, accordingly (no second was ever issued), Ilgen printed in separate sections the documents out of which he believed Genesis to have been composed. The result was highly interesting. In addition to the Yahwist J he fell upon the distinction already indicated (chap VI 1a) between two Elohist writers within the same book^c. But he did not work it out in the same manner as his modern successors. Like Eichhorn he founded his argument on the frequent presence of repetitions and doublets, on incongruities of fact and diversities of style, on variations in character and portrayal. But he was more rigid in the application of his criteria. His E^1 and E^2, therefore, by no means correspond to the P and E of current recognition. The story in 20 of Abraham and Abimelech, for example, now assigned to E, he ascribed to the author of 1, and placed it in the tol^edhoth group. In the artless repetitions in 22$^{1-13}$ he found traces of two hands, and he even applied this treatment to the narrative of the creation in 1-2^{4a}. Placing the tol^edhoth formula 2^{4a} at the head of the section, he noted that the story was cast into an impossible succession of days; there were evenings and mornings before there was any sun. He therefore eliminated 1$^{5\ 8\ 13\ 19\ 23\ 31}$ 2^1 as the handiwork of E^2. To E^2 further, on the ground chiefly of the frequent occurrence of θεός in the Greek versions, he ascribed the second creation story and its pendants in 2^{4b}-4, the statement in 4^{26} having been remoulded by a later hand, and the divine names generally amalgamated or

---

^{a} Other insertions, according to Eichhorn, would be found in 2^1-3, which Astruc had more correctly attributed to J, 33^{18}-34^{31} and 36$^{1-43}$, where again Astruc came nearer to the modern view
^{b} Cp Cheyne, *Founders of OT Criticism* 26.
^{c} Behind these writers lay the materials out of which their documents were composed, which were referred to numerous sources.

confused. This partition was carried to the end of 11, and the Yahwist was not allowed to make his entry till 12^1. Ilgen's E^1 and E^2, therefore, are hardly to be recognized in the modern P and E; and the eccentricities of his distribution involved his book in unmerited obscurity. The work abounded in shrewd and penetrating remarks, and was the first to point out that two narratives are blended in the stories of Joseph 40–48 which Astruc and Eichhorn (as far as 47^{27}) had agreed in assigning to the Elohist alone[a]. When the existence of E^2 was again demonstrated by Hupfeld, more than fifty years later, he made a generous acknowledgement of his indebtedness to his neglected predecessor.

3. The investigations of Ilgen were confined like those of Astruc to the Book of Genesis. But it became more and more apparent that this limitation must be abandoned. The composition of Genesis could not be separated from that of the middle books. In these Eichhorn had recognized a collection of separate and discontinuous pieces, though he insisted that they all originated in the Mosaic age. This was a revival of the view of some of the seventeenth-century critics, and it was soon applied to the entire Pentateuch and Joshua.

(a) The application was made in this country by a learned Roman Catholic priest, Dr Alexander Geddes[b], who published in 1792 the first volume of a new translation of the Scriptures with explanatory notes and critical remarks[c]. In an introductory chapter Dr Geddes laid down three propositions: '(1) the Pentateuch in its present form was not written by Moses: (2) it was written in the land of Canaan and most probably at Jerusalem: (3) it could not be written before the reign of David, nor after that of Hezekiah:' and he suggested 'the long pacific reign of Solomon' as the most suitable. But the date of the present form of the Pentateuch is one thing, and the antiquity of its materials is another: and on this distinction Dr Geddes wrote as follows[d]:—

> But although I am inclined to believe that the Pentateuch was reduced into its present form in the reign of Solomon, I am fully persuaded that it was compiled from ancient documents some of which were coeval with Moses, and some even anterior to Moses. Whether all these were written records, or many of them only oral traditions, it would be rash to determine. It is my opinion that the Hebrews had no written documents before the days of Moses, and that all their history prior to that period is derived from monumental indexes or traditional tales. Some remarkable tree under which a patriarch had resided; some pillar which he had erected, some heap which he had raised, some ford which he had crossed, some spot where he had encamped, some field which he had purchased, the tomb in which he had been laid—all these served as so many links to hand his story down to posterity, and corroborated the oral testimony transmitted from generation to generation in simple narratives or rustic songs. That the marvellous would sometimes creep into these we can easily conceive; but still the essence, or at least the skeleton of history, was preserved.

Whether Moses was the first collector, Geddes was willing to leave uncertain, though his own opinion leaned decidedly to the later date. He included the book of Joshua with the Pentateuch in his first volume because he 'conceived it to have been compiled by the same author.' But the volume which was to have contained the justification of his view was never published.

(β) The Biblical study of Great Britain at the beginning of this century did not contribute much to the development of research in Germany; but the work of Geddes had the rare distinction of incorporation into an elaborate commentary on the Pentateuch by J S Vater, published at Halle (in three volumes) in the years 1802 and 1805. Vater carried out the 'fragment-hypothesis' to its fullest extent, and

---

[a] Ilgen divided the whole group 39–50 between his two Elohists. The last passage he allotted to J was 38.

[b] Cheyne, *Founders of OT Criticism* 4.

[c] A second volume appeared in 1797, but the enterprise was never completed, though a volume of *Critical Remarks* (Gen—Deut) was issued in 1800.

[d] Vol I p xix.

regarded the Pentateuch as a huge aggregate of separate compositions varying naturally in extent, but not capable of classification into groups or of union into single wholes. The strongest evidences for this were found in the obvious fact that small collections of laws have been thrown together, as was proved (for instance) by the closing formulae of Lev 7 26 27. Even Deuteronomy which presented 'most appearance of unity' did not escape his dissection. He pointed, with penetrating insight, to the different titles traceable in 1^{1-4} 4^{45-49} and 12^1: he insisted that $1-4^{40}$ was not written by the author of $4^{45}-11$; he declared that 12–26 was a piece by itself, subsequently united with the preceding discourses by 11^{32}; he even affirmed that within this collection duplicates might again be discovered, such as 12^{13-16} and 12^{20-24}, while $31^{1-8\ 9-12}$ formed a parallel to $31^{14-23\ 24}\ldots$. But his eye for superficial differences was much keener than his perception of their underlying unity. He had a brilliant vision for the discrepancies of the adjacent; but he could not discern the affinities of the remote. He could concede that some pieces in the same book might belong to a common source; he could hardly admit it when they were found in separate books. It was possible to distinguish passages in Genesis marked by the use of Yahweh from those which only employed Elohim; but this simple test could not prove identity of authorship on the basis of the occurrence of similar names; and he apparently despaired of discovering other and more satisfactory criteria. It was much easier (as other malcontents have since found) to ridicule Astruc, Eichhorn, and Ilgen, for their different distributions of a difficult passage like Gen 30. Which division, he asked triumphantly, is right? for all three disagree (iii 726). The arrangement of the Pentateuch as a whole Vater was disposed to place rather later than Dr Geddes. The age of David or Solomon was no doubt appropriate for a legislative collection such as he conceived to lie at the basis of Deuteronomy. Lost for a time in obscurity, this was discovered under Josiah; and the series of documents of history and law which had come into existence in the meantime, were gradually united with it towards the close of the monarchy. Not till the exile did the Pentateuch as a whole rise into view.

4. If the ponderous volumes of Vater had done nothing more than waken the interest of the young De Wette, they would not have been written in vain. In the year 1806 W M L De Wette, then only five-and-twenty years of age, published at Halle the first part of a remarkable little treatise which he modestly entitled *Contributions to the Introduction to the Old Testament*[a]. With singular freshness and independence of judgement this masterly book opened up a new line of inquiry, and inaugurated the investigation of the religious institutions of the Pentateuch.

(*a*) De Wette conceived of his problem as really twofold. As it had been stated by Astruc, Eichhorn, and the analytical school, it had a literary side. What were the materials of which the Pentateuch was composed? Could they be arranged in continuous documents, or were they nothing but unconnected fragments? Or were they, as Eichhorn had asserted, continuous in Genesis, but afterwards separate and unrelated? The answer of De Wette to these questions was somewhat cautious and reserved. On the one hand he accepted Vater's 'proof' that all the books of the Pentateuch were composed of single independent and often contradictory documents (i 265). Not even Deuteronomy was an exception, though this book was undoubtedly distinguished by a greater uniformity of tone. It was possible, indeed, that each book had its own compiler; but De Wette regarded the attempts of the critics to recover the constituents of the sources as inevitably unsuccessful. There was no security that the compiler had not made large omissions. The materials for the analysis were insufficient. With regard to the divine names he asked (as

---

[a] *Beiträge zur Einleitung in das Alte Testament*. The second part followed in 1807. Cp Cheyne, *Founders of OT Criticism* 31.

Klostermann has done since) what guarantee there was that they had remained unimpaired by accidental corruption or intentional change: and he laid it down that they were not so much the distinctive property of different writers as the marks of different periods or religious schools (ii 29–30). Nevertheless De Wette did recognize a fundamental Elohist document in Genesis, continued in the middle books, which was concerned with the origin of the national religion and its ceremonial expression. He described it as the Epos of the Hebrew theocracy (ii 31). Into this document were from time to time inserted small collections of laws which had grown up independently, such as the Covenant-book in Ex 21–23, the ritual of sacrifice Lev 1–7, the groups which had been thrown together in 11 13-14 15, or the short code to which 26 formed an obvious close. Similarly it would seem, the Yahwist narratives in Genesis were successively incorporated in the Elohist groundwork, though De Wette did not formulate any clear view of the process.

(β) The main strength of his work lay on the historical side. Putting aside the literary questions which had been raised concerning Genesis, De Wette turned to the examination of the institutions implied or described in the Pentateuchal codes. How far were these institutions, he asked in effect, consistent with each other, and how far did the history of Israel show evidence of their existence? Like another young student sixty years later, Graf, he opened his inquiry with an investigation of the differences between the books of Chronicles and Kings; which ended in the rejection of the former as evidence for the religious usages of Israel under the early monarchy. The real testimony was to be found in the unconscious witness supplied by the indications of Judges, Samuel, and Kings. When these proved that the requirements of the Pentateuch were continually ignored or violated by the responsible leaders of the nation, did not such neglect or violation constitute good grounds for believing that the requirements in question had not yet been definitely imposed? For example, the cultus enjoined at the Dwelling (Ex 25–30, and Leviticus *passim*) assumed that sacrifice could be offered only in one place. That also was the fundamental law of Deut 12. Yet the whole history after the age of Joshua was one continuous demonstration that this principle had in no way controlled the religious practice of the nation. The book of Judges showed that Mizpah, Bethel, and Shilo were all of them accredited sanctuaries. Samuel and the first kings had not been at all confined to a single altar. Mizpah, Bethel, Zuph (1 Sam 9^{12}), Gilgal, Bethlehem, Nob, Hebron, Gibeon, each witnessed again and again the sacred acts which the law permitted on one spot alone. Even after the erection of the temple this freedom was still maintained. The worship of the royal sanctuary was in fact a court function, and by no means superseded that of the ancient centres of hallowed tradition. So far indeed as the description of the Levitical Dwelling was concerned Ex 25 , it could not be reconciled with that of the Tent of Meeting in 33$^{7\cdots}$; and it was plainly modelled on the edifice in Jerusalem (ii 268). But with it was inseparably connected the Aaronic priesthood and the entire corpus of Levitical law. That was, indeed, the product of a long development; the history of the removal of the ark in 2 Sam 6 showed how free and even lawless (from the later point of view) were the proceedings of David (i 244) The Pentateuch, then, contained within itself indications of the successive development of legislation (i 265); and a comparison with history was the only satisfactory basis for conjectures concerning the origins of its different codes. In laying down this principle De Wette flung out a number of brilliant suggestions which were then little more than clever and courageous guesses, but have since become widely accepted. In the narrative of the golden calf he saw the prophetic condemnation of the worship of the Ten Tribes. From Jer 7^{21} · he inferred that there was then no body of ceremonial legislation claiming (like the Levitical) a Sinaitic origin and a Mosaic authority (i 184). This pregnant hint, however, he did not further pursue. He made no detailed comparison between successive strata which he recognized in the Pentateuch, (1) the Covenant-book, (2) the institution of the Dwelling and its priesthood with the associated Levitical ritual, and (3) Deuteronomy. He did not investigate with any minuteness the question of priority between the last two[a], though he plainly regarded the first as the earliest. But he did endeavour (and in the main successfully) to fix the age of Deuteronomy. In a striking chapter on the 'Relation of Deuteronomy to the preceding books of the Pentateuch' he argued that the law of the unity of the sanctuary in Deut 12 certainly referred to Jerusalem; before the temple there was no trace of a general national centre of religious worship. The book belonged therefore to the monarchy, and this was confirmed by its express sanction of the royal power 17^{14}... To what reign, then, could it be assigned? In some passages like 14 23^{21}· 24^8 it presupposed other legislation behind it, but in 4^{19} 17^3 it forbade a worship prohibited in no other laws, which Manasseh was first recorded to have practised 2 Kings $21^{3\ 5}$, the cultus of the host of heaven. De Wette, then, assigned the book without hesitation to the seventh century, and by this result the majority of critics still to-day abide.

5. The work of De Wette was so far in advance of its time that it had all to be done over again two generations later. But the progress of investigation went slowly on. A succession of scholars discussed the literary problem with unwearied zeal. Various hypotheses were propounded as it became more and more clear that the facts were more complicated than had yet been realized. One great name stands out in the middle of the century as that of a master, for the pre-eminence of his genius, the immense extent of his labours, and (it must be added) the seeming arbitrariness of his judgements, Heinrich Ewald[b]. In the *History of Israel* Ewald endeavoured to do for the Hebrew people what Niebuhr had done for Rome. He saw that historical construction was only possible when the literary materials on which it was based had been carefully classified, and their worth thoroughly sifted. He opened his narrative, accordingly, with a survey of the documents from which it was derived. The Pentateuch was resolved into a variety of literary groups, but he gave no clue to the method by which any given passage was referred to its source, or the age and characteristics of that source were discovered. His exposition was consequently somewhat oracular; in the twenty years which elapsed between the first edition (1843) and the third (1864) it underwent some slight modifications; its general features, however, remained the same, and in spite of occasional indistinctness in detail, his main conception exercised a commanding influence over a whole generation of scholars. Earliest in date he recognized a few scanty traces of Mosaic works such as the Ten Words in their primitive form, fragments from a biography of Moses, and a Book of Covenants (the latter including, for instance, the two Beer-sheba incidents in Genesis, and the Covenant-book in Ex 21^2–23^{19}). None of these, however, were continuous. The remainder might be distributed into three groups. There was first the Book of Origins (*tol^edhoth*), a treatise of universal history and priestly legislation, opening with the creation in Gen 1, and coincident with the modern P. This was the literary foundation of the whole, extending into Joshua, and was assigned to the age of Solomon. Secondly, Ewald recognized a series of prophetic narratives running through Genesis, Exodus, and Numbers. They were finally distributed among three different writers, who flourished in the eighth and ninth centuries, from the

---

[a] He seems to have considered Leviticus as the older on the ground that Lev 26 had been imitated in Deut 28, cp Lev 26^{19} Deut 28^{23}, 26^{29} Deut 28^{53-57}, 26^{16} Deut 28^{22} &c, i 272.

[b] Cp Cheyne, *Founders of OT Criticism* 66. His first work, *Die Composition der Genesis kritisch untersucht*, appeared in 1823, and maintained the unity of Genesis in narrative, plan, and language

days of Elijah to the age preceding Amos. To these were assigned the documents already designated **J** and **E** (chap VI 2β), one of the prophetic narrators being credited with portions of each. The oldest was an Ephraimite; the other two belonged to Judah, and the last was supposed to have partially supplemented the work of his predecessors and united the documents into a whole. Finally, the book of Deuteronomy, written in the reign of Manasseh, was attached to the preceding collection before the close of the seventh century, the final editor revising the whole. According to this scheme not only the literary but also the historical composition of the Pentateuch would be expressed in modern symbols by the formula **PJED**. The arrangement brought into strong relief the distinction between the priestly and prophetic elements in the Pentateuch, but gave the priority to the former. It placed beyond doubt the existence of that 'epic of the theocracy' which De Wette had recognized in the welter of Vater's fragments, and treated it as the groundwork of the whole. It conceived the prophetic narratives as in the main independent original sources, not merely designed as 'supplements' to the brief introduction to the Priestly law. And it admitted that a hand in sympathy with Deuteronomy had put the finishing touches to the combined work. The view of the growth of Israel's religious institutions which resulted from the ascription of the sacerdotal organization in the Book of Origins to the age of Solomon, was naturally widely different from that of De Wette who regarded it as of much later date. Yet both asserted that Deuteronomy was the latest of the Pentateuchal Codes, and agreed in assigning it to the seventh century.

CHAPTER VIII

THE JUSTIFICATION OF THE PARTITION

The modern form of the documentary theory of the Hexateuch really dates from Ewald's contemporary Hupfeld, whose treatise on the 'Sources of Genesis[a]' finally proved the existence of the three independent narrators now designated **P J** and **E**. The details of his analysis have been frequently set aside by subsequent investigation[b]. But his main results have stood the test of further inquiry. His view of the historical relations of the documents, which approximated to that of Ewald, has indeed been rejected in favour of a hypothesis which may be regarded as now established in the critical schools. His literary partition, however, dating just a century from Astruc's, still provides the clue to the distribution of the Pentateuch into its constituent parts.

On what grounds does that partition rest? It is still sometimes represented as little more than a whim or caprice of learned industry, which found no better occupation than that of counting up the occurrences of words and grounded its analysis on a purely linguistic basis. This has been called the philological theory[c]. It must, however, be remembered, as the foregoing sketch has endeavoured to indicate, that the hypothesis of different documents was only slowly evolved as a means of explaining the presence of multitudes of conflicting facts, which were inconsistent with unity of authorship. These facts remained at first isolated and disconnected. When they were compared, it was found that unexpected links of idea or phrase could be detected among them. The suggestion then naturally arose that they might be grouped around

[a] *Die Quellen der Genesis*, Berlin, 1853   Cp Cheyne, *Founders of OT Criticism* 149.
[b] Thus he restored E^1 (P) in Exodus after 6^{2-9} as follows, $12^{40\ 51}\ 12^{37}\ 13^{20}\ 15^{22\ 23a\ 27}\ 16^1\ 17^1\ 19^1$, $20^{1-17}\ 21-23^{19}\ 24^{3-8}\ 25-31\ 35-40$ Lev 8 &c.
[c] Sayce, *Early History of the Hebrews* 105.

these criteria. Certain conceptions tended to recur in similarities of language, but not till the conceptions were recognized as harmonious, were the affinities of expression observed. The 'philological method' is therefore not the beginning but one of the results of the whole process. Doubtless, in its turn, it becomes an instrument for the analysis of passages which there is reason, on other grounds, to regard as composite. It may even in conspicuous cases, such as the relation of Deuteronomy to Num 26–36, serve at the outset to create a presumption in favour of difference of origin. But at the best it is only one among several criteria, which may not, indeed, be all capable of application to any given section, still less to any particular verse, but which are founded on an examination of the Pentateuch as a whole. These criteria are of various kinds. The Pentateuch contains a collection of laws and histories, which depict the origins of Israel's religious institutions. What are those institutions? Are they consistently represented in the same forms? Do the regulations concerning them make the same assumptions and enjoin the same practice? Do the narratives which describe them always agree with the ordinances which have preceded? If not, cannot the usages be classified, and the narratives which cohere with them be arranged in groups? The different institutions of the Pentateuchal codes thus supply the first criterion. Positive religious commands of course embody definite beliefs. These beliefs constantly determine the form in which special requirements are expressed or particular events are understood. The view of Israel's early history, offered by any writer, will largely depend upon his thought of Israel's God. The specific institutions of a later day bear a definite relation to the past. If the institutions are conceived differently, the past will be conceived differently also, and vice versa. A second criterion may therefore be found in the agreement or diversity of religious ideas. Diversity of religious ideas implies the existence, synchronously or in succession, of different schools of thought. Thus Jeremiah and Ezekiel belonged to the same period and were members of the same priesthood. They took similar views of the causes of the national ruin in which they were both involved. But in spite of occasional community of thought and utterance, each has a devotional idiom of his own. When similar differences are discovered in the Pentateuch, when one set of laws and exhortations shows marked affinities with the language of Jeremiah, and another with the phraseology of Ezekiel, how is the fact to be explained? Doubtless more than one explanation is possible, but the historian is bound to inquire which is the most probable. These facts claim recognition as strongly as the parallel between the legal style of the record of Abraham's purchase of the cave of Machpelah Gen 23 and the contract tablets of ancient Babylonia[a]. Both have their basis in general correspondences of expression or in the specific usage of words. If the method be legitimate in the one case, it cannot be pronounced futile in the other. The resemblances of language, then, constitute a third branch of inquiry, first of all for documentary identification within the Pentateuch itself, and subsequently for historical comparison in the wider field of Hebrew literature. In the following section illustrations are offered of this threefold argument. In fixing its attention first on the Pentateuchal institutions, recent investigation owes most, of course, to the brilliant analysis of Wellhausen in the *Prolegomena to the History of Israel*[b].

i. *The Argument from Religious Institutions*

1. The central act of ancient Israelite worship consisted in sacrifice. Around this rite various questions gradually arose. By whom might it be offered? In what places

---

[a] Sayce, *Early History of the Hebrews* 57; *Expository Times*, Jan 1898.
[b] Edinburgh, 1885. First published in Berlin, 1878, under the title *History of Israel*. The significance of this work will be more fully indicated hereafter.

and under what forms? The answers to these questions in the Pentateuch, direct or implied, are by no means identical.

(*a*) The sketch of primaeval history in Gen 4 depicts sacrifice as the earliest form of religious homage. Cain and Abel both bring their offerings to Yahweh. When Noah and his family have left the ark, his first act is to build an altar to Yahweh 8^{20}. On Abram's arrival at Shechem he offers his first sacrifice to Yahweh in the land of promise 12^7, and repeats his worship between Bethel and Ai ^{8}, a stage further south, cp 13^4. At Hebron he dedicates another altar to Yahweh 13^{18}, and at Beer-sheba plants a sacred tree 21^{33}. There Isaac also rears an altar to Yahweh 26^{25}. J therefore recognizes the patriarchal practice from the first days. Nor does E take any different view. His Abraham follows the usage of his counterpart in J, but with a more precious victim 22^9. Jacob offers a sacrifice in the mountain (Gilead) 31^{54}. On reaching Shechem, he renews to El, the Elohim of Israel, the devotion which his grandfather had paid 33^{20}; and at Bethel he builds an altar to the El of the sacred place $35^{7\,a}$. Both J and E then freely attribute the right of sacrifice to the patriarchs, as heads of families. Nay even race is no limitation. Jethro takes a burnt offering for Elohim Ex 18^{12}, and Aaron and the elders of Israel are invited to the hallowed meal. And when Moses prepares to solemnize the covenant between Yahweh and his people, he sends 'young men of the children of Israel, which offered burnt offerings, and sacrificed peace offerings of oxen unto Yahweh' 24^5. Were there, then, no priests? They are, indeed, named in $19^{22\ 24}$ (assigned in the analysis to J), as though their functions might be taken for granted ^{b}. But of their origin there is no hint. The view of P, however, is entirely different. In the *Tol^edhoth* book in Genesis the perfect Noah makes no thank offering when the peril of the flood is past. Abraham, Isaac, Jacob, move through the land; but they never commemorate, by the ritual of the altar, the 'place' where El Shaddai appears. No sacrifice was legitimate which was not offered according to divine command. The cultus of P is not the spontaneous offering of man to his Maker, old as the human race. It is the express ordinance of God himself; it must be performed by the persons whom he chooses and at the spot which he selects. Not till the Dwelling was reared was the place prepared Ex 40^{29}; not till Aaron and his sons were consecrated could sacrifice properly begin Lev $8^7 \cdots$.

(β) The place, then, according to one conception, is as important as the persons. The patriarchs of J and E felt no reserve in this matter. Wherever Yahweh or Elohim appeared, the divine condescension evoked its natural response. And this view was embodied in the earliest legislative rule Ex 20^{24}:—

An altar of earth thou shalt make unto me, and shalt sacrifice thereon thy burnt offerings, and thy peace offerings, thy sheep, and thine oxen in every place where I ^{c} cause my name to be remembered I will come unto thee and I will bless thee.

The passage proceeds to sanction, as an alternative to the earth-altar, an altar of unhewn stone. Neither of these, it is plain, can be identified with the altar of the Dwelling, which is made of wood with bronze plates $27^1 \cdot$. The rule cannot possibly be limited to the period preceding the construction of the Desert sanctuary, for it is announced as of universal application. It receives its historic interpretation only in connexion with the usage of Israel in Canaan as reflected alike in the patriarchal narratives and in the period following the settlement, and an interesting application of it is

---

^{a} This passage is plainly connected with 28^{17}, and necessarily implies another Elohistic writer in Genesis besides P, when compared with 35^{9-15}. So Hupfeld, *Quellen* 38.

^{b} Cp 'Aaron the Levite,' i e priest 4^{14}.

^{c} 𝔖 and the *Jerusalem Targum* read 'thou shalt cause' This reading is defended by Kuenen, *Rel of Isr* ii 82, and has been supported by Geiger, Hitzig, Merx, and more recently by Bruston.

seen in Deut 27⁵, cp Josh 8³¹. But D lays down a very different principle. The Deuteronomic code opens in 12 with the demand that all local sanctuaries shall be abolished, and sacrifice shall be restricted only to the single place which Yahweh shall choose 12⁵. :—

⁵ Unto the place which Yahweh your God shall choose out of all your tribes to put his name there, even unto his habitation shall ye seek, and thither thou shalt come ⁶ and thither ye shall bring your burnt offerings, and your sacrifices, &c.

The permission which is thus expressly granted in Ex 20²⁴ is here withdrawn. The worshipper may only 'remember Yahweh's name' in a single spot. That which was legalized in Sinai is denounced in Moab ⁸ :—

Ye shall not do after all the things that we do here this day, every man whatsoever is right in his own eyes

The Deuteronomic law was understood to refer to Jerusalem (1 Kings 8¹⁶, where 𝔊 adds, 'but I chose Jerusalem that my name should be there,' cp 2 Chron 6⁶ 1 Kings 8⁴⁴ ⁴⁸ &c^a), and its reiteration in various forms throughout the code shows what stress it was felt necessary to lay upon it, cp 14²² 15²⁰ 16⁵. &c. It is not a little surprising that the Deuteronomic formula concerning the place which Yahweh would choose to make his name 'dwell' there (שכן), should make no allusion to the 'Dwelling' (משכן) which had been already erected for that precise purpose^b. In this Dwelling alone might sacrifice be offered. Throughout the manual of ritual Lev 1–7 which precedes the account of the dedication of Aaron and his sons, the possibility of sacrifice elsewhere than on the altar, at the entrance of the tent of meeting, is nowhere recognized. There is but one sanctuary and one altar. In a strange passage (which will become more intelligible subsequently) 17⁵⁻⁷, the sacrifices which are offered 'in the open field' are treated as no better than offerings to satyrs. The illegitimacy of all cultus, save at the central sanctuary, no longer needs demonstration or enforcement, it is throughout assumed.

(γ) It may be added that the classes of sacrifice which these three sets of documents recognize are not entirely identical. When Cain brings his offering Gen 4³, it is a *minhah*, i e a 'present' (cp 32¹³.. 33¹⁰ 43¹¹). Such gifts were conveyed to Deity upon the altar by fire, and hence were called burnt offerings, *'olah*. Besides the 'burnt offerings' the law of the earthen altar Ex 20²⁴ recognizes also 'peace offerings,' and both these formed part of the covenant sacrifice by the 'young men' 24⁵. In Deut 12⁶ ¹⁷ the list is increased by the 'heave offering,' besides tithes and vows and freewill offerings and firstling dues (cp Ex 22²⁹. 34¹⁹ ²²), the term *minhah* being absent^c. In P, however, the name reappears with a limited meaning, that of 'meal offering.' It forms only one of a long series (P118) which may be summed up under the general term 'oblation' (*qorbân*). Not only is this word peculiar to the Levitical law in relation to the other Pentateuchal codes, it occurs only twice in the rest of the whole literature of Israel (Ezek 20²⁸ 40⁴³). Moreover the Priestly list includes two kinds of offerings which find no place in D, the guilt offering and the sin offering. In view of the place which these occupy (especially the sin offering in the solemn ritual of Israel's most sacred day Lev 16), their total exclusion from the great recapitulation naturally awakens some surprise.

2. It has already been pointed out (chap IV 2β) that the books of Exodus and Numbers contain two incompatible representations of the sanctuary in the wilderness. In Ex 33⁷.. Num 11²⁴.. 12⁴ . the Tent of Meeting is pitched outside the camp. The first of

^a Cp Driver, *Deut* 140.
^b Ex 25⁸ 'that I may dwell among them' 29⁴⁵ 'and I will dwell among the children of Israel.'
^c Deut 18¹ also mentions the 'fire offerings.'

these passages assumes the existence of the tent and describes the sacred usage connected with it: the others supply incidental confirmation by depicting incidents which happened at its door. With these conceptions Deut 31^{14} is in harmony. It is a singular circumstance that (in the present text) the first mention of the place of this Tent Ex 33^{7}.. represents it as in actual use before it was made. It is a part of the sanctuary which is to be constructed 27^{21} 28^{43} 29^{4}... 30^{16}... 31^{7}; but its preparation is not begun till after the second sojourn of Moses on the mount 34, its erection being solemnly completed 40$^{2-33}$. Must it not be admitted that the two long corresponding sections 25–30 and 35–40 together with Num 2–3 present an account which is entirely independent of the story in Ex 33^{7} and inconsistent with it? It is true that P occasionally employs the designation 'tent of meeting' which marks the references to the sanctuary outside the camp. But P also coins his own name for it, the 'Dwelling' Ex 25^{8} (cp p 54). The probable origin and religious meaning of this term will demand consideration hereafter (chap XIII 3ε): at present it may suffice to remark that the employment of two titles where one alone is invariably used elsewhere, itself suggests another hand. Various differences will be found to gather round the two accounts: attention will be speedily called to the widely separated views of the sacred ministry connected with it (*infra* 4), and of the modes by which the divine presence was manifested at it (*infra* ii 2β).

3. The sacred tent was doubtless designed as a shelter or abode for the ark, which was in its turn the receptacle for the stones bearing the Ten Words. Of these Ten Words there are, in the opinion of some recent investigators, two versions, which cannot by any means be harmonized. One version is cited in two closely corresponding though not identical forms Ex 20 and Deut 5. Another is apparently contained in Ex 34, where ^{28} is understood by many interpreters^a to identify the preceding commands as the Ten Words (cp note *in loc*). Whatever view may be taken of this hypothesis, there can be no doubt that the account of the origin of the ark in Deut 10^{1}.. is entirely incompatible with that in Ex 25^{10}.. 37^{1} · (cp *ante* p 30). But what was the source of the Deuteronomic version? It occurs as the sequel of a recital of the apostasy of the golden calf Ex 32. The dependence of Deut 9^{12}.. on Ex 32^{7}.. will be illustrated hereafter: it is sufficient to point to their common continuation:—

Ex 34	Deut 10
^{1} And Yahweh said unto Moses, Hew thee two tables of stone like unto the first and I will write upon the tables the words that were on the first tables, which thou brakest ^{2} And be ready by the morning, and come up in the morning unto mount Sinai, and present thyself there to me on the top of the mount... ^{4} And he hewed two tables of stone like unto the first; and Moses rose up early in the morning, and went up unto mount Sinai, as Yahweh had commanded him, and took in his hand two tables of stone	At that time Yahweh said unto me, Hew thee two tables of stone like unto the first, and come up unto me into the mount, and make thee an ark of wood. ^{2} And I will write on the tables the words that were on the first tables which thou brakest, and thou shalt put them in the ark ^{3} So I made an ark of acacia wood, and hewed two tables of stone like unto the first, and went up into the mount, having the two tables in mine hand.

Obviously the passage in Deut 10 is based upon Ex 34. But the second contains an important item which is absent from the first, the preparation of the ark in readiness to receive the hallowed stones. A study of the passages in which D reproduces the narrative of the previous books justifies the conclusion that D did not himself insert the reference to the ark, but found it in the sources which he employed. In other words, the narrative in Ex 34^{1}.. also once recorded the divine command and its fulfilment by Moses. Why, then, should it have been eliminated? The answer is not far to seek. In the combination of 34^{1}.. with 25 and 37 the incongruity was too glaring. Just as it

---

^{a} So Wellhausen, Stade, Cornill, Bacon; cp Briggs, *Higher Criticism* 189, Driver, *LOT*^{6} 39

is probable that 33 once possessed an account of the preparation of the Tent of Meeting before the description of its use, which had to make way for the more elaborate delineation of the Dwelling, so, with even greater confidence in view of Deut 10$^{1..}$, it may be argued that Ex 34$^{1..}$ also provided an ark as well as stones.

4. Another important series of divergences is connected with the ministry at the sanctuary. To whom was this entrusted, and under what conditions? The code which opens with the recognition of a plurality of altars Ex 20^{24}-23 lays down no rules concerning their service. Nor do the covenant words of 34 assign the right of sacrifice to any special class of sacred persons. In the Tent of Meeting outside the camp 33^{11} Joshua, an Ephraimite, minister of Moses, was appointed to its custody, and remained in it when Moses himself used to return to the camp. According to Deut 10^8, after the death of Aaron at several stages from the sacred mount, the tribe of Levi was set apart to carry the ark (it is not stated who had borne it until then), and to stand before Yahweh to serve him. Within this tribe D recognizes no distinctions of rank. All Levites possess the priesthood, and have equal rights of ministry 18$^{1-7}$. But in the service of the Dwelling fresh distinctions are introduced. The priesthood is limited to Aaron and his house Ex 28. The sacred vestments are perpetually ordained for him and for his seed after him 28^{43}. The priests in general are designated 'Aaron's sons' Lev 1^5 (cp p130); the responsibility for the holy office falls on them alone Num 18^1; theirs is the charge of sanctuary and altar ^{5}; and any attempt at usurpation of this privilege will involve death ^{7}. Of this terrible doom a conspicuous example is afforded in the fate of Korah and his two hundred and fifty followers 16. What remains, then, for the rest of the tribe of Levi? The rights which according to the present arrangement of Deut 10 were conceded at Jotbathah $^{7..}$, had already according to Num 3 been refused at Sinai. The Levites are there assigned to Aaron to keep his charge $^{6..}$, but the priesthood is expressly reserved for Aaron and his sons ^{10}, and whoever infringes their privileges rushes on his own fate. With the legal theory that the Levites represented the first-born males of the nation, and were accepted by Yahweh in satisfaction of his claim, we have at present no concern: it is enough to observe that the other codes in dealing with the redemption of first-borns (Laws 8ab) make no allusion to it. But the influence of the Levitical conception in exalting the dignity of Aaron beside that of Moses is highly instructive. In one series of plague-stories, for example, Moses acts alone; in his own person he announces to the stubborn king Yahweh's intent; the wonder follows, as Yahweh's will fulfils itself. Or, it may be, he stretches forth his hand with the 'rod of God,' and the threatened sign takes place. But in a third series (cp Ex 7^{8N}) Moses is not charged with executive power. He does but transmit the divine command to Aaron, who stretches out *his* rod, and the expected judgement is accomplished. When the thirsty people at Marah murmur against Moses Ex 15$^{24.}$ he cries to Yahweh; but when the whole congregation of the children of Israel murmur against Moses and Aaron 16^2 Moses calmly bids Aaron summon them before Yahweh ^{9}. In the first Meribah story 17$^{2-7}$ the people strive with Moses; in the second Num 20$^{2-13}$ they assemble against Moses and Aaron. Similarly, in D (which mentions no high-priest) Moses is instructed to charge Joshua Deut 3^{28}, and the pair present themselves at the Tent of Meeting 31$^{14. 23}$. But in P the transfer of authority is only valid when it is effected before Eleazar the high-priest and the congregation Num 27$^{19..}$; before the former that Eleazar may inquire for him by the judgement of Urim before Yahweh; and before the latter, that they may obey. Corresponding differences will be found in the book of Joshua, where, on the one part, Joshua acts on his own initiative, and on the other Eleazar 14^1 takes the lead.

5. The calendar of the annual feasts is repeated no less than four times. It is ordained in nearly parallel terms in the two collections of Covenant-words Ex 23 and 34. It is

enjoined with rich hortatory additions in Deut 16. It is elaborately expounded in Lev 23, where two new items of high significance are added to the list. The cycle in the two groups of Covenant-words is plainly based upon the agricultural year. Whatever may be the precise import of the feast of unleavened bread, it was probably connected with the earliest produce of the soil. The feasts of harvest and of ingathering leave no doubt of their dependence on cornfield and vineyard. Such simple festivals took place all over the country at the times which local circumstance made fittest. They varied with the season year by year. The variation naturally fell within calculable limits, and allowed a sufficient margin for the vicissitudes of crops which might not all ripen equally at one date. No place of celebration is specified; it is only enjoined that every male shall 'see Yahweh's face' three times a year. The nearest sanctuary, therefore, was the natural scene, so that the householder could the more easily combine the homage to his divine Lord with the family or village merrymaking. In Deut 16, however, a striking modification is introduced. Not only is the passover formally joined with the feast of unleavened bread, but the domestic celebrations are peremptorily forbidden. The law of the unity of the sanctuary requires that the appropriate sacrifice shall be offered there and there alone $^{5-7}$. The same demand is made in the other cases also $^{11\ 15}$: and the feast of 'booths,' as the ingathering is now called, becomes a special season of rejoicing for the poor and dependent. In the Levitical code new interests appear in the sacred year Lev 23 Num 28-29. In the first place, the number of the feasts is increased. The first day of the seventh month is a 'memorial of blowing of trumpets' Lev 23^{24}; and on the tenth of the same month is the day of atonement ^{27}. Concerning the place of celebration of the festivals the legislator assumes it to be needless to lay down rules. It is self-evident that there is but one altar where sacrifice can be offered. He is more interested about the time. The Deuteronomic code had assigned the combination of unleavened bread and passover to the old 'ear' month, Abîb, when the earliest corn ripened. The joint celebration is now connected with the first month of the year^a, and the passover is slain 'on the fourteenth day at even.' This is in obvious accordance with the instructions in Ex 12$^{2-6}$, where the injunctions, though issued on a specific occasion, have the character of a perpetual ordinance ^{14}. It is therefore worthy of note that the festal victim is a 'lamb' (or kid), whereas **D** permits the passover to be sacrificed 'of the flock and the herd' Deut 16^2: moreover the lamb is to be roasted Ex 12^8, and it is expressly forbidden to boil it, the very mode which Deut 16^7 enjoins ^{b}. The succeeding feasts in Lev 23 are all dated as rigidly as the passover, and specific directions are given for the observance of 'booths.' To this feast alone does the term *hagg* which the Covenant-words applied to all three Ex 23^{14} still adhere Lev 23$^{39\ 41}$. It is to be celebrated for seven days, with an eighth day of solemn rest ^{39}, of which **D** makes no mention. When these several series are set side by side, they naturally display significant differences in phraseology. The Levitical 'set feasts' 'holy convocations' and 'solemn rest' have no parallels in the codes of Exodus or Deuteronomy. The prohibitions of 'servile work,' the reiteration that the ordinances are 'statutes for ever' $^{14\ 21\ 31\ 41}$, the threat to 'cut off from his people' whoever does not join in the atonement-fast ^{29}, reappear again and again in the priestly law, but no echoes of them are heard in **D**. The precepts of Sinai are couched in new forms in Moab.

6. Another interesting illustration of this divergence is to be noted in the social arrangements for the relief of the poor. The first series of Covenant-words Ex 23^{10}. enforces on the land the principle of a sabbatical 'release.' Every seventh year it is to lie fallow, the vineyard and oliveyard being treated in like manner. The spontaneous

---

^{a} On the significance of this calendar, cp chap XIII.
^{b} The word which *RV* translates 'roast' in this passage is the same which is rendered 'sodden' in Ex 12^9. Cp Driver, *Deut* 193

produce was not to be collected by the owner; it was to be reserved for the poor; and anything which they might leave was abandoned to the 'beast of the field.' The Deuteronomic law is silent about the land. But it applies the same principle under the name of the 'year of release' to debts 15^1··. In the legislation of Exodus it does not appear clear whether the observance would be uniform over the whole country, or whether differing districts or even different holdings might follow their own septennates. But D provides that 'Yahweh's release' shall be publicly proclaimed ^{2}, and it covers all cases, therefore, alike. Its precise scope, however, is difficult to determine. Did the creditor permanently forgo all claim upon the debtor, or did the 'release' only suspend his rights for twelve months? The legal and archaeological bearings of this question need not be here discussed. They are only of importance in so far as they concern the inquiry whether these two laws issued from the same hand, or whether they do not represent two separate efforts to provide help for the suffering poor, corresponding to different stages of social development^a. This argument may be reinforced by a consideration of a kindred law in Lev 25. Without employing the term 'release,' it is ordained that every seventh year the land shall 'keep sabbath to Yahweh'^{2}. The poor, indeed, are not in the author's view. Attention appears to be concentrated on the value of the sabbatical observance. Contrary to the implied provision of Ex 23, the householder is himself to gather in the produce, and he and his labourers, bondmen and hired, may all enjoy it together. On the basis of this periodic rest, however, a further institution is established. After seven sabbaths of years the fiftieth shall be hallowed ^{10}, and liberty shall be proclaimed throughout the land. Bondmen will regain their freedom, and land that has been sold shall go back to its ancient proprietors. The religious theory underlying this arrangement asserts ^{23} that the sole ownership is vested in Yahweh; the land cannot therefore be perpetually alienated by the tenants whom he has placed upon it, for it is not theirs to sell. The connexion of this law in its present form with the Levitical calendar is indicated by the rule that the trumpet which announces the advent of the jubile, shall be sounded through the country on the day of atonement ^{9}. Is it not clear that the 'release' of Deut 15 and the 'liberty' of Lev 25 lie in different planes, are founded on different social theories, and are animated by different religious conceptions?

7. The jubile privileges were not limited to the recovery of land by its former occupants. The Hebrew slave on this occasion regained his freedom Lev 25^{40}··. The bondmen and bondmaids of other nations remained in servitude, and could be bequeathed to the next generation $^{44-46}$; but the person of the Israelite was not his own to sell; like his land, it belonged to Yahweh who had himself emancipated his people from Egypt ^{42}; and it could not become the permanent possession of another. The incompatibility of this conception with the laws of Exodus and Deuteronomy which expressly sanctioned voluntary enslavement for life, has been already noticed (cp chap IV 2γ p 31). A smaller divergence between the modes of effecting the contract for family bondage may be now made clear. The Judgement-book Ex 21^6 ordains that the master shall bring his slave 'to God'; there at the door of the sanctuary, the centre of the administration of justice, the master shall bore his ear through with an awl, affixing it momentarily to the door-post, so that under the authority of religion he becomes a slave 'for ever.' The corresponding law in Deut 15$^{12-18}$ introduces some interesting modifications. It is extended to women; it lays emphatic stress on generous recognition of the six years' forced labour; and in conclusion it retains the symbolic action with the awl. But it omits all reference to 'God.' The door-post to which the slave is attached is that of the householder's own dwelling. The public and

---

^{a} Cp Driver, *Deut* 178 D further provides a triennial tithe 14^{28}· for the Levite, the stranger, the fatherless, and the widow.

official ceremony is converted into a private and domestic incident. The meaning of this change is not obscure. The law of Exodus belongs to the code which admits a plurality of sanctuaries: the Deuteronomic principles recognize but one. Important ceremonies, like the annual festivals, are transferred (as has been shown in 5 p 54) to the only centre of worship. There, too, must tithes be consumed 14^{23}·, an express provision being inserted for those who lived too far off to take their tithes thither in kind. The case of the household slave, however, was not important enough to require the intervention of the supreme authorities in the capital, and the reference to justice and religion dropped.

ii. *The Argument from Religious Ideas*

The foregoing examples have been cited to show that the religious institutions of the Pentateuch are variously conceived in its several codes. The issues of these differences have been occasionally traced in the narratives related to the laws, while their roots have been in some cases discovered in their fundamental ideas of the relation of Israel to Yahweh. To further variations in these ideas it may now be worth while to invite attention. When they become mutually exclusive they cannot proceed from a common source, while if they are mutually coherent a presumption of unity or connexion is established.

1. It has already been observed (chap V 2 p 34) that more than one theory of religious history can be traced in the delineations of the pre-Mosaic age. On the one hand the knowledge of Yahweh existed from primaeval times; and sacrifice and prayer were continuous from generation to generation. On the other, the sacred name was first made known to Moses as the prelude and assurance of Israel's deliverance. This conception, in its turn, was capable of being worked out in two ways. It was consistent with views of revelation by angel or by dream, making specific places holy, where the remembrance of the divine appearing might be cherished by the altar-rite. But it might also imply an earlier stage of religious development, when no cultus was offered because none had been ordained. These three representations may all be discerned in the patriarchal narratives of J E and P, and they can hardly be ascribed to a single mind. A number of other peculiarities follow in their train. The genealogical method of the *tol^edhoth* sections is naturally unfavourable to the delineation of character. The human race at its first appearance shares with the rest of creation the divine approval of blessing, and it is with surprise that we learn in the tenth step from Adam that the inspection of Elohim now finds the earth corrupt Gen 6^{12}. The cause of decline is nowhere indicated; it does not come within the writer's plan to deal with it. The patriarchs pass across the stage, but no lights or shadows fall upon their way; they are the types of an ideal perfection 6^9 17^1, before the law had begotten the offences for which the sin offering could atone. To the author of the Eden story on the other hand, the first act of disobedience and its consequences are matters of absorbing interest. He records the rise of each new art, and notes the social dangers it involves, sketching in few but powerful strokes the significance of the inner life as the true sphere of moral action where 'evil imagination' does its deadly work. The patriarchal stories thus acquire a kind of dramatic significance, as the purpose of Yahweh, disclosed in the call of Abraham, moves steadily forward to its fulfilment. That purpose is expressed in the election of Israel to be the people of Yahweh, and occupy the land of Canaan. This conception is, indeed, common to both narrators, J and P. But it is portrayed in different modes, as the study of the two covenants in Gen 15 and 17 will show. In the one case, the agreement is celebrated with ancient form; the covenant-victims are cut in twain, and after Abraham has watched beside them all day long, and the sun has set, a mysterious flame, symbol of Deity, passes

between them 15^{17}. In 17, however, the covenant is 'established' simply by being announced. Such outward sign as it requires is performed on the human not on the divine side: it is the part of Abraham and his descendants to show in their own person the token of El Shaddai's demands. So impressive is this covenant form of the tol^edhoth writer, that he carries it back to the days of Noah, and presents by its aid the promise of Elohim that there should not be another flood 9^{11}. On the other hand, he does not employ it where it might have been confidently expected, to express the solemn relation instituted at Sinai. Two covenants are there described Ex 24 and 34; and the conditions of Israel's tenure of the land of promise are set forth in the 'Words' which are issued on occasion of them. But they do not quite coincide with each other, nor with the retrospect of Deuteronomy. For that book also is based upon the Covenant conception. There had been a covenant with the fathers 4^{31} 7^{12} 8^{18}; there was a covenant in Horeb; there was another in Moab. The covenant in Horeb consisted of the declaration of the Ten Words $5^{2..}$, so that the stones on which they are engraved receive the name of 'tables of the covenant' $9^{9\ 11\ 15}$, and the ark in which the stones are deposited is called the 'ark of Yahweh's covenant' 10^8. No other covenant words are recognized by **D** as given in Horeb 5^{22} cp ^{31}. But the statutes and judgements recited in the land of Moab form the basis of a second covenant 29^1, made not only with the assembly that heard Moses' words $^{10-12}$, but also with the distant posterity who were not there that day ^{15}, so that all generations might be knit by a common bond of obedience and trust. This conception is not present in the Priestly Law. Whether or not this law recorded the announcement of the Ten Words is not clear; at any rate it does not relate the revelation at Sinai under the form of a covenant[a]. When Moses descends from the mount he carries in his hand the 'tables of the testimony' Ex 34^{29}. The ark is designated in advance 'the ark of the testimony' 25^{22}, and after it has been constructed the 'testimony' is duly placed within it, and the sacred chest is brought into the Dwelling $40^{20..}$, which may even be entitled the 'Dwelling of the Testimony' 38^{21} Num $1^{50\ 53}$ 10^{11}. Nor is there any declaration before Moses has solemnly appointed Joshua his successor Num 27 ∥ Deut 31 analogous to the Deuteronomic scene[b]. Alike, therefore, in its representations of the religious history of antiquity and of the Mosaic age, the Priestly Code differs profoundly from the other constituents of the Pentateuch.

2. As the religious facts of Israel's past were differently presented by different writers, so also were the manifestations of its God varyingly conceived.

(a) The action of Yahweh in the early history of mankind according to **J**, was marked by definite human characteristics. The production of the first man is accomplished by forming or moulding him out of the clods of the ground, and blowing into his nostrils living breath. Yahweh walks in the garden at the cool of the day, shuts Noah into the ark, smells the sweet savour of his sacrifice, comes down to see the tower built towards the sky Gen 11^5, and similarly proposes to visit Sodom and Gomorrah and ascertain by personal inspection whether the guilty cities are really as wicked as rumour alleges 18^{21}. Similarly in the range of moral feeling he is apprehensive lest the man who has 'become as one of us' should also gain the power to live for ever 3^{22}; he 'repents' 6^6 that he has made man on the earth; he condescends to expostulate with Sarah and prove himself in the right 18^{14}. A more advanced stage appears to be indicated by the conception of the angel of Yahweh (or Elohim) who is the manifested presence of the Deity, identical with and yet differentiated from him. The angel appears to Hagar in the wilderness, but she knows that it is

---

[a] The only allusion to a Sinaitic covenant concerns the sabbath Ex 31^{16}, cp Lev 2^{13} Num 18^{19} salt; Lev 24^8 shewbread.

[b] A minor reference is found to a covenant of priesthood given to Phinehas Num $25^{12..}$.

Yahweh who speaks 16^{13}. Two angels escort Lot out of Sodom, yet in some mysterious way one of them holds in his hand the power to overthrow or to deliver 19^{20}.. Jacob beholds the angels of Elohim ascending and descending on the ladder, and he knows that he has been sleeping in the 'house of Elohim.' None of these representations appears in the *Tol^edhoth* book. In the sublime story of the heavens and earth with which it opens, the creative utterance realizes itself; speech calls forth the external fact to match the inner thought: 'Elohim said, Let there be light, and light was.' Mankind arises, male and female simultaneously 1^{27} in obedience to the energizing word; rightly did the Psalmist seize on this mark of the divine activity, 'for he spake, and it was done.' Accordingly in his intercourse with men Elohim's part is commonly indicated only by his commands 6^{13} 8^{15} 9^{1} ^{8} &c. Not till the covenant is announced to Abram does Elohim 'appear' $17^{1\,a}$. But the form of his manifestation is carefully held in reserve. No flaming torch moving between the halves of slaughtered victims is needed to reveal him; nor does he arrive attended by companions like himself ready to accept the patriarch's hospitality. Before his august presence Abram 'fell upon his face ^{b}'; and when the interview was over, Elohim 'ascended' 17^{22} cp $35^{13\,c}$. The conception of P thus disengages itself from the peculiar anthropomorphisms which pervade the narrative of J, and to a less extent that of E. He nowhere represents God as 'trying' or 'tempting' man; nor does man in his turn 'tempt' or 'try' God. In modern language it may be said that his representation is more abstract.

(β) It is natural to look for parallel phenomena in the continuations of the documents through the Mosaic age, and they are certainly to be found. In the first revelation to Moses in Ex 3, Yahweh in the person of his angel appears in flame out of a bush; in the second, he does not 'appear' at all, he only speaks 6^2. Plainly this latter utterance is not from the same hand as that which relates that Yahweh had already encountered Moses and sought to kill him $4^{24\,d}$. The Horeb-Sinai scenes are in the same manner marked by distinctive features. In one series Yahweh 'comes down' on to mount Sinai $19^{11b\;18\;20\;23}$ with fire and smoke; in another Elohim 'comes' to 'try' or 'prove' his people with thunders and lightnings and a thick cloud 19^{16} 20^{18-20}. D combines the fire, the cloud, and the thick darkness 5^{22}, though Horeb was ablaze ^{23}. To P, however, filled with awe for the supreme majesty, the conception of actual flame is too concrete. The presence of Deity was indicated by his 'glory' Ex 24^{16}; and the 'appearance of the glory' resembled consuming fire to human sight ^{17}, but what the transcendent reality was in itself could not be told. It can hardly be supposed that the writer who thus symbolizes the divine advent, could just before have described the seventy elders as 'beholding Israel's God,' or as eating and drinking at his feet ^{10}.. Nor could he have recorded the promise that Moses should see his 'back' 33^{23}, or even related that Yahweh passed by before him 34^6. Such language carries with it inevitable implications of some external (if not human) shape. Against this the Deuteronomic exhortations vehemently protest: 'ye heard the sound of words, but ye saw no form, only a sound' 4^{12} cp $^{15\;36}$ 5^{24}. Yet to Moses at least the form was displayed in super-prophetic privilege Num 12^{6-8}:—

⁶ If there be a prophet among you, I Yahweh will make myself known unto him in a vision, I will speak with him in a dream. ⁷ My servant Moses is not so, he is faithful in all mine house ⁸ with

---

^{a} It is admitted on all hands that 'Yahweh' in this passage is contrary to the usage of P, and must be regarded as accidental error, or (more probably) editorial harmonizing.
^{b} So afterwards do Moses and Aaron, cp $^P67$.
^{c} This is the counterpart in P of Yahweh's descent, cp $^{JE}19$.
^{d} A story which, according to Prof Sayce, *Early History of the Hebrews* 165, 'belongs to the folk-lore of a people still in crude barbarism.'

him will I speak mouth to mouth, even manifestly, and not in dark speeches; and the form of Yahweh shall he behold[a].

The scene is outside the camp before the Tent of Meeting, at the entrance of which stands Yahweh in a pillar of cloud, addressing Aaron and Miriam. What is the pillar? When the Israelites started on their march for liberty, it contained the person of their divine guide Yahweh, who went before to show the way, in a column that looked by day like cloud and by night like fire Ex 13^{21}. It had for its counterpart the angel of Elohim 14^{19} [b], who, on the desperate night of the Egyptian approach, fulfilled the same protecting function as the pillar, and stood between the camp of Israel and its foes. When the Tent of Meeting was pitched, whenever Moses entered it, the pillar descended, stood at the entrance, and spoke with him 33^9 ..:—

[10] And all the people saw the pillar of cloud stand at the door of the Tent .... [11] And Yahweh spake unto Moses face to face, as a man speaketh unto his friend.

So was it when Moses and the seventy elders were gathered around Num 11^{24}; so was it when Moses took Joshua with him to receive the divine charge Deut 31^{14}.. The Priestly Code, however, does not allude to the pillar, and its conception of Yahweh's intercourse with Moses is different. When Yahweh fulfils his promise to be God to Israel Ex 6^7, he does so by taking up his abode in the Dwelling which he charges Moses to construct for him. Within the Dwelling, the most holy place shelters the ark. Upon the ark stands the 'covering' bearing a cherub at each end with outspread wings. They are the supporters of Yahweh, who declares that there he will meet with Moses and will speak with him, issuing his commands to the children of Israel 25^{22}. Thither accordingly Moses used to repair, and there in the darkness and the silence he listened to the Voice Num 7^{89}. Was there, then, no outward sign of Yahweh's nearness? When the Dwelling is reared, when the first incense has been burned before the veil, when the first sacrifice has been offered on the altar in the court, Yahweh himself deigns to enter. The cloud covers the holy Tent, and the entire Dwelling is filled with his glory Ex 40^{34}. As long as the sanctuary remains in one place, this cloud remains spread over it from day to day. At even it assumes 'as it were the appearance of fire until morning' Num 9^{15}. Its ascension is the signal for departure, and it must be understood to have accompanied the march, for its settlement determines the place of the next camp [17]. Such was the manifestation to Israel, according to P, of Yahweh's sacramental presence in its midst.

3. When the manifestations of Deity thus vary, it is not surprising that the modes of conceiving his being and character should vary also. In tracing the successive incidents of history the 'prophetic narrators,' to use Ewald's nomenclature, feel the hand of their God at every turn. The first pair are under Yahweh's immediate control. He sets his mark on Cain; he pronounces his doom upon a guilty humanity; the origins of language are due to his interference; Abram marches from the east by divine monition, and his servant relies on Yahweh his master's God, for an omen in the choice of a bride. This relation is again and again presented in vivid forms of dramatic intervention and appeal. It involves ethical demands, summed up as 'the way of Yahweh' Gen 18^{19}, or doing justice and right, the lofty attribute of Yahweh himself, conceived as 'judge of all the earth' [25]. The obedience of Abraham draws out a solemn oath from Yahweh 22^{17}. to bestow blessings on his posterity; and Yahweh, as the God of Abraham and Isaac and Jacob, may be confidently reminded of his promises

---

[a] The Greek translators, in dread of anthropomorphism, render 'and the *glory* of the Lord shall he behold.' Jerome, with a different punctuation, 'not in dark speeches (riddles) and figures does he behold the Lord.' [b] Cp 23^{20}.

Gen 32^{9-12}, or on the other hand may justly claim the trust of his people Ex 3^{16}. Beside his faithfulness is presented his compassion 34^{6-7}:—

⁶ And Yahweh passed by before him, and proclaimed, Yahweh, Yahweh, a God full of compassion and gracious, slow to anger, and plenteous in mercy and truth ; ⁷ keeping mercy for thousands, forgiving iniquity and transgression and sin and that will by no means clear *the guilty*, visiting the iniquity of the fathers upon the children, and upon the children's children, upon the third and upon the fourth generation.

In this there is, indeed, an element of the unforeseen ; 'I will be gracious to whom I will be gracious' 33^{19} ; but even in its repeated acts of disobedience Israel may implore his pardoning mercy, and its prayer is granted Num 14^{17}..[a]. The counterpart of this is Yahweh's jealousy Ex 34^{14} 20^5, which is at once excited when Israel offers homage to another God. These conceptions are not unrepresented in D, but the reader is conscious of a different emphasis. In the Deuteronomic homilies the oath to the fathers is repeatedly brought to the remembrance of a later generation: Yahweh is 'the faithful God which keepeth covenant and mercy with them that love him and keep his commandments to a thousand generations, and repayeth them that hate him to their face, to destroy them' 7^9. But a new stress is laid on his unity and his transcendence: 'he is God in heaven above and upon the earth beneath: there is none else' 4^{39} : 'hear, O Israel: Yahweh our God, Yahweh is one' 6^4: the 'heaven of heavens' is his 10^{14}, and he is 'God of gods and Lord of lords' ^{17}. It is only by an unfathomable mystery of grace that Israel is elected for the love of such a Being 7^7.. In elder time, the worshipper might seek to contract with the object of his homage for 'bread to eat and raiment to put on' Gen 28^{20}, and his worship depended on the satisfaction of these demands. The relation is now inverted. Israel's continued possession of the land is contingent on its obedience ; life and death are offered them, welfare or destruction, let them choose life and live. With a new thought of God, therefore, comes a new duty: 'thou shalt love Yahweh thy God with all thy heart and soul and might.' It will be observed that in the Deuteronomic discourses Moses continually speaks to Israel of 'thy God[b].' The phrase is in reality a survival in prophetic speech from the days when it was possible to conceive Yahweh of Israel pitted against Chemosh of Ammon : 'wilt not thou possess that which Chemosh thy god giveth thee to possess?' inquires Jephthah Judg 11^{24}, 'so whomsoever Yahweh our God hath dispossessed from before us, them will we possess.' D employs his formula over three hundred times in a single book. But in the main portions of the Priestly Code it occurs but rarely[c]. This is not simply a matter of accidental diction ; it points to a different religious attitude, further indicated in the solemn address 'God of the spirits of all flesh' Num 16^{22} 27^{16}. For P conceives of humanity as a whole. The first covenant with Noah is made with the entire race Gen 9^{15}.; and this term, found outside P only in Deut 5^{26}, echoes through the whole story from the Flood to Moses[d]. Elohim then, as he is presented in the Priestly Code, is universal. Had not his spirit brooded in the darkness on the deep, and out of it brought forth the heavens and earth? The brief *tol^edhoth* sections scarcely allow of any delineation of his attributes. Natural causes account for the diversities of race and language ; and Abram's migration takes place without a superhuman call. But power and beneficence shine through the creation : on Enoch and Noah who walked with God, the divine approval was signally bestowed : P alone describes one patriarch as already perfect, and in the name of El Shaddai demands perfection of another Gen 6^9 17^1. The covenant-observance which wins for Yahweh elsewhere the epithet

---

[a] Cp the social conduct required among Israelites in consequence Ex 22^{27}, and connected laws 22^{21}–23^9.

[b] Cp ^D1.   [c] Cp ^P179^c. It is more frequent in P^h 203^{bc}.   [d] Cp ^P21^b.

of 'faithful,' is here assumed as matter of course, and expressed in the phrase 'remembering the covenant' ᴾ135. One word suffices, in fact, to sum up the complex total of the manifold aspects of God's being: he is holy. A remarkable section of the Priestly Code enforces this conception with especial emphasis [a], but it is not limited to a particular group of laws. The holiness of Yahweh is the central idea of the whole of the religious institutions delineated by P, which have for their aim to produce or to preserve corresponding holiness in his worshippers. There were, indeed, various forms of this requirement. The First Code Ex 22³¹ had its own view of its application:—

And ye shall be holy men unto me therefore ye shall not eat any flesh that is torn of beasts in the field, ye shall cast it to the dogs.

On a similar ground D forbids personal mutilation in mourning for the dead 14¹·, and the eating of anything that has died naturally ²¹; for Israel is already a dedicated people, hallowed by Yahweh's choice which has singled it out from all the other nations of the earth 7⁶. The whole Deuteronomic Code has for its real aim to set forth the conduct which alone could maintain Israel in this relation. That conduct is summarized by P in one single pregnant demand, founded on an equally pregnant reason Lev 19² 'Ye shall be holy: for I Yahweh your God am holy.' The cultus, with its various grades of consecrated persons, Levite, priest, high-priest; the sanctuary, with its holy vessels, its outer court, its holy place, and its most holy; the sacrifices by which atonement was made for injuries to this supreme relation—all ministered to a common end, the maintenance of Yahweh's sacramental presence in Israel's midst unimpaired. The legislative codes thus reflect different aspects of God's being, as the histories illustrate varying modes of his action in the world. On this ground, also, therefore, as on that of matter of fact, the hypothesis of diversity of source is confirmed.

iii. *The Argument from Language and Style*

The discovery of incongruities in narrative and law was naturally followed by comparisons of language. In the account of the deluge, for example, Eichhorn already observed that one set of expressions tended to recur where the name Elohim was employed, while another set presented themselves in connexion with Yahweh [b]. What light does such an argument throw on the documentary hypothesis? To what extent can it be pressed in favour of the process of partition?

1. It is obvious that differences of matter will naturally be marked by differences of terminology. The account of the Dwelling, its furniture, its ritual, and its sacred officers in Ex 25-30 35-40 Lev 1-9 is of so highly specialized a kind that it is crowded with peculiar words. On these it would be unsuitable to found a special theory of authorship. But by the side of the technicalities of construction and usage a brief survey speedily discovers other expressions which reappear elsewhere, alike in legal connexions or in independent narrative. For example, the purpose of the whole is to provide for Yahweh a 'sanctuary' Ex 25⁸. This word occurs altogether in twelve other passages of the Levitical code cp ᴾ91. It is found also in a somewhat different application in Ex 15¹⁷, and it is employed of a sacred place at Shechem Josh 24²⁶. But it is not used in either the First Code or in D. It may be said, therefore, to be a favourite word of the Priestly Law. The 'sanctuary' constitutes a place for Yahweh to 'dwell' in, and is called the Dwelling. This term also D never names. Apart, however, from the title of the sanctuary, the word 'dwell' is repeatedly used to express the presence of Yahweh in the midst of his people Ex 29⁴⁵· cp ᴾ54ᵃ. It is not the common word in the Pentateuch for inhabiting a house or land, and is only found outside the Priestly Law in the poetical 'Blessing of

---

[a] The 'holiness legislation,' cp chap XIII 8.   [b] Cp Gen 6⁵ᴺ.

Moses' Deut 33¹² ²⁰. But **D** is curiously fond of it in a derived conjugation (Piel) in the formula 'the place which Yahweh shall choose to put [cause to dwell] his name there' cp ᴾ87. Why should the Dwelling which was already in their midst be so persistently ignored? The priestly vestments are ordained as a 'statute for ever' Ex 28⁴³ (like the oil for the lamp 27²¹) to Aaron and 'his seed after him.' The 'everlasting statute' (= 'perpetual statute' 29⁹, 'due for ever' 29²⁸) recurs elsewhere twenty-seven times in the Priestly Code: the same epithet being applied ᴾ62 to the words 'covenant,' 'generations,' 'possession,' in the *tolᵉdhoth* sections of Genesis, and to the terms 'possession,' 'priesthood,' and 'redemption' in the Priestly Law. But neither the prophetic narrators, nor the First Code, nor **D**, ever thus employ it. The description of posterity by the phrase 'and his seed after him' ᴾ162 again finds its counterpart in the *tolᵉdhoth* sections and the Priestly Law, and is not found elsewhere. The examination of the formula 'throughout your generations' 27²¹ 29⁴² ᴾ76ᵇ (thirty-nine times) yields the same result.

2. The inquiry thus suggested brings many remarkable phenomena to light.

(α) It reveals in the first place that in passages which are based on different historical and religious assumptions, different words are used for the same thing. The *tolᵉdhoth* sections in Genesis, for instance, as regularly call Hebron Kiriath-arba ᴾ3 as they call God El Shaddai and Elohim in contrast with Yahweh: similarly they designate the Mesopotamian home of Jacob's kindred Paddan-aram ᴾ6 instead of 'Aram of the two rivers' Gen 24¹⁰ Deut 23⁴, or the 'land of the children of the east' Gen 29¹. Their continuation in the Priestly Code names the sacred mountain Sinai ᴾ7; to **D** the mountain of the first covenant is always Horeb ᴾ7ᵃ. The organization of the children of Israel around the Dwelling is founded on the tribes (מטה) which are divided into 'fathers' houses,' their chiefs being 'princes ᵇ,' and the whole constituting the 'congregation ᶜ.' The Deuteronomic code also recognizes the tribes, though it calls them by another name (שבט): their chiefs are 'heads' and 'elders' 5²³: and the entire people forms an 'assembly ᵈ.' Where **P** describes the 'establishment' of a covenant, in **JED** it is 'cut' or 'given.' When **P** expresses 'possess' and 'possession' by the root *'aḥaz*, **D** always prefers *yarash*. The ark and the tables of the 'testimony' in **P** become the ark and the tables of the 'covenant' in **D**. Again while **P** and **D** describe Yahweh as *bringing* Israel *out* of Egypt (הוציא), **JE** (twenty times) write 'bring up' (העלה) ᴶᴱ136). These peculiarities do not seem reconcilable with unity of authorship: and their force is increased when it is observed that in large numbers of other cases there is a preponderant use of particular expressions discernible in one document even though they are not entirely absent from another ᵉ.

(β) Another class of indications is found in the presence or absence of grammatical peculiarities, common turns of speech, and simple phrases of narrative and dialogue. Attention was long ago called to the fact that **P** employs only one form of the pronoun 'I' (אני), while **J** and **E** set a second by its side (אנכי) ᶠ. On the other hand **D** habitually uses the latter form (fifty-six times) ᵍ. Whether these differences have any significance for the history of language, and so (by implication) for the date of the documents, may be for the present ignored; that they are consistent with the hypothesis of uniformity of origin can hardly be maintained. Two forms of the word 'heart' appear throughout the Pentateuch. In **E** both are employed indifferently: **J** and **P**ᵍ always prefer the

---

ᵃ A similar distinction divides **J** (Sinai) and **E** (Horeb)
ᵇ Ct another term for 'prince' ᴶᴱ191.
ᶜ For the usage of these terms the reader is referred to the tables of words
ᵈ 'Assembly' is also employed by **P**: but 'congregation' never by **D**.
ᵉ This is especially the case in comparing the phraseology of **J** and **E**.
ᶠ Cp Briggs, *Higher Criticism of the Hexateuch* 71
ᵍ On the exceptions, 12³⁰ and 29⁶, see Driver, *Deut* 150 and 321. אני is also found in the Song of Moses 32²¹ 39ᵃᵇᶜᵈ and in the brief extract from **P** 32⁴⁹ ⁵²

shorter לב ; D and P^h use the longer לבב ^a. Can this distribution be explained otherwise than by diversity of source? Again, for 'beget' P uses the form הוליד while J employs ילד. The connexion of words or clauses by the repetition 'both . . . and' (גם . . גם) occurs seventeen times in JE and but once in P; while P sometimes effects a similar combination by other means ^P35: the particle גם 'also' being used with overwhelming predominance in JE (a total of 141 occurrences compared with fifteen in P). For 'one' and 'another' J and E predominantly employ 'a man' and 'his neighbour' ^JE188; P invariably uses 'a man' and 'his brother' ^P184 cp ^JE112. The speaker's words are introduced in P (over 100 times) with the formula 'And (Elohim) spake unto (Noah) . . . saying.' This phrase never occurs in JE (though both use a corresponding expression 'said . . . saying' ^P185d) and very rarely in D ^P185a; with it are associated two others exclusively the property of P, 'speak unto . . . saying,' and 'speak and say.' On the other hand the enclitic נא, 'now,' 'I pray you,' is common in JE (102 times ^JE186), but in P occurs only twice Num 16^8 Josh 22^26 (cp לו Gen 17^18 23^13). The adverb 'now,' or 'and now' (= 'therefore'), may be found eighty-six times in JE, twelve times in D, and but three in P ^JE187. J uses the polite periphrasis 'thy servant' &c forty-four times; in P it is found only twice in passages exhibiting other peculiar phenomena ^JE73. The curious reader may study in the Tables of Words the singular statistics concerning the use of the idiom 'and it came to pass' 'and it shall come to pass' (in various grammatical connexions), giving a total to JE of sixty-nine against eight in P ^JE3 and 127. Other significant particulars will be found in connexion with the words 'before' (טרם ^JE6 and בטרם ^JE132), 'but' (בלתי ^JE138), 'whether . . . or not' ^JE229, 'wherefore' ^JE228. The prophetic narrators freely use two words for 'young man' (ילד thirty times, נער forty-two times, ^JE234, 235): in P each occurs (in the same passage, regarded on independent grounds as secondary) only once. The touches which give so much life to the stories of JE, fixing the time of events to the morning, daybreak, sunrise, noon, heat of the day, high day, cool of the day, sunset, evening, night, may be counted by several score ^JE236, they are poorly represented by such a passage as Num 9^15...in P, where a general practice is described and all vividness of individualization is lost.

(γ) In the foregoing illustrations attention has been invited to characteristics of common usage. It would be easy to cite lists of peculiar words occurring but once or twice. These, however, must be necessarily rare, and can hardly be expected to throw light on the relations or origins of the several documents. A special interest, however, attaches to the variations in religious phraseology. Such variations have already been pointed out in connexion with the divine names, and the institutions of the sanctuary. But they are not confined to these limits. In the tol^edhoth record of the covenant of El Shaddai with Abraham, it is stated to be his purpose to 'be for a God' to him and to his seed Gen 17^7. ℌ. The phrase goes ringing on through P *in the mouth of Yahweh* ten times. But it is never so found elsewhere ^P26. The same is true of the repeated declaration 'I am Yahweh' ^P179 ^b. On the other hand D loves to describe Yahweh (in address to Israel) as 'thy God,' 'our God,' or 'God of thy fathers' ^D1: while JE designate him in various ways as 'God of heaven' of Shem, of Abraham, &c ^JE120. The same narrators further use the prophetic style 'Thus saith Yahweh' (in communications with Pharaoh, &c) which P never employs, and for which D has no occasion ^JE87. If P lays stress on the purpose that Israel or Egypt may 'know' the Deity who is dealing with them, JE emphasize the merit of 'believing,' and the guilt of mistrust

---

^a Briggs, *Higher Criticism* 72. Deut, however, has לב in 4^11 28^65 29^4 19, all of them passages which on independent grounds are regarded as secondary.
^b Cp the associated 'know that I am Yahweh.'

^{JE}134. The closeness of the relation of Yahweh to those whom he has chosen to carry out his purposes is expressed in various ways. **P** announces that Elohim (after Ex 6² Yahweh) will 'be for a God.' **JE** affirm (fifteen times before Ex 3) that Deity is 'with' the patriarchs, and the phrase, often on the lips of Moses, is finally handed on by him to Joshua ^{JE}130. This is otherwise indicated during the wanderings by describing Yahweh as 'in the midst' of Israel (בקרב ^{JE}58). The thought is likewise familiar to **P**, but he must needs use another word: in the Priestly Code Yahweh always dwells 'among' his worshippers (בתוך ^P22).

(δ) The foregoing specimens are all of them examples of many occurrences, amounting sometimes to scores in number. Their effect is cumulative. For each fresh case, taken by itself, some other explanation might conceivably be allowable. But for the aggregate, when the total phenomena are reckoned by hundreds (representing thousands of separate instances) only one explanation seems to be possible. It may be well, however, to approach the question from another side, and examine the application of the general results above described in a few definite cases. For instance, it has been suggested that the record of Abraham's purchase of the cave of Machpelah Gen 23 reads like 'a translation into Hebrew from a Babylonian cuneiform document, the phrases and style being those of Babylonian texts and the Tel-el-Amarna tablets [a].' The particular expressions on which this view is based have not been adduced. But it is plain that if it is lawful to compare the phraseology of a passage in Genesis with a cuneiform tablet, it must be equally legitimate to collate it with other sections of the same book. A glance at the table of words belonging to **P** will at once reveal a number of expressions which recur continually in that great collection of narrative and law. The designations 'Kiriath-arba' and 'land of Canaan'; the formulae of age and length of life [1]; the introduction of Abraham as speaker [3]; the personal pronoun 'I' [4]; the terms 'sojourner' [4], 'possession' [4], 'prince' [6]; the legal phrases 'even of all' [10], and 'were made sure' [17] ($\mathfrak{H}$ 'stood'); the unusual 'I pray thee' [13] (לו cp 17[18]); all establish literary points of contact with other parts of the Pentateuch, themselves marked by many similar characteristics, and intertwined with further portions by fresh threads of agreement in matter of fact, in religious ideas, or in technical language. It is impossible in such a case to isolate a score of verses and pronounce them a 'translation' from a foreign tongue. The chapter stands or falls, not indeed with its context, but with other passages with which it is found to cohere both by substance and form. Some further illustration of this method may not be inappropriate.

(ε) Two separate announcements are made to Abraham of the birth of a son to Sarah Gen 17 and 18, the first on the part of El Shaddai 17[1], the second by Yahweh 18[14]. By the principle of Ex 6². it is at once clear that these narratives cannot be from the same hand. Each step reveals further evidence. The first is careful to announce the date of the occurrence, but omits to mention the scene: the second neglects the year in order to fix the time of day. In the one case, Abraham falls on his face in awe: in the other he runs to meet his visitors before he bows (as Jacob bowed before Esau Gen 33³) to the ground. The presence of El Shaddai is revealed only by speech, and his final ascension. Yahweh, on the other hand, as one of three men, washes his feet and rests beneath the tree, and finally eats of the meal which the hospitality of a pastoral sheikh at once provides. It is worthy of note that the promise of this second story is couched in the utmost simplicity, 'Sarah thy wife shall have a son.' But the language of El Shaddai is much more copious: it contains not only the announcement that Sarah shall be mother of kings but the covenant-promise of multitudinous posterity and the gift of the land. Yahweh had already made similar declarations: the following table shows how the language of the two groups is reiterated on various occasions through the Pentateuch:—

[a] Sayce, *Expository Times*, Jan 1898, p 177.

P	JE
Gen 17^2 I [Elohim] will multiply thee, . . . ^{6} and I will make thee exceeding fruitful. ^{20} And as for Ishmael, I [Elohim] have heard thee behold, I have blessed him, and will make him fruitful, and will multiply him exceedingly. 1^{22} And Elohim blessed them, saying, Be fruitful, and multiply, and replenish the waters in the seas ^{28} And Elohim blessed them · and Elohim said unto them, Be fruitful, and multiply, and replenish the earth. 8^{17} (And Elohim spake saying) . . that they may breed abundantly in the earth, and be fruitful, and multiply upon the earth 9^1 And Elohim blessed Noah and his sons, and said unto them, Be fruitful, and multiply, and replenish the earth. ^{7} And you, be ye fruitful, and multiply. 28^3 And El Shaddai bless thee, and make thee fruitful, and multiply thee. 35^{11} And Elohim said unto him, I am El Shaddai : be fruitful and multiply. 47^{27} And they gat them possessions therein, and were fruitful, and multiplied exceedingly. 48^4 (El Shaddai) blessed me, and said unto me, Behold, I will make thee fruitful, and multiply thee. Ex 1^7 And the children of Israel were fruitful, and increased abundantly, and multiplied. Lev 26^9 And I will have respect unto you, and make you fruitful, and multiply you.	Gen 13^{16} I [Yahweh] will make thy seed as the dust of the earth so that if a man can number the dust of the earth, then shall thy seed also be numbered 15^5 Look now toward heaven, and tell the stars, if thou be able to tell them and he [Yahweh] said unto him, So shall thy seed be. 16^{10} And the angel of Yahweh said unto her, I will greatly multiply thy seed, that it shall not be numbered for multitude. 22^{16}. By myself have I sworn, saith Yahweh, . . . that in blessing I will bless thee, and in multiplying I will multiply thy seed as the stars of the heaven, and as the sand which is upon the sea shore 26^3 (And Yahweh said) . . . I will establish the oath which I sware unto Abraham thy father ; ^{4} and I will multiply thy seed as the stars of heaven. ^{24} And Yahweh said . . . fear not, for I am with thee, and will bless thee, and multiply thy seed for my servant Abraham's sake 28^{14} (And Yahweh said) . . . and thy seed shall be as the dust of the earth. 32^{12} And thou (Yahweh) saidst, I will surely do thee good, and make thy seed as the sand of the sea, which cannot be numbered for multitude. Ex 32^{13} Remember Abraham, Isaac, and Israel, thy servants, to whom thou swarest by thine own self, and saidst unto them, I will multiply your seed as the stars of heaven.

The connexion of the passages in each of these two series is obvious at once. The Elohim group repeats with an unvarying combination the formula 'be fruitful and multiply,' to which is sometimes prefixed 'bless.' The Yahweh catena is less monotonous in form ; it presents comparisons with the dust of the earth, the stars of heaven, and the sand of the sea shore. The members of each series are bound together by community of thought and expression, but differenced from their counterparts on the alternative religious base. Can they be harmonized within a common source ?

(ζ) The theory of Astruc and Eichhorn conciliated the partition of Genesis with the authorship, or at least the authority, of Moses, by supposing him to have compiled the book out of pre-existing documents. But it has been already observed that the records of his own life exhibit similar phenomena. The following instances are selected from its last months (cp the double charge to Joshua, chap VI 2γ p 41). In Num 28 29 Yahweh issues through Moses a solemn command to the children of Israel concerning the altar dues throughout the year. This law is addressed, not to the priesthood, nor to the wider Levitical order, but to the whole people. There is about it nothing secret or reserved. In its ritual language it follows the manual of sacrifice Lev 1-7. The catalogue of its annual feasts agrees with that announced in the second year of the Exodus in Lev 23. Shortly after, according to Pentateuchal chronology^a, Moses recites to Israel the law of the second covenant. This also contains a calendar of feasts, Deut 16. The material differences between these lists are the same as those already cited between Deut 16 and Lev 23 (chap VIII i 5): the most prominent is the limitation of **D** to three celebrations 16, whereas **P** includes five. The variations in form are no less significant. The regular term in **P** for 'set feasts' Num 28^2 29^{39} is never used by **D**, while **P** avoids the form 'appear before Yahweh' (originally, 'see Yahweh's face' ^{JE}203) Deut 16^{16}. The Priestly Code does not think it necessary to specify where the altar is on which the elaborate offerings are to be consumed : only a single

---

^{a} See Chap VI 2γ p 41.

passage alludes to the 'holy place' Num 28⁷. **D**, on the other hand, lays the utmost emphasis on the duty of attendance at the 'place which Yahweh thy God shall choose' ² ⁶· ¹¹ ¹⁵·. **D** is little concerned, however, to fix the times: 'ear-month' suffices to determine the season for the Passover and Unleavened Bread; seven weeks from the cutting of the first ripe ears lead to Weeks; while Booths depends on the completion of threshing and vintage. But to **P** the months in numbered succession, and the days within them, must all be properly counted: nothing is elastic, all is fixed. The terminology of celebration is different: **P** requires 'holy convocations' 28¹⁸ ²⁵, at the opening and close of Passover and Unleavened Bread (cp ²⁶ 29¹ ⁷ ¹²), and abstinence from 'servile work': to **D** these expressions (which pervade the Priestly Code) are wholly unknown. Equally foreign to **D** are the 'sin offering,' 'atonement,' and 'afflicting of the soul,' prescribed by **P** 28²² 29⁷, in this connexion as in so many others: while **P** never provides either for the historic 'remembrance' Deut 16³, or for the participation of the necessitous poor, after the customary exhortations of **D** (see parallels to 16³ ¹¹ ¹⁴ ¹⁵ ¹⁷). Can it be supposed that these two passages were addressed in succession to the same readers by the same writer after he had already received notice of approaching death?

(η) One further instance is perhaps yet more significant. Under similar conditions to the foregoing, Moses is commanded to issue a law for the appointment of six cities of refuge, three on the east of Jordan and three in Canaan Num 35⁹⁻³⁴. They are intended as places of resort in cases of accidental homicide to secure immunity from pursuit by the *Goel* until the manslayer 'stand before the congregation for judgement.' The conditions for determining whether the homicide was after all accidental or not, are carefully specified. If the case is decided against the manslayer on adequate testimony ³⁰, he is delivered over to death. If the verdict is in his favour, he is restored to the city of refuge, and must remain there till the death of the high priest. Then he is at liberty to go where he will. In Deut 19¹⁻¹³ the same theme is again treated, on a different basis and in a different form. The land which Israel is to occupy in future is to be divided into three parts ³, with a city in each. Hither the manslayer in any one of the three divisions may flee. No tribunal is mentioned before which he may be cited to appear: but a trial is obviously implied, for in the event of his guilt being made clear, the elders of his city are charged with the duty of fetching him from his place of shelter and delivering him to the *Goel*. It is added parenthetically, that if Yahweh shall enlarge their border, they may assign three more cities for similar asylum. Why should the leader, already divinely warned that he must die, issue two such laws in a few weeks' interval? What causes could have intervened to make such repetition necessary? And if they were repeated, why should the arrangements of the first be modified in the second? The situation itself seems to create a presumption against the hypothesis of unitary authorship, and this is confirmed by the respective literary characteristics. The initial formula in Num 35¹⁰ 'speak unto the children of Israel and say unto them,' frequent in **P**, is unknown to **D**. The opening statements characteristically differ:—

Num 35 **P**	*Deut* 19 **D**
¹⁰ When ye pass over Jordan into the land of Canaan, ¹¹ then ye shall appoint you cities to be cities of refuge for you; that the manslayer which killeth any person unwittingly may flee thither. ¹² And the cities shall be unto you for refuge from the avenger, that the manslayer die not, until he stand before the congregation for judgement. ¹³ And the cities which ye shall give shall be for you six cities of refuge.	¹ When Yahweh thy God shall cut off the nations, whose land Yahweh thy God giveth thee, and thou succeedest them, and dwellest in their cities, and in their houses, ²thou shalt separate three cities for thee in the midst of thy land, which Yahweh thy God giveth thee to possess it. ³ Thou shalt prepare thee the way, and divide the borders of thy land, which Yahweh thy God causeth thee to inherit, into three parts, that every manslayer may flee thither.

The law in **P**, in accordance with the regular usage of the main Priestly Code, is addressed in the plural; that of **D**, following its almost invariable practice, in the singular. **P** designates the future country of Israel as the land of Canaan ($^P4^a$); **D** never so names it, but describes it by numerous circumlocutions $^{1\ 2\ 3\ 10}$. **P** promptly calls the cities 'cities of refuge,' a title which **D** persistently ignores. The terminology of **P**, 'person,' 'congregation,' 'high priest anointed with the holy oil,' 'stranger and sojourner,' 'statute of judgement' ^{29}, 'throughout your generations,' 'in all your dwellings,' these have all vanished. For **P**'s 'killeth any person^a unwittingly,' **D** writes 'killeth his neighbour unawares, and hated him not in time past,' laying stress on the hatred, $^{4\ 11}$. The conditions of guiltless homicide are stated in widely different terms Num 35^{22} and Deut 19^5; and the characteristic phrases at the close, each pointing to numerous recurring parallels elsewhere, are clearly based on independent modes of religious thought:—

Num 35 P	*Deut* 19 D
^{33} So ye shall not pollute the land wherein ye are: for blood, it polluteth the land and no expiation can be made for the land for the blood that is shed therein, but by the blood of him that shed it. ^{34}And thou shalt not defile the land which ye inhabit, in the midst of which I dwell · for I Yahweh dwell in the midst of the children of Israel.	^{10} That innocent blood be not shed in the midst of thy land, which Yahweh thy God giveth thee for an inheritance, and so blood be upon thee ... ^{13} Thine eye shall not pity him, but thou shalt put away the innocent blood from Israel, that it may go well with thee.

Could any legislator, anxious to use his last days for the utmost benefit of his people, devote himself to the preparation of two similar laws thus bound by numerous connecting links with two separate codes, issued on the same spot, yet marked by so many differences both in contents and form?

iv. *The Development Hypothesis*^{b}

The foregoing argument has been directed to prove that the Pentateuch is a great collection of sacred laws and corresponding narratives. These laws and narratives fall on examination into separate groups, which may be discriminated by criteria of substantial fact, of historic assumptions, of religious ideas, and finally of language. Such groups are necessarily the product of different minds; it may even be of different social and religious conditions. It becomes important then to inquire what are their mutual relations. Do they show any marks of interdependence? How far can one be said to presuppose another? Is it possible to connect them into a coherent scheme of historic development?

1. The inquiry thus opened has a twofold aim. If the documents are by various writers, it may be assumed that they do not all belong to the same decade, and it is quite conceivable that they may be separated by centuries. When the analysis has been provisionally effected, the first step, therefore, is to discover the sequence in which the several groups of material arose. If a definite order can be established among them, so that they can be arranged in a series or progression, a clue to their relations is obtained as a working basis for further advance. For it is plain that the mere linear distribution of the elements is quite independent of the actual literary chronology; it fixes nothing in positive time, it only exhibits a certain conception of the stages in the growth of the complex whole. The second step, therefore, is to ascertain the relation of such stages to the actual facts of history. Is there any definite evidence connecting any of the documents with particular events, or even with important periods, in the national life of Israel? If a single book can be clearly associated with any specific incident, and its date assigned within reasonable limits, those which

---

^{a} Cf this use of נפש with that in D's phrase 'smite him mortally' $^{6\ 11}$.
^{b} This title will be found applied and expounded by Dr Briggs, *Higher Criticism* IX.

follow it in the Pentateuchal series cannot be placed before this date; and those anterior to it cannot be set later. The older criticism did not clearly disengage this twofold problem. It assumed that the document which appeared to be the literary foundation first of the book of Genesis, and then of the entire Hexateuch, was the earliest in time. It was embarrassed by theories of supplementation, and sought for its chief basis in the connexions of the narratives rather than of the laws. Not until the various codes were carefully studied in their relations with each other, and with the facts of Israel's religious history, could a clearer view be reached. The establishment of this method has been the work of the last thirty years.

2. It has already been mentioned that the sacred law as conceived by Ewald and most of his contemporaries practically started with the Priestly Code in the age of Solomon. The great Book of Origins (**P**) containing the Levitical legislation was an early product of the organization of the national worship in the Temple. It was followed by a group of documents, partly of Ephraimite and partly of Judean origin, marked by strong affinities with prophetic thought, descending through the tenth and ninth centuries and perhaps touching the eighth. These corresponded with the modern **JE**. To these were added, lastly, the book of Deuteronomy, first published in the reign of Josiah. A number of distinguished scholars adopted this view of the succession, though with various modifications in detail. In this country it lay at the back of the early investigations of Bishop Colenso; it gleamed through the lectures of Dean Stanley; it was systematically expounded by Dr S Davidson; while the publication of the translation of Ewald's great *History of Israel* displayed its historical significance in full to the English reader. In the land of its birth, however, it was felt less and less possible to maintain so early a date for the Priestly Law, and first Noldeke and then Dillmann admitted that it contained later elements [a]. The place of Deuteronomy, in the seventh century, remained practically unchallenged; nor did any critic wish to shift **JE** from the ninth and eighth centuries, whatever views might be cherished as to the relative antiquity of **J** and **E**. The controversy really settled around the Priestly Code: was it older or younger than Deuteronomy?

3. The suggestion that **D** had been composed earlier than **P**, and afterwards inserted into it, was made, though in a somewhat grotesque form, by Spinoza. But it had no critical or historic basis, and remained unfruitful. De Wette, who placed **D** in the reign of Josiah, conjectured that the Levitical law came gradually into existence after the reign of Solomon, but he did not seriously investigate its constituents, or compare them with the law-book of Josiah. As early as 1833, however, Reuss was elaborating in his lectures at Strassburg the thesis that much of the priestly legislation in the middle books was posterior to Deuteronomy. Two scholars, Vatke and Georg, working on wholly independent lines, arrived simultaneously in 1835 at the same result. They were in advance of their age, and were so bitterly opposed by the dominant school that no further progress was made in that direction for a quarter of a century. In 1861, however, Kuenen ventured to publish the view [b] that the priestly law contained passages (such as Lev 16 17 Num 16 18 31) which could only be understood as further developments of the demands formulated in **D**. The decisive attack on the established critical tradition was made by Graf, a pupil of Reuss, in two essays published at the close of 1865 [c]. The study of the historical records, from the period of the Judges to the fall of the monarchy, convinced him that the Levitical code was not in existence between the settlement in Canaan and the capture of Jerusalem. That code, however, was not all of one piece; it contained earlier and later elements.

---

[a] So, at the present day, Kittel, *History of the Hebrews* 1 132, Baudissin, Strack, and others.
[b] *Historisch-Kritisch Onderzoek* 1, Leiden, 1861
[c] *Die Geschichtlichen Bücher des Alten Testaments*, Leipzig; the work bore the date of 1866.

The older were chiefly comprised in a group of chapters Lev 17–26 (since designated the Holiness legislation P[h]), which Graf connected with the prophet Ezekiel. The younger were incorporated by Ezra after the captivity. The views of Graf did not at once make way, and they were encumbered at the outset by a critical difficulty. He adhered to the early date of the *Tol*e*dhoth* sections in Genesis, and thus cut Ewald's Book of Origins in two. It was not long before the reviewers seized upon this inconsistency, which Kuenen also pointed out in private[a], and he subsequently accepted the correction, with the result that the *Tol*e*dhoth* sections, and the code to which they served as introduction, were assigned to a common date. Dr Kalisch in this country was at the same time reviving the views of Georg in his learned commentary on Leviticus[b]; and in Holland Kuenen adopted the main conceptions of Graf as the basis of his history of the 'Religion of Israel[c].' From this time, the 'Grafians,' as they were sometimes contemptuously called, began slowly to increase in number[d]; and in 1876 their little band received the powerful support of Wellhausen, whose brilliant series of articles on the composition of the Hexateuch at once awoke the attention of Germany. These were followed in 1878 by the first volume of a *History of Israel*[e], which contained a searching examination of the entire tradition of the cultus, involving a comparison of the Pentateuchal codes with the historical records. These two works, together with the elaborate treatise on the Hexateuch issued by Kuenen in 1885[f], have formed the basis of all subsequent exposition for their school, while the great series of commentaries by Dillmann represent the modifications which have been found needful by the continuators of the current hypothesis of fifty years ago[g]. By his admirable lectures on 'the Old Testament in the Jewish Church,' the late Prof W Robertson Smith familiarized the results of Kuenen and Wellhausen for English readers: this view lay at the back of his profound researches into the origin of Semitic institutions, and by his influence it was adopted as the foundation for the general treatment of the Old Testament in the last edition of the *Encyclopaedia Britannica*. To it, also, Prof Driver has given his weighty support[h]: and his eminent American colleagues in the preparation of the new edition of the Hebrew Lexicon of Gesenius, Prof C H Briggs and Prof Francis Brown, have incorporated it into their work. A crowd of scholars in Germany, Holland, France, Great Britain, and the United States, are ranged side by side in its defence. No other critical hypothesis has won so large a variety of adhesions in so short a time. It may be safely said at present to command the field. On what grounds does it rest? The answer is twofold, (1) on a comparison of the documents with each other, and (2) on a comparison of the documents with history. The first yields the order, **JE**, **D**, and **P**; the second leads to the negative result that **D** was unknown before the seventh century, and **P** not in existence in its present form before the exile; while positively it connects **D** with a promulgation of sacred law under Josiah in 622, and **P** with a similar promulgation by Ezra, the date commonly assigned being 444 B.C.

[a] Bishop Colenso still championed it in the last instalment of his *Pentateuch*, part vii, though he finally acquiesced in the modern view.
[b] Dr Kalisch had previously advocated the Mosaic authorship of Genesis and Exodus. *Leviticus*, vol i, appeared in 1867.
[c] Issued in Dutch, 1869–70, and in English, 1874.
[d] Bishop Colenso adopted the late date of the Levitical legislation in his *Pentateuch* Part vi, 1872.
[e] Issued in English in 1885 under the title *Prolegomena to the History of Israel*. In 1894 this was succeeded by his *Israelitische und Jüdische Geschichte*.
[f] As the first vol of a new edition of the *Onderzoek*. An English translation by Mr P H Wicksteed appeared in 1886.
[g] Dillmann's position is still held in the main by scholars like Kittel, Baudissin, and Strack.
[h] See his well-known *Introduction to the Literature of the OT*. With this book must be named Prof Ryle's essay on *The Canon of the OT*.

CHAPTER IX

THE ORDER OF THE DOCUMENTS

THE reader who has followed the exposition in the foregoing section will not be surprised to find **D** chosen as a suitable basis for the twofold comparison just indicated. Its well defined place in the Pentateuch permits it to be easily isolated for literary purposes; while its mingled contents of narrative and legislation secure for it numerous points of contact with the books which have preceded it. Further, its central ideas are simple; their application to Israel's life is also simple; and they furnish, therefore, a ready clue to the inquirer who interrogates history to ascertain the first traces of their recognition.

i. *The Antecedents of Deuteronomy*

The book of Deuteronomy opens with a recital of the events of the wanderings of Israel since their departure from Mount Horeb. It thus covers the narrative of Num 10^{11}–36. But the exhortations which follow carry back the story to the Covenant of the Ten Words, and recall by many an allusion the wonders of the Exodus and of ancient time. The former days of the fathers are open to its survey, as well as the latest incidents of the wilderness: and the inquiry into the precursors of **D** concerns itself accordingly on the one hand with the traditions, and on the other with the laws.

1. The most prominent reference in **D** to the ancestors of Israel concerns the divine promise of the land. This is always cited in the terms of **JE**. It is repeatedly described $^D 107$ as an oath in a form nowhere employed by **P**:—

1^8 Go in and possess the land which Yahweh sware unto your fathers, to Abraham, to Isaac, and to Jacob, to give unto them.

A comparison with the passages enumerated in $^{JE}217$ at once establishes them as the source of **D**'s allusion:—

Deut	*Gen*
1^{10} Yahweh your God hath multiplied you, and, behold, ye are this day as the stars of heaven for multitude.	22^{16} By myself have I sworn, saith Yahweh, ^{17} that in multiplying I will multiply thy seed as the stars of heaven.

Yahweh is thus to **D** pre-eminently the 'God of the fathers,' a title recalling his providential guidance in a manner familiar to **JE** $^{JE}120$ but avoided by **P**. In describing the descent of Israel into Egypt, however, **D** specifies the number seventy persons 10^{22} in accordance with **P**. The references to the increase of the people and to their sufferings $26^{5..}$ (see margin) seem to follow the narrative of **JE**, and we are thus brought to the period of Moses' own career.

(a) The retrospect never touches the hour of his divine call; nor does it specify the separate strokes of the wrath of Yahweh against Pharaoh. It frequently recalls the 'signs and wonders' $^D 101$ and the 'mighty hand' $^D 80\,^a$: but when it introduces

---

^{a} The affinities of these expressions may be studied in the word-lists. For 'signs and wonders' cp Ex 7^3 **P**; 'stretched out arm' 26^8 cp Ex 6^6 **P**; 16^3 'haste' cp Ex 12^{11} **P**. Do these parallels require us to suppose that **D** derived them from **P**? In an inquiry concerning literary and historical dependence, the evidence must be viewed in various lights Until a definite result is reached on other grounds, linguistic parallels may be conceivably read both ways if **D** may be founded on **P**, may it not also be argued that **P** may have caught up the expressions of **D**? Or may they not both draw from a larger range of literary and religious tradition? Something will depend on context, or on frequency of usage Thus **D** only uses 'signs and wonders' once, but **D** six times · in **P** the words are associated Ex 7^4 with 'judgements' which **D** never employs: the same word appears in Ex 6^6 where **P** has 'stretched out arm and great judgements' (once) in place

detail concerning the month of the deliverance 16¹, it is the detail (ear-month) of
J contrasted with that of **P**. The allusions to the overthrow of Pharaoh 11⁴ and to the
manna 8³ ¹⁶ are not decisive (though there is a critical presumption in favour of **E**, see
marginal references and notes *in loc*). But on the march the references are clear;
Massah 6¹⁶ 9²² and the attack of Amalek 25¹⁷⁻¹⁹ belong to **E**[a]. At Horeb (**E**'s name
for the sacred mountain) it is the narrative of **E** which is mostly followed. The
recital of the Ten Words contains a marked difference in the commentary on the fourth
commandment (Deut 5¹⁵ ct Ex 20¹¹). The version in Exodus is obviously related to
Gen 1-2⁴ᵃ **P**. Can it be supposed that **D** set aside the solemn appeal to the creative
week crowned with divine rest, to introduce a historic reminiscence which had no
practical connexion with the observance of the seventh day? The representations
of the terrified people Deut 5²³⁻²⁷ expand those in Ex 20¹⁸⁻²⁰ **E**; and the recital of the
great apostasy Deut 9, and its sequel in the reinscription of the Ten Words 10¹⁻⁵, runs
a similar though not identical course with **JE** in Ex 32-34. It has already been pointed
out that the account of the construction of the ark Deut 10¹⁻⁵ is irreconcilable with that
of **P**[b] (chap VIII i 3). Nor are there any allusions to the chief features of **P**'s narrative:
the 'glory' does not cover the mount, and no Dwelling arises to receive the 'ark of the
covenant' into its holy place, and provide a throne for Yahweh in the centre of his
people.

(β) Before leaving Horeb Moses appoints assistant judges 1⁹⁻¹⁸, his recital being
strangely blended (see the margin) from passages in Ex and Num belonging to **E**.
When the people quit the sacred mountain, the narrative of **D** still recognizes only
the incidents of **JE**, such as are connected with the names of Taberah and Kibroth-
hattaavah 9²², the leprosy of Miriam 24⁹, the march round Seir 2¹, the passage through
Edom 2⁴⁻⁸, and the fiery serpents 8¹⁵. The first step in the Trans-jordanic conquest
is related 2²⁶⁻³⁷ in obvious dependence on **JE**, which does not seem originally to have
included the defeat of Og and the capture of Bashan[c]. The mention of Balaam 23⁴ and
of Baal of Peor 4³ shows the familiarity of **D** with the contents of **JE** up to the Jordan
camp. The view which it takes of the ideal boundaries of Israel's land 1⁷ 11²⁴ coincides
with **JE** in Gen 15¹⁸, and not with the limits then so recently defined by **P** Num 34¹⁻¹².
Of **P**, indeed, there is no trace. The accounts of the death of Aaron 10⁶ and the charge
to Joshua 31¹⁴, ²³ now incorporated in **D**, cannot be reconciled with it. To the striking
episodes of the second census, and (still more) the Midianite war, which have happened
but yesterday, **D** makes no reference: and his account of the divine refusal to permit
Moses to enter the promised land 1³⁷, cp 3²³⁻²⁶ does not harmonize with the cause
assigned by **P** Num 20¹². The silence of **D** concerning the objects of most prominent
interest to **P** may be variously interpreted: but in view of the constant references to
JE they excite a presumption that **D** was not acquainted with **P**'s narrative. That
presumption is heightened by the fact that various statements now incorporated in **D**
concerning the construction of the ark, the death of Aaron, the selection of the tribe

---

of **D**'s frequent 'mighty hand and stretched out arm.' Again, 'haste' Deut 16³ occurs in connexion
with a time-specification different from **P**'s (see above) So 'hard service' Deut 26⁶ is found in
Ex 6⁹ **P**, but in another context Cp 'create' 4³² and Gen 1¹ ²⁷. Above all the phrase 'be for
a God' Deut 26¹⁷ 29¹³ recalls the terminology of **P**. But a reference to ᴾ26 suggests caution. In
the two passages in **D** the words are associated with a counterpart 'be for a people' These are
found together in almost all the prophetic passages (where alone the phrase appears outside the
Pentateuch), but only twice in **P** Ex 6⁷ and Lev 26¹² The usage, therefore, points to derivation
from the devotional language of a religious school, rather than to the adoption of a phrase from one
document into another

[a] In 8¹⁵ water is brought out of the rock (*sûr*) as in Ex 17⁶ **E**. In **P**'s story Num 20¹ the rock
is *çela'*.

[b] They agree, however, that the ark was made of acacia wood.

[c] On peculiar difficulties connected with 3¹⁸⁻²⁰ and Num 32, cp Num 32¹ᴺ. It will be noticed
that **D**'s language is consistently clear of the characteristic terms of **P**.

of Levi, the charge to Joshua, cannot be brought into accord with their counterparts in **P**. Two singular instances point definitely to this conclusion. It has already been shown (chap IV 2δ) that some of the narratives in the Pentateuch are combined out of two independent stories which have been woven into one. The texture is loose, and ragged edges betray the imperfect union. Two such narratives are found in Num 13-14 and 16; the first relates the mission of the spies, the second the fate of Korah, Dathan, and Abiram. To each of these **D** makes reference. In their present form they are blended out of materials belonging to **JE** and **P**, which originally constituted independent narratives. The allusions of **D** are in both cases coincident with **JE**. Thus in recounting the expedition of the spies and its sequel Deut 1^{22-46}, **D** follows **JE** in limiting their journey to the valley of Eshcol, instead of reporting with **P** their arrival at the furthest boundary of the north. Their impression of the country ^{25} agrees with that recorded by **JE**; so does the oath of doom uttered by Yahweh ^{34}. and the special exemption of Caleb. Joshua was evidently not one of the twelve in **D**'s conception ^{38}, though **P** formally includes him in the number, and joins him with Caleb both in resistance to the popular fears and in survival beyond the guilty generation. But **D** like **P** represents the spies as twelve in number, and both describe their mission by a common word, *tûr*^{a}. In 11^6 **D** cites the fate of Dathan and Abiram. That of Korah would have been no less apposite to his argument. Why is it, then, ignored? The obvious answer is that it was unknown; it was not in **D**'s reach because it had yet not been put where it now stands.

(γ) Three facts emerge from this brief survey. (1) In an enormous majority of cases, **D** founds himself on **JE** (whether separately or in combination cannot be at present determined) as against **P**. (2) Nevertheless he occasionally adopts an independent course: Jethro is unnamed in the story of the institution of the Judges; Moses himself takes the initiative, and the choice is referred to the people themselves. Similarly, it is the people who propose the dispatch of the spies (this statement may have been found in Num 13 in **JE**'s version, and eliminated in the union with **P** as out of harmony with it): the victorious enemies are Amalekites and Canaanites Num 14^{43}, where **D** has Amorites: Edom who refused to allow the passage of Israel Num 20^{14-21}, permits it in Deut $2^{4-7\ b}$. (3) Three items only, unnamed by **JE**, are found in **P**, the seventy souls of Israel when Jacob went down into Egypt, the construction of the ark out of acacia wood, and the reckoning of the spies as twelve. These, it is clear, cannot be treated as proof of **D**'s acquaintance with **P** in face of the large amount and variety of indications opposed to that hypothesis. The numbers in question, and the material of the ark, might easily have been part of a common tradition, or might even have been appropriated by **P** from **D**. The evidence will be differently valued according to the judgement based on the relations of the laws: but it is worthy of note that in maintaining on other grounds the priority of **P** Dillmann concedes that these coincidences are insufficient to prove the employment of **P**'s narrative by **D**^{c}.

2. The legislation of Deuteronomy is distributed under two covenants, one at Horeb 5^1 comprised in the Ten Words, the other in Moab 6^1–29^1. The limitation of the Mosaic teaching at Horeb is definite and precise. Moses is summoned by Yahweh 5^{31} to stand with him and hear the commandment which he is in future to impart to his people. But the promulgation of these 'statutes and judgements' in Israel does not begin at once; it is reserved till they are on the eve of entering the promised land 6^{1-3}. There is thus no place in **D**'s narrative for the subsequent declaration of

---

^{a} Any argument based on this verbal identity must be subject to the cautions already offered, ante p 70^a.

^{b} Driver, unlike most recent commentators, Dillmann, Oettli, Steuernagel, regards these passages as referring to different incidents.

^{c} *NDJ* 610

THE ANTECEDENTS OF DEUTERONOMY

the 'Words and Judgements' of Ex 20^{22}–23 24^{3-8}, nor for the Covenant Words announced in 34. Still less does **D** conceive that Israel carried about with it on the march a Dwelling containing a permanent seat of revelation Ex 25^{22} Num 7^{89}. The entire legislative code of **P** is practically excluded by the scheme of **D**.

(a) Nevertheless while **D** contains a large amount of legislation peculiar to itself[a], it naturally also contains numerous parallels with laws in the preceding books. The study of these parallels reveals many interesting facts. In one set of cases the laws may be regarded as substantially identical, yet they differ in expression, and each is enforced by characteristic phrases belonging to its own group. A passage from the social statutes will illustrate these affinities:—

Ex 22 **E**	*Deut 24* **D**	*Lev 19* **P**[h]
^{25} If thou lend money to any of my people with thee that is poor, thou shalt not be to him as a creditor; neither shall ye lay upon him usury ^{26} If thou at all take thy neighbour's garment to pledge, thou shalt restore it unto him by that the sun goeth down: ^{27} for that is his only covering, it is his garment for his skin · wherein shall he sleep? and it shall come to pass, when he crieth unto me, that I will hear; for I am gracious.	^{10} When thou dost lend thy neighbour any manner of loan, thou shalt not go into his house to fetch his pledge. ^{11} Thou shalt stand without, and the man to whom thou dost lend shall bring forth the pledge without unto thee. ^{12} And if he be a poor man, thou shalt not sleep with his pledge . ^{13} thou shalt surely restore to him the pledge when the sun goeth down, that he may sleep in his garment, and bless thee · and it shall be righteousness unto thee before Yahweh thy God.	
	^{14} Thou shalt not oppress an hired servant that is poor and needy, whether he be of thy brethren, or of thy strangers that are in thy land within thy	^{13} Thou shalt not oppress thy neighbour, nor rob him the wages of a hired servant shall not abide with thee all night until the morning.

[a] In the following table laws are reckoned as peculiar when they introduce some wholly fresh principle, such as the unity of the sanctuary, or the application of 'release' to debts.

12^{1-28} The concentration of sacrifice at Jerusalem.
$^{29-31}$ Against imitation of Canaanite rites.
13 Against seduction to idolatry.
15^{1-11} The year of Release
16^{18} Appointment of Judges.
17^{2-7} Against the worship of the host of heaven
$^{8-13}$ Appeals to be carried to a supreme court.
$^{14-20}$ The Monarchy.
18^{9-22} Prophecy
19^{14} Against removal of boundary stones.
20 Military service and war 24^5.
21^{1-9} Expiation for undiscovered murder.
$^{10-14}$ Treatment of female captives
$^{15-17}$ Primogeniture.
$^{18-21}$ Treatment of an undutiful son.
$^{22-23}$ Treatment of the body of a malefactor.
22^5 Against wearing the garments of another sex.
$^{6-7}$ Regulation of bird's nesting.
^{8} Parapets on roofs
$^{13-21}$ Slander against a newly married woman.
23^{1-8} Admission into Yahweh's assembly.
^{15}. Humanity to escaped slave
^{17}. Against religious prostitution.
^{24}. Regard for neighbour's crops.
24^{1-4} Divorce
^{16} Criminals' children not to suffer.
25^{1-3} Limit to bastinado.
^{4} Against muzzling a threshing ox.
$^{5-10}$ The Levirate marriage.
^{11} Modesty in women.
$^{17-19}$ Remember Amalek
26^{1-15} Liturgical directions at offerings

Ex 22 E	*Deut* 24 D	*Lev* 19 P^h
	gates ¹⁵ in his day thou shalt give him his hire, neither shall the sun go down upon it, for he is poor, and setteth his heart upon it: lest he cry against thee unto Yahweh, and it be sin unto thee	
²¹ And a stranger shalt thou not wrong, neither shalt thou oppress him: for ye were strangers in the land of Egypt. ²² Ye shall not afflict any widow, or fatherless child. ²³ If thou afflict them in any wise, and they cry at all unto me, I will surely hear their cry; ²⁴ and my wrath shall wax hot, and I will kill you with the sword; and your wives shall be widows, and your children fatherless. 23⁶ Thou shalt not wrest the judgement of thy poor in his cause ... ⁹ And a stranger shalt thou not oppress: for ye know the heart of a stranger, seeing ye were strangers in the land of Egypt.	¹⁷ Thou shalt not wrest the judgement of the stranger, *nor* of the fatherless; nor take the widow's raiment to pledge: ¹⁸ but thou shalt remember that thou wast a bondman in Egypt, and Yahweh thy God redeemed thee thence: therefore I command thee to do this thing.	³³ And if a stranger sojourn with thee in your land, ye shall not do him wrong: ³⁴ The stranger that sojourneth with you shall be unto you as the homeborn among you, and thou shalt love him as thyself; for ye were strangers in the land of Egypt: I am Yahweh your God.
	¹⁹ When thou reapest thine harvest in thy field, and hast forgot a sheaf in the field, thou shalt not go again to fetch it: it shall be for the stranger, for the fatherless, and for the widow: that Yahweh thy God may bless thee in all the work of thine hands. ²⁰ When thou beatest thine olive tree, thou shalt not go over the boughs again: it shall be for the stranger, for the fatherless, and for the widow. ²¹ When thou gatherest *the grapes of* thy vineyard, thou shalt not glean it after thee: it shall be for the stranger, for the fatherless, and for the widow. ²² And thou shalt remember that thou wast a bondman in the land of Egypt: therefore I command thee to do this thing.	⁹ And when ye reap the harvest of your land, thou shalt not wholly reap the corners of thy field, neither shalt thou gather the gleaning of thy harvest. ¹⁰ And thou shalt not glean thy vineyard, neither shalt thou gather the fallen fruit of thy vineyard; thou shalt leave them for the poor and for the stranger: I am Yahweh your God 23²² And when ye reap the harvest of your land, thou shalt not wholly reap the corners of thy field, neither shalt thou gather the gleaning of thy harvest: thou shalt leave them for the poor, and for the stranger: I am Yahweh your God.

The contents of these regulations for social welfare are not differentiated from each other by references to distinctive religious ideas or institutions. The simpler forms of Exodus compared with the hortatory expansions in Deuteronomy certainly suggest priority, especially when it is observed that the phraseology of the additions in **D** repeatedly occurs elsewhere. Thus in Exodus 22^{23 27} 'cry' cp ^{JE}141; 23⁹ 'ye know' ^{JE}174. But the passages from **D** yield the following parallels: ¹³ 'and it shall be righteousness unto thee' 6²⁵; ¹⁴ 'brethren' ^D25, 'within thy gates' ^D51; ¹⁵ 'lest he cry (ᛉ *call*) against thee' 15⁹, 'and it be sin to thee' ^D102; ^{18 22} 'remember that thou wast a bondman' ^D97, 'redeem' ^D95, 18 22 'therefore I command thee' 15¹¹; ^{19–21} 'the stranger, the fatherless, and the widow' ^D105; 'that Yahweh may bless thee' ^D22, 'the work of thine hands' ^D119. The passages from Leviticus also show traces of an independent hortatory framework in the repeated phrases 19^{10 34} 'I am Yahweh'

'I am Yahweh your God' p203. They further display a separate legal terminology, 19⁹ 23²² 'poor and stranger,' 19³⁴ 'stranger that sojourneth with you' p145ᵇ, 'homeborn' p34. But it appears difficult to come to any conclusion with respect to the antiquity of these passages compared with **D**: the variations of style point to their formulation and arrangement in another school, but the criteria are insufficient to suggest any definite order of antecedence or sequence.

(β) Further inquiry into the relations of **D** to the First Code supplies ample evidence that much of the material embodied in the legislation of Ex 21–23 has been utilized in **D**. In view of the fact that considerable portions of this Code (Ex 21¹⁷⁻²² ²⁶⁻³⁶ 22¹⁻¹⁵ ¹⁹ ²⁸) have no counterparts in **D**, it may be doubted whether **D** may be even broadly described as a new edition of it. But of the relation of other parts there can be no doubt. The laws of slavery and the series of the feasts are obviously in close connexion; so are those concerning the restoration of lost property and seduction. Many of these Deuteronomic reproductions, however, introduce important new features with the aim of extending, defining, or modifying, the earlier usage. Thus the law of temporary servitude and septennial manumission is applied in Deut 15¹² ¹⁷ to women as well as to men, and the Deuteronomic law-giver enforces on the householder a generous treatment of the outgoing bondman. In the following parallel ordinances the principle applied to strayed animals is extended to lost articles of clothing and generalized finally as of universal application:—

Ex 23	Deut 22
⁴ If thou meet thine enemy's ox or his ass going astray, thou shalt surely bring it back to him again ⁵ If thou see the ass of him that hateth thee lying under his burden, and wouldest forbear to help him, thou shalt surely help with him.	¹ Thou shalt not see thy brother's ox or his sheep go astray, and hide thyself from them: thou shalt surely bring them again unto thy brother ² And if thy brother be not nigh unto thee, or if thou know him not, then thou shalt bring it home to thine house, and it shall be with thee until thy brother seek after it, and thou shalt restore it to him again. ³ And so shalt thou do with his ass, and so shalt thou do with his garment; and so shalt thou do with every lost thing of thy brother's, which he hath lost, and thou hast found · thou mayest not hide thyself. ⁴ Thou shalt not see thy brother's ass or his ox fallen down by the way, and hide thyself from them: thou shalt surely help him to lift them up again

These passages further exhibit a suggestive change in nomenclature: the 'enemy' of Exodus becomes the unknown 'brother' in Deuteronomy cp p25: within the tribe or the nation all members of the race are 'brothers.' On the other hand instead of enlarging the older regulation by fresh cases, **D** sometimes limits it, as when the ancient *lex talionis* Ex 21²³⁻²⁵ is restricted in Deut 19¹⁹⁻²¹ to the punishment of false witness. The law enjoining the gift of firstlings to Yahweh can hardly be said to show any literary dependence on the First Code Deut 15¹⁹⁻²³ cp Ex 22³⁰; but it adds a number of important particulars, such as the prohibition to employ the firstling of the ox in labour, and the rejection of blemished animals for sacrifice. In the case of the sabbatical fallow year for the land, the principle is applied in Deut 15¹·· in a new form (cp chap VIII i 6), though a literary link is supplied in the retention of the term 'release.' Had it been intended to preserve the older law, it seems improbable that it should not have been specified.

(γ) The most important modifications, however, are due to the fundamental law of the unity of the sanctuary. It has been already shown (chap VIII i 1β) that the three chief Codes of the Pentateuch treat the place at which sacrifice may be offered to Yahweh from different points of view. The First Code sanctions an altar anywhere, but lays stress on its material. Deuteronomy abolishes the local altars, centralizes the cultus at the metropolitan temple, and appears expressly conscious that the step is revolutionary 12^8. This view is only intelligible if the Deuteronomic law was designed to promote the reform of an older usage which had fallen into abuse. It is inconceivable that the same legislator should issue a permission in one place, then withdraw it in another, and yet allow both the rule and its revocation to stand side by side. The conditions which rendered such a reform needful will be sought hereafter: at present it is only necessary to observe that the concentration of worship at one sanctuary, and the abolition of all others, involved different kinds of modification in customs founded on the ancient law of Ex 20^{24}. This has been noted already in connexion with the feasts (chap VIII i 5 p 53): the pious householder who comes to 'see Yahweh's face,' and pay his seasonal dues, must seek him only in the place where he has chosen to set his Name. Similarly, the old practice of judicial resort to Elohim Ex 22^8 falls to the ground, and a supreme tribunal is to hear appeals at Jerusalem Deut 17^{8-12}. A different consequence was noted in the case of the manumitted slave (chap VIII i 7 p 55): when it was no longer practicable to require his attendance at the temple in Jerusalem, the sanction of religion was invoked no more. A modification of yet a third kind may be traced in the application of this principle to the right of asylum in case of homicide. The law of the First Code Ex 21^{14} recognizes such a protection in the altar, though the conditions under which it may be claimed are carefully guarded. The existence of the local sanctuaries spread ample possibilities of refuge through the land. But when they were declared illegal, it was necessary to provide some substitute. The old law is dropped without reserve, but a new law takes its place. The antique phraseology, 'if a man lie not in wait, but Elohim deliver him into his hand,' passes into the illustrative case of a man going into the forest with his neighbour to hew wood Deut 19^5; and the manslayer flees, no longer to the altar, but to one of three cities appointed for such shelter. These different types of modification all result from a common cause, the application of a fresh and definite principle to varying religious and social customs; they are wholly independent of the 'philological method,' though they receive important confirmation from it; they are concerned with the history of institutions, and the changes which are rendered inevitable by new ideas and hitherto unformulated demands. In the field of legislation, then, as of narrative, **D** must be regarded as posterior to **JE**.

3. The continual reiteration in **D** of the new rule that sacrifice can only be offered in the place of Yahweh's choice, is difficult to reconcile with the Levitical representation that Yahweh had been continuously dwelling in Israel's midst for wellnigh forty years. It has been already noted (p 51) that the assumption of the unity of the sanctuary in the main portions of **P** implies that the principle for which **D** so strenuously contends has been effectively established, and is no longer in dispute. If this view be correct, the priority of **D** before **P** is clear. It is supported by the fact that while **P** is not without its traces of controversy[a], the subject is no longer the sacred place, but the right of ministry. The differences to which attention has been already directed (chap VIII i 4 p 53) need some further exposition and development.

(a) The Deuteronomic law repeatedly identifies the Levites with the priesthood. Its customary phrase 'the priests, the Levites' 17^9 ^{18} 24^8 27^9, i e the Levitical priests, contrasts them at once with priests of other orders. Elsewhere they are styled 'the priests, the sons of Levi' 21^5 31^9. This tacitly implies that all members of the tribe are priests. But as if to render doubt impossible, the Levitical priests 18^1 are expressly equated with 'the whole tribe of Levi.' They are set apart originally to minister to Yahweh 10^8 21^5 18^5: they bless the people in his name 10^8 21^5: they share in the

---

[a] See the notes on the story of Korah Num 16.

supreme administration of justice 21^5 17^{8-12} 19^{17}. There is no reference to any distinction of rank, office, or duty. The Levites are depicted as scattered over the country in town and village; they are also to be found of course in the metropolitan sanctuary. Throughout the land they have served at the local altars, and the rites of household and clan were in their hands. What was to be their future if the Deuteronomic principle of one place of sacrifice were adopted? They would be at once deprived of their means of livelihood. This danger did not escape the advocates of the reform, and they introduced a bold provision intended to meet it. Let the disestablished Levites come up to Jerusalem and exercise their ministry there Deut 18^6.:—

⁶ And if a Levite come from any of thy gates out of all Israel, where he sojourneth, and come with all the desire of his soul unto the place which Yahweh shall choose, ⁷ then he shall minister in the name of Yahweh his God, as all his brethren the Levites do, which stand there before Yahweh.

How far the Levites were allowed to avail themselves of this permission will be seen hereafter. It need only be observed now that the arrangement could never have been proposed if the legislator had not regarded the Levites as all possessed of equal rights, whether they served a distant hamlet or belonged to the temple-guild. But the Levitical legislation makes a fundamental cleavage through the tribe. The family of Aaron is selected for the dignity of the priesthood, and the priests are entitled 'Aaron's sons.' Their personal purity is guarded with the utmost care Lev 21, and at their head stands the 'high priest' 21^{10} or the 'anointed priest' 4^3 ^{5} ^{16} 6^{22} 16^{32}. His office is hereditary, Num 20^{28}; his special functions are to consult the Urim and Thummim Ex 28^{30} Lev 8^8, and to perform the expiation for the nation on the great annual day of atonement 16: and his death marks a social era, when the innocent homicide may leave his city of refuge and return home without fear of the *Goel* Num 35^{25}. Sharply marked off from this consecrated order is the lower function of the Levites. They are not allowed to 'stand before Yahweh, to minister unto him' Deut 10^8: such presumption would expose them to the avenging fire Num 16^{35}. Theirs is a lower ministry, that of the priests Num $3^6 \cdot \cdot 18^2$. The charge of the sacred tent with all its vessels is entrusted to them on the march, but they may not lift the hallowed furniture till the priests have first packed it up, that no inferior touch may profane the holy things, for such touch brings death Num 4^{15-19}. To such servants of the sanctuary aspiration after the priesthood is absolutely forbidden. They may not approach the altar or enter the holy place and remain alive Num $18^{3\ 7}$. Had these severe restrictions been in force when the Deuteronomic code was compiled, could its author have so persistently ignored them? Is it conceivable that rules so stringent could have completely fallen into disuse, and that a later legislator should have quietly dropped the claims of an earlier and austerer day? The question cannot be completely discussed apart from the testimony of history (cp *infra* ii 1β, and chap XIII 3). Moreover, it is only one among a number which are discovered to be intertwined by innumerable links of idea and even of phrase, as the complex fabric of the Levitical legislation is slowly unravelled. A strong probability at least, however, is established that the Priestly Code in enforcing by the direst threats a distinction to which D pays throughout not the slightest heed, is in reality its successor and not its antecedent.

(β) The priority of D is further implied in the regulations for the priestly maintenance. Various sacred dues are specified from time to time in D, the principal being the following: (1) At any ordinary sacrifice 18^3 the priest may claim the shoulder, the two cheeks, and the maw. (2) The firstlings of the flock and herd are to be eaten annually at a sacred feast at Jerusalem 15^{19}. $12^{6.\ 17}$. by the householder and his family with his bondmen and his local Levite. In this feast the temple-priests would doubtless receive a share. (3) A similar festal character was to mark the consumption of the yearly tithe of the produce of the ground 14^{22}·, the Levite within the gates being again expressly commended on this occasion also to the householder's goodwill. But this observance was to be suspended every third year, and the triennial tithe was wholly reserved for the Levite, because he had no inheritance, together with the stranger, the fatherless, and the widow, 14^{28}·. The corresponding prescriptions in **P** provide a much larger revenue for the priests. From (i) the peace offerings they may appropriate the breast and the right thigh Lev 7^{33}·; theirs, too, were the heave offerings, the wave offerings, and others corresponding to the richer ritual of the Priestly Code compared with **D**, meal offering, sin offering, and guilt offering Num 18$^{9-11}$; and they were entitled also to every thing that fell under the ban ^{14}. The firstlings (ii) were handed over entirely to the priests (except the fat) ^{17}·; the first-born of men and unclean beasts being redeemed, and the proceeds belonging to the sanctuary. Similarly the first-fruits of cornfield and vineyard ^{12}· fell to them. The tithe (iii) underwent a similar aggrandizement on behalf of the Levites ^{21}··, who in their turn surrendered a tenth to the priests ^{26}··. Its consumption by the householder who paid it, is set aside: it is no longer even to be eaten in the sanctuary: it supplies maintenance for the Levite and his family in their own home. Moreover it is to be levied additionally on the herd and the flock Lev 27^{32}. The triennial tithe dedicated to the poor has disappeared. (iv) The Levitical demands appear to have been formulated originally on the theory that the Levites had no inheritance in the land Num 18^{20} cp Deut 10^9. But one immense benefaction remains to be mentioned. The regulation contained in Num 35$^{1-8}$ contemplates the endowment of the order with forty-eight cities and measured pasture-lands around. It does not seem likely that any priesthood would have submitted voluntarily to the curtailment of their privileges involved in the view that **P** was really anterior to **D**^{a}. If the priestly revenues had been so carefully provided and so clearly defined, how is it that the poor Levite of the homestead is represented as dependent on the householder's charity, and is grouped with the destitute and forlorn? Must it not be conceded that the higher demands of the Priestly Code constitute a more advanced claim, so that in this matter as in others **D** occupies the middle place between **JE** and **P**?

(γ) It is natural, therefore, to interpret the other prominent divergences between **D** and **P** in the same manner. The enrichment of the Calendar of the feasts in Lev 23 by the feast of trumpets and the atonement-day (chap VIII i 5 p 54) suggests a ritual and religious development analogous to the introduction of a distinction within the Levitical ranks, and the increase in the priestly revenues. The division of the sacred tribe into two orders, one higher and the other lower, and the separation of both from the laity, corresponded to a deepening consciousness of the requirements of the service of Yahweh, which found expression in another form in the organization of the sin and guilt offering, and the ceremonies of atonement. The details of the feasts are marked by new precision of time, and fresh prescriptions are announced for 'Booths.' A similar comparison may be instituted between the jubile law Lev 25 in its twofold application to the land and the person of the Israelite. On the basis of a principle formulated there for the first time the arrangements of tenure are revised (a notable difference being enjoined in the treatment of land and of house property), and the conditions of Hebrew slavery are remodelled. In the latter the usage of the septennate is tacitly withdrawn, much to the disadvantage of the slave: theoretically, his position is improved, inasmuch as he is recognized to belong to Yahweh: practically he loses by the postponement of his manumission to a jubile which he may not live to see. Finally, the right of asylum as conceived by **P** is

---

^{a} It is no longer necessary to argue that the date of Num 35 brings it in Pentateuchal chronology into open conflict with **D** at a few weeks' interval.

expressed in a terminology unknown to **D**; it is regulated by institutions and based upon ideas with which he appears unacquainted. The relative time-order of the two laws in Num 35^{9-34} and Deut 19^{1-13} may be at first sight indistinct, though the facts that **P** supplies the name 'cities of refuge' which **D** leaves unused, and that **P** positively enjoins the separation of six while **D** only requires three, indicate that here, too, a process of development has been at work. But the setting of **P**'s law in close connexion with the other great Levitical conceptions supplies a definite key to its phenomena, and fresh confirmation that **P** follows **D** is thus obtained[a].

ii. *The Testimony of History*

The twofold comparison on the basis of the Narratives and the Laws thus yields the chronological sequence **JE, D, P**. In turning to the records of Israel's history for the purpose of determining, if possible, the actual dates of these documents, inquiry may take one of two directions. Assuming their diversities of origin, it may found itself on positive evidences of their first appearance, or starting from the Mosaic age in which sacred tradition has so long located them, it may ask what indications are presented of their observance, and what circumstances bring them definitely into view. Following the method slowly wrought out by the scholars whose patient labour has gradually fixed the stages of Israel's religious development, a sketch is here offered of the witness supplied by history to the principles and institutions of the Pentateuchal Codes[b]. For test-purposes two leading features are selected: (1) the place at which sacrifice may be offered, and (2) the persons who may perform it. A preliminary caution, however, is necessary. It has become abundantly clear that many of the books of the Old Testament have undergone continuous editorial manipulation. Older materials have been recast, additions have been inserted in the text, and earlier accounts have been expanded to bring their representations into harmony with later standards of pious usage. The books of Judges and Kings especially exhibit clear traces of Deuteronomic influence; this was the form of Mosaic *torah* by which the compilers of the national annals judged the persons and the events of the past[c]. The evidence, therefore, must sometimes be read in another light than that in which it is actually presented. And the unconscious testimony of the record may be of more significance than the historian's positive assertion. The chief fact to be explained is the repeated and systematic violation of the Deuteronomic and Levitical demands on the part both of the people and their responsible leaders, without any attempt to make royal, priestly, or prophetic practice conform to the plainest requirements of the law.

1. Two circumstances come clearly into view during the early history of Israel's settlement in Canaan, (1) the variety of local sanctuaries, and (2) the frequent performance of sacrifice by laymen.

(*a*) Prior to the Jerusalem temple there is no trace of any exclusively authorized sanctuary. The Mosaic tent is fixed at Shiloh Josh 18^1, but there is even in Joshua's time a holy place at Shechem[d] with its solemn stone and oak in its enclosure 24^{26}, where a national assembly is held, a covenant is made and laws are issued. What relation this bore to the temple of the 'Baal of the League' Judg 9^4 it is not necessary to conjecture. It is sufficient to point out that sacrifice might be offered in almost any spot, and for sacrifice an altar of some sort was indispensable. The country was covered with sacred places, many of them doubtless connected with the cultus of the Canaanite

---

[a] This conclusion is not impaired by a comparison of Deut 14 with Lev 11; see note on Deut 14^4.
[b] A slightly different view will be found in Dr Briggs' chapter on this subject, *The Higher Criticism* xi.
[c] Cp Driver, LOT^6 166–7, 177, 185.
[d] 𝔊 reads Shiloh in Josh 24^1, and this reading is adopted by Gratz.

occupants [a], at which the Israelites soon learned to worship. Such was the great 'high place' at Gibeon 1 Kings 3^4, one of a small group of Canaanite towns which retained their independence till after the monarchy had been established. Such, probably, was the Gilgal or Stone-circle near Jericho (there was a second in the neighbourhood of Bethel, and a third is named near Megiddo Josh 12^{23}). Others were founded by the new settlers. Gideon built an altar at Ophrah Judg 6^{24}, and devoted a portion of the Midianite booty to his sanctuary 8^{27}. The Danites plant themselves with the grandson of Moses for their priest in the far north 18^{29}. The boy Samuel is dedicated to the service of the house of Yahweh at Shiloh. This is no wandering tent, it is a stationary temple 1 Sam 1^9. A later annotator has, indeed, attempted to identify it with the Levitical Dwelling, by inserting a clause 2^{22b} referring to the women that did service at the door of the Tent of Meeting Ex 38^8. But this passage is recognized as an addition by the fact that it is not contained in the original Greek text [b], and its testimony cannot therefore be accepted. In the Shiloh temple, Samuel, himself no Levite, still less priest, sleeps in the chamber of the ark 1 Sam 3^3: and in after days he ministers at the high place in Ramah, his own home 9^{12}. Sacrifice is equally legitimate upon a rock Judg 6^{19}, or on an extemporized altar in the open field 1 Sam 6^{14} 14^{35}. The permanent sanctuaries are not all, however, of equal importance. Shiloh and the ark no doubt took the lead. But the overthrow of the temple there did not affect the local worships elsewhere. Bethel is an important place of pilgrimage 10^3. Nob emerges out of obscurity for a moment, and falls back into the gloom. Ramah must have been lifted into eminence by Samuel 7^{17}, but of any successor in his ministry at the 'high place' there is no record. Even after the removal of the ark to Zion, the right of sacrifice elsewhere is still open in the neighbourhood of Jerusalem. David offers the oxen on Araunah's threshing-floor 2 Sam 24^{25}; and when Adonijah prepared to claim the succession, he is supported by the priest Abiathar in a festive sacrifice at the 'serpent stone' beside the 'Fuller's well [c]' 1 Kings $1^{7\ 9}$, a public act which could not have involved a flagrant violation of sacred law likely to prejudice his bid for the throne. But the first step towards a new order had been taken by David, and Zion naturally tended more and more to become a religious centre, as Jerusalem focussed the civil life of the nation.

(β) The Deuteronomic demand for a single sanctuary being thus unrecognized, it is not surprising to find Levitical principles ignored or defied with equal regularity and persistence. Whatever may be the early history of the tribe of Levi, and no branch of the history of Israel is more obscure, it appears plain that religious usage in the age immediately following the settlement is entirely unconscious of the requirements of the Priestly Code. There is no trace of any exclusive sacred order. The chief authority is civil, not ecclesiastical: the 'congregation' is dissolved and the 'high priest' disappears: the people have no proper unity, they are scattered tribes, and the work of establishing a political and religious bond requires hundreds of years. All through the main narrative of Judges 3–16 there is no mention of professional priests. Gideon and Manoah sacrifice 6^{26} 13^{19}. after the fashion of the patriarchs of elder time. A wealthy Ephraimite who piously establishes a household sanctuary, instals one of his own sons as its priest 17^5. Even the wandering Levite whom he engages on the small annual stipend of ten pieces of silver, a suit of clothes, and his board ^{10}, was not of Aaronic descent. At Shiloh the priesthood has become hereditary in Eli's family [d], but a youth from another tribe is

---

[a] Such were the three sun-sanctuaries (Beth-shemesh) Judg 1^{33} Josh 15^{10} 19^{22}; Beth-anath and Anathoth, deriving their names from the Mesopotamian Anath, and many more. Cp von Gall, *Altisraelitische Kultstatten*, 1898. [b] Cp Driver, *Notes on the Text of Samuel* p 26.
[c] Cp W Robertson Smith, *Religion of the Semites* 157.
[d] The connexion of Eli with the house of Levi is nowhere affirmed in the oldest narratives 1 Sam 2^{27-36}, having been 'recast by the narrator, and in its new form coloured by the associations with

admitted into the sanctuary, and in defiance of all Levitical prescription sleeps beside the ark. Others among the larger sanctuaries doubtless had permanent priesthoods. The numerous guild at Nob 1 Sam 22^{18} seems to have been connected with the house of Eli 22^{11} 14^3. At Dan the sacred office was transmitted by descent from the grandson of Moses Judg 18^{30}, just as afterwards at Jerusalem the temple-guild was derived from Zadok. But though Levitical priests might be preferred, they appear to have been few in number and impoverished in condition, and their presence was certainly not required to legitimate a sacrifice. Samuel conducts it regularly at Ramah and frequently elsewhere, as at Mizpah, Bethlehem, and Gilgal, 1 Sam 7^9. 9^{12}. 12^{15} 16$^{2\ 5}$; and Saul does the same 13^9 14^{35} 15$^{15\ 22}$; over the family sacrifice once a year at Bethlehem, Jesse or some other elder probably presided. No series of incidents brings into clearer light the habitual and unconscious violations of the order delineated in the Priestly Code than the story of the treatment of the ark. When it is sent back by its Philistine captors 1 Sam 6^{12}, the kine bring the cart in which it has been placed into the fields of Beth-shemesh, where the villagers are gathering the wheat-harvest. The cart stops beside a great stone; the grateful reapers immediately extemporize a sacrifice; the cart is chopped up to kindle the altar fire, and the kine are burned as an offering to Yahweh. When the sacrifice is over, the Levites appear and take down the ark from the cart already burned, and the men of Beth-shemesh repeat the rite. This singular incongruity is only explicable on the view that ^{15} is an editorial insertion after the manner of 2^{22b}, though in this case the Greek text does not betray it [a]. The sequel proves that the Levites could have had no share in the proceedings. The men of Beth-shemesh, afraid to retain the ark in their midst, propose its removal to Kiriath-jearim. There it is placed in the house of Abinadab, and the townsmen consecrate his son to guard it. The fact that the ark was thus permitted to remain for many years in lay custody, is one of the most singular circumstances in this singular age. Samuel shows no concern for it. The descendants of its former guardians, the priestly house at Nob, are indifferent to it. Saul is not interested in it; and it is not till David is firmly established in Jerusalem that he prepares with great solemnity to transport it to Jerusalem 2 Sam 6. An unhappy disaster interrupted the procession, and with an extraordinary violation of Levitical propriety the ark was carried into the house of an alien, bearing the name of a foreign god, Obed-edom of Gath. Its final transfer was effected three months later, David himself assuming a priestly vestment ^{14}, conducting the sacrifices ^{18} and pronouncing the benediction in the name of Yahweh. The older narrative records no participation by priest or Levite in these proceedings. What share they ought to have taken according to the Pentateuchal standard may be inferred from the representation of the Chronicler in the spirit of pious observance of the Law 1 Chron 15, where Obed-edom is converted into a Levitical harper ^{21}. At the court of David, Abiathar, who alone had escaped from the massacre of the ill-fated house of Eli at Nob, is associated with Zadok, 2 Sam 8$^{17\ b}$. But this does not hinder David from appointing his own sons priests likewise ^{18}, as well as Ira of the Manassite clan Jair [c] settled on the east of the Jordan 20^{26}. That Absalom should pay his vow at the ancient sanctuary of Hebron 15$^{7-9}$, and offer sacrifices there ^{12}; that Solomon should sacrifice at the great *Bamah* at Gibeon 1 Kings 3^4, and before the ark at Jerusalem ^{15}, that he should nominate Zabud, Nathan's son, to be priest 4^5, that he should himself consecrate the temple court 8$^{62-64}$ and utter the blessing ^{14}, is entirely in accordance with the usages

which he was himself familiar,' Driver, *LOT*^{6} 174. Budde, *SBOT*, assigns the passage to R^d On the general question cp Nowack, *Hebr Archaol* 11 91, and Benzinger, *Hebr Archaol* 411.

[a] Budde ascribes it to a late priestly Redactor
[b] 𝔊 reads *Abiathar son of Ahimelech*, and this correction is universally accepted.
[c] 𝔊 reads Jattir, in Judah, 1 Sam 30^{27} Josh 15^{48}.

of the time, though by no means in accordance with the sanctuary-ordinance of Deuteronomy or the clerical distinctions of the Priestly Code. The Levitical institutions, however, appear to be implied in the ceremonial at the dedication of the Temple 1 Kings 8$^{1-5}$. But the same witness which has already proved the presence of interpolation in favour of the Levitical dwelling 1 Sam 2^{22b} comes forward again to testify that the specific references to the sacerdotal Law had no place in the original story. The Greek version represents an older text than the Hebrew which has descended to us from the Synagogue; and a comparison of the two reveals that the Hebrew underwent late Levitical enrichment, carrying back the sacred order of the second temple to honour the dedication of the first:—

Hebrew	*Greek*
^{1} Then Solomon assembled the elders of Israel, and all the heads of the tribes, the princes of the fathers' *houses* of the children of Israel, unto king Solomon in Jerusalem, to bring up the ark of the covenant of Yahweh out of the city of David, which is Zion. ^{2} And all the men of Israel assembled themselves unto king Solomon at the feast, in the month Ethanim, which is the seventh month. ^{3} And all the elders of Israel came, and the priests took up the ark. ^{4} And they brought up the ark of Yahweh, and the tent of meeting, and all the holy vessels that were in the Tent; even these did the priests and the Levites bring up ^{5} And king Solomon and all the congregation of Israel, that were assembled unto him, were with him before the ark, sacrificing sheep and oxen, that could not be told nor numbered for multitude.	Then Solomon assembled the elders of Israel, to bring up the ark of the covenant of Yahweh out of the city of David which is Zion, in the month Ethanim. And the priests took up the ark and the tent of meeting and the holy vessels that were in the tent. And the king and all Israel were before the ark sacrificing sheep and oxen that could not be numbered

It will be noted that some of the insertions (though not all) are dependent on the ideas and phraseology of P. Such are the 'princes' ^{P}131 of 'the fathers' houses' ^{P}66, the 'priests and the Levites' as separate orders, and the 'congregation' ^{P}45; the identification of Ethanim as the seventh month being another sign of later modes of reckoning^a. But when these are withdrawn, there is nothing characteristically Levitical in the remainder, and the proof that Solomon's dedication ceremony followed the demands of P falls to the ground. A comparison with the narrative in Chronicles here provides a suggestive clue. According to the statement of 1 Kings 8^3 the ark was carried by the priests, following ancient usage (cp Josh 3^3 6^6 8^{33}). But 2 Chron 5^4 assigns this duty to the Levites, under the regulations of the Priestly Code. Does it not seem as if P must have come into view between the compilation of the two records of the monarchy^b?

2. The erection of the temple at Jerusalem was not exclusively a religious act; it had a political significance as well; the splendour of the royal sanctuary was the symbol of the royal power, but it was not a substitute for the local altars hallowed by the piety of generations. The editor of the Book of Kings, it is true, writing under the influence of Deuteronomic principles, does so regard it. In his view the establishment of a central cultus at Jerusalem invalidated all others. Before that time they might be excused; after it, they could only be condemned (cp 1 Kings 3^2.). In Jerusalem alone did Yahweh set his name (1 Kings 8^{16} 𝔊, 2 Chron 6^6); there only was worship legitimate.

(*a*) But there is no sign that this was the opinion of Solomon's own time. The age did not lack prophets; and the importance of the temple must have given special prominence to Zadok, whom Solomon installed as his chief priest, and to the priestly guild which afterwards bore Zadok's name. Yet neither prophet nor priest is recorded to have made any protest against the 'high places.' In the long succession of kings who

---

^{a} Cp chap XIII 4δ.
^{b} For a confirmation of this conclusion founded on the comparison of 1 Kings 8^{65}. with 2 Chron 7$^{8-10}$, see chap XIII 4a.

maintained the continuity of the Davidic house in Jerusalem, while the northern kingdom saw one line after another abruptly closed by murder and revolution, distinguished piety again and again secures the historian's commendation (Asa 1 Kings 15^{14}, Jehoshaphat 22^{43}, Joash 2 Kings 12$^{2.}$, Amaziah 14^4, Uzziah 15$^{3.}$, Jotham 15$^{34.}$). But a qualifying clause is added: 'Howbeit the high places were not taken away; the people still sacrificed and burned incense in the high places.' It is plain, then, that there was no demand for their abolition, and the local worships were practised without objection. This was naturally the case, also, in the northern kingdom. At Dan was a priesthood which claimed descent from Moses, though they served Yahweh in the form of a golden bull. Bethel, hallowed in tradition by the theophanies to the patriarchs, a place of pilgrimage in Samuel's day, had been raised to the rank of a 'royal sanctuary' Amos 7^{13} by Jeroboam. Shechem and Gilgal in middle Canaan, and Beer-sheba in the far south, were also favourite places of religious resort for the worshippers of Israel. The prophetic guilds raise no cry for their suppression. In the great struggle with the house of Omri, Elijah hurls all his force against the cultus of the Tyrian Baal, but he is content to leave the high places, their sacred pillars, and their images, unchallenged. On Carmel he rebuilds the fallen altar 1 Kings 18^{30}; and he witnesses without rebuke the un-Levitical proceedings of Elisha 19^{21}, where the word 'slew' is, strictly, 'sacrificed.'

(β) These conditions seem to be plainly reflected in the patriarchal stories recited by **J** and **E**, and in the altar-law of the First Code Ex 20^{24}. The narratives of the altars commemorating the theophanies to the ancestors are unconsciously intended to account for the time-honoured repute and sanctity of places which afterwards became important centres of cultus. Beer-sheba and Hebron in the south, Bethel and Shechem among the central heights, Mizpah and Peniel on the east of Jordan, were thus incorporated into the traditions of the past[a]. The sacred stones, the trees, the wells, which a later prophetic age found heathenish, were unmistakably marked as hallowed by divine approval in the stage of thought and feeling out of which the narratives emerged. The allusions of the prophet Hosea 12$^{3.\ 12}$ show that he was well acquainted with the stories of the Jacob cycle; and the more general references of Amos point in like manner to the account of the wanderings presented in **JE**. His question concerning the cultus of the desert, 'Did ye bring unto me sacrifices and offerings in the wilderness forty years, O house of Israel?' 5^{25}, seems directly to exclude the complicated ritual of the Priestly Code. Had such a body of sacrificial statutes been recognized as in actual operation on the march, he could not have thus easily assumed that it did not exist. Yet Amos prophesied in the sixth century from Sinai. The denunciations of the worship at the northern sanctuaries which break from Amos and Hosea, are not founded upon its illegality, but upon its unspiritual character. Neither because it is offered at the wrong place, nor on the ground of its performance by the wrong persons, do they condemn it. It is not affirmed that Yahweh cannot be found at Bethel, because he has set his name in Jerusalem; nor are the sacrifices worthless because the Levitical distinctions are not observed. There is 'teaching' in plenty Hos 8^{12}, though it has been forgotten 4^6; but its object is not ceremonial but moral 6^6; the 'knowledge of God' which is its proper purpose, lies not in offerings but in judgement, righteousness, and brotherly love.

3. In Jerusalem under the stimulus of prophetic thought Zion began to gain a new place in religious imagination. True, her priests were drunken and venal, yet the city which held the earthly counterpart to the heavenly sanctuary (Is 6^1) rose higher and higher as the seat of Yahweh's decrees Amos 1$^{2\,b}$. Here was the supreme court of

---

[a] A parallel instance may be found in the legends which cluster around Glastonbury. Cp the sanctuary stories so frequently reported by Pausanias.

[b] Cheyne, introduction to W R Smith's *Prophets of Israel*^{2} xvi, proposes to strike out this verse. But cp Wellhausen, *Die Kleinen Propheten* (1892) 67; G A Smith, *Twelve Prophets* i (1896) 93; Nowack, *Die Kleinen Propheten* (Handkommentar, 1897) 122.

appeal for the administration of justice which had been so intimately connected with religion from the earliest Mosaic days; here was the centre of the priesthood whose recognized duty it was to give 'teaching.' So to Isaiah Zion is the seat of Yahweh's sovereignty over Israel, the dwelling of the heavenly king 8^{18}. If the prophetic oracle which appears so curiously duplicated in Is 2^{2-4} and Mic 4^{1-3}, may still be regarded as ancient[a], Yahweh's mountain was already destined to become the religious centre for the world; thither would the nations resort for teaching, thence should Yahweh's word go forth among the peoples. But this future exaltation of the temple hill does not depend on its sole right to the cultus. It is even compatible in Micah 4^5 with the continuance of polytheism. Like their earlier contemporaries, Isaiah and Micah do not condemn the worship of their countrymen as illegal. It is worthless, it is true, but not because the plurality of altars is a defiance of the law; the hands that offer it are 'full of blood,' and the images before which it is performed are fit only for the moles and bats. Accordingly the eighth-century prophecy does not seem to have formulated any call on the civil power for the destruction of the high places. A movement in that direction is, however, ascribed to Hezekiah 2 Kings 18^{3-6}. The statement is couched in the language of the Deuteronomic editor of the whole book, and belongs to a time when the roll of the kings was completed [5]. In the retrospect of the exile, in full view of the Deuteronomic principle enforcing the limitation of the cultus to one place, the reforming zeal of Hezekiah could only be conceived in one direction,—the overthrow of the agencies of idolatry, and the purgation of worship. He is said, therefore, not only to have shattered the brazen serpent which tradition connected with Moses (Num 21^8.), but also to have removed the high places and broken the sacred pillars. What precise facts this general statement covers, cannot now be ascertained. The date of the reform is unknown; it has been even supposed (in spite of Is 36^7 [b]) to have been the fruit of Isaiah's influence on Hezekiah after the retreat of Sennacherib[c]. But it is plain from the records of Josiah's proceedings that Hezekiah could not have gone very far[d]. In the temple precincts he did not disturb the altars on the roof of the upper chamber of Ahaz, intended probably for star-worship; across the valley on the Mount of Olives the high places erected by Solomon for the foreign worships remained untouched 2 Kings 23^{12}.. It is hardly likely, therefore, that there was any attempt at the general suppression of the local altars to Yahweh. The time for such a movement was not ripe; it lacked an adequate impulse. When Josiah actually accomplished it in the next century, it has the air of a startling novelty. It does not appear that any predecessor had really prepared the way. Up to the end of the eighth century, therefore, no clear trace of the special institutions of either **D** or **P** can be discovered. Usage, sanctioned by the leaders of the people, political and religious, continually conflicts with them. The language of prophecy shows no definite acquaintance with their devotional phraseology[e]. The inference inevitably follows: their demands were unrecognized because they had not yet been made.

[a] So Kuenen, *Onderzoek*² (1889); Duhm, *Jesaia* (1892) 15; König, *Einleit* (1893) 312; similarly Cornill⁴, Wildeboer, Driver, *LOT*⁶ 207; on the other hand cp Stade, *ZATW* 1 165 ff, iv 292; Wellhausen, *Skizzen* v 139 (1892), Cheyne, *Introd to the Book of Isaiah* (1895) 9 and *Isaiah* in *SBOT* 18; Nowack, *Die Kleinen Propheten* (Hdkomm) 206; indeterminate, G A Smith, *Twelve Prophets* 1 367.

[b] On this narrative cp Cheyne, *Introd to Isaiah* 226, and Driver, *LOT*⁶ 227.

[c] So Stade, *Gesch des Volkes Israel* 1 608, cp Montefiore, *Hibb Lect* 163; Wellhausen, *Isr und Jud Gesch* 91.

[d] Cp Kuenen, *Hex* 200.

[e] On the affinities of **D** cp chap X 2a, and of **P** chap XIII 4γ.

CHAPTER X

DEUTERONOMY

The foregoing summary of the earlier testimony of history concerning the different requirements of the Pentateuch indicates that the religious institutions of Israel up to the end of the eighth century were in general harmony with the ideas and ordinances of **JE**. The argument from silence is overwhelmingly strong against the public recognition, or even against the private existence, of important legislative collections such as **D** and **P**. Further evidence, however, is needed to account for the first appearance and the subsequent authority of these codes. Such evidence is, happily, forthcoming. But before inquiring for it in the case of **D**, it may be well to ask whether the book itself contains any clues to the secret of its date.

1. The critics of the seventeenth century like Hobbes early made an attempt to distinguish between the central Law and the historical and hortatory setting. It was pointed out that the opening words which described Moses as addressing all Israel 'on the other side of Jordan' implied a writer in Palestine. The time-language, also, was unfavourable to Mosaic authorship: the events of the preceding months were repeatedly described in terms implying distant retrospect, and their results were linked to the present by the formula 'unto this day.' Such remarks affect only the framework of the actual laws. But the laws themselves are devised to meet conditions distant by centuries from the Mosaic age; they prohibit practices which are first recorded under the influence of foreign cults when the religion of Israel was exposed to new dangers, and unexpected rivals imperilled the national homage to Yahweh. Thus not only do the general regulations of the book assume the settlement of Israel after the conquest,—the boundaries of property fixed in ancient time 19^{14}, the life of the homestead with its local priest 'the Levite that is within thy gates,' the sacred festivals of the agricultural year,—but specific laws are designed to regulate the political and religious circumstances of a much later day. (i) The monarchy is described 17^{14}·· in terms which plainly recall the reign of Solomon, with its definite allusions to the royal horse-trade ^{16} (cp 1 Kings 10^{28}. Is 31^1) and the royal harem. (ii) The prophetic order is strong and active, but its activity must be watched and its claims must be scrutinized. These conditions at once place the laws on prophecy far below its rise in the age of Samuel. They point to the conflicts revealed in the language of Isaiah and still more of Jeremiah, when the temple was the scene of open struggle between rivals who each claimed to speak in the divine name. Two passages are concerned with this theme. The first 13^{1-5} at once rejects all prophecy inviting to the worship of other gods; the second 18^{20-22} considers the case of the prophet who announces 'Thus saith Yahweh' when Yahweh has not bidden him. It is not a little singular—and probably points to composition by more than one hand—that the criterion proposed in the second case has already been disallowed in the first. The prophet of other gods may promise a sign or a wonder, and the promise may come to pass, but he deserves no credence. For the prophet who speaks in Yahweh's name, however, there is no other test: 'if the thing follow not, that is the thing which Yahweh hath not spoken.' His doom is certain, 'that same prophet shall die.' It was the test which Jeremiah proposed to Hananiah Jer 28^{16} 'this year thou shalt die.' (iii) Beside the monarchy and prophecy the provision for appeals 17^{8-13} assumes the existence of a supreme authority for hearing and deciding them. It is suggested in the analysis that the difficulties in the description of the arrangement arise from the combination of two orders, one civil delivering 'judgements,' the other religious, pronouncing *torah*. Two bodies appear to exist side by side, cp 19^{17};

both are located in the capital; but their precise mutual relations and the particulars of their jurisdiction are not defined. The law, however, which refers to them as already in action must be posterior to their establishment. Little indeed is known of the constitution of such tribunals: but the Chronicler ascribes to Jehoshaphat in the ninth century a supreme judicial organization in which priests and Levites on the one hand, and the laity on the other, were both represented 2 Chron 19^8 ^{a}. (iv) The language of Deut 2$^{4\cdot}$ appears to contain an allusion to the independence of Edom, which is part of the divine purpose. Some critics have seen in this passage a political reference to the events of the reign of Ahaz. Conquered by David 2 Sam 8^{14}, Elath at the head of the gulf of Akabah became an important port for Solomon's eastern trade 1 Kings 9^{26}. His successors failed to hold it, but it was regained by Uzziah 2 Kings 14^{22}. With the help of Rezin, however, Edom threw off the suzerainty of Judah 2 Kings 16^6 ⓖ 2 Chron 28^{17}; and after the fall of Rezin maintained its own liberties, like the little neighbouring kingdoms of Moab and Ammon, cp Jer 9^{26} 25^{21} 27^3. This argument practically places the book in the seventh century. (v) Weightier evidence is found in the enforcement of the unity of the sanctuary. The fundamental law of Deut 12 requires the abolition of the high places. The word, indeed, is not employed; but the meaning of the statute admits of no doubt. Couched in the dramatic form of a command issued by Moses before the Conquest, it regards the local sanctuaries as Canaanite, and the usages of religion practised there as Canaanite also. That view was no doubt in many cases correct. Particular altars might be ascribed to Samuel or to Saul; but the majority were the time-honoured foundations of generations older still. The worship celebrated there perpetuated the same sacred objects, image and pillar and tree-pole; it was associated with some of the same rites ^{b}. At the same altar, it is quite possible, homage was offered alternatively to Yahweh or to the Baals Hos 2$^{8-13}$. As the sequel shows, the high places that were destroyed were high places of Yahweh, and the priests who served them were priests of Yahweh, for whom the new code provided equal rights at the temple-altar (cp Is 36^7 Deut 18$^{6\cdot}$ 2 Kings 23^9). But the proposal to suppress these local sanctuaries after the earlier law had so long recognized them, could only arise when there was no longer any hope of relieving them of their abuses and purging their worship of its corruption. Even the prophecy of the eighth century only called for their reform, it did not contemplate their extinction ^{c}. The code which starts with sweeping them entirely away must belong, therefore, to a still later age. (vi) Beside the altar it was common to erect a sacred pillar, or plant a hallowed tree-pole known as an Ashérah ^{d}. Such pillars were sometimes regarded as having antique sanctity. The pillar at Bethel was ascribed to Jacob himself Gen 28$^{18\ 22}$; another famous pillar at Mizpah in Gilead was also attributed to him 31^{45}; and so was the pillar near Bethlehem known as the pillar of Rachel's grave 35^{20}. The narratives which relate their origin conceived them as venerable objects of Israel's sacred past. To the precursors of D, however, they had already become intolerable. The code includes an older law on the basis of a plurality of altars, forbidding their erection beside an altar of Yahweh 16^{22}. But it further enjoins the destruction of those already in existence 12^3, and thus severs itself altogether from the patriarchal traditions recited by JE. What interval of time was necessary to effect this change? Other forms of unhallowed

---

^{a} Cp Dillmann and Driver *in loc*; Nowack, *Hebr Archaol* 1 323, Benzinger, *Hebr Archaol* 330. The form of the Chronicler's statement is open to question, but many critics believe it to be founded in some important legal arrangement.

^{b} The ritual language of Israel has many affinities with that of Phenicia, as is proved by inscriptions from Cyprus to Marseilles

^{c} Save, indeed, this might be involved in the general ruin of the whole nation. On the language of Mic 1$^{5-7}$ cp G A Smith, *Twelve Prophets* 1 380

^{d} On the Ashérah cp Driver, *Deut* 202.

worship are no less stringently forbidden, and carry with them a more specific date. Witchcraft and numerous arts of necromancy had been always secretly popular in Israel; but the reign of Manasseh, the successor of Hezekiah (B C 686-641), is said to have witnessed a remarkable recrudescence of these practices on the part of the king himself. The statement of the historian may be compared with the prohibition in the law:—

2 Kings 21	Deut 18
^{6} And he made his son to pass through the fire, and practised augury, and used enchantments, and dealt with them that had familiar spirits, and with wizards.	^{10} There shall not be found with thee any one that maketh his son or his daughter to pass through the fire, one that useth divination, one that practiseth augury, or an enchanter, or a sorcerer, ^{11} or a charmer, or a consulter with a familiar spirit, or a wizard, or a necromancer.

This is probably one of the numerous cases where the Deuteronomic phraseology has coloured the narrative of Kings. But such influence was only possible because the writers were not after all so far apart, and the compiler of Kings made Deuteronomy his base. But **D**, in its turn, was not unconcerned with the abominable rites fostered by Manasseh. His grandfather Ahaz had made his son to pass through the fire 2 Kings 16^3. But Manasseh was himself the first to introduce a new cultus to 'the host of heaven' for which he built altars in the two temple courts 2 Kings 21$^{5\,a}$. It seized hold of the imagination of Jerusalem and became popular Jer 8^2 19^{13}. It is plain that it would not be legally forbidden centuries before it had arrived from Mesopotamia; and its severe treatment in **D**—the penalty of death by stoning is affixed to it 17$^{3-5}$—is an indication of the indignation which it excited in the minds of the prophetic champions of Yahweh, who saw Manasseh desecrating the 'place which he had chosen to set his name there.' (vii) These considerations may further be reinforced by the general warnings of the danger of deportation abroad and of captivity in a foreign land. Some peculiar phenomena in 4 28-30 will be found discussed in the notes; it is sufficient to allude to the familiarity of the writer with the characteristics of the invader and the most ghastly scenes of siege and famine. The description of 28^{49} plainly has the Mesopotamian tyrant in view, whether Assyrian Is 5^{26} 28^{11}, or Chaldean Jer 5^{15} (with Deut 28^{51} cp Jer 5^{17}). And the portrayal of the hopeless weariness of exile 28$^{64-67}$ implies a background of real experience hardly conceivable at least before the fall of Samaria in 722 B C, and the forced march of its prisoners beyond the Tigris. The language of 29^{23} can already describe the expatriation of Israel as a present fact.

2. A number of considerations thus point to the seventh century, with the possibility that some of the hortatory discourses may be even later still. This conclusion is further strengthened by the affinities of language discernible between **D** and the writings of Jeremiah. A comparison of the tables of characteristic words at once reveals the striking differences between the religious expression of **D** and the other books of the Pentateuch. The nearest approach to its style is to be found in some parts of **JE**. It is reasonable to expect that the technical sections of the Priestly Code shall be marked by peculiarities of terminology. But neither the narratives nor the exhortations of **P** (e g Lev 26) show any real approximation to the Deuteronomic counterparts; they have their own strongly marked features, but they are not those of **D**^{b}. The language of eighth-century prophecy, also, contains none of its recurring phrases^c, and

---

^{a} This cultus seems to have been derived from Assyria. In the retrospect of the idolatries of the Ten Tribes 2 Kings 17^{16} this worship is also attributed to them. But the statement about it is vague: its introduction is not referred, as in the case of Manasseh, to a particular period: it is nowhere mentioned by contemporary observers like Amos or Hosea: and it seems, therefore, to be included in a general condemnation (cp Judg 10^6) of all known idolatries. Cp Kuenen, *Hex* 218.

^{b} Cp chap IX i 1a p 70.

^{c} The passage in Deut 28^{68} cited by Hommel, *The Ancient Hebrew Tradition* 11, to prove that **D** was known to Hosea, does not seem conclusive. Hosea says 8^{13} 'they shall return to Egypt': **D** says 'Yahweh shall bring thee into Egypt again with ships.' If one is a quotation from the other, why may not Hosea be the source, and **D** make the citation? There is obviously no certainty of

the long roll of Deuteronomic oratory finds no echoes amid the thunders of an Amos or an Isaiah[a]. But in the writings of Jeremiah, and to a less extent in those of his younger contemporary Ezekiel, as well as in the books of Judges and Kings, the presence of the Deuteronomic phraseology is strikingly apparent. As the evidence is best appreciated when it is exhibited in sequence to the reader's eye, a series of parallels is here transcribed[b]:—

Deut	*Jer*
10^{17} the great God (El), the mighty, and the terrible.	32^{18} the great, the mighty God [so Neh 1^5 9^{32} Dan 9^4].
7^{21} a great God and a terrible.	
4^{34} by trials, by signs, and by wonders, and by war, and by a strong hand, and by a stretched out arm, and by great terrors.	21^5 by a stretched out hand and by a strong arm, even in anger, and in fury, and in great wrath.
5^{15} by a strong hand and by a stretched out arm.	27^5 by my great power and by my stretched out arm.
7^{19} the great trials which thine eyes saw, and the signs, and the wonders, and the strong hand, and the stretched out arm	32^{17} by thy great power and by thy stretched out arm.
9^{29} by thy great power and by thy stretched out arm.	[Ezek 20^{33}. by a strong hand, and by a stretched out arm, and by fury poured out.
11^2. his greatness, his strong hand, and his stretched out arm, and his signs, and his works.	1 Kings 8^{42} ‖ 2 Chron 6^{32} they shall hear of thy great name, and of thy strong hand, and of thy stretched out arm.
26^8 by a strong hand, and by a stretched out arm, and by great terribleness, and by signs, and by wonders.	2 Kings 17^{33} by great power and by a stretched out arm
	Ps 136^{12} by a strong hand and by a stretched out arm.]
1^{38} he shall cause Israel to inherit it.	3^{18c} the land that I gave for an inheritance unto your fathers.
3^{28} he shall cause them to inherit the land.	12^{14} the inheritance which I have caused my people Israel to inherit.
12^{10} the land which Yahweh your God causeth you to inherit	
19^3 thy land, which Yahweh thy God causeth thee to inherit	
31^7 thou shalt cause them to inherit it.	
[Josh 1^6 thou shalt cause this people to inherit the land]	
4^{10} that they may learn to fear me all the days that they live upon the earth.	32^{39} that they may fear me all the days.
5^{29} that they would fear me, and keep all my commandments all the days	[1 Kings 8^{40} ‖ 2 Chron 6^{31} that they may fear thee all the days that they live in the land which thou gavest unto our fathers]
6^2 that thou mightest fear Yahweh thy God, ... all the days of thy life	
6^{24} to fear Yahweh our God, for our good all the days	
14^{23} that thou mayest learn to fear Yahweh thy God all the days	
31^{13} and learn to fear Yahweh your God all the days that ye live.	
[Josh 4^{24} that they may fear Yahweh your God all the days. cp 4^{14}.]	
8^{19} if thou shalt forget Yahweh thy God, and go after other gods, and serve them, and worship them.	11^{10} they are gone after other gods to serve them.
11^{16} lest ye turn aside, and serve other gods, and worship them.	13^{10} which are gone after other gods to serve them, and to worship them.
13^2 Let us go after other gods and serve them.	16^{11} Because your fathers have forsaken me, saith Yahweh, and have gone after other gods, and have served them, and have worshipped them.
6^{13c} Let us go and serve other gods	
17^3 hath gone and served other gods, and worshipped them.	22^9 Because they forsook the covenant of Yahweh their God, and worshipped other gods, and served them.
28^{14} to go after other gods to serve them.	

dependence either way. 'Proof' in such a case is impossible. It is significant that according to the Masoretic text Hosea's view varied 11^5 'he shall not return into the land of Egypt.' Does Hosea here correct D?

[a] On Amos 2^4 cp Driver, *Joel and Amos* 117   Cornill and Nowack also reject the verse.
[b] Further lists will be found in Colenso, *Pent* pt III chap 11, pt VII appendix 149; Driver, *Deut* xciii.

	Deut	Jer

Deut | *Jer*

29^{18} to go to serve the gods of those nations.
26 went and served other gods, and worshipped them.
30^{17} be drawn away, and worship other gods, and serve them.
[Josh 23^{16} go and serve other gods, and worship them.]

| 25^6 go not after other gods to serve them, and to worship them, and provoke me not to anger with the work of your hands.
35^{15} go not after other gods to serve them.
[Judg 2^{12} and went after other gods . . . and worshipped them.
19 going after other gods to serve them, and worship them.
1 Kings 9^6 go and serve other gods, and worship them.
9 laid hold on other gods, and worshipped them, and served them. ‖ 2 Chron 7^{22}.]

4^{20} brought you forth out of the iron furnace, out of Egypt.

11^4 brought them forth out of the land of Egypt, out of the iron furnace.
[1 Kings 8^{51} which thou broughtest forth out of Egypt, from the midst of the furnace of iron.]

30^{15} See, I have set before thee this day life and good, and death and evil.
19 I have set before thee life and death.

21^8 Behold, I set before you the way of life and the way of death.

28$^{63\text{c}}$ as Yahweh rejoiced over you to do you good.
30^9 Yahweh will again rejoice over thee for good.

32^{41} I will rejoice over them to do them good.

10^{16} Circumcise the foreskin of your heart.
30^6 Yahweh thy God will circumcise thine heart.

4^4 Circumcise yourselves to Yahweh, and take away the foreskins of your heart.
9^{26} the house of Israel are uncircumcised in heart.
[Lev 26^{41} if then their uncircumcised heart be humbled.
Ezek 44$^{7\ 9}$ uncircumcised in heart.]

4^{29} But if from thence ye shall seek Yahweh thy God, thou shalt find him, if thou shalt search after him with all thy heart and with all thy soul.

29^{13} And ye shall seek me, and find me, when ye shall search for me with all your heart.

12^2 upon the high mountains, and upon the hills, and under every green tree.

2^{20} upon every high hill and under every green tree.
3^6 upon every high mountain and under every green tree.
3^{13} under every green tree.
17^2 by the green trees upon the high hills.
[Ezek 6^{13} upon every high hill, in all the tops of the mountains, and under every green tree.
2 Kings 16^4 on the hills, and under every green tree.
17^{10} upon every high hill, and under every green tree.]

12^{11} 14^{23} 16$^{6\ 11}$ 26^2 the place which Yahweh thy God shall choose to cause his name to dwell there.

7^{12} my place which was in Shiloh, where I caused my name to dwell at the first.
[Neh 1^9 the place which I have chosen to cause my name to dwell there.]

10^{16} Be no more stiffnecked (lit. make not your neck stiff).

7^{26} 17^{23} 19^{15} made their neck stiff.
[2 Kings 17^{14} Neh 9$^{17\ 29}$ made their neck stiff.
2 Chron 30^8 make not your neck stiff, 36^{13} made his neck stiff, cp Prov 29^1.]

13^5 because he hath spoken rebellion against Yahweh your God.

28^{16} 29^{32} because thou hast spoken rebellion against Yahweh.

29^{19} walk in the stubbornness of mine heart.

3^{17} neither shall they walk any more after the stubbornness of their evil heart.
7^{24} walked . . . in the stubbornness of their evil heart.
9^{14} have walked after the stubbornness of their heart.

Deut	Jer
	11^8 walked every one in the stubbornness of their evil heart.
	13^{10} walk in the stubbornness of their heart.
	16^{12} ye walk every one after the stubbornness of his evil heart
	18^{12} we will walk after our own devices, and we will do every one after the stubbornness of his evil heart
	23^{17} every one that walketh in the stubbornness of his heart.
	[Ps 81^{12} So I let them walk after the stubbornness of their heart.]
26^{18}. Yahweh hath avouched thee this day to be a peculiar people unto himself . . . to make thee high above all nations which he hath made, in praise, and in name, and in glory.	13^{11} that they might be unto me for a people, and for a name, and for a praise, and for a glory.

These parallels, which might be extended still further, are insufficient to prove identity of authorship^a, in view of other divergent phenomena. But they certainly indicate a relation of no common closeness. Of this some other passages may be reproduced in illustration :—

Deut	Jer
28^{49} Yahweh shall bring a nation against thee from far, from the end of the earth, as the eagle flieth, a nation whose tongue thou shalt not understand ; ^{50} a nation of fierce countenance, which shall not regard the person of the old, nor shew favour to the young ^{51} and he shall eat the fruit of thy cattle, and the fruit of thy ground, until thou be destroyed which also shall not leave thee corn, wine, or oil, the increase of thy kine, or the young of thy flock, until he have caused thee to perish. ^{52} And he shall besiege thee in all thy gates, until thy high and fenced walls come down, wherein thou trustedst, throughout all thy land and he shall besiege thee in all thy gates throughout all thy land, which Yahweh thy God hath given thee.	5^{15} Lo, I will bring a nation upon you from far, O house of Israel, saith Yahweh it is a mighty nation, it is an ancient nation, a nation whose language thou knowest not, neither understandest what they say. ^{16} Their quiver is an open sepulchre, they are all mighty men. ^{17} And they shall eat up thine harvest, and thy bread, *which* thy sons and thy daughters should eat they shall eat up thy flocks and thine herds they shall eat up thy vines and thy fig trees they shall beat down thy fenced cities, wherein thou trustest, with the sword.
29^{24} All the nations shall say, Wherefore hath Yahweh done thus unto this land ? what meaneth the heat of this great anger? ^{25} Then men shall say, Because they forsook the covenant of Yahweh, the God of their fathers, which he made with them when he brought them forth out of the land of Egypt ; ^{26} and went and served other gods, and worshipped them.	22^8 And many nations shall pass by this city, and they shall say every man to his neighbour, Wherefore hath Yahweh done thus unto this great city ? ^{9} Then they shall answer, Because they forsook the covenant of Yahweh their God, and worshipped other gods, and served them.

What is the historic significance of these resemblances? They may be interpreted in two ways, connected though not identical. It is possible that Jeremiah was powerfully under the influence of the book of Deuteronomy considered as a literary whole; that he had absorbed its spirit and also its language; and that even if not consciously quoting it, he nevertheless instinctively reproduced its striking phrases. The references to the covenant in Jer 11$^{1-6}$ seem certainly best interpreted in connexion with the promulgation of Deuteronomy and the national agreement founded upon it by Josiah (*infra* 3)^b. On the other hand, if Jeremiah had thus identified himself with the actual book, it might have been expected that he would show more definite sympathy with its leading idea, the unity of the sanctuary, on which, however, he lays no stress at all. And it would be natural to look for other Deuteronomic expressions in his writings, which are not, however, to be found. It is further probable that the book of Deuteronomy is not all from the same hand. Even within its laws there are traces of the amalgamation of different materials; and its homilies exhibit

---

^{a} This view was maintained by Colenso, who cites altogether about 200 words and expressions.
^{b} Cp Cheyne, *Jeremiah* (Pulpit Comm) 1 293 ; Giesebrecht, *Jeremia* (Hdkomm) 67.

still further signs of diversity (*infra* 4). The book may thus be regarded as the product of a prophetic school whose members were bound together by common aims, and used a common vocabulary of religious thought and speech, yet still preserved their own individuality both of treatment and expression. These thinkers had sufficient cohesion, continuity, and literary force, to impress their view powerfully upon the national histories (Judges and Kings) as they had previously done upon the national religion by the medium of a new book of sacred law. Jeremiah stood in close fellowship with them, while his younger contemporary Ezekiel was in much less intimate relations. Jeremiah shared many of their ideas, though his own work was different from theirs, and his emphasis was consequently thrown upon fresh elements of prophetic teaching. If this be so, the explanation of the parallels of language is not to be sought so much in Jeremiah's familiarity with the actual words of D, as in his sympathy with some of its dominant conceptions of Israel's duty and destiny, and his acquaintance with the leading members of the Deuteronomic school.

3. The circumstances presupposed in Deuteronomy and the peculiarities of its language alike point to its composition in the seventh century. It is certain that it is in this age that it first comes definitely into view.

(α) The story of the discovery of the law-book under Josiah is so well known that it need not be repeated in detail. In the eighteenth year of the king, usually identified with 621, some repairs were needed in the temple (2 Kings $22^{3\cdot\cdot}$), and the king's secretary Shaphan was sent to Hilkiah, the high priest, with directions concerning the required funds. Hilkiah then placed in his hands a book of law which he had found in the sanctuary. Shaphan read it, and in his turn communicated it to the king. Deeply moved by its threats, the king sent a deputation to the prophetess Huldah, for the purpose of inquiring the will of Yahweh. The reply of the prophetess gave the divine sanction to the book, but expressly exempted the king from the doom on the unfaithful city[a]. Josiah lost no time in convoking a national assembly in the temple. City and country, priest and prophet, great and small, were all represented, and the law-book was solemnly read in the presence of the whole concourse. A formal covenant for its observance was made by the king, and the people ratified it with their assent.

(β) What was this law-book? It is expressly called a 'covenant-book' 23^2. This could not be the whole Pentateuch which nowhere bears that name, and is moreover too long to be publicly read aloud at one meeting. Nor can it be identified with the covenant-book of Ex $24^{3\cdot 7 b}$, for this, so far as the covenant-words can be traced, contains no threats resembling those specified in 2 Kings 22^{16-20}, nor does it by any means account for the king's acts, such as the suppression of the local sanctuaries, and the celebration of the passover in a new style. The *bibliotheca* of the ancient Church, as Jerome was afterwards fondly called, had early identified it with Deuteronomy[c]; Hobbes in the seventeenth century, and De Wette a hundred and fifty years later, repeated the same identification. The proof lies in the fact that the proceedings of Josiah correspond step by step with D's demands[d]. The covenant promise (in the language of the historian) pledged the king to 'keep Yahweh's commandments' $^D 82^c$, 'with all his heart and with all his soul' $^D 59$. The temple was first purged of all idolatrous emblems. The vessels dedicated to the Baal and the Ashérah and the heavenly host

---

[a] The words (22^{16-20}) assigned to Huldah are the expression of the historian's view of her counsel they are themselves coloured, especially ^{17}, by the Deuteronomic language.
[b] The view of Vatke, *Bibl Theol* 504^2 (1835), cp chap VIII iv 3 p 68.
[c] Chap III 1 p 21.
[d] The narrative in 2 Kings 23 shows some traces of expansion by various additions, cp Stade, *Gesch* 1 649, and *ZATW* (1885) 292 ff, Klostermann, in the *Kurzgefasster Commentar*.

were carried out and burned. The Ashérah itself was burned Deut 12³ 7⁵. The houses of the forbidden sodomites (Deut 23¹⁷) within the temple precincts were destroyed. The horses and chariots of the sun were removed, and the chariots burned. The altars for the worship of the heavenly host were overthrown Deut 12³ 4¹⁹ 17³, and the Topheth where the grim fire-sacrifice of children had been performed, was desecrated Deut 12³¹ 18¹⁰. Alike in the city and country the high places and their altars were broken down, the sacred pillars were shattered, and the Ashérahs hewn in pieces Deut 12³. Their priests were not indeed allowed to come up to the temple altar, as Deut 18⁷ had provided; but they received their maintenance in accordance with **D**'s demands from the temple dues. With the symbols of the idolatrous cults, witchcraft and necromancy were suppressed Deut 18¹¹. And the whole reformation received its final sanction in a passover celebrated on the new principle of the unity of the place of sacrifice 2 Kings 23²¹, a celebration such as had never been seen before, drawing the people together from town and hamlet throughout the land. Each stage of the movement thus bears upon it the impress of the Deuteronomic code.

4. The previous inquiry has tended to establish the identity of Josiah's law-book with **D**, to show that such a law had been till then unrecognized, and to make it probable that it was first compiled in the seventh century.

(*a*) But it may be further asked whether it comprised the entire work as we possess it. The book is at present incorporated at its opening and its close into the general framework of the Priestly Code. Do the intervening contents constitute a homogeneous literary whole? Even a casual inspection reveals many curious phenomena. The poems ascribed to Moses in 32 and 33 are wholly unlike in style both to each other and to the exhortations which precede. After the initial title and the retrospect of the march from Horeb, a second title is inserted 4⁴⁵⁻⁴⁹ with a summary of the historical situation. This is followed in its turn by a recital of the Horeb covenant, so that in 5 the speaker describes events which preceded the introductory discourse. The homilies in 6-11 appear to suspend the announcement of the laws communicated to Moses at Horeb 5³¹, the formal declaration of them being postponed till 12¹⸳⸳. The nucleus of the entire book is found in the legislative sections 12-26 and the great exhortation 28 which is connected with it (cp 28¹ and 26¹⁹). But there are traces of more than one final oration*ᵃ*; and the reduction of the book to writing and its deposition in the care of the Levites is recorded twice over 31⁹⸳⸳ and 31²⁴⸳⸳. As there are two titles and two introductory collections of discourse, so there seem also to be two conclusions. Are all these different passages due to the same hand? or do these duplications point to variety of origin? The literary analysis of **D** opens up highly interesting problems, to which brief answers will be found in the notes upon successive sections. The general conclusion which emerges out of manifold and complicated phenomena suggests that **D** like other great constituent documents of the Pentateuch presents numerous marks of growth. Unlike the collections designated **J E** and **P** it remains (apart from the Joshua sections, see Introd to Joshua) undivided, and occupies a separate place of its own. That is due to the obvious fact that it throughout assumes a single historical situation. But this outward unity does not by any means exclude some amount at least of internal diversity. The phenomena which lead to the view that the homilies in 5-11 may be assigned to the hands which prepared 12-26 (though not necessarily all prefixed at the same time), while the retrospect in 1⁶⁻3 is with much probability referred to another edition of the book, are discussed elsewhere (cp notes to 1⁶ 5¹); and a summary of the literary history of the whole work (as conceived by the present Editors) will be found at the close of the analysis 34¹²ᴺ. On some other questions, however, a further word must be said.

ᵃ Cp notes on 27⁹ 28 29² 30

(β) Assuming that the elements of **D** are not entirely homogeneous, it is natural to ask in what relation they stand to the law-book as it was found in the temple. The question reaches further than might at first sight appear. There is no apparent appropriateness, so far as the programme of the Deuteronomic reforms is concerned, in the historical retrospect 1^6–3. But neither is there, for example, in the laws which regulate bird's-nesting or parapets upon a roof 22^{6-8}. With what feelings could Josiah have listened to these details? If there is ground for believing that the historic and hortatory elements of **D** show traces of gradual accretion, may not the collection of the statutes 12–26 do so too? It is plain that the contents of the Code, at least in its later portions, are very miscellaneous, cp $12^{1\aleph}$. It would be absurd to expect of an ancient document the strict logical order which a modern jurist might adopt as the basis of the codification of older laws. But the distribution of subjects in the principal legislative section 12–26 is very perplexing. Continuity of arrangement is repeatedly broken; allied elements are separated, and the disconnected joined. Even in the first great group 12–19 a passage occurs 14^{4-21a} which by diversity of substance and style may be plausibly referred to a source quite different from the adjacent laws in 13 and 15. Similar phenomena may be observed in later portions of the code 20–25. They indicate that the collection has been compiled from various antecedent elements, which have been incorporated with more or less of hortatory expansion. The attempts hitherto made to resolve the laws into definite series of smaller groups have not appeared successful[a], but it is quite possible that such groups existed though they can no longer be reconstructed, and supplied the materials from which the present code has been compiled. Traces of such groups may perhaps be found in common conceptions and recurring formulae (for illustrations see $12^{1\aleph}$); and other traces of prior or independent collections have been already discussed in considering the affinities of **D** with the First Code and with the Holiness Legislation in Lev 17–26 (chap IX i 2a p 73). In some cases the method of **D** is clear enough. The old law is recast to suit the new conditions, and invested with a hortatory expansion suitable to the Deuteronomic spirit. A comparison of the ordinance on slavery in 15^{12-18} with Ex 21^{2-6} shows that $^{12\ 16}$ are founded on the prior statute, while $^{13-15\ 18}$ constitute fresh additions. A similar treatment has been applied to the festival cycle in 16.

(γ) Other cases, however, present more difficulty. They are not obviously new, like the great laws of 12 and 13, which can hardly be treated as fresh versions of Ex 20^{24} or 22^{20}. They are not modifications of older usage caused by the adoption of a central principle hitherto unknown, like the law of asylum in 19^{1-13}. They may not be directly connected with it at all. If they deal, for instance, like the laws of the administration of justice, or the laws regulating the relations of the sexes or the rights and duties of family life, with some common subject, it would have been not unreasonable to expect that they should all be placed together. Yet they may occur in detached groups, separated from each other by unrelated material. Thus the proper practice of the judges is enforced in the following series, 16^{18-20} 17^{8-13} 19^{15-21} 24^{17}. 25^{1-3}:—

16^{18} Judges and officers shalt thou make thee in all thy gates, which Yahweh thy God giveth thee, according to thy tribes and they shall judge the people with righteous judgement. ^{19} Thou shalt not wrest judgement; thou shalt not respect persons · neither shalt thou take a gift; for a gift doth blind the eyes of the wise, and pervert the words of the righteous. ^{20} That which is altogether just shalt thou follow, that thou mayest live, and inherit the land which Yahweh thy God giveth thee

17^8 If there arise a matter too hard for thee in judgement, between blood and blood, between plea and plea, and between stroke and stroke, being matters of controversy within thy gates. then shalt thou arise, and get thee up unto the place which Yahweh thy God shall choose; ^{9} and thou shalt come unto the priests the Levites, and unto the judge that shall be in those days and thou

---

[a] Cp introductory note to **D**

shalt inquire; and they shall shew thee the sentence of judgement ¹⁰ and thou shalt do according to the tenor of the sentence, which they shall shew thee from that place which Yahweh shall choose; and thou shalt observe to do according to all that they shall teach thee · ¹¹ according to the tenor of the law which they shall teach thee, and according to the judgement which they shall tell thee, thou shalt do thou shalt not turn aside from the sentence which they shall shew thee, to the right hand, nor to the left ¹² And the man that doeth presumptuously, in not hearkening unto the priest that standeth to minister there before Yahweh thy God, or unto the judge, even that man shall die · and thou shalt put away the evil from Israel. ¹³ And all the people shall hear, and fear, and do no more presumptuously.

19¹⁵ One witness shall not rise up against a man for any iniquity, or for any sin, in any sin that he sinneth : at the mouth of two witnesses, or at the mouth of three witnesses, shall a matter be established. ¹⁶ If an unrighteous witness rise up against any man to testify against him of wrong doing; ¹⁷ then both the men, between whom the controversy is, shall stand before Yahweh, before the priests and the judges which shall be in those days; ¹⁸ and the judges shall make diligent inquisition : and, behold, if the witness be a false witness, and hath testified falsely against his brother; ¹⁹ then shall ye do unto him, as he had thought to do unto his brother : so shalt thou put away the evil from the midst of thee ²⁰ And those which remain shall hear, and fear, and shall henceforth commit no more any such evil in the midst of thee. ²¹ And thine eye shall not pity ; life *shall go* for life, eye for eye, tooth for tooth, hand for hand, foot for foot.

24¹⁷ Thou shalt not wrest the judgement of the stranger, *nor* of the fatherless ; nor take the widow's raiment to pledge ¹⁸ but thou shalt remember that thou wast a bondman in Egypt, and Yahweh thy God redeemed thee thence · therefore I command thee to do this thing.

25¹ If there be a controversy between men, and they come unto judgement, and *the judges* judge them , then they shall justify the righteous, and condemn the wicked ; ² and it shall be, if the wicked man be worthy to be beaten, that the judge shall cause him to lie down, and to be beaten before his face, according to his wickedness, by number. ³ Forty stripes he may give him, he shall not exceed lest, if he should exceed, and beat him above these with many stripes, then thy brother should seem vile unto thee.

The general affinities of this group are sufficiently marked to justify their consideration together. But their distribution is peculiar. The paragraphs in 16¹⁸⁻²⁰ and 17⁸⁻¹³ appear closely connected in substance, yet they are interrupted by a law forbidding tree-poles and pillars, by another prohibiting the sacrifice of blemished animals, and a third denouncing the worship of other gods. Can such a collocation be regarded as natural, or at least as the work of a compiler grouping his materials round certain leading ideas? A closer examination brings further facts to light. The nucleus of 16¹⁸⁻²⁰ is discernible in ¹⁹, 'thou shalt not wrest judgement,' 'neither shalt thou take a gift . . . ,' two precepts already enjoined in the First Code, Ex 23⁶ ⁸. The re-enforcement of the spirit of judicial duties apparently suggests the prior provision of persons to discharge them; and ¹⁸ with its Deuteronomic phrases 'in all thy gates,' 'which Yahweh thy God giveth thee,' may be ascribed to the compiler, together with the concluding exhortation in ²⁰ in the same well-known style. A new phenomenon attracts attention in 17⁸⁻¹³. The analysis renders it probable that two laws concerning a supreme court of appeal have here been combined (cp 17⁸ᴺ), one couched in the name of the 'judges,' the other in that of the 'Levitical priests,' as if they were independent drafts of the same regulation. Such an amalgamation at once points to other literary sources besides the older collection lying behind 16¹⁹. Nor is it without example elsewhere in **D** (cp notes on 12, and the independent though unamalgamated laws in 13 and 17²⁻⁷), or even in the series now under consideration. It is perhaps to be traced, but it may be admitted much less clearly, in the next section on evidence 19¹⁵⁻²¹ founded on 17⁸⁻¹³, where the margins indicate the hortatory expansions, while the last phrases of ²¹ are based on the older legislation, cp Ex 21²⁴, though they limit its scope. In 24¹⁷· the opening words 'thou shalt not wrest the judgement . . .' at once connect the passage with 16¹⁹: a specific case of especial danger is cited in language steeped in Deuteronomic phrases—the imperilled persons are the usual group of suffering poor, 'the stranger, the fatherless and the widow,' and the reason for their just treatment is the favourite Deuteronomic plea that Israel likewise had once known the bitterness of oppression. The sequence of this law on 24¹⁴· is natural enough; but the connexion is strangely interrupted by ¹⁶. This has the air of a prophetic protest (cp Jer 31²⁰ Ezek 18⁴) which it was desired to insert somewhere, but which was lodged at this point by accident. Finally the law which defines the maximum infliction of the bastinado 25^{1-3}, may well have been derived from some older source. The opening clause in the third person contrasts with the more characteristic form of **D** in 17^8. But in 3^b the hand of **D** is again to be discerned in the explanation of 3^a. As the 'enemy' of Ex 23^4 became a 'brother' in Deut 22^1, so the 'wicked man' in 25^1 is presented as a 'brother' in 3^b. By such criteria it might be possible conjecturally to restore the possible antecedents of some of the laws in **D** for which there are no obvious precursors in the First Code, and which do not flow directly or indirectly from the doctrine of the unity of the place of sacrifice, and the duty of worshipping Yahweh alone[a]. But it appears beyond the limits of any critical instrument now available to sort these into groups, or determine their affinities, still less to carry such partition through the homilies and thus account for the production of the entire book[b].

5. The preceding suggestions perhaps suffice to make it probable that the compilation even of the legislative code in 12-26 was not effected at one time, nor perhaps by one person. The inclusion among the laws of the priestly teaching about forbidden foods 14^{4-21a}, or the regulations for admission into the assembly of Yahweh 23^{1-8}, points in the direction of editorial sympathy with ritual ideas of which there is elsewhere little trace; but conjectures as to the time or mode of their adoption into **D** seem vain. Nevertheless, the question once more recurs whether Josiah's law-book contained the whole of **D**, and if not whether it is possible to indicate what it may have comprised, and when it was actually compiled.

(*a*) No answers to such questions can possess more than different degrees of probability. The clues are scanty and the indications necessarily slight. One clue is found in the reformation carried out by Josiah, which aimed at the entire suppression of the homage offered to other gods and the expulsion of every form of idolatry. This purpose rendered it necessary to prohibit the cultus of Yahweh everywhere save at the one spot in which it might be rigidly controlled. The law-book, therefore, must have included the fundamental statutes of 12-13, and the numerous other regulations dependent on them, especially those affecting all religious duty (such as tithes $14^{22..}$, the three annual pilgrimages 16^{1-17}), and the functions of the three great theocratic powers, the judges and the king, the prophets, and the priests. These criteria practically cover the main contents of 12-19. But they do not touch the miscellaneous congeries of laws in 20-25. In 26, however, the Josian **D** may be again clearly recognized, and a slight link connects it with the group already isolated. The condition stated in 26^1 is analogous to that in 17^{14} 18^9 19^1, but it does not recur in 20-25. If this section be removed 26 would be brought into line with the series of paragraphs preceding it. To 26 was no doubt attached the original form of the Blessings and the Curses in 28, which now bear numerous marks of amplification[c]. The code and its final discourse must have been introduced by some title connecting it with Moses and specifying the circumstances of its promulgation. The title in $4^{45.}$ (see note *in loc*) may have served as the opening; and the discourse in 5 may have recalled the covenant of Horeb to prepare the way for that of Moab. The homilies in 6-11 (or at least the first in 6-8) may have been prefixed by the authors of the code to prepare for the great assembly convened by Josiah; and the book would naturally have closed with a description of the making of the covenant in Moab which might have served as type for that in Jerusalem. To such a ceremony

---

[a] Cp the list, chap IX i 2*a* p 73 note.
[b] Since the above was written Steuernagel's *Deut* in the *Handkommentar* has appeared. Some remarks on his position will be found in the analysis at the opening of **D**.
[c] See notes *in loc*.

there is more than one allusion, 27^9 $29^{1\ 12-15}$, but of the actual rite there is no word[a].

(β) If these conjectures be regarded as too hazardous, there still remains the problem concerning the date, if not the actual contents, of Josiah's law-book. The foregoing argument has proceeded on the assumption that the book was designed to serve as the basis of a movement corresponding to that which Josiah actually founded upon it. In that case, it is most natural to suppose that it was only compiled a comparatively short time before it was found in the temple[b]. It belonged, that is to say, to the reign of Josiah; and may be plausibly attributed to the party of reform who saw in the young king a promising agent of their hopes. Such promise could hardly have been discerned in a child who began to reign at the age of eight. He must have been some time on the throne before those around him could have felt confident of his readiness to use the opportunity if it were afforded him. These considerations receive some confirmation from the remarkable parallels already noticed between the language of D and the phraseology of Jeremiah. The Deuteronomic code is universally admitted to be profoundly marked by the prophetic spirit. Had it originated in an earlier age, it is difficult to understand why the contemporary prophetic literature should have been completely unaffected by so powerful a school of religious thought. This is the real reason why the proposal to place it under Hezekiah[c] appears unsatisfactory. It cannot be proved to have suggested Hezekiah's reforms[d]; there are no traces of Isaiah's acquaintance with it; Micah is equally clear of allusion to it. So many eminent critics have placed it in the reign of Manasseh that this cannot be called an improbable opinion[e]. It rests largely on the supposition that a book which was 'found' must have been previously lost. For such disappearance some time is required before the era of discovery, and this interval might well throw the origin of the book into a preceding generation. On the other hand this view is confronted with the difficulty of explaining how such a work, once composed, should have passed out of sight. Of the causes which involved it in obscurity and neglect we are wholly ignorant. A writer who so passionately advocated a particular series of reforms could scarcely have been indifferent to the prospect of their effectual realization; and it is hard to conceive that he should have calmly acquiesced in the frustration of his design, and have made no attempt to rescue the endangered work. But there is a further consideration of another kind. We are not without indications of the religious difficulties of the reign of Manasseh. It was a time of persecution and suffering, endured by some with a lowly patience Mic 7^{1-6}, while it evoked from others the most vehement of protests. The homely but vigorous figure of 2 Kings 21^{13} expressively indicates the view of impending doom which seemed alone possible in the crisis of prophetic despair. It is true that the wrath of the Yahwist party may not have been concentrated in such white heat of passion during the whole fifty-five years of Manasseh's long reign. But Deuteronomy betrays neither agony nor resignation.

[a] Cp Gen 15^{17} Ex 24^{6-8} Jer 34^{18}..

[b] On 'finding in the temple' as a mode of publication in Egypt, cp Cheyne, *Jeremiah, his Life and Times* 84.

[c] So Delitzsch, Westphal, Oettli, Konig, G A Smith, H L Strack.

[d] Reasons have been already offered for believing these to have been less extensive than the narrative of 2 Kings suggests, cp chap IX 11 3 p 84.

[e] This view is held by Dr Driver, and stated by him, *Deut* xlix–liv, with admirable insight into the religious history of the time. To his list of authorities for the respective dates the following may be added for the last years of Hezekiah, or early in Manasseh's reign, from 690 to 650, Steuernagel, *Das Deuteronomium* (1898) xii, the book being the result of a complicated literary process. Addis, *Documents of the Hexateuch* ii 9 (1898), suggests that the book may be the outcome of the reforms of Hezekiah, and thinks conjecture is free to move as it will between 701 and 621 B C For Manasseh, Kautzsch, *Literature of the OT* (1898) 65; Ryle, *Dict of the Bible* (ed Hastings), art 'Deut', for Josiah, Staerk, *Das Deuteronomium* (1894) 96 ff.

It is a book of confident faith, of joyous exultation, of ardent assurance that Israel has still a future. Was this conviction possible in the midst of men who expected to see Jerusalem cleaned out like a dish in punishment for its sins? Does not the irrepressible hopefulness of the greater part of the Deuteronomic exhortations imply a revival of the consciousness of Yahweh's favour which can only be explained by the changed circumstances of the new reign? It may be added that the ascription of the book to the age of Manasseh is less easy to harmonize with the literary conditions which point to its gradual growth at the hands of a little group of men interested in enforcing its ideas, and from time to time enriching it with new discourses. Whether or not Hilkiah was in their secret it is impossible to determine. The narrative gives no hint of his own feeling about the contents of the book. Shaphan's duty was discharged when he had communicated it to the king. But Hilkiah took the lead in the deputation to Huldah, of which Shaphan also was a member; and this step must have been taken with their concurrence, if not by their direct advice. Hilkiah, therefore, was favourable to the proposed reform; but it seems hardly likely that he was concerned in the preparation of the book, or even privy to its composition and discovery. For it was provided, on behalf of the disestablished priests 18^{6-8}, that they should come up to Jerusalem and have the right to serve at the temple-altar. Such an arrangement was naturally distasteful to the metropolitan guild, and they succeeded in frustrating it 2 Kings 23^9. Had Hilkiah sanctioned the Deuteronomic proposal beforehand, it is probable that he would have exerted his authority to give it effect. His apparent indifference to the position of the country priests in their vain effort to assert the rights which the new law conferred upon them, seems best explained upon the view that he had not been consulted about the plan. That the promoters of the Deuteronomic code were in connexion with the priesthood, even if there were no priests actually among them, may be inferred from their references to the priestly *torah* 24^8 cp $14^{4..}$, and to their assignment of supreme judicial duties to them 17^{9-11}. The importance conferred on the metropolitan sanctuary is explicable from either the priestly or the prophetic side cp Am 1^2 Is 6^1. Its definite enunciation of monotheism and its dependence on the Mosaic tradition set the book in line with the prophetic schools; and Deuteronomy, therefore, which is pervaded by a spirit of human sympathy, for which an Amos, an Isaiah, a Micah, had apparently not pleaded in vain, may be regarded as the first great effort of prophecy to reduce its demands to practical shape, and embody its ideals in a scheme of religious and social reform[a].

CHAPTER XI

THE ORIGINS OF J

The book of Deuteronomy is essentially a book of law and not of history. The collection of J, on the other hand, forms a book of history and not of law. Its scope is to relate the origin of the people of Israel, and connect it with the purpose of Yahweh in human things.

1. With this aim it opens with the formation of the first man, and the woman who is made, after the animals, to match him. It is possible that it had previously related the 'making' of the earth and sky Gen 2^{4b}, but no vestiges of such a narrative remain. After the expulsion of the pair from Eden, the early history of mankind

---

[a] The foregoing exposition has necessarily left some important questions untouched, such as the precise relations of D to J and E, or the extensions of D in Joshua. For a discussion of some connected topics, and a sketch of the literary history of D as conceived by the present editors, the reader is referred to chap XVI 1, to a note on Deut 34^{12}, and to the Introduction to Joshua.

is sketched in darkening colours, as the increased command of weapons gives freer range to human passions. The strange episode of the intercourse between the sons of Elohim and the daughters of men leads to the story of the flood and the preservation of Noah and his family. Released from the ark, Noah discovers the secret of husbandry and the culture of the vine. His descendants people the earth, and the writer apparently presented a catalogue of nations grouped under the names of his three sons, portions of which are now incorporated in the similar distribution of P. An independent cause is next assigned for the great dispersion 11^{1-9}, and the line of Abraham is then selected. One by one the collateral branches are dismissed from view; Lot settles at Sodom, and becomes the ancestor of Moab and Ammon; the mother of the unborn Ishmael passes out of sight to make way for Isaac; the family of Nahor is enumerated to prepare for Isaac's union with Rebekah; the descendants of Keturah complete the roll of Abraham's progeny; and the story is then concentrated on Isaac alone. With his twin sons it again momentarily divides, but Esau returns on his way to Seir and is seen no more, while the twelve sons of Jacob enter the field. The sale of Joseph, first to the Ishmaelites, and then to an Egyptian master, transfers the interest to Egypt. His appointment as Pharaoh's minister of state, the arrival of his brothers to buy corn, the tests to which they are subjected, and his final disclosure of himself, supply some of the most beautiful examples of J's art as narrator. The settlement of Jacob in Goshen follows, and the recital passes from the record of his funeral and the subsequent death of Joseph to the oppression, when Moses slays the Egyptian. His flight to Midian, his marriage and the birth of his son are the prelude to his great commission to lead his countrymen into the land of their fathers. His return awakens his people's faith; Pharaoh's resistance is at last subdued by the most terrible of the signs of Yahweh's power, and the Israelites hastily depart. The passage of the Red Sea frees them from their pursuers, and they march without hostile interruption, though not without desert trials, to Sinai. There, at the sacred mountain, Yahweh makes a covenant with Moses and Israel, and after an obscure episode of revolt severely punished with massacre by the Levites, the journey is again resumed. Spies are sent to explore the land, but the attempt to reach the promised country from the south is frustrated. After a long but indeterminate interval the resolve is taken to make the entry from the east. It involves the circuit of Edom and Moab and the conquest of Sihon and his kingdom. Lingering over the episode of Balaam, the story passes to the arrangements for the settlement of Reuben and Gad[a] and the death of Moses on the top of Pisgah. The leadership is assumed by Joshua, who conducts the Israelites across the Jordan, captures Jericho and Ai, crushes the kings at Beth-horon and Merom, and prepares to distribute the land. From the account of the actual settlement of the Israelites only a few fragments remain[b]. Such is the general scheme of J, which has been recited at length to serve as a subsequent basis of comparison with E and P. What light is thrown by its contents and characteristics on its probable origin?

2. It is natural first to inquire into its modes of religious and historic representation. Whatever clues it may supply to the place and time of its production must be found in its own treatment of the sacred past.

(a) Foremost among the distinctive features of its conception of the pre-Mosaic ages is its view of the primaeval character of the worship of Yahweh Gen 4^{26}. This unbroken continuity of revelation is assumed as the basis of the whole narrative[c]. It

---

[a] Probably to be found at the basis of Num 32.
[b] For the continuation of J in Judges, see Moore, *Judges*, in *Internat Comm*, and in Haupt's *SBOT*.
[c] When Abraham enters the story, the use of the name Yahweh is usually limited to his descendants, though not invariably cp Gen 26^{28} 39^3.

is repeatedly emphasized in the titles appended to the divine name. He is the 'God of Shem' 9^{26}, or the God of heaven who took Abraham from his father's house 24^7; to Isaac he is the 'God of Abraham' 26^{24}; to Jacob the 'God of Abraham and the God of Isaac' 28^{13}; to the suffering Israelites the God of their fathers, 'the God of Abraham, of Isaac, and of Jacob' Ex 3^{16}. He is emphatically also the God of heaven and earth Gen 24^3, and in like manner he is universal judge 18^{25}. But beside these exalted attributes stand other representations which ascribe to him various modes of human action. To some of these attention has already been invited (cp chap VIII ii 2a p 57): the repeated description of Yahweh as 'coming down' may be here specified. As he comes down to examine and then to frustrate the purpose of the tower 11^5, or to investigate the guilt of Sodom 18^{21}, so does he also come down to deliver Israel from its bondage Ex 3^8, and personally descend upon the sacred mount 19$^{11\ 18\ 20}$ 34^5. So, it would seem, it is **J** who describes the mysterious visitant with whom Jacob wrestles Gen 32^{24}··, as it is also **J** who relates the struggle when Yahweh sought to kill Moses Ex 4^{24}··. It may indeed be difficult to believe that this latter story is told by the same narrator who relates the awful theophany on Sinai 34^5. But the steps of transition, whether few or many, seem all to be made within the same group, and the differences find an explanation when the extremes are viewed as earlier and later elements of the same great religious school. In some cases (cp chap VIII ii 2β p 58), however, Yahweh does not appear or act himself in the fullness of his heavenly personality. He is represented by his angel, who calls to Hagar from the sky Gen 16^7··, precedes Abraham's servant to prosper his way 24$^{7\ 40}$, addresses Moses from the flaming bush Ex 3^2, and confronts Balaam and his ass Num 22^{22}··. The 'captain of Yahweh's host' who stands over against Joshua with drawn sword Josh 5$^{13-15}$, has probably a similar function to mediate between the older conception of Yahweh's direct presence and agency, and the later view of his higher spirituality and abode in heaven. To this same category belong the pillar of cloud and fire in which Yahweh went before the Israelites as leader and guide Ex 13^{21}, and the 'Presence' (or 'face') whose sustaining companionship would give Moses rest 33^{14}··.

(β) These conceptions suffuse the whole series of narratives, and form a continuous setting for the events which they relate. By their aid the writer expounds the significance of human labour and suffering, and justifies the oriental conception of marital rule. He depicts the growth of evil which accompanies progress in the arts of life Gen 4; recognizes that the new humanity which will start from Noah will not share his righteousness, for evil imagination will beset it from its youth; and throughout contrasts the chosen hero strenuously fulfilling a divine plan, like Abraham, Joseph, or Moses, with the opposite types of worldly self-indulgence, family jealousy, or national unbelief. To Abraham comes the word of promise, and he obeys in faith 12^1·· 15^6; and to him is announced alike the gift of the land and of blessing such as shall make the families of the earth invoke his name 12^3 18^{18} 28^{14}. The divine oath 15^{18} resounds through the whole story, which has (from one point of view) no other meaning than to justify Yahweh by giving it effect. This purpose can only be fulfilled by the training of a people to keep his way 18^{19}; it is for this end that Yahweh has in the language of prophecy 'known' Abraham as Amos declared that he had 'known' Israel alone among the nations of the earth Am 3^2. In such 'knowledge' on the part of Yahweh lies the clue to Israel's destiny, and the distant vision of a 'great and mighty nation' illuminates the darkness and dangers of the course. The obscure connexions of remote events are continually found in the determinations of Yahweh's will; the subjugation of the Canaanites is announced by Noah Gen 9^{25}; the wild future of Ishmael 16^{12}—the submission of Edom 25^{23}—the sovereignty over nations realized in one brief age of empire $27^{29\,a}$—all these are but distant glances at the mode in which Yahweh's intent works itself out for Israel's benefit. The constancy of this energy is expressed by saying that Yahweh was 'with' the agents of his choice (Isaac $26^{3\ 24\ 28}$, Jacob 28^{15}, Joseph $39^{2\ 21\ 23}$, Moses Ex 4^{12} cp $^{JE}30$); while in the case of Israel his presence takes a more intimate form, he condescends to dwell and act in its midst (בקרב). The unbelieving people try his long-suffering with the scornful question 'Is Yahweh in our midst or not?' Ex 17^7. The severest threat of punishment is couched in the phrase 'I will not go up in thy midst' 33^3; when Moses pleads for his stiff-necked countrymen, he prays 'let the Lord go in our midst' 34^9; when he addresses them, it is to complain 'ye have rejected Yahweh which is in your midst' Num 11^{20}; 'how long,' exclaims Yahweh, 'will they not believe in me for all the signs which I have wrought in their midst' 14^{11} (cp $^{JE}58$). In these characteristics of divine faithfulness contrasted again and again with the weariness, the mistrust, the open rebellion, of the Israelites, it is impossible not to recognize in the field of national tradition the profound influence of the motives and conceptions which appear elsewhere in the sphere of early prophecy.

(γ) In the treatment of the patriarchs the interest of J plays largely around the scenes of their life, their family relations, and the localities hallowed by their worship. It is not needful to catalogue the contents of its rich budget of stories, or to dwell on the skill displayed unconsciously in the portrayal of character. But its conceptions of the early cultus cannot be ignored, for in them is partly to be sought the real clue to its origin. Thus Abram signalizes his entry into the country by building an altar at Shechem close to the 'Teacher's oak' Gen 12^7, and another between Bethel and Ai 12^8 cp 13^4. In the south he sacrifices by the oaks of Mamre in Hebron 13^{18} cp 18^1, and on the confines of the desert beside the well at Beer-sheba he plants a tamarisk and invokes his God 21^{33}. At Beer-sheba likewise Isaac builds an altar 26^{25}; Jacob erects a pillar at Bethel which he hallows with a drink offering and anoints with oil 35^{14}; and by another pillar he marks Rachel's grave on the way to Bethlehem 35^{20}. No single spot is exclusively sacred; the rites of the altar may be celebrated anywhere, especially in the spots which Yahweh has marked by his appearing. The offering is the worshipper's 'present' 4^3 cp 32^{13} 43^{11}, it may be of the fruits of the ground, or of the firstlings of the flock. It must be clean; the unclean beast is unfit for sacred gifts; and it is made over to Yahweh by fire. In this simple cultus there is no need of priest. Dimly in the background he may wait to receive those who 'go to inquire of Yahweh' 25^{22}, for the management of the oracle was from of old his duty; but he is not named, and the solitary reference leaves all detail obscure. Thus under the shade of venerated holy trees, or near the sacred wells, or by the consecrated pillars, is the patriarchs' worship practised. They themselves emerge from the antique gloom of consecrated tradition with forms moulded by generations of recital, as the tales concerning them had been told by the priests at ancient sanctuaries, or the warriors round the camp-fires, or the shepherds at the wells. They are full of incident and character; and they are firmly rooted in the soil. When the scene changes to Egypt, the sense of locality is less distinct, but it is still present. Israel is settled in Goshen $^{JE}38$, but he yearns to be buried in the grave he has dug in his own land; and no story of his life has a deeper pathos than that of the splendid funeral train which escorts his mummy to Canaan in the fulfilment of his dying wish $50^{1-11\,a}$.

(δ) The interest of J in the Mosaic age, like his interest in the patriarchs, is national and historic rather than institutional[b]. He does not seek in it the origins of his faith or of his worship. These have about them an immemorial antiquity: he knows of no time when men could not call upon the name of Yahweh Gen 4^{26}. But the deliverance from

---

[a] The account of his actual interment, however, is suppressed in favour of P's.
[b] On the other hand, cp *infra* 3β p 103

Egypt first made Israel feel itself a people, and the story of its liberation, like that of its long wandering and its final entry into the land of Yahweh's promise, has its own value for the demonstration of his power. The demand that is to be first raised by Moses and the elders Ex $3^{16..}$ is limited to permission to go three days' journey into the wilderness. Whether Aaron was originally associated with Moses in J's narrative, there is some doubt. According to the view indicated in the Analysis, which has the support of Wellhausen, Julicher, Cornill, and even Kittel, the association of Aaron with Moses as his spokesman 4^{14-16} is an afterthought cp $4^{13\aleph}$. In the narrative of the plagues cp $7^{8\aleph}$, the successive punishments inflicted on the obdurate Pharaoh and his people are effected by the direct agency of Yahweh. Moses has only to announce them, and Yahweh does the rest, though the details of his method are occasionally mentioned, as when a strong west wind is employed to remove the locusts 10^{19}, and a strong east wind blowing all night makes the sea dry land 14^{21b}. It is characteristic of J's view of Israel's God that he describes him 14^{25}, as 'taking off' the chariot wheels of the Egyptians. The purport of the entire series of plagues is to prove the deity of Yahweh 7^{17} cp $8^{10\aleph}$, to display his power 9^{14-16}, and spread his name throughout the earth. The issue is not represented as an actual victory over the gods of Egypt, but it leaves Jethro in the profound conviction that Yahweh is greater than all gods 18^{11}. In the highly complicated narrative of the events at the sacred mountain, it is only possible to rescue fragments which may with more or less probability be ascribed to J, without attempting to reconstruct his original story. The detail of justification must be sought in the Analysis. Any attempt at restoration would start from the general anticipation that the covenant-narratives of J and E ran here (as elsewhere) a fairly parallel course. All critics agree to find in 34 the substance of J's covenant-words, and with these may perhaps be associated the solemn meal in the divine presence $24^{1-2\ 9-11}$, which may be regarded as the equivalent to E's ceremony of ratification $^{3-8}$. The reason for the separation of the sections which are thus supposed to be connected, is probably to be found in the combination of J with E. The harmonist sought to preserve as far as possible the materials of both documents. Each related a covenant-ceremony, each contained a summary of the covenant-words. The covenant-ceremonies might be more or less incongruously united, but there was no place for two versions of the 'words' side by side. One of them, therefore, must be either suppressed or postponed. For the latter alternative an opening was afforded by the prior insertion of E's narrative of the golden calf and the destruction of the tables. The renewal of the tables is employed by the compiler as the occasion for the introduction of J's recital of the covenant-terms. Such is in brief the view of J's narrative which emerges from the resolution of the text of the combined documents in 19-24 and 32-34 cp $34^{28\aleph}$. For two only of the Mosaic institutions does J provide an origin at Sinai. A comparison of $34^{1..}$ with Deut $10^{1..}$ makes it practically certain that J originally narrated the construction of the sacred ark; which appears (contrary to E's view of the sanctuary, chap XII 2ϵ) to have been habitually guarded in the centre of the camp Num 14^{44}. Concerning the priesthood, his representations are somewhat conflicting. In Ex $19^{22\ 24}$ priests are assumed, though nothing has been said of their appointment or their duties. Like the patriarchal cultus, it is perhaps supposed that they were always there. But in 32^{29} there is an express reference to the consecration of Levi as the priestly tribe. No further allusion presents itself, until at the crossing of the Jordan the priests are charged with the transport of the ark of Yahweh. It is thus apparent that the questions of the sanctuary and its ministers were not of supreme or even prominent interest for J^a: on the other hand he attached great importance to the Passover, and expounds its origin and significance with much

---

^{a} It will be noted that in the story of Dathan and Abiram Num 16, the J element is concerned with a resistance to the secular leadership of Moses.

detail $12^{21}\cdot\cdot$ $13^{3}\cdot\cdot$. But whatever bears on the possession of the land appeals at once to his imagination. To him first belongs the phrase 'flowing with milk and honey' ^{JE}34. He relates with characteristic vividness the scene on the return of the spies cp Num 13-14, dwells on the rich produce of the country, and depicts Caleb's urgency that they should go up at once. Again, moreover, he enforces the greatness of Yahweh's power 14^{17}. Yet the manifestation of it is to be found not in his victorious might over a hostile king, but in his pardoning mercy towards his own disobedient people. In spite of the singular mixture of appeal implied in the attempt to persuade Yahweh on the ground of his sensitiveness to Egyptian criticism 14^{13-16}, the writer nowhere reaches a greater religious elevation than in $^{17}\cdot\cdot$. The episode is important on other grounds, for it contains the earliest statement of the view that the generation which effected the settlement in Canaan was not the generation which had quitted Egypt. The period of the wanderings is not yet formulated as forty years; but the germ of the idea is to be found in the declaration that the children only shall occupy the land which the fathers have rejected 14^{31}. Towards this consummation the narrative presses rapidly forward, concerned with incidents of conquest, but indifferent to details of legislation. No trace remains of any farewell by Moses; he leaves no legacy of law to meet the changes from the desert to the city or the hamlet with its corn-fields and vineyards. He passes, and Joshua steps into the vacant command unsummoned, for there is no other leader. But his assumption of authority is not without warrant. The celestial visitant who bears in his hand the drawn sword of victory, bids Joshua put off his shoes Josh 5^{15}. The same act of homage had been imposed on Moses at the flaming bush Ex 3^5. The scene is doubtless in the writer's mind invested with the same significance. Joshua receives the commission to complete his predecessor's work. The land has yet to be conquered, and Jericho holds the key of entry. Not till Israel is in possession will the oath to the fathers be fulfilled.

3. To the foregoing indications of **J**'s general view of Israel's history, some remarks on the method and spirit of his narration may be added.

(*a*) The sources of **J** are doubtless to be found partly in traditions often repeated, and transmitted orally for many generations as a kind of sacred deposit. Such traditions are gradually shaped into definite and well marked types by the accumulated experience of those who propagate them. Fresh touches are added, irrelevant matter is sifted out, and attention is concentrated on the central elements in each successive situation. They thus produce impressions of character such as no single writer, perhaps, could have achieved. The story-teller's art is nowhere illustrated more strikingly in the Old Testament than in many of the scenes and personalities presented in **J**. That some of his narratives are intentionally didactic can hardly be questioned: the first man, the woman, the serpent, and Yahweh, all play their part in the Eden drama with a profound purpose underlying it: yet the simplicity of the story and the clearness of the characterization are unmarred. But there are others, like the account of the mission of Abraham's steward Gen 24, which have no such specific aim, and are unsurpassed in felicitous presentation, because they are unconsciously pervaded by fine ideas. The dialogues especially are full of dignity and human feeling; the transitions in the scenes between Abraham and his visitors 18, or between Joseph and his brethren, are instinctively artistic; for delicacy and pathos what can surpass the intercession of Judah, or the self-disclosure of Joseph? The vivid touches that call up a whole picture, the time-references from daybreak through the heat to evening-cool and night, the incidents that circle round the desert wells, the constant sense of the place of cattle alike in the landscape and in life, the tender consideration for the flock and herd (cp ^{JE}18, **32, 33, 227, 236**)—all these belong to a time when the pastoral habit has not ceased, and the tales that belong to it are told from mouth to mouth.

The breath of poetry sweeps through them; and though they are set in a historic frame which distinctly implies a reflective effort to conceive the course of human things as a whole, they have not passed into the stage of learned arrangement; they still possess the freshness of the elder time. The phraseology of **J**, especially in all that concerns the divine action, is still direct, vigorous, and varied. It has its distinctive turns of speech, but it does not fall into set formulae; it coins new phrases for new situations, frequently uses uncommon words, and possesses a wide range of vocabulary. **J**, moreover, loves to incorporate snatches of ancient song, the sayings—half proverb, half poem—in which long observation of national or tribal circumstances was condensed; and with this spontaneous reproduction of antiquity it presents alike the moral and the immoral, the ideal piety of Abraham and the selfish craft of Jacob, in the unconsciousness of their primitive creation, before incident and character have been examined and sifted by the severer conceptions and higher standards of a more reflective age.

(β) It is due to the conditions under which the document gradually took shape that **J** is concerned much more with places and names than with chronology. In his love of etymologies, indeed, he is not peculiar, but in his use of them he sometimes differs from the other writers. All three narratives **J P E**, for example, have a common play on the name Ishmael Gen 16^{11} 17^{20} 21^{17}; and Isaac, similarly, suggests allusion three times over 17^{17} 18^{12-15} 21^6. But these instances do not properly illustrate the method by which again and again the name is made to suggest some real feature in the person who bears it, as in the case of Jacob, or some illuminating incident which called it forth, as in the series of names given in 29 to Jacob's sons. Often, indeed, the story has apparently grown out of the name, as in the interpretations offered by both **J** and **E** of Beer-sheba 21 and 26, or the explanations of Beer-lahai-roi 16^{13}., Marah Ex 15^{23}, and Kibroth-hattaavah Num 11^{34}. Other stories account for the origin and sanctity of particular hallowed objects or places, such as the sacred pillars at Bethel and on Rachel's grave, the sanctuaries at Shechem and Hebron, at Mizpah in Gilead, and at Penuel. A still further group is connected with the supposed significance of some rite or usage. The Wrestler touches Jacob's thigh so that he limps; 'therefore the children of Israel eat not the sinew of the hip which is upon the hollow of the thigh, unto this day' Gen 32^{32}. Through the mysterious purpose of Yahweh who meets Moses on his way back to Egypt and seeks to kill him Ex 4^{24-26}, may perhaps be discerned a reference to the first practice of circumcision. Bacon has characterized stories of this class as 'aetiological[a].' A similar instance may be seen in the connexion of the death of the first-born and the passover 12^{21}..; and another illustration still is supplied in the account of the massacre by the Levites 32^{25-29} which obscurely results in the consecration of the tribe to Yahweh, as the blessing of the priesthood is bestowed upon them. The difference in spirit between these narratives and those of **P** will be noted subsequently (cp chap XIII 2ϵ p 125).

(γ) The interest of **J** in the early history of mankind has been already signalized. He explains the gloomy meaning of human toil and suffering. He concerns himself with the development of the arts, cattle-breeding and agriculture, building, music, and metal-working. He gathers up the stories of remote antiquity concerning the origin of the giants of old time Gen 6^{1-4}; he relates the flood 6^{5-8}; he ascribes husbandry and the culture of the vine to Noah 9^{20}... He is the first to attempt a classification of other nations; he explains the diversities of language; and he notes the movements of peoples, the rise of mighty cities, and the foundation of great empires (cp **J** in 10-11). These ancient narratives have received the powerful impress of the religion

---

[a] *Triple Tradition of the Exodus* 27. he interprets $^{10-16}$ in the same manner as a reference to the interpretative function of the priesthood.

of Yahweh, and the form in which they are presented by **J** accommodates them to Hebrew thought. How far they imply a process of collection or investigation on the author's part cannot of course be exactly determined. But it is probable that the mode in which they are grouped and correlated owes much to a systematic purpose, and in this aspect it is not altogether inappropriate to speak of the narratives prefixed to his account of the origins of Israel as the product of something analogous to modern research. But what is chiefly noticeable is the large view of human affairs which is thus indicated. Contrasted with the hostility to Canaanite idolatries manifested in **D**, the relations of the patriarchs to their neighbours in **J** are for the most part not unfriendly ^{a}. And in the single story Gen 34 which points to conflict, the conclusion ^{30} indicates no auspicious result for Israel, while the language of 49^{5-7} is still more unfavourable. Beyond the limits of Israel the writer's judgements naturally vary. An odious origin is assigned to Moab and Ammon; but the magnanimity of Esau is described with full recognition of his generous and chivalric temper. Traditions of intercourse with the east are still reflected in the pictures of the descendants of Nahor; while the connexions with remoter Arab tribes are twice specified, being mentioned both in the lineage of Joktan $10^{26..}$ and in the descendants of Keturah $25^{2..}$. **J**, therefore, does not hesitate to give to Joseph an Egyptian bride 41^{45}, or to provide Moses with a Midianite wife Ex $2^{21.}$, whom **P**, however, repeatedly ignores ^{b}. Moreover, he takes a sympathetic attitude towards the religious institutions of other nations. The knowledge of Yahweh is not limited to the chosen race; homage is paid to him in the land of the two rivers; the fame of Nimrod is sheltered under his name Gen 10^9; his benediction is invoked by Laban upon Abraham's servant 24^{31}. Rebekah inquires of him apparently at some local oracle 25^{22}; and Balaam becomes the organ of his spirit. No rigid line yet separates Israel as the instrument of Yahweh's purpose from the peoples round.

4. The inquiry into the origins of **J** encounters a very delicate problem in the attempt to determine the place of its composition. The data do not appear to be decisive, and each possibility finds eminent advocates.

(*a*) The question largely depends for its solution on the view which may be formed concerning the source of the patriarchal narratives. That they have arisen out of traditions is conceded by all. But how did the traditions themselves arise? The answer which naturally suggests itself is that they were formed in the localities with which they are primarily concerned. A story concerning Bethel would not be framed in Hebron; nor an incident east of the Jordan be first told on the edge of the wilderness in the south. The insight of Geddes pointed a hundred years ago to these connexions with particular places and objects (chap VII 3*a* p 44); but when attention is directed to them, they are discovered to partake for the most part of a common character. They are found to be sacred places, and the stories associated with them have for their purpose either avowedly or implicitly to explain the mode by which they acquired this sanctity. The most striking instance of this may be found in the narratives grouped around Bethel cp Gen 28^{10-22}. But this is by no means a solitary case. At Shechem 12^7 in middle Canaan, among the oaks of Mamre at Hebron 13^{18}, at Beer-sheba 26^{25}, at Beer-lahai-roi in the south 16^{14}, at Penuel across the Jordan $32^{24-29\ 31}$, altars are reared or divine manifestations occur. These stories, therefore, are sanctuary-stories. They were doubtless current at the different sacred places where they had been so long recited, and whence they had passed out among the

---

^{a} On the other hand, cp the doom on Canaan in Gen $9^{25..}$.

^{b} She is not named, nor her sons, either in Ex 6 or Num 3, though Aaron's family is twice chronicled. The last passage, which is expressly entitled the *tol^{e}dhoth* of Aaron and Moses, stops abruptly with the enumeration of Aaron's four sons.

people at large. Ultimately they may perhaps be traced to the local priesthoods[a]; and their collection into J may not unfairly perhaps be taken to imply that these sanctuaries were still places of repute when his narratives were first arranged. That many of them retained their popularity into the eighth century is abundantly evident from the references of Amos and Hosea[b]. Now some of these sanctuaries belong to the central country in contrast to the south; and even a southern sanctuary like Beer-sheba might retain a powerful attraction for the worshippers of the north, as the pilgrimages from Ephraim in the age of Jeroboam II sufficiently attest. Hebron, however, does not seem to have had any such connexion with middle Palestine. Again, while Abraham and Jacob are associated with both central and southern localities, Isaac is fixed exclusively in the Négeb 24^{62}; he is described at Gerar and at Beer-sheba, but nothing attaches him to Hebron. Among the wives of Jacob, on the other hand, Rachel is the best beloved; and her death and burial (marked by a sacred pillar) alone are mentioned. Round her son Joseph gathers the most striking group of stories; and the tribes that spring from him belong to the middle and the east. Yet the chief actor next to Joseph in J's cycle is Judah 37^{26} 43^8 $44^{16\ 18}$, who takes the lead instead of Reuben 37^{21} 42^{37}. The singular tale concerning Judah in 38 has been differently interpreted: does it convey an unfavourable judgement; or is it merely the product of a friendly interest such as a neighbour might not unnaturally show; or can it be cited as the witness of a descendant to the character of the founder of his tribe? At any rate in $49^{10\cdot\cdot}$ the function of sovereignty seems ascribed to Judah. Of the remoter figures little need be said. J associates Lot with Abraham and depicts his residence in Sodom; after the overthrow of the cities of the plain he is the progenitor of Moab and Ammon, the Hebrew peoples beyond the Dead Sea. In the Mosaic age, Caleb, who settles at Hebron Josh $15^{14\cdot\cdot}$, is foremost in attempting to persuade Israel to go up and take possession of the land (cp J in Num 13–14); and yet later still, the language of one of Balaam's oracles Num 24^{17} seems to point to the brilliant reign of David.

(β) To neither of the principal divisions of later time—geographical or political—do the predominant interests of J decisively point. Critical judgement has consequently been much divided, according to the importance attached to different items of evidence. Thirty years ago Schrader placed J in Ephraim, relying largely on the interest shown in Shechem Gen 34, on the censure implied in 38 on Judah, and on linguistic points of contact which he believed himself able to detect with E and with Hosea. On these and other grounds Reuss, Kuenen, and Kautzsch, while partially modifying Schrader's judgement in detail, adopted substantially the same view, though Kuenen and Kautzsch allowed that J^2 (see 6 p 108) must be assigned to Judah. For the southern kingdom a long catena of opinions might easily be cited. Starting from Ewald this view might be traced through Dillmann on the one hand and Wellhausen and Stade on the other. It is supported by a large consensus of scholars, among whom it is sufficient to mention as representatives of different lands, Budde, Cornill, and Kittel in Germany, Wildeboer in Holland, Driver in this country, and Bacon in America. It is further strengthened on grounds of general probability by the fact that E is unanimously assigned to Ephraim. Is it likely, it may be asked, that two separate documentary collections would be made at no great distance of time in the same general locality, founded on different conceptions of the patriarchal history? The two groups are in many ways allied, so as to be connected by all critics with the same general influences of prophetic thought. But they are distinguished by widely divergent conceptions

---

[a] Cp *ante* p 83^a
[b] Thus, Bethel Am 4^4 5^5 Hos 4^{15} 12^4; Beer-sheba Am 5^5 8^{14}; Shechem Hos 6^9; Gilead Hos 6^8 12^{11}.

concerning the period at which the personal name of Israel's God became known. Is not such divergence more easily interpreted as due to the existence of separate religious schools in the two kingdoms independently than as the product of irreconcilable views within the same area of traditions gathered from the same localities and dealing with similar subject-matter? The peculiarities of the case seem best met if it be supposed that while J may contain many legends of Ephraimitic origin, they were nevertheless wrought into shape and connected with others gathered from Judean sources by a southern hand.

5. For convenience of exposition J has hitherto been treated as at once a writing and a writer. A single person could have but a single date; or at least he could belong only to a single period. But the question of the date of J has become, under the influence of modern inquiry, increasingly complex, as it has been recognized with more and more decision that its constituents cannot be regarded as uniformly of the same literary age.

(a) In its general aspects J has been designated as a book of national history. The endeavour to account for Israel's place in Canaan, his origin and ancestry, the mutual relations of his tribes, their wanderings and settlement, could hardly have arisen until the nation had acquired a firm hold of its possessions. Before it could tell its own story, it must have established its unity and consolidated its strength. The continuation of the narrative of the Mosaic age into the days of Joshua at once carries the date below Moses himself, and its reappearance at the opening of Judges[a] points lower still. The literary evidence for the continuation of J through the books of Judges and Samuel must be sought elsewhere[b]. Its recognition of course practically involves one of two views: either an ancient document descending from a much earlier age was imitated and supplemented in successive centuries, at the hands of a distinct literary school, or the entire work only came into existence at a later time. General considerations plead strongly for the latter. The conception of national unity which underlies the representations of Jacob and his twelve sons can scarcely have been formed in the midst of the difficulties and disorganization which followed the settlement. Never once, in the age of the Judges, is there any combined movement among the scattered tribes. No leader ever succeeds in uniting them to act as a whole. After the great rising under Deborah and Barak, Judah is not even named in the triumph-song. Gideon only leads the central group. Jephthah has no influence save on the east of the Jordan; Samson hardly ever quits the slopes on the south-west[c]. Not till the monarchy were the tribes really welded into one people; and only then could the historians begin the systematic arrangement of the traditions into coherent form. Historical record naturally commences with what is nearer, and only slowly advances to the more remote, as reflexion constantly inquires after more distant causes, and at each step suggests the question 'what happened before?' Much of the materials of the books of Samuel concerning the reign of David must have come into existence in his own age or soon after. Their reduction to writing would gradually lead to the collection and organization of the

---

[a] On Judg 1 see Moore, *Judges*.

[b] See especially Budde, *Richter und Samuel*, whose main results have been widely accepted. Cp Driver, LOT^6 162 ff.

[c] The mention of the Philistines in both J Gen $26^{1.14}$. and E 21^{32} suggests some curious problems. It appears to be established by the Egyptian monuments that the Philistines did not settle in the cities of the Shephéla until the reign of Rameses III (cp Sayce, *Higher Criticism* 183, *Patriarchal Palestine* 164, 182, *Early Israel* (1899) 90; Maspero, *the Struggle of the Nations* 470) at a date considerably later than the Exodus. The Israelites suffered severely from them until the reign of David But in the book of Genesis the relations of Abraham and Isaac with them are friendly How much time must be allowed after the Philistine oppression, before the remembrance of it could have been so far lost that a patriarch could be represented as enjoying the friendship of a Philistine king, or making a covenant with him in the name of Yahweh Gen 25^{28}..?

traditions of an earlier time[a], and the fluctuating mass would at length acquire greater consistency by being cast into a series starting with the first man and presenting a continuous view of the history of the race[b].

(β) On general grounds it thus becomes probable that the book of national history designated J did not acquire written shape till the period of the monarchy. Its production must therefore be fixed in the interval between David and Solomon on the one hand and Josiah and the book of Deuteronomy on the other. Many other indications tend to confirm this general view. (i) In the first place the book is based on the idea that the name Yahweh is of primaeval antiquity and wide-spread use. But the names of the ancient story do not support this belief. In the Mosaic age names compounded with Yahweh are exceedingly rare: among the patriarchs they do not appear at all. Their names are compounded with El, such as Israel 'may El strive,' Ishmael 'may El hear[c].' Only with the time of David do names compounded with Yahweh begin to enter more freely[d]. May it not be inferred that a construction of the world's history which regards this divine name as a universal possession of the human race from the first days cannot have been framed until the name had been for some time commonly employed in Israel? This argument points definitely to an age not earlier than the monarchy[e]. (ii) The administration of Solomon is regarded by the historian as the period when the subjugation of the Canaanites was practically complete cp 1 Kings 9^{20}; and to this condition there seems to be a reference in the curse pronounced on Canaan Gen 9^{25}. The traditional boundaries of the empire of Solomon 1 Kings 4^{21} are those indicated in Gen 15^{18}. Edom, on the other hand, reduced by David cp Gen 25^{23} Num 24^{17}. in the ninth century regains its freedom; and so when Esau returns on his way into Seir Gen 32^{16}, he retires into a stately independence[f]. To this age, likewise, does Brugsch on contemporary monumental grounds assign the origin of such names as Zaphenath-paneah and Poti-phera Gen 41^{45}[g], while Lagarde believes them to be still later, ascribing them to the time of Psammetichus I and Necho, 663–595 B C[h]. To the ninth century also, does the language of Josh 6^{26} point, when Jericho was rebuilt in the days of Ahab 1 Kings 16^{34}. (iii) How far the references to the past in eighth-century prophecy rest definitely on present literary forms cannot be decided with certainty; the data are too few. Amos 2^{10} already specifies forty years as the period of the wanderings, a number which J does not name, though it is implied in the doom pronounced on the generation that left Egypt Num 14. It must be recognized as possible that such allusions as those contained in Am 2^9· Hos 12^3· ^{12}· 9^{10} Mic 6^4· might be founded on traditions still orally transmitted[i]. But the general religious development implied in the preaching of Amos and Hosea in Ephraim, of Isaiah and Micah in Judah,

[a] On the 'Book of the Wars of Yahweh' Num 21^{14}, cp chap II 1ε p 19.
[b] The progress of Greek historiography confirms this general view. The logographers with their schemes of genealogy and their systematic conception of the distribution of the Greeks in the shape of a pedigree of Hellen and his three sons, follow instead of preceding the recorders of nearer events. On the growth of the Anglo-Saxon Chronicle, cp *ante* p 4 At first extremely brief, it becomes fuller in the ninth century. Subsequently it is used as the basis of a new work by Marianus Scotus. Asser's *Life of Alfred* is incorporated into it. Then Florence of Worcester builds upon Marianus Scotus, and sets the whole in a frame of universal history, beginning with the creation and embracing a survey of all nations ancient and modern
[c] Monumental evidence gives us also Jacob-El and Joseph-El, with the probability that Isaac and other similar forms have been truncated Cp Gray, *Hebrew Proper Names* 214.
[d] Gray, *ibid* 259, reckons seventeen. [e] Cp König, *Einleit in das AT* (1893) 206
[f] Edom revolted under Joram 2 Kings 8^{20}.., was again conquered by Amaziah $14^{7\,10}$, but finally broke loose from Judah in the reign of Ahaz 16^6.
[g] Brugsch, *Steinnschrift und Bibelwort* (1893) 83.
[h] Lagarde, *Mittheilungen* III 229 See on the other hand Sayce, *Academy*, Jan 23, 1892, p 91, *Early History of the Hebrews* 84, and *Expository Times* x 173 (Jan 1899). For further discussion see Tomkins, *Life and Times of Joseph* (1891) 50, Holzinger, *Genesis* (in the *Kurzer Hand-commentar*, 1898) 227 237; Dillmann, *Genesis* 11 341 375; Lieblein, *PSBA* (1898) 204-208
[i] Cp Driver, LOT^6 123.

points to a well-established background of usage and phraseology which is best explained on the supposition of recorded narrative familiar to the people whom they addressed; and this is supported by the side glance of Hosea at written laws 8^{12}. These phenomena converge on a date between 850 and 750 B C as the probable period of the first reduction of **J**'s traditions into written form.

6. A further question, however, arises when the contents of **J** are examined. It has already been suggested that they cannot be regarded as altogether homogeneous. One passage only, the covenant-words of Ex 34$^{10-26}$ cp ^{28}, is formally ascribed to a written source[a]. The materials of the rest betray abundant diversity. There are snatches of antique song; there are popular sayings about the ancient tribes and tales of their tribal sires; there are dim allusions to the origins of religious customs and institutions; and earlier still there are traces of literary dependence (so we are assured) on actual cuneiform record[b]. Contrast with these the lofty passages proclaiming the name and attributes of Yahweh, announcing his sovereignty over the world and the righteousness of his government of the earth. Obviously the materials out of which the narrative has been wrought, whether for the patriarchal or the Mosaic age, have not been all of one piece: they have sprung from different minds at different times. This was the truth which lay behind the fragment-hypothesis of the older criticism; is it possible to restate it in more suitable form? The detailed proof must be sought in the notes appended to the Analysis: a few general observations only are here offered. The investigations of Wellhausen, Budde[c], Bruston[d], Kuenen, and subsequent scholars[e] have disclosed a number of significant phenomena.

(α) In the early history of mankind as related by **J** Gen 2^{4b}-11, there are various traces of incorporation or addition. Such perhaps is the description of the four rivers and their mysterious connexion with the Garden of Eden 2$^{10-14}$; and such also the reference to the tree of life 2^9 3$^{22\ 24}$. A contrast, again, is discernible between some of the elements of 4; where Cain is presented in two quite different characters, the murderer doomed to wander an exile from Yahweh's face $^{3-16a}$, and the successful father of the inventors of the arts $^{17-24}$. How, moreover, is the progress of civilization to be explained after the flood? Did Noah and his family possess all the crafts? A study of the fragments of the table of the dispersion set forth in 10 by the side of the united peoples all speaking one language in 11$^{1-9}$ again suggests a diversity of source, the story of Noah and his deliverance being independent of that of Cain and his posterity. In this view the narrative of the Deluge has been added from an independent cycle, and did not form part of the series in the earliest **J**[f]. Whether the additions to the Eden story were also derived from the source which yielded Noah cannot be positively determined; but it may be at least regarded as not improbable[g]; and the secondary symbol **J**^{s} may denote them.

(β) The narratives of the patriarchal age occasionally indicate similar diversity of source. It can hardly be supposed, for example, that the story of Abram passing off Sarai as his sister at Pharaoh's court, and that of Isaac dealing similarly with

---

[a] These 'words,' however, are clearly post-Mosaic, as is shown by their injunction of the three feasts of the agricultural year adopted after the settlement, and the mention of the house of Yahweh ^{26}, an expression not elsewhere used of the Mosaic tent (unless in Josh 6^{24}? cp 2 Sam 12^{20}).

[b] On Milcah and Iscah Gen 11^{29} cp Sayce, *Higher Criticism* 160.

[c] *Die Bibl Urgeschichte* (1883).   [d] *Les Deux Jéhovistes* (Montauban, 1885).

[e] Cp Cornill, *Einleitung in das AT* § 11 6-7, and the two works of Bacon.

[f] Budde further conjectures that this cycle also started with a narrative of creation on which P afterwards based the story now found in Gen 1-2^{4a}. A genealogy in ten steps then led through Seth to Noah, of which he finds traces in 4^{25}. 5$^{22\ 24\ 29}$. After the flood a similar genealogy led in seven stages from Shem through Terah to Abraham. For these incorporations Budde suggests the reign of Ahaz. It is significant in this respect that there is no allusion to Noah till the exile Ezek 14$^{14\ 20}$ Is 54^9.

[g] Cornill, however, *Einl* § 11 7, denies it.

Rebekah at Gerar, belonged originally to the same series of traditions. How, then, are such duplicates to be explained save as the literary product of earlier and later hands? In this case the second story seems the simpler. Isaac announces Rebekah as his sister Gen 26^7, but her real relationship is discovered before any casual infringement of it has occurred ^{10}. The story of Abram exhibits everything upon a grander scale. The court is in no little Philistine city; it is that of the sovereign of the Nile. Sarai is the observed of princes 12^{15}, and her entry into the royal palace secures for Abram abundant wealth. No accidental disclosure brings the truth to light; strokes of supernatural chastisement alight upon the throne whose occupant has unwittingly violated the rights of a guest ^{17}. So dangerous a visitor must be courteously dismissed, and a royal escort conveys Abram with his wife and his possessions across the frontier ^{20}. The heightened detail of this story, and the introduction of the direct intervention of Yahweh on Abram's behalf, were no doubt designed for the patriarch's honour; and they indicate a more reflective view of the whole transaction than the simple naturalism of 26$^{7-11}$. Attention has been already directed to the probability that the Mosaic story has received similar additions by the association of Aaron beside Moses as his spokesman in Ex 4$^{13-16}$ and kindred passages.

(γ) A third group of enlargements will be found in the occasional hortatory expansions of varying length which make their secondary character felt by delicate indications of disturbance in the text such as lack of proper grammatical sequence, or variations in the Greek version, these latter presenting themselves with peculiar frequency when there is often reason upon other grounds to suspect intrusions into the original narrative. Illustrations of such insertions may be found in the repeated lists of Canaanite nations Ex 3^{8N}, or in the religious declarations ascribed to Moses in his interviews with Pharaoh cp 8^{10N}. Such expansions often appear in narratives where a cruder and more primitive style of representation passes suddenly into one of loftier thought, so that even without evidence of textual disturbance, spiritual incongruity suggests the presence of a fresh hand. This is the probable explanation of passages like Gen 18$^{17-19\ 22b-33a}$ Ex 34$^{6-9}$ Num 14$^{17\cdots}$.

(δ) The union of **J** and **E** seems to have begotten another series of extensions, which are, however, so far in the style of **J**'s own thought that they may be included in a general survey of additions to his original cycle. Thus Gen 22$^{15-18}$ is plainly dependent on the narrative of **E** which precedes, yet its solemn recitation of Yahweh's oath places it in connexion with **J**. Its language also recalls, though not without slight differences, the divine promises previously reported by **J** in 12^3 and 13^{16}. A series of later references to the form or to the contents of this oath falls into the same group of editorial enlargements 26^{3b-5} 31^{7b-12} Ex 32$^{9-14}$ (cp chap XVI 1).

(ε) Finally the two brief collections of law in **J**, one connected with the passover Ex 13$^{3\cdots}$, the second founded on the covenant-words 34$^{10\cdots}$, both show marks of amplification bringing them into closer conformity with later style. But in these cases (as in the exhortation in 19^{3b-6}) the peculiar parallels with **D** point in the direction of a Deuteronomic redaction (cp chap XVI 2a). It does not seem possible to determine how far the various series indicated in β–δ may really be ascribed to a common editorial hand. The language of many of these passages shows a gradual approximation to the school of **D**, whose striking phraseology can hardly have been a new and sudden creation. The roots of **D**'s copious hortatory style may be sought not unnaturally in the religious vocabulary of its immediate predecessors, and many of the secondary elements of **J** and **JE** (if not all) may with great probability, therefore, be carried into the seventh century.

Concerning the process of union more will be said hereafter (chap XVI). It may be sufficient to observe at present that other books, notably those of the eighth-century prophets—and pre-eminently the writings of Isaiah among these—are now generally acknowledged to have undergone at various seasons, early or late, similar editorial treatment, by the insertion of explanatory clauses, or of longer passages designed to fill up intervals and effect new connexions. The ancient collections were not rigidly closed. It was a pious work to adorn them with fresh material illustrative of the purposes or contributing to the honour of Yahweh. There is no record of the production of **J** analogous to that of the Deuteronomic code; but there is no reason to regard it, when it first became known, as limited to a single copy. It is quite possible that the collection may have existed in different forms in different places. The Anglo-Saxon Chronicle, for example, appears to have been continued by divers hands in divers monasteries. Up to the reign of Alfred the texts appear in tolerably close agreement; after his time variations become more frequent and more material. It is even possible to infer from special circumstances in a particular MS, in what monastery it may have been prepared[a]. In a similar manner the two great versions of the patriarchal story **J** and **E** can with great probability be ascribed to the two kingdoms of Judah and Ephraim. But each may have existed in more than one form; and the peculiar phenomena of aggregation which they both display (though **J** presents them in larger measure) may be provisionally explained by the supposition that the documents, even before their union, had passed through various stages, so that **J** may be the issue of perhaps two centuries of literary growth (850–650 BC).

CHAPTER XII

CHARACTERISTICS AND ORIGINS OF E

Side by side with **J** in the combined narrative of **JE** runs the second document (cp chap VI 1) designated **E**. In actual quantity it is much smaller, as in scope it is more contracted, than the parallel story with which it is so closely united. Moreover the two forms of the tradition exhibit so many common features of style and expression that their discrimination is often difficult; much uncertainty must frequently attach to the partition; and even where there can be no doubt that the narrative is composite, in consequence of the presence of conflicting detail, the allotment of the several passages can only claim varying degrees of probability. In many cases, therefore, the analysis of **E** out of **JE** cannot attain the security with which **P** may be separated from the total product **PJE**. Yet it will be found on examination that this uncertainty only affects the items of less importance; the main contents and character of the document can be determined with sufficient clearness.

1. The entry of **E** into the field of Israel's early history is apparently reserved till the age of Abraham. No clear trace of this source can be discovered before[b]. Had it contained a view of the world's history, similar to that of **J**, it is probable that some portions of it would still survive, as in other cases (e g the story of the plagues, or the passage of the Red Sea) where three sets of representations **P J E** can all be detected. The critical schools are, therefore, almost unanimous in their conclusion that **E** made no attempt to connect the traditions of Israel with any survey of the progress of humanity or the distribution of the nations. Yet some beginning was necessary, and the language of Gen 20^{13} and Josh 24^2 seems to carry the story of Abraham back to the ancestral connexions in Mesopotamia before his 'wandering' into Canaan. Once in the land which

---

[a] Cp chap I 2a p 4.
[b] For Dillmann's view of possible **E** elements in Gen 4 see note on Gen 4^1.

his descendants were to occupy Gen 15^5, the account of his family relations proceeds side by side with that of J. In the story of Abraham and Sarah at the court of Gerar 20, of the expulsion of Hagar 21$^{8-21}$, of the covenant with Abimelech 21$^{22-27\ 31-33}$, E runs parallel with J (cp the *Synoptical Tables*), while in the account of the intended sacrifice of Isaac a fresh element is contributed to the delineation of Elohim's dealings with the patriarch. Similarly the rivalry of Esau and Jacob, the flight of the latter and his vision at Bethel, follow in both narratives; and E relates at length the marriages of Jacob, and the incidents of his intercourse with Laban. After Jacob's return with his sons to the land of his youth, the interest of E is concentrated on Joseph, whose fortunes in Egypt are described with great fullness. The migration of Jacob in answer to Joseph's summons is divinely sanctioned, and he goes down to Egypt under Elohim's protection 46$^{2-5}$, where his last act is to predict the return of his descendants to the land which he had conquered with sword and bow 48$^{20-22}$. The dying Joseph exacts a promise from his people that they will carry up his mummy with them when they depart, and the narrative then passes to the oppression of the Israelites, the birth of Moses, the great commission entrusted to him to bring forth the children of Israel to serve Elohim at Horeb Ex 3^{12}, and the solemn revelation of Elohim by the new name Yahweh ^{15}. In the delineation of Moses and his age, E takes again and again a highly independent course. But the main outlines of his story are naturally drawn on the same general plan as those of J. The demand for Israel's liberation, the resistance of Pharaoh, the consequent plagues, the final hour of escape, the dangers of pursuit, the triumph on the other side of the waters when the Egyptians are engulfed, all follow in rapid succession. The march to Horeb carries out the divine command, and there the Ten Words are solemnly proclaimed, and a covenant instituted on the basis of a series of 'words' running closely parallel with those of J cp 20$^{22\text{N}}$. With these 'words' a book of 'judgements' is now combined, which has the appearance of having been inserted among them from some other place. After the covenant-ceremony 24$^{3-8}$ Moses and Joshua ascend the mountain that Moses may receive the tables of stone $^{12-15\text{a}}$, and thence in 32 they descend to find the people dancing round the golden calf. The great apostasy led to the institution of the Tent of Meeting 33$^{7-11}$, the description of its construction having been apparently withdrawn in favour of the longer and more elaborate account of the Levitical Dwelling 25-30 35-40. Two striking scenes at the Tent illustrate E's conception of the prophetic gift and the eminence of Moses Num 11$^{24\text{b}-30}$ 12$^{1-15}$, while in the subsequent narratives of the mission of the spies, the revolt of Dathan and Abiram, and the request for permission to pass through Edom, E runs side by side with J. After the passage of the Arnon Num 21$^{11\text{b}-15}$ E, like J, relates the overthrow of Sihon, the visit of Balaam to Balak, and the Israelite worship of the Baal of Peor; and the story of Moses' leadership concludes with the charge by Yahweh to Joshua at the sanctuary Deut 31$^{14.\ 23}$, the Blessing which Moses bestows upon the tribes 33, and the brief mention of his death and burial in the land of Moab 34$^{5\cdot}$. Joshua then institutes preparations for the passage of the Jordan; Jericho is reconnoitred by spies, and after the solemn crossing of the river the city is attacked and falls. By the capture of Ai and the subsequent battle of Beth-horon Joshua secures the possession of middle Canaan; in the south he allots Hebron to Caleb the Kenizzite in the midst of the children of Judah; and after arranging for a distribution of the land among the tribes not yet settled, he finally takes a solemn leave of his people at Shechem when they pledge themselves by covenant to the loyal service of Yahweh Josh 24. But the narrative did not stop there: it was continued, so it would seem probable, through the age which followed the settlement, into the early history of the monarchy[a].

---

[a] On the presence of E in Judges and Samuel cp Moore, *Judges*, and Budde, *Samuel* (in Haupt's *SBOT*), cp *Richter und Samuel*.

2. The narrative whose chief contents have been thus enumerated, has not escaped repeated editorial handling, analogous to that already traced in **J**. In the successive combinations which it has sustained with other Pentateuchal documents, **J D P**, it has undergone transpositions and curtailments which place its original form beyond our reach. But these do not affect its spirit, nor disguise its style; it may be impossible to determine the precise order of all its contents, but its chief affinities can still be securely traced. These place it unmistakably by the side of **J**, in contrast on the one hand with **D**, and on the other with **P**. Its patriarchal narratives deal with the same episodes and repeatedly use the same terminology as **J**^{a}. Its covenant-words run parallel with those of **J**, and its law of the plurality of altars Ex 20^{24} differentiates it at once from the central conceptions of **D** and **P**^{b}. But amid these general resemblances there are numerous and important divergences of detail, to some of which attention must be invited.

(α) To **E**, in the first place, belongs a peculiar and highly interesting view of the progress of revelation. Three stages of religious development are clearly marked in his narrative. While **J** regards the progenitors of the race and the Mesopotamian kindred of Abraham as alike worshippers of Yahweh, **E** affirms that the forefathers of Israel 'beyond the river' were idolaters Josh 24^2. The wives of Jacob, accordingly, bring their 'strange gods' with them Gen 35^{2-4}, among them being the household images which Rachel 'stole' from her father to bear away with her to her distant home 31^{19}. By what means Abraham had learned the higher truth, and become a 'prophet' 20^7, the existing narrative does not relate. But he is conscious that he acts under the will of Elohim 20^{13}, who vouchsafes so manifestly to be 'with him' that even the king of Gerar can recognize the divine aid in his life 21^{22}. To Jacob, however, the vision of Elohim's angels makes known his presence in such wise that as he returns to the place of revelation he can no longer endure the homage offered by his family and their dependants to 'strange gods,' and the first act of religious reformation takes place when they are buried under the oak at Shechem 35^4. The revelation of Elohim is followed by that of Yahweh Ex 3^{15} in whose name Moses is instructed to announce his mission to lead forth his people. In the subsequent narrative, therefore, this name is freely used by **E** as well as **J**, though there still remain passages marked by the preferential employment of the designation Elohim (e g 13^{17-19} 18^{12}) besides its repeated occurrence in phrases such as 'the angel of Elohim,' the 'mount of Elohim,' and even 'the rod of Elohim.'

(β) Corresponding to this ascending sequence is the change in the form and method of divine communication. The anthropomorphic character of the appearance and action of Deity in **J** is far less prominent in **E**. He relates no stories of personal conflict, such as that of the mysterious wrestler with Jacob, or the attempt of Yahweh to kill Moses in the inn upon the way to Egypt. He does not even describe the gracious visit to Abraham's tent, or the protecting presence which stood by the sleeping fugitive Gen 28^{13} on the way from Beer-sheba to Haran; when Elohim comes it is in vision 15^1, or in a dream by night 20^3 31^{24} 46^2 ^{c}. The prominence of the dream in **E** (cp ^{JE}101) is especially characteristic; and marks in particular the story of Joseph alike in Canaan 37 and in Egypt 40 41. But there are other revealing agencies. Though Elohim does not himself appear, save to the eye that is veiled in nightly sleep from outward things, his 'angel' can call out of heaven by day to the weeping Hagar 21^{17}, or warn Abraham to do no harm to his son 22^{11}. At other times this manifestation of the divine personality is pluralized, as in the dream of Jacob at Bethel 28^{12} by which he recognizes the 'place' as the 'house of Elohim' ^{17}, and again at Mahanaim 32^2 where he identifies them as 'Elohim's host (Mahaneh).' In the Mosaic age the angel of Elohim marches in front of

---

^{a} Cp the table of ^{JE} words 120. ^{b} Cp chap VIII i 1β p 50.
^{c} Cp Balaam Num 22^9

the host (or camp, ⲘMahaneh) of Israel Ex 14^{19}, but withdraws to the rear in the shape of cloud and darkness to check the Egyptian advance [20]. In thick darkness also does Elohim abide upon the mount, when thunder and lightning, trumpet-blast and smoke, reveal his presence $20^{18\ 21}$. But at the Tent of Meeting, when Moses has passed within, the cloudy pillar descends and stands at the entrance to speak with him $33^{9\cdot}$; it is the signal for worship, as Deity thus appears before his people. With Moses, indeed, his communion is of the closest kind. He speaks with him face to face, as one man to another 33^{11}; 'mouth to mouth' is their intercourse, so that Moses is privileged to behold his very form Num 12^8. But this is reserved for Moses alone, in a task of exceptional labour and difficulty. Yet even in the future the gracious presence of Elohim will not be wholly withdrawn. His angel will accompany Israel to the place which he has prepared for them Ex 23^{20}: and when they are established in the land of his gift, Elohim will be still at hand in the sanctuary to preside over the functions of justice and solemnize the contract of master and slave 21^6 22^8. Moreover the prophetic function, recognized in Abraham Gen 20^7, prominent in Miriam Ex 15^{20}, and conferred by the gift of the spirit on the seventy elders Num 11^{25-29}, constitutes the true goal of Israel's development as a people. But it is not even confined to them: for Elohim can put his word into what mouth he pleases, and communicates as freely with Balaam in his distant home among the 'mountains of the east' 22^{38}, as with the agents of his choice in Israel.

(γ) Highly interesting, in partial contrast with J, is E's view of the great personalities of the national story. Less vividness of dramatic movement, perhaps, marks the narratives of successive incident: yet the heroes of the past seem conceived in some respects on a grander scale, and anticipate the glories of Israel's future. Abraham is already a prophet Gen 20^7; Jacob is the first conqueror with sword and bow 48^{22}; in Joseph is the spirit of Elohim 41^{38}. Moses rises above all his contemporaries, as the recipient of revelation, the instrument through whom the covenant of Yahweh is made with Israel Ex 24^8, the tried and faithful servant who is superior to prophets and is the trusted guardian of Yahweh's house Num $12^{6\cdot}$. His work is continued, though on a less exalted scale, by Joshua, his 'minister.' To him, and not to Aaron, is the care of the Tent of Meeting assigned Ex 33^{11}: from being keeper of the sanctuary he rises to the dignity of successor to Moses, designated for this high function by a divine charge Deut $31^{14\ 23}$: as conqueror of Canaan he presides over the settlement of the tribes Josh 18^{8-10} 24, and after making a covenant to ensure the loyalty of Israel to their God, he dies as 'servant of Yahweh,' and finds a sepulchre on his own estate in Ephraim. The scenes of blessing and farewell are again and again invested by E with a special significance and solemnity; he loves to depict the dying patriarch, Isaac or Jacob Gen 27 48, revealing the mysteries of the future, or Joseph foretelling the divine visitation and yearning for burial in the land of his fathers 50^{25}. The parting address of Moses has perhaps been removed to make way for the great group of orations now embraced in Deuteronomy (so Bacon, cp Deut $16^{N\ [2]}$); but the discourse assigned to Joshua in Josh 24 is a noble specimen of his stately retrospect and hortatory eloquence. By such episodes is the continuous purpose of Deity for Israel brought into repeated prominence; they partially take the place in E of the revelations related again and again in J promising abundance of posterity and the possession of the land. Once indeed to Abram is the announcement made of seed as the stars of heaven Gen 15^5; and Jacob is to become a great nation $46^{3\cdot}$; but of the oath to the fathers recorded by J, on which D dwells with such loving insistence, there is no mention.

(δ) The scene of Abraham's story seems to have lain for E in the south. He is located first at Gerar Gen 20^1, and then at Beer-sheba 21^{32} 22^{19}. In the wilderness of

Beer-sheba Hagar wandered with Ishmael 21^{14}; and thither Jacob, after his residence at Shalem and the purchase of a plot of ground in middle Canaan 33^{18}, migrated with his family and his flocks, so that the summons to Egypt found him there 46^5. But Hebron, which plays so important a part in J and P, is not named in any extant passage. As in J, so also in E the patriarchal cultus is freely recognized. Abraham builds an altar in the 'land of Moriah' on 'one of the mountains' $22^{2\ 9}$. Jacob erects sacred pillars at Bethel 28^{18}, in Gilead 31^{45}, and at Shalem (if Wellhausen's correction be adopted) 33^{20}; he builds an altar at Bethel $35^{3\ 7}$, and offers sacrifices at Beer-sheba 46^{1b}. The traditions thus explain the origin of the hallowed spots of later time, and place under patriarchal sanction some of the holy stones which a later stage of cultus-law was to repudiate. The story of Rachel's theft of her father's teraphim $31^{19\cdot\cdot}$, and the plaintive question of Laban ^{30} 'Wherefore hast thou stolen my gods,' recall the episode of Micah's loss of his ephod and teraphim Judg 18, and his pitiful appeal to the roving Danites ^{24} 'Ye have taken away my gods which I made.' Both narratives belong to a mode of thought and worship in which the teraphim still played an important part. In a cultus thus elementary sacrifices are classed under two heads Ex 20^{24} 'burnt offerings and peace offerings.' When Moses prepares to solemnize the covenant between Yahweh and Israel 'under the mount' 24^4 · at Horeb, he builds an altar, erects twelve pillars 'according to the twelve tribes of Israel,' and appoints young men to perform the altar-rites. There is as yet no consecrated order: the representatives of the nation belong to no sacred caste: their sacrifices are naturally those which the Covenant-words have just enjoined.

(ϵ) These Covenant-words (cp Ex $20^{22\aleph}$) form the basis of the 'First Legislation' 20^{22}-23 in union with the 'Judgements' 21^1. They are preceded in the present arrangement of E by the Ten Words, which D afterwards selects as the basis of the Horeb-covenant Deut 5. These lay down no law as to the place at which Yahweh may be worshipped, but the subsequent collection of Words opens with permission to erect an altar of earth or unhewn stones in every place where Yahweh causes his name to be remembered Ex $20^{24\ a}$, a rule which recognizes the legitimacy of the traditional sanctuaries of old time. The Mosaic sanctuary, however, is of a different order. It is a tent, fit for the conditions of nomad life in the desert, pitched outside the camp $33^{7\cdot\cdot}$, bearing the name of the Tent of Meeting. The account of its construction has been apparently eliminated in favour of the more detailed account of P's Dwelling $25\cdot\cdot$. It was no doubt intended to enshrine the ark, which in its turn held the sacred stones. The story of the ark likewise has disappeared; but its original presence in E may be inferred both from the parallel narrative of J, and from the summary in Deut 10^8 in close proximity to a fragment of E $^{6\cdot}$ (see notes *in loc*). The Tent of Meeting, however, when first instituted, needed the service of no sacred tribe. It was not even placed under the care of Aaron and his sons. An Ephraimite, Moses' minister, the young Joshua, was installed as its guardian; and when Moses returned into the camp, Joshua remained within the Tent. Nevertheless E does apparently contain traces of an Aaronic priesthood in the statement that on Aaron's death at Moserah, Eleazar his son succeeded him in the priestly office Deut 10^6. Of the circumstances under which the tribe of Levi was dedicated to Yahweh's ministry no account seems to have been preserved from E. The narrative in Ex 32^{25-29} which, in its present position, ascribes their consecration to their participation in the massacre following the worship of the golden calf, does not seem to be in its original setting, and is assigned in the analysis to J rather than E: while the allusions in Deut 33^8· do not appear to be explained by any form of the traditions now included in J E or P; and if the poem be rightly attributed to E it may be inferred that that document

---

^{a} Cp chap VIII 1 1β p 51

connected Levi with incidents of which the record has been lost[a]. On the other hand, a very full account of the institution of judges on a decimal organization of the people is preserved in Ex 18^{12-26}. It is apparent from the data of the narrative that in the compilation of the several documents this episode has been placed too soon cp 12^N, and it seems natural to connect with it in some way the collection of 'Judgements' now inserted into the midst of the Covenant-words $21^{1}\cdot\cdot$ (cp 20^{22N} *ad fin*). Whether the Horeb-covenant was supplemented in **E** by a Moab-covenant, according to the representation of Deuteronomy, depends upon the estimate of the probabilities of transposition suggested by the study of Ex 20–24. The view offered in the analysis (see notes *in loc*, and 34^{28N}) does not find it necessary to resort to the bold hypothesis of Kuenen that the whole Covenant-book once occupied the place which Deuteronomy now holds as a corpus of Moabite legislation. Yet **E** was deeply impressed with the covenant-idea as the expression of the relation between Yahweh and Israel. He does not, it is true, carry it back like **J** to Abram; no oath to the fathers is recorded in his narrative. But the nation which has taken possession of the land through which their sires had been led Josh 24^3, finds in this form the appropriate mode of declaring its choice to serve Yahweh, and the retrospect of the settlement in Canaan concludes with the solemn covenant at Shechem $24^{25\ b}$.

3. The narrative which has thus been briefly surveyed seems to have been somewhat narrower in scope than **J**. It does not attempt to link the history of Israel into the wider history of the world. It is not concerned with the remoter affinities even of Israel's own kindred; Ishmael and Esau are reckoned in the line of descent from Abraham, but no others. Nevertheless the attitude to non-Israelites is not unfriendly. Abimelech of Gerar is divinely protected from the consequences of his unintentional violation of Abraham's marriage rights. Jethro celebrates a sacrifice to which Aaron and the elders of Israel are invited: Balaam receives prophetic words from Elohim The language of **E** with respect to Deity does not run through so wide a range of variation as that of **J**: it is neither marked by the crudeness and simplicity of early imagination, nor does it glow with the spiritual fervour of more advanced and ethicized thought. Passages there are, indeed, still marked by signs of antique use. Such, probably, is the explanation of the occasional employment of the plural with the divine name Elohim, as though the conception of Deity still wavered between unity and an undefined plurality of powers, Gen 20^{13} $31^{53\ c}$ 35^7 Ex 22^9 Josh $24^{19\ d}$. The unique designation 'the Fear of Isaac' Gen $31^{42\ 53}$ is also stamped with ancient awe; and to the same order of primitive sentiment belong the apparent identification of the sacred stone with the actual abode of the *Numen* of Bethel 28^{22}, the view of the pillar at the Tent-door as so completely embodying the divine presence that it could be said to speak Ex $33^{9\ e}$, or the audience of the witnessing-stone at Shechem Josh 24^{27}. Yet the general effect of **E**'s representation is distinctly less anthropomorphic than **J**'s. In admitting into his written narrative the cruder expressions of antique tradition, he may well have placed a broader interpretation upon them, just as the phrase 'a sweet savour' passes from **J** Gen 8^{21} into the Levitical legislation $^P1^58$, and still finds a place in modern language of devotion. One expression, however, deserves notice in this connexion, according to which first Elohim and afterwards Yahweh is described as 'trying,' proving. or tempting his people, cp $^{JE}192$. A conspicuous instance of this appears in Gen 22^1, where the simple pathos of the recital, the restraint of Abraham and the

[a] Cp Driver, *Deut* 399.
[b] On the **E** sections in Joshua, cp the *Introduction to Joshua*
[c] If the unifying words 'the God of their fathers' be omitted with Ⓖ and some Hebrew MSS, the plural will imply that the Gods of Abraham and Nahor were not identical. Cp note *in loc*
[d] Cp König, *Einl* 203, who also notes the parallels between Ex $32^{4\ 8}$ and 1 Sam 4^8 1 Kings 12^{28} 19^2.
[e] 'The pillar of cloud descended, stood . and spake.'

artlessness of Isaac, show that E like J possesses in an eminent degree the capacity for narration, though the fragmentary character of many of his stories partially conceals it. In the Joseph cycle, however, it is well displayed; while on the other hand the E elements in the plague-series lack the dramatic character which distinguishes J's colloquies between Moses and Pharaoh, and the recurring use of the rod on the part of Moses seems less direct and impressive than the immediate agency of Yahweh described by J cp Ex 7^{8N}. The large amount of phraseological material common to J and E is illustrated in the Tables of Words; it arises naturally from the fact that they constantly run side by side, describing the same persons and the same incidents in the same general way. E like J has his own etymological explanations; he cherishes the detail of names; he can call Abram's heir Eliezer Gen 15^2, and Rebekah's nurse Deborah 35^8 (in 24^{59} J she is only 'her nurse'), and the Hebrew midwives Shiphrah and Puah Ex 1^{15}. More conspicuously than in J is the chronological dependence of one event on another marked by the phrase 'after these things' ^{JE}95. So E emphasizes the periods of Jacob's service Gen $31^{38\ 41}$; carefully reckons the famine years 45^6; and specifies the ages of Joseph $50^{22\ 26}$ and Joshua Josh 24^{29}, cp 14^{10}. This exactitude leads him to enrich his narrative with literary references, as in the case of the Amalekite defeat Ex 17^{14}, or the book of Yahweh's wars Num 21^{14}: he can quote the *Mosh^{e}lim* Num 21^{27}, and beside the survey of the tribes attributed by J to Jacob he can set a counterpart in the mouth of Moses Deut 33.

4. By general consent among the critical schools, E is assigned to the northern kingdom. The interests which predominate in his narrative seem to be those of middle Canaan. There are Bethel and Shechem with which the Jacob stories are so closely connected. The principal locality in the south, with which both Abraham and Jacob are associated, is Beer-sheba (cp 2δ), to which in the days of Amos the men of Israel still went on pilgrimage Am 5^5 $8^{14\ a}$. Of Hebron, which belonged peculiarly to Judah, no notice is taken. Similarly in the story of Joseph the lead is attributed in E to Reuben, whereas J assigns it unmistakably to Judah: while in the Mosaic age, Joshua who plays so many parts—minister of Moses, guardian of the sanctuary, leader in war, and legislator in peace—is an Ephraimite by descent, convokes the tribes in the hill country at Shechem, and receives both inheritance and burial Josh 24^{30}. The graves of the famous dead are, indeed, objects of special interest to E. Under the great oak below Bethel lay Deborah Gen 35^8; the bones of Joseph at last find a resting-place at Shechem 50^{25} Josh 24^{32}; Miriam is buried far in the wilderness at Kadesh Num 20^{1b}, Aaron at Moserah Deut 10^6, Moses in Moab 34^6, and Aaron's son Eleazar in the family estate on Phinehas' hill Josh 24^{33}. Several of these lay in the range of Ephraim, and the attention drawn to them confirms the general ascription of E to this locality. The tithes at Bethel Amos 4^4 seem to be explained in Gen 28^{22}: and Hosea, who certainly knows some of the stories now embodied by J (cp Hos 12^{3}.), was probably also acquainted with E. The Bethel allusion Hos 12^4 is hardly decisive (though it might seem to point to Gen $35^{3\ b}$); but the rare term 'memorial' ^{5} is probably founded on Ex $3^{15\ c}$. E, unlike J, calls Laban the 'Aramean' Gen $31^{20\ 24}$; and Hosea 12^{12} refers to Jacob's flight into the field of Aram, where his service for wife and flocks recalls E's language Gen $29^{20\ 30}$ 31^{41}. The whole conception of the Mosaic history in E is steeped in sympathy with the prophetic function; and if Moses is differentiated from the prophets, it is only to set him above them: to Hosea also 12^{13} Moses is a prophet by whom Yahweh 'brought up' (^{JE}136) Israel out of Egypt. The literary affinities of E are thus not out of harmony with its assignation to Ephraim. If the descriptions of the tribes in Deut 33 may be referred to E, the glowing picture of Joseph (which seems to have contributed some

---

a Cp Elijah's flight thither 1 Kings 19^3. *b* Read in Hos 12^{4b} 'spake with him'
c Nowack (*Handkommentar*) proposes to strike out $^{4b-7}$ as post-Hosean, and ^{13}. is similarly excised

elements to Gen 49), apparently reflecting the prosperity of the northern monarchy under Jeroboam II, supplies at once a double clue to its place and date (cp chap XIV 5).

5. The materials of J were found to be of various ages, and it became a probable view that the document after its first reduction to writing had received successive enrichments. The growth of E may be regarded as not dissimilar.

(α) It is no doubt true that the present mutilated condition of E through incorporation first with J and then with P renders it by no means easy to determine its original form and contents. But enough assuredly remains to justify the student in applying to its history the same general considerations already specified in the case of J. The patriarchal narratives of E are the product of similar influences: they reflect the same national conceptions first organized under the powerful stimulus of the Davidic monarchy (cp chap XI 5a). The twelve tribes ranged under Jacob, and the relations of Israel and Edom, represent in both documents the view that emerged under the political conditions of a later age, when the traditions of the past were wrought into systematic form. The parallel stories connected with eminent religious centres such as Bethel or Beer-sheba, no doubt had a common origin in sanctuary-lore[a]. Moreover they imply a similar attitude to the holy places of antiquity, and to the cultus-practices in sacrifice and festival. They have the same sacred year with its three feasts: and both give the sanction of the past to the sacred pillars which a later age was to denounce. Especially noteworthy is the emphasis in E on the function of the prophet. Abraham is already presented in that capacity to Abimelech of Gerar Gen 20^7, though an important note in 1 Sam 9^9 assures us that the word first came into use in the days of Samuel. The date thus indicated confirms for E the view above expressed concerning the connexion of both J and E with the conditions of the monarchy[b]. The citation from the Book of the Wars of Yahweh Num 21^{14} and the Blessing of Moses Deut 33 point in the same direction (cp chap II 1ε). And if the reference to successful Edomite revolt Gen 27^{40} be correctly ascribed to E, the passage receives its best explanation from the efforts of Edom to assert its independence, which culminated in the ninth century in the reign of Joram 2 Kings 8^{22}: Uzziah recovered Elath for a short time, but under Ahaz all was again lost.

(β) The investigation of the age of E thus reaches a date not far from that already claimed for J, and the further question arises whether it is possible to determine more closely their mutual relations. Can a decisive priority be asserted for either? The opposite impressions of Dillmann and Kuenen in this matter raise at first a natural doubt whether this question can be definitely answered. And if the two documents were homogeneous wholes this doubt might be difficult of solution. But the seeming contradictions are at least partially reconciled when it is recognized that each contains elements of various dates, so that even if J were actually the first to acquire consecutive literary form, it might yet have continued to receive fresh incorporations after the composition of E. Thus it has been already argued (chap XI 6β p 108) that J's story of Abram at the court of Pharaoh Gen 12^{10-20} is of secondary origin compared with the similar story of Isaac at Gerar 26^7... What is the relative place of E's narrative in 20? The scene is the same as in Isaac's case, the little court of Gerar. Abraham, like Isaac, alleges on his wife's behalf 'she is my sister' 20^5 26^7, in fear of his life 20^{11} 26^7 (parallels of phrase may be noted in the words 'place' and 'kill' = 'slay' ⓗ). Abimelech's indignation expresses itself in almost identical questions 20^{10} 26^{10}. But the story of Abraham advances much further. Sarah is actually taken into Abimelech's court. The danger which is only possible in 26^{10} has been incurred by the king himself in 20. In vindication of his innocence he is supernaturally protected, and Elohim goes so far as to suggest that the prayers of Abraham may be efficacious in his behalf 20^7. Does not all

---

[a] On the Philistines Gen 21^{32} cp ante p 106c.   [b] On E in Judg-Sam cp 1 p 111a.

this heightened detail imply a more developed and so later form of the incident ^{a}? In J the beauty of Sarai is especially emphasized, and the divine protection of Abram is still more signally manifested, in Egypt. At Gerar the intervention of Elohim only suspended for a time in Abimelech's harem the ordinary incidents of nature 20^{17}. The court of Pharaoh suffers severer strokes 12^{17} inflicted directly by Yahweh. As with Sarai's beauty so with Abram's wealth; the enumeration in 12^{16} seems to advance on 20^{14} just as on $26^{.4}$, though the connexions are not quite the same. A sequence may thus be established in which the Rebekah-Abimelech story stands first; next follows the Sarah-Abimelech narrative, and the Sarai-Pharaoh incident concludes the series. E will then occupy a middle place between J and J^s. Other parallels suggest but do not clearly determine a similar order. The flight of Hagar in 16 and her subsequent wanderings seem to belong to a simpler story than the expulsion in 21. In the former Abram yields to Sarai's demand without a pang: in the latter his grief is deep, and is only relieved by a divine promise of future greatness for the bondwoman's son. The provision for the hapless pair, the scene in the wilderness as the mother sits with eyes averted from the dying boy, are new elements; and the angelic intervention, though fixed in the narrative, enters it on a new plane. The angel does not himself find Hagar as in 16^7; he calls to her out of heaven 21^{17}; he does not walk the ground like a man (cp 18-19), he is only the impersonation of a voice from the sky. Similarly in the Bethel visions 28 J depicts Yahweh as himself standing beside the sleeper; but in E Jacob does not behold the Deity who dwells above, he sees only the wondrous ladder on which Elohim's messengers go up and down. The conception is less simple; between man and God are ranged a host of superhuman powers; and in such interposition there seem plain marks of later thought ^{b}. It must however be remembered that the literary record may not always follow the order of origin. Stories may have been told and retold for generations before they were reduced to writing; and J's stories, even though recognized as being of an earlier type, may conceivably be posterior in their ultimate arrangement in consecutive form. But the same observation may be applied also to the cruder elements already noted in E (3 p 115): they may be of ancient derivation yet retained without open rejection in later narrative. These considerations, however, have less bearing on the general scheme of the whole. And in this aspect the work which takes for granted the worship of Yahweh from the beginning, implies a naiver conception of human things than the document which divides the history of Israel's religion into successive stages, and traces a progress culminating in the revelation of Yahweh at Horeb. On the other hand, E seems to have sustained less hortatory amplification (though traces of it are not wanting, cp Ex 23^{23-33}), and in narrative, at least, to be more nearly homogeneous than J ^{c}.

(γ) The general impression suggested by E is that of a period of considerable national prosperity. Abraham enters into a covenant on equal terms with Abimelech and the captain of his host. The blessing which Jacob wrests from Isaac emphasizes the 'fatness' of the earth and the abundance of corn and wine Gen 27^{28}. The dreams of Joseph reflect the future sovereignty of his house 37^8: in the elaborate organization sketched in Ex 18^{21} the military as well as the judicial administration of the people is implied: and the descriptions of the tribes in the Blessing of Moses Deut 33 contain no more allusions to the catastrophe which practically wiped out Simeon and Levi Gen 49^{5-7}: while the royal power of Ephraim seems fully recognized $^{16.}$. This poem may not, indeed, be an integral part of E; but it is at least in general harmony with its main delineation. The

---

^{a} Cp Kuenen, *Hex* 235
^{b} Kuenen and others find further illustration in Gen $30^{17.}$ compared with $^{14-16}$; and in 31^{4-13} and 30^{23-43} (*Hex* 235').
^{c} On secondary elements in E, however, see below δ p 119

Balaam songs imply the same delight in the number and the victorious prowess of Israel Num 23; and the conquests of Joshua also take for granted the secure possession of the land from north to south. In the farewell address of the Ephraimite hero the choice which is set before the people takes no notice of the Tyrian Baal, but lays stress on the temptations of Mesopotamian cults and the rites of Canaan Josh 24^{15}. The struggle with the house of Ahab is over, and the revolutionary work of Jehu is complete: on the other hand, new influences from the land of Israel's ancestry are beginning to endanger their allegiance to Yahweh[a]. The Gilead-covenant in like manner points to an age of peace between Israel and Aram; the Syrian wars have ended, and Jacob and Laban can respect each other's boundaries Gen 31^{51-53}. These conditions seem to be fulfilled in the first half of the eighth century B C during the long and prosperous reign of Jeroboam II. If the reduction of E to writing be placed before 750 B C, a written base is then provided for Hosea's allusions[b].

(δ) The attempt to determine the age of E, however, soon encounters a difficulty analogous to that already presented by J. (i) The narratives of the patriarchal age do not indeed, like those of J, offer clear marks of diversity of date, so that secondary elements may be discerned within them. But after Ex 3 there are occasional passages where the divine name Elohim is still regularly employed, as in the E sections of Genesis, instead of Yahweh, e g Ex 13^{17-19} 14^{19} 18^{12-27} $19^{3a\ 17\ 19}$ 20^{19-21} 31^{18b}, and in the Balaam story Num $22^{9\ 12\ 20\ 38}$ 23^4. It seems most natural to explain such a peculiarity by reference to a source marked by this usage; but if so, it must be admitted that the materials of which E is composed have not been uniformly reduced in the editorial process to a common type.   (ii) Again the Horeb-scenes in Ex 19-24 and 32-33 appear highly complex, and suggest numerous and embarrassing problems, which seem to require the hypothesis of different strata of literary deposit. Thus the First Legislation in 20^{22}-23 contains diverse elements, the Covenant-words and the collection of Judgements. The Covenant-words appear to have undergone considerable manipulation to bring them into closer harmony with J (see notes *in loc*); but the whole group, and the ceremony founded upon them 24^4· with its laymen at the altar and its twelve pillars ct 23^{24}, seem to belong to an early stage of cultus usage. The phrases of 21^6 22^8 'bring him to Elohim,' 'come near to Elohim' (and possibly also the language of 22^{28}) are moulded on a primitive religious practice. It may be noticed also that the law of the theocratic dues assimilates the gift of male human first-borns to that of sheep and oxen $22^{23b\ 30}$ without introducing the provisions conspicuous in J 34^{20}; it had not apparently been yet found necessary to formulate the equivalents for animals (like the ass) which could not be offered on the altar, nor to prescribe the redemption of children. In such relative crudeness and simplicity it is natural to find evidence of great antiquity[c]. Much of the material of the 'Judgements' may in like manner depend on ancient custom. Both Words and Judgements, it is true, rest upon agricultural rather than nomad life: but some of the regulations concerning personal injuries and property may be founded on tribal tradition derived from the remotest past.   (iii) On the other hand the literary analysis renders it probable that the Ten Words in Ex 20 were not included in the original E. It cannot be proved that Hos 4^2 is founded on them: it is admitted that the commentaries attached to them show the influence of the hortatory additions in which the schools of JE approximate to that of D[d]: and an increasing body of critical opinion regards them as showing in their existing arrangement the influence of the

---

[a] Cp Amos 5^{26}.
[b] Unless with Nowack the integrity of the text be denied
[c] Some critics have supposed that Gen 22 contains a protest against the sacrifice of the first-born analogous to that of Mic 6^7. That the sacrifice of the first-born son was not unknown in the ninth century is plain from the action of the king of Moab 2 Kings 3^{27} Cp Ahaz 2 Kings 16^3.
[d] Cp Driver *LOT*[6] 35.

seventh century (cp Ex 20¹ᴺ). In the present state of the documents it does not appear that their source, or the date of their incorporation in **E**, can be determined. But it has been usual to connect in the closest manner with the Ten Words the episode of the golden calf 32, which has in its turn been regarded as a prophetic polemic against the worship at Bethel and at Dan. In the announcement of a divine visitation ³⁴ᵇ some interpreters find an allusion to the overthrow of the kingdom of the Ten Tribes in 722 B C, and the whole story is then assigned to a Judean edition of **E** in the seventh century [a]. There is no doubt an awkwardness in the present collocation of the text by which (as Cornill points out) the departure of Israel to the promised land 32³⁴—an advance to take possession of the gift to their sires—is represented as a part of Yahweh's penal doom. But reasons are alleged in the analysis for regarding ³⁰⁻³⁴ as supplemental; and the passage which follows 33¹⁻⁶ has undergone too much manipulation to permit of its serving as a secure foundation for any criticism concerning the writer's intention in describing the origin of the sanctuary. It may, however, be remarked that though the story of Moses' action implies the inscribed stones, it does not necessarily imply the Ten Words of 20. The Covenant-words of **J** 34¹⁷ contained the prohibition of images; and according to one view these were supposed to have been written on the tables 34²⁸. In what the record on **E**'s tables consisted, the narrative (as we have it) is not clear, for both 24¹² and 32¹⁵ show traces of later treatment. But it is possible that **E**'s original view of the stones (like **J**'s) may have been independent of the Ten Words of 20, for **D** is the first to assert definitely that these were actually written by Yahweh Deut 5²². In that case the supposed dependence of the narrative of the great apostasy on Ex 20⁴ can hardly be enforced as an argument for the later date of **E**'s share in 32. Moreover, it may be argued that the polemic against idolatry[b] is entirely in harmony with the prophetic attitude of Amos and Hosea; and though these prophets do not cite the Ten Words, yet Hos 4² 12⁹ᵃ 13⁴ᵃ at least show some affinity with them. The possibilities in different directions offer sufficient warning against a too exclusive judgement. (iv) Clearer evidence of secondary character is perhaps to be found in Num 11–12, where the prophetic activity of Moses is exalted in the highest degree. In the account of the Seventy Elders the spirit upon Moses suffices on its distribution 11²⁵ to excite them all to prophecy: in 12 the jealousy of Aaron and Miriam is rebuked by the declaration of their brother's lofty dignity as Yahweh's servant with whom he speaks mouth to mouth ⁷. . The first of these narratives is certainly related to that of the institution of the judges in Ex 18 (cp Num 11¹⁶ᴺ); and appears to be the prophetic rather than the judicial version of the provision of aid for Moses' overtasked strength. But though Num 11¹⁶. ²⁴ᵇ⁻³⁰ and 12²⁻¹⁵ may be plausibly regarded as late elements in **E**, they do not bear a specifically Judean character, and the time and place of their addition to the main document must be left uncertain. The example of Hosea's own writings shows that the literary products of the northern kingdom passed easily into the southern: but we do not know enough of the religious conditions to do more than affirm that **E**, like **J**, contains elements of various date, some of which may have been contributed to it after it had been adopted into the record of history and law preserved in Judah.

[a] So Kuenen, Cornill, and others.   [b] Cp Gen 35¹⁻⁴ Josh 24

CHAPTER XIII

THE PRIESTLY CODE

The large extent and the complicated character of this great collection raise many problems. It will be convenient first to consider its main features, and their relation to the other documents J E D and to the history; and at a subsequent stage to inquire how far it is itself homogeneous, or how far different elements can be traced within it.

1. To whatever period this document is assigned, it is unanimously regarded as the groundwork of the present Pentateuch. The elimination of its contents is for the most part rendered easy by its definite characteristics both in matter and form; and the study of its relations to the other sources employed in Genesis makes it clear that P has been adopted as the basis of the entire compilation. The clue to its separation has been already indicated in the declaration of Ex $6^{2..}$ concerning the appearances of El Shaddai to the patriarchs Abraham, Isaac, and Jacob (chap V 2 p 34). In the search for the record of these revelations it became apparent that the basis of the book of Genesis was formed by a series of ten *tol^edhoth* sections divided into two groups, five tracing the history of the world from the Creation to the posterity of Shem, and five concerned with the immediate circle to which the people of Israel belonged, Terah the father of Abraham Nahor and Haran, Ishmael and Isaac, Esau and Jacob. This series ends with the death and burial of Jacob Gen 49^{33} 50^{12}. The narrative then passes to the fortunes of his descendants in Egypt, their increase and their oppression by the Egyptians, and the divine observance of their sufferings. At this point Moses enters, and the name Yahweh is revealed to him, with the commission to announce to his people Yahweh's purpose of deliverance. As Moses has not previously been mentioned, either the account of his origin has been omitted by the compiler in favour of the record of JE, in Ex 2–5, or the writer assumed such a knowledge of him as might justify his introduction undescribed [a]. This seems the more likely as a later hand has apparently sought to supplement the deficiency by inserting some genealogical particulars in 6^{20}. The abstract treatment which marks P's early narratives is here conspicuous. There is no flaming bush, no sacred mount. The sequel of the story 7^6 implies that the revelation took place in Egypt; the demand which Moses is instructed to address to Pharaoh is confined to simple permission to depart; of the sacrifice in the wilderness J 3^{18}, or the service on the mountain E 3^{12}, not a word is said. The struggle with Pharaoh follows, and in preparation for the last great incident, the death of the first-born and the departure of the Israelites, the Passover Law is introduced 12. The narrative then relates the march through the waters in which the Egyptian pursuers are overwhelmed, and brings the people to Sinai $19^{1..}$, where the glory of Yahweh dwells on the mount, and Moses in answer to the divine summons ascends and enters into the cloud $24^{16..}$. The camp at Sinai is the scene at which the great theocratic institutions of Israel are founded. The Dwelling is first elaborately described, and then with equal elaboration constructed, 25–30 35–40. The Aaronic priesthood is established; the ritual of sacrifice is ordained; and a vast mass of legislation is issued enumerating the priestly duties and privileges in various connexions, as well as defining the methods of maintaining the purity and holiness of the people. After a census of the tribes has been taken, the Levites are solemnly dedicated to the service of the sanctuary, and in the second month of the second

---

[a] Cp the reference in Gen $19^{'9}$ to the well-known episode of the 'overthrow' of Sodom and Gomorrah.

year after the Exodus Num 10¹¹ the signal is given for departure. In accordance with **JE** the result of the mission of the spies evokes the discontent of the 'congregation,' and a doom of forty years of wandering falls on the rebellious people. During the fortieth year Aaron dies upon Mount Hor, and the children of Israel encamp in the 'plains of Moab' on the east of the Jordan, opposite Jericho 22¹. There a second census is taken; Moses is commanded to ascend the mount of Abarim and die; and he prepares for his departure by securing the appointment of Joshua as his successor. But the fulfilment of the divine intent is unexpectedly postponed. Not only is the whole of the book of Deuteronomy inserted at the close of the prophet's career, but a number of supplemental incidents and laws prolong Moses' last days, and display the aged leader as solicitous for every detail to the end. To him are revealed the boundaries of the land which he has never seen; he is instructed to prepare for its distribution; to regulate the offerings at the feasts; to make arrangements for the provision of cities for the maintenance of the Levites and the refuge of the homicide; and his last act is to settle the law for heiresses 36. The record of his death in Deut 34 brings the Pentateuch to a close. Yet, as might be expected from the language of Ex 6⁸, the document whose contents have been thus briefly sketched, did not end there. It is continued in the book of Joshua. But it no longer serves as the literary base of the story of the conquest and settlement in Canaan, as it has previously served as the groundwork of Gen-Num. The significance of this fact for the process by which the books were finally compiled as we have them, will be discussed hereafter (chap XVI 3δ): it need only be noted now that in the union of **P** with **JE** and **D** in Joshua no formal close to its narrative has been preserved.

2. The aim and significance of **P** are revealed with sufficient clearness in the stages of its history and legislation, its main object being to present a systematic view of the origin and working of the great theocratic institutions of Israel. Some of the distinctive features of the execution of this design deserve special notice.

(*a*) In commencing his narrative with the origin of humanity **P** follows the path already traversed by **J**. His view of the primaeval history, however, is by no means the same. Instead of deriving the race from a single pair, he regards the original creation, male and female, as plural Gen 1²⁷. He knows no Eden, he relates no temptation, he does not seek to explain the stern conditions of human labour or suffering. The world, as Elohim beholds it, is 'very good.' The progress of mankind is traced in ten steps to Noah, under the genealogical form already employed by **J**, who was, however, content with seven. That common material has been employed may be inferred from the parallels in 4 and 5, Enoch being found in both lists 4¹⁷ 5¹⁸⁻²⁴, while Methushael and Lamech 4¹⁸ are obviously represented by Methuselah and Lamech 5²¹⁻²⁸ [a]. No details save those of age accompany these names. The interest which **J** shows in the development of social affairs is suppressed, though the actual line is extended, and the reader learns with surprise 6¹¹ that violence and corruption filled the earth. Through what causes the joy and gladness of creation had been overcast by this moral gloom is nowhere indicated. To those who can read between the lines a singular indication is afforded by a comparison of the numbers of the patriarchs' ages in the Massoretic and Samaritan texts [b]. In the latter the ages of the patriarchs from Adam onwards regularly decline, and in view of the well-known connexion in Hebrew thought between excellence and length of days, a suspicion is at once aroused that the diminution of the duration of life implies

---

[a] A further connexion may be suspected between Cain and Cenan, Mehujael and Mahalalel, Irad (עירד) and Jared (ירד).

[b] See Dillmann's argument in favour of the Samaritan numbers, *Genesis* 1 217–221.

the growth of evil. The sixth patriarch, whose name Jared has been interpreted as 'descent,' ie decline or degeneration [a], begins a second group of five, whose varying fates imply different characters. Enoch and Noah both walked with God. The first is removed from this world by a divine act of assumption; the second is delivered from destruction to become the sire of a new race, and lives actually longer than Adam. The other three all die in the year of the flood. But the flood is the punishment of sin; and by their participation in a common doom, the author delicately suggests that the wickedness which called it forth was no sudden growth, but extended back for generations [b]. The incidents of the Deluge are conceived upon a grander scale by P, who ascribes it to something more severe than continued rain: windows are opened in heaven, and the fountains of the great deep broken up 7^{11}. At its close Noah offers no sacrifice, but Elohim 'establishes' or 'sets up' his covenant with him not to destroy the earth again by water, and puts his bow in the clouds as a sign. The share of P in the table of nations presented in 10 includes a wider range than J: and in its recognition of diversities of language as the natural result of the dispersion, it stands in the same contrast with the ancient story in 11^{1-9} as is afforded by J's (cp XI 6a p 108).

(β) The delineation of the patriarchal age in P follows in outward succession the stages of JE. There are the same 'fathers,' Abraham, Isaac, and Jacob; and the nation is constituted out of the same twelve tribes. But the difference in spirit is very striking. Like J, so P slowly concentrates his view on the special line of Israel; and first Ishmael, and then Esau, passes out of sight. But in JE these family incidents resulted from conflicts of interest, from outbursts of feeling, from all the mingled play of character, which led Abram to acquiesce in Sarai's demand for Hagar's expulsion, or incited Rebekah and Jacob to outwit Esau. P is content to enumerate the twelve sons of Ishmael 25^{12}·, or to relate the migration of Esau 36^6· on the simple ground that the possessions of the two brothers were too numerous for the same land to bear them. The 'fathers' have thus become ideal types, of whom nothing must be related that does not become the dignity of progenitors of a race which God will hereafter summon to be holy like himself. To Abraham is addressed the command to realize what Noah had already achieved, the walk with God, the perfect life 17^1 cp 6^9. This abstract character is intensified by the singular absence of geographical detail. It is said of Abram that 'he dwelt in the land of Canaan' 13^{12}, almost as though he were its only inhabitant. The localities on which J and E love to dwell, the altars, the wells, the sacred trees and stones, are all ignored, as well as the theophanies which hallowed them. One spot only is named with repeated emphasis, Kiriath-arba (Hebron), and the adjacent grave at Machpelah which Abraham purchases first of all for his dead wife 23: and to this may be added Bethel 35^{15}, the importance of which in ancient story secured its recognition also by P [c]. Save Ephron the Hittite, no person outside the charmed circle of the kinship of Israel is named. Even when Lot settles in the cities of the 'Circle,' the writer refrains from commenting on their character 13^{11}·; and when the 'overthrow' is mentioned 19^{29}, it is apparently assumed that its cause is known. Again and again does the brevity of the narrative imply that the author relies on the previous acquaintance of his readers with the facts. The artifice in 5 by which the increase of corruption was indicated, would have been unintelligible to one who was not already prepared for this feature in the story. In the brevity of the record of Isaac's marriage 25^{20}, in the curt enumeration of Jacob's twelve sons 35^{23-27},

---

[a] For this explanation, and the interpretation to which it belongs, cp Budde, *Urgeschichte* 100 ff.
[b] Cp Addis, *Hexateuch* II 199
[c] The massacre of the Shechemites in 34 was probably not part of the original P.

in the abrupt introduction of Moses Ex 6², as well as in other cases, the writer seems to summarize episodes so familiar as to need no further elaboration. If this impression be just, if (in other words) P writes for those who are already familiar with JE, the later origin of his narrative is confirmed.

(γ) Between his two predecessors, in his theory of religious history P approximates to E rather than J. True, he recognizes no idolatry among the patriarch's kindred; but with E he postpones the revelation of the name Yahweh till the age of Moses. True, also, he admits neither cultus nor prophecy in the ancient days. Noah may build no altar, Abraham offer no sacrifice, Jacob erect no sacred pillar. No offering is recorded till Aaron and his sons are ready Lev 8. Nevertheless, when the sanctuary is established, it bears the name familiarized by E, and is called not only the 'Dwelling,' but also the Tent of Meeting. The priesthood, as in E, is connected with Levi; and Aaron is succeeded by Eleazar, cp E in Deut 10⁶. Yet though P thus rigidly postpones all acts of worship till the appropriate place could be constructed and the right persons chosen for its performance, he makes his own preparation step by step for the enforcement of the sacred law. Even the order of creation has its ritual significance. The heavenly bodies serve to mark the festal times Gen 1¹⁴; and after the production of the universe and its contents in six days, Elohim keeps sabbath on the seventh day and hallows it 2²˙˙. On Noah is laid the first ordinance concerning flesh-food. Primitive humanity was vegetarian 1²⁹; but the new race is to be carnivorous 9³, subject, however, to the prohibition of eating the blood in which lay life. Noah also receives the first social command authorizing capital punishment for homicide. A further advance is made with Abraham, when the covenant to give the land of Canaan to him and his seed is enforced by the sign of circumcision 17: while the future possession of the sacred soil is symbolized by the grave to which the mummy of Jacob is carried up from Egypt. Yet another step is taken when the Passover is instituted on the eve of the Exodus Ex 12¹⁻²⁰, and rules are added which define the conditions under which slaves and strangers shall be entitled to partake of it, the limits of the 'congregation' (first mentioned in ³) being thus incidentally determined. A new conception is here introduced, and the theocratic penalty which was formulated as cutting off a soul 'from his people' Gen 17¹⁴, is now expressed in the phrase 'that soul shall be cut off from the congregation of Israel' Ex 12¹⁹. It was, indeed, no new term; in the popular tales about Samson it denoted a 'swarm' of bees Judg 14⁸; it served to describe the national assembly at Shechem which made Jeroboam king 1 Kings 12²⁰ [a]; but in P it possesses a peculiar and technical sense as the designation of the 'meeting' of Yahweh's people in whose midst he dwelt [b]. Round this conception does the Priestly legislation gather.

(δ) The religious progression thus indicated culminates in a twofold purpose. When the Deity, known to Abraham, to Isaac, and to Jacob, as El Shaddai, reveals himself as Yahweh Ex 6³˙˙, he first recites his covenant to 'give them the land' into which he subsequently promises to bring the children of Israel. To describe their permanent settlement where their fathers had been only sojourners, to explain the divine design and to relate its subsequent fulfilment, is the first and prominent aim of the writer. But he has also in view the solemn act of adoption by which Yahweh will take Israel to him as a people, and will be to them a God. The establishment of this relation is the central idea of the entire Code. What institutions expressed it, what conduct it required, what character it sought to train—these questions find their answer in the Sinaitic law. In such a relation the people were throughout regarded as a religious

---

[a] The passage in Hos 7¹² is probably corrupt.
[b] Cp the use of the same root in the ancient name of the sanctuary, 'Tent of Meeting,' with P's allusion Ex 29⁴³. D uses a quite different word, 'assembly' D20.

rather than as a political community. Of its secular government not a word is said. The crown and the judiciary are never named. On the side of civil administration all is blank. But while there is no allusion to any aspect of Israel's life among the nations of the world (save in the implication Gen 17⁶ 35¹¹ that the monarchy was a distinction and a blessing), its calling as a dedicated people is repeatedly emphasized. The most signal manifestation of Yahweh's favour is the institution of his Dwelling among them, by which the promise in Egypt is fulfilled Ex 29⁴⁵, and Yahweh becomes Israel's God. The construction of the sanctuary, the ranks of its officers, the laws of its service, its daily or its annual ritual, these are all divinely ordained. They are not the product of the age-long homage of mankind, assuming new forms with fresh stages of human advance; they are the realization of Yahweh's own ideas; Moses can make nothing of which he has not first seen the pattern in the mount. Nevertheless these ideas when they are imparted to Moses, are for communication to Israel. The laws are issued to the entire nation. They are not reserved for a special sacred caste. In the details of rites and the particulars of ceremonies the people are invited to see the expression of their supreme religious privilege. For their sanctuary they make willing offerings: they witness the consecration of the priests: they sanction by their attendance the presentation of the Levites as the equivalent of their own first-born: and they are never without some share in the story until their inheritances are distributed under the superintendence of Eleazar and Joshua before Yahweh in Shiloh. From first to last P is designed not as a manual prepared for priests, but as a text-book of history and law for a whole people.

(ε) The execution of this design is marked by many peculiar features of style. The narratives of J and E seem to spring out of oral tradition; they are full of dramatic variety; in snatches of song and folk-tale they gather up the fragments of immemorial antiquity. But P is constructed on a definite literary method. The historical introduction is cast into ten *tolᵉdhoth* sections. The writer is not without graphic power or skill in dialogue, as the sublime opening of Gen 1 or the description of the purchase of the cave of Machpelah 23 makes clear; but he does not permit himself to linger over episodes such as those contained in 20 or 24 with an artless pleasure in the mere narration. Everything is subordinated to definite ends. Hence titles are frequent and regular, cp ᴾ188; every description is precise; and when once the proper form of words has been selected, it is unfailingly reproduced on the next occasion[a]. Similarly the issue of a divine command is constantly followed either by the recitation of its fulfilment in parallel words (as in the creative utterances and acts of Gen 1), or by an often repeated formula of execution, e g 'thus did Noah, according to all that Elohim commanded him, so did he' ᴾ189. 'Particularly noticeable,' says Prof Driver[b], 'is an otherwise uncommon form of expression, producing a peculiar rhythm, by which a statement is first made in general terms, and then partly repeated, for the purpose of receiving closer limitation or definition[c].' Especially significant is the love of the writer for fixed numerical conceptions which are often worked with simple artifice into his narrative. Thus the height of the ark is reckoned at 30 cubits Gen 6¹⁵; the waters rise 15 cubits above the highest mountain-summits 7²⁰; the ark, apparently half-submerged, rests on the peak of Ararat[d]. In the patriarchal narratives the interests of place are subordinated to those of time, and the age of the hero at each main event

[a] Thus cp the use of the migration-formula Gen 12⁵ 31¹⁸ 36⁶ 46⁶; or the Machpelah description Gen 23¹⁹ 25⁹ 49³⁰ 50¹³.
[b] *LOT*⁶ 130.
[c] Gen 1²⁷ 6¹⁴ 8⁵ 9⁵ 23¹¹ 49²⁹ᵇ⁻³⁰ Ex 12⁴ ⁸ 16¹⁶ ³⁵ 25² ¹¹ ¹⁸. 26¹ Lev 25²² Num 2² 18¹⁸ 36¹¹. &c.
[d] Cp the forty days of the journey of the spies, Num 14³⁴, and the forty years of wandering. For another curious example in making up the traditional seventy who went down into Egypt see Gen 46⁸ᴺ*.

is carefully noted (e g Gen 12^4 $16^{3\ 16}$ $17^{1\ 17\ 25}$ &c). This fondness for detail gives rise, indeed, in the accounts of the Mosaic age to unexpected difficulties. The dimensions of the Dwelling have their own significance[a], but they are too small to accommodate the Congregation which is conceived on a totally different scale[b]. The growth of some of the tribes involves a rate of multiplication which the author evidently did not work out to its consequences in his own mind[c]; and a comparison of the figures in the second census Num 26 with those of the first 1 shows that large excess in some cases is artificially balanced by decline in others, while yet others under precisely similar conditions maintain a stationary position[d]. It was observed by Gutschmid and Noldeke[e] that the period from the Creation to the Exodus amounted to 2666 years, two-thirds of a round number of 100 generations of 40 years each. But this calculation rests on the present Masoretic text, and if the Samaritan numbers be preferred (cp **2**a p 122) as the more original, it only implies that in the later handling a new systematic arrangement was introduced[f].

3. Evidence has been already offered to show that **P** represents a more advanced stage of ritual organization and hierarchical order than **D**[g]. Nor is this conclusion impaired by a comparison of Lev 11 with Deut 14. Even if the regulations concerning clean and unclean animals in **D** were decidedly of a later type than those in the Levitical *torah*, no satisfactory inference could be drawn from this single case as to the relative ages of the two great collections. It would still be possible to regard the main principles of **D** as prior to those of **P** which had, in this particular instance, preserved an earlier rule. In reality, however, the comparison points to the opposite view (see Deut $14^{4\text{N}}$), and the general presumption already established is not invalidated.

(a) Is there, then, any evidence to show by what steps the conceptions of **D** were carried forward into more fully developed forms? The testimony of a whole generation of scholarship finds a link of the utmost importance in the writings of Ezekiel. The Deuteronomic legislation was designed for a people whose election by Yahweh had made them 'holy' Deut 7^6; it laid down the conduct which such a relation required; it described the joyous service which a dedicated nation could render to its heavenly Lord. But the political catastrophe which brought the monarchy of Judah to an end, might be regarded from one point of view as injuring if not destroying the force and closeness of this hallowed tie. In the language of Ezekiel, when Israel went into captivity and the nations around declared that Yahweh was impotent to save his own, his holy name was 'profaned' Ezek 36^{20}, and a fresh demonstration of his Deity was needed ^{23}. This would be effected by the restoration of the scattered captives, their purification from their ancient sins, the gift of a new heart, and the bestowal of power through the spirit to walk in the statutes and judgements of Yahweh. So should they dwell in the land which he gave to their fathers; they should be his people, and he would be their God 36^{24-28}. For an Israel thus regenerated Ezekiel provides a scheme of religious life, in the shape of a description of the sanctuary and its worship designed to portray the service of the future 40-48. It opens with an elaborate account of a new temple set on the sacred hill. The 'law of the house' is expounded with much detail $40-43^{12}$, and the prophet then announces the ordinances of the altar. These are followed in their turn by regulations for the priesthood and the appropriate sacrifices, and a scheme of cultus is thus displayed by which the people, once more consecrated,

[a] Cp below 3ϵ.   [b] Colenso, *Pentateuch* 1 31
[c] Thus Kurtz and Colenso (*ibid* 84) showed that the number of boys in every family must have been about forty-two, and they were from the same mother. Dan's male descendants in the fourth generation through his son Hushim amount to 62,700 Num 2^{26} cp *ibid* 107.
[d] Cp Noldeke, *Untersuchungen* 117   [e] Ib 111.
[f] Cp Dillmann. *Genesis* 1 221   [g] Cp chap IX 2-3.

shall be preserved from further temptation to unfaithfulness and shall secure the presence of Yahweh in their midst for ever.

(β) When this scheme is examined, it is found to stand in very interesting and remarkable relations on the one hand with D and on the other with P. To the Israel of the future, living in the spirit, it is unnecessary to address warnings against idolatry. The impassioned exhortations of Deuteronomy are reiterated no more. There are no longer any other sanctuaries in view but the temple on the holy mount: the principle of the centralization of the worship of Israel is assumed. But this worship is still based essentially on sacrifice, and the ritual of the altar acquires a prominence which was not assigned to it in D. In demanding the abolition of the local shrines the Deuteronomic legislators had found it needful to make provision for the disestablished Levitical priests. They did so by stipulating that any Levite might come up to Jerusalem and claim the right to minister at the altar and share in its dues Deut 18⁷·. This arrangement was frustrated by the Temple-guild, but it is clear that D recognized no clerical distinctions, and conceded the same functions to all. Ezekiel, however, announces for the future a division of the sacred tribe into two orders, one of which shall minister to Yahweh and the other not. This partition is expressly grounded on their past conduct; and those who have been unfaithful suffer the penal deprivation of the privilege which they have hitherto enjoyed. Some of the menial duties of the Temple had been laid on uncircumcised heathen who had been employed within the precincts of the sacred house, and allowed to officiate in its services Ezek 44⁷·. 'Ye have broken my covenant ^{a},' cries the indignant prophet in the name of Yahweh, 'ye have set them as keepers of my charge in my sanctuary ^{b}.' The first requisite for the new worship, therefore, is the strict exclusion of all aliens, and the next is the withdrawal from the guilty Levites of the priestly functions which they had abused. They are to be confined henceforth to the inferior duties; they must keep the gates, slay the victims, cook the sacrificial food, as the servants of the people who bring their offerings: but they may no longer approach Yahweh.

44¹³ And they shall not come near unto me, to execute the office of priest unto me, nor to come near to any of my holy things, unto the things that are most holy but they shall bear their shame, and their abominations which they have committed.

For one group of Levitical priests, however, the sons of Zadok, a different lot is provided. They are exempted from the doom of exclusion pronounced upon the rest. As the reward of faithfulness they will retain the right to minister to Yahweh, and make the sacred offerings 44¹⁵, duties involving access to the altar, admission to the actual sanctuary, and approach to the shew-bread table 41²² :—

44¹⁵ But the priests the Levites, the sons of Zadok, that kept the charge of my sanctuary when the children of Israel went astray from me, they shall come near to me to minister unto me ; and they shall stand before me to offer unto me the fat and the blood, saith the Lord Yahweh ¹⁶ they shall enter into my sanctuary, and they shall come near to my table, to minister unto me, and they shall keep my charge

It is not necessary to inquire whether Ezekiel here correctly apportions the merit or the blame. The Levites who went far from Yahweh when Israel erred ¹⁰ ^{c}, were the priests who had once served at the local sanctuaries. To these Ezekiel metes out a punishment which the Deuteronomic code never contemplated: they are to be deprived of the rights which they had perverted to disloyal ends, and forbidden again to minister to the Deity whose service they had corrupted. They may still have a place in his house, but it is a place of degradation not of privilege. It is otherwise

^{a} So 𝔊 𝔖 𝔏, Ewald, Wellhausen, Smend, Cornill, Bertholet, &c, cp Davidson *in loc.*
^{b} Amended text after 𝔊, cp Smend, Cornill, Bertholet.
^{c} Cornill strikes out the words 'which went astray from me.' Smend and Bertholet refer them to the Levites, which Davidson also admits as possible cp 48¹¹

in the Priestly Code, where the choice of the tribe of Levi and its elevation to the sanctuary-duties are throughout regarded as the gracious election of Yahweh. Ezekiel is apparently ignorant that any distinction in the sanctuary-duties had ever been made before. He proposes it for the first time. Had it been of Mosaic origin and established through centuries of use, his words would have had no meaning, for he would have proposed to punish the guilty Levites by depriving them of the right to exercise functions already forbidden under pain of death. The inference can by no means be avoided that Ezekiel, though a priest of the temple, was unacquainted with the Levitical law.

(γ) Other noteworthy facts point to a similar conclusion. The deviations of Ezekiel from the Mosaic rules long ago excited the surprise of the Rabbis. At the head of the priestly order stands 'the priest' $45^{19\,a}$; he is not indeed designated 'high priest,' cp Lev 21^{10} 2 Kings 22^4, but he is the chief officer of the guild. No special vestments are ordained for him; and the priestly attire described in Ezek 44^{17}. seems unrelated to the garments named in Ex $28^{40.\,b}$. 'The priest' of Ezekiel is only *primus inter pares*; he is not the symbol and embodiment of the consecration of the whole people, bearing over his brow the motto 'Holiness unto Yahweh' Ex 28^{36}. In the calendar of the festivals in which he must officiate, a singular divergence is presented. Ezekiel ordains two annual ceremonies of atonement, one at the opening of the first month, the other six months later, $45^{18-20\,c}$. In each case a young bullock is offered for a sin offering. But P is satisfied with but one day, the tenth of the seventh month instead of the first, Lev 16. In the Levitical law the ceremonies of this day gather round them the most solemn meaning; and the prescribed ritual is far more complicated. Ezekiel requires only one bullock as a sin offering for all who have erred. P specifies the bullock as the sin offering for the high-priest alone, and for the people two goats must be provided. The blood of Ezekiel's solitary victim is sprinkled on the temple doorposts but is not taken inside: but in the Dwelling the blood was to be carried into the inmost shrine, and the ceremony of aspersion performed over the 'covering' on the ark Lev 16^{14}. Such differences as these point to growing elaboration of ceremonial, and they may be traced in other cases also. Thus in Ezek 46^6. and Num 28^{11}. the following sacrifices are demanded at new moons:—

Ezek	*Num*
1 young bullock.	2 young bullocks
1 ram.	1 ram.
6 lambs	7 lambs
1 ephah for the bullock.	$\frac{3}{10}$ fine flour mingled with oil for each bullock.
1 ephah for the ram.	$\frac{2}{10}$ for the ram.
'for the lambs according as he is able'	$\frac{1}{10}$ for each lamb.
1 hin of oil to an ephah	$\frac{1}{2}$ hin of wine for each bullock.
	$\frac{1}{3}$ for the ram
	$\frac{1}{4}$ for each lamb.
	1 he-goat for a sin-offering.

These discrepancies can hardly be regarded as due to prophetic correction on the part of Ezekiel. They imply differences of usage, and it is natural to regard the simpler as the earlier. The Rabbis, indeed, were of another mind. Some proposed to remove the offending book from the Canon: others denied its authenticity and attributed it to the 'Men of the Great Synagogue': while after the fall of the Temple Eleazar ben Hananiah, belonging to the strictest Shammaitic school, was supposed, after expending 300 measures of oil in protracted vigils, to have succeeded in reconciling the two

---

[a] Cp 2 Kings 11^{15} 16^{11} Jer 21^1 29^{21}.

[b] The words 'linen' and 'tires' do not represent the same $\mathfrak{H}$ as in Ex 28^{40}. The prohibition of wool ^{17} implies that it had been sometimes used

[c] The reading of $\mathfrak{G}$ in RV^m is now generally accepted

authorities. But no solution was permanently satisfactory, and the synagogue left the contradictions to be harmonized 'when Elijah shall come ^{a}.'

(δ) Prominent among the institutions of P is the 'Dwelling.' Like the new temple of Ezekiel it has for its function to provide a place where Yahweh may reside in the midst of his people. To Ezekiel came the divine promise ^{b} :—

37^{26} And I will make a covenant of peace with them an everlasting covenant shall it be with them and I . . . will set my sanctuary among them for evermore. ^{27} And my dwelling shall be with them ^{c}, and I will be their God, and they shall be my people

With a similar aim is the Dwelling to be constructed :—

Ex 25^8 And let them make me a sanctuary; that I may dwell among them. . . . 29^{45} And I will dwell among the children of Israel, and will be their God (cp Ex 6^7).

The actual sacred house of Ezekiel stands in a court one hundred cubits square, facing the east. Within the porch is the holy place, containing only a wooden table 41^{22} 44^{16} for the shew-bread: a door led into the holy of holies in the rear, a chamber twenty cubits square. The returning exiles will not occupy their ancient inheritances, they will divide the land by lot. Among the tribes the priests will have no possession 44^{28}: but two large tracts of land of equal area immediately adjoining the sanctuary are to be set apart for the priests and the Levites, not apparently for tillage and maintenance but to preserve the holiness of the Temple. Similar in general arrangement is the structure of the Levitical Dwelling. The camp is so pitched that it can always look to the east. The court, the holy place, and the holy of holies, correspond to grade above grade in sanctity. This was the plan also of Solomon's Temple; and that there was a relation between them may be inferred from the fact that the lineal dimensions of the Dwelling in the desert were just half those of the House in Jerusalem ^{d}. This relation may be illustrated in other ways. The shrine in the Temple contained two large cherubim made of olive wood with outspread wings which protected the ark 1 Kings 6$^{23-27}$ 8^6. Such figures were unsuitable to a portable tent: in the Dwelling they are accordingly represented as diminished in size, but of gold instead of wood, affixed to the 'covering' laid upon the ark Ex 25$^{18-22}$ ^{e}. Cherubim likewise were carved upon the Temple walls: in the Dwelling they are wrought into the hangings which line the sides. The great brazen altar in the Temple-court 1 Kings 8^{64} 9^{25} is represented by an altar adapted to the travelling sanctuary. It is of no solid metal, but of wood overlaid with bronze Ex 27$^{1-8}$ which, however, when heated, must soon have charred the acacia planks beneath ^{f}. A great variety of considerations thus combine to affect the historical character of the Levitical Dwelling, which a long line of critics has challenged since the eighteenth century. The circumstances of the wanderings could not have been favourable to the production of such a structure, in the year following the Exodus. Even in Solomon's day, after centuries of more settled life, artists in metal could not be found in Israel, and it was necessary to seek them in Phenicia. The incompatibility of the delineation of E's tent of Meeting outside the camp with P's Dwelling in its centre has been already displayed, p 30; and a similar incompatibility exists between the earthen altar, reared where it might be needed Ex 20^{24}, and the plated altar of acacia-wood carried on the shoulders of Levites from encampment to encampment. Tradition is almost entirely silent: and its silence is only broken by uncertain and

^{a} Cp Kalisch, *Levit* ii 269; Derenbourg, *Hist* 255. ^{b} Cp Cornill's text and the commentaries
^{c} Or 'over them,' ie in the ideal sense, cp 'dove-like, sat'st brooding o'er the vast abyss.'
^{d} Cp Ex 26^{15}.. and 1 Kings 6$^{17\ 20}$.
^{e} The only reference to this 'covering' outside P is found in 1 Chron 28^{11}, cp ^{P}47.
^{f} The golden incense-altar in Ex 30^1.. seems to be supplemental (note *in loc*). The temple of Solomon probably had but one altar, like that of Ezekiel, cp Stade, *ZATW* iii 146 168, Benzinger, *Hebr Arch* 401; Nowack, *Hebr Arch* ii 40

jarring tones. It is said indeed Josh 18¹ that the Levitical sanctuary was erected in Shiloh. But the Judges-book contains no reference to it (at 'the house of God in Shiloh' 18³¹). The allusion in 1 Sam 2²²ᵇ is of very late origin ᵃ. When the ark is brought by David to Jerusalem 2 Sam 6, it is placed in a tent pitched for it ¹⁷, but the Dwelling-place is ignored ᵇ. Only in 2 Sam 7⁶ does the word occur in a passage which can hardly be correct as it stands, Klostermann and Budde proposing to read after 1 Chron 17⁵ 'from tent to tent, and from dwelling to dwelling.' That the Levitical arrangements ascribed to the dedication of the Temple 1 Kings 8¹ᐧᐧ were not part of the original text, has been already shown (chap IX ii 1β p 82). Not till the days of the Chronicler, however, was it found necessary actually to account for the Levitical sanctuary. Then it is located at Gibeon 1 Chron 21²⁹ 2 Chron 1³⁻⁶, in spite of the frank recognition of the editors of 1 Kings 3²⁻⁴ that Gibeon was only the seat of one of the high places which D had declared to be unlawful. The story of the Dwelling-place at Gibeon was thus unknown to the compilers of Kings: and it first enters the sacred tradition in the interval between Kings and Chronicles. Its relations to the temple of Solomon and to the holy house of Ezekiel are thus explained. Moses, like Ezekiel, was believed to have seen the pattern on the mount Ezek 40⁴ Ex 25⁹: and the Dwelling in the camp is the place where Yahweh's sacramental presence hallows his people. One of the sublimest passages in Hebrew prophecy Ezek 43¹⁻⁶ describes the return of the glory of Yahweh from the east to occupy the sanctuary ('and the glory of Yahweh filled the house'). A similar manifestation had consecrated Solomon's temple, when 'the glory of Yahweh filled the house of Yahweh' 1 Kings 8¹¹. Alone among the Hexateuchal documents does P describe the 'glory' as the symbol of Yahweh's advent. When the sacred tent was finished and the court reared up around it, 'the glory of Yahweh filled the Dwelling' Ex 40³⁴ᐧᐧ.

(ε) It is observed by Dillmann that P casts no prophetic glances into a Messianic future ᶜ; but the remark is only true with qualifications. The revelation of El Shaddai to Abraham announces the establishment of an 'everlasting covenant' with Abraham and his posterity to be God unto them Gen 17⁷ᐧᐧ. This phrase had acquired a peculiar significance, as it was used in later prophecy. It had once expressed the close relation in which Yahweh and Israel were knit together at Horeb Deut 26¹⁷ cp Jer 7²³. But it came to sum up the faith and hope of the future Jer 30²² (where 𝔊, however, omits it). The union which it denoted would usher in the great restoration Ezek 36²⁸; it would mark the presence of Yahweh's Dwelling among the exiles in the restoration 37²⁷; it would ensure the replenishing of Jerusalem with an abundant population Zech 8⁸. Hence its appearance in the scheme of P carries with it the implications of the ideal future. In Abraham's day that future is, indeed, remote. But it draws nearer and nearer. When Elohim declares himself to Moses to be Yahweh Ex 6³ᐧᐧ, he promises by his new name to take Israel to him for a people, and to be to them a God; and this promise is realized through the Dwelling at Sinai 29⁴⁵. According to P's conceptions, therefore, the type of Israel's holiness for which prophets had yearned, was actually established in the past. The theocratic institutions are depicted, by an act of imaginative faith, as founded in the early history of the nation. But they are designed to serve as the rule of present practice. The blessings and graces of which they were the vehicle in elder time, will stream forth again on the people which lives by their law. In other words, by dutiful obedience the 'church-nation' may enter at once into the religious communion with its God in which prophecy had discerned the purpose of its election and the goal of its history. Using the word

---

ᵃ Cp Chap IX ii 1a p 80. ᵇ The description in ² has probably been enlarged. ᶜ *NDJ* 653

'Messianic' in its widest sense, it may be said that for **P** the Messianic future has arrived, and Israel is bidden to avail itself of its advent[a].

4. The conclusion suggested by the foregoing argument is supported by numerous indications which converge upon a common result.

(a) It has been already shown that some of the allusions to Levitical institutions in pre-exilian history are later additions to the text (1 Sam 22^b cp chap IX ii 1a; 1 Kings 8^{1-5}, *ibid* 1β). In the account of the dedication of Solomon's temple, the king's prayer betrays no acquaintance with the language of **P**, while the Deuteronomic influence is everywhere apparent. The sacrifices include peace offerings on a colossal scale, the burnt offering and the meal offering 1 Kings 8^{63}. But one class is conspicuous by its omission, the sin offering, which, according to **P**'s record, constituted the first sacrifice ever performed in the history of Israel Lev 8^{14}. cp 9^2. Ezekiel afterwards prescribed for the temple of the future a seven-days' atonement at the consecration of the altar 43^{18-27}. A corresponding ceremony is enjoined by **P** for the purification of the altar in the Dwelling Ex 29^{37} Lev 8. Had this ritual been already known in Solomon's day, it could not possibly have been ignored. The description of the dedication-feast supplies further evidence that the ordinances of **P** were not then in force. It coincided with the great autumn festival 1 Kings $8^{2\ 65}$. The parallel narrative in Chronicles is here very suggestive:—

1 *Kings* 8	2 *Chron* 7
^{65} So Solomon held the feast at that time, and all Israel with him, a great congregation, from the entering in of Hamath unto the brook of Egypt, before Yahweh our God, seven days and seven days, even fourteen days ^{66} On the eighth day he sent the people away, and they blessed the king, and went unto their tents joyful and glad of heart for all the goodness that Yahweh had shewed unto David his servant, and to Israel his people.	^{8} So Solomon held the feast at that time seven-days, and all Israel with him, a very great congregation, from the entering in of Hamath unto the brook of Egypt. ^{9} And on the eighth day they held a solemn assembly for they kept the dedication of the altar seven days, and the feast seven days ^{10} And on the three and twentieth day of the seventh month he sent the people away unto their tents, joyful and glad of heart for the goodness that Yahweh had shewed unto David, and to Solomon, and to Israel his people.

The statement in 1 Kings 8^{66} that on the eighth day the people were dismissed is in obvious conflict both with ^{65}, which reckons the duration of the combined festival at fourteen days, and with 2 Chron 7^9, which fixes a 'solemn assembly' (**M** 'closing festival') on the eighth day. Chronicles follows the rule of the Levitical calendar, according to which Lev 23^{34-36} the autumn feast of Booths began on the fifteenth of the seventh month, lasted seven days, thus extending to the twenty-first, and concluded on the twenty-second with a 'holy convocation' described as a 'solemn assembly': the people are accordingly dismissed on the twenty-third. But Chronicles recognizes an altar-dedication lasting seven days, and running synchronously with the seven days of the feast. The Levitical annotator of Kings has accordingly added to 1 Kings 8^{65} the words 'and seven days,' but in spite of ^{66} he has regarded the two periods as successive, 'even fourteen days.' The omission of the words in $\mathfrak{G}^{B^3}$ confirms the belief that they did not belong to the original text, which is then consistent with itself and harmonious with Deut 16^{15} where the autumn feast lasts only seven days. Once more, therefore, the evidence points to the appearance of the Levitical Law between the compilation of Kings and Chronicles (cp *ante* 3δ p 130, and chap IX ii 1β p 82). It is congruous with this result that Jeremiah should still recognize lay rights of sacrifice, at least in the person of the prince $30^{21\ b}$, and that in 33^{18-22} ($\mathfrak{G}$ omits $^{14-26}$) the Deuteronomic view of the Levitical priesthood should

---
[a] Cp Stade, *Gesch* ii 142 ff, Holzinger, *Einleit* 389.
[b] Stade, Smend, and Cornill all regard 30–31 as exilian or even later But Kuenen accepts 30 as pre-Babylonian, and Giesebrecht allows that at least the nucleus of 30^{18-21} is Jeremiah.

be adopted as the rule for the future. The prophetic promise Is 66^{21} that some of the restored captives shall be admitted to the priesthood ('for priests for Levites') is variously understood according to the reading which is preferred. Are we, with 𝔊 and *RV*, to understand 'priests and Levites' as separate orders; or with Dillmann and Konig to treat 'for Levites' as an interpolation or modifying gloss; or with Kuenen, Duhm, and Cheyne to read 'for Levite priests[a]'? Neither of the two latter suggestions carries the passage beyond the range of **D**.

(β) The theological conceptions of **P** are in many respects characteristically divergent from those of **J** and **E**. It is generally recognized, for example, that his descriptions of the action of Deity are far less anthropomorphic. The method of creation needs no delineation; it suffices for Elohim to speak, and his word immediately realizes itself. Mankind are, indeed, made in his 'image' Gen 1^{27}; and Elohim rests upon the seventh day 2^2. In the descriptions of his intercourse with the patriarchs some physical implications were inevitable. But they are reduced to the lowest practicable amount: the divine commands are conveyed to Noah by speech 6^{13} 8^{15} 9^1. To Abraham and Jacob Elohim does, indeed, 'appear,' but the only allusion to his form is that contained in the close of the interview by his ascension 17^{22} 35^{13}. The language of **JE** according to which Yahweh 'repents' $^{JE}20$, or his 'nostril grows hot' $^{JE}233$, or Moses 'strokes his face' Ex 32^{11}, or the worshipper, visiting the sanctuary, 'sees his face' $^{JE}203$, is carefully avoided. Allusions to the divine wrath cannot, indeed, be suppressed, but the formula 'that there be no wrath' (and kindred expressions) $^P178$, veils its source. For the nation in the wilderness the manifestation of Yahweh is effected by his 'glory' $^P79$. This 'dwells' upon Mount Sinai Ex 24^{16}, and fills the Dwelling when it is first reared 40^{34}, where it is connected with **E**'s older tradition of the cloud. But the cloud as conceived by **P** does not 'come down' and stand at the Tent-door; still less does it speak. It covers the Dwelling, and 'dwells' over it 40^{34}. Num $9^{15..}$, having the aspect of fire by night. It is a permanent symbol of Yahweh's presence, not its occasional manifestation. When the camp is to be broken up, it is 'made to ascend' ^{17} (the counterpart of Yahweh's descent $^{JE}19$) $^P159$, much as the 'glory' was 'made to ascend' Ezek 9^3, in preparation for its departure from the polluted temple cp Ezek 11^{23}. The actual nature of the 'glory' is nowhere defined, but its 'appearance' is pictured like fire, for **P**, like Ezekiel, refrains from identifying Yahweh with any physical element, and is satisfied with reserved comparisons[b]. The word 'likeness' Gen 1^{26} $5^{1\,3*}$ is also of special frequency in Ezekiel (sixteen times), and Ezekiel further associates the mysterious forms which bear the holy Presence with a 'firmament' $1^{22.\,25}$ cp $^P70$. But though the communion of Deity with his people is thus freed as far as possible from the associations of human personality, it is always direct. No mediating agencies are employed; no dream or vision brings guidance or warning; no angel calls from heaven or walks the earth. The conceptions of prophecy (as well as its declaratory formula 'thus saith Yahweh' $^{JE}87$) are absent. In the wilderness Yahweh addresses Moses by a voice from between the cherubim over the ark Ex 25^{22} Num 7^{89}, but no 'spirit' is ever lifted off him to be distributed upon chosen elders Num $11^{17\,25}$. A rather different doctrine of the 'spirit' seems, indeed, to be contained in **P**. It is not specially named as the source of human life Gen 6^3, but on the other hand it broods in the beginning over the primaeval waters. Nor is it connected with prophetic power, though it is the medium of the gift of wisdom and understanding and knowledge for the artist to whom is entrusted the preparation of the Dwelling Ex 35^{31}. Lastly it may be noted that if the *tolᵉdhoth* sections do not describe the origin of evil and the entry of sin and suffering, they are not indifferent

---

[a] Cp Cheyne, *Introd to Isaiah* 377–379
[b] Thus, for the word 'appearance' cp Ex 24^{17} Num 9^{16} with Ezek $1^{5\,13.\,16\,20-28}$ $8^{2\,4}$ $10^{1\,9}$. 40^3 43^3 &c.

to them, rather does the method of Gen 5 presuppose them, and 6¹³ records their consequences. In the patriarchal narratives the writer admits no stories unfavourable to the characters of his heroes; but the picture of life under the Law has its own lights and shadows of holiness and sin. Here for the first time in sacred legislation, as in Ezekiel for the first time in prophecy, do we meet with the conceptions of the sin offering and of atonement (ᴾ118ᶠʲ 25). Here also, and here alone, are ceremonial offences divided into two classes, those that are committed 'unwittingly ᵃ,' and those that are wrought consciously 'with a high hand' Num 15²⁴⁻³¹. Nowhere else is the great ritual of national atonement enforced Lev 16ᵇ; and no other Old Testament writer recognizes the theocratic penalty by which an erring soul is 'cut off from his people' ᴾ50.

(γ) A great literary and legal collection like **P**, which is distinguished by so many marks of independence both in history and institutions, may be expected to manifest peculiar characteristics in language and phraseology. An inspection of the table of its words and formulae shows that these peculiarities are twofold. They affect the narratives in comparison with **JE**, and the laws in comparison with **D**. Moreover in the latter case they are not exclusively due to differences of subject matter, as in the descriptions of special ritual acts; they pervade the entire body of legislation, as an examination (for example) of the two calendars of the feasts Lev 23 and Deut 16 abundantly proves. It is no doubt true that much of the sacrificial terminology may be of high antiquity ᶜ. The instinct of established priesthoods is always in favour of perpetuating the ancient language endeared by traditional usage. It may be assumed, therefore, that the phraseology of **P** was gradually formed on the basis of elements long current in the sacerdotal communities. But this process implies the continuous enrichment of the vocabulary by the introduction of fresh expressions. And from the literary side this process can be partially traced by comparing the characteristic turns of **P** with those of other portions of Hebrew literature which can be definitely dated. Stress has been already laid on the affinities of thought between **P** and Ezekiel. Such affinities carry with them many resemblances of language; and these are not confined to parallels in ritual or ceremonial terms, they have a wide range through descriptive relations of many kinds ᵈ. Under the hypothesis of a united Pentateuch in Ezekiel's day, how are these coincidences to be explained? Can it be supposed that Ezekiel sifted out the vocabulary of a particular document, and absorbed it into his own style, leaving the phraseology of other portions (such as **D**) unassimilated? There are some other expressions which do not find place in his prophecies but appear in literature later still ᵉ. The most natural explanation of such phenomena is that the style and usage of **P** were formed under influences common to Ezekiel and his successors. Thus, for example, a peculiar expression for the number 'eleven ᶠ' recurs in **P**, which first enters Hebrew literature in the days of Jeremiah and Ezekiel, and is found after the exile in Zechariah and Chronicles. With this may be cited another fact of similar significance. In **P** the months of the year are never cited by their names, but by their numbers ᵍ. The first legislation apparently sets the beginning of the year in the autumn, after the feast of ingathering Ex 23¹⁶ 34²² ʰ. This reckoning still prevailed in the days of Josiah, who celebrated the passover in the eighteenth year of his reign 2 Kings 23²³ cp 22³ according to the new Deuteronomic principles, after the reformation had been accomplished. This would have been impossible had the calendar which

---

ᵃ Outside **P** only in Eccles 5⁶ 10⁵ cp ᴾ168.
ᵇ With other passages in **P** depending on it   On the silence of **D** cp chap VIII § 5 p 54.
ᶜ Cp Driver, *LOT*⁶ 156.
ᵈ Thus illustrations may be found in the following numbers, ᴾ28 42 43 46 55ᶜ 56ᵇ 63 70 80 91 96 99 104 109 110 118ᵇ 138 139 142 143 145 153ᵇ 157 158 164 179ᵇ
ᵉ Cp ᴾ51 77 82 93 155   ᶠ Cp ᴾ57   ᵍ Cp ᴾ183
ʰ Wellhausen, *Proleg* 108, Benzinger, *Hebr Archaol* 199

placed the feast on the fifteenth of the first month been then in use. D still employs the ancient name for the spring month, Abib (i e 'ear-month') Deut 16¹. Only three other names survive, Ziv 1 Kings 6¹, Ethanim 8², Bul 6³⁸. In the books of Jeremiah and Ezekiel, however, a new method of reference appears, by which the months are cited in their numerical order[a], beginning no longer in the autumn but the spring. In the Persian age this usage is established Hagg 1¹ ¹⁵ 2¹ ¹⁰ Zech 1¹ ⁷ 7¹ ⁵ (where the new names, derived from Babylonia, are probably editorial additions[b]). The definite institution of the new year in the spring Ex 12² thus seems to depend on that form of Mesopotamian calendar which opened after the vernal equinox with the month Nisan, and the view which connects P with the priestly schools in Babylonia after the age of Ezekiel thus receives additional support[c].

(δ) It has been already argued that the general distribution of the Pentateuch into its constituent documents rests on a number of converging lines of evidence which all point to a common conclusion. The proof of the origin and date of any single document in the same manner rests on a variety of indications which all demand consideration, and the most probable hypothesis is that which reconciles them most successfully. Thus, it is stated by Prof Sayce[d], on cuneiform evidence, that the mention of Gomer Gen 10². involves a later date than 680 B C. It would be unreasonable to assert that this single item fixed P not earlier than the seventh century, for it would be conceivable that the names of Gomer and his descendants had been inserted into an older document, as Prof Sayce suggests. But when this fact is taken into connexion with other circumstances, some more and others less prominent, it is found to fit appropriately into the general evidence above expounded. The same result is reached along a quite different line. It has been argued by Mr G B Gray[e] that several of the names contained in P, especially such forms as Ammishaddai, Zurishaddai, Shaddaiur, Pedahzur, are only artificial creations, which were never current in ordinary life at all. The systematic list of tribal princes and other enumerations do not represent the arrangements of the Mosaic age; and whatever may have been the sources from which some of them were derived, others appear to have been provided to complete the numbers. Of the twenty-nine names entirely peculiar to P, Mr Gray regards seventeen as probably post-exilic[f].

(ε) The general bearing of archaeological discovery on the theory of the composition of the Pentateuch is discussed by Prof Cheyne in chap XV; but it may be worth while to point out here some items in which distinguished cuneiform scholars have seen signs of dependence on the part of P on Babylonian data. That the numbers in Genesis seemingly fit into certain large chronological schemes has been already indicated (*ante* 2ε p 126). Following out various suggestions of system and adjustment, such as the apparent distribution of the period of the flood over a solar year[g], Oppert has endeavoured to show that P's view of the pre-diluvian and post-diluvian patriarchs is clearly based on certain broad divisions in early Chaldean mythic history[h]. His combinations certainly have a curiously artificial air, and some of them depend on the

---

[a] Thus Jer 39¹. 41¹ Ezek 1¹ 8¹ &c, and similarly the compiler of Kings 1 Kings 6¹ ³⁸ 8² 2 Kings 25¹ ⁸ ²⁷.

[b] Cp Nowack *in loc*. For the Babylonian origin of the names afterwards regularly used among the Jews, see Schrader, *Cuneif Inscr and the OT* ii 68–70

[c] On other indications, such as the use of אני 'I,' and דוליד 'beget,' cp König, *Einl in das AT* 229. The counter-argument of Hommel, *Ancient Hebrew Tradition* and *Expository Times* vol ix 235, has been met in the *Expository Times* vol ix 286 430 474, by Prof König.

[d] *Early History of the Hebrews* 131

[e] *Studies in Hebrew Proper Names* 190–211.

[f] Op cit 210   See further, in reply to Hommel, Mr Gray's essay in the *Expositor* (1897) vol vi 173

[g] Cp Dillmann, *Genesis* i 252

[h] 'Die Daten der Genesis,' in *Nachrichten von der Konigl Gesellsch der Wissenschaften zu Gottingen* (1877) p 201.

numbers in the Masoretic text which (as already stated) some modern investigators belonging to different critical schools think less original than those of the Samaritan. But the precision of the coincidences between the two schemes suggests something more than accidental resemblance, at whatever date the correspondences may have been introduced. Thus it is alleged that the Chaldean chronology assigned to the pre-human period 168 myriads of years. Now 168 is the number of hours in a week, and each hour of the creative week prefixed to the beginning of the history of mankind thus represents a myriad years. Between Adam and Noah the line of ten patriarchs is analogous to the ten prehistoric kings from Alorus to Xisuthrus (Hasisadra) under whom the flood took place; and the total duration of the patriarchs' lives compared with the monarchs' reigns is in the proportion of one Biblical week to one Chaldean 'soss' of months[a]. From the Flood to the birth of Abraham P again reckons ten patriarchs, 292 years; from the birth of Abraham to the death of Joseph, 361 years[b], making a total of 653 years. The Chaldean chronology placed after the flood a mythic cycle of 39,180 years, or 653 × 60, i e 653 sosses of years. Moreover, on astronomical grounds this cycle is divisible into two periods of 17,520 and 21,660 years respectively, or 292 × 60 and 361 × 60. The adherence of P to this scheme in which the longer space had to be filled only by four patriarchs, and the shorter by ten, explains (in Oppert's view) why the patriarchs between Noah and Abraham beget sons at so early an age compared with their successors, and why Shem and Eber live on (as the Rabbis said) to teach the little Jacob his letters. If Oppert's data be accepted[c], it may fairly be argued that the numerical relations which they imply are too precise to be explained out of independent versions of ancient tradition; they involve actual acquaintance with the contents of cuneiform records. A similar conclusion has been founded on the peculiar term *kopher* 'pitch' in Gen 6^{14}: it is the equivalent of the word *kuupr-i* in the Assyrian text[d]. Items such as these may be contrasted with the existence in ancient Israelite literature of terms like the 'deep' 1^2, belonging to the general stock of mythological conceptions derived from Babylonia[e]. Yet other features of P's narrative of the creation appear to show closer kinship with Mesopotamian sources; and if such relations should be definitely established, it would be most natural to seek occasion for them during the residence of the exiles and their descendants beyond the Euphrates, when fresh influences poured in upon the seers and thinkers of Israel[f].

5. The inquiry into the origin and antecedents of P may be pursued from the days of Ezekiel and the Captivity into the age of the Second Temple without discovering any definite traces of the Levitical Law.

(*a*) When the gloom and suffering which descended on Judah in 586 begin at last to clear away, and the voices of Haggai and Zechariah are heard in the first years of Darius summoning their countrymen to rebuild the sanctuary, there is still no proof that the usages of the Priestly Code were as yet established. The restoration of the

---

[a] The figures are worked out thus. From Adam to the Flood 1,656 years = 72 × 23 years. Now 23 solar years (reckoning in 5 intercalary days) = 8,400 days or 1,200 weeks · hence 1,656 years = 86,400 weeks. The Chaldean period was 432,000 years = 72 × 6,000 5 years or 60 months was reckoned as one 'soss' of months 6,000 years = 1,200 sosses of months 432,000 years = 72 × 1,200 sosses of months, or = 86,400 sosses of months, so that one Biblical week matches one soss of months.

[b] Cp Abraham, Isaac, and Jacob Gen 21^5 25^{26} 47^9, Joseph 41^{46-48} 45^5 $50^{22\ 26}$. These dates are partly derived from JE, which has in some cases replaced P in the final compilation; but their presence in P also may be inferred from 37^2 and from the sequel.

[c] They were criticized by Bertheau, *Jahrb fur Deutsche Theol* xxiii (1878) 657–682, who supplied other examples of numerical artifice in Gen 5 11. Cp Schrader, *Cuneif Inscr and the OT* 1 49

[d] Schrader, *COT* 1 48; Jensen, *Kosmologie der Babylonier* 374 l 62; Dillmann, *Gen* 1 270.

[e] Cp Gunkel, *Schöpfung und Chaos* 114 · cp 169 .

[f] Cp Jensen, *Kosmol* 306; Jastrow, *Rel of Bab and Ass* (1898) 451, 696. For the text of the cuneiform fragments, cp Friedr Delitzsch, *Das Babylonische Weltschopfungsepos* (Leipzig, 1896). Halévy, *Recherches Bibl* (1895) 1 49–52, while admitting the dependence of Gen 1–2^{4a} on cuneiform material, ascribes it to the age of Solomon Cp *Analysis* Gen 1^{1N}.

Temple is to be the work of Zerubbabel Zech 4^9; the ideal future is at hand, Yahweh has returned to Jerusalem and will dwell in its midst 1^{16} 2^{10}. 8^3. In the 'city of faithfulness' two powers will rule side by side, the priestly and the civil, represented by Joshua and Zerubbabel respectively[a], united in harmonious action. But **P** has no secular head. Unlike the Deuteronomic code which recognizes the monarchy, the Levitical code is silent on the political institutions of Israel. Ezekiel had contemplated a lay 'prince,' though he had rigorously curtailed his duties and privileges; but though the term appears in **P** in connexion with tribal organization $^{P}131$, there is no reference to any permanent civil authority. May not this be due to the fact that the community in Jerusalem possessed no national independence, and lived under a foreign rule? Other indications point to the conclusion that Levitical usage was not yet codified in the form in which it is now presented in **P**. Thus Haggai 2^{11-13} suggests that the priests should be consulted for 'teaching[b]' concerning the conditions under which the contagion of holiness or uncleanness was propagated. As in the days of the Deuteronomic code, it was still their duty to give decisions in doubtful cases. Such utterances are still based on priestly tradition, not on written law. The inquirer does not consult a book, but the living exponents of sacred custom cp Lev 5^{10} 9^{18} 10^{10} Num 15^{24} 29^{18}. Even yet later, in the days of Malachi[c], this function remains to the priest Mal 2^7; his lips guard knowledge, from his mouth do men seek 'teaching,' instruction, or revelation; and the abuse of this right exposes the guilty to the severest condemnation 2^{8}.

(β) It is no doubt true that the writings of Zechariah and Malachi show occasional points of linguistic contact with the vocabulary of **P**[d]. But these are by no means decisive of acquaintance with the existing Levitical law. Such affinities may be explained in various ways. It is evident from the book of Ezekiel that there was a considerable body of priestly usage in his day marked by its own terminology, and closely related to the sources from which much of the Priestly Code has been derived. There is no ground for surprise therefore that similar resemblances of language should be discovered at Jerusalem. But these resemblances are insufficient to countervail the evidence which the book of Malachi presents that **P** was not yet known as a rule of religious practice. For Malachi identifies the law of Moses 4^4 with the legislation in Horeb, the 'statutes and judgements' summed up by **D**. The priests are 'sons of Levi' 3^3, as though the right of altar-service still belonged (as in **D**) to the whole tribe cp 2^{4-8}. The worshippers of Yahweh shall be his 'peculiar treasure' 3^{17} cp Ex 19^5 Deut 7^6. In harmony with the view that Malachi has not before him the codified demands of **P**, it may be noted that he employs the term *minḥah* (which **P** uses in the restricted sense of meal offering) to cover the larger range of sacrificial victims $1^{10.13}$; while in 1^8 the verbs 'offer' and 'present' do not correspond to **P**'s technical phraseology. The reference to tithes and heave offerings $3^{8\ 10}$ may seem to go beyond Deut 12^{11}. 14^{23}..26^{12}, where tithes were to be eaten in festive meals at Jerusalem. The heave offering was assigned by Ezekiel to the priests 44^{30}: and in the covenant made under Nehemiah Neh 10^{38}, the Levites are instructed to bring the tithe of the tithe up to the temple treasury (𐤀 = 'storehouse' Mal 3^{10}) for the use of the priests, the priestly law only recording the endowment of the tribe of Levi with the tithes, without specifying how or where they should be paid Num 18^{21-24}[e]. The references of Malachi may thus

---

[a] On Zech 6^{9-15} cp G A Smith, *The Twelve Prophets* ii 308, Driver, *LOT*⁶ 346
[b] G A Smith, *The Twelve Prophets* ii 245 'ask of the priests a deliverance'
[c] On the date cp G A Smith, *The Twelve Prophets* ii 335-338, Driver, *LOT*⁶ 357.
[d] Thus Zech $2^{5\ 10}$ 3^7 6^{14} 7^{12} $8^{3\ 8}$ Mal $2^{10\ 12}$ 3^{14}.
[e] Neh 10^{37} implies that the Levites' tithes were collected from city to city According to Kosters' view of the priority of the covenant recited in Neh 10 before the promulgation of the law described in Neh 8, the 'ordinances' which the signatories 'made for themselves' ^{32} were not founded on the new code (which they preceded), but were based on usage to which it was thus proposed to give new and general force See below 6δ p 140.

belong to an intermediate stage of practice out of which the regulations of P finally emerged. A similar remark may be applied to the denunciation of the carelessness or greed which offered imperfect or unsound victims at the altar 1^8. It does not seem necessary to insist that this presupposes the prohibition of Lev $22^{20-25\,a}$; there is no linguistic point of contact, and there must have been some priestly rules about animals which could be rejected as unfit. Not yet have we discovered unmistakable indications of the existence of the Levitical Code.

6. The Priestly Law first enters clearly into the history of Israel under the combined leadership of Ezra and Nehemiah. The great Dutch scholar Kuenen was the earliest to recognize the importance of the narrative in Nehemiah's memoirs describing the promulgation of a book of sacred law ^{b}. The events which led to this decisive movement may be briefly summarized as follows :—

(*a*) In the year 458 B C, according to the received chronology ^{c}, Ezra arrived in Jerusalem at the head of a caravan of laymen, priests, Levites, and temple-servants. The expedition had started at the end of March or the beginning of April, and reached the holy city in August. They brought with them gifts for the temple, and royal letters to the Persian governors west of the Euphrates, for the promotion of the service of the sanctuary. Ezra had not, however, been long in the capital before he was informed that the 'holy seed' had violated the sacred law by intermarriage with alien wives. The discovery caused him the utmost distress. The community was threatened with all the dangers which had brought down the chastisements of the past, and the severest measures were needed to save it from sinking hopelessly into pollution. A national assembly was convoked in December; a commission was appointed, and the terrible inquisition house by house began. Three months were occupied by the investigation, and by the spring New Year 457 the lists of the guilty were complete. With the expulsion of the hapless women and their children Ezra $10^{7..}$, darkness and silence fall upon the scene. More than twelve years later, in December 445 ^{d}, Nehemiah receives news at Shushan of the desolation of Jerusalem. In the spring of the following year, 444 (or 445 Neh 2^1), he obtains leave from the king to go to Jerusalem and rebuild the walls. The narrative proceeds with breathless haste, recounting his arrival at Jerusalem, his midnight ride three days later to inspect the ruins, his summons to the priests and nobles to begin the work of reconstruction, and the triumphant conclusion of their labour in fifty-two days Neh 6^{15}. Meantime Ezra had taken advantage of Nehemiah's arrival to prepare for the measure which had probably been planned long before as the cause and object of his own journey. He was at least believed in a later age to have brought with him the law of his God in his hand ^{e}: why did he take no immediate steps to make it known? The question has received a twofold answer, founded on the circumstances of the time. The troubles which followed the expulsion of the foreign women involved Judah in serious difficulties with its neighbours, so that the attempts to produce a new code could meet with no success; and Ezra may himself have needed opportunity for the further adaptation of his legal enactments to the conditions of the community in Palestine. The new zeal awakened by the energy of Nehemiah brought

---

^{a} On the other hand cp Kuenen, *Hex* 181; Holzinger, *Einleit* 428

^{b} Cp Kuenen, *Religion of Israel* ii 226.

^{c} This date depends on Ezra 7^7.. On the views of van Hoonacker and Kosters see p 141 note ^{c} On the literary structure of Ezra–Nehemiah as a continuation of Chronicles, cp Driver, *LOT*^{6} 544, Ryle, *Ezra and Nehemiah* (Cambr Bible) xxvi–xxix. A fresh and highly suggestive presentation of Ezra's activity has just been offered by Prof Cheyne, *Jewish Religious Life after the Exile* (American Lectures) 11. The statements in the text are based on the view generally received.

^{d} So Kuenen, Stade, and Driver, 446, Wellhausen, Meyer, Bertheau-Ryssel, Ryle.

^{e} Ezr 7^{14}; how far this document is based on a genuine royal commission cannot be exactly determined. It is commonly regarded as having an actual historic foundation; but the language may be that of the compiler.

the favourable moment. On the old New Year's day, the first of the seventh month, immediately (it would seem) after the walls were completed, i e at the end of September 444, the people met in the great square before the water-gate Neh 8¹. A large wooden pulpit had been erected, and there from early morning till midday in the presence of Nehemiah, Ezra read to the assembly*a*, both men and women, out of the book of the law. The meeting was renewed the following day, and preparations were then made for the solemn observance of the feast of booths which was duly kept for eight days with joyous celebration unknown since the time of Joshua the son of Nun Neh 8¹³⁻¹⁸.

(β) What was the law-book which was thus promulgated? The analogy of the great meeting with the national assembly in the eighteenth year of Josiah is unmistakable; and naturally suggests that the law-book now promulgated stood in the same general relation to the age of Ezra as that which marked the Deuteronomic code in the seventh century. Among the incidents of the reformation under Josiah was the celebration of a passover on principles such as had been unknown in Israel during the whole period of its historic occupation of the country 2 Kings 23²²; they were the principles defined in the 'book of the covenant' Deut 16. That calendar also ordained the annual observance of the feast of booths for seven days without, however, fixing its date; the harvest festival arrived at its natural place in the agricultural year. But the 'ordinance' now promulgated placed the feast in the seventh month Neh 8¹⁴ and enjoined the preparation of booths out of branches and boughs ¹⁵ which should be occupied for seven days, till the proceedings closed with a solemn assembly on the eighth ¹⁸. These requirements are found only in the Priestly Code. In Lev 23³⁴ the feast is assigned to the seventh month; it is to last for seven days with a solemn assembly on the eighth ³⁶; and the worshipping people are to live in booths made of 'branches of palm and boughs of thick trees, and willows of the brook' ⁴⁰⁻⁴². The 'ordinance' belongs beyond question to **P**. It had been unobserved since Israel entered Canaan. But no reason for this neglect could be assigned, had this law been in the possession of the responsible leaders of the nation. It was not known to Solomon (cp *ante* 4*a* p 131). In the age of Ezra it is an obvious novelty, and is enforced for the first time. The inference seems to be inevitable that the legislation of which it is a part had never been promulgated before. And if it had not been published, and no clear trace can be found that it was privately known, does not the probability reach almost positive certainty that it had not been earlier made the basis of united action because in this form up to this age it did not exist?

(γ) But a further inquiry arises concerning the contents of Ezra's Law-book. Was it limited to **P**, or did it also include the other documents of our present Pentateuch, **JE** and **D**? The answer to this question is not perhaps so simple as it has sometimes been regarded. It depends to some extent on the view which may be formed of the significance of the covenant recorded in Neh 10. The celebration of 'booths' was followed by a solemn fast on the 24th of the month 9¹·, when the seed of Israel purged themselves of their national guilt by confessing their sins, and pledged themselves to fulfil certain definite religious demands. These demands appear to be enumerated in 10³⁰⁻³⁹, where the Chronicler introduces a document which has all the air of a direct extract from a contemporary source. The general phrases of ²⁹ are probably due to an editorial preface *b*, for if the signatories to the covenant had actually undertaken to

---

a Neh 8³. the rendering 'congregation' suggests the technical term ᴾ46, the word is, however, that used in **D** as well as **P** ᴰ20, ᴾ24, and denotes here not so much a religious fellowship or community as an actual meeting; in ¹⁷ it is employed somewhat differently, being equated by apposition with 'those that had returned' &c.

b For 'enter into a curse' cp Deut 29¹², 'walk in God's law,' 'observe and do,' 'commandments, statutes, and judgements,' show affinities with **D**. But the Chronicler was evidently well acquainted with Deuteronomy The use of Elohim in preference to Yahweh ('God's law,' 'servant of God') finds a parallel in the Chronicler's manner; as he constantly describes the temple as the 'house of Elohim,' e g 2 Chron 3³ 4¹¹ ¹⁹ &c where the parallels in Kings read 'Yahweh.'

observe all the commandments of Yahweh, it would have been needless to specify the details that follow. These comprise a number of engagements affecting the social and religious life of Israel. Marriages with aliens will be no longer tolerated: sabbath trading will be suppressed: the seventh-year remission will be enforced: and a variety of arrangements concerning the maintenance of the temple-services, and the payment of the priestly dues, will be carefully observed. On what do these several undertakings rest? The language of ^{30} cp 13^{25} approximates to that of Deut 7^3. cp Ex 34^{16}: **P** does not formally prohibit intermarriage with foreigners, though it may be argued that various provisions (e g Num 33^{51-56} Lev $18^{3\ 24..}\ 20^{23\ 26}$) practically exclude it even more absolutely than **D** itself, which allows marriage with captives in war 21^{10}.. The refusal to hold sabbath markets is an application of the general rules for the sanctification of the sabbath (*Laws* **9 b**), but finds no specific law on its behalf*a*: while the term 'holy day' doubtless points to recognized festivals but is not actually employed by **P** *b*. The promise to 'forgo the seventh year' cites the language of Ex 23^{11} ($\mathfrak{H}$ = 'let lie fallow'); and the 'exaction of every debt' rests on a technical expression in Deut 15^2. So far the evidence rather suggests a basis in **JED** than in **P**. In ^{32}, however, a poll-tax of the third of a shekel is adopted in terms akin to **P**'s phraseology; but with the peculiar difference that in Ex 30^{11-16} **P** fixes the contribution of every Israelite from the age of twenty at *half* a shekel *c*. The parallels of ^{33} with the Levitical arrangements are obvious; while the language of ^{34} has probably been supplemented editorially, as the law contains no definite prescriptions concerning the wood-supply, but only enjoins the maintenance of an ever-burning fire Lev 6^{12}.. The demand for first fruits of the ground ^{36} is emphasized in every legislative stage (cp *Laws* **8 c**), though not even Num 18^{12}. specifies 'the first fruits of all fruit of all manner of trees.' Firstlings in like manner ^{36} were claimed for Yahweh in each code (*Laws* **8 b**); while the first fruits of the 'dough' ^{37} are enjoined as a heave offering Num 15^{20}. cp Ezek 44^{30}, and the tithes of the ground, paid out of corn, wine, and oil $^{37\ 39}$ are specified both in Deut 14^{23} and Num 18^{21}.., the tithe of the tithes ^{38} being further ordained Num 18^{26-28}. Tithes of cattle, however, which are imposed in Lev 27^{30-32}, are here ignored, though the Chronicler himself recognizes them 2 Chron 31^6. It would thus seem probable that if the covenant is to be regarded as having a basis in written law, that law must have included the several codes of **JE, D,** and **P**, in which case it would be most natural to suppose that the documents were no longer separate, but were already united into something resembling our present Pentateuch. This view is not inconsistent with a recent date for the Priestly Code: it only assumes that the editorial combination of the various materials had already taken place *d*.

a The Sabbath laws are concerned chiefly with the prevention of labour and the enforcement of rest, rather than with the prohibition of trade
b In Lev 23 and Num 28-29 the 'holy convocations' are enumerated.
c On the difficulty that this is not enjoined as an annual contribution, see note *in loc.*
d Thus it is held by Wellhausen, *Isr und Jud Gesch*^{2} (1895) 176, as well as by Dillmann, *NDJ* 671 ff. With them may be named Ryle, *Ezra and Neh* (Cambr Bible) on Neh 10^{31} p 273, König, *Einleit* 241, and Addis, *Hex* 1 xciii and ii 189 On the other hand, the view adopted in the text has the support of Kuenen, Stade, Cornill, Holzinger, Wildeboer, Cheyne, Bennett, Kautzsch, *Literature of the OT* 118, and others, among whom must now be counted Piepenbring, *Hist du Peuple Israel* 559, and Schurer, *Gesch des Jud Volkes*^{3} ii 306 Those who regard Ezra's law-book as the whole Pentateuch support themselves chiefly on the terms of Nehemiah's covenant, but they are by no means in accord as to the place and circumstances of the union of **JED** with P, König supposing it to have been effected in Babylonia, and Wellhausen insisting that P must have been drawn up in sight of the temple Wellhausen, therefore, ascribes to Ezra a double task, (1) the compilation of the Priestly Code, and (2) the incorporation into it of the previous collection **JED** This was his occupation during the silent years from 458 to 444 The problem is complicated by the place of Joshua in the scheme, cp chap XVI 3δ and the *Introd to Josh*. Putting this difficulty for the present aside, it seems only needful to observe (in addition to the general considerations offered above) that the effect of the promulgation of the Priestly Code would be far more impressive if it were published alone, than if it were only part of an amalgam of familiar documents The attention of the people could be most easily concentrated on the new law, if it were offered them by itself, and they were not required to pick out the novelties as the reading proceeded

The likelihood that this was accomplished so early is differently estimated by different critics. According to the received view of the chronology an interval of fourteen years elapsed between Ezra's arrival and the covenant under Nehemiah: and it is suggested that this period would have amply sufficed to effect the amalgamation. Or it is even conceivable that the literary process might have been conducted still earlier by the Babylonian scribes, and that the law-book which Ezra brought with him was actually complete. On the other hand, evidence will be offered hereafter to show that the Priestly Code itself contains earlier and later elements; so that there is reason to regard it as a growth to which additions could still be made even after the time of Ezra (cp 7). Moreover it will appear that the task of redaction was by no means simple; it probably advanced only by successive stages, and needed the labours of more than one single editorial hand (cp chap XVI). These considerations are unfavourable to the view that Ezra's law-book consisted of **JEDP**. But there is a further circumstance to be taken into account. Is it likely that **P** would have been combined with the earlier codes until it had obtained general recognition? The Deuteronomic law was not enforced until the king with an assembly of the people had covenanted to observe it. It became the standard for the worship of the future by a solemn national act. May it not be conjectured that any fresh code could only become valid by a similar method of public adoption? In face of the traditional authority possessed by **D**, can it be supposed that a private group of scribes would have ventured to associate with it a new law which had as yet received no popular sanction? Does not the analogy of the two promulgations under Josiah and Nehemiah lead to the inference that the law-book made known by Ezra was as fresh as that which was brought to light by Hilkiah? And if so, how can it have included anything beyond the limits of **P**?

(δ) This argument, however, fails to explain the singular circumstance that Ezra's covenant appears to show dependence on mixed sources, **JED** as well as **P**. It may, however, be possible that it has been wrongly connected with the promulgation of the law. The document Neh 10^{30-39} really falls into two parts. In ^{30} three great objects are secured, (1) the suppression of foreign marriages, (2) the prohibition of sabbath trade, and (3) the relief of distressed Israelites. The second portion consists of 'ordinances' ($\mathfrak{H}$='commandments') which the signatories 'made to stand' (cp ^{p}141) upon themselves. They were, therefore, voluntary and self-imposed obligations, which there was as yet no law to enforce[a]. It has accordingly been argued with great skill by the late Prof Kosters[b], that the terms of the covenant really preceded instead of following the public acceptance of the Levitical law. The first three objects were entirely explained out of the circumstances of the time. How could the condition of things described in Neh 13^{23-25} have arisen after the solemn engagement of 10^{30}? Did not, on the other hand, the terms of 10^{30} express Nehemiah's effort to terminate the situation which appeared so intolerable 13^{25}? Similarly, the resolve to abstain from sabbath trading 10^{31} was the outcome and not the antecedent of the traffic in fruit and fish and other wares which Nehemiah so rigorously suppressed 13^{15-21}[c] cp Jer 17^{19-27}. And, once again, the provisions about the treatment both of land and of debtors in the seventh year Neh 10^{31b} find a base in the measures which Nehemiah found necessary for the protection of the impoverished people who had been reduced

---

[a] The phrase 'as it is written in the law' $^{34\,36}$ may be regarded as an editorial addition. It will be noticed also that ^{34} breaks the grammatical continuity of ^{33} and ^{35}. and in ^{33}, after specifying firstlings of cattle ('beasts'), the text adds 'the firstlings of our herds and of our flocks' (two plurals unknown to the laws).

[b] Successor of Kuenen at Leiden, see his essay *Het Herstel van Israel in het Perzische Tijdvak*, Leiden (1894) 91-104.

[c] It may be noticed that his expostulation contains no reference either to specific law or to the covenant.

to mortgaging their property, and even selling their children into slavery 5^{3-13}. This view implies, no doubt, considerable chronological disorder in the present arrangement of the documents. But of such dislocation there is sufficient evidence elsewhere in these books[a], and the hypothesis of misplacement by the compiler cannot be considered arbitrary. Kosters would thus put 13^{4-31} before 9-10^b; and 9-10 in its turn before 8. The covenant would thus represent the prior movement which made the subsequent promulgation possible. Its aim was to secure the formation of a strict community which might afterwards be ready to receive and adopt a new law. But that law would not be absolutely strange. It would be founded on usage and expressed in phraseology already sanctioned by the custom of generations. The 'ordinances,' therefore, would naturally run parallel to a considerable extent with the code which was shortly after to be made known, since this code sought to embody and co-ordinate the religious practices on which the 'commandments' were based. The compiler then confused the narrative of the covenant and the account of the acceptance of the law, and blended the items of the one with the results of the other. This view seems sufficiently to explain the dependence of 10^{30-39} on other sources besides P without resort to the assumption that the law-book of $8^{1..}$ comprised the entire Pentateuch nearly in its present form, which has been already rejected as improbable[c].

7. The law-book of Ezra, then, may be regarded as limited to the Priestly Code. But a further question at once arises, was that code itself a complete and homogeneous whole? The other great documents of the Pentateuch have disclosed indications that they were not each compiled at one date; they contain materials of various ages, successively incorporated during a long literary process. Does P show any traces of a similar growth?

(a) The answer to this inquiry cannot be doubtful. Apart from the historical introduction contained in Gen 1-Ex 6, the phenomena of the laws seem sufficiently clear. Thus a comparison of the account of the preparation of the sanctuary Ex 35-40 with the ideal description of it in 25-28 reveals a number of peculiarities (see notes *in loc*) which appear only explicable on the hypothesis that the second section is a later elaboration of an earlier and simpler account of the execution of the divine commands. The directions for the consecration of Aaron and his sons 29 are not fulfilled until Lev 8, where there are again traces of a secondary and dependent narrative. But in the interval, a short manual of sacrifice has been interposed 1-7, itself exhibiting manifold marks of composite origin. Similar groups of law on specific subjects will be found embodied in Leviticus, such as the regulations concerning clean and unclean beasts 11, leprosy 13-14, uncleanness of men and women 15, while other formulae seem to mark the termination of small codes $18^{26..}$ 19^{37} 22^{31-33} 23^{43}. 24^{22} 25^{55} 26^{46} 27^{34}. These point clearly to the aggregation of shorter collections, which may be expected, therefore, to reveal occasional diversities of

---

[a] Cp Driver, LOT^6 547-8, on Ezra 4^{6-23}.
[b] He regards $13^{10..}$ as prior to 10^{33}.
[c] In his treatise *De Entstehung des Judenthums* (1896) 208-215, Meyer defends Kuenen's hypothesis that the Ezran law-book consisted only of P while accepting the traditional order of the documents in Nehemiah. Kosters' criticism further questions the present place of Ezra 7-10, and locates it between Neh 13^{4-31} and 9-10. This involves the abandonment of the date in Ezra 7^7. According to this arrangement Ezra and his caravan did not reach Jerusalem till Nehemiah's second administration, soon after 432 B.C., and the publication of the Priestly Code was not separated by any long interval from the proceedings which followed Ezra's arrival. In this case the displacement of the date of the New Year's assembly is not necessarily very great. Prof van Hoonacker (Louvain) has, however, proposed to place the mission of Ezra in the seventh year of Artaxerxes II, 398-7; but this suggestion has not met with any general support. Cp Driver, LOT^6 552. The treatment of the Ezran age by Kosters is wholly independent of his plea concerning the rebuilding of the temple and the supposed restoration under Cyrus, the two subjects being entirely distinct.

conception and language as the result of different processes of codification. Other indications may be discerned in Numbers. Apart from more delicate signs of expansion such as those which may be traced in the first census (see notes to Num 1), the curious repetitions involved in the choice and dedication of the tribe of Levi, e g 3^5-4 and 18, are only explicable on the assumption of the amalgamation of various materials. The story of Korah 16 will be found to contain two independent representations of Levitical claims; while the group of laws and narratives in 28-36 bears numerous marks of secondary character. A presumption is thus established that **P** no less than **JE** and **D** is rather the product of a priestly school than of a single author.

(β) It becomes, then, the critic's task to discover, if possible, the sources out of which **P** has been compiled, and the stages of its growth. The analysis of Genesis soon isolates the *tol^edhoth* sections as a continuous narrative leading up to the great revelation in Ex $6^{2..}$. The commission to Moses creates the expectation that this narrative will be continued through the story of the deliverance from Egypt, the solemn institution of a special relation between Yahweh and Israel as God and people, and the fulfilment of the promises to the patriarchs by the settlement of their descendants in the land of Canaan. This anticipation is realized by the discovery of passages undoubtedly belonging to **P** describing the plagues, the Exodus, the march to Sinai, and the ordinance of the Dwelling. Around this central conception **P** then proceeds to group a number of connected institutions, concerned with the priesthood Lev 9 10^{1-5} 16, the calendar of sacred feasts 23, the appointment of the Levitical order and its duties Num 3, until the time arrives for the break-up of the Camp and the resumption of the journey to the promised land. The narrative reproduces with fresh representations some of the incidents already related by **JE**, such as the mission of the twelve explorers 13 and the consequent refusal of the people to advance 14, or the clamour for water at Meribah 20^{1-13}. The death of Aaron on Mount Hor and the investiture of Eleazar with his robes of office follow in the fortieth year, and the story then moves on rapidly without hint of opposition or conquest to the encampment by the Jordan in the plains of Moab 22^1. There Moses is warned that he must shortly die $27^{12..}$, and Joshua is solemnly ordained as his successor. But the story is still incomplete. The gift of the land of the ancestral sojournings has yet to be fulfilled, and when the Jordan has been crossed, and the passover celebrated in Gilgal as the first act of entry, the account of the settlement of the people and the distribution of the tribal inheritances realizes at last the divine design originally announced to Abraham, and repeated to Moses. The groundwork of **P** (indicated by the symbol **P**^g) is thus a continuous narrative from the creation to the establishment of the chosen nation in the abode providentially selected for it. In this respect it is analogous to **J**; but it differs from its earlier prototype in the stress which it lays on the sacred institutions of Israel, and the minute detail with which it describes the sanctuary, its holy persons, and its consecrated rites; while other elements in the story, such as the incidents arising out of the family relations of the patriarchs, or the military operations of the conquest, are apparently kept in the background, if not wholly suppressed.

(γ) Into this framework have been from time to time inserted numerous groups of laws and narrative extensions, distinguishable by various marks, both in contents and form. They may be roughly classed in three groups, each probably composed of material of various dates. Oldest of these, undoubtedly, as regards some of its ultimate constituents, is the series of laws now known as the Holiness-legislation **P**^h, chiefly comprised in Lev 17-26. A second subsidiary collection may be traced in the priestly teaching (*torah*) **P**^t, on subjects connected with sacrifice, the clean and unclean, and occasional ritual and social usage. And to these must be added a miscellaneous set of secondary enlargements, ranging over a wide variety of topics, genealogical expansions, legislative elaborations, illustrative narratives, which do not seem to belong to the original groundwork, and may be distinguished by various marks under the general head of **P**^{s}. On each of these groups a few words of further explanation may be desirable.

8. The peculiar phenomena of Lev 17-26 early attracted the attention of critics who accepted the general solution of the date of **P** put into their hands by Graf. That lamented scholar had, indeed, already discussed them [a]. But it was reserved for Klostermann in 1877 to attach to this section the special name of Holiness-legislation which has since become generally adopted [b]. The exposition by Prof Driver might seem to make separate treatment of this group needless, but completeness appears to require that it should not be ignored.

(a) Various distinctive features may be readily noted in Lev 17-26. The colophon in 26^{46} at once suggests that a collection of laws is there brought to a close, though the Sinaitic legislation is by no means complete. This conjecture is confirmed by the character of the preceding exhortation 26$^{3-45}$; it is analogous to the great discourse appended to the Deuteronomic code in Deut 28, and to the little homily which concludes the First Legislation in **E** Ex 23$^{20-33}$. But this exhortation does not stand alone: it finds briefer parallels in other passages such as Lev 18$^{2-5\ 24-30}$ 19$^{2-4\ 36}$. 20$^{22-26}$ 22$^{31-33}$. These have a common resemblance to each other; but they do not correspond to **P**'s customary usage in the enunciation of laws. They are especially designed to emphasize the duty of the maintenance of holiness; they continually refer to Yahweh's 'statutes and judgements'; they warn Israel with repeated urgency against defiling themselves with the practices of the Canaanite nations; and they dwell on the Deity of Yahweh who brought Israel out of the land of Egypt. These exhortations are naturally marked by their own characteristic phraseology (see the margins and ᴾ**192–220**). Of especially frequent recurrence is the reiteration of what has been termed 'the divine I' in the formula 'I am Yahweh' (sometimes expanded by additional words or clauses) ᴾ**203**, this affirmation recurring no less than seventy-eight times in Ezekiel while it is found only once in Jeremiah (32^2). Moreover it evidently serves in some cases to mark off specific groups or series of laws, as in 19$^{10\ 12\ 14\ 16\ 18}$, the contents of which are different both in substance and in form from the bulk of the Priestly Legislation. In other cases **P**^{h} employs words or phrases unused elsewhere in the Hexateuch [c], or occasionally forms of words or expressions having analogies in **JE** or **D** but not current in **P** [d]. These peculiarities clearly carry back the contents of the Holiness laws to Lev 18. But an examination of the previous chapter affords strong grounds for associating it with the group in 18-26. For 17 lays down rules concerning the place of sacrifice which are altogether superfluous after the institution of the Dwelling, and are apparently directed to a wholly different ceremonial condition (cp δ p 145). Now both the Covenant-words of **E** Ex 20$^{24..}$ and the Moab legislation Deut 12$^{..}$ open with a law concerning the place of sacrifice. In Lev 17, then, it seems natural to discern a similar beginning, and an examination of its literary characteristics at once discloses numerous affinities with the rest of this peculiar collection. It is probable that the original compilers were not acquainted with the Levitical Dwelling, the appearance of this term in 17^3 being probably due to editorial redaction; the holy place is elsewhere termed the 'sanctuary' 21^{12}. The same point of view is not, in fact, consistently maintained. While some of the laws are

---

[a] *Die Geschichtlichen Bücher des ATs* 75-83

[b] See the most recent discussions in Baentsch, *Das Heiligkeits-Gesetz* (1893); Paton, 'The Original Form of Lev 17-19,' *Journ of Bibl Lit* (1897) 31-37, Driver, *LOT*⁶ 47-59 145-152; Addis, *Documents of the Hexateuch* ii 170-186.

[c] Cp 195 202ⁿ 204 205 206 210 216 220   [d] Thus cp 199 201 213 215.

prefaced by the formula 'When ye be come into the land' e g 19^{23} 23^{10} 25^{2b}, other phrases in the hortatory passages seem to imply that the Israelites are already established there, and the conquest and ejectment of the Canaanite peoples is complete cp 18^{24-28} 20^{23}. Accordingly there are no traces of the adaptation of the laws to the circumstances of the desert or the conditions of camp life ct 13^{46} 14^8 : while the social legislation plainly assumes the settled pursuit of agriculture 19^9. $^{23-25}$ 25^{2b}..., on which also the calendar of the feasts is based 23^{10}.. ^{39}... The priesthood is clearly in view, but it is doubtful if it was connected with the line of Aaron. The phenomena of 21 are somewhat complicated, and must be studied in the text. The superscription does not appear properly to fit the contents, which are themselves hardly continuous and betray occasional editorial touches, though the extent of the redaction may be variously estimated. The general effect of the priestly regulations is certainly different, for instance, from that of Ex 29 Lev 9 in P^g. The 'high priest,' no doubt, stands out at the head of the entire order. But he is only the chief 'among his brethren' Lev 21^{10}; the references to his unction and sacred robes do not necessarily carry with them the special Aaronic dignity of Ex 29. The list of sacrifices is more limited than that of P; the sin and guilt offering are never mentioned[a]; 'burnt offering' and 'sacrifice' Lev 17^8. seem to sum up the remaining classes cp 22^{18} ^{21} ^{29} 19^5. In the regulations concerning the consumption of the 'holy things' 22, no distinction is drawn corresponding to that in Num 18^8.. between the 'most holy things' which may be eaten by priests alone ^{10}, and the 'holy things' $^{8\ 11}$ of which all clean members of the priestly families male and female may alike partake. The clause in Lev 21^{22} may therefore be eliminated as a harmonizing addition.

(β) The indications just enumerated suffice to establish the probability that Lev 17-26 comprises materials bound together by common ideas and phraseology representing an earlier stage of codification than P^g. But the analogy with D suggested by the opening law of sacrifice and the closing exhortation opens up further questions. From what antecedents was this legislation compiled? Is it throughout self-consistent and homogeneous? Are there any traces of similar legislation elsewhere, and to what date may the collection be referred? A brief inspection suffices to prove that the contents have been brought together from divers sources. The feeling for order and connexion which marks the first half of the Deuteronomic code (12-18) is far less prominent here, and the signs of the incorporation of various legislative items are clearer and more numerous. The miscellaneous group in 19 contains an amalgam, apparently, of numerous smaller sets, exhibiting manifold repetition both within itself (cp 19^{2N}) and in comparison with adjoining laws. Thus :—

19^{3b} Ye shall keep my sabbaths.
^{30} Ye shall keep my sabbaths, and reverence my sanctuary. I am Yahweh.
26^2 Ye shall keep my sabbaths, and reverence my sanctuary I am Yahweh
19^4 Turn ye not unto things of nought, nor make to yourselves molten gods. I am Yahweh your God.
26^1 Ye shall make you no things of nought, neither shall ye rear you up a graven image, . . . for I am Yahweh your God.

Similarly 23^{22} reproduces 19^9..; while the prohibition of eating anything with blood 19^{26a} has been already elaborately imposed in 17^{10-14}. In like manner 24^{21} repeats 24^{17}.. Some difference of usage has been noted between 19^6 and 22^{20}, while diversity of expression may certainly be observed between 18^{13} and 20^{18}; nor can it be supposed that the two lists of forbidden sexual relations 18^{6-23} and 20^{10-21} were drawn up by the same hand. They seem best explained as different redactions founded on

---

[a] On the insertion Lev 19^{21}. see note *in loc*

similar bases. The priestly laws in 21-22 are apparently drawn from another legislative cycle compared with the social regulations of 19: while in 23-25 it becomes plain that the earlier materials of P^h have been wrought into the more rigid and elaborate forms of P^g and P^s with large loss in the process. In the entire group, therefore, it is natural to recognize the product of continuous editorial activity working upon elements of various origin and date.

(γ) The characteristic phraseology of P^h is not, however, exclusively confined to Lev 17-26. It reappears in scattered passages throughout the Priestly Code, and thus raises the question whether any fragments of P^h are still extant in other connexions, and what may have been its original scope. Thus Driver[a] ascribes to this document Ex 6^{6-8} 12^{12}. 31^{13-14a} Lev $10^{9a. 10}$. 11^{44} Num 15^{37-41}, while Addis[b] allows only Lev 11^{43-45} and Num 15^{37-41}. Other scholars, again, like Wurster, Cornill, and Wildeboer, further propose to include within it a considerable group of Levitical laws more or less cognate in subject and style[c]. Reasons will be given hereafter for associating these and other legislative sections in a body of Priestly Teaching originally conceived independently of the main conceptions of P^g (cp 9β p 152), and occasionally exhibiting important analogies with P^h. But greater difficulty is presented by passages of narrative like Ex 6^{6-8} and 12^{12}.. The chief indication of P^h here would seem to be the formula 'I am Yahweh.' But this recurs elsewhere as in 29^{46}; and with 12^{12} it would be natural to associate the language of Num $3^{12. 45}$ and perhaps ^{41}. Are all these to be regarded as relics of P^h? In that case it must have contained historical as well as legislative matter on an extensive scale. It must have related the commission to Moses, the death of the first-born, the establishment of the Dwelling, and the dedication of the Levites to Yahweh's service. Even if the latter passages be denied to P^h, the implications of Ex 6^{6-8} suggest that the document to which it belonged comprised an account of the Exodus, the great religious institutions, and the settlement in the land promised to the forefathers. If so, it may naturally be asked why there are no further traces of so comprehensive a story; what were the antecedents of the commission given to Moses; how much more should we attempt imaginatively to reconstruct? It does not appear necessary on general grounds to assume such a complete predecessor of the narrative of P^g. Some brief introduction may have been needed to the opening law of sacrifice in Lev 17, analogous to that which must originally have preceded the corresponding opening of the Deuteronomic code. But just as D belongs to a single situation, and did not relate the whole career of Moses, so it seems safer to confine P^h to a collection of laws and exhortations in the wilderness independent of any lengthy historical recital, and the following passages only are assigned to it in the text outside Lev 17-26, viz Ex 31^{13-14a} Num 10^9. 15^{38b-41}.

(δ) The age of the Holiness-collection has been differently estimated according to the stress laid on its respective elements. A distinction immediately arises between the various materials of which it is composed, and the hortatory framework in which they are set. The former are obviously not all of one date. The repetitions and duplicates sufficiently prove diversity of source, and diversity of source involves variety of age. Some of the social regulations may be of very great antiquity. The lists of forbidden intercourse in Lev 18 and 20 find strange parallels in the ancient Penitentials, which represent the efforts of the Church[d] to control the passions of a period of rude violence not without its occasional analogies in the early history

---

[a] LOT^6 151.   [b] *Hexateuch* ii 178.
[c] Thus Cornill attributes originally to P^h Lev 12 13^{1-46} 14^{1-8a} 15 Num 5^{11-31} 6^{2-8} 19.
[d] See the Penitential ascribed to Theodore in Thorpe, *Laws and Inst* ii 9-22; Haddan and Stubbs, *Councils* iii 178

of Israel. Again, Lev 19 contains laws which show occasional contact with the Judgement-book of E; and there are similar indications of acquaintance with the usage of J cp ²ᴺ. The conjecture, therefore, rises whether J could have originally contained any short legislative code similar to E's judgements, which might have served as one of the sources of Pʰ. P follows J in the use of the designation Sinai instead of Horeb employed by ED: Aaron is significant in J as in the later P (cp the basis of Ex 6^{12} 7^1· in 4^{10-16}): Nadab and Abihu are reckoned in his family in both 24^1 Lev 10^1. The ordinances of P admittedly rest on older usage: they are plainly compiled from manifold sources: it would not be surprising, therefore, that they should incorporate fragments of legislative material which might have been derived from the school of J. Further evidence of their antiquity is perhaps to be found in the traces of arrangement in series or groups of fives, winding up with the customary formula 'I am Yahweh' cp $19^{9. \ 11. \ 13. \ 15 \ 17}$.. Other laws have counterparts in Deut 22 24· cp Lev 19^{2N}. They are enclosed in different formulae, but they point to derivation from common originals (cp chap IX i 2*a* p 74). Is it possible to determine their relative age? The evidence can rarely if ever be decisive, for even if there be clear marks in one or other of more primitive or more comprehensive character, it might still be possible that the later collection had (from some unexplained cause) employed the earlier type. Thus the opening law in Lev 17 concerning the slaughter of animals for sacrifice has obviously gone through successive stages on the way to its present form. It is apparently issued in the wilderness and adapted to the camp ³, but it is soon clear that it was really designed for the settled life of Israel: it speaks of the 'open field' or country ⁵ (as contrasted with the city), and recognizes the aliens ⁸ who lived in Israel's midst. The reference to the camp, therefore, must be regarded as editorial. The original purport of such a law appears to have been to secure to Yahweh the proper portion of sacrificial animals which might be killed for food. In the oldest usage the ordinary slaughter of one of the flock or the herd had its votive side; the flesh might not be eaten unless the blood or life had been poured out before Yahweh [a]. That rule is modified in Deut 12^{20}·· in the case of distance from the central sanctuary. It is ignored also in Lev 7^{22} · which implies that ox or sheep or goat may be freely eaten on condition of abstinence from the fat and the blood. But the Holiness-legislation emphatically requires that every Israelite who kills one of his domestic animals shall bring an offering from it to Yahweh. Under what conditions was this practicable? On the one hand it is urged [b] that such a rule was only intended to apply to a territory of limited extent, such as might be occupied by the settlers who should return from the captivity, and establish themselves in the neighbourhood of Jerusalem. If it be admitted as probable that Lev 26 belongs to the exile (cp ζ p 149), this law would then rank among the later elements of Pʰ. But on the other hand, it may be argued that the law is appropriate rather to that stage of religious organization in which the numerous local sanctuaries provided each worshipper with the opportunity of paying his sacrificial dues near his own home. In this view the ordinance of 17 belongs to the earlier circumstances recognized by E in Ex 20^{24}··. It has then been accommodated by a later editor to the camp-form which is the base of Pᵍ, but not elsewhere recognized in Pʰ; and has taken up into itself the references to P's central sanctuary, the Tent of Meeting or Dwelling. This is the view adopted in the text [c]: but it is by no means free from difficulties. The phraseology of ³⁻⁷

---

[a] W Robertson Smith, *OTJC*² 249

[b] Baentsch, *Heiligkeits-Gesetz* 116, Addis, *Hexateuch* ii 337. Kalisch, *Lev* ii 343, 'we are brought far into the Persian period, when the above command . . . was at least not quite impracticable, for at that time the Jews lived together in a comparatively small circle round Jerusalem.'

[c] Cp Driver, *LOT*' 51. Baentsch is supported among earlier writers by Wellhausen and Kuenen; and more recently by Holzinger, *Einl* 447 The latter, like his predecessors, also admits much 'working over.'

does not show any indications of an early type of ceremonial rule; it contains numerous points of contact with other laws both in P^h and more generally in P (see the margin); while the rare term 'he-goats' or 'satyrs' occurs only elsewhere in exilian prophecies. If, however, 17³· be recognized as originally prior to D, it is possible that some of the social and humanitarian laws may in the same way be earlier than the compilation of the Deuteronomic code. On the other hand P^h may present them in a form presumably later. The fragments of the Holiness-calendar in Lev 23 do not seem to yield sufficient data for comparison with Deut 16; but a suggestive instance may be found in the following parallels :—

Lev 19	Deut 25
³⁵ Ye shall do no unrighteousness in judgement, in meteyard, in weight, or in measure. ³⁶ Just balances, just weights, a just ephah, and a just hin, shall ye have. I am Yahweh your God, which brought you out of the land of Egypt.	¹³ Thou shalt not have in thy bag divers weights, a great and a small ¹⁴ Thou shalt not have in thine house divers measures, a great and a small. ¹⁵ A perfect and just weight shalt thou have, a perfect and just measure shalt thou have: that thy days may be long upon the land which Yahweh thy God giveth thee.

D deals only with the stones used for weight, and the ephah for measure. But P^h enters into more detail. It specifies 'meteyard, weight, and measure ^{a},' and beside the ephah it names the hin. The larger elaboration suggests a more advanced type.

(ϵ) A more important group of evidences is to be found in the peculiar relations subsisting between the Holiness-legislation and the prophecies of Ezekiel. It has been already pointed out that marked affinities may be observed between the Deuteronomic discourses and the language of Jeremiah (chap X 2 p 88). Similar resemblances may be noted between the substance and phraseology of P^h and the writings of the 'father of Judaism' by the river Chebar. It may be convenient to exhibit first some of the parallels in the legislation, and then proceed to the examination of their hortatory envelopments. The opening law starts with a formula found elsewhere only in Ezekiel :—

Lev	Ezek
17³ Every man of the house of Israel.	14⁴ Every man of the house of Israel.
⁸ ¹⁰ Every man of the house of Israel, or of the strangers that sojourn among them. Cp 20² The strangers that sojourn in Israel.	⁷ Every man of the house of Israel, or of the strangers that sojourn in Israel, . . . †
¹⁰ I will set my face against that soul . . and will cut him off from among his people.	⁸ I will set my face against that man, . . . and will cut him off from the midst of my people. Cp 15⁷.
¹³ He shall pour out the blood thereof, and cover it with dust.	24⁷ She poured it [the blood] not upon the ground, to cover it with dust
¹⁶ He shall bear his iniquity ^{b}.	14¹⁰ 44¹⁰ ¹² They shall bear their iniquity.

Again and again does Ezekiel dwell on the offences prohibited especially in P^h, as in the following examples :—

Lev	Ezek
18⁸ The nakedness of thy father's wife shalt thou not uncover: it is thy father's nakedness. 20¹⁰ And the man that committeth adultery with another man's wife, even he that committeth adultery with his neighbour's wife, the adulterer and the adulteress shall surely be put to death. ¹¹ And the man that lieth with his father's wife hath uncovered his father's nakedness: both of them shall surely be put to death;· their blood shall be upon them ¹² And if a man lie with his daughter in law, both of them shall	22¹⁰ In thee have they uncovered their fathers' nakedness. in thee have they humbled her that was unclean in her separation ¹¹ And one hath committed abomination with his neighbour's wife; and another hath lewdly defiled his daughter in law; and another in thee hath humbled his sister, his father's daughter.

a The word 'measure' occurs elsewhere only in Ezek 4¹¹ ¹⁶ and 1 Chron 23²⁹
b Also 19⁸ 20¹⁷ ¹⁹ 22¹⁶ P₁93

Lev	Ezek
surely be put to death : they have wrought confusion; their blood shall be upon them . . ¹⁷ And if a man shall take his sister, his father's daughter, or his mother's daughter, and see her nakedness, and she see his nakedness, it is a shameful thing ; and they shall be cut off in the sight of the children of their people. he hath uncovered his sister's nakedness ; he shall bear his iniquity ^{a}.	
¹³ Thou shalt not oppress thy neighbour, nor rob him. Cp 6$^{2\ 4}$.	
¹⁵ Ye shall do no unrighteousness in judgement.	18^7 And hath not robbed any. ¹² Hath robbed the poor and needy. ¹⁶ Neither hath robbed any. 18^8 Hath withdrawn his hand from unrighteousness, hath executed true judgement 33^{15} Doing no unrighteousness [The word occurs ten times in Ezek.]
²⁶ Ye shall not eat any thing with the blood.	²⁵ Ye eat with the blood. [Cp 18^6 hath not eaten with the blood. So W R Smith, Smend, and others.]
³⁶ Just balances, just weights, a just ephah, and a just hin, shall ye have.	45^{10} Ye shall have just balances, and a just ephah, and a just bath.
20^9 Every one that curseth his father or his mother.	22^7 In thee have they cursed father and mother
21^{1b} There shall none defile himself for the dead among his people ; ^{2} except for his kin, that is near unto him, for his mother, and for his father, and for his son, and for his daughter, and for his brother ; ^{3} and for his sister a virgin, that is near unto him, which hath had no husband, for her may he defile himself.	44^{25} And they shall come at no dead person to defile themselves: but for father, or for mother, or for son, or for daughter, for brother, or for sister that hath had no husband, they may defile themselves
^{5} They shall not make baldness upon their head, neither shall they shave off the corner of their beard, nor make any cuttings in their flesh.	²⁰ Neither shall they shave their heads, nor suffer their locks to grow long ; they shall only poll their heads
¹⁴ A widow, or one divorced, or a profane woman, an harlot, these shall he not take : but a virgin of his own people shall he take to wife.	²² Neither shall they take for their wives a widow, nor her that is put away but they shall take virgins of the seed of the house of Israel, or a widow that is the widow of a priest.
22^8 That which dieth of itself, or is torn of beasts, he shall not eat to defile himself therewith : I am Yahweh.	³¹ The priests shall not eat of any thing that dieth of itself, or is torn, whether it be fowl or beast. 4^{14} Then said I, Ah Lord God ! behold, my soul hath not been polluted. for from my youth up even till now have I not eaten of that which dieth of itself, or is torn of beasts . . .
¹⁵ And they shall not profane the holy things of the children of Israel, which they offer unto Yahweh.	22^{26} Her priests . . . have profaned my holy things
25^{18} Ye shall dwell therein in safety.	28^{26} They shall dwell therein in safety. Cp 34$^{25\ 28}$ 38$^{8\ 11\ 14}$ 39$^{6\ 26}$.
³⁶ Take thou no usury of him or increase. ³⁷ Thou shalt not give him thy money upon usury, nor give him thy victuals for increase.	18^8 He that hath not given forth upon usury, neither hath taken any increase. Cp $^{13\ 17}$ 22^{12} Prov 28^8†.
⁴³ Thou shalt not rule over him with rigour.	34^4 With rigour have ye ruled over them. Cp Ex 1^{13}†.

These illustrations imply a large community of thought and feeling between P^h and Ezekiel ^{b}. Especial stress is laid by both on the 'sanctuary' Lev 19^{30} 20^3 21$^{12\ 23}$ 26^2 cp

---

^{a} Cp 'uncover the nakedness' ^{P}215 ; 'their blood shall be upon them' ^{P}195 ; where the parallels in Ezekiel are enumerated.

^{b} Further parallels may be found : Lev 18^{17} 'wickedness' ^{P}220 ; 18^{19} 'separation' ^{P}139 ; 18^{20} 'defile' ^{P}167^d ; 18^{21} 'profane the name' ^{P}210 ; 18^{22} 'abomination' ^{P}192 ; 19^3 'my sabbaths' ^{P}211 ; 19^7 'abomination' 7^{18} Ezek 4^{14} Is 65^4† ; 19^{14} 'put a stumblingblock' Ezek 3^{20} cp 7^{19} 14$^{3,\ 7}$ 18^{30} 21^{15} 44^{12} ; 19^{16} 'tale-bearer' or 'slanderer' Ezek 22^9, 'peoples' ^{P}208 ; 19^{35} 'measure' Ezek 4$^{11\ 16}$ 1 Chron 23^{29}† ; 21^6 'bread of thy God' ^{P}196 ; 21^7 'put away' Ezek 44^{22} ; 21^{13} 'virginity' Ezek 23$^{3\ 8}$, 22^2 'separate themselves' Ezek 14^7 ; 23^{40} 'thick trees' Ezek 6^{13} 20^{28} Neh 8^{15}† ; 25$^{14\ 25}$ ה 'sell that which is sold' cp $^{27-29\ 33\ 50}$ Ezek 7^{13} Neh 13^{20} ct Deut 18^8† ; 26^1 'figured stone' Num 33^{52} Ezek 8^{12} (where Cornill, however, strikes it out as an intrusion from Lev 26^1) Prov 25^{11} and metaphorically Ps 73^7 Prov 18^{11}†.

Ezek 5^{11} 8^6 23^{38f} 25^3 $43^{7\cdots}$, which must be carefully guarded from profanation ^{a}. Both emphasize the necessity for maintaining ceremonial purity, and preserve the priesthood rigidly from defilement: the ancient rules of abstinence from blood and from animals not properly slaughtered are enforced by both; and Ezekiel is hardly less concerned than P^h to secure purity in family relationships, justice in mutual dealings, uprightness in trade, and generous consideration for the poor. In the social and moral legislation of Lev 18-20 the compiler has collected together rules which may well be of far older date than Ezekiel. Similarly in 23 the fragments of the festival calendar, as yet unattached to specific months and days, doubtless imply a prior type compared with the fixed dates of Ezekiel $44^{18\cdots b}$. The brief fragment in Lev 24^{15b-22} ranges itself alongside of 18-20: while the base of 25 belongs in like manner to the same general humanitarian series. But the priority of the ceremonial legislation in 21-22 is less easy to decide. On the one hand P^h sanctions for the priesthood generally that marriage with widows which Ezekiel forbids 44^{22}: in Lev 21^{14} ct ^{7} this is disallowed for the high priest alone. Moreover P^h makes no distinction between higher and lower ranks within the sacred order, while Ezekiel for the first time divides the functions of the Levites from those of the priests. On the other hand Lev $21^{10\cdots}$ recognizes a 'high priest' for whom Ezekiel apparently makes no provision. Does this passage require the assumption of a later date than Ezekiel's ideal legislation? It may be noted that while in the eighth century under Ahaz the chief officer of the temple, Urijah, simply bears the distinctive title 'the priest' 2 Kings 16^{10}, Hilkiah, a hundred years later, is designated expressly 'the high priest' $22^{4\ 8}$ 23^4 (cp Seraiah 25^{18}). It does not seem, therefore, unreasonable to suppose that the usage of Lev $21^{10\cdots}$ may be founded on the practice of the last century of the monarchy, when the head of the temple guild, who was 'high priest among his brethren,' was already distinguished perhaps by special unction and robes ^{c} and bound by more rigid obligations of personal purity. Between such a functionary and the heir of the Aaronic dignity Ex 28-29 there is yet a wide gap, and Ezekiel supplies no intermediate link, his 'prince' being entrusted with some of the functions which might otherwise have been assigned to the sacerdotal chief cp Ezek $45^{17\ 22\cdots}$ $46^{2\cdots d}$. There remains, however, a peculiar expression in Lev $21^{17\ 21}$ 22^4, which designates the priests as the 'seed of Aaron.' This term appears unknown to Ezekiel, who traces their origin no further back than Zadok 40^{46} &c. If it be allowed to P^h, it must be regarded as a distinct advance on Ezekiel's view of the priesthood; but the general critical judgement of recent scholars unanimously rejects it, and it seems on the whole wiser to ascribe it to early editorial redaction. In this view, the earlier materials of P^h will be found originally in the ancient nucleus of Lev 17 and the legislative collections of 18-20 23-25, while later ceremonial rules are embodied in 21-22, the whole having probably undergone repeated elaboration by the scribes of the second temple.

(ζ) But the inquiry into the age of the Holiness-legislation is compelled to take account of a further fact. The separate collections are in some cases preceded and followed by short exhortations, and the entire collection closes with a long and notable discourse Lev 26^{3-45}. The date of the code as a whole must depend on the union of the legal and the homiletic elements. To what period, then, may the latter be probably referred? Whether these are all of one date cannot, indeed, be positively affirmed. But there can be no doubt that they are all of one school. A survey of the parallels

---

a Cp $^P210^b$.
b There is no trace, moreover, of the atonement ceremonies or the sin or guilt offerings
c Cp ^{10N}. Driver, in Haupt's *SBOT*, regards the reference to the unction and vestments as supplemental So Addis, *Hex* ii 349.
d On the other hand Addis, *Hex* ii 183, like Baentsch and Kuenen, places Lev 21-22 after Ezekiel

between 26^{3-45} and the preceding group 18-25 soon reveals numerous affinities of thought and language. Thus in 26^3 'walk in my statutes' cp 18^4 ^{30} 20^{23}: 'keep my commandments and do them' 18^4. ^{26} 19^{37} 20^8 ^{22} 22^{31} 25^{18}: ^{4} 'yield their fruit' 25^{19}: ^{5} 'dwell in your land safely' 25^{18}.: ^{9} 'I will have respect [$\mathfrak{H}$ will turn] unto you' 19^4 ^{31} 20^6: ^{10} 'old store' 25^{22}: ^{13} 'I am Yahweh thy God which brought you out of the land of Egypt' 19^{36}: ^{35} 'dwell upon it' 25^{18}: ^{45} 'I am Yahweh' $^{P}20^3$: on the other hand the peculiar phrase in 18^{25} ^{28ab} 20^{22} ('the land vomiteth out her inhabitants') does not occur in 26 where it might certainly have been expected. It is natural therefore to inquire whether the exhortations show the same parallels with Ezekiel which have been already discovered in the laws 17-25. They are assuredly not difficult to find, as the following table shows:—

Lev	Ezek
18^{2b} I am Yahweh your God.	$20^{5\ 7\ 19}$ I am Yahweh your God. Cp ^{20} 28^{26} $39^{22\ 28}$, not in Is Jer.
^{3} After the doings of the land of Egypt . . . shall ye not do.	20^7 Defile not yourselves with the idols of Egypt.
^{3} In their statutes ye shall not walk ^{4} My judgements shall ye do, and my statutes shall ye keep, to walk therein . . ^{5} Ye shall therefore keep my statutes, and my judgements which if a man do, he shall live by them. Cp ^{26} 19^{37}.	^{18} Walk ye not in the statutes of your fathers, . . . ^{19} walk in my statutes, and keep my judgements, . ^{21} they walked not in my statutes, neither kept my judgements to do them, which if a man do, he shall live by them. Cp 5^6 $11^{12\ 20}$ $18^{9\ 17}$ $20^{11\ 13}$ 36^{27}.
^{24} Defile not yourselves in any of these things. ^{30} That ye defile not yourselves therein.	20^7 Defile not yourselves with the idols of Egypt. ^{18} Defile not yourselves with their idols. Cp 14^{11} 37^{23}.
^{25} The land is defiled. Cp ^{27}. $^{'8}$ When ye defile it [the land]. ^{26} Do any of these abominations. Cp $^{27\ 29}$ 20^{22}. Cp 18^{24}…	36^{17} They defiled it [the land] . . . by their doings. Cp ^{18}. 8^6 The great abominations that the house of Israel are doing here. Cp $^{9\ 13\ 17}$ 9^4 $18^{13\ 24}$.
^{24} Ye shall possess their land [ירש, for P's אחז]	35^{10} We will possess it
^{25} Ye shall separate between the clean beast and the unclean Cp 11^{47} To separate between the unclean and the clean	$22^{2)}$ They have not separated between the holy and the common, neither have they caused men to discern between the unclean and the clean. 42^{20} To separate between that which was holy and that which was common.
^{25} Ye shall not make your souls abominable by beast, or by fowl, or by anything wherewith the ground creepeth. Cp 11^{4J}.	8^{10} Behold every form of creeping things, and abominable beasts. [With שקץ cp Ezekiel's frequent use of שקוץ 5^{11} 7^{20} $11^{18\ 21}$ $20^{7\ 30}$ 37^{23}.]

Here also the vocabulary approaches Ezekiel's, though it is by no means identical with it. Ezekiel does not use the words 'vomit' Lev 20^{22} or 'abhor' ^{23} (קוץ, ct געל 26^{11}): and his characteristic addition to the description of the 'land flowing with milk and honey' ^{24} 'which is the glory of all lands' Ezek $20^{6\ 15}$ is not employed by P^h. The language of Lev 26^{3-45}, however, shows still closer approximation to the usage of the priest-prophet of the first years of the captivity: and the resemblances are often so close as to have given rise to the suggestion that this discourse must have been actually composed by him. It will suffice, perhaps, to collect the parallels in the first section $^{3-13\ a}$:—

Lev 26	Ezek
^{3} [Cp $18^{3-5\ 26}$ 19^{37}] ^{4} I will give your *rains in their season, and the land shall yield her increase, and the trees of the field shall yield their fruit.* ^{5} And your threshing shall reach unto the vintage, and the vintage shall reach unto the sowing time and ye shall eat your bread to the full ^{b}, and *dwell* in your land	$20^{18.\ 21}$ &c. 34^{25} And I will make with them a covenant of peace, *and will cause evil beasts to cease out of the land* and they shall *dwell safely* in the wilderness and sleep in the woods . . ^{26} And I will cause the *rain to come down in its season*, . . ^{27} *And the tree of the field shall yield its fruit, and the land shall*

---

^{a} Similar enumerations will be found in Colenso, *Pent* vi 5-7, and among more recent critics in Baentsch, *Heiligkeits-Gesetz* 121, and Driver, *LOT*^{6} 147, cp Zunz, *ZDMG* xxvii 682-4.

^{b} Cp Ezek 39^{19} 'and ye shall eat fat to the full.'

Lev 26	Ezek
safely. ⁶ And I will give *peace in the land, and ye shall lie down, and none shall make you afraid and I will cause evil beasts to cease out of the land,* neither shall the sword go through your land.	*yield her increase,* and they shall be *safe* on their ground ; . . . ²⁸ *and they shall dwell safely, and none shall make them afraid* Cp 39²⁶ᵇ. 14¹⁷ . . . and say, Sword, go through the land.
⁹ And I will have respect [Ⴙ turn] unto you	36⁹ And I will turn unto you.
⁹ And I will make you fruitful and multiply you.	¹⁰ And I will multiply men upon you, . . ¹¹ and I will multiply upon you man and beast ; and they shall multiply and be fruitful. Cp Jer 3¹⁶ 23³
⁹ And I will establish my covenant with you.	16⁶² And I will establish my covenant with thee. Cp ⁶⁰.
¹¹ And I will set my dwelling among you	37²⁶ And I will set my sanctuary among them, . . . ²⁷ and my dwelling shall be over them.
¹² And I will walk among you. ¹² And I will be your God, and ye shall be my people.	43⁷ ⁹ I will dwell among the children of Israel ᵃ. 37²⁷ And I will be their God, and they shall be my people. 36²⁸ And ye shall be my people, and I will be your God. 11²⁰ 37²³ And they shall be my people, and I will be their God. Cp 14¹¹ 34²⁴ ³⁰.
¹³ I am Yahweh your God, which brought you forth out of the land of Egypt. Cp 19³⁶.	20⁵ᵇ I am Yahweh your God, ⁶ in that day I lifted up mine hand unto them, to bring them forth out of the land of Egypt.
¹³ I have broken the bars of your yoke	34²⁷ And they shall know that I am Yahweh, when I have broken the bars of their yoke.

Similar parallels may be traced (see the margins of Lev 26) through the rest of the discourse. Dr Colenso reckoned that twenty-two expressions were common to Lev 26 and Ezekiel, which occurred nowhere else in the Old Testament; and he added thirteen more which were not found in the rest of the Pentateuch. From these peculiar phenomena he inferred that Ezekiel might be regarded as the author of this exhortation; and the parallels already cited suggested the extension of this inference to the redaction of the entire group of Holiness-laws ᵇ. Reasons have been already advanced for regarding the laws as derived from other sources; and the same conclusion is rendered probable for their hortatory framework. Distinctive expressions have been noted in 18²⁴·· 20²²·· which Ezekiel does not employ. This is true to a much larger extent of 26, which not only contains an unusual number of single words found nowhere else ᶜ, but freely uses other words which Ezekiel avoids. Though he repeatedly mentions 'statutes' and 'judgements,' he never specifies 'commandments' ³ ¹⁴: the word 'abhor' occurs in Ezek 16⁵ ⁴⁵, but the phrase 'my soul abhors' Lev 26¹¹ ¹⁵ ³⁰ ⁴³ does not appear. Similarly 'chastise' ¹⁸ ²³ ²⁸ : 'walk contrary' ²¹ ²³· ²⁷· : 'smell' ³¹ : 'enjoy her sabbaths' ³⁴ ⁴³ : 'confess' ⁴⁰ : 'be humbled' ⁴¹ : 'reject' (with Yahweh as subject) ⁴⁴— are none of them found in his writings. To these instances may be added the reiterated אַף 'also' ¹⁶ ²⁴ ²⁸ ³⁹ ⁴⁰ ⁴¹ ⁴²ᵃᵇ ⁴⁴, which only occurs three times in the whole book of Ezekiel. These peculiarities appear sufficient to establish independence of authorship, but it is hardly possible to infer the relative ages of the two writers from the mere study of these literary phenomena; though the argument that if Lev 26 was known to Ezekiel, some of its many unusual phrases might have been expected to present themselves in some part of his copious writings, is not altogether without weight. The decision must, however, be founded rather on the consideration of the substance of the discourse, especially of the section ²⁷⁻⁴⁵. Does that seem more suitable to the approach of exile, or to the hope that its close is near? Different estimates have been formed of its significance ᵈ. On ³⁴··· Kalisch remarked in 1872: 'Now the author no longer delineates the past but the woful present.' Dillmann frankly recognizes the

---

ᵃ For the phrase 'walk among' (though not of Yahweh) cp Ezek 19⁶ 28¹⁴
ᵇ So already Graf in 1866, *Gesch Bucher* 81–83 ; in 1874, Kayser, *Das Vorexilische Buch* 176.
ᶜ Cp margin in ⁵ ⁷ ¹³ ¹⁶ ³⁶ ³⁷ ⁴⁴ and ²¹ ²³· ²⁷·.
ᵈ See the opinions cited by Driver, *LOT⁶* 149–50.

later character of $^{34.\ 39\ 40..}$, but conjectures that these passages are due to expansion at the hand of younger prophets in the course of the exile[a]. The general unity of style, however, is so well maintained that this suggestion has met with little support: and it appears on the whole probable that the great exhortation must be placed rather after Ezekiel than before or during his age[b].

9. It has been already indicated (7γ) that other elements beside the Holiness-legislation may be recognized in the general collection of **P**. Among these attention may be drawn to a group of laws only distantly connected with the main conceptions of **P**^{g}, which appear to represent the priestly teaching on subjects peculiarly under the control of the sacred order.

(*a*) Many of the religious institutions of **P**^{g} are attached to specific incidents in his narrative. Thus the observance of the sabbath, the prohibition of the eating of blood, and circumcision, are introduced at successive stages of the history of the race. Similarly the passover is first celebrated on the night of the Exodus; the preparation of the Dwelling and the dedication of Aaron and his sons embody the principles of the sanctuary and the priesthood; on these depend the laws of sacerdotal duty and atonement alike for the consecrated order and the whole people Lev 10 and 18. In like manner the regulations for Priests and Levites, the definition of their spheres of action, and the provision for their maintenance, follow the story of the rising of Korah Num 16-18. But in other cases a different method is adopted. The law of leprosy, for example, is not called forth by the necessity of dealing with a particular sufferer: it is not designed for the wilderness at all: it contemplates the life of the city and the 'open field' Lev 14$^{7\ 53}$, and has apparently been adapted to the situation in the desert by an occasional reference to the camp and the tent of meeting $^{3\ 8\ 11\ 23}$. It will be observed that these regulations are occasionally summed up by the formula 'This is the *torah* of . . .' 13^{59} 14$^{2\ 32\ 54\ 57}$. Parallel phrases will be found in the little manual of sacrifice 6$^{9\ 14\ 25}$ 7$^{1\ 11}$; and they occur in connexion with other topics such as unclean food 11^{43}, personal impurity 12^7 15^{32}, marital suspicion Num 5^{29}, the Nazirite vow 6$^{13\ 21}$, defilement caused by death 19^{14}. In some cases there seems reason to believe that these laws are themselves compiled from antecedent materials (see notes on Lev 11 and Num 5). But in general they may be regarded as derived from a *corpus* of priestly teaching originally independent of the wanderings. That such 'teaching' was one of the special functions of the priesthood is well known. As early as the Blessing of Moses, Levi is endowed with two privileges, the service of the altar and the teaching of the people Deut 33^{10}. On its judicial side this 'teaching' had the character of decisions which might become the basis of law cp 17^{11}; while on its ritual side it was largely concerned with the means of preserving ceremonial purity. Thus **D** already recognizes a priestly teaching about leprosy 24^8, which may be now incorporated in Lev 13-14. Ezekiel reckons among the functions of the priesthood the 'teaching' of the difference between the holy and the common, the unclean and the clean Ezek 44^{23} cp Lev 10^{10}. It is in accordance with this method that he sums up the description of the ideal sanctuary with the corresponding formula 'this is the *torah* of the house' 43^{12}. To such a source we may assign Lev 1-7 in its earlier form, 10^{10}. 11-15 Num 5-6 15$^{1-31}$ 19$^{14-22}$.

(β) These 'teachings' like the Holiness-legislation seem anterior to the theory of the

---

[a] Cp *Ex Lev*^{3} 677.
[b] So Wellhausen, Kuenen, Baentsch, and recently Addis, *Hex* ii 367. Addis further proposes to place Lev 18-20 between 621 and 591 B C, *Hex* ii 182. Baentsch, *Heiligkeits-Gesetz* 94 pointing to 18^{24}.. 20^{22} ., suggests a date shortly before the first deportation, about 600 B C. The second group 21-22 Baentsch assigns, *ibid* 113, to a date after Ezek 40-48 while he ascribes 17 to an indeterminate place in the exile before P, *ibid* 120, and the conclusion in 26 follows (at least in its present form) last of all, *ibid* 127.

Aaronic priesthood. The process of adaptation cannot, indeed, be always securely traced. But the peculiar phenomena noted in Lev 1–3, see 1⁵ᴺ, show that the text has probably passed through a series of minute alterations which have not always been completely carried out, so that occasional traces of them remain. The laws of sacrifice 1–7 do not name the Dwelling; they habitually employ the designation 'tent of meeting.' But they are occasionally brought up to the standard of its arrangements, as in the references to the veil and incense-altar 4⁶·, and the court 6¹⁶. It is probable that materials of different dates have here been amalgamated, and that the various 'teachings' may have been expanded or developed by successive hands. That they rest on anterior usage is both in itself reasonable, and may be further inferred from the peculiar phrase 'according to the ordinance' (𝔊 'judgement') 5¹⁰ Num 15²⁴ cp Lev 9¹⁶ Num 29¹⁸*, which suggests the existence of a recognized body of customs grounded on the settlement of disputed cases. As they are largely occupied with related topics a certain community of phraseology may be observed among them, which does not reappear elsewhere ^{a}: and notable parallels occur in comparison with P^h. Thus in Lev 7¹⁸ the peculiar word 'abomination' (פגול) is found otherwise in the Hexateuch only in P^h Lev 19⁷ cp Ezek 4¹⁴ Is 65⁴†. The language of Lev 11⁴⁴· is of a common type with hortatory passages in P^h: and further points of contact may be noticed in Lev 15¹⁶·· cp 19²⁰ 22⁴; 15³¹ 'dwelling' in the ideal sense cp 26¹¹ Num 19¹³; Num 5² cp Lev 24² 19²³: Num 5⁹ 'holy things of the children of Israel' cp Lev 22². In Num 5⁵⁻⁸ it may not be too bold to recognize a supplement to earlier regulations, and a connexion may be thus inferred between some parts of the Holiness-legislation and the Priestly teaching which was afterwards still further defined. But the greater portion of this group appears to belong to a stage anterior to the form given by P^g to the sanctuary and the sacred order.

10. There remain a number of passages both in narrative and law which do not seem congruous with their context, and must be regarded, therefore, as secondary extensions. In this view, the groundwork of **P** has been enriched from time to time by additions conceived more or less in its spirit, after the manner already indicated in the older documents **J** and **E** (chap XI 6 p 108 and chap XII 5δ p 119).

(a) The historical introduction shows occasional signs of the incorporation of materials from other sources ^{b}, as in the story of the massacre of the Shechemites Gen 34, the genealogy of Edom 36, the list of Jacob's descendants 46⁸⁻²⁷, and the pedigrees in Ex 6¹³⁻³⁰. The narrative of the gift of manna in 16 betrays at once the hand of the compiler in its curious dislocations, while the sabbatical arrangements seem to imply later developments. Occasional traces of addition may be discerned in the account of the Dwelling and its furniture 25–31. Thus the incense-altar 30¹⁻¹⁰ does not seem to have been among its sacred objects, as conceived by the first narrator. The Samaritan Pentateuch, it is true, places this section between 26³⁵ and ³⁶. But it is exposed to suspicion on two grounds. In the first place it is ignored in other connexions where it would have been natural to mention it had it been recognized among the contents of the sanctuary, e g Lev 16 cp Ex 30¹⁰ and Lev 8 cp 4⁷; while on the other hand it appears in passages whose secondary character is confirmed by independent evidence cp Num 3³¹ 4¹¹. Moreover, the contiguous matter in Ex 30¹¹–31¹¹ suggests further presumptions of addition, for the omission by 𝔊 of the reference to the anointing oil and the incense-ingredients in 25⁶ makes

---

^{a} Thus קמץ Lev 2² 5¹² ‖ Num 5²⁶†: Lev 4⁶ cp 14⁶ ¹⁶ ⁵¹ Num 19¹⁸: Lev 4¹³ 'err' Num 15²²*, 'be hid' Lev 5²⁻⁴ Num 5¹³* Lev 4²⁰ ²⁶ ³¹ ³⁵ 'be forgiven' 5¹⁰·· 19²² Num 15²⁵⁻²⁸ Niph†. Lev 6²⁸ 'rinsed' 15¹¹⁴* Lev 13³³ 'shaven' 14⁸· 21⁵ Num 6⁹ ¹⁸·: Lev 14⁷ ⁵³ 'open field' 17⁵ Num 19¹⁶* Lev 15¹⁶⁻¹⁸ ³² 'seed of copulation' 19²⁰ 22⁴ Num 5¹³† Lev 15³¹ 'defile my dwelling' cp Num 5³ 19¹³ 35³⁴ Num 5⁷ cp Lev 6⁵· Num 5¹⁵ cp Lev 14²¹· Num 15¹⁵ cp Lev 7⁷· Num 19²⁰ cp ¹ᵈ Lev 15³¹.
^{b} See the notes *in locc.*

it probable that these sections also did not belong to the original description. This description, further, seems to have limited the priestly unction to Aaron $29^{7\ 29}$. But another series of passages extends it also to his sons, i e to ordinary priests 28^{41} 29^{21} 30^{30} 40^{15} Lev 7^{36} 8^{30} 10^{7} Num 3^{3}, several of these being associated with groups otherwise viewed as later in form. These extensions are thus marked by a general tendency towards the heightening of ritual and the elaboration of detail: they sometimes enforce earlier demands with increased stringency and precision; they apply principles to fresh cases, or they seek to harmonize differences, and modify old rules apparently to suit unforeseen circumstances. The directions for the double burnt offering, morning and evening Ex 29^{38-41}, were rejected by Kuenen[a] partly on the ground of their incompatibility with the arrangements of the covenant in Neh 10^{33}. That difficulty is relieved if it may be supposed with Kosters (cp 6δ p 140) that that covenant actually preceded instead of following the promulgation of the law related in 8: but there seem to be other reasons cp Ex $29^{38\text{N}}$ for regarding the passage as an editorial insertion. In Lev 4 the rite of the sin offering includes the sprinkling of the altar of incense in the holy place, and is thus dependent on the section in Ex 30^{1-10}. Lev 16 appears to introduce into a more general ritual a special element of atonement for the priestly order; while another remarkable case of expansion on an older basis will be found in the arrangements for the jubile in 25. Supplemental laws may be observed in the ordinance imposing tithes of animals in addition to the requirement of their first-born 27; in the secondary passover Num 9^{1-14}; in the law of the drink offering 15^{1-16} apparently dependent on Lev 2; and the firstling of dough Num 15^{17-21}; while 8^{23} modifies the age of Levitical service specified in 4^{3}. Indications of another kind may be discerned in the repetitions which describe the execution of the divine commands. The accounts of the preparation of the Dwelling Ex 35-40, and of the consecration of Aaron and his sons Lev 8, are both secondary to Ex 25-29 and $30-31^{11}$. Various phenomena in Num 1-4 imply that the census in 1, the camp-order in 2, and the Levitical arrangements in 3-4 owe their present form to this kind of expansion. The monotonous repetitions of 7 and its chronological discords cp $^{1\text{N}}$ point to an adapter of late date, while the dedication of the Levites in 8 is a counterpart to the ceremony of Lev 8, and Num 9^{15-23} seems a supplement to Ex 40. A secondary stratum in the Korah story in Num 16 has been recognized since Kuenen pointed out[b] that Korah and his associates appeared in two capacities, on the one hand as laymen vindicating the rights of the whole congregation, and on the other as Levites protesting against priestly exclusiveness. The second census 26 presents even more decisive marks of later origin than the first, and carries with it the case of Zelophehad's daughters 27^{1-11}. At this point a strong presumption is raised that the original injunctions concerning the death of Moses, represented in the text by 27^{12-14} were followed after $^{15-23}$ by the actual record of his death[c]. That event, however, is postponed by the insertion of a miscellaneous group of laws and narratives, by no means altogether congruous with each other, or all specially adapted to the situation of the great leader. Their heterogeneous character, as well as numerous minute linguistic and textual indications, seem best explained on the supposition that a series of additions was made at this point by later hands. What stage in the redaction of the Pentateuch was most suitable for such augmentations, cannot be determined. They may have been rendered easier by the incorporation of the Deuteronomic Code, which interposed a large collection of addresses and narrative between the divine warning of Moses' death and its execution. In some

---

[a] *Hex* 310.   [b] *Theol Tijdschr* XII 139-162, *Hex* 95 334.
[c] On the immediate fulfilment of the divine commands, cp Noah Gen 6^{22}; Abraham 17^{23}; Moses Ex 12^{28}, Aaron Num 20^{27}.. &c.

cases, e g in Ex 35-40, there is evidence that the final redaction may even have been deferred till the third century before our era.

(β) The general evidence for the secondary character of these and other passages is thus of various kinds. It is gathered from incongruities of fact and representation; from the supplemental character of different ordinances; from implications of mutual dependence, and irregularities of time-order. To these may be added a number of peculiarities in phrase and formula, some of which are tabulated below[a]. In particular P^s appears to show much greater freedom in the handling of older materials. Thus the vocabulary of narrative in P^g seems very definitely marked; the description of the creation, the revelation of El Shaddai to Abraham, the purchase of the cave of Machpelah, Gen 1 17 23, do not show any approximation to the usual style of JE. But in P^s the older type of language is employed much more freely, as the margins of Num 31-32 sufficiently show, and in Gen 34 Wellhausen and Cornill believe that the basis of the story of P^s was derived from E. In a similar manner some of the legislation of P^s may rest on older forms of P^h. This seems to be clearly indicated in the manner in which the jubile law is superposed on that of the older Sabbath year Lev 25: and some curious linguistic traces may be noted in Num 9^{1-14} 30 and 33^{51}... In abandoning the strict usage of P^g, P^s allows himself greater latitude of expression; and he occasionally employs some of the characteristic words of D for which P^g prefers other terms, cp 'tribe' 32^{33} 36^3, and 'possess' 27^{11} 36^8: parallel phenomena will be found in Josh 20 and 22. The linguistic evidence (with its occasional correspondences in later literature) thus distinctly confirms the view that these sections may be ascribed to a later and reproductive age of legal codification.

11. The analysis of the Priestly Code leads to the conclusion that it consists of smaller collections P^h P^t P^s incorporated into one principal document P^g whose carefully arranged narrative offered numerous points at which insertions of various kinds could be introduced. But under what conditions did this fusion take place?

(a) The time and mode in which the various elements were combined, cannot of course be determined within any fixed limits. The secondary materials represented by P^s are so plainly diverse in age (the description of the Dwelling Ex 35-40 being apparently the latest of all) that their addition to the great law-book may naturally be conceived rather as a literary process than as a specific editorial act. But the union of P^h and P^t with P^g admits perhaps of somewhat clearer, though still largely conjectural, presentation. The Holiness-legislation is plainly connected, through its affinities to Ezekiel, with the priestly schools in Babylonia. To the same general

---

[a] Among the formulae specially characteristic of P^s may be noted the following 'This is (Anah) who...' 188^c 'as Yahweh commanded Moses' 189^c 'by the hand of . ' and 'command by the hand of . .' 180^{ad} · 'take the sum,' 'heads of fathers' 84^{ac} · 'purify oneself' 143^b. Unusual expressions, not occurring in P^g, may be of two kinds : they may arise out of the peculiar subject-matter of the narrative or law, as the words 'bond' Num $30^{2-5\ 8\ 10-14}$†, 'rash utterance' 6^8†, 'lying in wait' $35^{20\ 22}$†; or they may have a more general significance, as replacing common phrases, or perhaps involving combinations of familiar terms which are not discoverable elsewhere (or only occasionally so) in such connexions. Thus cp ⌂, 'cords' Ex 35^{18} 39^{40} Num $3^{26\ 37}$ $4^{26\ 32*}$ 'cloud of Yahweh' Ex 40^{38} Num 10^{34}† 'are poured out' Lev 4^{12}† 'in perpetuity' $25^{23\ 30}$† 'sold as bondmen' 25^{42}†. 'expressed by name' Num 1^{17} 1 Chron 12^{31} 16^{41} 2 Chron 28^{15} 31^{19} Ezr 8^{20}† 'declared their pedigrees' Num 1^{18}†: 'oversight' $3^{32\ 36}$ 4^{16} ct 16^{29*} 'covering' $4^{6\ 14}$† 'table of shewbread' 4^7† 'for a moment' 4^{20}† · 'covered wagons' 7^3 cp Is 66^{20}†. 'dedication' Num $7^{10\ 84\ 88}$ cp Ps 30 (title) 2 Chron 7^9 Ezr 6^{16}. Neh 12^{27} Dan 3^2.† 'water of expiation' Num 8^7†. 'service of Yahweh' 8^{11}†. 'sometimes' 9^{20}. cp Neh 5^2† 'this is the statute of the law' Num 19^2 31^{21}†: 'speak right' 27^7 36^5 cp Ex 10^{29*}. 'statute of judgement' Num 27^{11} 35^{29}†. 'drink offering' 28^7. 'day of firstfruits' 28^{26}†. 'heads of the tribes' 30^1 cp 1 Kings 8^1 2 Chron 5^2† cp Num 32^{28} Josh 14^1 21^1: 'disallow' Num $30^{5\ 8\ 11}$ 32^7 ^{9} Ps 33^{10} 141^5†. 'arm ye' Num 31^3 $32^{17\ 20*}$. 'vengeance of Yahweh' 31^3† Jer Ezek† 'were delivered' Num 31^5†. 'prey' $31^{11.\ 26\ 32}$ Is 49^{24}†: 'service of the war' Num 31^{14*}· 'which went to the battle' 31^{21} 32^6 1 Chron 19^7†. 'skilled in war' Num 31^{27}† cp Jer 2^5 'tribute' Num $31^{28\ 37}$†: 'drawn out' $31^{3)\ 47}$ 1 Chron 24^6†. 'people of the host' Num 31^{32}. 'captains of thousands and of hundreds' 31^{54} 1 Chron 13^1†: Num 33^{51} ‖ 35^{10} 34^2 ‖ 35^2 : 36^2 'my lord' cp J47.

origin may the laws embraced in the Priestly teaching be ascribed. Numerous small points of contact link the two groups together, though it is plain that the present contents of P^t are by no means all of the same date (e g in Lev 1–7). It may be surmised, then, that when P^g was drawn up, P^h and P^t were embodied in it. The amalgamation was probably not due to the original author. It can hardly be supposed that the great designer of the Levitical Dwelling, with all its associated institutions, would have himself interpolated into his work a law originally so incongruous with it as that which regulates sacrifice in 17; or again, that he would have sought to combine the flexible arrangements of the older calendar with the fixed order of months and days in 23. It is probable, therefore, that these related elements were introduced by other hands. Not unnaturally did the critics who had so clearly recognized the diversity of materials in P, ascribe to Ezra the labour of unification, and suggest that it was that which engrossed him between the eventful years 458 and 444 B C [a]. But the confidence with which this view was once entertained, is moderated by other considerations. On the received view of the chronology the severe measures which Ezra sanctioned and carried through, must have roused against him bitter hostility. This lasted long and checked all further effort. He can take no further step until he has the support of Nehemiah. Is it likely that such a period of failure and defeat was occupied with the literary labours of codification? Does it not seem on the whole more probable that Ezra brought the new law-book with him from Babylonia, and that the promulgation followed without long delay? The view of Kosters to which attention has been already invited (ante 6δ p 140), shortens indefinitely the interval between Ezra's arrival and the great publication. The share which we may then ascribe to him and Nehemiah somewhat resembles the parts of Hilkiah and Josiah in connexion with D. save that the relative significance of the sacerdotal and the civil powers is reversed. The function of Ezra was not that of the subsequent editors of the Deuteronomic documents; his duty was not to compile but to proclaim; the practical task devolved upon him of securing the acceptance of a code which he had received from others, and of which he probably no more knew the personal authors than Hilkiah knew the original preachers of the Deuteronomic law [b].

(β) The inquiry as to the exact scope of the post-Ezran additions is necessarily unable to attain definite results. Different critical judgements may be passed on the regulation for the daily burnt offering, morning and evening Ex 29$^{38\cdots}$, according as the covenant of Neh 10 is supposed to follow or to precede the actual introduction of the new code: but it is clear that the adoption of Kosters' arrangement does not obviate all difficulties. The textual phenomena render the passage suspicious; and the supposition that this and other sections found their way into P between the covenant and the promulgation would imply an activity on the part of Ezra and his friends which can hardly under the circumstances be ascribed to them. It may, therefore, be plausibly regarded as of later date. An argument of another kind may be applied to Lev 16. The immediate consequence of the reading of the new code is the splendid celebration of Booths for eight days beginning on the fifteenth of the month Neh 8$^{14\cdots}$. But between the first and the fifteenth the calendar assigns the solemn day of atonement to the tenth Lev 23$^{27-32}$. Why is no notice taken of this hallowed fast, imposed on the whole nation under the severest theocratic penalties? The 'argument from silence' impresses different critics differently. The significance of it, however, in this case seems heightened by the description of the fast-day and confession which followed

---

[a] So Graf, in Merx's *Archiv* 1 476, Reuss, *Gesch der Heil Schr ATs* § 377 p 462; Kuenen, *Rel of Isr* 11 233 and *Hex* 304, Wurster, *ZATW* iv 128. Cp ante 6a–γ

[b] So also Holzinger, *Einl* 453, on the basis of the traditional chronology Addis, *Hex* 11 189, supposes that Ezra's law-book included the whole Pentateuch, without the later additions (P^s).

on the twenty-fourth Neh 9¹·... Why should this have been needful? Why was no notice taken of the peculiar rites of the 'Day' (as it came afterwards to be called by distinction), which would have rendered such national humiliation superfluous? There seems good reason, therefore, on the basis of the received order, to question the inclusion of Lev 16 in Ezra's law-book, at least in the form which constitutes it an annual celebration*a*. It is possible that (as Wurster has argued) the present rite has been converted into an annual ceremony by later modifications, the original ordinance with its narrower application having been contained at the outset in **P**. Or it may be that in the misplaced order of the documents in the books of Ezra and Nehemiah, the narrative in Neh 9 belonged really to the events in Ezra 10, and had no relation to the reading of the Law. Kuenen's plea that there was a difference between the enthusiastic celebration of an ancient popular festival and the immediate acceptance of a wholly new ceremony, would then have considerable weight. But on the whole it seems easiest to suppose that Lev 16 as it stands now is of later date, and to accept the inevitable inference that passages which rest upon it, such as Ex 30^{1-10} Lev 23^{26-32} $25^{9...}$, are of still more recent origin, and did not enter the Priestly Code till after Ezra's promulgation. Other sections in P^s are probably yet younger; but the question of their incorporation may perhaps be more suitably discussed in examining the general process of the reduction of the whole Pentateuch into one continuous collection (cp chap XVI).

CHAPTER XIV

UNCLASSIFIED DOCUMENTS

BESIDE the main collections, **JE**, **D**, **P**, into which the Hexateuch may be resolved, there remain a few passages, chiefly poetical, which seem to be of independent origin.

1. Gen 14 is admitted on every hand to show many peculiarities. These are seen alike in the subject-matter—the invasion of the Mesopotamian kings, Abram's victorious pursuit, and his interview with Melchizedek—and in the details of phrase and name.

(*a*) To neither of the two documents traceable in Genesis up to this point can it be assigned with any probability: not (1) to **P**, for it is not in his manner (in spite of some terms cited below), and, in admitting the use of the name Yahweh by Abram ²², it violates **P**'s fundamental canon of the progress of revelation Ex 6^3 (cp chap XIII 1*a*); nor (2) to **J**, for the picture which it gives of Abram and his surroundings does not agree with **J**'s habitual representations. In **J** Abram lives among the Canaanites 12^6 13^7, here he is called a Hebrew and is leagued with Amorites: Mamre, in 13^{13} 18^1 apparently a place, is here a chieftain (cp Eshcol 'grape-cluster' Num 13^{23}): and whereas in **J** Abram is a wealthy sheikh who moves through the country on terms of independent amity with his neighbours, here he displays military resources and capacity which enable him to overwhelm a league of kings. The margins, however, show affinities of style with both **J** and **P**. To the latter, in particular, belong the terms 'goods' ¹¹· ¹⁶ ²¹ ^{P}155, 'born in his house' ¹⁴ cp $17^{12.\ 23\ 27}$ Lev 22^{11*}, and 'persons' ²¹ ^{P}146; and the force of these connexions is hardly weakened by Dillmann's observations that 'goods' appears again outside **P** under the hand of **R** in Gen 15^{14}, that 'born in his house' is an editorial gloss, while the designation 'persons' was hardly to be

---

a So Zunz, *ZDMG* xxvii 682; Kalisch, *Lev* ii 272; Reuss, *Bible* i 260 On the other hand cp Kuenen, *Hex* 312.

avoided. These phenomena would point to a writer acquainted with the linguistic usage of both **J** and **P**.

(β) The narrative is further distinguished by a large number of names occurring nowhere else in the Hexateuch, or even in the Old Testament. Besides those of the Mesopotamian kings and of the five tributaries in the Jordan valley, with Aner and Melchizedek, a whole map of localities is unrolled here for the only time, Bela [2], the vale of Siddim [3], Ham [5], Shaveh [5] [17], El-paran [6], En-mishpat [7], Hobah [15], King's Vale [17]. In the critical impossibility of attributing the narrative to **J** or **P**, Dillmann and Kittel fall back on **E** (cp chap XII 1). The justification appears hardly adequate. The league with the three Amorites [13] (cp the Amorite in **E** [JE]96) is compared with the covenant in 21[32] between Abraham and Abimelech; on the strength of Hos 11[8] the names Admah and Zeboiim [2] are assigned to the Ephraimitic source; while a similar origin in **E** is asserted for the archaeological detail in [5], to which such curious parallels are found in Deut 2[10] [12] [22]. These indications are scarcely conclusive. **E**'s Abram is a prophet Gen 20[7] not a general, and Dillmann is further obliged to admit a continuous editorial manipulation by **R** culminating in the insertion not only of 'Yahweh' [22], but of the whole Melchizedek episode by a Judean editor, perhaps **R**[d]. König, with clearer perception of the individual character of the narrative, attributes it[a] like Eichhorn a century ago, Ewald in the last generation, and Driver to-day[b] to a special source; but he fixes its origin in the Book of the Wars of Yahweh Num 21[14], **P**'s 'goods' being introduced by an editor. Kuenen, Wellhausen, Cornill, Budde, Bacon, Wildeboer, Ball, on the other hand, having regard to the linguistic indications already cited, as well as to the difficulties in the story itself (first emphasized by Noeldeke[c], who dated it about 800 B C), refer it to a writer later than **P**, and group it with the Midrash literature of later Judaism.

(γ) Recent cuneiform investigation has thrown much light on the names of the Mesopotamian kings, and on the general relations of Syria to the Eastern empire. But nothing has as yet been discovered which gives any support to the story of Chedorlaomer's overlordship, or to that of an expedition terminating in the total rout of himself and all his allies [17][d]. On the results of archaeological research, cp Meyer, *Gesch des Alterthums* (1884) i 166, Sayce, *Higher Criticism* 161··, *Patriarchal Palestine* 64··, *Early History of the Hebrews* 24-30, Maspero, *Struggle of the Nations* 47··, Driver, *Guardian*, March 11 and April 8, 1896, Hommel, *Ancient Hebrew Tradition* v, *Church Times*, March 18, 1898; and below, chap XV (contributed by Prof Cheyne, where a reference will be found to King's recent edition of the letters of Khammurabi). The narrative as it stands cannot possibly be coeval with the events which it describes, for it employs names to which subsequent narratives assign a much later origin. The Amalekites [7] are specified in 36[12] among the descendants of Esau. Dan 14[14] points to a date posterior to the Danite conquest narrated in Judg 18[29]. There are also grave chronological embarrassments affecting the contemporaneousness of Abraham with the Mesopotamian kings. These princes are placed by the monumental evidence in

---

[a] *Einleitung* (1893) 182. [b] *LOT*[6] 15. [c] *Untersuchungen* (1869) 156-72

[d] *RV* speaks of the 'slaughter of Chedorlaomer and the kings that were with him' The rendering is doubtful, for ה ('smite') may only mean their complete overthrow without involving their actual death 𝔊 translates by κοπή which represents equivalent ה in Josh 10[20], where the massacre of the Canaanites is certainly implied by the following clause; and the same word is naturally employed by the author of Hebrews 7[1], where *RV* again renders 'slaughter' From the point of view of the cuneiform records and their supposed confirmation of the Hebrew narrative, the question is not without significance, for Prof Sayce infers from the Mesopotamian texts that the kings survived to make war on each other nearer home (*Early History* 27). In Num 31[7], twelve thousand Israelites (a vastly greater number than Abram's little force) with Phinehas the priest slay (הרג) the five Midianite kings together with every male the women and children are captured, the maidens alone numbering 32,000 [35]. Apparently no Israelite is lost on either occasion Are these the contemporary records of real fighting?

the twenty-third century BC*a*, and the Exodus is dated in the thirteenth*b*. Between Abraham and Moses there is thus an interval of a thousand years. Yet according to the testimony of Gen 15^{16}, though this is not free from difficulties on other grounds, the return of Israel to Canaan was to take place in the fourth generation from Abraham, and with this the genealogies of the Mosaic age are in substantial accord. Prof Hommel, indeed, proposes to reduce the gap by placing Khammurabi (Amraphel) about 1900 BC. Apart from the question whether this result can be harmonized with the view just named, it must be pointed out that it is only gained by striking out a whole dynasty of kings named on the tablets as 'entirely apocryphal.' This process of elimination may be justifiable on other grounds, but it cannot be overlooked that it is offered as an alternative to hypotheses concerning which Prof Hommel observes that 'the acceptance of any one of them would be merely bringing grist to the mill of the modern critics of the Pentateuch' p 133. At present, therefore, it can only be affirmed that the author of 14 employed names and perhaps other materials ultimately derived from ancient cuneiform texts. It is possible that he was himself acquainted with them; but he may only have worked up hints or suggestions not immediately dependent on cuneiform sources. Prof A A Bevan has remarked*c* that 'in the East fragments of historic tradition may be transmitted from age to age and from nation to nation in a great variety of ways; and it is particularly important to observe that historical romances are much more likely to be transmitted than genuine historical narratives.' Nothing has yet refuted the suggestion of Meyer*d* and Tiele*e* that a Hebrew author may have utilized a tradition first learned in Babylon to glorify the great ancestor of Israel. In that case we may suppose that the numerous explanatory notes are not the product of later editorial activity, but are part of the writer's own method. The names of the kings of Sodom and Gomorrah were understood by the Rabbis to be derived from the Hebrew nouns 'evil' and 'wickedness': and it is a curious circumstance that the number of Abraham's 'trained men' 14 corresponds to the sum of the numerical values of the letters of the name Eliezer 15^2. Is this an instance of the cypher known as Gematria*f*?

2. The 'Blessing of Jacob' in Gen 49$^{2-27}$ can hardly be regarded as a single composition. The inequalities in style, and the different treatment of the tribes, first suggested to Renan that it had arisen out of a collection of proverbial or poetical sayings*g*. These appear to be founded on different incidents, and to belong to various dates. Thus in $^{5-7}$ the recollection of some ancient act of violence by Simeon and Levi (the latter being as yet no dedicated tribe) is clearly preserved: and the doom pronounced upon them may go back to the early days of the settlement cp 34^{30}. On the other hand the monarchy of Judah seems to be implied in ^{10}. Dillmann, indeed, with whom König and Wildeboer substantially agree, ascribes the whole poem to the age of the Judges; Reuss thinks the conditions appropriate to the rise of David against Saul; Driver discerns a reflexion of the social circumstances under the Judges, Samuel, and David*h*. Kautzsch*i* notes the divergence between the language concerning Levi ^{7}, too early for the monarchy, and the ascription to Judah of an eminence before unknown. The problem is further complicated by the reference to Joseph. On the one hand he has been seriously wounded ^{23}; on the other, his wealth and prosperity are described in glowing terms ^{25}. But the originality of this passage is open to doubt; it may be a harmonistic insertion from Deut 33$^{13-16}$. In that case the apparent

---

a *Higher Criticism* 165; *Early History* 12; other views in *Ancient Hebr Trad* 121.
b *Early History* 151, 1277 BC   *c* *Critical Review* vii 411
d *Gesch des Alterthums* i 166.   *e* *Bab-Assyr Gesch* (1886) 123   *f* Wellhausen, *Comp* (1889) 310–11.
g *Hist Gen des Langues Semitiques* (1858) 120   Cp Kuenen, *Hex* 240
h *LOT*^{3} 19   *i* *Literature of the OT* 15–16.

allusion to the northern kingdom [26] falls away. Yet there remains the recognition of his power [22] impaired but not destroyed by hostile attack. This finds a widely received explanation in the Syrian wars of the ninth century, before the victories of Jeroboam II [a]. The poem may have really grown out of a smaller nucleus describing the fortunes of some of the most prominent of the tribes. In its present form it expresses that fuller national consciousness which first emerged under the Davidic monarchy, and is reflected in the systematized scheme of the patriarchal traditions [b]. Reuben, Simeon, Levi, Judah (cp 29^{31-35}) sons of Leah, stand first; while Joseph and Benjamin, offspring of Rachel and the latest born, wind up the list. The compiler thus stands on the basis of J's original order, and may be supposed to represent the southern view. But he is not to be identified with J, for the alternations of Jacob and Israel [2] and [24] are hardly in his manner [c], and the poem seems to stand apart by its rugged style from his general narrative [d].

3. The 'Song of Moses' in Ex 15^{2-18} is obviously a poem of a very different class. It does not show any close relation to either of the documents in which the passage of the Red Sea is described, J E P in 14 [e]. On the contrary, it seems to stand at a distance from the triumph which it commemorates. It is not marked by any personal or local allusions. Contrast the vivid touches of the 'Song of Deborah' Judg 5, or the lament of David over Saul and Jonathan 2 Sam 1. All early poetry, fresh from the scene and the event, is full of concrete detail. The poet of Judges 5 leaves the fate of Sisera in no doubt: but in Ex 15^4 it is uncertain whether or not Pharaoh perished with his host. Moreover, such definite references as there are, point to a much later age. They describe the pangs of Philistia, the amazement of Edom, the panic of Canaan [14]. But this excitement and terror are not caused by the overthrow of the Egyptian troops: they arise from the victorious march of Israel under its divine leader into his 'holy habitation' [13]. In other words, the poet looks back on the settlement in Canaan as already accomplished. Nor is this all, for the language of [17] has been often supposed to refer to the temple. The first clause may, indeed, describe the whole land rather than the sacred house; and the second may be regarded with Wellhausen [f] as a later and limiting addition [g]; but even in this case the evidence of [13] would still be decisive of post-Mosaic origin. Some echoes of [1] are to be heard in Is $12^{2\ 5}$, but the late character of this composition is no guarantee of an early date for the phrases which it seems to reproduce. The general affinities of the poem both literary and religious (cp the parallels in the margin) seem to class it with the psalms of a subsequent age; and the emphatic assertion of Yahweh's eternal sovereignty with which it concludes implies an advanced stage of the doctrine of the divine Kingship such as had found fresh expression during and after the exile [h]. The prophets of the Captivity deeply felt the parallel between the deliverance under Cyrus and the escape from the Egyptian servitude; and their own hope of return and of the restoration of their sanctuary may have generated the language of $^{13-17}$. The evidence is rather general than specific: the place of the poem will be judged rather in connexion with a wide view of Israel's religious and literary development than on the more definite ground of particular historic allusion [i].

[a] So Wellhausen, Kuenen; Stade (*Gesch Isr* 1 150) suggests the reign of Ahab. Cornill, Ball (*PSBA* xvii 179-180), Holzinger (*Genesis* 263) accept this general date.
[b] Cp chap XI 5 p 106.   [c] Cp Holzinger, *Genesis* 264. the text of 24^b is doubtful.
[d] Some linguistic peculiarities are noted in the margins
[e] Cp, however, 'host' 15^4 with P in $14^{4\ 17\ 28}$; 'pursue' 15^9 with P in $14^{4\ 8}$
[f] *Prolegomena* 22^N.
[g] The word 'place' occurs elsewhere only in 1 *Kings* $8^{13\ 39\ 43\ 49}$, of Yahweh's heavenly dwelling-place.
[h] Mic 4^7 is probably part of a later addition (so Stade, Cornill, Wellhausen, Nowack; 'another hand, of what date we cannot tell,' G A Smith)
[i] Cp Cheyne, *Origin of the Psalter* 31^g

4. The 'Song' in Deut 32 is attached like the code to the name of Moses, but it is plainly not by the author either of the laws or of the homilies of **D**. The introduction in 31$^{16-22}$ is shown in the analysis to be derived from another school; and the language of the poem has scarcely any points of contact with the distinctive Deuteronomic phraseology. The retrospect in $^{7-14}$ carries it below the period of conquest and settlement: the description of Israel's idolatries $^{15-22}$ implies a historical reflexion analogous to that now found in the framework of the Book of Judges. Chastisement, however, is at hand, nay it has already overtaken the unsteadfast children; and the poet desires that his people may still have wisdom to understand the discipline by which they are being tried ^{29}. The historical situation is not defined by any clear local or secular allusions: but the 'foolish nation' ^{21} (i.e the ungodly conquerors) can hardly be the Syrians in the time of Elisha (Dillmann, Westphal, Oettli), nor even the Assyrians attacking Samaria (Ewald, Kamphausen, Reuss), for the religious atmosphere of the poem is not that of the ninth century, or even of the eighth, and the most striking literary parallels occur in writings of a much later date.

(a) Thus the theological characteristics and phraseology seem to belong to the movement led by Jeremiah, which culminated in the later prophecies of the Babylonian age. (1) The emphatic assertion of monotheism in ^{39} resembles the affirmations of 4$^{35\ 39}$ in substance, while the phrase 'I even I am he' recalls the style of Is 41^4 43$^{10\ 13}$ 46^4 48^{12} (for the repetition 'I, I' cp 43$^{11\ 25}$ 51^{12}). (2) Prominent among the titles of Deity is the name 'Rock' $^{4\ 15\ 18\ 30.\ 37}$*, so that the God of Israel is contrasted with the God of Israel's foes as 'our Rock' with 'their Rock.' This usage (not quite identical with that in Is 17^{10} 30^{29}) is seen in Hab 1^{12} Is 44^8, and in poems like 1 Sam 2^2 Ps 18$^{31\ 46}$ 19^{14} &c. (3) Another title '*Eloah* $^{15\ 17}$ (now accepted as an artificially formed singular from the older plural Elohim, cp Ges-Brown, *Hebr Lexicon* אֱלוֹהַּ) also appears in Ps 18^{31} and in writings of the Jeremian age or later Hab 1^{11} 3^3 Is 44^8 Ps 50^{22} &c (forty-one times in Job). (4) To these must be added '*Elyon*, 'Most High' ^{8} cp Gen 14^{18} · Num 24^{16}. The name does not belong to the prophetic theology before the Exile cp Is 14^{14} and, as used in the later Psalms, seems to carry with it the implication of exalted sovereignty over the various ranks of the angelic hosts, e.g Ps 97^9. If the reading of 𝔊 in ^{8} 'according to the number of the angels of God [i.e "sons of El" for "sons of Israel"]' be adopted (with Kuenen, Cheyne, Cornill, Stade, Schultz, *OT Theol* i 227), the writer's view of the divine election of Israel is compatible with the providential allotment of the other nations to patron angels cp 4^{19}. (5) The concern attributed to Yahweh for 'the provocation of the enemy' who would misinterpret his dealings with Israel ^{26}·, is analogous to the 'pity for his holy name' which Ezekiel ascribes to him 36$^{20-23}$; and the punishment of his adversaries is conceived in the fierce style of later prophecy e.g Ezek 39 Is 34 63$^{1-6\ a}$. (6) Israel, on the other hand, is to be righted (for the judgement ^{36} cp 1 Sam 2^{10}), for Yahweh will 'repent himself of his servants' ^{36}. The use of this term (cp ^{43}) deserves attention. In pre-exilian prophecy it is limited to the prophetic order Am 3^7 Jer 7^{25} 25^4 26^5 29^{19} 35^{15} 44^4 Ezek 38^{17} cp Is 44^{26}. Only later does it come to include the holy people Is 54^{17} 65$^{13\ 15}$ 66^{14}, and in that sense it is frequent in the Psalter 34^{22} 69^{36} 79$^{2\ 10}$ 89^{50} 90$^{13\ 16}$ 102$^{14\ 28}$ 105^{25}. (7) The language of the opening of the poem $^{1.}$, and the stress repeatedly laid on 'understanding' $^{6\ 28.}$, point to the view of religion as 'wisdom' represented pre-eminently in Prov 1-9, and several rare words find parallels in the Wisdom literature cp $^{5\ 6\ 20\ 24}$. (8) The appeal to the nations with which the poem concludes, implies a universalism hardly possible until the Exile, when it first received lyric utterance in prophecy, as in Is 42$^{10-12}$

---

^{a} For the 'vengeance' of God ^{35} cp Lev 26^{25} Num 31^2· Mic 5^{15} Jer 11^{20} 20^{12} 46^{10} 50$^{15\ 28}$ 51$^{11\ 36}$ Ezek 24^8 25$^{12-17}$ Is 34^8 35^4 47^3 59^{17} 61^2 63^4 Ps 58^{10}. 'Avenge' Is 1^{24} &c, cp Driver, *Deut* 374 cp Ps 47^1 67 &c These illustrations justify Cornill's brief description of the poem as a 'compendium of the prophetic theology.' And that theology must be already at a relatively advanced stage, for the chastisement of the enemy announced in $^{41-43}$ could only be invoked when Israel's cup of suffering was full (cp Is 13-14^{23} beside the parallels already cited). In other words, the poem can not be dated before the Captivity.

(β) With this result the parallels of language are in entire accord. The argument founded on coincidences of phrase and similarities of expression may be often read in two ways when it cannot be certain to which side priority belongs. But in this case the significance of the correspondences of phrase lies in the proof which they afford that the poem belongs by its verbal affinities to the schools of Jeremiah, Ezekiel, and their successors, rather than to the eighth century. The evidence is of course cumulative. When Yahweh is said to have 'made' Israel ^{6}, or Israel to have forgotten Yahweh ^{18}, it cannot be definitely affirmed that these passages bear any direct relation to Hos 8^{14} either of antecedence or sequence: but when Is 45^{18} employs the two terms 'make' and 'establish' cp ^{6}, there is an additional probability of phraseological suggestion, which is increased in the case of ^{13} cp Is 58^{14}, 'days of old' and 'generations' ^{7} Is 63^{11} cp 58^{12} 61^4 (the same terms of the future instead of the past Is 13^{20} 34^{17} 60^{15} Jer 50^{39}). The Song no doubt shows a strong literary individuality, for it contains an unusual proportion of words found nowhere else (cp Driver, *Deut* 348 and margin); but it also employs a considerable number of words and phrases more or less frequent in the last days of the monarchy and onwards, but not before. Among these may be noted the following in the order of their occurrence:—(1) 'strange god' ^{12} Mal 2^{11} Ps 81^9†; (2) 'lambs, rams, and goats' ^{14} (in combination) Jer 51^{40} Ezek 27^{21} 39^{18} Is 34^6†; (3) 'moved him to jealousy' $^{16\ 21}$, 1 Kings 14^{22} Ps 78^{58}, 'with strange ones' (applied to foreign gods) Jer 2^{25} 3^{13} Is 43^{12} Ps 44^{20} 81^9†; (4) 'abominations' ^{16} (pl) Deut 18^9 ^{12} 20^{18} Lev $18^{26\cdot 29}$ Jer 7^{10} 16^{18} 44^{22} 1 Kings 14^{24} 2 Kings 16^3 $21^{2\ 11}$ Ezek [38] Prov 6^{16} 26^{25} Chron Ezr†; (5) 'provoked him to anger' ^{16} Deut 4^{25} 9^{18} 31^{29} Jer $7^{18.\ 8^{19}}$ 11^{17} 25^6. $32^{29.\ 32}$ $44^{3\ 8}$ Ezek 8^{17} 16^{26} Judg 2^{12} 1-2 Kings [17] Is 65^3 Ps 78^{58} 106^{29} Chron cp Hos 12^{14}†; (6) 'dreaded' ^{17} = 'be horribly afraid' Jer 2^{12} Ezek 27^{35} 32^{10}†; (7) 'vanities' ^{21} (pl) Jer 8^{19} 10^8 14^{22} 1 Kings $16^{13\ 26}$ Jon 2^3 Ps 31^6†; (8) 'a fire is kindled' ^{22} Jer 15^{14} cp 17^4 Is 50^{11} 64^2†; (9) 'done' ^{27} פעל of the divine action Ex 15^{17} Num 23^{23} Hab 1^5 Is 26^{12} 41^4 43^{13} Ps 7^{13} 31^{19} 44^1 68^{28} 74^{12} Prov 16^4 Job 22^{17} 33^{29} 36^{23}†; (10) 'sold' ^{30} (figuratively) Ezek 30^{12} Judg 2^{14} 3^8 4^2 ^{9} 10^7 1 Sam 12^9 Ps 44^{12}†; (11) 'day of their calamity' ^{35} Jer 18^{17} 46^{21} Obad ^{13} Ps 18^{18} Prov 27^{10} Job 21^{30}† cp 'time of their calamity' Ezek 35^5 ('calamity' only in these books); (12) 'shut up or left at large' ^{36} 1 Kings 14^{10} 21^{21} 2 Kings 9^8 14^{26}†; (13) 'lift up my hand' ^{40} Ezek 20^5 $^{15\ 23\ 28\ 42}$ 36^7 44^{12} 47^{14} Ex 6^8 Num 14^{30} P Ps 106^{26}†; (14) 'as I live' ^{40} Jer 22^{24} 46^{18} Zeph 2^9 Ezek 5^{11} &c [17] Is 49^{18} Num 14^{21} J^{E} ^{28} P†; (15) 'avenge the blood' ^{43} 2 Kings 9^7 cp Ps 79^{10}†. Other peculiarities of phraseology may also be noted, such as 'doctrine' ^{2} Is 29^{24} Prov 1^5 4^2 7^{21} 9^9 $16^{21\ 23}$ Job 11^4†; 'ascribe ye to Yahweh' = 'give' Ps 29^1. 96^7. (1 Chron 16^{28}.)†; 'perverse' ^{5} 2 Sam 22^{27} (∥Ps 18^{26}) Ps 101^4 Prov 2^{15} 8^8 11^{20} 17^{20} 22^5 28^6† (cp Prov 4^{24} 6^{12} 10^9 28^{18}); 'bought thee' ^{6} cp Ex 15^{16}, or in the meaning 'formed thee' Gen $14^{19\ 22}$ Ps 139^{13} Prov 8^{22}; 'increase of the field' ^{13} Lam 4^9† cp Ezek 36^{30}; 'Jeshurun' ^{15} 33^5 ^{26} Is 44^2†; 'demons' ^{17} Ps 106^{37}†; 'give birth' or 'travail' (of God) ^{18} cp Ps 90^2 Prov 8^{24}, and (with a different word) Is 42^{14}; 'froward' ^{20} Prov $2^{12\ 14}$ 6^{14} 8^{13} 10^{31}. $16^{28\ 30}$ 23^{33}†; 'foundations of the mountains' ^{22} Ps 18^7†; 'devoured' ^{24} = 'eaten' Prov 4^{17} 9^5 $23^{1\ 6}$ Ps 141^4†; 'with burning heat' ^{24} Hab 3^5 Ps 76^3 78^{48} Cant 8^6 Job 5^7; 'things that are to come upon them' ^{35} cp Is 10^{13} Job 3^8 15^{24} Esth 3^{14} 8^{13}† cp Driver *Deut* 374. These affinities of thought and language seem, on the whole, to point to the origin of the Song in the age which possessed the prophetic vocabulary of Jeremiah, Ezekiel, and the Editors of the Books of Kings[a]. It probably issued from the same general school of lyric composition which produced the Song of Hannah and Ps 18; but whether it was originally written in the person of Moses, or only assigned to him later, cannot be clearly determined. As the poem contains no allusions to Moses himself, the latter hypothesis seems the more suitable.

5. The 'Blessing of Moses' in Deut 33 forms a counterpart to the 'Blessing of Jacob' in Gen 49, with which some verses are closely connected cp $^{13-16\ 22}$. The order of enumeration, however, is different, and the circumstances implied are by no means the same. Reuben is nearly extinguished ^{6}; Simeon has disappeared altogether; Judah is apparently separated from his people and praying for reunion ^{7}; Levi is no longer denounced for its share in a cruel crime, but exalted as the priestly tribe; and Yahweh has taken up his dwelling in the temple at Jerusalem in the territory of Benjamin ^{12}. The enthusiastic description of Joseph $^{13-17}$, combined with the isolation of Judah, has led most critics to seek the origin of the poem in the Northern Kingdom[b]. With this inference the references to the mountain-sanctuary of Zebulon and Issachar ^{19} are also in harmony. The general character of the sayings in $^{6-25}$ is less abrupt and rugged than that of Gen 49, and they have more the air of a continuous composition instead of being collected from the popular speech of different ages and localities. A more definite religious atmosphere pervades the whole, and the references to the cultus $^{10\ 19}$ and to the blessing or the judgements of Yahweh $^{10\ 12\ 13\ 21\ 23\ 24}$ impart to the series a clearer sense of unity. Accepting the ascription to Ephraim, the Blessing has been attributed to a period 'shortly after the rupture under Jeroboam I' (Schrader, Dillmann, Westphal; Driver, *Deut* 387); or to the prosperous reign of Jeroboam II about 780 B C, with which the references to Levi in $^{9\cdot}$ would seem more in harmony (Graf, Kuenen, Stade, Baudissin, Cornill, Wildeboer, Ball in *PSBA* 1896 April 137)[c]. Under this aspect it has been usually treated as originally incorporated into the northern version of the traditions, E, the phrase 'before his death' also recurring Gen 27^7 50^{16}; on the other hand the designation 'Moses the man of God' occurs elsewhere only in later passages Josh 14^6 Ps 90^{title}†, so that its occurrence awakens some suspicion. But it is possible that the poem as now presented is in fact composite. The historical retrospect in $^{2-5}$ and the lyrical conclusion in $^{26-29}$ bear no particular relation to the 'sayings' which they thus include. The central group $^{6-25}$ is quite independent of the opening and close of the poem. This is especially clear in ^{6}. The tribal descriptions are usually introduced with the formula 'And of (Levi) he said' $^{8\ 12\ 13\ 18\ 20\ 22\ 23\ 24}$. This renders it probable that a similar preamble originally stood before Reuben ^{6} and Judah ^{7}. The missing preface for Reuben may possibly be found curtailed in ^{2a}; in ^{7} 𝔊 (as if conscious of the awkwardness of the double formula) omits 'and he said.' An examination of the linguistic affinities of $^{1-5}$ and $^{26-29}$ supports the suggestion that they are of later origin. The beginning $^{2\cdot}$ seems modelled on the description in the Song of Deborah Judg 5^4 cp Hab 3^3. In spite of the corrupt state of the text the following points may be noted:—^{2} 'shined forth' Ps 50^2 80^1 94^1 Job 3^4 10^3 ^{22} 37^{15}†; 'Mount Paran' Hab 3^3†; ^{4} 'inheritance' = 'heritage' Ex 6^8 = 'possession' ℌ Ezek 11^{15} 25$^{4\ 10}$ 33^{24} 36$^{2\cdot\ 5}$†; 'assembly' ℌ Neh 5^7†. The phrase in ^{4} 'Moses commanded us a law' points

---

[a] Driver, *Deut* 378, thinks that Is 43$^{11-13}$ shows acquaintance with Deut 32^{39}. Such literary dependence can hardly be demonstrated; but the parallels at least point to common modes of thought and expression, cp 'servants' ^{36}, *ante* p 161.

[b] An ancient Rabbinical conjecture has, however, been recently adopted by some scholars, according to which the prayer in ^{7a}, 'hear' שמע, really referred to Simeon שמעון cp Gen 29^{33}, who stands next to Levi in 49^5 So, among others, Bacon, *Triple Tradition* 271; cp Driver, *Deut* 397. Bacon then emends Deut 33^{7b}, and inserts it in ^{11} where it is referred with its new context to Judah By this device the poem is placed in the Southern Kingdom and ascribed to J

[c] The allusion to Judah's difficulties in ^{7} is too vague to supply any clear suggestion.

to an age which already recognized a Mosaic *torah* (such as is now contained in **D**) and is rejected by Dillmann as a post-Deuteronomic gloss, *NDJ* 419: while the occurrence of the name 'Jeshurun' $^{5\ 26}$ supplies a point of contact with 32^{15} (elsewhere only in Is 44^2). The imagery of $^{26-29}$ is full of phrases found only in compositions much later than the age of Jeroboam II, and yet further removed from the popular calf-worship of Jeroboam I. With ^{26a} cp Ex 8^{10} 9^{14} 15^{11} 2 Sam 7^{22} Deut $4^{35\ 39}$ 32^{39}. The expression 'rideth upon the heaven' does not occur elsewhere, but cp Is 19^1 Hab 3^{8b} Ps 18^{10}..; 'excellency' (of Yahweh) Ps 68^{34}; 'skies' Is 45^8 Jer 51^9 Ps 18^{11} 36^5 57^{10} ($\|108^4$) 68^{34} 77^{17} 78^{23} $89^{6\ 37}$ Prov 3^{20} 8^{28} Job 35^5 36^{28} $37^{18\ 21}$ 38^{37}='clouds'†. The designation 'God of old' ^{27} ($\mathfrak{H}$='ancient' ^{15}) has no exact parallel, though cp Hab 1^{12} Ps 55^{19}, nor has the phrase 'everlasting arms'; for the idea of duration and the dwelling-place cp Ps 90^1.. ^{28} 'dwelleth in safety' Prov 1^{33} $\mathfrak{H}$ cḅ ^{12} cp Deut 12^{10}; 'fountain of Jacob' cp Ps 68^{26}†; 'alone' $\mathfrak{H}$ 32^{12} Lev 13^{46} Is 27^{10} Jer 15^{17} 49^{31} Lam 1^1 3^{28}†; 'a land of corn and wine' 2 Kings 18^{32} ($\|$Is 36^{17}) cp ᴅ30; 'drop down' 32^2†. ^{29} 'saved by Yahweh' Is 45^{17}†; 'shield of thy help' cp 'shield of thy salvation' Ps 18^{35}†; 'submit themselves unto thee' $\|$ Ps 66^3 cp 18^{44} 81^{15}†; 'tread on their high places' Am 4^{13} Mic 1^3 Hab 3^{19} Job 9^8† cp Deut 32^{13} Is 58^{14} Ps 18^{33}. These general affinities seem best explained on the hypothesis that the 'sayings' have been extended by later additions of a post-Deuteronomic type (i e exilian or later)^a. In this view the title receives fresh light, while the incorporation into **E** becomes slightly less secure. The difficulty may be overcome by regarding the designation 'man of God' as a subsequent insertion.

CHAPTER XV

CRITICISM AND ARCHAEOLOGY

1. SLOWLY, and for ardent spirits far too slowly, the critical study of the Hexateuch has been passing into an archaeological phase, and now that younger men are coming to the front we may expect a more thorough treatment of the relation between archaeology and literary or analytic criticism. To give the lay-student a clear idea of this relation while the researches of the few special scholars are still in such an unfinished state, is difficult in the extreme. The great want of those who aspire to become special scholars is at present a commentary on Genesis in which the problems which are now emerging are treated with some degree of fullness and courage. But there are very good reasons why we should wait a little longer for such a work, and chief among these reasons is one which will also justify the present writer in his omission of many interesting subjects—viz the want of more carefully tested Assyriological evidence.

It is perfectly true that there are in existence a number of popular works summarizing the results of Assyriology, ranging from Mr Ch Edwards' *Witness of Assyria*, on the heterodox side, to Prof A H Sayce's *The Higher Criticism and the Verdict of the Monuments* on the side of orthodoxy. But very few of these works can be relied upon^b, not only because they have a theological colour, but because they are necessarily based on trans-

---

^{a} So also Steuernagel, *Deut* 123. He appears to regard $^{2-5}$ and $^{26-29}$ as parts of a post-exilian Psalm.

^{b} Mr Basil T A Evetts' *New Light on the Bible and the Holy Land* (London: Cassell and Co, 1892) is probably the most to be recommended of the popular works referred to.

literations and translations which need much rectification. My disappointment is great in making this statement, but Prof Sayce will fully bear me out in it, for in his address as President of the Semitic Section of the Orientalists' Congress held in London in 1892, he expressly affirmed that the time for strictly philological treatment of the inscriptions had not yet come. This does indeed appear to me an exaggeration; certainly, other special scholars, such as Delitzsch, Jensen, and Zimmern, would not altogether assent to it. It must at any rate be admitted that many meritorious Assyriological books are now antiquated, and that works based upon them (whether critical or popular) must consequently be pronounced inadequate.

2. I pass at once to the narratives of the creation of the world and of man in Gen 1^1-2^{4a}. From each of the three scholars mentioned above we have translations of the most famous of the Babylonian creation-myths[a]. It is unnecessary for me to trace minutely the coincidences between the Babylonian and the best-known Hebrew account, or to argue in favour of the view that there is a historical connexion between the narratives. The question on which I have to offer some suggestions is this, Does the discovery of a Babylonian cosmogony, similar in form to the chief Hebrew cosmogony, though very different from it in spirit, tend to confirm or to refute the conclusions of critical students of Genesis?

(a) One conceivable answer is this. It is certain from the Amarna Tablets[b] that even before the Egyptian conquests and the rise of the kingdom of Assyria, Babylonian culture had spread to the shores of the Mediterranean. Religious myths must have travelled to Palestine as a part of this culture. It is, therefore, intrinsically probable that a Babylonian cosmogony penetrated into Canaan before the fifteenth century B C, and that the Israelites as soon as they became settled enough borrowed and Hebraized this story. And then the student may leap to the conclusion that the so-called Priestly Record, which contains this Hebraized Babylonian story, must be not only a pre-exilic, but an early pre-exilic work.

(β) The author of this inference, however, would show that he was a very inexperienced critic. The more closely we scrutinize the story in Gen 1^1-2^{4a}, the more clearly we see that it stands at or near the close and not at the beginning of a development of imaginative thought on the origin of things. When the Israelites adopted from their Canaanitish neighbours the tale of creation which the latter had received from the Babylonians or from some people in close contact with the Babylonians, they certainly did not at once proceed to omit the most interesting details, and so deprive it of almost all its colour and intelligibility, and to use it as a means of illustrating an extremely refined idea of God, and of leading up to an advanced theory of 'covenants.' There must have been earlier Hebrew forms of the same cosmogony, and it is the business of the critic to find out in the Old Testament itself any traces which may exist of such earlier forms. So that the discovery made by George Smith among the remains of Assurbanipal's library is no death-blow to modern criticism, but a friendly message to critics that their critical theories were still too simple, and needed to be expanded so as to correspond better to the complex character of true historic development. That the Priestly Record is a very late work is all the more certain now that we have the great Babylonian 'Creation-epic.' A particular critical theory—viz that the narrative in Gen 1 is the product of the reflexion of a late priestly writer[c]—is no doubt refuted, but this theory has at no time within the last five-and-twenty years been generally accepted.

[a] Jensen, *Die Kosmologie der Babylonier* (1890) pp 268-300; Zimmern, in Gunkel's *Schopfung und Chaos* (1895) pp 401-417, and Delitzsch, *Das Babylonische Weltschopfungsepos* (1897).
[b] See Evetts, *New Light* &c pp 163-185.
[c] Wellhausen, *Prolegomena* Eng Transl p 298.

3. Omitting the story of Paradise and of the expulsion of the first human pair from this happy abode, I pass on to the narrative of the Deluge. Translations of the chief Babylonian Deluge-story, recent in date and critical in character, are referred to below [a]. Again I have to ask, Is the discovery of what is popularly but incorrectly known as '*the* Babylonian Deluge-story' subversive of modern critical views of the composition of the Hexateuch? I will endeavour to treat this question as seriously as the similar question which I have already, as I hope, answered. There is again much that I must omit, because the subject is so new to lay-students, and we have no introductory work on Genesis (Dillmann's lately translated commentary is not quite satisfactory) which will take them into the heart of the present critical problems. In the case of the Deluge-story, it is remarkable that we should possess two distinct accounts of the Deluge, which have been worked together by a compiler—such at least is the view of critics. The main narrative comes from the Priestly Record P, but the elements introduced from the Yahwist J, when put together, form a pretty complete narrative, as the reader of this work will have seen.

(a) It is not impossible that some student may answer the above question thus. The account assigned by critics to the Priestly Record is so strongly Babylonian in character that we cannot help supposing it to have been borrowed by the Israelites directly or indirectly from the Babylonians. Granting that religious myths were a part of the culture received by the Canaanites from the Babylonians, and by the Israelites from the Canaanites, we may reasonably infer that the Record containing the principal Hebrew Deluge-story was an early pre-exilic work. This is not quite such a difficult proposition as that which I had to dismiss at the opening of this discussion. For the account taken from the Priestly Record is much more of a narrative than the cosmogony in Gen 1^1-2^{4a}. And yet it would be a mistake. The arguments which tend to show that the framework of our chief Deluge-story is artificial cannot be refuted simply by the discovery that that Deluge-story itself has strong Babylonian affinities. The fact that the Deluge-story of the Priestly Record leads up to a second covenant between God and man 9^{1-16} should of itself restrain us from placing the composition of that story in its present form early in Israelitish history. And now let us note this circumstance. The Yahwistic Deluge-story, as presented to us by the compiler referred to above, begins with the words, 'And Yahweh said to Noah, Go thou with all thy house into the ark' 7^1. It is in the highest degree probable that the Yahwist's account contained information on all these points on which at present we are dependent entirely on the other narrative, and not much less probable that on all these points the Priestly Writer was really himself indebted to the Yahwist. There is much more that might be added. But it must suffice to say here with regard both to the Creation- and to the Deluge-stories that if they were in circulation in early pre-exilic times it is difficult to understand the absence of any direct allusion to them in the undoubted pre-exilic writings. We can well believe that they were told and retold in certain circles, but the great prophets, and the historical writers of their school, *appear* not to have known them, at any rate, as moralized and edifying stories to which they could venture to refer.

4. To make the above clear, it may be well to mention the periods in which an interest in Babylonian myths may be presumed to have existed among the Israelites. The first is the period of their first settlement in Canaan (a period not to be computed with exactness). The second is that of David and Solomon. The former king not improbably had as his secretary a Babylonian, or at any rate a foreigner who had been

---

[a] Paul Haupt, in Schrader's *Die Keilinschriften und das Alte Testament*, 2nd edition (1883) pp 56-64 (not in Whitehouse's translation), Jensen, *Kosmologie* pp 368-383, Zimmern, in Gunkel's *Schopfung* pp 423-428; Muss-Arnolt, *Biblical World* iii (1894) pp 109 ff. The last of these is in English.

trained in Babylonian culture^a; the latter erected at Jerusalem a temple containing sacred objects of Babylonian origin^b. The third is the period of the eighth and seventh centuries B C, when Aramean, Assyrian, and neo-Babylonian influences were, as it appears, strongly felt in Palestine in some of the chief departments of life. The fourth and fifth periods are the exilic and post-exilic, when a revival of interest in mythology appears to have taken place among the Jews which the religious authorities could to some extent neutralize but not extinguish^c. It was abundantly possible for stories to have been taken by the Israelites at any one of these periods, and if taken at one of the early periods, they might easily be revived and amplified, after a temporary decline, at one of the later periods. There is evidence enough, in the present writer's opinion^d, to refute the view of Dillmann (in his commentary on Genesis and elsewhere) that the Hebrew and Babylonian accounts of the origin of things are independent developments of a mythic tradition common to the north-Semitic races.

5. We may now proceed to ask whether the personal and quasi-personal names contained in the Priestly Record (Arphaxad and Ammishaddai are two notable examples) supply evidence as to the date of that Record. The question has been treated in a controversial spirit by Prof Hommel in his *Ancient Hebrew Tradition* (1897), who returns an affirmative answer. Unfortunately this scholar is sometimes too hasty in his statements respecting Assyriological facts. Instances of this have been lately produced by the Rev C H W Johns^e and Mr L W King^f. It is far from my thoughts to cast stones at Prof Hommel, whose real disposition towards critics of the Hexateuch I know to be more genial than readers of the popular book referred to will suppose. But till the cuneiform and the Sabaean epigraphic material has been more completely mastered, it would have been better to abstain from basing such far-reaching theories upon it, though it must be added, that even accepting all the alleged evidence, it proves but little. On this and other grounds I need not here undertake the large task of examining Prof Hommel's statements in detail. He has certainly given a fresh stimulus to the inquiry into the sources from which the Priestly Writer drew—sources which were evidently not so limited as earlier critics very naturally supposed. This is title enough to highly honourable mention. But it must be plain enough to those who have no controversial bias that the existence of some ancient material does not prove the early date of the compilation in which the material is found^g. The amount of late material (both in names and in narratives) may be reduced, but even so there will remain superabundant evidence of the recent origin of this great introduction to the post-exilic Church History.

6. The simplification produced in critical research by frankly rejecting the controversial spirit and pressing on towards truth on strictly critical lines is nowhere more manifest than in dealing with Genesis 14.

(*a*) The controversial spirit requires us to take up one of two positions. (i) Gen 14 is an old pre-exilic document, based upon still more ancient Canaanitish archives, and

---

^a 'Shavsha was scribe' (M 'secretary') 1 Chron 18¹⁶. For the facts on which this theory is based see *Encyclopaedia Biblica*, s v 'Shavsha.'

^b See *Encyclopaedia Biblica*, s vv 'Sea, Molten,' 'Nehushtan.'

^c Suggestive remarks have been made on this subject by Stade. The present writer, in a series of works, has indicated some of the exegetical evidence for the above conclusion. The latest and fullest source of information is Gunkel's *Schopfung und Chaos* (1895). See also the *Encyclopaedia Biblica* (in preparation).

^d It is willingly admitted that only in a commentary could this opinion be thoroughly justified to those who take the opposite view.

^e 'Note on Ancient Hebrew Tradition,' *Expositor* Aug 1898 158-160.

^f *Letters of Khammurabi*, Introduction, xxviii ff.

^g See G B Gray, 'The Character of the Proper Names in the Priestly Code; a Reply to Prof Hommel,' *Expositor* Sept 1897 173-190; and the same scholar's book, *Studies in Hebrew Proper Names* (1896). See also various articles in the *Encyclopaedia Biblica*.

thoroughly to be trusted for what it tells us both about Abram 'the Hebrew' and about Chedorlaomer king of Elam and his allies, and (ii) Gen 14 is from beginning to end a pure romance, the work of the post-exilic period. If we have to defend the former view we shall of course approach any primitive Babylonian documents which have come down to us with the expectation of finding in them the names of the kings given in Gen 14, in connexion with events closely resembling those described in the Hebrew writing. If on the other hand the latter view be our thesis, we shall do our utmost to avoid accepting such identifications of names and such a parallelism of historical narratives. Modern critics however—those who are actually working on these subjects—are not controversialists; they are committed to neither of these positions. Kittel and König may hold Gen 14 to be in the main of early pre-exilic origin; Wellhausen, Stade, Meyer, Kautzsch, with whom I am in accord, hold it to be a post-exilic Midrash. But though Kittel recognizes a degree of historicity in the narrative which is to some of his critical brethren startling in the extreme, he fully admits that the passage relative to Melchizedek, the priest-king of Salem, has been 'very largely worked over by a redactor[a].' And though the more advanced school of critics thinks the narrative as a whole to be unhistorical, it is quite willing to accept the truth (if it be a truth) that historical names and even historical events had come down to the late writer who composed the quasi-historical Midrash. It was merely a working hypothesis which was put forward by E Meyer[b] in 1884 that 'the Jew who inserted Gen 14 in the Pentateuch had obtained in Babylon minute information as to the early history of the land.' It is open to any one to suppose that, not only myths, but names and events of remote historical origin had come down to the later Jews[c], and also that if we had the text of Gen 14 in an entirely correct form there would be no ground for the rather weak criticism which has been based on the form of the names Bera, Birsha, Shinab, Shemeber[d].

(β) Critics, then, are not controversially minded. But they are on that account all the more interested in the investigation of the primitive history of Babylonia and Elam. It has a direct bearing on Biblical archaeology, and therefore on the researches into the origin of the Old Testament. Anything which throws light on the course of Israelitish and indeed of Canaanitish history, and on the early traditional material which the Israelitish narratives may have used, is welcome to them. Let us then ask, what confirmation is given by Babylonian inscriptions to the view that the author of Gen 14 used traditional material? Putting aside for the present Father Scheil's recent discovery (as it at first appeared to be), we may safely affirm so much as this. In the twenty-third century B C a king of Elam named Kudur-nanḫundi, ravaged southern Babylonia. Kudur-mabug is the name of another Elamite prince who somewhat later conquered the old kingdom of Larsa (probably the Ellasar of Gen 14), which was supreme over south and central Babylonia. The name Kudur-lagamar has not been found, but Lagamar(u) occurs as the name of an Elamite deity. Arioch seems to be Eri-aku (otherwise called Rim-sin), king of Larsa, and son of Kudur-mabug. Whether in a very remote period Canaan as well as Babylonia fell under the Elamite rule, we cannot say, the alleged evidence being inadequate. It seems, however, not an improbable view. It is also plausible to identify the name Amraphel with the name Ḥammurabi.

[a] *Geschichte der Hebraer* (1888) 1 p 162; English Translation 1 179.
[b] *Geschichte des Alterthums* 1 166.
[c] This consideration renders it possible to hold that 'Nimrod' is really a corruption of the name Nazi-maiattaš, a conquering Babylonian king of the Kassite dynasty. That the writer of Gen 14 used an old native Palestinian tradition, or rather elements of such a tradition, is the view of Lehmann, *Zwei Hauptprobleme der altoriental Chronologie* (1898) p 84. Lehmann accepts all the equations, Amraphel = Ḥammurabi, Arioch = Eri-Aku, Tidal = Tudḫula, Chedorlaomer = Kudur-nuḫ-gamar.
[d] See articles in *Encyclopaedia Biblica*.

But if Shinar is, as Schrader holds *a*, a Hebraized form of Šumer, Amraphel (Ḥammurabi) was not king of Shinar till he had put down the Elamite rule in Babylonia. But then it became impossible for an alliance to exist between Amraphel and Arioch. Tidal remains a mystery; Goyim (in the phrase 'king of nations,' *melek gōyim*) is certainly a corruption of a name, possibly of Guti or Kuti, a people of whom Prof Hommel has much that is interesting to say in his *Ancient Hebrew Tradition*.

(γ) A sensation was caused in 1896 by Father Scheil's report *b* that he had discovered a mention of Chedorlaomer in a text in the Constantinople Museum. The name was read by this scholar Ku-dur-la-a'g-ga-mar; it occurred in a letter from Ḥammurabi king of Babylon to Sin-idinnam king of Larsa. Unfortunately the passage rendered by Father Scheil 'on the day of (the defeat of) Kudurlagamar' is, according to Mr L W King, only capable of being translated 'the troops under the command of Inuḫsamar.' The letter of Ḥammurabi is quite as interesting historically as Father Scheil represents, but not on the ground that it contains a mention of Chedorlaomer. Mr T G Pinches had at a somewhat earlier date found a cuneiform tablet in the British Museum which seemed to him to contain the names of no less than three of the kings mentioned in Gen 14, viz *Kudur-lagamar* or Chedorlaomer, *Eri-aku* or Arioch, and *Tudḫula* or Tidal *c*. It is true, the date was not earlier than the fourth century B C, but it might be conjectured that the inscription was copied from one made in the primitive period. Schrader *d* inclined to agree with Pinches in the reading and identification of the names, but the uncertainty of the identifications could not be denied. It was not Eri-aku, but Eri-[E]aku and Eri-Eku (or -Ekûa) which occurred, and the name identified with Chedorlaomer was not read with perfect certainty. Mr L W King reads the latter name Ku-dur-ku-mal and Ku-dur-ku-kŭ-mal, and, while admitting that this personage is called a king of Elam, finds no reason to suppose that he was a contemporary of Ḥammurabi. All Biblical critics will be disappointed at this result. The larger the traditional element in Gen 14, a document which, as it now stands, is undoubtedly due to an editor, the better they will be pleased. But appearances are very much against the view that Kittel's theory of a narrative derived from Canaanitish archives can stand. There may possibly have been a dim tradition of an Elamite invasion of Canaan, but we can lay no stress on details, and the historical character of Abraham, and much more, of Melchizedek king of Salem (or Shiloh?), remains unproved.

Mr King, whose important work, *The Letters and Inscriptions of Khammurabi* only lies before me in part, does not claim the distinction (for as such it may be justly viewed) of being a Biblical critic; he does not wield the two-edged sword which Schrader, at any rate formerly, could wield. But his testimony to facts is all the more valuable, whether it happens to make for or against any of the current theories.

With some regret I pass over the questions arising out of the story of Joseph. To deal with them properly, I should need to be able to refer the reader to some commentator, keener in criticism and more deeply interested in archaeology, than Dillmann. But I may at least record the opinion that archaeological (Egyptian) evidence favours the view that that fascinating story continued to be worked over and revised rather late in the pre-exilic period. My next halt must be made at the Exodus.

7. It must unfortunately be admitted that we have as yet no external information which throws light on the triple Hebrew tradition of the Exodus given by the Yahwist J, the Elohist E, and the Priestly Writer P. An Egyptian account is indeed given in

---

a *Cuneiform Inscriptions* &c (edited by Whitehouse) i 103 f.
b See *Recueil de Travaux* (edited by Maspero) xiv 4 ff, and cf Hommel, *Anc Heb Trad* pp 173-180.
c Paper before the Victoria Institute, Jan 20, 1896.
d *Sitzungsberichte der Akad der Wissenschaften* (Berlin 1895) No XLI.

the fragments of Manetho (Jos *c Ap* i 26 f), but we can hardly help observing in it the influence of the Jewish tradition, and it is a reasonable view of E Meyer [a] that Manetho has confounded Moses with the reforming or heretical king commonly known as Khu-en-aten (Amenhotep IV). The famous 'Israel-stelè' discovered by Mr Flinders Petrie creates fresh difficulties for the historical critic, and throws no light on the question, Can we detect early traditional material in the accounts handed down to us by J, E, and P? The reader will doubtless remember the description given by the eminent discoverer of the circumstances under which 'the ruthless Merenptah' inscribed a noble slab of black syenite with a long semi-poetical semi-historical composition [b]. We have now Spiegelberg's translation of this 'Triumphal Song [c].' The passage relating to Israel runs thus, 'Devastated in Tehenu, Kheta is quieted, led away is Askelon, taken is Gezer, Yenoam is brought to nought, the people of Israel is laid waste—their crops are not, Khor (Palestine) has become as a widow for Egypt, all lands together—they are in peace.'

Moreover in 1885 and again in 1891, M Naville could confidently maintain that his researches at Tell el-Maskhutah and elsewhere had brought strong confirmation to the view (which is certainly at first sight a natural one) that the statement in Ex 1¹¹ is strictly correct, that the Israelites were in Egypt, that they were oppressed under Rameses II, and escaped from Egypt under Merenptah [d]. This, however, does not accord with what we read on the stelè of the latter king. Hypotheses to reconcile the inscription with the current view can easily be and have been formed. But clearly we are not entitled to say that archaeological discovery has revealed to us the traditional facts which, when coloured and reshaped by gifted Hebrew writers, became the narratives with which we are so familiar. A shock—doubtless a wholesome shock—has been given by this discovery to all students of Hebrew antiquity, but the shock is less painfully felt by those who have adopted the methods of literary and historical criticism than by those whose main object is to prove the historical trustworthiness at all points of the Hebrew narratives.

8. It is not the present writer's object to discuss the points of historical criticism which naturally arise to the mind in this connexion, the work to which this chapter belongs being of the nature of Prolegomena to historical criticism, and not a specimen of that criticism, which may, we hope, some day arise out of this and kindred works on English soil. The only question which may fairly be asked here is a literary one. Is it possible that Lieblein's view may not be without a certain element of truth, and that an old Hebrew tradition of the Exodus was modified and expanded in the time of Rameses II, when the political and social influence of Egypt was predominant in Syria [e]? That the story of Joseph was thus modified at a still later date is certainly a not improbable view. And did that old Hebrew tradition mean by Mizrim [f] the land of Egypt, or the North Arabian region known, as Winckler has proved, by the same name?

The object of this chapter has now been attained. The points in which the literary criticism of the Hexateuch is affected by archaeology have been referred to, so far as this is possible in the absence of a thoroughly adequate commentary on this portion of the Old Testament literature. A complete conspectus of the facts of archaeology,

---

[a] *Geschichte des Alterthums* 1 270 § 226

[b] See 'Egypt and Israel,' *Contemporary Review* May 1896

[c] Flinders Petrie, *Six Temples at Thebes* chap ix, by W Spiegelberg (1897)

[d] See Naville, *The Store City of Pithom and the Route of the Exodus* (Egypt Exploration Fund, 1885); *Route of the Exodus* (Victoria Institute, 1891).

[e] 'L'Exode des Hébreux,' *Proceedings of the Society of Biblical Archaeology* xx (1898) pp 277 ff.

[f] *Altorientalische Forschungen* 1 pp 241 ff, *Musri, Meluḫḫa, Ma'in*, Parts I and II (Berlin 1898) (Mittheilungen der Vorderasiatischen Gesellschaft). Cp *Encyclopaedia Biblica*, s v 'Mizraim.'

which bear not only on questions of the analysis and the date of documents, but on the credibility of the facts related in the documents, will no doubt be given in a perfectly satisfactory form by Dr Driver in his expected contribution to Mr Hogarth's large work on Archaeology in its relation to Literature.

CHAPTER XVI

THE UNION OF THE DOCUMENTS

IF the Pentateuch consists of different documents of varying age, is it possible to determine the process by which they were combined? And how far do the traces of this process support or impair the view of the origins of the constituent sources which has been expounded in the foregoing Introduction? Some brief answer must be given to these questions. Did the documents remain separate till their final union, or, if not, in what order were they amalgamated? The inquiry has been answered along opposite lines according to the main division between the critical schools founded on divergent conceptions of the age and significance of the Priestly Code. And within these groups other modifications display themselves from time to time, so that a number of schemes may be suggested, each having some kind of justification[a]. The following outline only attempts to indicate the main stages of what was probably a long and intricate labour conducted by unknown hands through many centuries.

1. A number of passages indicate the activity of the harmonist who combined the early narratives of J and E into the prophetic history of Israel's ancestry.

(a) Thus in Gen 16^9 the narrative appears to have received two independent insertions. The promise of the multiplication of Hagar's seed ^{10} prematurely anticipates the announcement of the birth of a son in ^{11}, while in form and language it resembles another addition 32^{12}. But in 16^9 Hagar is enjoined to return to her mistress and submit to her harshness. Yet the description of Ishmael in ^{11} is certainly not founded on the assumption that he will be brought up in Abram's tent. Why then should Hagar be sent back? Plainly in order to prepare the way for E's story of her expulsion in $21^{10\cdots}$. At the close of E's story of Abimelech's intended marriage with Sarah 20, the Yahwist editor has felt it needful to supply an explanation ^{18} of the statements made in ^{17}. The explanation is obvious enough, but it is equally plain that it was not part of E's original story, and was added by the harmonist. By similar devices $26^{15\ 18}$ room is found for a second account of the origin of the name Beer-sheba. In $22^{15-18}\ 26^{3b-4}\ 32^{12}$ the compiler has connected together a series of prophetic promises of Israel's future greatness. The method of fusing the two documents, however, is not always the same. Sometimes a portion of one narrative is shorn clean away to make room for the corresponding account of the other, the narrative of Abraham's migration 20^{13} having been removed from E to make room for that of J $12^{1\cdots}$. Sometimes the two are blended into one, as in the accounts of the theophany at Bethel $28^{10\cdots}$, or the births of Jacob's sons.

[a] For convenience of representation the different processes described below may be expressed in notation thus: J + E, the union of J and E, resulting in the combined document JE: JE + D, the further combination of JE with D producing the Law-book of the Restoration JED: JED + P, the amalgamation with Ezra's Code, forming our Pentateuch, designated JEDP. But this result might be reached by other methods: thus if P took shape first, its union with J and E or JE would yield PJE, and the subsequent incorporation of D would produce PJED. Or the process might be conceived as J + E + D = JED, &c

In the treatment of the three great patriarchs, Abraham, Isaac, and Jacob, R^{je} appears to take the narrative of **J** for his base, and only to introduce appropriate supplemental sections from **E**. On the other hand, in relating the fortunes of Joseph, the more copious materials supplied from Ephraim led to a reversal of this method, and in 40–41^{28} the main narrative is drawn from **E** with occasional brief insertions (e g in 40$^{5\ 15}$ 41^{14}) founded on a corresponding account in **J**. The amalgamation of **J** and **E** did not prevent the combined document from receiving further additions, and it has been already argued that 12$^{10-20}$ is a secondary passage in **J** probably later in date than either of the narratives in 20 or 26 (cp chap XI 6β p 108). Whether such passages were the work of **R** himself, it is impossible definitely to decide: nothing hinders the supposition that they were inserted gradually, as part of the general literary growth of the whole. It may, however, be noted that their phraseology falls entirely within the range of the characteristic style of **JE**: they assume that knowledge of the name Yahweh which **E** practically disowns and **P** formally denies: while their prophetic outlook emphasizes the greatness of Israel's destiny and the condescension of the divine choice^a. In both these aspects R^{je} is wholly independent of **P**, a consideration which is highly unfavourable to Dillmann's view that the editorial process began with the union of **P J** and **E** ^{b}.

(β) The narratives of the Mosaic age undoubtedly present many complicated phenomena, so that the exact amount of the share of R^{je} in the production of the present text cannot be specified with any certainty. The presumption established by his treatment of the patriarchal traditions seems, however, to be justified by the analysis. He did not, according to these results, found a new narrative on the basis of older materials, he followed his previous method and contented himself with the simple reproduction of his sources in continuous union. The curious irregularities in the occurrence of the divine name in sections independently ascribed to **E**, at once, however, suggest further problems. Did **E** continue to use the name Elohim even after recording the revelation in Ex 3, and has **R** sometimes altered it and sometimes left it unchanged^c? Again, to whom are due the expansions, the hortatory additions, the lists of nations, and other similar passages, which do not seem to have belonged originally to either **J** or **E** ^{d}? The earlier narratives contain, no doubt, occasional touches due to the editorial combination cp Ex 3^{19} 4^{14b} 18$^{2-4}$ &c. But the recital is on the whole clear and intelligible, and does not show any serious traces of dislocation. On the other hand, the Sinai-Horeb scenes in 19–24 and 32–34 have undergone more than one series of transpositions and alterations, on their way to their present form. Some recent conjectures are discussed in 34^{28N}: it must suffice at present to point to the indications of harmonizing activity in the two sets of covenant-words in 23 and 34; to the additions to the story of the great apostasy in 32, and to the changes in order which have probably taken place between 33^{12} and 34^9. The original **JE** no doubt contained accounts of the preparation of the Tent of Meeting and the sacred ark which have been eliminated to make way for **P**'s elaborate description 25–31^{18a}: while the act of religious devotion by which Israel sought to provide material for the sanctuary has been editorially converted into a punishment for its crime against Yahweh 33^5. In the events of the march the hand of R^{je} or of J^s

---

a Thus compare Gen 22$^{16-18}$ with other similar passages ^{16} 'By myself have I sworn' Ex 32^{13*}; 'oracle' or 'utterance of Yahweh' Num 14^{28} 24$^{3.\ 15.*}$; 'because' Deut 1^{36} Josh 14^{14*}; notice the aggregation in ^{17}, with the double comparison to the stars of the sky and the sand on the shore in ^{18} the 'families' of 12^3 have become 'nations,' while נברך has been changed into התברך cp 26^{4*}: 'because' 26^{5*}.

b Cp *NDJ* 675 Dillmann's chief object is to determine whether **P** was incorporated in **JED** or **D** in **PJE** As his result depends almost wholly on some peculiar phenomena of Joshua (which are considered separately in an introduction prefixed to that book), further argument may be reserved.

c Cp Chap XII 5δ (1) p 119. d Cp Chap XI 6 p 108

is clearly to be traced in Num 14$^{11-24}$; but the account of the conquest of the Trans-jordanic country has probably suffered little modification beyond the actual process of blending the two sources, which may be followed through the Balaam story to the death of Moses[a]. As in the patriarchal narratives so in the traditions and laws of the Mosaic age, the entire absence of any evidence that R^{Je} was acquainted with **P** is not favourable to the view that **P** was united with **JE** before **D**. On that hypothesis how can **D**'s use of the opening of Ex 34 in Deut 10$^{1..}$ be explained? Why should **D** build upon a statement which had been entirely set aside by the fuller and more explicit accounts of **P**? If the author of Deut 10$^{1..}$ made use of a form of **J** (or **JE**) no longer extant, and ignored **P**, may it not be safely inferred that the combination **PJE** did not exist?

(γ) Did **D**, however, possess **JE** or only **J** and **E** in separation? Had the union of **J** and **E** taken place before the discovery of the 'book of the law'? In other words, at what date were **J** and **E** combined? The answers to these questions depend on somewhat delicate considerations, arising out of the relation of **D** to the previous documents. It has been already demonstrated that **D** rested in general terms upon **JE** (cp chap IX i 1-2), but the inquiry whether **J** and **E** were still separate or already united, was left undetermined. On the one hand **D**'s invariable use of the name Horeb in preference to Sinai allied him with **E** rather than **J**; and his employment of the laws in **E**'s 'Judgement-book' supplied another strong link of connexion. On the other hand the repeated allusions to the 'oath which Yahweh sware to the fathers' provided an equally clear reference to a characteristic incident of **J**. But these and similar instances are not decisive. There is nothing in them to show whether the documents from which they were derived were still distinct, or had already undergone amalgamation. Kuenen, accordingly, still maintained that the author of Deut 5-26 need only be supposed to have used the separate sources, **J** and **E**, the latter in a revised Judean edition[b]. The case can only be decided if clear evidence can be produced proving **D** to have been acquainted with their combined form. Fortunately such evidence is at hand. It is shown in the analysis that Deut 9$^{13..}$ rests upon Ex 32$^{9..}$. But Ex 32^{13} in its turn is founded on Gen 22$^{16.}$, as the following parallels prove:—

Ex 32	Gen 22
^{13} To whom thou swarest by thine own self, and saidst unto them, I will multiply your seed as the stars of heaven	^{16} By my own self have I sworn, . ^{17} that . . . I will multiply thy seed as the stars of heaven

Now Kuenen himself (*Hex* 254) assigns Gen 22$^{15-18}$ to R^{Je}, and if the author of the Deuteronomic homilies 5-11 was also (as he contends) the compiler of the code 12-26, it must be conceded that he possessed **J** and **E** already in union, though it is not impossible that they may have also been still in circulation separately. Another instance will be found in the relation of Deut 10$^{1..}$ and Ex 34$^{1..}$. This conclusion receives some confirmation from the peculiar manner in which the language of **J** and **E** seems again and again combined in reminiscence by **D**. Two examples are here offered. The interesting liturgical recital prescribed for the Israelite who brings his firstfruits to the temple at Jerusalem 26$^{5-8}$, presents a curious series of alternate parallels to the phrases of both sources:—

Deut 26^5 He went down into Egypt, . . . and became there a nation. ^{5} And sojourned there.	^{E} Gen 46^3 Fear not to go down .. for I will make of thee a great nation. ^{E} Num 20^{15} Our fathers went down into Egypt. ^{J} Gen 47^4 To sojourn in the land.

---

[a] The overthrow of Og king of Bashan Num 21$^{33-35}$ is a later insertion, based on Deut 3$^{1..}$.

[b] *Hex* 253. But he admitted that Deut 1-4 presupposed **JE**, for Deut 1$^{9..}$ draws from both Ex 18 and Num 11$^{4-34}$ (see Analysis).

⁵ Mighty, and populous	ᴊ Ex 1⁹ More populous and mightier.
⁶ And the Egyptians evil entreated us	ᴇ Num 20¹⁵ And the Egyptians evil entreated us.
⁶ And afflicted us.	ᴊ Ex 1¹² They afflicted them.
⁶ Hard service.	ᴊ ¹⁴ Hard service.
⁷ We cried unto Yahweh, . : and Yahweh heard our voice.	ᴇ Num 20¹⁶ And we cried unto Yahweh, and he heard our voice.
⁷ Saw our affliction	ᴊ Ex 3⁷ I have . . seen the affliction.
⁷ And our toil.	ᴇ Gen 41⁵¹ My toil cp ᴇ Num 23²¹ 𝔇*.
⁷ And our oppression	ᴇ Ex 3⁹ I have seen the oppression.
⁹ A land flowing with milk and honey	ᴊ ⁸ cp ᴊᴇ33

D thus accumulates the expressions of both **J** and **E**. Did he do so by way of reminiscence from separate narratives, or did he draw from their combined form? The presumption established by the foregoing instances points to the latter hypothesis, and is supported by another case, the reference to Dathan and Abiram Deut 11⁶:—

Deut 11⁶ Dathan and Abiram, the sons of Eliab	ᴇ Num 16¹·¹².
⁶ The earth opened her mouth, and swallowed them up, and their households.	ᴇ ³²ᵃ The earth opened her mouth, and swallowed them up, and their households.
⁶ And every living thing	ᴊ Gen 7⁴·²³ Every living thing †
⁶ That followed them (𝔇 at their feet).	ᴊ Ex 11⁸ That follow thee Cp ᴊ Gen 30³⁰ Num 20¹⁹ ∥ Deut 2²⁸*.

The relationship thus indicated appears best explained by the suggestion that **J** and **E** had been already united before the Deuteronomists began to write. It can hardly be imagined that a new religious vocabulary of so striking a kind was a wholly fresh creation. In the secondary passages of **J**, and in those which may with great probability be ascribed to **Rᴶᵉ**, the language and ideas approximate more and more to those of **D**. Instances of this may be noticed in the lists of the Canaanite nations Ex 3⁸ᴺ, in the monotheistic affirmations of Moses to Pharaoh cp 8¹⁰ᴺ, or in the sublime revelation of Yahweh's character on the mount 34⁶⁻⁹. Even the narratives of Genesis are not without signs of this tendency, as may be seen in Gen 18¹⁷⁻¹⁹ and 26³ᵇ⁻⁶; but it is difficult to know how many of these passages can be definitely assigned to the literary activity of **Rᴶᵉ**, or how many may have been thus expanded by other hands before he began his task. In any case there is probably no very long interval between them. They mark the transition between the directness of the earlier narratives and the later and more devotional style: and as they may be regarded as prior to **D**, the first stage of documentary redaction with which they are associated may be ascribed to 650 B C ᵃ.

2. The foregoing argument has tended to show that **J** and **E** were combined before their union with Deuteronomy. It has, indeed, been suggested that they were still separate when this amalgamation took place ᵇ; but the evidence of the acquaintance of **D** with passages resting on the fusion seems only explicable on the supposition that while they may still have been in circulation apart, they had also been wrought into a single whole ᶜ. The next step therefore was to fit **D** into this book of prophetic history. The work was naturally effected by a member of the Deuteronomic school; and the process—for more than one hand may have taken part in it—may be designated by the expression **Rᵈ**.

(*a*) It was formerly supposed by Colenso that this process was of a very extensive character. It involved, in his view, large additions to Genesis, Exodus, and Numbers. In Genesis he attributed no less than 117 verses to this source; in Exodus he

---

ᵃ Kuenen, *Hex* 249, places **Rᴶᵉ** between 621 and 586 B C. This is chiefly on the ground that **Rᴶᵉ** may be supposed to have incorporated the Song of Moses Deut 32¹⁻⁴³. But both the poem and the introduction in 31¹⁵⁻²² seem to be of later date See Analysis and Chap XIV 4.

ᵇ Kittel supposes that the combined JED was reached rather by J + E + D than by JE + D

ᶜ The suggestion of Bacon has been already mentioned, that the introductory discourse of **D** was founded on a farewell exhortation of Moses in **E**, cp chap XII 2γ and Deut 1ᶜᴺ⁽²⁾.

recognized 138½, and in Numbers 156½ ᵃ. There seems, however, no sufficient reason for regarding it as so far-reaching. The approximation of the later **J** (including **R**ᴶᵉ) to the Deuteronomic position, both in thought and language, sufficiently accounts for the stylistic resemblances; and the tendency of recent criticism has been to confine the revision of **R**ᵈ within much narrower limits. It is suggested in the analysis that his activity prior to the Sinai-Horeb scenes may be traced in Gen 15^{18-21} 26^5 Ex 12^{25}.. 13^3 $^{14-16}$ 15^{26}, but it does not appear that he actually recast any extensive passages, or made any serious changes in the order of the narrative. With 19, however, in the estimation of many distinguished critics, he enters on a more thorough treatment. His hand is probably to be seen in ^{3b}..: the commentaries on the Ten Words in 20 may owe something to him: and to him is assigned the amalgamation of the 'Judgements' $21-22^{17}$ with **E**'s Covenant-words cp 20^{22N} and 34^{28N}. The harmonist of **J** and **E** had been already at work to bring the Covenant-words of his two documents into closer accord. The process of revision and extension was probably continued by **R**ᵈ in 22^{21b} ^{22} ^{24} 23^9 ^{13} (possibly ^{15}) from the Deuteronomic point of view; while the remarkable affinities of 23^{23-25a} ^{27} $^{31b-33}$ with Deut 7 suggest considerable extensions in **E**'s hortatory conclusion. But here, as in other cases, the possibility must always be kept open that the same result might have been reached by different means. Similar signs of expansion seem traceable in **J**'s Covenant-words in Ex 34. The Sinai-Horeb narratives have therefore passed through two distinct stages, the first in the union of **J** and **E**, the second in the combination of **JE** and **D**. Each of these brought hortatory additions or alterations into the text. Further changes—not of expansion but of omission—were required when **JED** was incorporated in **P**.

(β) No conspicuous instance of **R**ᵈ's presence is to be traced in the story of the wanderings between Sinai and Moab, save the brief episode of the conquest of Og Num 21^{33-35}, which appears to be founded on the longer version in Deut 3. This at once connects the editorial revision in Gen-Ex-Num with the process by which Deuteronomy itself assumed its present form (cp chap X 4 and Deut 34^{12N}). The analysis renders it probable that **D** is itself composite. The union of its different introductions, its homilies, and its final exhortations, may not all have taken place at once. But there is reason for regarding at least one stage of it as linked with the process of working up **JE** and **D** into one whole, for curious fragments of **E** seem incorporated unexpectedly in 10 and 31. Bacon has even supposed that the hortatory retrospect 1^{6-3} was founded on a farewell discourse of Moses contained in **E** cp $1^{6N\,[2]}$; while Dillmann ib $^{[3]}$ regards it as the result of the conversion of an earlier narrative into the form of direct address, consequent on the proximity of the combined story of **JE**. Fresh problems are introduced by the signs of **R**ᵈ's activity in Joshua, where his manipulation of **JE** seems much more extensive and penetrating (cp *Introd to Joshua* vol ii), so as to give rise to the conjecture that an important break was already recognized in the death of Moses at the close of Deuteronomy.

(γ) Under these conditions it is plain that it is only possible to assign a date to **R**ᵈ within wide limits. Even within the book of Deuteronomy itself a considerable range must be allowed. In parts of 4 28 29 30 there are not a few indications of exilian origin, both in substance and in phraseology (see margins and notes). The work of **R**ᵈ can hardly have begun before the end of the monarchy of Judah was approaching; and Kuenen accordingly suggested the deportation of Jehoiachin in 597 B C, as the first practicable date, while he supposed that **JED** was complete by 536. The phenomena

---

ᵃ *Pent* vii, Synopt Table, and App 145 ff.

of the Song of Moses in 32 with its introduction in 31$^{16-22}$ point to a later rather than an earlier age, the preface containing some expressions (cp margins on ^{16} ^{18}) analogous to the characteristic phraseology of P^h. The well-known marks of Deuteronomic editorship in the series of national histories, Judges, Samuel (to a much less extent) and Kings, suggest that R^d belonged to the group which gathered up the remains of the national literature, and found in the editing of the sacred traditions and laws the means of keeping alive the fires of patriotism and religion. There is no certain proof that this task was completed in 536 B C. One curious passage in Josh 20 shows so peculiar a blending of the characteristics of D and P as to suggest that even post-exilian materials might still be elaborated in Deuteronomic style^a. In that case, the process represented by R^d must be recognized as still unfinished when the Priestly Code itself was promulgated.

3. The third great step in the composition of our present Pentateuch was the union of **JED** with **P**. Of the various elements now traceable in **P**, it has been argued that Ezra's Law-book contained P^{ght}, and possibly some of the secondary additions P^s. Under what circumstances and by what plan did this final combination take place?

(α) The light thrown on the age of Ezra and Nehemiah by their memoirs fades away into obscurity. But from the subsequent course of literary and religious development, as well as from the phenomena of the Pentateuch itself, a sufficiently definite picture can be formed of the mode in which the last amalgamation of the documents took place. Ezra was a 'scribe'; he belonged to a class which made the sacred Law its chief concern; he no doubt found others round him in Jerusalem (e g Zadok Neh 13^{13}) who were ready to share his plans, and promote his aims. Of their activity in later times there is abundant evidence: the *Chronicles*, in which the story of the monarchy of Judah is retold on the basis of the Priestly Law, issued a hundred years or more after the first promulgation of **P** out of their midst. In their schools, no doubt, did the Pentateuch pass through the final stages of editorial treatment. The first impulse would rise out of the desire to combine in one collection all the materials connected with the name of Moses. The Deuteronomic code, with its great historical introduction in **JE**, itself containing ancient covenant-words, had already acquired the sanctity of long tradition. In the two centuries since its publication the reverence of the community had gathered round it; and into that homage the new law-book was now to be admitted. The hold which the older book possessed may be partly measured by the care taken to preserve its sacred law. Though much of the fresh code was really incompatible with the prior institutions, these were not set aside; they remained as precious monuments of the past.

(β) The literary process of R^p can be traced in its general outlines without much difficulty. The chronological framework of **P**'s early history, with the well-marked stages of its successive *tol^{e}dhoth* sections, made it a suitable base for the entire collection. But when **P**'s story of the creation was placed at the head, the superscription was probably transposed to form the link between the narrative of the production of the heavens and the earth with all their host, and that of the garden of Eden and the first Man^b. In the early sections R^p seems to have aimed chiefly at keeping his document intact; he does not himself introduce fresh material, or add hortatory expansions after the manner of R^{je} and R^d. So anxious was he to include his text uncurtailed that he even retained a summary such as that in Gen 19^{29} in the midst of the longer narrative of **J**. On the other hand the birth of Esau and Jacob could not be accom-

---

^{a} The influence of D long remained powerful, as the style of the confession in Neh 9 sufficiently shows Speaking broadly it may be said that the prophetic school preceded the priestly but this does not exclude the possibility of their coexistence after the rise of the latter

^{b} If J^2 had a creation story this was of course removed to make way for P's.

modated with **J**'s prophecy, and has accordingly disappeared. In the story of Jacob and Joseph, moreover, the curt genealogical method was less easily combined with the rich variety of **JE**, and considerable rents were consequently caused in the continuity of **P**. In the cycle of Joseph narratives, however, from Gen 40 onwards, there are curious indications of a revision by a hand kindred to **P** cp 40^{2N}, though this kind of interference with an older work is rarely to be traced elsewhere. The Mosaic sections of **P** do not appear to have lost much, though there must have been some introduction of Moses himself before Ex 6^2, and **P** also would seem to have had some account of the 'Testimony' containing the Ten Words cp 25^{21}. **JE**, on the other hand, has suffered serious loss. From the history of primitive humanity it is conjectured that a creation-story analogous to that in Gen $1-2^{4a}$, the Sethite table cp 4, and the antecedent of the rainbow after the flood in J^s, have all been withdrawn[a]. The account of Abram's arrival in Canaan has been replaced by **P**'s migration-formula 12^{4b}; while **JE** no doubt originally contained mention of the birth and naming of Ishmael, and the deaths of Sarah and Abraham. The preparation of the Mosaic Tent of Meeting and the sacred ark has also given way before the elaborate narratives of **P**; while the people's initiative in the mission of the twelve spies Num 13 cp Deut 1^{22} has been suppressed in favour of a more august commission. In these cases incidents which from their very nature could only be related once, are usually preserved in the form given to them by **P**; or, as in the Deluge narratives, or the passage of the Red Sea, the several sources are combined. On the other hand, two versions of the origin of the name Bethel are preserved, as they are assigned to different periods in Jacob's career Gen 28^{11-22} and 35^{9-15}: two revelations of Yahweh's name are made to Moses: while the quails appear twice in the wilderness under varying conditions Ex 16^{13} and Num 11^{31}, and the 'strife' at Meribah is allowed to occur on the way to Sinai Ex 17^7 and at Kadesh Num 20^{13}. On the whole, the method of R^p was as conservative as possible; and to this tendency are we indebted for the retention of numerous incongruities which throw significant light on the contents and relations of the documents.

(γ) But the process of harmonizing **JE** and **P** had another instrument at its command besides either omission or amalgamation. Particular clauses, or whole sections, might be transposed. Thus the analysis shows that Gen 7^{16b} has been detached from its rightful connexion. The narrative of the birth of Esau and Jacob $25^{21\cdot\cdot}$ should apparently follow $26^{33\cdot\cdot}$. Ex 16 assumes the institution of the sanctuary and is consequently placed too soon: in 18 the visit of Jethro finds Moses encamped at the mount of God ^{5}, which he does not reach before 19^2. The intricate combinations of **J** and **E** in 19-24 and 32-34 are made more bewildering still by the insertion of a fresh account of Moses' sojourn on the mount and the instructions for the preparation of the Dwelling 25-31, which involve the elimination of the earlier account of the sanctuary. On the other hand, wherever it is possible, differences are softened by harmonizing touches. In Gen $2^{4b}-3$ the planter of Eden seems to be identified with the creator of the world in $1-2^{4a}$ by the addition of Elohim after the name Yahweh. After 17 Abram and Sarai become Abraham and Sarah in **JE** as well as **P**. In 27^{46} it is usual to see the reason by which R^p prepares the way for the transition from Esau's wrath and Jacob's danger to the tranquil blessing with which Isaac sends his younger son to the home of his ancestors to find a bride. Similar harmonistic indications appear in $34^{13\ 25\ 27}\ 35^5\ 37^{14}$ cp 40^{2N} &c. To the same method is probably to be ascribed the addition of Aaron in Ex 4^{23} and a series of subsequent passages cp 4^{13N} with the purpose of heightening the importance of the

[a] Cp Holzinger, *Einleit* 496

priestly dignity by associating him with Moses as the agent of Israel's deliverance cp Num 1¹ˣ. This harmonizing activity also seems to be the source of the curious blending of the phraseology of **P** with that of **JE** which marks Ex 12²¹⁻²³, of the late touches in 13⁹, or of the intrusion of **P**'s characteristic language in Num 13²⁶ᵇ 14¹⁴ &c. In general the usage of **P** is carefully observed by the compiler. In one conspicuous case, however, it is curiously violated, where the term otherwise exclusively applied to the Dwelling of Yahweh is associated with Korah, Dathan, and Abiram Num 16²⁴ ²⁷. Does this neglect of a distinction otherwise carefully emphasized imply that **R**ᵖ stood at some distance from the original designer of the Levitical sanctuary? It is at least arguable that this curious lapse betrays a considerable interval between the author of Ex 25–29 and the editor of the combined documents.

(δ) The Priestly Code was apparently designed to include the record of the settlement in Canaan, according to the promise of Yahweh Ex 6⁸. It may be naturally anticipated, therefore, that the **P** sections in Joshua belong to its main narrative. But they show several curious features, and doubts have been consequently expressed concerning their original character (e g by Wellhausen ᵃ). Some passages, it is certain, belong to the later group designated **P**ˢ (cp *Introd to Josh* 5 (1), ii 316). But it is clear that the editorial process in the compilation of Joshua was not identical with that which may be traced elsewhere (cp ii 315), and this suggests that the fusion was not effected by the same redactors, or at the same time, as was formerly supposed (for example) by Kuenen and Stade. Additional support has been sought for this conclusion in the circumstance that the code promulgated by Ezra was known subsequently as the 'law of Moses ᵇ,' from which it has been inferred that the book could not have included the narrative of the settlement under Joshua ᶜ. But too much stress must not be laid on this term, which is probably due to the editor of Nehemiah's memoirs. The general description 'the law of Moses which Yahweh, the God of Israel, had given' Ezr 7⁶ does not necessarily imply Mosaic authorship, and fixes no definite limits of adjacent narrative: it only describes the legislative contents as Mosaic. If a historical introduction, beginning with the Creation, might be comprised under the term *torah*, why not also a historical sequel? But the peculiarities of the redaction remain, and these are not lightly to be set aside. In view of these difficulties, Prof Holzinger and Prof W H Bennett arrived independently at the belief that the union of **P**'s Joshua with **JED** was accomplished independently of the combination of the preceding books ᵈ. How, then, may the whole process be conceived? Two main possibilities are open. Did the compiler of the Five Books, **R**ᵖ, simply cut off Joshua from **JED** and **P**, and leave them to some successor to be dealt with as might seem fit? Or did he already find **JED** divided into two parts, the main portion terminating with the record of the law by Moses and the narrative of his death, and a supplement carrying on the story through the conquest and settlement? The latter seems on the whole the more probable view. For the Deuteronomic redaction of Joshua itself displays a much freer treatment of older materials than the records of the Mosaic age (cp *Introd to Josh*), and this fact, analogous to what has been already observed in connexion with the compound Joshua **JEDP**, points to the separation of **JE**'s Joshua and its expansion by **D** under different conditions from those which determined the form of the united documents **JED** as far as the death of Moses. That event made an obvious pause in the national story. So also, at a later stage, did the death of Joshua. The Deuteronomic redaction of the Judges-book early in the sixth century ᵉ already found in it a point of new

---

ᵃ *Israel und Jud Gesch*² 172.   ᵇ Neh 8¹ cp 10²⁹ 13¹.
ᶜ So Holzinger, *Einleit* 501; and cp Addis, *Hex* ii 189
ᵈ Holzinger, *Einleit* 502, Bennett, *Primer of the Bible* 90, and *JQR* x 649
ᵉ Cp Cornill, *Einleit*; Moore, *Comm on Judges*; Driver *LOT*⁶

departure 2^6... From the phenomena of Judges it may be tentatively concluded that Joshua in the shape given to it by R^d existed in similar isolation. But though this tends to confirm the theory that **P**'s Joshua was not amalgamated with its predecessor **JED** by the hand which arranged the Pentateuch, it cannot be said to give equal support to the hypothesis that 'the Priestly Code, as Ezra promulgated it, no longer contained the Joshua-sections[a].' There is everything to lead us to expect that it originally did so, and nothing to prove that they had been already detached in the year 444 B C. It is still possible, therefore, to ascribe the actual severance to R^p, while another hand undertook the task of introducing the new material into the Deuteronomic Joshua-book. To R^p also may be attributed with much plausibility the existing divisions of the Pentateuch. The Deuteronomic law with its hortatory and historical introductions formed an obvious whole, and is brought into the chronological scheme of **P** by an editorial insertion in 1^{1b-3}. Natural pauses were also suggested by the death of Joseph, and the erection of the Dwelling; while the first census supplied a suitable point of fresh departure, at the close of the Holiness-legislation. Whether the supplemental law in Lev 27 had been already inserted, or (in other words) how much of P^s had been then incorporated, there is no means of determining. But the evidence offered in connexion with Ex 35-40 shows that the Pentateuch continued to receive additions long after the union of **P** with **JED**.

(ϵ) To what date is the product **JEDP** to be referred? The question can only be answered provisionally and within wide limits. The Chronicler, writing early in the Greek age, founds himself on what is practically the present Pentateuch (apart from the possibility of occasional subsequent expansion). Before the fall of the Persian sovereignty the Samaritan schism supplies a still earlier testimony. Its exact year, indeed, is not known; neither can we trace the circumstances under which the Pentateuch was adopted as its sole religious authority. Moreover, the era of Ezra himself is still in dispute, the range of variation extending through no less than sixty years. The traditional view, however, even when modified by Kosters, would find ample room for the union of the documents before 400 B C[b]. Assuming (as already argued, chap XIII 6γ p 138) that Ezra's law-book was confined to **P**, it is natural to conjecture that steps would be taken speedily after its adoption to lift it into canonical eminence by uniting it with the older work which already possessed Mosaic authority; and Prof Ryle, accordingly, in view of the Samaritan schism regards the Pentateuch as substantially complete before 432 B C[c]. But whatever be thought the most probable date for the first amalgamation, the possibility of subsequent additions, whether in the shape of small glosses and antiquarian explanations, or of larger passages like Gen 14 or Ex 35-40, must not be excluded. The Pentateuch as we have it is the result of long and laborious scribal activity, extending through perhaps two centuries from the time of Ezra.

[a] Bennett, *JQR* x 651.   [b] So Kuenen, Holzinger, Wildeboer.   [c] *Canon* 90.

TABULAR APPENDICES

A. SELECT LISTS OF WORDS AND PHRASES.
   INTRODUCTORY NOTE.

  I. THE PROPHETIC NARRATORS, JE.
   ^{J}1–93 ^{E}94–119 ^{JE}120–237.

  II. THE DEUTERONOMIC SCHOOL, D.

  III. THE PRIESTLY LAW AND HISTORY BOOK, P.
   ^{Pgs}1–191 ^{Ph}192–220.

B. LAWS AND INSTITUTIONS.
  INTRODUCTORY NOTE.

C. ANALYSIS AND CONSPECTUS OF THE HEXATEUCH.

APPENDIX A

THE DOCUMENTARY VOCABULARIES

THE reader who has considered 'the argument from language and style' (*ante* pp 61–67), is already acquainted with the fact that the discovery of the existence of different documents in the Pentateuch led to the observation that they each had their own characteristic phraseology. The following lists have been compiled to exhibit some of these peculiarities, and a few words may be offered in explanation of their significance. Their main object is to present the broad facts illustrating the differences of topic and style in the several documents, so far as these could be appreciated by the English reader. Minuter shades of meaning in the use of particular Hebrew words have been disregarded.

In the first place it did not seem desirable to include words which occurred only two or three times, perhaps in places where the distribution was uncertain. Such appearances are too few to establish a distinctive use, and they are therefore only noted in the margin of the text. A minimum number of five occurrences was accordingly adopted as the basis, and this limitation has been only once or twice abandoned. As, however, the documents are combined in very different proportions, the total amount recoverable for E being very much smaller (for example) than that of P, this rule has excluded some words which might have been found sufficiently often had more of E's materials been preserved.

The same difficulty affects the question of preponderance. Words have been regarded as 'characteristic,' when they occurred in the proportion of 3 to 1. It is obvious that the existing ratios might easily be disturbed if any of the discarded passages, thrown out in the process of compilation, could be reproduced. This is especially the case in the comparison of J and E, which often relate the same stories (such as that of Rebekah's guile in Gen 27) much in the same manner. But here, also, some numerical principle was necessary, and it is hoped that the proportion selected has secured a fair representation. Some of the results, however, must be regarded as accidental. Genuine characteristics of style are probably to be seen in **2 3 6 7 9** &c on the part of J, or in **95 96 99 102 104 105 107** &c on the part of E. The predominance in J of such words as 'camels' 'cattle' 'run' 'thy servants' points to a different way of telling the story, an interest in the persons, the animals, the successions of the action, not displayed by E. That E should regularly employ the names 'Amorite' and 'Horeb' in specific uses may be claimed as distinctive; but the frequent appearance of the words 'dream' and 'interpret' is mainly due to the fact that the Joseph-cycle seems largely derived from him, though J may also have related the same domestic or Egyptian incidents. Similarly the references to 'garden' or 'bricks' in J have no more value than to point to stories not included in E or P. On the other hand, J's description of Yahweh as 'in the midst' of Israel **58**, or

E's employment of the words 'offer' 'pray' and 'prophet,' implies a different emphasis on elements of religious action or thought.

It must be also remembered that any one of the four documents **J E D P** may be compared with any of the other three. Several words, accordingly, in the lists of **J** and **E** must be tested not by their respective predominance in one or other of these two sources only, but by their further occurrence in **D** or **P**. A third section of the **JE** list contains a large number of words some of which reappear under **D**. The reason is that they mark both **JE** and **D** as possessing certain common historical or theological conceptions contrasted with **P**. The chief use of the words in this section, however, is to illustrate the differences of topic and style between **JE** on the one hand and **P** on the other. Though **JE** and **P** relate the same general history from Abraham to Moses (**J** and **P** actually running parallel from the origin of the human race), yet their modes of treatment vary so widely that two wholly separate lists can be quickly collected. Only a selection of these words has been thought necessary, and to some students this branch of the evidence will seem superfluous. In some cases the comparison is expressly limited to the corresponding sections in Genesis, as in the case of the words 'know' ^{JE}174, 'word (matter, or thing)' ^{JE}232. In others the stylistic peculiarity runs through the whole story, and may show itself either in special phrases of narrative or conversation—the mode of asking a question or of making an announcement or of recording the connexion of events—or in the choice of specific terms for the same idea, or in the frequent reference on the part of **JE** to objects or incidents which do not fall within the scope of **P**. Examples of these having been already quoted (*ante* pp 62–64) the lists may be left to the reader's inspection with only one further comment. A distinction must be made between frequency of usage and repetition in one single passage. Thus the terms 'servant' 'servants' ^{JE}207 occur over 140 times in the narratives (and the brief legislation) of **JE**, 88 times in Genesis alone. The **P** sections of Genesis do not contain the word once; of its eighteen appearances ten are in the laws (eight being accounted for by the jubile-emancipation Lev 25), leaving only eight for narrative, all except Ex 7^{10} presenting themselves in passages regarded on other grounds as secondary. **J** and **E** employ the phrase 'build an altar' 16 times and **P** 7. But **P**'s occurrences are all in a single story at the end of the Conquest and Settlement Josh 22: while those in **JE** are distributed over fourteen occasions.

The homiletic vocabulary of **D** has been illustrated on the same general basis, the Deuteronomic sections of Joshua being included. But it has not seemed possible to classify the results as between **D** and **D**^{r}, cp Deut 1^{6N} (4) v.

The terminology of **P** includes a very large number of phrases employed in descriptions of the altar-ritual and other ceremonies. Of these only a few, such as the specific names for the various sacrifices ^{P}118, have been tabulated. The technicalities of the construction of the Dwelling, Ex 25–28 and 35–40, have been in like manner omitted, peculiar terms (with their parallels in the accounts of Solomon's temple and Ezekiel's ideal sanctuary) being noted in the margin with their number of occurrences in brackets. Only one group within the Priestly Code seemed sufficiently distinct to deserve separate treatment. Specimens of the vocabulary of **P**^{h} will be found in ^{P}192–220. In this section owing to the relatively small amount of material three occurrences were held to secure a place on the list. Illustrations of the language of **P**^{t} and **P**^{s} will be found *ante* pp 153 and 155.

Errors there must inevitably be in these lists; passages may have been overlooked, and totals wrongly computed. Where the occurrences are numbered by many scores the figures must be regarded as approximate rather than exact. But it is believed that such accidental inadvertences will not affect the general value of the evidence which is here accumulated.

I. Words and Phrases characteristic of JE

§ 1. J

On the use of the divine name *Yahweh* prior to the revelations to Moses Ex 3^{15} (E) and Ex 6^2 (P) see *Introd* pp 34 38.

1 *Abroad* (or *into the street* החוצה)
 J Gen 19^{17} 24^{29} $39^{12.\,15\,18}$ Josh 2^{19} ..   7 J
 E Gen 15^5 .. ..   1 E
 D Deut 24^{11} 25^5 .. ..   2 D
 Cp 'without' בחוץ Gen 9^{22} 24^{31} Ex 21^{19} =10*
 Deut 24^{11*}: ct P חוצה Ex 12^{46} Num 35^{4*}.

2 *According to these words* (*the word of* .., *after this manner,* דבר *with* כ)
 J Gen 18^{25} 24^{28} 30^{34} 32^{19} $39^{17.\,19}$ 44^2
  7^{ab} 10 47^{30} Ex $8^{10\,13\,31}$ 32^{28} Josh 2^{21} ..   16 J
 R^{je} Ex 12^{35} Num 14^{20} .. ..   2 R^{je}
 D Deut 4^{32} 13^{11} 19^{20} (these three cases
  are somewhat different) Josh 8^8 ^{27} ..   5 D
 P Lev 10^7 .. ..   1 P
          =24*

3 (a) *And it came to pass when* .. (ויהי כי, cp **127**)
 J Gen 6^1 26^8 27^1 43^{21} 44^{24} Josh 17^{13} 6 J
 E Ex 1^{21} .. ..   1 E
 R^d Ex 13^{15} .. .. ; ..   1 R^d
          =8*
 (b) *And it shall come to pass when* .. (והיה כי)
 J Gen 12^{12} 46^{33} Ex 1^{10} $12^{25\,r}$ $13^{5\,11}$
  Num 10^{c2} Josh 8^5 .. ..   9 J
 E Ex 3^{21} 22^{27} .. ..   2 E
 D Deut 6^{10} 11^{29} 15^{16} 26^1 30^1 Ex 13^{14} 6 D
 R Deut 31^{21} .. .. ..   1 R
 P Lev 5^5 6^4 Josh 22^{28} .. ..   3 P
          =21*

4 *Angel of Yahweh* (מלאך י׳) cp 'Angel of Elohim' **97**
 J Gen 16^7 $^{9.\,r}$ ^{11} $22^{11r\,15r}$ ($24^{7\,40}$ 48^{16})
  Ex 3^2 (33^{2r}) Num $22^{22-27\,31.\,34}$. (cp
  Gen 18^2 $19^{1\,15}$) .. ..   17 J
 R^{je} Ex 23^{23} 'mine angel' ..   1 R^{je}
          =18*

5 *As thou comest* (באכה)
 J Gen $10^{19ab\,30}$ 13^{10} 25^{18} .. ..   5 J
  1 Kings 18^{46} 'to the entrance of' ..   1
          =6†

6 *Before* (*ere, not yet,* טרם בטרם) see **132**
 J Gen 2^{5ab} 19^4 $24^{15\,45}$ Ex 9^{30} 10^7 12^{34}
  Num 11^{33} Josh 2^8 3^1 ..   11 J*

7 *Beget, to* (ילד) ct ^{P}**30**
 J Gen 4^{18abc} 10^8 $^{13\,15\,24\,26}$ 22^{23} 25^3 ..   10 J*

8 (a) *Begin, to* (החל)   **J**
 J Gen 4^{26} 6^1 9^{20} 10^8 11^6 44^{12} Num 25^1 7 J
 E Gen 41^{54} .. ..   1 E
 D Deut $2^{24.\,31}$ 3^{24} 16^9 Josh 3^7 ..   6 D
 P Num 16^{46}. .. .. ..   2 P
          =16*
 (b) *Beginning, at the* (or *at first* בתחלה)
 J Gen 13^3 $43^{18\,20}$ (cp Judg 1^1) ..   3 J
 E Gen 41^{21} .. ..   1 E
 Ct Gen 1^1 ⸻ P.   =4*

9 *Behold now* (הנה נא) cp **186**
 J Gen 12^{11} 16^2 $18^{27\,31}$ 19^2 $^{8\,19}$. 27^2 ..   9 J*

10 (a) *Bless, to* (of the patriarchs and their descendants by Yahweh) ct ^{P}**33**
 J Gen 12^2 24^1 26^3 $^{12\,24}$ 30^{27} 39^5 Josh
  17^{14} .. ..   9 J
 R^{je} Gen 22^{17} .. .. ..   1 R
          =10*
 (b) *Bless themselves, to* (נברך and התברך)
 J Gen 12^3 18^{18} 28^{14} (or *be blessed* Niph)   3 J
 R^{je} Gen 22^{18} 26^4 (Hithpa) .. ..   2 R^{je}
 D Deut 29^{19} (Hithpa) .. ..   1 D
          =6*
 (c) *Blessed* (ברוך) cp **24**
 J Gen 9^{26} $24^{27\,31}$ 26^{29} $27^{29\,33}$ Ex 18^{10}
  Num 22^6 (מברך) 24^9 ..   9 J
 E Num 22^{12} Deut $33^{20\,24}$ ..   3 E
 D Deut 7^{14} 28^{3-6} .. ..   7 D
  Gen 14^{19}.   2
          =21*

11 *Both .. and* (גם .. גם, with negative, *neither .. neither*) cp **126**
 J Gen $24^{25\,44}$ 32^{19} 43^8 44^{16} 46^{34} $47^{3\,19}$
  50^9 Ex 4^{10} 5^{14} 12^{31}. 34^3 ..   14 J
 E Gen 21^{26} Ex 18^{18} Num 23^{25} ..   3 E
  Deut 32^{25} (Song of Moses) ..   1
 P Num 18^3 (ct ^{P}**35**) .. ..   1 P
          =19*

12 (a) *Bow to the earth, to* (*ground,* השתחוה ארצה)
 J Gen 18^2 19^1 24^{52} 33^3 43^{26} ..   5 J
 E Gen 37^{10} 42^6 48^{12} .. ..   3 E
          =8*

J (b) *Bow the head and worship, to* (*make obeisance*, קדד והשתחוה)
  J Gen $24^{26\ 48}$ 43^{28} Ex 4^{31} 12^{27} 34^8
  Num 22^{31} ('and fell on his face') . . 7 J*

13 *Brick* (*and make brick*, לבן לבנה)
  J Gen 11^{3abc} Ex 1^{14} $5^{7ab\ 8\ 14\ 16\ 18}$. (cp 24^{10}) 11 J*

14 *Brother, his* (the second of two, after the first has been named)
  J Gen 4^{21} 10^{25} 22^{21} 25^{26} 38^{29}. . . 6 J*
  Ct 'the second' Gen 41^{52} E.

15 (a) *Call upon the name of Yahweh, to* (קרא בשם י׳)
  J Gen 4^{26} 12^8 13^4 21^{33} 26^{25} Ex 34^5 . . 6 J*

  (b) *Therefore he called the name* . . (or *was his name called,* על־כן קרא שם׳) cp **85**
  J Gen 11^9 (cp 16^{14}) 19^{22} 29^{34}. 30^6 31^{48}
  33^{17} 50^{11} Ex 15^{23} Josh 7^{26} . . 10 J
  E Gen 25^{30} (cp 21^{31}) . . . . 1 E
  =11*

16 *Camels*
  J Gen 12^{16} 24^{10}. . (18) 30^{43} 31^{17} $32^{7r\ 15}$
  37^{25} Ex 9^3 . . . . 25 J
  E Gen 31^{34} . . . . 1 E
  D Deut 14^7 ∥ Lev 11^4 . . . . 2 DP
  =28*

17 (a) *Canaanite, the* (as the occupant of the country)
  J Gen 10^{18}. 12^6 24^3 37 50^{11} Num $14^{43\ 45}$ 8 J

  (b) *Canaanite and Perizzite, the*
  J Gen 13^7 34^{30} . . . . 2 J

  (c) *Canaanite, the* (at the head of an enumeration) cp Exod 3^{8N}.
  Ct Num 13^{29} 14^{25}.

18 *Cattle* (מקנה)
  J Gen 4^{20}—Num 20^{19} . . . . 33 J
  E Gen 31^9 . . . . 1 E
  R^{je} Ex 9^{19-21} . . . . 3 R^{je}
  D Deut 3^{19ab} Josh 1^{14} 22^{8r} . . 4 D
  P Gen 31^{18} 34^{23} 36^6. 46^6 Num 31^9
  $32^{1ab\ 4ab\ 16\ 26}$ Josh 14^4 . . 13 P
  =54*

19 *Come down, to* (or *descend*, of Yahweh to the earth, ירד)
  J Gen $11^{5\ 7}$ 18^{21} Ex 3^8 $19^{11\ 18\ 20}$ 34^5 . . 8 J
  E Num $11^{17\ 25}$ 12^5 (in the pillar of cloud, cp Ex 33^9) . . 3 E
  =11*

20 (a) *Comfort, to* (נחם Pi Niph and Hithpa)
  J Gen 5^{29} 24^{67} 27^{42} 37^{35ab} 38^{12} 50^{21}. 7 J*

  (b) *Repent, to* (נחם Niph and Hithpa)
  J Gen 6^6. (of Yahweh) Ex $32^{12r\ 14r}$. 4 J
  E Ex 13^{17} (the people) Num 23^{19} (God) 2 E
  Deut 32^{36} Hithpa (Song of Moses) . . 1
  =7*

21 *Conceive, to* (הרה), and adj. *with child* (הרה)
  J Gen 4^1 17 16^4. 11 19^{36} 21^2 25^{21} 29^{32-35}
  $30^{5\ 7\ 23}$ 38^3. 18 24. 49^{26} Num 11^{12}. 22 J
  E Gen $30^{17\ 19}$ Ex 2^2 21^{22} . . 4 E
  =26*

22 *Consume, to* (or *destroy*, ספה)
  J Gen 18^{23}. $19^{15\ 17}$ Num 16^{26} . . 5 J
  D Deut 29^{19} . . . . 1 D
  =6*

23 *Cry* (צעקה) cp **141**
  J Gen 18^{21} 19^{13} 27^{34} Ex $3^{7\ 9}$ 11^6 12^{30} 7 J
  E Ex 22^{23} . . . . 1 E
  Similarly זעקה J Gen 18^{20*}. =8*

24 *Cursed* (ארור) cp 10°
  J Gen $3^{14\ 17}$ 4^{11} 9^{25} 27^{29} 49^7 Num 24^9
  Josh 6^{26} 9^{23} . . . . 9 J
  D eighteen times, cp ^{D}**32** . . 18 D
  'To curse' ten times in seven different passages in JE. In P six times in one passage, Num 5^{18}. $22\ 24ab\ 27$. =27*

25 *Dry, to be, and dry land* (חרב and חרבה)
  J Gen 7^{22} 8^{13b} Ex 14^{21b} Josh 3^{17a} 4^{18} . . 5 J
  D Josh 3^{17b} . . . . 1 D
  P Gen 8^{13a} . . . . 1 P
  =7*

26 *Dwell in the midst* (or *among*, ישב בקרב)
  J Gen 24^3 Josh 6^{25} 9^7 16^d 22^b 13^{13} 16^{10}
  Judg $1^{29.\ 32}$. . . . 11 J
  D Deut 23^{16} . . . . 1 D
  Cp בקרב, of Yahweh in Israel, **58**;
  and ct שכן ^{P}**54**, בתוך ^{P}**22**. =12*

27 *Eastward* (or *at the east*, מקדם)
  J Gen 2^8 3^{24} 11^2 12^{8ab} 13^{11} Josh 7^2 . . 7 J*

28 *Fall on the neck and weep, to*
  J Gen 33^4 45^{14ab} 46^{29} cp 50^1 . . 5 J*

29 *Famine was sore* (or *grievous*, כבד) cp **78**
  J Gen 12^{10} 41^{31} 43^1 47^4 13 . . 5 J*

30 *Father* ('he was the father of' . . in genealogical tables)
  J Gen 4^{20}. 10^{21} 11^{29} 22^{21} . . 5 J*

31 (a) *Find favour, to* (or *grace*, מצא חן)
  J Gen 6^8 18^3 19^{19} 30^{27} 32^5 $33^{8\ 10\ 15}$ 34^{11}
  39^4 $47^{25\ 29}$ 50^4 Ex $33^{12\ 13ab\ 16}$. 34^9
  Num $11^{11\ 15}$ . . . . 21 J
  D Deut 24^1 . . . . 1 D
  P^s Num 32^5 . . . . 1 P^s
  =23*

  (b) *Give favour* (נתן חן)
  JE Gen 39^{21} Ex 3^{21} 11^3 12^{36} . . 4 JE*

32 *Flock* (or *drove*, עדר)
  J Gen $29^{2ab\ 3\ 8}$ 30^{40} $32^{16abcd\ 19}$ . . 10 J*

33 *Flocks and herds* (or *sheep and oxen*, צאן ובקר)
  J Gen 12^{16} 13^5 24^{35} 26^{14} 27^{7r} 33^{13} 45^{10}
  46^{32} 47^1 50^8 Ex 9^3 10^9 24 $12^{32\ 38}$ 34^3
  Num 11^{22} . . . . 17 J
  E Gen 20^{14} 21^{27} Ex 20^{24} ct Num 22^{40} 3 E
  D Deut 16^2 ct 8^{13} 12^6 17 21 $14^{23\ 26}$ 15^{13} 1 D
  P Gen 34^{28} ct Lev 1^2 27^{32} Num 15^3
  31^{28}. . . . . 1 P
  =22*

CHARACTERISTIC OF J

34 *Flowing with milk and honey* (זבת חלב
    ודבש)
    J Ex $3^{8\ 17}$ 13^5 33^3 Num 13^{27} 14^8 16^{13}.   8 J
    D Deut 6^3 11^9 26^9 ^{15} 27^3 $31^{20!}$ Josh 5^6 7 D
    P^h Lev 20^{24} .. ..   1 P^h
    Elsewhere Jer 11^5 32^{22} Ezek 20^6 ^{15}†.   =16*

35 *Forasmuch as* (כי־על־כן) cp **85**^{a}
    J Gen 18^5 19^8 33^{10} 38^{26} Num 10^{31} 14^{43} 6 J*

36 *From the time that .. (or since,* מאז)
    J Gen 39^5 Ex 4^{10} 5^{23} 9^{24} .. ..   4 J
    R^d Josh 14^{10} .. .. ..   1 R^d
       =5*

37 *Garden* (of Eden, Yahweh, &c)
    J Gen $2^{8-10\ 15}$. $3^{1-3\ 8ab\ 10\ 23}$. 13^{10} ..   14 J
    D Deut 11^{10} .. .. ..   1 D
       =15*

38 *Good, to do* (היטיב)
    J Gen 4^{7ab} 12^{16} $32^{9r\ 12abr}$ Num 10^{29} 32^{ab} 9 J
    E Ex 1^{20a} Josh 24^{20} .. ..   2 E
    D Deut 5^{28} 8^{16} 18^{17} 28^{63} 30^5 cp $^p116^c$ (5)   10 D
    P Ex 30^7 ('dress') Lev 5^4 ..   2 P
       =23*

39 *Goshen (land of,* גשן *in Egypt)*
    J Gen 45^{10} $46^{28ab\ 29\ 34}$ $47^{1\ 4\ 6b\ 27a}$ 50^8
    Ex 8^{22} 9^{26} (ct Josh 10^{41} 11^{16} 15^{51})..   12 J†

40 *Ground, face of the* (פני האדמה)
    J Gen 2^6 4^{14} 6^1 ^{7} 7^4 ^{23} 8^8 13^b Ex 32^{12r}
    or R^{je} 33^{16} .. .. ..   10 J
    E Num 12^3 .. .. ..   1 E
    D Deut 6^{15} 7^6 14^2 . ..   3 D
    'Ground' (in the sense of 'soil') thirty
    times in J and seventeen in D: only
    five times in P (Gen 1^{25} 6^{20} $7^{8!}$ 9^2 Lev
    20^{25}, all with 'creep' and 'creeping
    thing'): E and P preferring 'the
    earth' הארץ.   =14*

41 *Handmaid (or maidservant,* שפחה) ct **99**
    J Gen 12^{16} $16^{1.\ 5.\ 8}$ 24^{35} $30^{4\ 7\ 9.\ 12\ 18\ 43}$
    $32^{5\ 22}$ $33^{1.\ 6}$ Ex 11^5 .. ..   20 J
    R^{je} Gen 20^{14} .. .. ..   1 R^{je}
    D Deut 28^{68} .. .. ..   1 D
    P Gen 16^3 25^{12} 29^{24ab} ^{29ab} 35^{25}. Lev
    19^{20} .. ..   9 P
       =31*

42 *Harden, to (the heart,* some form of כבד, cp **78**)
    J Ex 7^{14} $8^{15\ 32}$ 9^7 ^{34} cp 10^{1r} ..   6 J*

43 (a) *Hasten, to (or make haste, do quickly,*
    מהר)
    J Gen $18^{6ab\ 7}$ 19^{22} $24^{18\ 20\ 46}$ 27^{20} 43^{30}
    44^{11} 45^9 ^{13} Ex 2^{18} 10^{16} 12^{33} 34^8
    Josh 4^{10b} 8^{14} ^{19} .. ..   19 J
    E Gen 41^{32} .. .. ..   1 E
    (b) adverbially, מהר, E Josh 2^{5b} R^{je} Ex
    32^8, D Deut 4^{26} 7^4 9^3 $^{12ab\ 16}$ 28^{20} 10
    (c) advbly, מהרה J Josh 8^{19}, E Josh 10^6,
    D Deut 11^{17} Josh 23^{16}, P Num 16^{46} 5
       =35*

44 (a) *Hearken to the voice of, to* (שמע לקול פ')
    J Gen 3^{17} 16^2 Ex 3^{18} 4^{8ab} ^{9} ..   6 J
    E Ex 18^{24} .. .. ..   1 E
    R^{je} Ex 15^{26} .. .. ..   1 R^{je}
       =8*

(b) With ב, frequent in JE cp $^p58$, never in P.

45 *Heart* (in the formula 'be grieved'
    'say' &c 'in his heart'; J habitually
    prefers לבב, לב Ex 14^5; $^p59$ usually
    לבב, P commonly לב)
    J Gen 6^6 8^{21} 24^{45} 27^{41} Ex 4^{14r} ..   5 J
    D Deut 7^{17} 8^{17} 9^4 18^{21} 29^{19} ..   5 D
    P Gen 17^{17} .. .. ..   1 P
       =11*

46 *Herb of the field* (עשב השדה)
    J Gen 2^5 3^{18} Ex 9^{25b} 10^{15c} ..   4 J
    R^{je} Ex 9^{22} .. .. ..   1 R^{je}
    Ct 'herb of the land' Ex $10^{12\ 15b}$* E.   =5*

47 *Ill, to deal (or do wickedly, hurt &c* הרע)
    J Gen $19^{7\ 9}$ 43^6 44^5 Ex 5^{22}. Num 11^{11}
    16^{15} .. ..   8 J
    E Gen 31^7 Num 20^{15} Josh 24^{20} ..   3 E
    D Deut 26^6 .. .. ..   1 D
    P Lev 5^4 .. .. ..   1 P
       =13*

48 *Intreat, to* (עתר)
    J Gen 25^{21ab} Ex $8^{8.\ 28-30}$ 9^{28} 10^{17} ..   10 J*

49 (a) *Israel* (as a personal name for Jacob)
    J Gen 32^{28} $35^{21\ 22ab}$ 37^3 13^a 42^5 $43^{6\ 8\ 11}$
    $45^{21a\ 28}$ $46^{1\ 29}$. $47^{27a\ 29\ 31}$ $48^{2b\ 10a}$
    13^{ab} ^{14} 50^2 .. .. ..   24 J
    R^{je} Gen $46^{2\ 5}$ $48^{8\ 11\ 21}$ ..   5 R^{je}
    P Gen 35^{10} .. .. ..   1 P
    [But cp Klostermann, *Pentateuch,* 40-41.]   =30*

(b) as a name for the people (contrasted
with 'all Israel' $^p2^a$), far more frequent in J than in E (eg in Ex
seventeen times J, and four times
E), where 'children of Israel' is
more common.

Kindred, see *Nativity.*

50 *Know, to* (euphemistically, ידע)
    J Gen $4^{1\ 17\ 25}$ 19^8 24^{16} 38^{26} ..   7 J*
    Ct P Num $31^{17.\ 35}$ ֻֻ.

51 *Little, a (few,* מעט)
    J Gen 18^4 $24^{17\ 43}$ 26^{10} $30^{15\ 30}$ $43^{2\ 11ab}$
    44^{25} Num 16^{13} Josh 7^3 ..   12 J
    E Ex 17^4 Num 13^{18c} ..   2 E
    D Deut 7^7 26^5 $28^{38\ 62}$ .. ..   4 D
    P Gen 47^9 Lev 25^{52} Num 16^9 $26^{54\ 56}$
    33^{54} 35^8 Josh 22^{17} .. ..   8 P
    'By little and little' E Ex 23^{30ab} =30*
    D Deut 7^{22ab}†.

WORDS AND PHRASES

J 52 *Little ones* (טף)
  (a) used absolutely for the dependent members of the household
    J Gen 43^8 $50^{8\ 21}$ Ex $10^{10\ 24}$ 12^{37} Num 14^{31} .. ..   7 J
  (b) with *wives, household,* &c
    J Gen 45^{19} $47^{12\ 24}$ Num 14^3 16^{27c} ..   5 J
    R^{je} Gen 46^5 .. . . . .   1 R^{je}
    D cp ^{p}118 .. ..   9 D
    P^s Gen 34^{29a} Num $31^{9\ 17}$. $32^{16.\ 24\ 26}$ ..   8 P^s
                          =30*

53 *Lodging* (מלון) cp *lodge,* **178**
    J Gen 42^{27} 43^{21} Ex 4^{24} Josh 4^3 8^b ..   5 J*

54 *Look, to* (שקף Hiph and Niph)
    J Gen 18^{16} 19^{28} 26^8 Ex 14^{24} Num 21^{20} 23^{28} ..   6 J
    D Deut 26^{15} .. .. ..   1 J
                          =7*

55 *Looked and beheld* (or *saw and behold,* or *beheld and lo,* וירא והנה)
    J Gen 8^{13b} 18^2 19^{28} 24^{63} 26^8 29^2 33^1 37^{25b} Ex 3^2 Josh 5^{13} 8^{20} ..   11 J
    E Gen 22^{13} .. .. ..   1 E
    Ct Gen 1^{31} 6^{12} P.   =12*

56 (a) *Lord, my* (אדני, as a periphrasis for 'you')
    J Gen 32^5—Josh 5^{14} ..   22 J
    E Gen 31^{35} Ex 32^{22} ..   2 E
    P^s Num $32^{25\ 27}$ 36^{2ab} ..   4 P^s
                          =28*

  (b) *Oh, my Lord* (בי אדני)
    J Gen 43^{20} 44^{18} Ex $4^{10\ 13r}$ Josh 7^8 ..   5 J
    E Num 12^{11} .. .. ..   1 E
                          =6*

57 (a) *Mercy and truth* (or *deal kindly and truly,* חסד ואמת)
    J Gen $24^{27\ 49}$ 32^{10r} 47^{29} Ex 34^6 Josh 2^{14} 6 J*

  (b) *shew mercy, to* (or, *do kindness, deal kindly,* עשה חסד)
    J Gen 19^{19} $24^{12\ 14}$ Josh 2^{12} Judg 1^{24} (cp Gen 39^{21}) .. ..   5 J
    E Gen 20^{13} 21^{23} 40^{14} .. ..   3 E
    R^{je} Ex 20^6 ǁ Deut 5^{10} .. ..   2 R^{je}

  (c) *Mercy* (alone)
    J Ex 34^7 Num $14^{18.r}$, D Deut $7^{9\ 12}$, Ex 15^{13} (Song of Moses) ..   6
    Ct Lev 20^{17} 'shameful thing' (cp Ges-Brown, *Heb Lex*).   =22*

58 *Midst, in the* (or *among,* of Yahweh in Israel or Egypt, בקרב) ct 'among' ^{p}22
    J Ex 3^{20r} 8^{22r} 10^1 17^{7c} 33^3 34^9 Num 11^{20} $14^{11r\ 14r\ 42}$ Josh 3^5 10^a ..   12 J
    R^{je} Ex 33^5 .. .. ..   1 R^{je}
    D Deut 1^{42} 6^{15} 7^{21} 23^{14} 31^{17} ..   5 D
                          =18*

59 *Mighty, to be* (and *mighty,* adj, עצם)
    J Gen 18^{18} 26^{16} Ex $1^{7\ 9\ 20b}$ Num 14^{12r} 22^6 7 J
    D Deut 4^{38} 7^1 $9^{1\ 14}$ 11^{23} 26^5 Josh 23^9 7 D
    P^s Num 32^1 .. ..   1 P^s
                          =15*

60 *Nativity* (or *kindred,* מולדת in the sense of 'birth' or 'birthplace')
    J Gen 11^{28} 12^1 $24^{4\ 7}$ 31^{3r} 32^{9r} 43^7 Num 10^{30} 8 J
    E Gen 31^{13} .. .. ..   1 E
    Ct P Gen 48^6 Lev 18^{9ab} ^{11}.   =9*

61 *Not* (before the infin, 'that .. not,' or *lest* לבלתי)
    J Gen 3^{11} 4^{15} 19^{21} 38^9 Ex $8^{22\ 29}$ 9^{17} ..   7 J
    E Ex 20^{20} .. .. ..   1 E
    D Deut 4^{21ab} 8^{11} 12^{23} $17^{12\ 20ab}$ Josh 5^6 11^{20} 23^6. ..   11 D
    P Lev 18^{30} 20^4 26^{15} Num 9^7 32^9 Josh 22^{25} ..   6 P
                          =25*

62 *Now* (or *this once, this time,* הפעם)
    J Gen 2^{23} 18^{32} 29^{34}. 30^{20} 46^{30} Ex 9^{27} 10^{17} ..   8 J*

63 *Old age* (*a son in his,* זקנים and זקנה)
    J Gen $21^{2\ 7}$ 24^{36} 37^3 44^{20} 5 J*

64 *Peradventure* (or, *it may be,* אולי)
    J Gen 16^2 $18^{24\ 28-32}$ 24^5 32^{20} 43^{12} Num $22^{6\ 11\ 33}$ 23^{27r} Josh 9^7 ..   16 J
    E Gen 27^{12} Ex 32^{30} Num 23^3 ..   3 E
    R^d Josh 14^{12} .. .. ..   1 R^d
                          =20*

65 *Place* (i e *home,* מקום)
    J Gen 18^{33} 29^{26} 30^{25} Ex 3^8 Num $24^{11\ 25}$ 6 J
    E Gen 31^{55} cp Ex 18^{23} 23^{20} (of Canaan as the home of the Israelites) ..   3 E
    D Deut 21^{19} .. .. ..   1 D
    P^s Ex 16^{29ab} Num 32^{17} ..   3 P^s
                          =13*

66 *Prosper, to* (i e 'make to prosper,' הצליח)
    J Gen $24^{21\ 40\ 42\ 56}$ $39^{2.\ 23}$ (cp Num 14^{41} צלח) ..   8 J
    D Deut 28^{29} Josh 1^8 ..   2 D
                          =10*

67 *Provender* (מספוא)
    J Gen $24^{25\ 32}$ 42^{27} 43^{24} (Judges 19^{19} cp Moore, *Judges,* pp 405, 407) ..   5 J†
    Ct מזון 'victual,' Gen 45^{23} E.

68 *Refuse to let Israel go,* cp **197** **205**^{d}
    J Ex 7^{14} 8^2 9^2 10^4 .. ..   4 J
    R^{je} Ex 4^{23} .. .. ..   1 R^{je}
                          =5*

69 *Remained not one* (or *was not left,* לא נשאר)
    J Gen 47^{18} 𝔖 Ex 8^{31} $10^{19\ 26}$ 14^{28b} Josh 8^{17}. Cp 𝔖 = *be left* Gen 42^{38} cp 7^{23} ..   6 J*
    D Ct Hiph 'he left none remaining' Josh 8^{22N}.

70 *Run, to* (רוץ, sometimes followed by *to meet* **183**)
  J Gen $18^{2\ 7}$ $24^{17\ 20\ 28}$ 29^{12} 33^4 41^{14}
    (Hiph) Josh 7^{22} 8^{19} .. .. 12 J
  E Num 11^{27} .. .. 1 E
  P Num 16^{47} .. .. 1 P
                                            = 14*

71 (a) *Sake of, for the* (or, *because*, בעבור prep)
  J Gen 3^{17} 8^{21} $12^{13\ 16}$ $18^{26\ 29\ 31}$. 26^{24}
    Ex 9^{16ab} 13^{8r} .. .. 12 J

 (b) *that* (or, *for this cause*, conj)
  J Gen 21^{30} $27^{4\ 19\ 31}$ 46^{34} Ex 9^{14} .. 6 J
  E Gen 27^{10} (ב' אשר) Ex 19^9 20^{20ab} .. 4 E
                                            = 22*

72 *Scatter, to* (or *spread*, פוץ Qal Niph Hiph)
  J Gen^a 10^{18} $11^{4\ 8}$. 49^7 Ex 5^{12} Num 10^{35} 7 J
  D Deut 4^{27} 28^{64} 30^3 .. .. 3 D
                                            = 10*

73 *Servant(s), thy* &c (as periphrasis for 'I' &c) cp **207**
  J Gen $18^{3\ 5}$—Josh 10^{6a} .. .. 33 J
  D Deut 3^{24} Josh 9^{24} .. .. 2 D
  P^s Num 31^{49} $32^{4\ 25\ 27\ 31}$ .. 6 P^s
                                            = 41*

74 *Set, to* (or *leave, present*, הציג)
  J Gen 30^{38} 33^{15} 43^9 47^2 Ex 10^{24} 5 J
  D Deut 28^{56} .. .. 1 D
                                            = 6*

75 *Sheol* (or *the grave, pit*, שאל)
  J Gen 37^{35} 42^{38} $44^{29\ 31}$ Num $16^{30\ 33}$ .. 6 J
    Deut 32^{22} (Song of Moses) 1
                                            = 7*

76 *Sinai, mount* (הר סיני) cp ^{P}7
  J Ex $19^{11b\ 18\ 20\ 23}$ $34^{2\ 4}$ .. .. 6 J
  Ct Horeb in E and D, cp 'mount' and
    'wilderness' ^{P}7^a.

77 *Sodom and Gomorrha*
  J Gen 10^{19} 13^{10} 18^{20} $19^{24\ 28}$ .. 5 J
    Gen $14^{2\ 8\ 10}$. Deut 29^{23} .. 5
  Ct P 'cities of the plain' Gen 13^{12a} 19^{21}.
                                            = 10*

78 *Sore* (to be, or *grievous, heavy, dim, rich, honoured, glorious* &c, כבד vb Qal Niph Pi Hiph and adj) cp **29** and **42**
  J Gen 12^{10}—Num 24^{11ab} . 31 J
  E Ex 17^{12} 18^{18} 19^{16} 20^{12} (∥ Deut 5^{16})
    Num 11^{14} 22^{15} .. .. . 6 E
  D Deut 5^{16} 28^{58} .. .. .. 2 D
  Ct P Niph Ex $14^{4\ 17}$. Lev 10^3 .. 4 P
                                            = 43*

79 *Sorrow, to* (or *grieve*, vb and noun, עצב *toil* עצבון)
  J Gen $3^{16ab\ 17}$ 5^{29} 6^6 34^7 45^5 .. 7 J*

80 *Spread abroad, to* (or *break forth, make a breach*, פרץ)
  J Gen 28^{14} $30^{30\ 43}$ 38^{29} Ex 1^{12} 19^{22} 24 .. 7 J*

81 *Spring* (or *fountain*, lit 'eye,' עין)
  J Gen 16^{7ab} $24^{13\ 16\ 20\ 30\ 42\ 45}$ 49^{22} Ex 15^{27} .. .. 11 J
  E^r Deut 33^{28} .. .. .. 1 E^r
  D Deut 8^7 .. .. 1 D
  P^s Num 33^9 (ct מעין Gen 7^{11} 8^2 Lev 11^{36}
    Josh 15^9 18^{15} P*) .. 1 P^s
                                            = 14*

82 *Take a wife, to* (for oneself or for another, לקח אשה)
  J Gen 4^{19} 6^2 11^{29} $24^{3\ 7\ 37\ 40}$ 25^1 31^{50} 38^6 .. .. 12 J
  E Gen 21^{21} Num 12^{1r} .. .. 2 E
  D Deut 20^7 22^{13} $24^{1\ 5}$ .. .. 4 D
  P Gen 26^{34} 27^{46} $28^{1\ 6ab}$ (34^4) Lev 18^{18}
    20^{14} $21^{7ab\ 13}$. .. 13 P
  Ct E who uses 'take' absolutely, as   = 31*
    in Ex 2^1 ᛘ.

83 *Task masters* (נגשים)
  J Ex 3^7 $5^{6\ 10\ 13}$. .. .. 5 J*
  Cp the vb נגש in Deut 15^2.*

84 *There is* (in various idioms, יש)
  J Gen 18^{24} $24^{23\ 42\ 49}$ 28^{16} $33^{9\ 11}$ $39^{4\ 5ab\ 8}$
    42^2 $43^{4\ 7}$ $44^{19\ 26}$ 47^6 Ex 17^7
    Num 22^{29} .. .. .. 20 J
  E Gen 31^{29} 42^1 Num 13^{20} (all passages
    where the documents are much inter-
    woven) .. .. .. 3 E
  D Deut 13^3 29^{15} 18^{ab} .. .. 4 D
  P Gen 23^8 Num 9^{20}. .. .. 3 P
                                            = 30*

85 (a) *Therefore* (or, *wherefore*, על כן) cp **35**
  J Gen 2^{24} 10^9 11^9 16^{14} 19^{22} 26^{33} 29^{34}.
    30^6 31^{48} 32^{32} 33^{17} 47^{22} 50^{11} Ex $5^{8\ 17}$
    15^{23} Josh 7^{26} .. .. 18 J
  E Gen 20^6 21^{31} 25^{30} 42^{21} Num $21^{14\ 27}$ 6 E
  D Ex 13^{15} Deut 5^{15} 10^9 $15^{11\ 15}$ 19^7
    $24^{18\ 22}$ Josh 14^{14} .. .. 9 D
  P Ex 16^{29} 20^{11} Lev 17^{12} Num 18^{24} .. 4 P
                                            = 37*

 (b) *Therefore* (or *wherefore*, לכן) J Gen 4^{15}
  30^{15}, P Ex 6^6 Num 16^{11} 20^{12} 25^{12}*

86 *Three days' journey* (דרך שלשת ימים)
  J Gen 30^{36} Ex 3^{18} 5^3 8^{27} Num 10^{33ab} .. 6 J
  P^s Num 33^8 .. .. 1 P^s
                                            = 7†

87 (a) *Thus saith Yahweh*, cp **222**^{b}
  J Ex 4^{22r} 7^{17a} 8^1 ^{20} 11^4, with *God of Israel* Ex 32^{27} Josh 7^{13} .. 7 J
  E with *God of Israel* Ex 5^1 Josh 24^2. 2 E
                                            = 9*

 (b) *Thus saith Yahweh, God of the Hebrews*
  J Ex $9^{1\ 13}$ 10^3 .. .. .. 3 J*

 (c) *Yahweh, God of the Hebrews*
  J Ex 3^{18} 5^3 7^{16} $9^{1\ 13}$ 10^3 .. 6 J†

---

^{a} On נפצה Gen 9^{19} cp Ges-Kautzsch, *Hebrew Grammar* (tr Cowley and Collins, Oxford 1898) § 67 dd, p 190.

J 88 *Towns* (or, *villages*, ⌂ 'daughters,' בנות)
  J Num 21^{25} ^{32} 32^{42} Josh 17$^{11\text{abcde}}$ (∥ Judg
    1$^{27\text{abcde}}$) Josh 17^{16} .. .. .. 9 J*
  R^p Josh 15^{45} $^{47\text{ab}}$ 17^{11} .. . .. 4 R^p
                                                   = 13*

89 (a) *What is this* (מה־זאת and מה־זה)
  J Gen 3^{13} 12^{18} 26^{10} 27^{20} Ex 4^2 14^5 11 .. 7 J
  E Gen 29^{25} 42$^{28\text{b}}$ .. .. .. 2 E
  R^d Ex 13^{14} .. .. 1 R^d
                                                   = 10*

(b) *Wherefore* (or, *why*, i e 'for what is
    this,' למה זה) cp **228**
  J Gen 18^{13} 25^{22} 32^{29} 33^{15} Ex 2^{20} 5^{22} 17^3
    Num 11^{20} 14^{41} Josh 7^{10} .. .. 10 J*

90 *Where* (and *whither*, אי and איה)
  J Gen 3^9 4^9 16^8 18^9 19^5 38^{21} Ex 2^{20} .. 7 J
  E Gen 22^7 .. .. 1 E
  Deut 32^{37} (Song of Moses) . .. 1
                                                   = 9*

91 (a) *While* (or *yet*, עוד, with pronom suff)
  J Gen 18^{22} 25^6 29^9 43^{27}. 44^{14} 46^{30} 48^{15}
    Ex 9^2 ^{17} Num 11^{33} 22^{30} .. .. 12 J
  E Ex 4^{18} .. .. 1 E
  D Deut 31^{27} Josh 14^{11} .. .. 2 D
                                                   = 15*

(b) *Yet alive* (עוד חי)
  J Gen 25^6 43^7 ^{27}. 45^{28} 46^{30} .. 6 J
  E Gen 45^3 ^{26} Ex 4^{18} .. .. .. 3 E
  D Deut 31^{27} .. .. 1 D
                                                   = 10*

92 *Younger*, (the, of two sons or daughters, צעיר)
  J Gen 19^{31} ^{34}. ^{38} 25^{23} 29^{26} (cp 43^{33})
    48^{14} Josh 6^{26} (cp Judg 6^{15}).. 8 J*

93 Peculiarities of Hebrew diction
(a) Dillmann (*Genesis*, ii 91) reckons the emphatic ending וּן—, 2 and 3 masc pl impf, e g five times in Gen 18$^{28-32}$ (J^s); but it also occurs in **E** Ex 18^{20}, is especially frequent in **D** and appears in **P**^{s}, cp Num 32^7 ^{15} ^{20} ^{23}: see Holzinger, *Einleitung*, 106.

(b) Dillmann and Holzinger further find in **J** a marked preference for attaching the accusative pronominal suffix to the verb instead of expressing it by את (as in **E**): thus in Gen 24 the verbal suffix occurs fourteen times, and את only three (24^{14} ^{47} ^{56}): in Judg 1 the proportion is ten to two: cp Holzinger, *Einleitung*, 107.

§ 2. E

E 94 (a) *God* (Elohim, אלהים)
  On the use of the name *Elohim* prior to the revelation of the name Yahweh to Moses Ex 3^{15}, cp *ante* p. 38. It also occurs in several sections of subsequent narrative with such frequency as to point to the employment of a distinctive source, e g Exod 13$^{17-19}$ 14^{19} 18$^{1\ 12-23}$ 20$^{1\ 19-21}$ (24^{11}?) Num 21^5 22$^{9.\ 12\ 20\ 22r\ 38}$ 23$^{4\ 27r}$ Josh 24^1; cp Deut 4^{32} 25^{18} Josh 22^{33}.

(b) *God* (אלהי) *of my* (*thy* &c) *father*
  E Gen 31^5 ^{29} ^{42} ^{53r} 46^{1b} ^{3} 50^{17} Ex 3^6 ^{13} ^{15} cp ^{JE}**120**.

(c) *God* (El, אל, as a proper name, without an adjective)
  E Gen 33^{20} 35^7 46^3 Num 12^{13} (ct 16^{22})
  In the Balaam Poems both in **E** Num 23$^{8\ 19\ 22.r}$ and **J** 24$^{4\ 8\ 16\ 23}$.
  Ct *El roi* Gen 16^{13}, *El 'Olam* Gen 21^{33}, *El 'Elyon* Gen 14$^{18-22}$, *El Shaddai* ^{P}**1**.
  האל Gen 31^{13} 35^1 ^{3} 46^3, Deut 7^9 10^{17}.

95 *After these things*
  E Gen 15^1 22^1 39^7 40^1 48^1 Josh 24^{29} .. 6 E
  R^{je} Gen 22^{20} .. .. .. 1 R^{je}
                                                   = 7*

96 *Amorite* (as a designation for the original occupants of the country)
  E Gen 15^{16} 48^{22} Num 13^{29} 21$^{13\text{ab}}$ 21 31
    Josh 10^{5a} ^{6d} 24^8 (12) 15 18 .. 13 E
  J Num 21^{25} ^{26r} ^{32} 32^{39} .. .. 4 J
  Cp ^{p}**3**. Otherwise in lists, e g Gen
    10^{16} 15^{21} &c.   = 17

97 *Angel of Elohim* (מלאך א') cp **4**
  E Gen 21^{17} (22^{11}) 28^{12} 31^{11} 32^1 Ex
    14^{19a} (cp 23^{20} 32^{34} Num 20^{16}) .. 5 E*

98 *Bereave, to* (שכל, Pi 'cast the young')
  E Gen 27^{45b} 31^{38} 42^{36} 43^{14ab} Ex 23^{26} .. 6 E
  Deut 32^{25} (Song of Moses) 1
  P^h Lev 26^{22} . .. . 1 P^h
                                                   = 8*

99 *Bondwoman* (or, *maidservant*, אמה) ct **41**
  E Gen 20^{17} 21^{10ab} ^{12}. 30^3 31^{33} Ex 2^5
    20^{10} ^{17} 21^7 ^{20} ^{26}. ^{32} 23^{12} .. .. 16 E
  D Deut 5^{14} ^{21} 12^{12} ^{18} 15^{17} 16^{11} ^{14} (ct
    28^{68} ^{JE}**41**) .. .. 7 D
  P Lev 25^6 ^{44ab} . .. . 3 P
                                                   = 26*

100 *Death, shall surely be put to* (מות יומת) ct $^P36^b$
    E Ex $21^{12\ 15-17}\ 22^{19}$ .. .. .. 5 E
    J Gen 26^{11} Ex 19^{12} . .. .. 2 J
    P Ex 31^{14}.—Num 35^{31} cp $^P52^b$ .. 20 P
                                              =27*

101 *Dream* (vb and noun)
    E Gen $20^{3\ 6}\ 28^{12}\ 31^{10.\ 24}\ 37\ 40\ 41\ 42^9$
       Num 12^6 .. .. .. 49 E
    D Deut $13^{1ab\ 3ab\ 5ab}$ .. .. 6 D
                                              =55*

102 *Fear* (towards God, vb, noun and adj ירא, יראה) cp $^D44$, $^P200$
    E Gen $20^{11}\ 22^{12}\ 42^{18}$ Ex $1^{17}\ 21\ 18^{21}$
       20^{20} Josh 24^{14} . . 8 E
    R^{je} Ex $9^{20\ 30}\ 14^{31}$ .. .. 3 R^{je}
                                              =11

103 *Hang, to* (תלה)
    E Gen $40^{19\ 22}\ 41^{13}$ .. .. 3 E
    J^a Josh $8^{29}\ 10^{26ab}$ .. .. 3 J
    D Deut 21^{22}. .. .. 2 D
                                              =8*

104 *Here am I* (preceded by *and he said*, or *saying*, הנני)
    E Gen $22^{1\ 7\ 11}\ 27^{1b\ 18a}\ 31^{11}\ 37^{13b}\ 46^2$
       Ex 3^{4b} Num 14^{40} .. .. 10 E*

105 *Horeb* (or, *the mountain of God*, חורב, הר האלהים) ct $^J76\ ^P7$ 'Sinai'
    E Ex $3^1\ 4^{27}\ 17^6\ 18^5\ 24^{13}\ 33^6$. 6 E
    D Cp $^D7$ . .. .. 9 D
                                             =15*

106 *Interpret* (and *interpretation*, פתר, פתרון)
    E Gen $40^{5\ 8ab\ 12\ 16\ 18\ 22}\ 41^{8\ 11\ 12ab\ 13\ 15ab}$ 14 E†

107 *Master* (in various idioms, e g 'men of Jericho' Josh 24^{11}, especially of marriage, בעל)
    E Gen $20^3\ 37^{10}$ Ex $21^3\ 22\ 28\ 29ab\ 34ab\ 36$
       $22^{8\ 11.\ 14}\ 24^{14}$ Num 21^{28} Josh 24^{11} 18 E
       Cp Gen $14^{13}\ 49^{23}$ (Lev 21^4) Deut 15^2
       $22^{22}\ 24^4$ 6
    Ct איש in the family relation, Gen $3^{6\ 16}$
    $29^{32\ 34}\ 30^{15}$ J, Gen $30^{18\ 20}$ E.   =24*

108 *Matter* (or *cause*, a subject of dispute, 𝔊 'word,' דבר)
    E Ex $18^{16\ 19\ 22ab\ 26ab}\ 22^{9ab}\ 23^7\ 24^{14}$ .. 10 E
    D Deut $1^{17}\ 17^{8ab}\ 19^{15}\ 22^{26}$ 5 D
                                           =15*

109 *Minister, to* (שרת, and ptcp משרת)
    E Gen $39^4\ 40^4$ Ex $24^{13}\ 33^{11}$ Num 11^{28}
       Josh 1^1 .. . 6 E
    Ct its use for the Levitical ministry
    Deut 10^8 &c, $^D90^c\ ^P129^c$.

110 *Offer, to* (העלה)
    E Gen $22^{2\ 13}$ Ex $24^5\ 32^6$ Num $23^{2\ 4\ 14\ 30}$
       Deut 27^6 .. .. 9 E
    J Gen 8^{20} .. .. 1 J
    D Deut 12^{13}. Josh 8^{31} .. .. 3 D
    P P^h Lev 17^8 P^t Lev 14^{20} P^s Ex 30^9
       40^{29} Josh 22^{23} ct $^P118$ .. 5 P
                                           =18*

111 *On account of* (or *concerning, for the sake of*, על אודות)
    E Gen $21^{11\ 25}$ Ex 18^8 Num $12^1\ 13^{24}$ 5 E
    J Gen 26^{32} .. .. 1 J
    R^d Josh 14^{6abr} .. 2 R^d
                                           =8*

112 (a) *One (to) another* (𝔊 'a man to his brother,' איש אל־אחיו)
    E Gen $37^{19}\ 42^{21\ 28b}$ Ex $10^{23}\ 16^{15}$ Num 14^4 6 E
    J Gen 26^{31} Ex 32^{27} .. 2 J
    P $^P184$ (9) .. 9 P
                                         =17*

(b) *One to another* (𝔊 'a man to his neighbour,' איש אל רעהו)
    E Ex $11^2\ 18^{16}\ 21^{14\ 18\ 35}\ 22^{7\ 10\ 14}\ 33^{11}$ 9 E
    J Gen $11^{3\ 7}\ 15^{10}\ 31^{49}\ 43^{33}$ Ex $18^7\ 32^{27}$ 7 J
    D Deut $19^{11}\ 22^{26}$ .. 2 D
                                      =18*

113 *Pray, to* (התפלל)
    E Gen $20^{7\ 17}$ Num $11^2\ 21^{7ab}$ .. 5 E
    D Deut $9^{20\ 26}$ .. 2 D
    Ct 'besought' Ex 32^{11} R^{je}.   =7*

114 *Prophet* (and *to prophesy*, נביא, התנבא)
    E Gen 20^7 Ex 15^{20} Num $11^{25-27\ 23}\ 12^6$ 7 E
    D Deut $13^{1\ 3\ 5}\ 18^{15\ 18\ 20ab\ 22b}\ 34^{10}$ 10 D
    P Ex 7^1 .. .. 1 P
                                        =18*

Prove, to (נסה with Deity as subject) see 192^a.

115 *River, the* (of the Euphrates)
    E Gen 31^{21} Ex 23^{31} Num 22^{5b} Josh $24^{2.\ 14}$ 7 E*
    Ct 'the (great) river, the river Euphrates' Gen 15^{18} Deut $1^7\ 11^{24}$ Josh 1^4.

116 *Speak with, to* (דבר עם) ct $^P185^e$
    E Gen $31^{24\ 29}$ Ex $19^9\ 20^{19ab\ 22}\ 33^9$ Num $11^{17}\ 22^{19}$ Josh 24^{27} . .. 10 E
    J Gen 29^9 .. 1 J
    D Deut $5^4\ 9^{10}$ .. .. 2 D
                                       =13*

117 *Steal, to* (גנב, *thief* גנב, *theft* גנבה)
    E Gen $30^{33}\ 31^{19.\ 26\ 30\ 32\ 39ab}\ 40^{15ab}$ Ex 20^{15}
       (‖ Deut 5^{19}) $21^{16}\ 22^{1-4\ 7ab\ 8\ 12}$ .. 20 E
    J Gen $31^{27}\ 44^8$ Josh 7^{11} .. 3 J
    D Deut $5^{19}\ 24^{7ab}$ . .. 3 D
    P^h Lev 19^{11} .. .. 1 P^h
                                       =27*

---

^{a} In the original analysis, on which this list was founded, these passages were assigned to E, in connexion with the law in Deut 21^{22}. In the last revision of Joshua, however, the distribution was changed; but it was then too late to remove the word from the list and alter the succeeding numbers.

E 118 *Suffer, to* (or *give leave*, a particular use of 'to give') נתן
    E Gen 20^6 31^7 Num 20^{21} 21^{23} 22^{13} .. 5 E
    J Ex 12^{23}, ... 1 J
    R^{je} Ex 3^{19} .. .. 1 R^{je}
    D Deut 18^{14} Josh 10^{19} .. .. 2 D
                                              =9*

119 Peculiarities of Hebrew Diction (cp Holzinger, *Einleitung*, 190)
  (a) Peculiar infinitive forms, Gen 31^{23} 46^3 48^{11} 50^{20} Ex 2^4 3^{19} 18^{18} Num 20^{21} (‖ Gen 38^9 J) $22^{13.\,16}$.

  (b) Unusual forms of suffixes in nouns, Gen 21^{29} ? 41^{21} 42^{36} cp 31^6.

  (c) Preference of את with pronominal suffix, instead of attaching the suffix to the verb, e g in Josh 24 את with suff fourteen times, vbl suff twice.

  (d) Preference in narrative for the *third day*, Gen 22^4 31^{22} $40^{13.\,19}$. 42^{17}. Ex 10^{22}. $19^{11a.\,16}$ Josh 1^{11} 2^{16} 22 3^2 9^{16a}; cp supposed E basis in Gen 34^{25}; Josh 9^{17} P.* Ct J's phrase **86**.

§ 3. JE

JE 120 *Yahweh* or *Elohim* as God of Shem, heaven, Abraham, &c
  (a) *Yahweh*, J Gen 9^{26} $24^{3.\,7.\,12.\,27.\,42.\,43}$ 26^{24} 28^{13} (43^{23}) Ex 3^{16} 4^5, 'God of Israel'^{a} Ex 32^{27} 34^{23} Josh $7^{13.\,20}$ (?), (without *Yahweh*) Ex 24^{10}, 'God of the Hebrews' Ex 3^{18} 5^3 7^{16} 9^1 10^3.

  (b) *God of my (thy &c) father* E Gen $31^{5.\,29.\,42}$ 31^{53} $46^{1b.\,3}$ 50^{17} Ex $3^{6.\,13}$, (with *Yahweh*) Ex 3^{15}.
  Cp 'El, the God of Israel' Gen 33^{20}, 'Yahweh, God of Israel'^{a} Ex 5^1 Josh 24^2
  R^{je} Gen 32^9 Ex 18^4
  Ex 15^2 (Song of Moses)
  D 'Yahweh, God of thy fathers' Deut $1^{11.\,21}$ 4^1 6^3 12^1 26^7 27^3 29^{25} Josh 18^3, 'Yahweh, God of Israel'^{a} Josh 8^{30} $10^{40.\,42}$ 13^{14} ‖ 33 14^{14} 24^{23} cp ^{D}1.
  Ct P 'God of Israel' alone, Num 16^9 Josh 22^{16}, with 'Yahweh'^{a} Josh 7^{19} 9^{18}. 22^{24}, 'El, God of the spirits of all flesh' Num 16^{22}, 'Yahweh, God of the spirits &c' Num 27^{16}.

121 *Afar off* (*far, a space*, &c, רחוק)
  JE Gen 22^4 37^{18} Ex 2^4 $20^{18.\,21}$ 24^1 Josh 9^6 9^a 22 .. .. 9 JE
  D Deut 13^7 20^{15} 28^{49} 29^{22} 30^{11} .. 5 D
  P Num 9^{10} Josh 3^4 .. .. 2 P
                                            =16*

122 *Afflict, to* (*deal hardly*, &c, ענה Pi)
  JE Gen 15^{13} 16^6 31^{50} 34^2 Ex 1^{11}. 22^{22}. 32^{18} Num 24^{24} .. .. 10 JE
  D Deut $8^{2.\,16}$ 21^{14} $22^{24.\,29}$ 26^6 .. 7 D
  Ct P 20 'afflict your souls.' =17

123 *Again* (ℌ add יסף Qal and Hiph, used idiomatically of the continuance or repetition of an action)
  JE Gen 4^2—Num 22^{25}. .. .. 24 JE
  D Deut 3^{26} 5^{22} 13^{11} 17^{16} 18^{16} 19^{20} 20^8 25^3 28^{68} Josh 7^{12} 23^{13} .. .. 11 D
  P Lev $26^{18.\,21}$ Num 32^{15} .. .. 3 P
                                            =38*

124 *All that he had* (ℌ *all [anything] which was to him [thee, &c]*) (כל אשר לו)
  JE Gen 12^{20}—Josh $7^{15.\,24}$ .. .. 26 JE
  D Deut 5^{21} 8^{13} .. .. .. 2 D
  P Lev 27^{23} Num 1^{50} .. .. 2 P
  Gen 14^{23} 1
                                            =31*

125 *Alone* (*only*, לבד, with pronominal suffix, 'by itself')
  JE Gen 2^{18} 21^{28}. 30^{40} 32^{16} 42^{38} 43^{32abc} 44^{20} 47^{26} Ex $18^{14.\,18}$ $22^{20.\,27}$ 24^2 Num $11^{14.\,17}$ .. .. 19 JE
  D Deut $1^{9.\,12}$ 4^{35} 8^3 22^{25} 29^{14} Josh 11^{13} 7 D
  P Ex 12^{16} .. .. 1 P
  Ct use of לבד without suffix ('by themselves') P Ex 26^9 36^{16}. =27*

126 *Also, and also* (*even*, גם וגם) cp **11**
  JE Gen 3^6—50^{23} eighty-nine times (thirty-two times before a pronoun, *I thou he*), elsewhere forty-nine .. 138 JE
  D Deut eighteen and Josh six times 24 D
  P Gen 17^{16} Ex 6^4. 7^{11ab} Lev 25^{45} $26^{24.\,44}$ Num 4^{22} 16^{10} 18^2 $3^{ab.\,28}$ 27^{13} .. 15 P
  Gen 14^7 16^{ab} Deut 32^{25ab} . .. 5
                                            =182*

---

^{a} Dillmann ascribes the phrase in Joshua (fourteen times) to R^d: Kuenen (followed by Holzinger, Addis and Steuernagel) attributes it to the final editor R^p, *Hex* 342. Cp Josh 7^{18}א

CHARACTERISTIC OF JE

127 *And it came (shall come) to pass when* (or *as*, ויהי or והיה, followed by כאשר) cp **3**

(a) JE Gen 12^{11} 20^{13} $24^{22\,52}$ $27^{30\,40}$ 29^{10} 30^{25} 37^{23} 41^{13} 43^2 Ex 17^{11} 32^{19} Josh 4^{11} .. .. .. 14 JE
    D Deut 2^{16} 28^{63} Josh 4^1 5^8 23^{15} .. 5 D
    P Num 33^{56} .. .. 1 P
    =20*

(b) *And it came (shall come) to pass when* (ויהי or והיה, with ב or כ and infin)
    JE Gen 4^8 11^2 12^{14} 19^{17} 24^{30} 29^{13} $35^{17.\,22}$ 38^{28} $39^{10\,13\,15\,18}$. 44^{31} Ex 13^{17} $33^{8.\,22}$ Num 10^{35} 11^{25} 16^{31} Josh 2^{14} 3^{13}. 4^{18} 5^{13} 6^5 $8^{14\,24}$ 10^1 $11\,20\,24$ 11^1 15^{18} .. .. .. 39 JE
    D Deut 5^{23} 17^{18} $20^{2\,9}$ 23^{13} 25^{19} 27^4 29^{19} 31^{24} Josh 5^1 6^8 9^1 .. 12 D
    P Gen 19^{29} Ex 16^{10} 34^{29} Num 15^{19} 16^{42} 5 P
    =56*

128 *Arise* (and he arose, &c, in the sense of 'starting' or 'setting out,' קום)
    JE Gen 13^{17} — Josh 18^8 (twenty-five times in Gen) .. 34 JE
    D Deut $2^{13\,24}$ 9^{12} 10^{11} 17^8 .. 5 D
    P Gen 28^2, ct legal use in P Gen $23^{17\,20}$ Lev 25^{30} (*be made sure*), $27^{14\,17\,19}$ (*stand*), Num $30^{4.\,7\,9\,11}$ (of vows) cp Deut 19^{15} .. .. 1 P
    =40*

129 *Ask, to* (שאל)
    JE Gen $24^{47\,57}$ 26^7 $32^{17\,29ab}$ 37^{15} 38^{21} 40^7 $43^{7ab\,27}$ 44^{19} Ex 3^{22} 11^2 12^{35}. 18^7 22^{14} Josh 4^6 9^{14} 15^{18} .. 22 JE
    D Deut 4^{32} 6^{20} 10^{12} 13^{14} 14^{26} $18^{11\,16}$ Ex 13^{14} Josh 4^{21} .. 9 D
    Deut 32^7 (Song of Moses) .. 1
    P Num 27^{21} Josh 19^{50} 2 P
    =34*

130 *Be with* (עם of Deity with Israel) cp **58**
    JE Gen 21^{22} $26^{3\,24\,28}$ $28^{15\,20}$ $31^{3\,5\,(42)}$ 35^3 $39^{2.\,21\,23}$ 46^4 48^{21} Ex 3^{12} $4^{12\,15r}$ 10^{10} 18^{19} Num 14^9 ^{43} 23^{21} Deut 31^{23} 24 JE
    D Deut 2^7 $20^{1\,(4)}$ $31^{(6)\,8}$ Josh $1^{5\,9\,17}$ 3^7 7^{12b} (ct 14^{12} §) .. 10 D
    =34*

131 *Befall, to* (or *meet*, קרה Qal and Niph)
    JE Gen 42^{29} 44^{29} Ex 3^{18} (cp 5^3) Num 11^{23} $23^{3.\,15}$.. 8 JE
    D Deut 25^{18} .. .. .. 1 D
    =9*

    הקרה (Hiph)
    J Gen 24^{12} 27^{20} .. 2 J
    P Num 35^{11} .. 1 P
    =3†

132 *Before* (בטרם) cp **6**
    JE Gen $27^{4.\,33}$ 37^{18} 41^{50} 45^{28} Ex 1^{19} .. 6 JE
    R^d Deut 31^{21} .. .. 1 R^d
    P Lev 14^{36} .. .. 1 P
    = 8*

133 *Behold* (with pronominal suffixes, הנה) cp **104**
    JE Gen 16^{11} 20^3 40^6 41^{17} 44^{16} 47^1 50^{18} Ex 8^{21} 9^{18} 10^4 16^4 17^6 34^{11} Num 23^{17} 24^{14} Josh 7^{21} .. .. 16 JE
    D Deut 1^{10} 31^{16r} Josh 9^{25} .. 3 D
    P Gen $6^{13\,17}$ 9^9 48^4 Ex 14^{17} Num 25^{12} (only in solemn asseverations of Deity) 6 P
    =25*

134 *Believe, to* (האמין)
    JE Gen 15^6. 45^{26} Ex $4^{1\,5\,8ab\,9\,31}$ 14^{31} 19^9 Num 14^{11} .. .. 11 JE
    D Deut 1^{32} 9^{23} (28^{66}) .. .. 3 D
    P Num 20^{12} .. .. .. 1 P
    =15*

135 *Blot out, to* (מחה used of people)
    JE Gen 6^7 $7^{4\,23}$ Ex 17^{14} 32^{32}. .. 6 JE
    D Deut 9^{14} $25^{6\,19}$ 29^{20} .. 4 D
    R^p Gen 7^{23} ct Num 5^{23} .. 1 R^p
    =11*

136 *Bring up, to* (Israel from Egypt, העלה)
    JE Gen 46^4 50^{24} (cp ^{25} Ex 13^{19} Josh 24^{32}) Ex $3^{8\,17}$ 17^3 $32^{1\,4\,7.\,23}$ $33^{1\,12\,15}$ Num 14^{13} 16^{13} 20^5 21^5 Josh 24^{17} .. 21 JE
    D Deut 20^1 (D habitually uses 'bring out,' $^D28^b$ cp Ex 20^2, P Ex 6^6 &c) 1 D
    P^h Lev 11^{45} .. .. .. 1 P^h
    =23*

137 *Build an altar, to* (בנה מזבח)
    JE Gen 8^{20} 12^7. 13^{18} 22^9 26^{25} 35^7 Ex 17^{15} 20^{25} 24^4 32^5 Num $23^{1\,14\,29}$ Deut 27^5. 16 JE
    D Josh 8^{30}? .. .. 1 D?
    P^s Josh $22^{10.\,16\,19\,23\,26\,29}$ .. 7 P^s
    =24*
    Cp in JE 'make an altar' Gen 13^4 $35^{1\,3}$ 'erect' Gen 33^{20}.

138 *But* (*save*, בלתי prep and conj) cp **61**
    JE Gen 21^{26} $43^{3\,5}$ 47^{18} Ex 22^{20} Num 11^6 .. .. 6 JE
    D Deut 3^3 Num 21^{35} Josh 8^{22} 10^{33} $11^{8\,19}$ (all with עד) Josh 11^{19} .. 7 D
    P Num 32^{12} .. .. .. 1 P
    =14*

139 (a) *Call, to* (or *cry*, often with *and say, bless, speak, tell,* &c, קרא, followed by ל or אל, or the accus)
    JE Gen 3^9—Josh 24^9 .. .. 51 JE
    D Deut 4^7 5^1 15^9 20^{10} 24^{15} 25^8 29^2 31^7 Josh 22^1 23^2 24^1. .. 11 D
    P Gen 28^1 49^1 Ex 7^{11} 24^{16} 34^{31} 36^2 Lev 1^1 9^1 10^4, אל except in Ex 7^{11} .. 9 P
    =71*

(b) *Call the name, to* (קרא שם) cp **15^b**
    JE Gen 2^{20}—50^{11} fifty-one times, Ex 2^{10} 22 15^{23} $17^{7\,15}$ Num 11^3 34 21^3 (32^{42}) Josh 5^9 7^{26} .. 61 JE
    D Deut 3^{14} 25^{10} ct 28^{10} (all passive) .. 2 D
    P Gen 5^2. 17^5 $15\,19$ 21^3 30^{21} $35^{10ab\,15}$ Ex 16^{31} Num 32^{38} .. 12 P
    =75*

JE 140 *Cease, to* (*leave off, forbear,* חדל)
    JE Gen 11^8 18^{11} 41^{49} Ex $9^{29\ 33}$. 14^{12}
        23^5 .. ..   8 JE
    D Deut 15^{11} 23^{22} .. .. 2 D
    P Num 9^{13} .. ..   1 P
                                  = 11*

141 *Cry, to* (צעק) cp **23**
    JE Gen 4^{10} 27^{34} 41^{55} Ex 5^8 8^{12} 14^{10}
       ^{15} 15^{25} 17^4 $22^{23\ 27}$ Num 11^2 12^{13} 20^{16}
       Josh 24^7 .. .. 16 JE
    D Deut $22^{24\ 27}$ 26^7 .. .. .. 3 D
                                  = 19*

142 *Day* (in different formulae)
  (a) *In that* (*the same*) *day* (or *night* ביום
    ההוא, בלילה ההוא) in narrative
    JE Gen 15^{18} $19^{33\ 35}$ $26^{24\ 32}$ $30^{16\ 35}$
      $32^{13a\ 21}$. 33^{16} 48^{20} Ex 5^6 8^{22} 14^{30} 32^{28}
      Num 14^1 Josh 8^9 $^{13\ 25}$ 9^{27} 24^{25} .. 22 JE
    D Deut 27^{11} Josh 4^{14} 6^{15} 10^{28} 35^{ab}
      14^9 ^{12ab} .. .. 9 D
    R^d Deut 31^{22} .. .. 1 R^d
    P Num 9^{6ab} 32^{10} .. .. .. 3 P
                                  = 35*

  (b) *Unto this day*
    JE Gen 19^{37}. 26^{33} 32^{12} 35^{20} 47^{26} 48^{15}
      Ex 10^6 Num 22^{30} Josh 5^9 6^{25} 7^{26ab}
      8^{29} 13^{13} 15^{63} 16^{10} .. .. .. 17 JE
    D Deut 2^{22} 3^{14} 10^8 11^4 29^4 34^6 Josh 4^9
      8^{28} 9^{27} 14^{14} 22^3 23^8. .. .. 13 D
    P Josh (10^{27}) 22^{17} .. .. .. 1 P
                                  = 31*

143 *Deliver, to* (or *take away*, נצל, Hiph and Niph)
    JE Gen $31^{9\ 16}$ $32^{11\ 30}$ 37^{21}. Ex 2^{19} 3^8
      5^{23} 12^{27r} $18^{4\ 8}$. ^{10ab} Josh 2^{13b} 9^{26} 24^{10}
      (cp Pi Ex 3^{22} 12^{36*} Hithpa Ex 33^{6*}E) 21 JE
    D Deut 23^{14}. 25^{11} .. .. .. 3 D
      Deut 32^{39} (Song of Moses) .. 1
    P Ex 6^6 Num 35^{25} Josh 22^{31} .. 3 P
                                  = 28*

144 *Dig, to* (*search out*, חפר)
    JE Gen 21^{30} $26^{15\ 18ab\ 19\ 21.\ 32}$ Ex 7^{24}
      Num 21^{18} Josh 2^2. .. .. .. 12 JE
    D Deut 1^{22} 23^{13} .. .. .. 2 D
                                  = 14*

145 *Discern, to* (*acknowledge*, הכיר)
    JE Gen 27^{23} 31^{32} $37^{32b\ 33a}$ 38^{25}. $42^{7\ 8ab}$
      Deut 33^9 .. .. 10 JE
    D Deut 1^{17} 16^{19} 21^{17} .. .. 3 D
                                  = 13*

146 *Do, to* (עשה, in various formulae)
  (a) *Do this, do* (*according to*) *this thing*
    JE Gen 3^{14} 18^{25} $20^{5.\ 10}$ 21^{26} 22^{16} 30^{31}
      34^{19} 42^{18} 43^{11} $44^{2\ 17}$ $45^{17\ 19}$ Ex 1^{18}
      8^{13} ^{31} 9^5 18^{23} 24^3 Num 16^{28} 22^{30} .. 24 JE
    R^d Josh 9^{24} .. .. 1 R^d
    P Gen 34^{14} Lev 26^{16} Num 4^{19} 14^{35} 16^6
      32^{20} Josh 9^{20} 22^{24} .. .. .. 8 P
                                  = 33*

  (b) *Do to, for, to* (עשה ל׳)
    In narrative in Genesis
    JE Gen 9^{24} 12^{18} 16^6 19^{8ab} 20^9 22^{12} 26^{10}
      $27^{37\ 45}$ 29^{25} 30^{31} $31^{12\ 43}$ 39^{19} 42^{25}
      28^b (and with other prepositions, עם
      &c, 19^{19} 20^9 ^{13} 21^{23ab} $24^{12\ 49}$ 26^{29ab}
      31^{29} 32^{10} 40^{14} 47^{29}) .. .. 30 JE
    P Gen 21^{1b} 50^{12} .. .. .. 2 P
    Frequent in JE's subsequent narrative   = 32
      and in the laws, **D** and **P**.

  (c) *Do, to* (or *make, of the divine action in*
    human life)
    JE Gen 12^2 21^6 42^{23b} Ex 3^{20} 6^1 $8^{13\ 24}$
      31 9^5. 13^8 $14^{13\ 31}$ $18^{1\ 8}$. 19^{4r} 20^{6r} 32^{10}
      33^{5r} 34^{10ab} Num $14^{11.\ 22}$ Josh 3^5 24^5 27 JE
    D Cp $^D12$ .. .. 20 D
    P Num $14^{28\ 35}$ 33^{56} Lev 26^{16} Ex 12^{12} 5 P
                                  = 52*

  (d) *What* (*is this that*) *thou* (&c) *hast done*
    JE Gen 3^{13} 4^{10} 12^{18} 20^9 26^{10} 29^{25} 31^{26}
      42^{28b} 44^{15} Ex $14^{5\ 11}$ Num 23^{11} Josh
      7^{19} .. .. 13 JE*

147 *Draw near, to* (*come near*, נגש)
  (a) Qal and Niph
    JE Gen 18^{23} 19^{9ab} $27^{21.\ 26}$. 29^{10} $33^{3\ 6\ 7ab}$
      43^{19} 44^{18} 45^{4ab} Ex $19^{15\ 22}$ 20^{21} 24^{2a}
      ^{14} Josh 3^9 8^{11} .. .. .. 24 JE
    D Deut 20^2 21^5 $25^{1\ 9}$ Josh 14^6 .. 5 D
    P Ex 28^{43} 30^{20} $34^{30\ 32}$ Lev $21^{21ab\ 23}$
      Num 4^{19} 8^{19} 32^{16} Josh 21^1 .. 11 P
                                  = 40*

  (b) Hiph, *to bring near*
    JE Gen 27^{25ab} $48^{10\ 13}$ Ex 21^{6ab} 32^6 .. 7 JE
    P Lev 2^8 8^{14} .. .. 2 P
                                  = 9*

148 *Drive out, to* (*thrust out*, גרש, Pi and Pu)
    JE Gen 3^{24} 4^{14} 21^{10} Ex 2^{17} 6^1 10^{11} 11^{1ab}
      12^{39} 23^{28-31} 33^{2r} 34^{11r} (Qal) Num 22^6
      ^{11} Deut 33^{27r} Josh $24^{12\ 18}$ .. .. 20 JE*
    (Ct P Qal ptcp pass *divorced* Lev $21^{7\ 14}$
      22^{13} Num 30^{9*}.)

149 (a) *Eat bread, to* (in narrative)
    JE Gen 3^{19} 31^{54} 37^{25} 39^6 $43^{25\ 32}$ Ex 2^{20}
      18^{12} 34^{28} .. .. 9 JE
    D Deut 8^9 $9^{9\ 18}$ 29^6 .. .. .. 4 D
    P Ex 16^3 ($^{15\ 32}$) .. .. 1 P
                                  = 14*

  (b) *Eat and drink, to*
    JE Gen 24^{54} 25^{34} 26^{30} Ex 24^{11} 32^6 34^{28} 6 JE
    D Deut $9^{9\ 18}$ 29^6 .. .. 3 D
                                  = 9*

150 *Edge of the sword, with the* (לפי חרב)
    JE Gen 34^{26} Ex 17^{13} Num 21^{24} Josh 6^{21}
      8^{24ab} 19^{47} cp Judg 1^8 ^{25} .. .. 7 JE
    D Deut 13^{15b} 20^{13} Josh $10^{28\ 30\ 32\ 35\ 37\ 39}$
      $11^{11.\ 14}$ .. .. 12 D
                                  = 19*

CHARACTERISTIC OF JE

JE

151 *Elders* (of Israel, &c)
    JE Gen 50^{7ab} Ex 3^{16} ^{18} 4^{29} (10^9) 12^{21}
    17^5. 18^{12} 19^7 $24^{1\ 9\ 14}$ Num $11^{16ab\ 24,\ 30}$
    16^{25} $22^{4\ 7ab}$ Josh 7^6 8^{10} 9^{11} ..   25 JE
    D Cp $^D42$ .. .. 23 D
    P Lev 4^{15} 9^1 Josh 20^4 .. .. 3 P
                                            = 51*

152 *Fair to look upon* (cp *pleasant to the sight, well-favoured, ill-favoured, &c*)
    JE Gen 2^9 12^{11} 24^{16} 26^7 29^{17ab} 39^{6ab} 41^2
    $^{3\ 4ab\ 18}$ 19^1 21 cp 3^6 .. .. 15 JE
    D Deut 21^{11} .. .. 1 D
                                            = 16*

153 *Father's house* (both dwelling and family)
    JE Gen 12^1 20^{13} 24^7 $^{23\ 38\ 40}$ 28^{21} 31^{14}
    ^{30} 34^{19} 38^{11ab} 41^{51} 46^{31ab} 47^{12} 50^8 ^{22}
    Josh 2^{12} 18 6^{25} .. .. 21 JE
    D Deut 22^{21ab} .. .. .. 2 D
    P Not in Genesis, but frequent afterwards in the expression 'fathers' houses' $^P66$. = 23

154 *Fear not* (אל תירא cp 102)
    JE Gen 15^1 21^{17} 26^{24} 35^{17} 43^{23} 46^3 50^{19}
    ^{21} Ex 14^{13} 20^{20} Num 14^9 Josh 11^6 .. 12 JE
    D Deut $1^{21\ 29}$ 3^2 20^3 31^6 (3^{22} 7^{18} 20^1 31^8
    לא) Num 21^{34} Josh 8^1 10^8 25 cp $^D44^c$ 13 D
                                            = 25*

155 *Feast, to make a* (עשה משתה)
    JE Gen 19^3 21^8 26^{30} 29^{22} 40^{20} .. 5 JE*

156 *Fight, to* (or *make war*)
    JE Ex 1^{10} $14^{14\ 25}$ 17^{8-10} Num 21^1 23 26^r
    22^{11} Josh 10^5 11^5 19^{47} 24^8 9^r 11 cp
    Judg $1^{1\ 3\ 5\ 8}$. .. .. 16 JE
    D Deut $1^{30\ 41}$. 3^{22} 20^4 $^{10\ 19}$ Josh 9^2 10^{14}
    $^{25\ 29\ 31\ 34\ 36\ 38\ 42}$ $23^{3\ 10}$ (cp $^D45$) .. 18 D
                                            = 34*

157 *Find, to*
    In narrative in Gen, JE fifty-five times 55 JE
    P Gen 36^{24} .. .. .. 1 P
                                            = 56

158 *Flee, to* (ברח)
    JE Gen $16^{6\ 8}$ 27^{43} $31^{20-22\ 27}$ $35^{1\ 7}$ Ex
    2^{15} 14^5 Num 24^{11} ct P Ex 26^{28} 36^{33*} 12 JE
    P uses נוס e g Lev $26^{17\ 26}$ Num 35^6, which is common also to JED.

159 *Forgive, to* (נשא)
    JE Gen 50^{17ab} Ex 10^{17} 23^{21} 32^{32} 34^7
    Josh 24^{19} .. .. .. 7* JE
    Ct סלח, Deut 29^{20} Lev 4^{20} Num 30^5 &c.

160 *Forsake, to* (*leave*, עזב)
    (a) Of Yahweh and Israel
        JE Gen 28^{15} Josh $24^{16\ 20}$ .. 3 JE
        D Deut 28^{20} 29^{25} $31^{6\ 8\ 16,r}$ Josh 1^5 .. 7 D
                                            = 10
    (b) Generally
        JE Gen 2^{24} 24^{27} $39^{6\ 12,\ 15\ 18}$ 44^{22ab} 50^8
        Ex 2^{20} 9^{21} (23^{5ab}) Num 10^{31} Josh 8^{17} 16 JE
        D Deut 12^{19} 14^{27} Josh 22^3 .. 3 D
        Deut 32^{36} (Song of Moses) .. 1
        P Lev 19^{10} 23^{22} 26^{43} .. 3 P
                                            = 33*

161 *Garment* (*clothes, raiment*, שמלה)
    JE Gen 9^{23} 35^2 37^{34} 41^{14} 44^{13} 45^{22ab} Ex
    3^{22} 12^{34}. $19^{10\ 14}$ 22^{26} Josh 7^6 .. 14 JE
    D Deut 8^4 10^{18} 21^{13} 22^3 ^{5} ^{17} .. 6 D
    Ct בגד in P as also in J. = 20*

162 *Go, get thee* (*come, &c*, especially to introduce another proposal or command, לכו לך &c)
    JE Gen 12^1—Josh 18^8 .. 57 JE
    D Deut 5^{27} 10^{11} Josh 22^4 .. 3 D
    P Gen 28^2 .. .. .. 1 P
                                            = 61*

163 *Go, come in unto* (euphemistically, בוא אל)
    JE Gen 6^4 16^2 4 $19^{31\ 33}$. $29^{21\ 23\ 30}$ $30^{3,\ 16}$
    $38^{2\ 8,\ 16ab\ 18}$ $39^{14\ 17}$ .. .. 20 JE
    D Deut 22^{13} .. .. .. 1 D
                                            = 21*

164 *Go to* (= *come, give, ascribe*, interjectional and with verbal meaning הבה)
    (a) As an interjection
        J Gen $11^{3,\ 7}$ 38^{16} Ex 1^{10} .. 5 J
    (b) Followed by an accusative
        JE Gen 29^{21} 30^1 47^{15}. Josh 18^4 5 JE
        D Deut 1^{13} .. .. .. 1 D
        Deut 32^3 (Song of Moses) .. 1
                                            = 12*

165 *Good and evil* (*bad or good, conjoined or opposed*, טוב ורע)
    JE Gen 2^9 ^{17} 3^5 ^{22} 24^{50} $31^{24\ 29}$ 44^4 50^{20}
    Num 13^{19} 24^{13} .. .. 11 JE
    D Deut 1^{39} .. .. .. 1 D
    Not in P, but cp Lev 5^4 $27^{10\ 12\ 14\ 33}$. = 12*

166 *Grow great, to* (or *long*), Pi *make great* (or *magnify*, גדל)
    JE Gen 12^2 $19^{13\ 19}$ $21^{8\ 20}$ 24^{35} 25^{27} 26^{13ab}
    $38^{11\ 14}$ 41^{40} 48^{19ab} Ex 2^{10}. Num 14^{17} 17 JE
    D Josh 3^7 4^{14} .. .. 2 D
    P Num 6^5 .. .. .. 1 P
                                            = 20*

167 *Hate, to* (שנא)
    JE Gen 24^{60} 26^{27} $29^{31\ 33}$ $37^{4,\ 8}$ Ex 1^{10}
    18^{21} 20^{5r} (|| Deut 5^9) 23^5 Num 10^{35}
    Deut 33^{11} .. .. .. 13 JE
    D Deut 5^9 $7^{10ab\ 15}$ 12^{31} 16^{22} $19^{4\ 6}$
    ^{11} $21^{15ab-17}$ $22^{13\ 16}$ 24^3 30^7 .. 17 D
    Deut 32^{41} (Song of Moses) .. 1
    P Lev 19^{17} 26^{17} Deut 4^{42} Josh 20^5 4 P
                                            = 35*

168 *Here* (בזה)
    JE Gen 38^{21}. 48^9 Ex 24^{14} Num 22^{19}
    23^{1ab} $29^{ab\ r}$ .. .. .. 9 JE*

169 *Heretofore* (כתמול, מתמול שלשום)
    JE Gen $31^{2\ 5}$ Ex 4^{10} $5^{7,\ 14}$ $21^{29\ 36}$
    Josh 4^{18} .. .. .. 9 JE
    D Deut $19^{4\ 6}$ (|| Josh 20^5) Josh 3^4 3 D
    R^P Deut 4^{42} Josh 20^5 .. 2 R^P
                                            = 14*

WORDS AND PHRASES

JE 170 *Hide, to* (חבא)
    JE Gen 3^8 ^{10} 31^{27} Josh (2^{16}) 6^{17r} 25^1
    $10^{16. 27}$ .. .. 8 JE*

171 *Hither* (הנה) in various combinations,
    this way and that way &c, with עד
    up till now, since)
    JE Gen 15^{16ab} 21^{23} 42^{15} 44^{28} $45^{5\,8\,13}$
    Num 14^{19r} Josh 2^2 3^9 8^{20} 18^6 .. 13 JE*

172 *Hunting* (*venison, provision, victual* ציד)
    JE Gen 10^{9ab} $25^{27.}$ $27^{5\,7\,19\,25\,30.\,33}$
    Josh $9^{5\,14}$ .. .. 13 JE
    P Lev 17^{13} .. .. 1 P
                                = 14*
    צידה
    JE Gen 27^3 42^{25} 45^{21} Ex 12^{39} Josh 1^{11}
    9^{11} .. .. 6 JE*

Kill (הרג) see *Slay.*

173 *Kiss, to* (נשק)
    JE Gen 27^{26}. $29^{11\,13}$ $31^{28\,55}$ 33^4 41^{40}
    45^{15} 48^{10} 50^1 Ex 4^{27} 18^{7a} .. 13 JE*

174 *Know* (*I, thou, ye,* with the pronoun
    expressed, אתה ידעת)
    JE Gen 20^6 $30^{26\,29}$ 31^6 44^{27} Ex 3^{19} 23^9
    32^{22} Num 20^{14} .. .. 10 JE
    D Deut 9^2 29^{16} 31^{27} Josh 14^6 .. 4 D
    In Gen 'to know' occurs in JE fifty-
    eight times, but not once in P. = 14*

175 *Lie with, to* (of the sexes) in narrative
    JE Gen 19^{32-35} 26^{10} 30^{15}. $34^{2\,7}$ 35^{22a}
    $39^{7\,10\,12\,14}$ .. .. 16 JE
    Found in all three codes, JE D P.

176 *Lift up, to* (נשא)
    (a) *the eyes and see* (*look, or and behold*)
    JE Gen $13^{10\,14}$ 18^2 $22^{4\,13}$ 24^{63}. $31^{10r\,12r}$ $33^{1\,5}$ 37^{25} 43^{29} Ex 14^{10}
    Num 24^2 Josh 5^{13} .. .. 16 JE*
    (b) *the voice and weep* (cp **226**) הרים
    JE Gen 21^{16}·27^{38} 29^{11} (cp $39^{15\,18}$
    45^2) cp Num 14^1 .. .. .. 3 JE*

177 *Light upon, to* (or *meet,* פגע)
    JE Gen 28^{11} 32^1 Ex 5^3 20^{23} 24^2 Josh 2^{16} 6 JE
    P Num $35^{19\,21}$ (otherwise, Gen 23^8,
    and in boundary formulae, Josh
    16^7. &c) .. .. 2 P
                                 = 8*

178 *Lodge, to* (or *tarry, be left,* לון)
    JE Gen 19^{2ab} $24^{23\,25\,54}$ 28^{11} 31^{54} $32^{13a\,21}$
    Ex 23^{18} 34^{25} Num 22^8 Josh 3^{1c} 4^{3b}
    6^{11} 8^9 .. .. 16 JE
    D Deut 16^4 21^{23} .. .. .. 2 D
    P^h Lev 19^{13} .. .. 1 P^h
                                 = 19*

179 *Look, to* (*behold,* הביט)
    JE Gen 15^5 $19^{17\,26}$ Ex 3^6 33^8 Num 12^8
    21^9 23^{21} .. .. 8 JE*

180 *Love, to* (אהב)
    JE Gen 22^2 24^{67} 25^{28ab} $27^{4\,9\,14}$ $29^{18\,(20)}$
    $30\,32$ $37^{3.}$ 44^{20} Ex 20^{6r} 21^5 .. 16 JE
    D Cp $^D74$ (Yahweh and Israel)
    P^{hs} Gen 34^{3b} Lev $19^{18\,34}$ .. .. 3 P^{hs}

181 *Make a covenant, to* (כרת ברית)
    JE Gen 15^{18} $21^{27\,32}$ 26^{28} 31^{44} Ex 23^{32}
    24^8 $34^{10\,12r\,15r\,27}$ Josh $9^{6b\,7\,11b\,15b\,16b}$
    24^{25} .. .. 17 JE
    D Deut 4^{23} 5^2 7^2 9^9 $29^{1ab\,12\,14\,25}$ .. 10 D
    R^d Deut 31^{16} .. .. 1 R^d
    Ct P 'establish a covenant' $^P60^a$.
                                 = 28*

182 *Man* (גבר)
    JE Ex 10^{11} 12^{37} Num $24^{3\,15}$ Josh
    $7^{14\,17}$. .. .. 7 JE
    D Deut 22^{5ab} .. .. 2 D
                                 = 9*

183 *Meet, to* (*over against, against,* לקראת)
    JE Gen 15^{10} 18^2 19^1 $24^{17\,65}$ 29^{13} 30^{16}
    32^6 33^4 46^{29} Ex $4^{14\,27}$ 5^{20} 7^{15} 14^{27}
    18^7 19^{17} Num $20^{18\,20}$ 21^{23} $22^{34\,36}$
    23^3 24^1 Josh 8^5 14 22 9^{11a} .. 28 JE
    D Deut 1^{44} 2^{32} 3^1 29^7 Num 21^{33}
    Josh 11^{20} .. .. 6 D
    P^s Num 31^{13} .. .. 1 P^s
    Gen 14^{17} 1
                                 = 36*

184 *Mighty* (גבור)
    J Gen 6^4 $10^{8\,9ab}$ Josh 10^2 .. 5 J
    D Deut 10^{17}, 'mighty men of valour'
    Josh 1^{14} 6^2 8^3 $10^{7\,b}$ .. .. 5 D
                                 = 10*

185 *Mischief* (אסון)
    JE Gen 42^4 $38.$ 44^{29} Ex 21^{22}. .. 5 JE†

186 (a) *Now* (*I pray you,* &c, נא)
    JE Gen 12^{11}—Josh 7^{19} .. .. 97 JE
    D Deut 3^{25} 4^{32} .. .. .. 2 D
    P^s Num 16^8 Josh 22^{26} (ct לו Gen 17^{18}
    23^{13} Num 14^2 20^{3b}) .. .. 2 P^s
    (b) *let not . . . I pray* (אל נא)
    JE Gen 13^8 $18^{3\,30\,32}$ 19^7 ^{18} 33^{10} 47^{29}
    Num 10^{31} 12^{11-13} 22^{16} .. .. 13 JE
                                = 114*

187 (a) *Now* (עתה)
    JE Gen 19^9—Josh 5^{14} .. .. 28 JE
    D Deut 2^{13} 12^9 Josh 14^{11} .. .. 3 D
    Deut 32^{39} (Song of Moses) .. 1
                                 = 32*

---

    ^{a} It does not seem possible to find a distinctive usage in the two documents: נשק (Qal) occurs with accus in Gen 33^4, text doubtful: with ל in Gen 27^{26}. 29^{11} 50^1 Ex 18^7 J, and Gen 48^{10} Ex 4^{27} E. על נשק Gen 41^{40} E: נשק ל (Piel) Gen 29^{13} J $31^{28\,55}$ 45^{15} E.

    ^{b} Prior to the last revision of Joshua, the occurrences in 6^2 8^3 10^7 were ascribed with hesitation to J.

(b) *Now, and* (*now then, now therefore, so now,* ועתה)
    JE Gen 3^{22}—Josh 24^{23} .. .. 57 JE
    D Deut 4^1 5^{25} $10^{12\ 22}$ 26^{10} Josh 9^{25}
        $14^{10ab\ 12}$ 22^4 . .. . 10 D
    R^d Deut 31^{19} .. .. 1 R^d
    P Gen 48^5 Num 31^{17} Josh 9^{19} .. 3 P
                                            =71*

188 *One* (אחד, in various phrases)
 (a) *The name of the one,*
    JE Gen 2^{11} 4^{19} 10^{25} Ex 1^{15} 18^3. Num
       11^{26} .. .. 7 JE*
    ('The one' in other idiomatic phrases,
    Gen 19^9 $42^{13\ 27\ 32}$. 44^{28}.)
 (b) *One of* (אחד in the constr state)
    JE Gen 21^{15} 22^2 26^{10} 37^{20} 49^{16} Josh
       10^2 .. .. 6 JE
    D Deut 12^{14} 13^{12} 15^{7ab} 16^5 17^2 18^6 $19^{5\ 11}$
       23^{16} .. .. 10 D
    Otherwise with מן Gen (2^{21}) 3^{22} Num =16*
    16^{15} Deut 25^5 28^{55} and always in P
    Lev $4^{2\ 13\ 22\ 27}$ $5^{4.\ 13\ 17}$ $6^{3\ 7}$ 13^2
    Deut 4^{42} Josh 20^4.
 (c) *One* (idiomatically, in the plural)
    JE Gen 11^1 27^{44} 29^{20} .. .. 3 JE*

189 *Only* (*but,* רק)
    JE Gen 6^5 19^8 20^{11} 24^8 26^{29} 41^{40} 47^{22}
       ^{26} 50^8 Ex. 8^9 $^{11\ 28}$. 9^{26} $10^{17\ 24}$ 21^{19}
       Num 12^2 20^{19} Josh 6^{17} .. .. 20 JE
    D Cp ^{p}**84** .. .. 33 D
    R^p Josh 6^{24} .. .. 1 R^p
    Gen 14^{24} 1
                                        =55*

190 *Peace* (or *welfare,* שלום)
    JE Gen 15^{15} $26^{29\ 31}$ 28^{21} 29^{6ab} 37^4 ^{14ab}
       41^{16} $43^{23\ 27ab\ 28}$ 44^{17} Ex 4^{18} $18^{7\ 23}$
       Josh 9^{15} $10^{(4)\ 21}$ .. .. .. 21 JE
    D Deut 2^{26} $20^{10\ 11}$ 23^6 29^{19} .. 5 D
    P Lev 26^6 Num 6^{26} 25^{12} .. 3 P
                                        =29*

191 *Prince* (or *captain,* שר)
    JE Gen 12^{15}—Josh 5^{14}. .. 47 JE
    D Deut 1^{15abcd} 20^9 .. .. .. 5 D
    P^s Num $31^{14ab\ 48ab\ 52ab\ 54}$ ct נשיא ^{p}**131** 7 P^s
                                        =59*

192 *Prove, to* (Piel נסה, with Deity as subject, and as object)
 (a) *Elohim or Yahweh proves* (or *tries*)
    E Gen 22^1 Ex 15^{25} 16^4 20^{20} Deut 33^8 5 E
    D Deut (4^{34}) $8^{2\ 16}$ 13^3 .. 4 D
 (b) *The people prove* (or *tempt*) *Yahweh*
    JE Ex $17^{2b\ 7c}$ Num 14^{22} .. .. 3 JE
    D Deut 6^{16ab} .. .. 2 D
                                        =14*

193 *Put, to* (*place, appoint,* שים) in Gen
    JE Gen 2^8—48^{20} .. .. .. 46 JE
    P Gen 6^{16} .. .. 1 P
    Elsewhere common in JE D and P. =47

194 *Put, to* (*appoint, lay,* שית)
    JE Gen 3^{15} 4^{25} 30^{40ab} 41^{33} 46^4 $48^{14\ 17}$
       Ex 7^{23} 10^1 21^{22} 30^{ab} $23^{1\ 31}$ 33^4 Num
       12^{11} 24^1 .. .. 18 JE*

195 *Rain, to* (*cause to,* המטיר)
    JE Gen 2^5 7^4 19^{24} Ex $9^{18\ 23}$ 16^4 .. 6 JE*

196 *Ready, to make* (or *prepare,* advbly *firm,* הכין)
    JE Gen $43^{16\ 25}$ Ex 23^{20} Num $23^{1\ 29}$
       Josh 1^{11} 3^{17} 4^4 .. .. .. 8 JE
    D Deut 19^3 Josh 4^{3b} .. .. 2 D
    P Ex 16^5 .. .. 1 P
                                        =11*

197 *Refuse, to* (מאן) cp **68**
    JE Gen 37^{35} 39^8 48^{19} Ex 4^{23} 7^{14} 8^2 9^2
       10^3. 22^{17} Num 20^{21} 22^{13}. .. .. 13 JE
    D Deut 25^7 .. .. 1 D
    P Ex 16^{28} .. .. 1 P
                                        =15*

Remove, see *Turn* **224** (b).
Repent, see *Comfort* **20**.

198 *Ride, rider* (רכב Qal and Hiph)
    JE Gen 24^{61} 41^{43} 49^{17} Ex 4^{20} $15^{1\ 21}$
       Num $22^{22\ 30}$ Deut 33^{26r} .. .. 9 JE
    Deut 32^{13} (Song of Moses) 1
    P Lev 15^9 .. .. 1 P
                                        =11*

199 (a) *Righteous* (adj, צדיק)
    JE Gen 7^1 $18^{23\ 24ab\ 25ab\ 26\ 28}$ 20^4 Ex 9^{27}
       23^7. .. .. 12 JE
    D Deut 4^8 16^{19} 25^1 .. .. 3 D
    Deut 32^4 (Song of Moses) .. 1
    P Gen 6^9 .. .. 1 P
                                        =17*
 (b) *Righteous, to be* (Hiph *justify,* Hithpa *clear ourselves,* צדק)
    JE Gen 38^{26} 44^{16} Ex 23^7 .. 3 JE
    D Deut 25^1 .. .. 1 D
                                        =4*
 (c) *Righteousness* (*justice,* צדקה)
    JE Gen 15^6 18^{19} 30^{33} Deut 33^{21} .. 4 JE
    D Deut 6^{25} 9^{4-6} 24^{13} .. .. 5 D
                                        =9*

200 *Rise up in the morning, to* (השכים)
    JE Gen 19^2 27 20^8 $21^{14\ 22}$ 26^{31} 28^{18}
       31^{55} Ex 8^{20} 9^{13} 24^4 32^6 34^4 Num
       14^{40} Josh 3^1 $6^{12\ 15}$ 7^{16} 8^{10} 14^r .. 20 JE*

201 *Roll, to* (גלל)
    JE Gen $29^{3\ 8\ 10}$ 43^{18} Josh 5^9 10^{18} .. 6 JE

202 *Sacrifice, to* (*offer, kill,* זבח)
    JE Gen 31^{54} 46^1 Ex 3^{18} $5^{3\ 8\ 17}$ $8^{8\ 25}$
       $^{26ab\ 27-29}$ 20^{24} 22^{20} 23^{18} 24^5 32^8 34^{15}
       Num 22^{40} Deut 27^{7a} 33^{19} .. .. 22 JE
    D Deut $12^{15\ 21}$ 15^{21} $16^{2\ 4\ 5}$. 17^1 18^3
       Ex 13^{15} (Josh 8^{31}) .. .. 11 D
    Deut 32^{17} (Song of Moses) .. 1
    P^h Lev $17^{5ab\ 7}$ 19^{5ab} 22^{29ab} .. 7 P^h
    P^s Lev 9^4 ct 'offer' ^{p}**118** .. 1 P^s
                                        =42*

198   WORDS AND PHRASES

JE 203 *See the face of, to* (ראה פנים)
  JE Gen $3^{12\ 5}\ 32^{20\ (30)}\ 33^{10ab}\ 43^{3\ 5}\ 44^{23\ 26}$
    $46^{30}\ 48^{11}$ Ex $10^{28}.\ 33^{20\ 23}$ .. .. 15 JE
  On the original meaning of Ex 23^{15}
  cp $^{17}\ 34^{21\ 23}$. Deut 16^{16} cp Geiger,
  Urschrift 337, Dillmann *in loc*,
  Driver on Deut 16^{16}. Ct **P** Ex 34^{35}*.

204 *Seed, to be multiplied* (הרבה) ct $^{P}73$
  JE Gen $13^{16}\ 15^5\ 16^{10}\ 22^{17}\ 26^4\ ^{24}\ 28^{14}$
    32^{12} Ex 32^{13} Josh 24^3 .. .. 10 JE*
  (a) like the dust of the earth, Gen 13^{16}
    28^{14}*.
  (b) like the stars, Gen $15^5\ 22^{17}\ 26^4$
    Ex 32^{13} cp Deut $1^{10}\ 10^{22}\ 28^{62}$*.
  (c) like the sand of the sea, Gen 22^{17}
    32^{12}*.

205 (a) *Send, to, put forth, let go*, &c (שלח)
  JE sixty-three times in Gen alone.
  P Gen $19^{29}\ 28^5$..
  (b) *put forth (lay) the hand, to* (שלח יד)
  JE Gen $3^{22}\ 8^9\ 19^{10}\ 22^{10\ 12}\ 37^{22}\ 48^{14}$
    Ex $3^{20}\ 4^{4ab}\ 9^{15}\ 22^8\ ^{11}\ 24^{11}$ .. 14 JE*
  (c) *send, to* (*away*, also of ceremonial escort,
    Pi שלּח)
    JE Gen 3^{23}—Josh 24^{28} .. .. 27 JE
    R^d Josh 22^6. .. .. .. 2 R^d
    P Gen $19^{29}\ 28^6$ .. .. .. 2 **P**
  (d) *let Israel go, to* (שלח את י״) =31
    JE Ex 3^{20}—14^5 .. .. .. 43 JE
    R^d Ex 13^{15} .. .. .. 1 R^d
    P Ex $6^{11}\ 7^2\ 11^{10}$ .. .. .. 3 **P**
                                              =47*

206 *Serpent* (נחש)
  JE Gen $3^{1.\ 4\ 13}.\ 49^{17}$ Ex $4^3\ 7^{15r}$ Num
    $21^{6.\ 9abc}$ .. .. 13 JE
  D Deut 8^{15} .. .. 1 D
                                              =14*

207 (a) *Servant* cp 72
  JE Gen 9^{25}—50^{18} eighty-eight times,
    elsewhere fifty-four.. .. 142 JE
  D Deut 5^{15}—Josh 22^5 Ex $13^{3\ 14}$ .. 44 D
  P Ex $7^{10}\ 12^{44}$ Lev $25^{6\ 39\ 42ab\ 44ab\ 55ab}$
    26^{13} Num $31^{49}\ 32^{4.\ 25\ 27\ 31}$ Josh 24^{17r} 18 **P**
    Song of Moses Deut $32^{36\ 43}$ Gen 14^{15} 3
  Cp 'to serve' in JE (23), **P** (0). =207*
  (b) Specially, of Yahweh's servant (Abraham,
    Moses, Caleb &c)
    JE Gen 26^{24} Ex $14^{31}\ 32^{13}$ Num $12^{7}.\ 14^{24}$
      Deut 34^5 Josh $1^1.\ 24^{29}$ .. .. 10 JE
    D Deut 9^{27} Josh $1^7\ 13^{15}\ 8^{31\ 33}\ 9^{24}\ 11^{12\ 15}$
      $12^{6ab}\ 13^8\ 14^7\ 22^{2\ 4}$. .. .. 16 D
    R^P Josh 18^7 .. .. 1 R^P
                                              =27*

208 *Shepherd* (*tend a flock* &c)
  JE Gen (twenty-three) 4^2—Ex 3^4 .. 27 JE
  P Num $14^{33}\ 27^{17}$ .. .. .. 2 **P**
                                              =29*

209 *Shut, to* (סגר)
  (a) Qal Niph Pual
    JE Gen $2^{21}\ 7^{16}\ 19^{6\ 10}$ Num 12^{14}. Josh
      $2^{5\ 7}\ 6^{1ab}$ .. .. 10 JE
    P Ex 14^3 .. .. 1 **P**
                                              =11*
  (b) Hiphil
    P Lev 13^{4}.—14^{46} (eleven) ct Deut 23^{15}
      32^{30} Josh 20^5*.

210 *Slay, to* (or *kill*, הרג)
  JE Gen $4^{8\ 14.\ 23\ 25}\ 12^{12}\ 20^4\ ^{11}\ 26^7\ 27^{41}.$
    $34^{26}\ 37^{20\ 26}\ 49^6$ Ex $2^{14ab}\ 15\ 4^{23}\ 5^{21}$
    $13^{15}\ 21^{14}\ 22^{24}\ 23^7\ 32^{12\ 27}$ Num 11^{15}
    $22^{29\ 33}\ 25^5$ Josh $8^{24}\ 9^{26}\ 10^{11}$ .. 33 JE
  D Deut 13^9 Ex 13^{15} .. .. .. 2 D
  P Gen 34^{25} Lev 20^{15}. Num $31^7\ ^{8ab\ 17ab}$
    ^{19} Josh 13^{22} ct $^{P}100$ .. .. 10 **P**
                                              =45*

211 *Sojourn, to* (גור, in narrative)
  JE Gen $12^{10}\ 19^9\ 20^1\ 21^{23\ 34}\ 26^3\ 32^4$
    47^4 Ex 3^{22} .. .. 9 JE
  D Deut $18^6\ 26^5$ .. .. 2 D
  P Gen 35^{27} Ex $6^4\ (12^{48}$ Lev 19^{33} Num 15^{14}) 2 **P**
  For the legal phrase 'Stranger that =13*
    sojourneth' cp $^{P}145^b$, 'land of so-
    journings' $^{P}145^a$.

212 *Spies, and to spy*
  JE Gen $42^9\ ^{11\ 14\ 16\ 30.\ 34}$ Num 21^{32}
    Josh $2^1\ 6^{22}.\ 7^{2ab}$ .. .. .. 13 JE
  D Deut 1^{24} Josh $6^{25}\ 14^7$ .. .. 3 D
                                              =16*

213 *Spring up, to* (or *grow*, Qal and Hiph צמח)
  JE Gen $2^{5\ 9}\ 3^{18}\ 41^6\ ^{23}$ Ex 10^5 .. 6 JE
  D Deut 29^{23} .. .. 1 D
  P Lev 13^{37} .. .. 1 **P**
                                              =8*

214 *Stand, to* (or *present themselves*, יצב
    Hithpa)
  JE Ex $2^4\ 8^{20}\ 9^{13}\ 14^{13}\ 19^{17}\ 34^5$ Num
    $11^{16}\ 22^{22\ 23}\ 3^{15}$ Deut 31^{14ab} Josh 24^1 13 JE
  D Deut $7^{24}\ 9^2\ 11^{25}$ Josh 1^5 .. .. 4 D
                                              =17*

215 *Stand, to* (נצב) (a) *over against, in the
    way, by* (Niph)
  JE Gen $18^2\ 24^{13\ 43}\ 28^{13}\ 45^1$ Ex $5^{20}\ 7^{15}$
    18^{14} Num $23^{6\ 17}$ .. .. .. 10 JE
  (b) in various other relations
    JE Gen 37^7 Ex (15^8) $17^9\ 33^8\ 21\ 34^2$
      Num $16^{27}\ 22^{23\ 31\ 34}$ .. .. 10 JE
    D Deut 29^{10} .. .. 1 D
  (c) *to set up* (Hiph and Hoph)
    JE Gen $21^{28}.\ 28^{12}\ 33^{20}\ 35^{14\ 20}$ Josh 6^{26} 7 JE
    Deut 32^8 (Song of Moses) .. 1
                                              =29*

216 (a) *Stone, to* (סקל) ct $^{P}152$
    JE Ex $8^{26}\ 17^4\ 19^{13}\ 21^{28.\ 32}$ .. 6 JE
  (b) *Stone with stones*
    D Deut $13^{10}\ 17^5\ 22^{21\ 24}$ Josh 7^{25} .. 5 D
                                              =11*

217 *Swear, to* (of Yahweh's oath to the patriarchs &c)
  JE Gen 22^{16} 24^7 26^3 50^{24} Ex $13^{5\,11}$ 32^{13}
    33^1 Num 11^{12} $14^{16\,23}$ Deut 31^{23} 34^4 .. 13 JE
  D Deut–Josh thirty-three times (cp ^{p}107) .. 33 D
  P Num 32^{10}. .. .. 2 P
  = 48*

218 (a) *Tell, to* (נגד Hiph)
  JE Gen thirty times, Ex 4^{28} 13^{8r} 19^{3r}
    ^{9} Num 11^{27} 23^3 Josh $2^{14\,20}$ 7^{19} .. 39 JE
  D Deut 4^{13} 5^5 17^{9-11} 26^3 30^{18} .. 7 D
    Deut 32^7 (Song of Moses) 1
  P Ex 16^{22} Lev 5^1 14^{35} .. .. 3 P
    Gen 14^{13} 1
  = 51*

  (b) *and it was told* (Hoph ^{a})
  JE Gen 22^{20} 27^{42} 31^{22} $38^{13\,24}$ Ex 14^5
    Josh 10^{17} .. .. .. 7 JE
  D Deut 17^4 Josh 9^{24} .. .. 2 D
  = 9*

219 *Tell, to* (or *shew*, ספר Pi, ct Qal Niph in the sense of 'count' **JDP**)
  JE Gen 24^{66} 29^{13} 37^9. 40^8. $41^{8\,12}$ Ex 9^{16}
    10^2 18^8 24^3 Num 13^{27} Josh 2^{23} .. 14 JE*

220 (a) *Tent* (otherwise than 'Tent of Meeting')
  JE Gen 4^{20} $9^{21\,27}$ 12^8 $13^{3\,5}$ $18^{1.\,6\,9.}$
    24^{67} 25^{27} 26^{25} 31^{25} $33^{(5)}$. 33^{19} 35^{21}
    Ex 18^7 $33^{8\,10}$ Num 11^{10} 16^{26}. 24^5
    Deut 33^{18} Josh 3^{14} 7^{21-23} .. 36 JE
  D Deut 1^{27} 5^{30} 11^6 16^7 Josh $22^{4\,6-8}$ .. 8 D
  P Ex 16^{16} Lev 14^8 Num $19^{14abc\,18}$
    Josh $7^{24?}$ .. .. .. 7 P
  = 51*

  (b) *Tent* (as a verb, i e 'remove')
    Gen $13^{12b\,18}$†.

That (for this cause), see 71^b.

221 *Then* (אז)
  (a) Of past time
  JE Gen 4^{26} 12^6 13^7 49^4 Ex 4^{26} 15^1
    Num 21^{17} Josh 10^{12} .. .. 8 JE
  D Josh 8^{30} Josh 10^{33} 14^{11} 22^1 .. 4 D
    Song of Moses Ex 15^{15} 1
  P Deut 4^{41} (ct Josh 22^{31}) ^{b} .. .. 1 P

  (b) With מן (מאז) *from the time that, since*
    J Gen 39^5 Ex 4^{10} 5^{23} 9^{24} .. 4 J
    D Josh 14^{10} .. .. .. 1 D
  = 5*

222 (a) *Thus* (כה *so, here*, with עד *hitherto*, adverb of place and time, manner)
  JE Gen 15^5—Josh 24^2 .. .. 43 JE
  D Deut 7^5 .. .. .. 1 D
  P Num 6^{23} 8^7 32^8 Josh 22^{16} .. 4 P
  Ct כן in the formula ^{p}189^a.
  = 48*

  (b) *Thus saith, Thus shalt thou say* cp 87
  JE Gen 32^{4ab} 45^9 50^{17} Ex 3^{14}. 5^{10} 19^{3r}
    20^{22} Num 20^{14} 22^{16} .. .. 11 JE
  P^a Josh 22^{16} .. .. 1 P^a
  = 12*

223 *Trespass* (or *transgression*, פשע) ct ^{p}164
  JE Gen 31^{36} 50^{17ab} Ex 22^9 23^{21} 34^7
    Num 14^{18} Josh 24^{19} (only in sing) .. 8 JE
  P Lev $16^{16\,21}$ (pl) .. .. .. 2 P
  = 10*

Tribe, see ^{p}112.

224 (a) *Turn aside, to* (*depart, remove*, סור Qal)
  JE Gen 19^2. 49^{10} Ex 3^3. $8^{11\,29}$ 32^8
    Num 12^{10} 14^9 16^{26} .. .. 11 JE
  D Cp ^{p}114 (chiefly of religious apostasy) 14 D
  P Ex 25^{15} Lev 13^{58} .. .. 2 P
  = 27*

  (b) Hiph *remove, take off, put away* (הסיר)
  JE Gen 8^{13b} $30^{32\,35}$ 35^2 $38^{14\,19}$ 41^{42}
    48^{17} Ex 8^8 ^{31} 10^{17} 14^{25} 23^{25} 33^{23}
    Num 21^7 Josh 7^{13} $24^{14\,23}$ .. 18 JE
  D Deut 7^4 ^{15} 21^{13} Josh 11^{15} .. 4 D
  P Ex 34^{34}, (ritually, of removing the remains of the victim) Lev 1^{16} $3^{4\,9}$
    $^{10\,15}$ 4^9 $31^{ab\,35ab}$ 7^4 .. .. 12 P
  = 34*

225 *Water, to* (or *give to drink*, השקה)
  (a) JE Gen $2^{6\,10}$ 19^{32-35} 21^{19} $24^{14\,18.\,43\,45}$
    46^{ab} $29^{2.\,7.\,10}$ Ex $2^{16.\,19}$ 32^{20} .. 23 JE
  D Deut 11^{10} .. .. .. 1 D
  P Num $5^{24\,26.}$ 20^{8c} .. .. 4 P

  (b) In partcp = *cupbearer* (*butler*)
    E Gen $40^{1.\,5\,9\,13\,20.\,23.}$ 41^9 .. 9 E
  = 37*

226 *Weep, to* (cp 28 and 176)
  JE Gen 21^{16} 27^{38} 29^{11} 33^4 37^{35} 42^{24}
    43^{30ab} $45^{14ab\,15}$ 46^{29} $50^{1\,3\,17}$ Ex 2^6
    Num $11^{4\,10\,13\,18}$ 14^1 .. .. 21 JE
  D Deut 1^{45} 21^{13} .. .. 2 D
  P Gen 23^2 Num 20^{29} 25^6 Deut 34^8 .. 4 P
  = 27*

227 *Well* (באר)
  JE Gen 14^{10} 16^{14} $21^{19\,25\,30}$ $24^{11\,20}$ 26^{15}
    $^{18.\,20.\,22\,25\,32}$ 29^{2abc} $^{3ab\,8\,10}$ Ex 2^{15}
    Num 20^{17} $21^{16.\,18\,22}$ .. .. 28 JE
  Gen 14^{10ab} 2
  = 30*

228 *Wherefore* (or *why*, למה) cp 89^b
  JE Gen 4^{6ab} 12^{18}. 24^{31} 25^{32} 27^{45} 29^{25}
    $31^{27\,30}$ 42^1 43^6 $44^{4\,7}$ $47^{15\,19}$ Ex 2^{13}
    5^4 $^{15\,22}$ 32^{11}. Num 11^{11ab} 14^3 20^5 21^5
    22^{37} Josh 7^7 9^{22} .. .. 30 JE
  D Deut 5^{25} .. .. .. 1 D
  P Gen 27^{46} Num 9^7 20^4 27^4 32^7 .. 5 P
  = 36*

---

^{a} Cp יאמר Niph Gen 10^9 22^{14} 32^{28} Num 21^{14} 23^{23} Josh 2^2 **JE***.
^{b} **P** uses it to prescribe conduct in the future, cp Ex $12^{44\,48}$ Lev $26^{34ab\,41ab}$ Josh 20^6 (so J Gen 24^{41})*.

JE 229 *Whether ... or not* (אם ... ה׳)
  JE Gen 24^{21} 27^{21} 37^{32} Ex 16^4 17^7 (cp 22^{11}) Num 11^{23} 13^{20} (אין) .. .. 7 JE
  D Deut 8^2 .. .. 1 D
  = 8*

230 *Why* (מדוע)
  JE Gen 26^{27} 40^7 Ex 1^{18} 2^{18} 3^3 5^{14} 18^{14} Num 12^8 Josh 17^{14} .. .. 9 JE
  P Lev 10^{17} Num 16^3 .. .. .. 2 P
  = 11*

231 (a) *Wicked* (רשע)
  JE Gen 18^{23} 25^{ab} Ex 2^{13} 9^{27} $23^{1\ 7}$ Num 16^{26} .. .. .. 8 JE
  D Deut 25^1 .. .. 2 D
  P Num 35^{31} .. .. 1 P
  = 11*

  (b) *Condemn, to* (i e declare wicked or guilty, הרשיע) Ex 22^9 Deut 25^{1}*.

232 *Word* (matter, thing, דבר)
  JE Gen 11^1—48^1 fifty-nine times, Ex 1^{18}—Josh 24^{29} seventy-seven .. 136 JE
  D Deut 1^1—Josh 23^{15} .. .. 116 D
  P Gen $34^{14\ 18}$, Ex 12^{24}—Josh 24^{26} 36 P
  = 288*

233 *Wroth* (angry), to be (or, anger be kindled, burn)
  (a) חרה אף
  JE Gen 30^2 39^{13} 44^{18} Ex 4^{14} 22^{24} $32^{10.\ 19\ 22}$ Num $11^{1\ 10\ 33}$ 12^9 $22^{22\ 27}$ 24^{10} 25^3 .. .. 17 JE
  D Deut 6^{15} 7^4 11^{17} 29^{27} 31^{17r} Josh 23^{16} 6 D
  P^s Num $32^{10\ 13}$ Josh 7^1 ct $^r17^8$ .. 3 P^s

  (b) חרה ל
  JE Gen 4^5 $18^{30\ 32}$ 31^{36} 34^7 Num 16^{15} 7 JE

  (c) חרה בעיני
  JE Gen 31^{35} 45^5 .. .. .. 2 JE
  = 35*

(d) *fierce wrath* (of Yahweh, חרון)
  JE Ex 32^{12} Num 25^4 Josh 7^{26} (always with the verb 'turn from').
  Cp Ex 15^7 Deut 13^{17} Num 32^{14}*.

(e) *hot anger* (or *heat*, חרי)
  Ex 11^8 Deut 29^{24}*.

234 *Young man* (lad, child, ילד)
  JE Gen 4^{23} 21^8 14—16 30^{26} 32^{23} $33^{1\ 2ab}$ $5^{ab\ 6.\ 13.}$ 37^{30} 42^{22} 44^{20} Ex $1^{17.}$ 2^3 $6^{ab-9ab\ 10}$ $21^{4\ 22}$ .. .. .. 31 JE
  P Gen 34^4 (fem ילדה, Joel 4^3 Zech 8^5†) 1 P*
  = 32*

235 *Young man* (fem *damsel*, נער נערה)
  JE Gen 19^4—48^{16} thirty-four times, Ex 2^6 10^9 24^5 33^{11} Num 11^{27} 22^{22} Josh $6^{21\ 23}$ .. .. .. 42 JE
  D Deut $22^{15ab\ 16\ 19-21\ 23-29}\ 28^{50}$ .. 15 D
  P^s Gen 34^3 .. .. 1 P^s
  Gen 14^{24} 1
  = 59*

236 The time of day defined (in narrative) 'morning' 'daybreak' 'sunrise' 'noon' 'heat of the day' 'high day' 'cool of the day' 'sunset' 'evening' 'night'
  JE Gen 3^8—46^2, forty-four times, Ex 7^{15} 8^{20} 9^{13} 10^{13} 11^4 $12^{29.}$ $13^{21.}$ $14^{20.\ 24\ 27b}$ 17^{12} 18^{13} 19^{16} 34^2 Num $11^{9\ 32}$ $14^{1\ 14}$ 22^8 $13\ 19-21$ Josh $2^{2\ 5}$ 3^1 4^3 $6^{12\ 15}$ $7^{14\ 16}$ 8^3 $10\ 29$ 10^9 $26.^r$
  Cp P Ex 40^{38} Num $9^{15.}$ 16^5.

237 Use of the indicat and infin for the expression of emphasis, e g 'freely eat' Gen 2^{16}, 'surely die' Gen 3^4
  JE Gen 2^{16}—$50^{24.}$ thirty-eight times 38 JE
  P Gen 17^{13} .. .. 1 P
  Frequent afterwards in all the documents, JE, D, P.

II. The Deuteronomic School, D ^{a}

D 1 (a) *Yahweh* (thy, our, your *God*)
  Deut $1^{6\ 19.}$ &c, my (3), thy (231), his (2), our (23), your (46) = 305, Josh (33).

  (b) *Yahweh, the God of thy* (our, &c) *fathers* cp $^{JE}120$
  Deut $1^{11\ 21}$ 4^1 6^3 12^1 26^7 27^3 29^{25} Josh 18^3.

  (c) *Yahweh*, followed by participles (with the definite article) describing his action, or as predicates
  Deut 1^{33} 3^{22} $8^{14-16\ 18}$ 9^3 20^4 $31^{6\ 8}$ Josh 23^3 (cp E Josh 24^{17}).

2 (a) *All Israel*
  Deut 1^1 5^1 11^6 13^{11} 18^6 21^{21} 27^9 29^2 $31^{1\ 7\ 11}$ 32^{45} 34^{12} Josh 3^7 17^b 4^{14} 7^{24} $8^{15\ 21\ 24\ 33}$ 10^{15} $29\ 31\ 34\ 36\ 38\ 43$ 23^2. Ct Ex 18^{25} Num 16^{34}*.

  (b) *Hear, O Israel*
  Deut 5^1 $6^{(3)\ 4}$ 9^1 20^3 27^9 cp 4^{1}†.
  Cp Is 44^1 48^{12} Am 3^1 4^1 5^1 Hos 4^1 Is 1^2 10 &c.

  (c) *Children of Israel*
  Cp Deut $4^{44\aleph}$: used freely by R^d in Josh $4^{12\ 21}$ $5^{1\ 6}$ $8^{31.}$ &c.

---

^{a} In the lists of D and P the verses only are cited, without specifying every occurrence.

THE DEUTERONOMIC SCHOOL, D

D

3 (a) *Amorites, the* (as occupants of the hill country of Canaan, and east of Jordan)
  Deut 1^7 $^{19.\ 27\ 44}$ 3^9 Num 21^{34} Josh 5^1 7^7 10^{12} cp Josh 24^{12} and $^{JE}96$.

(b) *The hill country of the Amorites*
  Deut $1^{7\ 19}$·†.

(c) *Two kings of the Amorites* (Sihon and Og)
  Deut 3^8 4^{47} Josh 2^{10} 9^{10} 24^{12}, 'kings of the Amorites' Deut 31^4 Josh 5^1 cp Josh 10^5 E*.

4 *Anakim*
  Deut 1^{28} $2^{10.\ 21}$ 9^2 Josh $11^{21.}$ 14^{12} 15^*. Elsewhere *Anak*.

5 *Rephaim, the*
  Deut $2^{11\ 20}$ $3^{11\ 13}$ Josh 12^4 13^{12} 17^{15r} (ct 'Vale of Rephaim' Josh 15^8 18^{16} P).

6 (a) *Arabah, the*
  D Deut 1^1 2^8 3^{17} 4^{49} 11^{30} Josh $12^{1\ 3}$ cp JE Josh 8^{14}, P 3^{16} 18^{18}.

(b) *Arabah, the* (followed by *the hill country, the lowland, &c*)
  Similar, though not quite identical, enumerations, in Deut 1^7 Josh 9^1 10^{40} $11^{2\ 16}$ 12^{8*}.

(c) *Land of Moab, the*, ct $^P 2^a$ 'Arboth Moab'
  Deut 1^5 29^1, E Deut 34^{5}.. In 32^{49} P probably a later geographical gloss.

7 *Horeb*, cp $^{JE}105$, ct Sinai $^P7$
  Deut $1^{2\ 6\ 19}$ $4^{10\ 15}$ 5^2 9^8 18^{16} 29^1.

8 (a) *Slopes* (of Pisgah)
  Deut 3^{17} 4^{49} Josh 10^{40} $12^{3\ 8}$. Cp Josh 13^{20} P†.

(b) *Pisgah*
  Deut 3^{27} 34^{1b}. Ct P 'Nebo' 32^{49} 34^{1a}.

9 (a) *Abomination to Yahweh* (תועבה ליי)
  Deut 7^{25} 12^{31} 17^1 18^{12} 22^5 23^{18} 25^{16} 27^{15} cp 24^{4*}. Elsewhere only in Prov ten times.

(b) *Abomination* (abominable thing, תועבה)
  Deut 7^{26} 13^{14} 14^3 17^4 18^9 ^{12} 20^{18} cp 32^{16}. In P only in Lev $18^{22\ 26.\ 29.}$ 20^{13}.

(c) *Abhor, to* (i e abominate, תעב)
  Deut 7^{26} 23^{7ab*}.

10 *All or any in explanatory appositions*
  Deut 2^{37b} $3^{4b\ 13\ 18}$ 4^{19} 5^8 15^{21} 16^{21} 17^1 18^1 20^{14} 25^{16} 29^{10} Josh 1^4 5^4 6^{3r} 13^6 ^{12}.

11 *All that thou puttest thine hand unto* (כל משלח ידך)
  Deut 12^7 ^{18} 15^{10} 23^{20} 28^8 ^{20}†.

12 *All that Yahweh did &c* (or *which* or *as he did*) cp $^{JE}146^c$
  Deut 1^{30} 3^{21} $4^{3\ 34}$ 7^{18} (10^{21}) 11^{3-7} 24^9 29^2 31^4 Josh 4^{23} $9^9.$ 23^3 $24^{7\ 31}$.

13 (a) *All the days* (always, as long as, for ever)
  Deut 5^{29} 6^{24} 11^1 14^{23} 18^5 19^9 $28^{29\ 33}$ (cp 31^{13} ☧) Josh 4^{24}. Cp Gen 43^9 44^{32} J*.

(b) *All thy (his) days* (as long as thou livest)
  Deut 12^{19} $22^{19\ 29}$ 23^{6*}.

(c) *All the days of thy life*
  Deut 4^9 6^2 16^3 17^{19} Josh 1^5 4^{14} cp Deut 4^{10} 12^1 31^{13}. J Gen 3^{14} 17^*.

14 *All the peoples*
  Deut 4^{19} 7^6 $^{7-14\ 16\ 19}$ 10^{15} 14^2 $28^{37\ 64}$ 30^3 Josh 24^{18}. E Josh 24^{17}, 'Of the earth' Deut 28^{10} Josh 4^{24*}.

15 *All the words of this law*, cp **70**
  Deut 17^{19} $27^{3\ 8}$ 28^{58} 29^{29} 31^{12} 32^{46} cp 27^{26} 31^{24} Josh 8^{34*}.

16 *Altar of Yahweh thy God*
  Deut 12^{27} 16^{21} 26^4 (27^6 Josh 9^{27})* ct JE Ex 20^{26} 21^{14} Deut 33^{10} and P Lev 17^6 Josh $22^{19\ (28)\ 29*}$.

17 *Anger of Yahweh* (אף יי)
  Deut 6^{15} 7^4 11^{17} $29^{20\ 27}$ Josh 23^{16}. Cp Ex 4^{14} R^{je}, Num 11^{10} J, 12^9 E, 25^3. J, $32^{10\ 13}$. Josh 7^1 P^s *.

18 *Angry, to be* (אנף, Hithpa)
  Deut 1^{37} 4^{21} 9^8 ^{20} cp 1 Kings 11^9 2 Kings 17^{18}†.

19 *Ark of the covenant of Yahweh*
  Deut 10^8 31^9 ^{25}. Josh $3^{3r\ 17r}$ $4^{7ar\ 18r}$ 6^{8r} 8^{33} cp Num 10^{33} 14^{44*}.

20 (a) *Assembly, the* (קהל)
  Deut 5^{22} 9^{10} 10^4 18^{16} 31^{30} Josh 8^{35}. Cp $^P24$, whereas D never uses *Congregation*, cp $^P24^{bcd}$.

(b) *Assembly of Yahweh*
  Deut $23^{1-3\ 8}$ cp P Num 16^3 20^{4*}.

(c) *Assemble, to* (הקהיל)
  Deut 4^{10} $31^{12\ 28}$ ct $^P24^a$ 'assemble the congregation' Lev 8^3 Num 1^{18} 8^9 16^{19} 20^{8a*}.

21 (a) *Beyond Jordan* (of the Eastern country, בעבר הירדן or עבר ה׳) ct $^P2^b$
  Deut 1^1 5 3^8 $4^{41r\ 46.\ 49}$ Josh $1^{14\ 15}$ 2^{10} 9^{10} 12^1 13^8 22^4. J Gen 50^{10}. Josh 7^7, E Josh 24^8 (cp ^{2}.).

(b) *Of the West*
  Deut $3^{20\ 25}$ 11^{30} Josh 5^1 9^1 12^7 22^7 (Q°rî).

22 (a) *Bless, to*, in the formula *that Yahweh may bless thee* (or *when, for, because,* &c.)
  Deut 1^{11} 2^7 7^{13ab} 12^7 $14^{24\ 29}$ 15^4 $^{6\ 10\ 14\ 18}$ $16^{10\ 15}$ 23^{20} 24^{19} 26^{15} 28^8 ^{12} 30^{16}. Cp E Ex 20^{24} 23^{25}.

(b) *Blessing* (contrasted with *curse*)
  Deut $11^{26.\ 29}$ 23^5 28^{28} $30^{1\ 19}$ Josh 8^{34}. Cp E Gen 27^{12}.

(c) *According to the blessing of Yahweh thy God*
  Deut 12^{15} 16^{17}†.

23 (a) *Bow down, to* (or *worship*, sometimes with *serve*, of other gods)
  Deut 4^{19} 5^9 (∥ Ex 20^5) 8^{19} 11^{16} 17^3 29^{26} 30^{17} Josh $23^{7\ 16}$. Once of Yahweh, Deut 26^{10}. Cp J Ex 34^{14}, R^{je} Ex 23^{24*}.

(b) *Serve other gods*, cp **85**
  Deut 7^4 (cp ^{16}) 8^{19} 11^{16} (cp 12^2 ^{30}) $13^{2\ 6\ 13}$ 17^3 $28^{14\ 36\ 64}$ $29^{18\ 26}$ 30^{17} (cp 31^{20}) Josh 23^{16}. Cp E Josh $24^{2\ 15.\ 20*}$.

D 23 (c) *Serve Yahweh*
Deut 6^{13} $10^{12\ 20}$ 11^{13} 13^4 28^{47} Josh 22^5. Cp R^{je} Ex 23^{25}, E Josh $24^{14.\ 18.\ 21.\ 24}$. Ct the specific use in the narratives of the demands addressed to Pharaoh, Ex 3^{12} 4^{23} 7^{16} $10^{3\ 26}$, and the term 'service' $^P140$.

24 *Bring in, to* (of Yahweh bringing Israel into Canaan הביא, cp בוא **53**). Ct 'bring up' $^{JE}136$
Deut 4^{38} $6^{10\ 23}$ 7^1 8^7 9^4 ^{28} 11^{29} 26^9 30^5 (31^{20}.). Cp J Ex $13^{5\ 11}$ Num $14^{8\ 24\ 31}$, E Josh 24^8, R^{je} Ex 23^{23}: also in P rarely e g Ex 6^8.

25 *Brother* (i e fellow-countryman, in the code)
Deut $15^{2.\ 7\ 9\ 11}$. $17^{15\ 20}$ $18^{2\ 15\ 18}$ 19^{18}. 20^8 22^{1-4} $23^{7\ 19}$. $24^{7\ 14}$ 25^3 cp 1^{16}. Not in the codes of JE : cp P^h Lev 19^{17} $25^{25\ 35.\ 39\ 46-48}$.

26 (a) *Choose, to* (of the divine election of Israel, Levi)
Deut 4^{37} 7^6. 10^{15} 14^2 18^5 21^5 cp 17^{15*}.

(b) Of the place chosen for the sanctuary, cp **87**.

27 *Cleave, to* (to Yahweh, דבק)
Deut 4^4 10^{20} 11^{22} 13^4 30^{20} Josh 22^5 23^{8*}.

28 (a) *Come out, to* (from Egypt, in the formula 'when ye (they) came forth,' &c, צאת)
Deut $4^{45.\ 16^3}$ 6 23^4 24^9 25^{17} Josh 2^{10} 5^4. Cp J Ex 13^{8*}. Ct in dates (rather differently, לצאת) P Ex 16^1 19^1 Num 1^1 9^1 33^{33}.

(b) *Bring out, to* (of Yahweh bringing Israel out from Egypt, הוציא)
Deut 1^{27} $4^{20\ 37}$ 5^6 (∥ Ex 20^2) 5^{15} $6^{12\ 21\ 23}$ $7^{8\ 19}$ 8^{14} $9^{12\ 26\ 28}$. $13^{5\ 10}$ 16^1 26^8 29^{25} Ex $13^{3\ 9\ 14\ 16}$. Rarely in JE, R^e Ex 18^1, R^{je} Ex 32^{11}., E Josh 24^5. Cp the formula in P 'know that I am Yahweh which brought you out' &c $^P179^c$.

29 (a) *Command*, in the formula *As* (or *that*) *Yahweh thy God hath commanded thee* (us &c)
Deut $1^{19\ 41}$ 4^5 $5^{12\ 16\ 32}$. 6^1 $17^{20\ 25}$ 10^5 13^5 20^{17} (24^8) 26^{14} Josh 10^{40*}.

(b) *Which I command thee* (or *you*, often with *to-day*)
Deut $4^{2\ 40}$ $6^{2\ 6}$ 7^{11} $8^{1\ 11}$ (9^{12}) 10^{13} $11^{8\ 13\ 22\ 27}$. $12^{11\ 14\ 21\ 28\ 32}$ 13^{18} 15^5 19^9 $27^{1\ 4\ 10}$ $28^{1\ 13-15}$ $30^{2\ 8\ 11\ 16}$. Cp J^r Ex 34^{11*}.

(c) *Therefore I command thee*
Deut (5^{15}) $15^{11\ 15}$ 19^7 $24^{18\ 22*}$.

(d) *The commandment* (collectively)
Deut 5^{31} $6^{1\ 25}$ 7^{11} $8^{1\ 11}$ 8^{22} 15^5 17^{20} 19^9 26^{13} 27^1 30^{11} 31^5 Josh $22^{3\ 5}$. Cp Ex 24^{12b*}.

(e) *Commandments* (often with *do, keep, remember*) cp **82**^{c}
Deut twenty-eight times, Josh 22^5.
Cp JE Gen 26^5 Ex 15^{26} 20^6 ; P Ex 16^{28} Lev $4^{2\ 13\ 22\ 27}$ 5^{17} 22^{31} $26^{3\ 14}$. 27^{34} Num $15^{22\ 39.*}$

30 *Corn and wine and oil*
Deut 7^{13} 11^{14} 12^{17} 14^{23} 18^4 28^{51*}.
Cp 'corn and wine' Gen $27^{23\ 37}$ Deut 33^{28}.

31 (a) *Covenant* (in relation of Israel and Yahweh)
Deut $4^{13\ 23\ 31}$ 5^2. 7^9 ^{12} 8^{18} $9^{9\ 11\ 15}$ 17^2 $29^{1\ 9\ 12\ 14\ 21\ 25}$ Ex 19^5. Cp $31^{16\ 20}$ 33^9, JE Ex 24^7. $34^{10\ 27}$. and $^P47$. Cp **19** 'ark of the covenant.'

(b) *Make, to* (ᵯ *cut* כרת $^{JE}181$) *a covenant*
Deut 5^2. $29^{1\ 12\ 14}$ cp Ex $34^{10\ 27}$.

32 (a) *Curse* (contrasted with *blessing*, קללה) cp **22**^{b}
Deut $11^{26\ 28}$. (21^{23}) 23^5 27^{13} $28^{15\ 45}$ (29^{27}) $30^{1\ 19}$ Josh 8^{34}. Cp E Gen 27^{12*}. A different word (אלה) in Gen 24^{41} 26^{28} Deut $29^{12\ 14\ 19-21}$ 30^7, and P Lev 5^1 Num $5^{21\ 23\ 27*}$.

(b) *Cursed* (ארור)
Deut 27^{15-26} 28^{16-19}, cp $^{JE}24$.

33 (a) *Day, as at this* (כיום הזה)
Deut 2^{30} $4^{20\ 38}$ 6^{24} 8^{18} 10^{15} 29^{28} cp E Gen 50^{20} (in a different sense J Gen 39^{11})*.

(b) *Unto this day*
Deut 2^{22} 3^{14r} 10^8 11^4 29^4 34^6 Josh 4^9 8^{28} 9^{27} 14^{14} 22^3 23^8. Cp $^{JE}142^b$, P Josh 22^{17}.

(c) *Which shall be in those days*
Deut 17^9 19^{17} 26^3 cp Josh 20^6†.

Deliver into the hand of, see **52**.

34 (a) *Destroy, to* (השמיר) ct **86**
Deut 1^{27} $2^{12\ 21-23}$ 4^3 6^{15} $7^{4\ 24}$ $9^{3\ 8\ 14\ 19.\ 25}$ $28^{48\ 63}$ 31^3. Josh 7^{12} 9^{24} $11^{14\ 20}$ 23^{15} 24^8. Cp Deut 33^{27} Lev 26^{30} Num 33^{52*}.

(b) *Be destroyed*, Niph
Deut 4^{26} 7^{23} 12^{30} $28^{20\ 24\ 45\ 51\ 61}$. Cp J Gen 34^{30*}.

35 *Devote, to* (or *utterly destroy*, החרים)
Deut 2^{34} 3^6 7^2 13^{15} 20^{17} Josh 2^{10} 6^{18} $10^{28\ 35\ 37\ 39}$. $11^{11.\ 20}$.. Cp J Num 21^2. Josh 6^{21} 10^1, E Ex 22^{20} Josh 8^{26}, P Lev 27^{28*}.

36 (a) *Die* (in legal condemnations, *that he* [or *they*] *die*, ומת)
Deut 13^{10} $17^{5\ 12}$ 18^{20} 19^{12} 21^{21} $22^{21.\ 24}$. 24^7. Ct conditionally E Ex $21^{12\ 20\ 28\ 35}$ $22^{2\ 10}$.

(b) *Shall be put to death* (יומת)
Deut 13^5 17^6 (cp 21^{22} 24^{16}) ct $^{JE}100$ $^P52^b$.

37 (a) *Do that which is right in the eyes of Yahweh*
Deut $6^{18\ 12\ (8)\ 25\ 28}$ 13^{18} 21^9 cp Josh 9^{25}. Cp R^{je} Ex 15^{26*}.

(b) *Do that which is evil in the eyes of Yahweh*
Deut 4^{25} 9^{18} (13^{11}) 17^2 $^{(5)}$ (19^{20}) 31^{29}. P^s Num 32^{13*}.

38 *Drawn away, be* (the same verb in various applications, נדח Qal Niph Hiph)
Deut 4^{19} $13^{5\ 10\ 13}$ 19^5 20^{19} 22^1 $30^{1\ 4\ 17*}$.

Dread not (or *be not affrighted*, ערץ), see **44**^{d}.

39 *Drive out, to* (*possess, dispossess, succeed*, ירש with 'peoples' as object, cp 'land' **88**)

(a) Qal, see **88**^{b}.

(b) Hiph, Deut 4^{38} 7^{17} 9^{3-5} 11^{23} 18^{12} Josh 3^{10b} $13^{6\ 12}$ 14^{12} $23^{5\ 9\ 13}$. Cp J Ex 34^{24r} Num 32^{39} Josh 13^{13} $15^{14\ 63}$ 16^{10} 17^{12}., P^s Num 32^{21} 33^{52*}.

THE DEUTERONOMIC SCHOOL, D

40 *Dwell, to cause his name to* (לשכן) cp **87**
Deut 12^{11} 14^{23} 16$^{2\ 6\ 11}$ 26^{2}*. Ct ^{P}**54**.

41 (a) *Eat before Yahweh*
Deut 12$^{7\ 18}$ 14$^{23\ 26}$ 15^{20}‹. Cp Ex 18^{12}.

(b) *Eat and be satisfied (full)*
Deut 6^{11} 8$^{10\ 12}$ 11^{15} 14^{29} 26^{12}. Cp 31^{20}*.
Ct 'eat to satisfaction' Ex 16$^{3\ 8}$ Lev 25^{19} 26^{5} **P***.

Edge of the sword cp ^{JE}**150**.

42 (a) *Elders of the city*
Deut 19^{12} 21$^{3.\ 6\ 19.}$ 22$^{15-18}$ 25$^{7-9}$, **R**^{p} Josh 20^{4}*.

(b) *Elders of Israel (your, his, &c)*
Deut 5^{23} 21^{2} 27^{1} 29^{10} 31$^{9\ 28}$ Josh 8^{33} 23^{2} 24$^{1\ 31}$.
Cp ^{JE}**151**.

43 (a) *Eyes, before your* (or *unto thee, in the presence of, &c,* lit. 'to your eyes' (לעיניכם)
Deut 1^{30} 4$^{6\ 34}$ 6^{22} 9^{17} 25^{3} 28^{31} 29^{2} 31^{7} 34^{12} Josh 10^{12} 24^{17}. Less frequent elsewhere.

(b) *Thine eye shall not pity*
Deut 7^{16} 13^{8} 19$^{13\ 21}$ 25^{12} cp Gen 45^{20} ⌂*.

(c) *Which thine eyes have seen (shall see)*
Deut 4^{9} 7^{19} 10^{21} 28$^{34\ 67}$ 29^{3}* cp 21^{7}.

(d) *Thine eyes have seen (what Yahweh did &c)*
Deut 3^{21} 4^{3} 11^{7} Josh 24^{7}* cp Dt 28^{32} Gen 45^{12}.

44 (a) *Fear Yahweh, to* (in the infin ליראה)
Deut 4^{10} 5^{29} 6^{24} 8^{6} 10^{12} 14^{23} 17^{19} 28^{58} 31^{13}*
cp the similar infinitives or verbal nouns 'to love' **74**^{b}, and 'to hate' 1^{27} 9^{28}.

(b) *In other parts of the verb*
Deut 6$^{2\ 13}$ 7^{21} 10$^{17\ 20}$ 13^{4} 25^{18} 28^{58} 31^{12} Josh 4^{24}.
Cp ^{JE}**102**, ^{P}**200**, **P**^{s} Josh 22^{25}.

(c) *Fear not neither be dismayed* (or *affrighted* or *dread* ירא) followed by חתת or ערץ) cp ^{JE}**154**
Deut 1^{21} 20^{3} 31$^{6\ 8}$ Josh 8^{1r} 10^{25}*.

(d) *Dread not* (or *be not affrighted* ערץ)
Deut 1^{29} 7^{21} 20^{3} 31^{6} Josh 1^{9} ⌂*.

45 *Fight, to* (of Yahweh for Israel)
Deut 1^{30} 3^{22} 20^{4} Josh 10$^{14\ 42}$ 23$^{3\ 10}$.
Cp **J** Ex 14^{14} 25*.

46 *Finished, until they were* (or *consumed* עד תמם)
Deut 2^{15} 31$^{24\ 30}$ Josh 8^{24} 10^{20} cp Deut 2^{14} Josh 4^{10} 5^{6} (Lev 25^{29}) Num 14^{33} 32^{13}*.

Flowing with milk and honey, see **69**^{a}.

47 *Foreigner* (נכרי)
Deut 14^{21} 15^{3} 17^{15} 23^{20} 29^{22}.
Cp Gen 31^{15} Ex 2^{22} ∥ 18^{3} 21^{8}*.

48 *Forget, to* (as caution to Israel, in reference to Yahweh and his commands) cp **97**
Deut 4$^{9\ 23}$ 6^{12} 8$^{11\ 14\ 19}$ 9^{7} 25^{19} cp 26^{13}*.
Otherwise, Deut 4^{31} 24^{19} (31^{21} 32^{18}) cp Gen 27^{45} 40^{23} 41^{3}*.

49 *Found, if there be* (in legal formulae, כי ימצא)
Deut 17^{2} 21^{1} 22^{22} 24^{7}† cp Ex 22$^{2\ 4\ 7}$. אם.

50 (a) *Fruit of thy (the) ground*
Deut 7^{13} 26$^{2\ 10}$ 28$^{4\ 11\ 18\ 33\ 42\ 51}$ 30^{9}.
Cp Gen 4^{3} Jer 7^{20} Ps 105^{35}†.

(b) *Fruit of thy womb (body)*
Deut 7^{13} 28$^{4\ 11\ 18\ 53}$ 30^{9}. Cp Gen 30^{2}*.

(c) *Fruit of thy cattle*
Deut 28$^{4\ 11\ 51}$ 30^{9}†.

51 *Gates, thy (your)*
(a) *Within thy gates*
Deut 5^{14} (∥ Ex 20^{10}) 6^{9} 11^{20} 12$^{12\ 17.\ 21}$ 14$^{21\ 27-23}$ 15^{22} 16$^{11\ 14}$ 17^{8} 24^{14} 26^{12} 28^{57} 31^{12}*.

(b) *One of thy gates*
Deut 15^{7} 16^{5} 17^{2} 18^{6} 23^{16}*.

(c) *All thy gates*
Deut 12^{15} 16^{18} 28$^{52\ 55}$*.

(d) *The gate as the place where justice is administered*
Deut 17$^{5\ 8}$ 21^{19} 22$^{15\ 24}$ 25^{7}*.

52 *Give into (thy) hand, to* (or *deliver,* נתן ביד, cp **100**)
Deut 1^{27} 2$^{24\ 30}$ 3^{2}. 7^{24} 19^{12} 20^{13} 21^{10} Num 21^{34} Josh 7^{7} 8$^{1\ 7\ 18}$ 10$^{8\ 19\ 30\ 32}$ 11^{8} 21^{44}.
Cp **J** Num 21^{2} Josh 6^{2}(?), **E** Josh 2^{24} 24$^{8\ 11}$, **R**^{Je} Ex 23^{31}*.

53 *Go-in and (to) possess* (בוא וירש) cp **88**
Deut 1$^{8\ 39}$ 4$^{1\ 5}$ 6^{18} 7^{1} 8^{1} 9$^{1\ 5}$ 10^{11} 11$^{8\ 10\ 29\ 31}$ 12^{29} 17^{14} 23^{20} 26^{1} 28$^{21\ 63}$ 30$^{(5)\ 16\ 18}$ Josh 1^{11} 18^{3}*.

54 (a) *Go-over and (to) possess* (עבר וירש)
Deut 4$^{14\ 22\ 26}$ 6^{1} 11$^{8\ 11\ (31)}$ (30^{18}) 31^{13} 32^{47}*.
Cp 12^{10} ('go-over and dwell') 1^{21} 9^{23} ('go-up and possess').

(b) *Whither thou (ye) goest over*
Deut 3^{21} 4^{14} 6^{1} 11$^{8\ 11}$ 30^{18}.

55 (a) *Great and terrible*
Deut 1^{19} 7^{21} 8^{15} 10^{17} 21*.

(b) *Greater and mightier* (or *great and mighty = strong*)
Deut 4^{38} 9^{1} 11^{23} 26^{5} Josh 23^{9}.
Cp Deut 7^{1} 9^{14} ⌂, **J** Gen 18^{18} Ex 1^{9}, **R**^{Je} Num 14^{12}*.

(c) *Greatness*
Deut 3^{24} 5^{24} 9^{26} 11^{2}. Cp 32^{3} Num 14^{19}, in Hex only of Yahweh. Ct Is 9^{9} 10^{12} Ezek 31$^{2\ 7\ 18}$.
Cp Ps 79^{11} 150^{2}†.

Hate, to. Cp ^{JE}**167**.

56 *He and (all) his people*
Deut 2^{32}. 3$^{1-3}$ Num 21$^{33-35}$ Josh 8^{14} 10^{33}.
Cp Ex 17^{13}‹. Ct Josh 8^{5}.

57 *Heads* (of tribes)
Deut 1$^{13\ 15}$ 5^{23} 29^{10} Josh 23^{2} cp 24^{1}.
Ct Deut 33$^{5\ 21}$, **J** 'heads of the people' Num 25^{4}, **E** 'heads over the people' Ex 18^{25}, **P** 'heads of fathers' houses,' cp ^{P}**84**^{a}.

WORDS AND PHRASES

D 58 (a) *Hearken to (ob-y) my (Yahweh's) voice* (שמע ב׳)
Deut 4^{30} 8^{20} 9^{23} 13^4 ^{18} 15^5 26^{14} ^{17} 27^{10} 28^1. ^{15} ^{45} ^{62} 30^2 ^{8} ^{10} ^{20} Josh 5^6. Of others, Deut 1^{45} 21^{18} ^{20} Josh 10^{14} (?) 22^2 cp $^J44^b$.

(b) *Hear* ($\mathfrak{H}$ = *hearken*) *and fear*
Deut 13^{11} 17^{13} 19^{20} 21^{21*} 'hear and learn and fear' 31^{12} cp ^{13}.

(c) *Hear, O Israel*, see **2**^{b}.

59 *Heart, with all your heart and with all your soul*
Deut 4^{29} 6^5 10^{12} 11^{13} 13^3 26^{16} 30^2 ^{6} ^{10} Josh 22^5 23^{14*} לבב 47 times in Deut, Josh 2^{11} 5^1 7^{5r} 14^7, לב only in 4^{11} 28^{65} 29^4 ^{19} cp Josh 11^{20} 14^8).

60 (a) *Holy people* (עם קדוש)
Deut 7^6 14^2 ^{21} 26^{19} 28^{9}† cp Ex 19^6 גוי קדוש and Is 62^{12} עם הקדש.

(b) *a peculiar people* (עם סגלה)
Deut 7^6 14^2 26^{18}† cp Ex 19^5.

61 *House of bondage* (i e *servants*, cp **97, 109**)
Deut 5^6 (∥ Ex 20^2) 6^{12} 7^8 8^{14} 13^5 ^{10} Ex 13^3 ^{14} Josh 24^{17*}.

62 *How* (איכה)
Deut 1^{12} 7^{17} 12^{30} 18^{21} (32^{30} Song of Moses)*.

63 *I* (אנכי)
More than fifty times in Deut (31^{23} **E**) Josh 13^6 14^7. ^{10} 23^{14}. אני only in 12^{30} 29^6 Josh 23^2. Cp 32^{21} ^{33} (Song of Moses), **P** 32^{49} ^{52} cp $^P94$.

64 *In thee* (or *among you, with, unto*, of Israel collectively, בך)
Deut 7^{14} 15^4 ^{7} ^{9} 18^{10} 23^{10} ^{14} ^{21}. 24^{15} 25^{13} 28^{46} ^{54} ^{56}. Cp **78**^{a}.

65 (a) *Inherit (to cause to*, הנחיל) cp **69**^{df}
Deut 1^{38} 3^{28} 12^{10} 19^3 21^{16} 31^7 Josh 1^6. Cp Deut 32^{8*}.

(b) *no portion or inheritance*
Deut 10^9 12^{12} 14^{27} ^{29} 18^1. Cp **E** Gen 31^{14*}.

Innocent blood, cp **92**^{bc}.

66 *Instruct, to* (or *chastise*)
Deut 4^{36} 8^{5ab} 21^{18} 22^{18}. Cp. Lev 26^{18} ^{28*}.

67 *Judges* (of Israel)
Deut 1^{16} 16^{18} 17^9 ^{12} 19^{17}. 21^2 25^2 Josh 8^{33} 23^2 24^1. Cp **E** Num 25^{5*}. Ct Ex 18^{21-26}.

Keep, see *Observe* **82**.

68 (a) *Know therefore* (or, *and thou shalt know* or *consider*, specially of the experience of life)
Deut 4^{39} 7^9 8^5 9^3 ^{6} 11^2 Josh 23^{14} $\mathfrak{H}$. Cp Ex 6^7 10^2 16^6 ^{12} Num 14^{34} 16^{30*}.

(b) *which thou knowest*
Deut 7^{15} 9^2 cp 1^{31}.

(c) *which thou (ye, they) knowest not* (sometimes with *thy fathers*)
Deut 8^3 ^{16} 11^{28} 13^2 ^{6} ^{13} 28^{33} ^{36} ^{64} 29^{26}. Cp 32^{17*}.

69 (a) *(Land) flowing with milk and honey*
Deut 6^3 11^9 26^9 ^{15} 27^3 31^{20r} Josh 5^6. Cp $^{JE}34$.

(b) *the good land*
Deut $1^{(25)}$ ^{35} 3^{25} 4^{21}. 6^{18} 8^7 ^{10} 9^6 11^{17} Josh 23^{13} ^{15} ('ground') ^{16}. Cp **J** Ex 3^8, **P** Num 14^{7*}.

(c) *The land (possession, cities, gates, &c) which Yahweh thy (our &c) God giveth (hath given) thee (us)*
Deut 1^{20} ^{25} 2^{12} 3^{20} 4^1 ^{40} 5^{16} (∥ Ex 20^{12}) 7^{16} 8^{10} 9^{23} 11^{17} ^{31} 12^9 $^{(10)}$ 13^{12} 15^4 ^{7} 16^5 ^{18} ^{20} 17^2 ^{14} 18^9 20^{14} 25^{15} 26^2 ^{10} ^{15} 27^2. 28^8 ^{52} 32^{52} Josh 1^{15} 18^3 23^{13} ^{15}..
Cp **E** Josh 1^2; ct **P** Lev 14^{34} 23^{10} 25^2 Num 13^2 15^2 32^7 ^{9} Deut 32^{49} ^{52}.

(d) *The land (cities) ... as an inheritance*
Deut 4^{21} 19^{10} 20^{16} 21^{23} 24^4 26^1† cp 4^{38} 12^9 29^8.

(e) *The land ... to possess it*, cp **88**
Deut 3^{18} $5^{31 (33)}$ 9^6 12^1 19^2 ^{14} 21^1 Josh 1^{11}†. Cp Gen 15^7.

(f) *The land ... as an inheritance to possess it*, cp **88**
Deut 15^4 25^{19}† 'causeth thee to inherit' 19^3.

(g) *The land whither thou goest in (over) &c*, cp **53, 54**.

(h) *The land which Yahweh sware*, cp **107**^{a}.

70 (a) *Law, this*, cp **15**
Deut 1^5 4^8 $^{(44)}$ 17^{18}. 27^3 ^{8} ^{26} 28^{58} ^{61} 29^{29} 31^9 $^{11.}$ ^{24} 32^{46}. Ct **P** Num 5^{30*}.

(b) *This (the) book of the law*
Deut $29^{21 (27)}$ 30^{10} 31^{26} Josh 1^8 8^{34*}.

(c) *The words of this law*
Deut 17^{19} 27^3 ^{8} ^{26} 28^{58} 29^{29} 31^{12} ^{24} 32^{46*}.

71 (a) *Learn, to* (למד Qal)
Deut 4^{10} 5^1 14^{23} 17^{19} 18^9 $31^{12.*}$.

(b) *Teach, to* (למד Piel)
Deut 4^1 ^{5} ^{10} ^{14} 5^{31} 6^1 11^{19} 20^{18} 31^{19} ^{22*}.

Levite, the, in the village household, cp 'Stranger' **105**, 'thou and thy son' &c **109**, 'Gates' **51**, 'Priests' **90**.

72 *Live, that thou (ye) mayest*
Deut 4^1 5^{33} 8^1 16^{20} 30^{16} ^{19}, cp 6^{24} 30^6 32^{47} and **73***.

73 (a) *Long, to be* (of the days of Israel), האריך (intrans)
Deut 5^{16} (∥ Ex 20^{12}) 6^2 25^{15}.

(b) *prolong, to* (האריך, trans)
Deut 4^{26} ^{40} 5^{33} 11^9 17^{20} 22^7 30^{18} 32^{47}. Cp Josh 24^{31*}.

74 (a) *Love* (of Yahweh for Israel)
Deut 4^{37} 7^8 ^{13} 10^{15} ^{18} 23^{5*}.

(b) *of Israel for Yahweh*
Deut 5^{10} (∥ Ex 20^6) 6^5 7^9 10^{12} 11^1 ^{13} ^{22} 13^3 19^9 30^6 ^{16} ^{20} Josh 22^5 23^{11*}. Note the infin לאהבה followed by יי׳ Deut 10^{12} $^{(15)}$ 11^{13} ^{22} 19^9 30^6 ^{16} ^{20} Josh 22^5 23^{11}†.

75 *Manservant and maidservant* (עבד, bondman, with אמה, cp ^{JE}99)
Deut 5^{14ab} (∥ Ex 20^{10}) 21 (∥ Ex 20^{17}) 12^{12} ^{18} (15^{17}) 16^{11} ^{14}. Ct Lev 25^6 44*.

76 *Thou mayest not* (lit 'canst not,' or *he may not*)
Deut 7^{22} 12^{17} 16^5 17^{15} 21^{16} 22^3 ^{19} ^{29} 24^4. 'A very uncommon use, cp Gen 43^{32},' Driver, *Deut* p lxxxii*.

77 *Men of war*
Deut 2^{14} ^{16} Josh 5^4 ^{6} 6^3.
Cp E Josh 10^{24} (𝔊 omits *men*), P^s Num 31^{28} ^{49}*.

78 (a) *Midst, in the midst of thee* (בקרבך) of Yahweh's presence in Israel cp ^{JE}58 130 ct ^{P}22)
Deut 1^{42} 6^{15} 7^{21} 23^{14} (31^{17}) : otherwise 13^1 ^{11} ^{14} 16^{11} 17^2 19^{20} 23^{16} 26^{11} 28^{43}.

(b) generally
Deut 4^5 11^6 17^{20} 18^2 19^{10} 21^8 29^{11} ^{16}. The general phrase בקרב occurs in all documents, JEDP, though most frequently in D.
Ct ^{P}22.

(c) *From the midst of thee* (or *the camp, people,* &c)
Deut 2$^{14-16}$ 4^3 ^{34} 13^5 ^{13} 15^{11} 17^7 ^{15} 18^{15} ^{18} 19^{19} 21^9 ^{21} 22^{21} ^{24} 24^7 Josh 7^{12}.
Cp Ex 23^{25} Num 14^{13} ^{44} Josh 7^{13}. Cp ^{P}50.

79 (a) *Midst of the fire, out of the* (מתוך)
Deut 4^{12} ^{15} ^{33} ^{36} 5^4 ^{22} $^{(23)}$ ^{24} ^{26} 9^{10} 10^4.
Cp Ezek 14†.

(b) *in the midst*, generally (תוך, sometimes with ב)
Deut 3^{16} 11^3 13^{16} 19^2 21^{12} 22^2 23^{10} Josh 4^9. 13^9.

80 (a) *Mighty (strong) hand and stretched out arm* (of Yahweh) cp 106
Deut 4^{34} 5^{15} 7^{19} 11^2 26^8*.

(b) *Mighty (strong) hand*
Deut 3^{24} 6^{21} 7^8 9^{26} 34^{12} cp Josh 4^{24}.
Cp JE Ex 3^{19} 6^1 (Pharaoh) 13^9 32^{11} Num 20^{20} (Edom)*.

(c) *Strength (𝔊 might) of hand*
Ex 13^3 ^{14} ^{16}†. חזק Am 6^{13} Hagg 2^{22}†.

(d) *Stretched out arm*
Deut 9^{29}. Cp P Ex 6^6*.

Minister, to, see 90^c.

81 *Multiply, to* (of Yahweh's action on Israel)
Deut 1^{10} 7^{13} 13^{17} 28^{63} 30^5. Cp J^r Gen 16^{10}, R^{je} Gen 22^{17}, E Josh 24^3, ^{JE}204 ct ^{P}73*.

82 (a) *Observe, to* (or *keep*) *to do* (שמר לעשות)
Deut 5^1 ^{32} 6^3 ^{25} 7^{11} 8^1 11^{22} ^{32} 12^1 ^{32} 15^5 17^{10} ^{19} 19^9 24^8 28^1 ^{15} ^{58} 31^{12} 32^{46} Josh 1^7. 22^5.
Cp 2 Kings 17^{37} 21^8 (∥ 2 Chron 33^8) 1 Chron 22^{13}†.

(b) *Observe (or keep) and do* (שמר ועשה) cp ^{P}199
Deut 4^6 7^{12} 16^{12} 23^{23} 24^8 26^{16} 28^{13} 29^9 Josh 23^6, cp 'observe and hear' Deut 12^{28}.

(c) *Keep my (his) commandments (statutes, &c)*
Deut 4^2 ^{40} 5^{10} (∥ Ex 20^6) 29 6^2 ^{17} 7^9 ^{11} 8^1. ^{6} ^{11} 10^{13} 11^1 ^{8} ^{22} 12^{28} 13^4 ^{18} 17^{19} 19^9 26^{17}. 27^1 28^9 ^{45} 29^9 30^{10} ^{16} Josh 22^2 ^{5}.
Cp Gen 26^5 Ex 16^{28} Lev 22^{31} 26^3 Num 15^{22}*.
Cp 'keep' occasionally with 'covenant' 'mercy' 'oath' &c.

(d) *Take heed* &c (השמר) cp 108.

83 *Officers* (שטרים)
Deut 1^{15} 16^{18} 20^5 ^{8}. 29^{10} 31^{28} Josh 8^{33} 23^2 24^1.
Cp J Ex 5^6 ^{10} ^{14}. ^{19} E Num 11^{16} Josh 1^{10} 3^2*.

84 *Only* (or *but, notwithstanding, surely,* רק)
Deut 2^{28} ^{35} ^{37} 3^{11} ^{19} 4^6 ^{9} 10^{15} 12^{15} ^{16} ^{23} ^{26} 15^5 ^{23} 17^{16} 20^{14} ^{16} ^{20} always at the beginning of a clause (cp 28^{13} ^{33}). So Josh 1^7 ^{17}. 6^{15} ^{18} 8^2 ^{27} 11^{13} ^{14} ^{22} 13^6 ^{14} 22^5.
Cp ^{JE}189. Not in P^g; but cp Josh 6^{24b} R^p.

85 *Other gods* (with *serve* cp 23^b) often with *go after (follow)*
Deut (4^3) 5^7 6^{14} 8^{19} 11^{28} 13^2 (after Yahweh ^{4}) 18^{20} 28^{14} cp 31^{16} ^{18} ^{20}. Cp Ex 20^3 23^{13}*.

86 (a) *Perish* (*to make* or *cause to, destroy* האביד)
Deut 7^{10} ^{24} 8^{20} 9^3 28^{51} ^{63} Josh 7^7.
Cp Num 24^{19} J, Lev 23^{30} P*.

(b) *Ye shall utterly (surely) perish*
Deut 4^{26} (cp 11^{17}) 8^{19} cp 20 30^{18}*.

(c) *until (they, ye) perish*
Deut 7^{20} 28^{20} ^{22} Josh 23^{13}*.

(d) *destroy* (אבד Piel)
Deut 11^4 12^2. cp Num 33^{52}*.

Pity, see 43^b.

87 *The place which Yahweh shall choose* (sometimes *to put* or *cause his name to dwell* [לשכן] *there,* 40 ct ^{P}54)
Deut 12^5 ^{11} ^{14} ^{18} ^{21} ^{26} 14$^{23-25}$ 15^{20} 16^2 ^{6}. ^{11} ^{15}. 17^8 ^{10} 18^6 26^2 31^{11} Josh 9^{27} cp Deut 23^{16} (of an escaped slave)*.

88 (a) *Possess it, to* (לרשתה usually with *give, go in, go over*)
Deut 3^{18} 4^5 ^{14} ^{26} 5^{31} 6^1 7^1 9^6 11^8 ^{10}. ^{29} 12^1 15^4 19^2 ^{14} 21^1 23^{20} 25^{19} 28^{21} ^{63} 30^{16} ^{18} 31^{13} 32^{47} Josh 1^{11}. Cp Gen 15^7 Josh 13^1 Ezr 9^{11}†. The inf לרשת otherwise D Deut 2^{31} 9^1 ^{4}. 11^{31} 12^{29} Josh 1^{11} 18^3 24^4; P Gen 28^4 Lev 20^{24} 25^{46} Num 33^{53}.
The verb in different forms sixty-two times in Deut alone (Qal). Once in P^g Gen 28^4 (*inherit*) five times in P^{hs} Lev 20^{24} 25^{46} Num 27^{11} 33^{53} 36^8. Ct ^{P}127.

(b) *to possess* peoples (i e succeed or dispossess them)
Deut 2^{12} ^{21}. 9^1 11^{23} 12^2 29^{ab} 18^{14} 19^1 31^3*. Cp 39.

(c) *Possess and dwell*
Deut 11^{31} 17^{14} Josh 21^{43}*.

(d) *Possession* (ירשה, with *give*)
Deut 2^5 ^{9} ^{12} ^{19} 3^{20} Josh 1^{15} 12^6.*

D 89 *Prey, to take for a prey* (בזז)
Deut 2^{35} 3^7 20^{14} Josh 8^2 ^{27} 11^{14}.
Ct 'spoiled' Gen 34^{27} ^{29} Num 31^9 ^{32} ^{53} **P**^{s*}.

90 (a) *The Priests, the Levites*
Deut 17^9 ^{18} 18^1 24^8 27^9 Josh 3^{3r} 8^{33}, 'the sons of Levi' Deut 21^5 31^{9*}. 'The priest(s)' 17^{12} 18^8 19^{17} 20^2 26^3. Josh 4^{3r} ^{9}. 'The tribe of Levi' 10^8 18^1 Josh $13^{14\ (33)}$.

(b) *to stand before Yahweh*, Deut $10^{(8)}$ 17^{12} $18^{(5)}$ ^{7}; of Israel generally, 4^{10}. 19^{17} $29^{(10)}$ ^{15}.
Cp **P** Lev 9^5 (Num 16^9 35^{12} Josh $20^{6\ 9}$), and $^P141$.

(c) *to minister* (*unto* or *before Yahweh*, שרת) Deut 10^8 17^{12} $18^{5\ 7}$ 21^5. Ct $^{JE}109$, $^P129^c$.

(d) *the Levite that is within your gates*, Deut $12^{12\ 18}$ 14^{27} $16^{11\ 14}$ cp $26^{11.*}$. 'The Levite(s)' 12^{19} 14^{29} 18^6. 26^{13} 27^{14} 31^{25}.

91 *Promised, as Yahweh hath promised* (or *spoken, to Israel, Levi, &c*, כאשר דבר 'ד 'א) or
Deut 1^{11} ^{21} 2^1 6^3 ^{19} 9^3 ^{28} 10^9 11^{25} 12^{20} 15^6 18^2 19^8 26^{18}. 27^3 29^{13} 31^3 Josh 11^{23} $13^{14\ (33)r}$ 14^{12} 22^4 $23^{5\ 10}$. Otherwise 13^2 Josh 4^{12}. Occasionally elsewhere, e g Gen 24^{51} Ex 7^{13} &c. **P** frequently adds 'by the hand of Moses' 180^c.

Prophet, see $^{JE}113$.

Prove (assay, tempt), see $^{JE}192$.

92 (a) *Put away the evil from the midst of thee*
Deut 13^5 17^7 ^{12} 19^{19} 21^{21} 22^{21}. ^{24} 24^{7}†.

(b) *Put away* (innocent blood, hallowed things)
Deut 19^{13} 21^9 26^{13}..
Ct ⑤ **JE** Ex 22^5 Num 24^{22}, **P** Ex 35^3 Lev 6^{12*}.

(c) *Innocent blood*
Deut $19^{10\ 13}$ 21^8. 27^{25} ⑤*.

93 *Quickly* (*soon*, מהר) cp **JE 43**
Deut 4^{26} 7^4 ^{22} $9^{3\ 12\ 16}$ 28^{20} cp **E** Ex 32^8 Josh 2^{5*}. מהרה Deut 11^{17} Josh 23^{16}.
Cp Josh 8^{19} 10^6, **P** Num 16^{46}.

94 *Rebel, to* (המרה)
Deut $1^{26\ 43}$ 9^7 ^{23}. 31^{27} Josh 1^{18*}. Qal, Deut $21^{18\ 20}$ Num $20^{10\ 24}$ 27^{14*}.

95 *Redeem, to* (of the deliverance from Egypt, פדה)
Deut 7^8 9^{26} 13^5 15^{15} 21^8 24^{18*} ct Ex 15^{13} 6^6.

96 *Rejoice, to* (שמח)
Deut 12^7 $^{12\ 18}$ 14^{26} $16^{11\ 14\ (15)}$ 26^{11} 27^{7b}.
Cp 33^{18} (Blessing of Moses) **R**^{je} Ex 4^{14}, **P** Lev 23^{40*}.

97 (a) *Remember that thou wast a bondman*
Deut 5^{15} 15^{15} 16^{12} $24^{18\ 22*}$.

(b) *Remember*, in other forms of appeal
Deut 7^{18} 8^2 ^{18} 9^7 16^3 24^9 25^{17} Josh 1^{13} cp 32^{7*}.

98 *Rest, to give* (Yahweh to Israel)
Deut 3^{20} 12^{10} 25^{19} Josh $1^{13\ 15}$ 22^4 23^1.
Cp Ex 33^{14*}.

Reubenites, the, &c, cp $^P11^c$ and Josh $1^{12א}$.

99 *See* (or *behold*, before a verb in perfect or participle, הנה, ct ראה, $^P94^b$)
Deut 1^8 ^{21} $2^{24\ 31}$ 4^5 11^{26} 30^{15} Josh 6^2 (?) 8^{1b} ^{8b} 23^4. Cp **J** Gen 39^{14} 41^{41}, **R**^{je} Ex 33^{12}, **P** Ex 7^1 31^2 35^{30*}.

Servant of Yahweh, cp $^{JE}207^b$.

Serve, to, see 23^{bc}.

100 (a) *Set before, to* (or *deliver*, נתן לפני, when Yahweh delivers up the enemy or the land, cp **52, 69**)
Deut 1^8 ^{21} $2^{31\ 33\ 36}$ $7^{2\ (16)\ 23}$ 23^{14} 28^7 ^{25} (lit *give up … smitten*) 31^5 Josh 10^{12}, **J** Josh 11^{6*}.
Cp Judg 11^9 1 Kings 8^{46} Is 41^2†.

(b) *Set before* (statutes, &c)
Deut 4^8 $11^{26\ 32}$ $30^{1\ 15}$ 19^*.
Ct ⑤ Deut 4^{44} Ex 19^7 21^1.

101 (a) *Signs and wonders*
Deut 4^{34} 6^{22} 7^{19} 26^8 29^3 34^{11}. Cp Ex 7^{3*}.

(b) *Sign and wonder*
Deut 13^1. 28^{46*}.

(c) *Signs and works*   (d) *Great signs*
Deut 11^{3*}.   Josh 24^{17r}.

102 (a) *Sin in thee, and it be*
Deut 15^9 23^{21} 24^{15}. Cp ⑤ 21^{22} 23^{22}†. **D** uses חטא elsewhere in 19^{15} 22^{26} 24^{16}. Cp **E** Gen 41^9, **P** only in the phrase חטא נשא, $^P28^{b*}$.

(b) *righteousness unto thee, and it shall be*
Deut 6^{25} 24^{13*}.

103 *Spoil* (שלל)
Deut 2^{35} 3^7 13^{16} 20^{14} Josh 8^{2a} ^{27} 11^{14} 22^{8r}.
Cp **J** Gen 49^{27} Josh 7^{21}, Ex 15^9, **P** Num $31^{11.*}$

Stand before Yahweh, cp 90^b.

104 (a) *Statutes* (with *judgements, commandments*, cp $^P213$)
Deut $4^{1\ 5\ 8\ 14\ 40}$ 5^1 ^{31} 6^1. 7^{11} 8^{11} 10^{13} 11^1 ^{32} 12^1 26^{16}. 27^{10} $28^{15\ 45}$ $30^{10\ 16}$.

(b) *Statutes* (alone), cp $^P217$.
Deut 4^6 6^{24} 16^{12}.

(c) *Statutes* with 'this law'
Deut 17^{19}. Cp Ex $18^{16\ 20}$.
(a) (b) (c) always in plural. For sing cp Ex 15^{25} Josh 24^{25}.

(d) *Testimonies and Statutes*
Deut 4^{45} 6^{17} 20^*.

Stone with stones (סקל), see $^{JE}216$.

105 (a) *The stranger, the fatherless, and the widow*
Deut 10^{18} $24^{17\ 19\ 20}$. 27^{19}. Cp Ex 22^{21}..

(b) *The stranger, the fatherless, and the widow* with *the Levite*
Deut 14^{29} $16^{11\ 14}$ $26^{12.*}$.

(c) *Thy stranger who is within thy gates*
Deut 5^{14} 14^{21} 24^{14} 31^{12}. Cp 26^{11} 28^{43} 29^{11*}.

THE DEUTERONOMIC SCHOOL, D

106 (a) *Be strong and of a good courage* (חזק ואמץ)
Deut 31^6. Josh $1^{6.\ 9\ 18}\ 10^{25}$. E Deut 31^{23}*.

(b) *Be strong* (חזק)
Deut 11^8 cp 12^{23} Josh 23^6.   J Josh 17^{13}
Not in this sense elsewhere.

(c) *Strengthen and encourage* (חזק ואמץ)
Deut 3^{28}, 'encourage' alone Deut 1^{38} cp Josh 11^{20}.

107 (a) *Sware, Which Yahweh* (*he* or *I* or *thou*) *sware*, &c cp ^{JE}**217**.
Deut $1^{8\ 34}$. $4^{21\ 31}\ 6^{10\ 18\ 23}\ 7^{8\ 12}$. $8^1\ 18\ 9^5\ 10^{11}$ $11^{9\ 21}\ 26^3\ 28^{11}\ 30^{20}\ 31^{7\ 20.r}$ Josh $1^6\ 5^6\ 21^{43}$..

(b) *As Yahweh sware unto them* (*thy fathers*, &c)
Deut $2^{14}\ 13^{17}\ 19^8\ 26^{15}\ 28^9\ 29^{13}$.
Cp J Ex 13^{11}*.

108 (a) *Take heed to thyself* (or *beware*) *lest* (השמר לך)
Deut $4^{9\ 23}\ 6^{12}\ 8^{11}\ 11^{16}\ 12^{13\ 19\ 30}\ 15^9$.
Cp JE Gen $24^6\ 31^{24\ 29}$ Ex $10^{28}\ 19^{12}\ 34^{12}$*.

(b) In another form more generally
Deut $2^4\ 4^{15}\ 23^9\ 24^8$ Josh 23^{11}.   Cp Ex $23^{13}\ 21$*.

Teach, see **71**.

Testimonies (עדת) Deut $4^{45}\ 6^{17\ 20}$, only with *Statutes*, see **104**^{d}.

109 (a) *Thou and thy son* (followed by other members of the household, daughter, bondservant, &c)
Deut 5^{14} (|| Ex 20^{10}) $6^2\ 12^{12\ 18}\ 16^{11\ 14}$*. Ct ^{P}**176**.

(b) *Thou and thy household*
Deut $12^7\ 14^{26}\ 15^{16\ 20}\ 26^{11}$ cp J Gen 45^{11}*.

110 *Time, at that*, or *the same time* (בעת ההוא)
Deut $1^{9\ 16\ 18}\ 2^{34}\ 3^{4\ 8\ 12\ 18\ 21\ 23}\ 4^{14}\ 5^5\ 9^{20}\ 10^{1\ 8}$
Josh $11^{10\ 21}$.   Cp E Gen 21^{22}, J Gen 38^1 Num 22^4 Josh $5^{2r}\ 6^{26}$*.

111 *Tread, to* (דרך)
Deut $1^{36}\ 11^{24}$. Josh $1^3\ 14^9$.
Cp J Num 24^{17}, Deut 33^{29r} (Blessing of Moses)*.

112 (a) *Tribe* (שבט).   Ct ^{P}**165**
Deut $1^{23}\ 3^{13}\ 5^{23}\ 10^8\ 12^5\ 14\ 18^{1\ 5}\ 29^8\ 18\ 21\ 31^{28}$ Josh $1^{12}\ 4^{12}\ 12^6$. $13^7\ 14\ 18^{7r}\ 22^7\ 23^4$..
Cp JE Gen 49^{16} Ex 24^4 Num 24^2 Josh $3^{12}\ 4^{2\ 4}$. $7^{14\ 16}\ 18^{2\ 4}\ 24^1$.

(b) *According to* (or *by*) *your tribes* (לשבטיכם).
Cp ^{P}**18**
Deut $1^{13\ 15}\ 16^{18}$ Josh 11^{23}.
Cp J Num 24^2 Josh $7^{14\ 16}$*.

113 *Turn, to* (of personal movement, פנה)
Deut $1^{7\ 24\ 40}\ 2^{1\ 3\ 8}\ 3^1\ 9^{15}\ 10^5\ 16^7$ (ct 29^{18} 30^{17}) Num 21^{33} Josh 22^4.
JE Gen $18^{22}\ 24^{49}$ Ex $2^{12}\ 7^{23}\ 10^6\ 32^{15}$ Num 12^{10} 14^{25b} (16^{15}) Josh 7^{12}.
Ct P, towards Yahweh's glory Ex 16^{10} Num 16^{42}, towards idols ^{P}**214** (cp Deut $31^{18\ 20}$), of the situation of land Josh $15^{2\ 7}$.

114 (a) *Turn aside out of the way, to* (סור)
Deut $9^{12\ 16}\ 11^{28}\ 31^{29}$ cp Ex 32^8*.   For 'way' cp also **115**.

(b) *Turn neither to the right hand nor to the left*
Deut 2^{27} (ct Num 20^{17} ⓖ) $5^{32}\ 17^{11\ 20}\ 28^{14}$ Josh $1^7\ 23^6$.   Cp *turn, depart* Deut $4^9\ 11^{16}\ 17^{17}$, Hiph 7^4 (otherwise $7^{15}\ 21^{13}$ Josh 11^{15}): *rebellion* (= 'turning aside' סרה) $13^5\ 19^{16}$.

115 (a) *Walk in his ways, to* (or *the way*, religiously)
Deut $5^{33}\ 8^6\ 10^{12}\ 11^{22}\ 13^5\ 19^9\ 26^{17}\ 28^9\ 30^{16}$ Josh 22^{5}*.   Cp Ex 18^{20}*.

(b) *Way, the* (of the journey of the Israelites)
Deut $1^{22\ 31\ 33}$ (2^{27}) $8^2\ 17^{16}\ 23^4\ 24^9\ 25^{17}\ 28^{68}$ Josh $3^{4b}\ 5^{4.\ 7}$.   Cp E Josh 24^{17}.

116 (a) *Well* (*That it may be well with thee*, יטב)
Deut $4^{40}\ 5^{16\ 29}\ 6^3\ 8^{18}\ 12^{25\ 28}\ 22^7$.
Cp J Gen 12^{13}, E 40^{14}*.

(b) *for good to thee* (with slight variation, טוב לך)
Deut $5^{33}\ 6^{24}\ 10^{13}\ 19^{13}$*.

(c) Adverbial infinitive (היטב) 9^{21} ('very small') $13^{14}\ 17^4\ 19^{18}\ 27^8$ ⓖ: elsewhere in this application only 2 Kings 11^{18}.

117 *Willing, to be* (consent, אבה)
Deut $1^{26}\ 2^{30}\ 10^{10}\ 13^8\ 23^5\ 25^7\ 29^{20}$.
Cp J Gen $24^{5\ 8}$, E Ex 10^{27} Josh 24^{10}, P Lev 26^{21}*.

118 *Women* (*wives*) *and little ones* (טף) cp ^{JE}**52**
Deut $2^{34}\ 3^6\ 19\ 20^{14}\ 29^{11}\ 31^{12}$ Josh $1^{14}\ 8^{35}$ (Deut 1^{39} || Num 14^{31}).

119 *Work of thy hands* (מעשה ידך)
(a) with the verb 'to bless' or 'make plenteous'
Deut $2^7\ 14^{29}\ 16^{15}\ 24^{19}\ 28^{12}\ 30^9$.   Cp 15^{10}*.

(b) of idols (*work of men's hands*)
Deut $4^{28}\ 27^{15}\ 31^{29}$*.

120 *Written in this book*
Deut 28^{58} cp $^{61}\ 29^{20.\ 27}\ 30^{10}$ Josh 1^8.
Cp 'written in the book of the law' Josh $8^{31\ 34}$ 23^6 2 Kings 14^6 (|| 2 Chron 25^4) cp 2 Chron 35^{12}†.

III. The Priestly Law and History Book, P

P 1 *El Shaddai* or *God Almighty*
Gen 17^1 28^3 35^{11} 48^3 Ex 6^3. Ct *Shaddai* alone J Gen 49^{25} Num 24$^{4\ 16}$, R *El Shaddai* 43^{14}*.

2 (a) *Arboth*^{a} (*Plains of*) *Moab*, sometimes with *beyond Jordan*, or *by the Jordan at Jericho*
Num 22^1 26^3 ^{63} 31^{12} 33 $^{48-50}$ 35^1 36^{13} Deut 34$^{1\ 8}$ Josh 13^{32}†.
Plains of Jericho, Josh 4^{13} 5^{10} 2 Kings 25^5 Jer 39^5 52^8†.

(b) *beyond Jordan* (מעבר לירדן) ct ^{P}21
Num 22^1 32^{19} (once with and once without ל) ^{32} 34^{15} 35^{14} Josh 13^{32} 14^3 17^5 18^7 20^8*.
Cp Josh 13^{27} 22^7 (K^{e}thîbh).

3 *Kiriath Arba*
Gen 23^2 35^{27} Josh 15$^{13\ 54}$ 20^7 21^{11} cp Josh 14^{15} Jud 1^{10} Neh 11^{25}†.

4 (a) *Land of Canaan*
Gen 11^{31} 12^{5ab} 13^{12} 16^3 17^8 23^2 ^{19} 31^{18} 33^{18} 35^{6a} 36^5. 37^1 46^6 ^{12} 48$^{3\ 7}$ 49^{30} 50^{13} Ex 6^4 16^{35} Lev 14^{34} 18^3 25^{38} Num 13^2 ^{17} 26^{19} 32^{30} ^{32} 33$^{40\ 51}$ 34^2 ^{29} 35$^{10\ 14}$ Deut 32^{49} Josh 5^{12} 14^1 21^2 22$^{9-11\ 32}$.
JE Gen 42^5 (cp 40$^{2\aleph}$) ^{7} $^{13\ 29\ 32}$ 44^8 45$^{17\ 25}$ 47$^{1\ 4}$ $^{(13-15\ r)}$ 50^5 Josh 24^3*.

(b) *Land of Edom*
Gen 36$^{16.\ 21\ 31}$ Num 20^{23} 33^{37} cp E Num 21^{4b} (Judg 11^{18})*.

5 *Machpelah*
Gen 23$^{9\ 17\ 19}$ 25^9 49^{30} 50^{13}†.

6 *Paddan-aram*
Gen 25^{20} 28$^{2\ 5-7}$ 31^{18} 33^{18b} 35^9 ^{26} 46^{15} (48^7)†.

7 *Wilderness of Sinai* (or *Mount*)
Ex 16^1 19$^{1.}$ 24^{16} 31^{18} 34$^{29\ 32}$ Lev 7^{38ab} 25^1 26^{46} 27^{34} Num 1^1 ^{19} 3$^{1\ 4\ 14}$ 9$^{1\ 5}$ 10^{12} 26^{64} 28^6 33^{15}. Cp ^{JE}76, and R^{ed} Deut 33^2*.

8 *Wilderness of Sin*
Ex 16^1 17^1 Num 33^{11}.*

9 *Wilderness of Zin*
Num 13^{21} 20^1 27^{14} 33^{36} 34^3. Deut 32^{51} Josh 15^1 3*.

10 (a) *Children of Heth* (בני חת)
Gen 23$^{3\ 5\ 7\ 10\ 16\ 18\ 20}$ 25^{10} 49^{32}†.

(b) *Daughters of Heth* (בנות חת)
Gen 27^{46} cp 26^{34} 36^2* cp Daughters of Canaan Gen 28^1 36^2*.

(c) *Ephron the Hittite*
Gen 23$^{8-16}$ 25^9 49^{29}. 50^{13}†.

11 (a) *Children of Israel*
Gen 46^8 Ex 1^{17} and onwards: never *Israel* alone as in JE Ex 4^{22} 5^2 &c.

Congregation of Israel, see **45**.

(b) *House of Israel*
Ex 16^{31} 40^{38} Lev 10^6 17$^{3\ 8\ 10}$ 22^{18} Num 20^{29} Josh 21^{45}*.

(c) *Children of Reuben* (and *Gad*)
Num 32$^{1.\ 6..}$ Josh 13$^{15\ 24}$ 22$^{9-11}$.. cp 4^{12r}.
Ct **D** *Reubenites* &c, Deut 3$^{12\ 16}$ 29^8 Josh 1^{12} 12^6 13^8 22^1.

12 (a) *Aaron the Priest*
Ex 31^{10} 35^{19} 38^{21} 39^{41} Lev 7^{34} 13^2 21^{21} Num 3$^{6\ 32}$ 4^{16} 16^{37} 18^{28} 25$^{7\ 11}$ 26$^{1\ 64}$ 33^{38} Josh 21^4 ^{13}*.

(b) *Eleazar* (*son of Aaron*) *the Priest*
Ex 6$^{23\ 25}$ 28^1 Lev 10$^{6\ 12\ 16}$ Num 3$^{2\ 4\ 32}$ 4^{16} 16^{37} ^{39} 19^3. 20$^{25.\ 28}$ 25^7 26$^{1\ 3\ 63}$ 27^2 $^{19\ 21}$. 31$^{6\ 12.\ 21}$ 26 29 31 41 51 54 32^2.

(c) *Eleazar the priest and Joshua the son of Nun*
Num 32^{28} 34^{17} Josh 14^1 17^4 19^{51} 21^1*.
Ct Josh 24^{33}.

(d) *Ithamar* (*the son of Aaron the priest*)
Ex 6^{23} 28^1 38^{21} Lev 10$^{6\ 12\ 16}$ Num 3$^{2\ 4}$ 4$^{28\ 33}$ 7^8 26^{60}*.

(e) *Nadab and Abihu* (*the sons of Aaron*)
Ex 6^{23} 28^1 Lev 10^1 Num 3$^{2\ 4}$ 26^{60}.. Ct Ex 24$^{1\ 9}$*.

(f) *Phinehas, son of Eleazar*, &c
Ex 6^{25} Num 25$^{7\ 11}$ 31^6 Josh 22$^{13\ 30-32}$.
Ct Josh 24^{33}*.

(g) *Aaron and his sons*, cp **130**
Ex 27^{21} 28$^{1\ 4\ 43}$ 29$^{4\ 9.\ 15\ 19\ (21)\ 24\ 27\ 28\ 32\ 35\ 44}$ 30^{19} ^{30} 39^{27} 40$^{12\ 31}$ Lev 2^3 ^{10} 6^9 $^{16\ 20\ 25}$ 7$^{31\ 34}$. 8$^{2\ 6}$ 14 18 22 27 30. 36 9^1 17^2 21^{24} 22^{18} 24^9 Num 3^9. 38 48 51 4^5 15 19 27 6^{23} 8^{19} 22*.

13 *Bezaleel*
Ex 31^2 35^{30} 36^1. 37^1 38^{22}*.

14 *Korah* (son of *Izhar*)
Ex 6$^{21\ 24}$ Num 16$^{1\ 5.\ 8\ 16\ 19\ 24\ 27a\ 32b\ 40\ 49}$ 26$^{9-11}$ 27^3*.

15 *Oholiab*
Ex 31^6 35^{34} 36^1. 38^{23}*.

16 *Able to go forth to war* (*host* צבא) cp **92**
Num 1$^{3-45}$ (fourteen times) 26^2.
Cp 1 Chron 7^{11} 12$^{33\ 36}$ 2 Chron 25^5 26^{11}†.

17 (a) *Accept, to* (or *enjoy*, רצה)
Lev 1^4 7^{18} 19^7 22$^{23\ 25\ 27}$ 26$^{34\ 41\ 43}$.
Cp J Gen 33^{10}, Deut 33$^{11\ 24}$*.

(b) *accepted* (*acceptable*, לרצן)
Ex 28^{38} Lev 1^3 19^5 22$^{19-21\ 29}$ 23^{11}.
Ct רצן otherwise Gen 49^6 (*self-will*) Deut 33$^{16\ 23}$ (*goodwill, favour*)*.

---

^{a} Plural of *Arabah*, cp ^{D}6.

18 *According to* (or *after, by, of, throughout,* &c ל) in numerous phrases, such as the following:
(a) *its borders* Num 34^2 ^{12} Josh 18^{20} 19^{49}: (b) *its cities* Num 32^{33}: (c) *their dukes* Gen 36^{30}: *their families* see **65**: (d) *their fathers' houses* Ex 12^3 Num $1-4$ $17^{2\ 6}$ 26^2 34^{14} Josh 22^{14} cp **66**: (e) *their generations* cp **76, 77**: (f) *their goings out* Num 33^2: (g) *their habitations* Gen 36^{43} cp **55**: (h) *the head* Ex 16^{16} 38^{26} Num 1^2 $^{13\ 20\ 22}$ 3^{47} cp **83**: (i) *their hosts* Num 1^3 ^{52} 2^3 $^{9,\ 16\ 18\ 24.}$ ^{32} $10^{14\ 18\ 22\ 25\ 28}$ 33^1 cp Ex 6^{26} **92**: (j) *their journeys* Ex 17^1 Num $10^{6\ 12}$ 33^2 cp Gen 13^3†: (k) *its kind* Gen $1^{11\ 12\ 21\ 24.}$ 6^{20} 7^{14} Lev $11^{14-16\ 19\ 22\ 29}$‖Deut $14^{13-15\ 18}$ cp Ezek 47^{10}†: (l) *the months* Num 28^{14}: (m) *the names* Num 26^{53}: (n) *their nations* (לגויהם) Gen 10^{31}: (o) *their nations* (לאמתם) Gen 25^{16}: (p) *their places* Gen 36^{40}: (q) *their standards* Num 2^{17} 31^{34}: (r) *the tribe* Num 1^4 31^{4-6}, '*the tribes of their fathers*' Num 33^{54} cp **165**: (s) *those that were numbered* Ex 30^{12} Num 3^{43} $26^{18\ 22\ 25\ 27}$ $37^{43\ 47}$ cp **115**^{b}: (t) *their tongues* Gen $10^{5\ 20\ 31}$. Rare in JED, e g *according to thy (your, his) tribes* שבט Num 24^2 Deut $1^{13\ 15}$ 16^{18} Josh $7^{14\ 16}$ 11^{23} (23^4) ^{D}**112**

19 (a) *According to* (כפי) Ex 16^{21} Lev 25^{52} Num 6^{21} $7^{5\ 7.}$ 35^8*.
(b) *according to* (לפי) Ex 12^4 $16^{16\ 18}$ Lev $25^{16\ 51}$ 27^{16} Num 9^{17} 26^{54} 35^{30} cp Gen 47^{12} Josh $18^{4\ \text{c}}$.
(c) *according to the word (at the mouth) of Yahweh, Moses, Aaron, Joshua* (על פי) Ex 17^1 38^{21} (Moses) Lev 24^{12} Num $3^{16\ 39\ 51}$ 4^{27} (Aaron) $^{37\ 41\ 45\ 49}$ $9^{18\ 20\ 23}$ 10^{13} 13^3 27^{21} (Joshua) 33^2 ^{38} 36^5 Deut 34^5 Josh 19^{50} 22^9. Cp Gen 45^{21} Ex 23^{13} Deut 17^6 19^{15} 21^5*.
(d) *according to the word of Yahweh* (אל פי) Josh 15^{13} 17^4 $21^{3\ \text{c}}$.

20 *Afflict your souls* (ענה את נפשכם) Lev $16^{29\ 31}$ $23^{27\ 29\ 32}$ Num 29^7 30^{13} cp Isa 58^3 ^{5}†.

21 (a) *All (of, as regards)* לכל Gen $9^{10\text{b}}$ $23^{10\text{b}}$ Ex 14^{28} 27^3 ^{19} 28^{38} $36^{1\text{b}}$ Lev 5^3 11^{26} ^{42} $16^{16\ 21}$ 22^{18} Num $4^{27\ 31\ 32}$ 5^9 $18^{4\ 8}$. (probably a juristic use, Driver *LOT*^{6} 132) cp ל Lev 7^{26}.
(b) *All flesh* (כל־בשר) Gen $6^{12.\ 17\ 19}$ $7^{15.\ 21}$ 8^{17} $9^{11\ 15-17}$ Lev 17^{14} Num 16^{22} 18^{15} 27^{16} cp Deut 5^{26}*.

22 *Among* (or *in the midst*, בתוך) ct ^{JE}**58** ^{D}**78**
(a) Of the Divine Presence in Israel Ex 25^8 29^{45}. Lev 15^{31} 16^{16} 22^{32} 26^{11}. Num 5^3 16^3 18^{20} 35^{34} Josh 22^{31}.
(b) With pron suffix, cp (a), Gen $23^{6\ 9}$ Ex 7^5 12^{49} 28^{32}. 39^{23} Lev 11^{33} 16^{29} 17^8 $^{10\ 12}$. 18^{26} 20^{14} 26^{25} Num 1^{47} 13^{32} $15^{14\ 26\ 29}$ 19^{10} 25^{11} 32^{30} 35^{15} Josh 14^3 19^{49} 20^9 22^{19}. Cp **E** Gen 35^2 41^{48}*. (בתוך) is used freely by all writers before nouns such as 'garden' 'city' 'sea' 'fire' 'children of Israel' &c.)

23 (a) *Anoint* (משח)
Ex 28^{41} $29^{2\ 7\ 36}$ $30^{26\ 30}$ $40^{9.\ 11\ 13\ 15}$ Lev 2^4 6^{20} $7^{12\ 36}$ 8^{10-12} 16^{32} Num 3^3 6^{15} $7^{1\ 10\ 84\ 88}$ 35^{25}. Cp Gen 31^{13}*.
(b) *Anointed* (1 e 'the anointed priest' משיח) Lev $4^{3\ 5\ 16}$ 6^{22}*.
(c) *Anointing* (משחה) Ex 29^{29} 40^{15} Num 18^8†.

24 (a) *Assemble, to* (or *be assembled*, Hiph Niph קהל) Hiph Lev 8^3 Num 1^{18} 8^9 10^7 16^{19} $20^{8\text{a}\ 10}$. Niph Lev 8^4 Num 16^3 ^{42} 20^2 Josh 18^1 22^{12}. Cp Ex 32^1 (Niph*) Deut 4^{10} $31^{12\ 28}$ (Hiph*).
(b) *Assembly* (of Israel, קהל) Ex 16^3 Lev $4^{13.\ 21}$ $16^{17\ 33}$ Num 10^7 15^{15} $16^{33\text{c}}$ ^{47} 19^{20} $20^{6\ 10\ 12}$. Cp Gen 49^6 Num 22^4 ^{D}**20**.
(c) *Assembly of peoples* (or *nations*) Gen 28^3 35^{11} 48^4†.
(d) *Assembly of the congregation* (**45**) Ex 12^6 Num 14^5†.
(e) *Assembly of Yahweh* Num 16^3 20^4 cp Deut $23^{1-3\ 8}$*.

25 (a) *Atonement, to make* (כפר) Ex 29^{33}—Num 35^{33}, seventy times. Cp **J** Gen 32^{20} (*appease*) Ex 32^{30}, **D** Deut 21^8 (*forgive*): Song of Moses Deut 32^{43}†.
(b) *Atonement* (כפרים) Ex 29^{36} $30^{10\ 16}$ Lev $23^{27.\ 25^9}$ Num 5^8 29^{11}†.

26 *Be for a God* (*be their God*, היה לאלהים) Gen 17^7. Ex 6^7 29^{45} Lev 11^{45} 22^{33} 25^{38} $26^{12\ 45}$ Num 15^{41} cp Gen $28^{21\text{b}}$ Ex 4^{16} Deut 26^{17} 29^{13}* cp Jer 7^{23} 11^4 24^7 30^{22} $31^{1\ 33}$ 32^{38} Ezek 11^{20} 14^{11} 34^{24} 36^{28} $37^{23\ 27}$ Zech 8^8†.

27 *Be for . . . shall* (or *become in numerous other formulae,* היה ל in the future)
Be for a charge (*keep it up*) Ex 12^6 Num 19^9; *be for an everlasting covenant* Gen 17^{13}; *be for dust* Ex 9^9; *be for a fringe* Num 15^{39}; *be for lights* Gen 1^{15}; *be for meat* cp **110**; *be for a memorial* (**112**) Lev 24^7; *be for a memorial* (**113**) Ex 12^{14} 13^9 30^{16} Num 10^{10} Josh 4^7; *be for nations* Gen 17^{16}; *be for one people* Gen $34^{16\ 22}$; *be for a portion* Ex 29^{26} Lev 7^{33} [8^{29}]; *be for a possession* Lev 25^{45} Num 32^{22}; *be for a priesthood* Ex 40^{15}; *be for a refuge* Num $35^{12\ 15}$; [*be for a sign* (נס) Num 26^{10}]; *be for signs* (cp **142**) *and for seasons and for days and years* Gen 1^{14}; *be for a statute* (*due,* לחק לחקה) Ex $29^{9\ 28}$ Lev 16^{29} ^{34} Num 10^8 $19^{10\ 21}$ 27^{11} 35^{29}; *be for a token* cp **142**; *be for wives* (*marry*) Num $36^{3\ 6}$. Occasionally elsewhere, cp **J** Gen 2^{24} 'be for one flesh,' 21^{30} 31^{44}, **E** 41^{36} &c. Also in past narrative Gen 2^7 20^{12} 24^{67} &c.

28 (a) *Bear his* (*their*) *iniquity* (נשא עןֺ) Ex $28^{38\ 43}$ Lev $5^{1\ 17}$ 7^{18} 10^{17} 17^{16} 19^8 $20^{17\ 19}$ 22^{16} Num 5^{31} 14^{34} $18^{1\ 23}$ 30^{15}, somewhat differently Lev 16^{22}. Ct same ה in sense of 'forgiving iniquity' Ex 34^7 Num 14^{18}*. Cp Ezek 14^{10} $44^{10\ 12}$ (with note by Wellh, *Comp*^{2} 341).

P

28 (b) *Bear (his) sin* (נשא חטא)
    Lev 19^{17} 20^{20} 22^9 24^{15} Num 9^{13} 18^{22} 32*.

29 *Beast of the earth* (חית הארץ, חיתו ארץ)
    Gen 1^{24}. 30 9^2 10*.
    Ct J Gen 2^{19a} 'beast of the field.'

30 *Beget, to* (הוליד) ct ^{JE}7
    Gen 5$^{3-32}$ 6^{10} 11$^{10-27}$ 17^{20} 25^{19} 48^6 Lev 25^{45}
    Num 26$^{29\ 58}$.   Cp Deut 4^{25} 28^{41*}.

    Beneath (מלמטה), see *Upward* **169**^{c}.

31 *Besides* (מלבד)
    Gen 46^{26} Lev 9^{17} 23^{38abcd} Num 5^8 6^{21} 16^{49}
    28$^{23\ 31}$ 29$^{6\ 11\ 16\ 19\ 22\ 25\ 28\ 31\ 34\ 38}$ Josh 22^{29}.
    Cp J Gen 26^{11}, D Deut 4^{35} 29^{1*}.

32 *Between the two evenings* (בין הערבים)
    Ex 12^6 16^{12} 29$^{39\ 41}$ 30^8 Lev 23^5 Num 9$^{3\ 5\ 11}$
    28$^{4\ 8}$†.

33 *Blessed (them), and Elohim* (as subject, in Gen 1–Ex 6^2)
    Gen 1$^{22\ 28}$ 2^3 5^2 9^1 25^{11} 35^9 48^3 cp 17$^{16\ 20}$.
    Ct ^{JE}10^a.

    Border, see **186**.

34 (a) *Born in the land* (home-born, אזרח הארץ)
    Ex 12$^{13\ 48}$. Lev 16^{29} 17^{15} 18^{26} 19^{34} 23^{42} 24$^{16\ 22}$
    Num 9^{14} 15$^{13\ 29}$. Josh 8^{33*}.

(b) *One law for the home-born* (or *Israelite*) *and the stranger*
    Ex 12^{49} Lev 24^{22} Num 9^{14} 15$^{15.\ 29}$†.

35 *Both* (followed by *and*, ב ... ב, or ב 'including')
    Gen 7^{21} 8^{17} 9$^{2\ 10\ 15}$ cp 10^5 20^{32} 17^{23} 23^{18} Ex 12^{19}
    13^2 Lev 17^{15} 22$^{19\ 21}$ Num 4^{16} 8^{17} 18^{15} 31$^{11\ 26}$.
    Cp **108**^{b} and Holzinger *Einl* 341.

36 *Bought* (*with money*, and so *a possession, price*, מקנה and מקנת כסף) cp **78**
    Gen 17$^{12.\ 23\ 27}$ 23^{18} Ex 12^{44} Lev 25$^{16\ 51}$ 27^{22}.
    Cp Jer 32$^{11.\ 14\ 16}$†.

    Break (*the covenant, commandment, vow, &c*), see **46**^{a}.

    Bring near (*offer, present*, הקריב), see **118**.

37 *Burn, to* (הקטיר)
    Ex 29^{13}—Num 18^{17} (sacrificially) forty-four times*.

38 *Burn with fire, to* (שרף באש, ritually)
    Ex 12^{10} 29$^{14\ 34}$ Lev 4^{12} 6^{30} 7$^{17\ 1)}$ 8$^{17\ 32}$ 9^{11} 13^{52}
    $^{55\ 57}$ 16^{27} 19^6 (penally 20^{14} 21^9 Num 31^{10}).
    Ct Ex 32^{20} Deut 7^5 ^{25} 9^{21} 12^3 ^{31} 13^{16} Josh 6^{24}
    7$^{15\ 25}$ 11$^{6\ 9}$ 11*.

    Burnt offering, see **118**^{c}.

39 (a) *Charge, and to be kept for a* (משמרת and with ל)
    Ex 12^6 16$^{23\ 32-34}$ Num 3$^{25\ 31\ 36}$ 4$^{27.\ 31.}$ 17^{10}
    18^8 19^9.

(b) *Charge, to keep the* (*my, his, &c*)
    Lev 8^{35} 18^{30} 22^9 Num 1^{53} 3$^{7.\ 28\ 32\ 38}$ 8^{26} 9$^{19\ 23}$
    18$^{3-5}$ 31$^{30\ 47}$ Cp Gen 26^5 Deut 11^1 Josh 22^{3*}.

40 *Circumcise, to*
    Gen 17$^{10\ (11)\ 12-14\ 23-27}$ 21^4 34$^{15\ 17\ 22\ 24}$ Ex
    12$^{44\ 48}$ Lev 12^3. Cp J Ex 4^{26}, JR^d Josh 5$^{2-8}$.
    Ct 'circumcise the heart' Deut 10^{16} 30$^{6\ e}$.

41 (a) *Cities with their villages*
    Josh 13$^{23\ 28}$ 15$^{32-62}$ 16^9 18$^{24\ 28}$ 19$^{6.\ (8)\ 15.\ 22\ 30.}$
    $^{38.\ 48*}$.

(b) *Cities with their suburbs*, cp **156**
    Josh 21$^{2.\ 8\ 19\ 26\ 33\ 41*}$.

42 (a) *Clean, to be* (with derivatives, *pronounce clean, cleanse*)
    Lev 11^{32}—Josh 22^{17} fifty-four times. Cp Gen 35^{2*}.

(b) *Clean* (adj)
    (1) Ceremonially, Lev 4^{12}—Num 31^{24} twenty-nine times; (2) *pure* (of the gold for the Dwelling) Ex 25^{11}–30^3 37^2–39^{37}, twenty-eight times.
    Cp Gen 7$^{2\ 8}$ 8^{20} Deut 12$^{15\ 22}$ 14^{11} 15^{22*}.

(c) *Cleansing* or *purifying* (טהרה)
    Lev 12^4. 13^7 ^{35} 14$^{2\ 23\ 32}$ 15^{13} Num 6^9. Cp
    Ezek 44^{26} 1 Chron 23^{28} 2 Chron 30$^{1)}$ Neh 12^{45}†.

43 *Close by* (לעמת)
    Ex 25^{27} 28^{27} 37^{14} 38^{18} 39^{20} Lev 3^{9*}, fifteen times in Ezekiel.

44 *Confess, to* (התודה)
    Lev 5^5 16^{21} 26^{40} Num 5^7.
    Only in Chron–Neh Dan, seven times†.

45 (a) *Congregation, the* (i e *of Israel*, עדה)
    Ex 12^3—Josh 22^{30} 125 times. Cp 'Congregation of Yahweh' Num 27^{17} 31^{16} Josh 22^{16}: 'thy congregation,' 'congregation of Korah' Num 16$^{5.\ 11\ 16\ 40}$ 26^9 27$^{3\ c}$.
    Not in JE or D.

(b) *Assemble the congregation* (הקהיל את העדה) cp **24**
    Ex 35^1 Lev 8^3 Num 1^{18} 8^9 16^{19} 20$^{8a\ *}$.

    Convocation, a holy, see **89**.

46 *Covenant*, in various peculiar phrases
(a) *Break the covenant* (הפר)
    Gen 17^{14} Lev 26$^{15\ 44}$ (cp הפר in Num 15^{31} 30$^{8\ 12.\ 15}$ Deut 31$^{16\ 20\ c}$).
    The phrase is common in later prophetic style, cp Judg 2^1 Is 24^5 33^8 Jer 11^{10} 14^{21} 31^{32} 33^{20} Ezek 16^{59} 17$^{15.\ 18.}$ 44^7.

(b) *Establish a covenant*, see **60**^{a}.

(c) *Everlasting covenant*, see **62**^{a}.

(d) *Covenant of peace* Num 25^{12}: *of priesthood* Num 25^{13}: *of salt* Num 18$^{19\ *}$.

(e) *Remember the covenant* (of Elohim), see **135**^{a}.

47 *Covering* (or *mercy-seat*, כפרת)
    Ex 25$^{17-22}$ 26^{34} 30^6 31^7 35^{12} 37$^{6-9}$ 39^{35} 40^{20}
    Lev 16$^{2\ 13-15}$ Num 7^{89}, cp 1 Chron 28^{11}†.

48 *Create, to* (the heavens and the earth &c, ברא)
    Gen 1$^{1\ 21\ 27}$ 2$^{3\ 4a}$ 5^1. 6^{7r}. Cp Deut 4^{32}.
    In different application Ex 34^{10} Num 16^{30} and (in sense of 'cut') Josh 17$^{15\ 18\ k}$.

49 (a) *Creep, to* (*move, teem*, רמש)
Gen 1$^{21\ 26\ 28\ 30}$ 7$^{81\ 14\ 21}$ 8$^{17\ 19}$ 9^2 Lev 11$^{44\ 46}$ 20^{25}.
Cp Deut 4^{18}*.

(b) *Creeping thing*
Gen 1$^{24-26}$ 6^{7r} 7^{20} 7$^{14\ 23\imath}$ 8$^{17\ 19}$ 9^3*.

50 (a) *Cut off from his people* (Israel &c), *that soul* (*he*) *shall be* (כרת) followed by מן and מקרב $^\text{P}78^\text{c}$)
Gen 17^{14} Ex 12$^{15\ 19}$ 30$^{83\ 38}$ 31$^{14\text{b}}$ Lev 7$^{20\ 25\ 27}$ 18^{29} 19^8 20^{18} 22^3 23$^{29\ (30)}$ Num 9^{13} 15^{30} 19$^{13\ 20}$†.

(b) *Be cut off* (similarly, of persons)
Gen 9^{11} Lev 17$^{4\ 9\ 14}$ 20^{17}.
Ct **J** Gen 41^{36} Josh 9^{23}*.

(c) *Cut off, to* (הכרית, from Israel theocratically)
Lev 17^{10} 20$^{3\ 5}$. Num 4^{18}; otherwise Lev 26$^{22\ 30}$.
Ct **J** Ex 8^9 Josh 7^9, **D** Deut 12^{29} 19^1 Josh 11^{21} 23^4*.

51 *Die, to* (or *yield up the ghost*, גוע)
Gen 6^{17} 7^{21} 25$^{8\ 17}$ 35^{29} 49$^{33\text{c}}$ Num 17^{12}. 20$^{3\text{b}\ 29}$ Josh 22^{20}.
Cp Zech 13^8 Ps 88^{15} 104^{29} Lam 1^{19} Job (8)†.

52 (a) *Die not, that he* (*ye, they*, ולא ימות) ct $^\text{D}$36
Ex 28$^{35\ 43}$ 30^{20}. Lev 8^{35} 10$^{6\ 9}$ 15^{31} 16^2 $^{13\ (22^9)}$ Num 4$^{(15)\ 19\ (20)}$ 17^{10} 18$^{3\ 32}$ (35^{12} Josh 20^9).
Ct **J** Gen 42$^{2\ 20}$ 43^8 47^{19}*.

(b) *Death, surely be put to* (מות יומת). Cp **E** $^\text{JE}$100, ct $^\text{D}$36
Ex 31^{14}. Lev 20$^{2\ 9-13\ 15,\ 27}$ 24^{16}. 27^{29} Num 15^{35} 35$^{16-18\ 21\ 31}$.

53 *Divide, to* (or *separate*, הבדיל)
Gen 1$^{4\ 6\ 7\ 14\ 18}$ Ex 26^{33} Lev 1^{17} 5^8 10^{10} 11^{47} 20$^{24-26}$ Num 8^{14} 16$^{9\ 21}$ (Niph) Deut 4^{41} cp 10^8 19$^{2\ 7}$ 29^{21}*. מבדלות Josh 16^9†.

Drink offering, see **118$^\text{d}$**.

54 (a) *Dwell, to* (or *abide*, שכן, of the presence of Yahweh, the cloud, the glory of Yahweh)
Ex 24^{16} 25^8 29^{45} 40^{35} (Lev 16^{16}) Num 5^3 9$^{17,\ 22}$ 10^{12} 35^{34} Josh 22^{19} (18^1, Hiph, of the Tent of Meeting). Cp Deut 33^{12} (Blessing of Moses). Ct **E** Ex 33^9 Num 12^5 Deut 31^{15}, and $^\text{D}$**40**.

(b) *The Dwelling* (משכן)
Ex 25^9—Josh 22$^{19\ 29}$ 106 times. Ct Deut 12^5.

(c) *Dwelling of Yahweh*
Lev 17^4 Num 16^9 17^{13} 19^{13} 31$^{30\ 47}$ Josh 22^{19}.

(d) *Dwelling of the testimony*
Ex 38^{21} Num 1$^{50\ 53}$ 10^{11}.

(e) *Dwelling of the Tent of Meeting*
Ex 39^{32} 40$^{2\ 6\ 29}$ cp Num 16$^{24\ 27}$.

(f) *Court* (*of the Dwelling*)
Ex 27^9.. 35^{17}. 38–40 Lev 6$^{16r\ 26r}$ Num 3$^{26\ 37}$ 4$^{26\ 32}$.

(g) *My* (*his*) *dwelling*
Lev 15^{31} 26^{11} Josh 22^{29}.
Ct plural, of Israel, **J** Num 24^5*.

(h) *Dwell, dwelling, in the midst of,* or *among* (בתוך)
Ex 25^8 29^{45}. Lev 15^{31} 16^{16} 26^{11} Num 5^3 35^{34}*.

55 (a) *Dwellings, in all your* (*habitations*, משבות)
Ex 12^{20} 35^3 Lev 3^{17} 7^{26} 23$^{3\ 14}$ (cp ^{17}) $^{21\ 31}$ Num 35^{29}. Cp Ezek 6$^{6\ 14}$ 34^{13}†.

(b) *Dwelling* (or *habitation*, sing מושב)
Ex 12^{40} Lev 13^{46} 25^{29}.
Ct **J** Gen 10^{30} Num 24^{21}, **E** Gen 27^{39}.

(c) *Dwellings* (pl in other formulae)
Gen 36^{43} Lev 23^{17} Num 15^2 31^{10}.
Cp **E** (?) Ex 10^{23}, Ezek 37^{23} 1 Chron 4^{33} 6^{54} 7^{28}†.

56 (a) *East side, on the* (followed by *eastward* or ৸ *toward the sun-rising*, קדמה מזרחה)
Ex 27^{13} 38^{13} Num 2^3 3^{38} 34^{15} Josh 19^{12}.†.
Ct **J** (קדמה alone) Gen 13^{14} 25^6 *al.*

(b) *Southward* (תימנה)
Ex 26$^{18\ 35}$ 27^9 36^{23} 38^9 Num 2^{10} 3^{29} 10^6.
Cp Deut 3^{27} Ezek 20^{46} 47^{19} 48^{28}† ct **J** (נגבה) Gen 13^{14} 28^{14} (as also **P** Ex 26^{18} &c).

(c) *West* and *North* as in Gen 13^{14}, ימה, צפנה).

(d) *Right* (ימני)
Ex 29^{20} Lev 8^{23}. 14$^{14\ 16,\ 25\ 27}$. (23)* 1 Kings 6^8 7$^{21\ 39}$ Ezek 47^1 *al*, ct Gen 13^9 24^{49} &c.

(e) *Left* (שמאלי)
Lev 14$^{15,\ 26}$.* 1 Kings 7^{21} Ezek 4^4 *al.*
Ct Gen 13^9 24^{49} &c.

57 *Eleven* (עשתי עשר)
Ex 26^7. 36^{14}. Num 7^{72} 29^{20} Deut 1^3 cp 2 Kings 25^2 (‖ Jer 52^5) Jer 1^3 39^2 Ezek 26^1 33^{21} (cp Cornill, Smend, Bertholet) 40^{49} Zech 1^7 1 Chron 12^{13} 24^{12} 25^{18} 27^{14}†. Ct אחד עשר **JE** Gen 32^{22} 37^9, **D** Deut 1^2, **P** Josh 15^{51} *al.*

58 *Enough* (or *sufficient*, די in different formulae)
Ex 36$^{5\ 7}$ Lev 5^7 12^8 25$^{26\ 28}$. Cp Deut 15^8 25^2*.

59 *Ephod*
Ex 25^7 28 (twelve times) 29^5 35$^{9\ 27}$ 39 (eleven times) Lev 8^7*.

60 *Establish, to* (or *set up*, הקים)
(a) *a covenant* (of Deity)
Gen 6^{18} 9$^{9\ 11\ 17}$ 17$^{7\ 19\ 21}$ Ex 6^4 Lev 26^9. Cp Deut 8^{18} Ezek 16$^{60\ 62}$†. Ct Gen 26^3 'oath,' and **JED** *make* (৸ *cut* כרת) $^\text{JE}$181 and *give* (נתן) *a covenant.*

(b) *the Dwelling*, cp **54**
Ex 26^{30} 40$^{2\ 17\ 18}$ Num 1^{51} 7^1 9^{15} 10^{21}*.
Cp Josh 24^{26}.

61 *Estimation* (ערך)
Lev 5$^{15\ 18}$ 27$^{2-8\ 12,\ 15-19\ 23\ 25\ 27}$ Num 6^6 18^{16}.
Cp *to value* (הֶעֱרִיךְ) Lev 27$^{8\ 12\ 14}$ 2 Kings 23^{35}†.
'Order' 'row' Ex 39^{37} 40^4 ^{23} Lev 24^6.*.

62 *Everlasting* (qualifying various nouns, עולם)
(a) *covenant*
Gen 9^{16} 17$^{7\ 13\ 19}$ Ex 31^{16} Lev 24^8 Num 18^{19} cp 25^{13}*. Cp **47**.

P 62 (b) *generations*
Gen 9¹²*. Cp **76**.

(c) *ordinance* (or *perpetual statute*, or *due for ever*)
Ex 12¹⁴ ¹⁷ cp ²⁴ 27²¹ 28⁴³ 29⁹ ²⁸ 30²¹ Lev 3¹⁷ 6¹⁸ ²² 7³⁴ ³⁶ 10⁹ ¹⁵ 16²⁹ ³¹ ³⁴ 17⁷ 23¹⁴ ²¹ ³¹ ⁴¹ 24³ ⁹ Num 10⁸ 15¹⁵ 18⁸ ¹¹ ¹⁹ ²³ 19¹⁰ ²¹*.

(d) *possession*
Gen 17⁸ 48⁴ Lev 25³⁴*. Cp **127**.

(e) *priesthood*
Ex 40¹⁵ Num 25¹³*. Cp **129**.

(f) *redemption* (*redeem at any time* ⓗ)
Lev 25³².
Ct J Gen 21³³ 'everlasting God'; E Deut 33¹⁵ (∥ Gen 49²⁶) 'everlasting hills,' ²⁷ʳ 'everlasting arms'; D Deut 13¹⁶ Josh 8²⁸ 'heap for ever,' Deut 15¹⁷ 'bondman for ever'*.

63 *Exceedingly* (במאד)
Gen 17² ⁶ ²⁰ Ex 1⁷ cp Ezek 9⁹ 16¹³†.
מאד מאד Gen 7¹⁹ Num 14⁷. Cp J Gen 30⁴³ 1 Kings 7⁴⁷ 2 Kings 10⁴ Ezek 37¹⁰†.

64 *Face of, on the* (in the sense of 'in front of,' 'over against,' 'before,' על פני)
Gen 1²⁰ 23³ ¹⁹ 25⁹ 49³⁰ 50¹³ Lev 10³ 16¹⁴ Num 3⁴ (16⁴³ 20¹⁰ אל) 21¹¹ 33⁷ Deut 32⁴⁹ 34¹ Josh 13²⁵ 15⁸ 17⁷ 18¹⁴ ¹⁶ 19¹¹.
Occasionally elsewhere, e.g. J Gen 18¹⁶ 19²⁸ 25¹⁸.

65 (a) *Family*
Gen 8¹⁹—21⁴⁰ 224 times. Elsewhere Gen 10¹⁸ 24³⁸ ⁴⁰. Num 11¹⁰ Deut 29¹⁸ Josh 7¹⁴ ¹⁷.

(b) *Families, after your* (*their*, with ל) cp **18**
Gen 8¹⁹ 10⁵ ²⁰ ³¹ 36⁴⁰ Ex 6¹⁷ ²⁵ 12²¹ Num 1 (thirteen times) 2³⁴ 3–4 (fifteen times) 26 (sixteen times) 33⁵⁴ Josh 13¹⁵ ²³ ²⁸. ³¹ 15¹ ¹² ²⁰ 16⁵ ⁸ 17² 18¹¹ ²⁰. ²⁸ 19 (twelve times) 21⁷ ³³ ⁴⁰. Cp J Num 11¹⁰ᵃ 1 Sam 10²¹ 1 Chron 5⁷ 6⁶². (∥ Josh 21³³ ⁴⁰)†.

66 *Fathers' house(s).* Ct ᴶᴱ**153**
Ex 6¹⁴ 12³ Num 1–4 7² 17². ⁶ 18¹ 26² 34¹⁴ Josh 22¹⁴.

67 *Fell upon his face* (*their faces*, נפל על פניו)
Gen 17³ ¹⁷ Lev 9²⁴ Num 14⁵ 16⁴ ²² ⁴⁵ 20⁶.
Cp J Josh 5¹⁴ (אל) [ct Ex 3⁶] 7⁶*.

Female, see *Male and female* **107**.

68 *Fifth part* (חמישית)
Lev 5¹⁶ 6⁵ 19²⁵ 22¹⁴ 27¹³ ¹⁵ ¹⁹ ²⁷ ³¹ Num 5⁷
Cp J Gen 47²⁴.

69 (a) *Full the hand, to* (or *consecrate*)
Ex 28⁴¹ 29⁹ ²⁹ ³³ ³⁵ Lev 8³³ 16³² 21¹⁰ Num 3³.
Cp J Ex 32²⁹ Judg 17⁵ ¹²*.

(b) *Fillings* (*consecration*, מלאים)
Ex 29²² ²⁶. ³¹ ³⁴ Lev 7³⁷ 8²² ²⁸. ³¹ ³³ (cp Ex 25⁷ ⓗ 35⁹ ²⁷ 1 Chron 29² and Ex 28¹⁷ ²⁰ 39¹³)†.

Fire offering, see **113**ᵉ

70 *Firmament* (רקיע)
Gen 1⁶ ⁷ ⁸ ¹⁴ ¹⁵ ¹⁷ ²⁰ Ps 19¹ 150¹ Dan 12³†.
Cp Ezek 1²². ²⁵. 10¹ Ps 19¹ 150¹ Dan 12³†.

Food, see *Meat* **110**.

71 *Forefront* (אל מול פני)
Ex 26⁹ 28²⁵ ³⁷ 39¹⁸ Lev 8⁹ Num 8² ³, 2 Sam 11¹⁵†.

Fountain (מעין), cp ᴶᴱ**81**.

72 *Frankincense* (לבנה), cp **95**
Ex 30³⁴ Lev 2¹. ¹⁵. 5¹¹ 6¹⁵ 24⁷ Num 5¹⁵ᵇ.

73 *Fruitful and multiply, to be* (or *make,* פרה ורבה Qal and Hiph). Ct ᴶᴱ**204**
Gen 1²² ²⁸ 8¹⁷ 9¹ ⁷ 17²⁰ cp 2⁶ 28³ 35¹¹ 47²⁷ 48⁴ Ex 1⁷ Lev 26⁹.
Cp Jer 3¹⁶ 23³ Ezek 36¹¹†.

74 *Gathered, to be* (*gathering,* קוה Niph, מקוה)
Gen 1⁹. Ex 7¹⁹ Lev 11³⁶*.

75 *Gathered to his people* (נאסף אל עמיו) cp **122**
Gen 25⁸ ¹⁷ 35²⁹ 49²⁹ ³³ᶜ Num 20²⁴ ²⁶ 27¹³ 31² Deut 32⁵⁰†.

76 (a) *Generations* (דורות)
Gen 6⁹ Lev 23⁴³ Josh 22²⁷. cp (b) and Judg 3² Is 41⁴ 51⁹ Job 42¹⁶†.
Ct (sing only) J Gen 7¹ Ex 1⁶, E Gen 15¹⁶ Ex 3¹⁵ 17¹⁶, D Deut 1³⁵ 2¹⁴ &c

(b) *Generations* (*your, their,* &c, with ל) cp **18**
Gen 9¹² 17⁷ ⁹ ¹² Ex 12¹⁴ ¹⁷ ⁴² 16³². 27²¹ 29⁴² 30⁸ ¹⁰ ²¹ ³¹. ³¹ ¹³ ¹⁶ 40¹⁵ Lev 3¹⁷ 6¹⁸ 7³⁶ 10⁹ 17⁷ 21¹⁷ 22³ 23¹⁴ ²¹ ³¹ ⁴¹ 24³ 25³⁰ Num 9¹⁰ 10⁸ 15¹⁴ ²¹ ²³ ³⁸ 18²³ 35²⁹†.

77 (a) *Generations* (תולדות), *these are the,* cp **188**
Gen 2⁴ᵃ 6⁹ 10¹ 11¹⁰ ²⁷ 25¹² ¹⁹ 36¹ ⁹ 37²ᵃ Num 3¹.
Cp Ruth 4¹⁸ 1 Chron 1²⁹†.

(b) *Generations* (in other formulae)
Gen 5¹ Ex 28¹⁰ Num 1²⁰⁻⁴² (twelve times)†.

(c) *According to their generations* (with ל), cp **18**
Gen 10³² 25¹³ Ex 6¹⁶ ¹⁹ 1 Chron (eight times)†.

78 *Getting* (or *possession* or *substance* or *purchase,* קנין), cp **36**
Gen 31¹⁸ᵇ 34²³ 36⁶ Lev 22¹¹ Josh 14⁴*.

79 *Glory of Yahweh.*
Ex 16⁷ ¹⁰ 24¹⁶. 29⁴³ 40³⁴. Lev 9⁶ ²³ Num 14¹⁰ 16¹⁹ 42 20⁶.
Ct Jˢ Ex 33¹⁸ ²², Rᴶᴱ Num 14²¹., D Deut 5²⁴ᵛ.

80 *Goings out* (in boundary-descriptions)
Num 34⁴ ⁸. ¹² Josh 15⁴ ⁷ ¹¹ 16⁸ 17⁹ ¹⁸ 18¹² ¹⁴ ¹⁹ 19¹⁴ ²² ²⁹ ³³.
Cp J Josh 16³, Ezek 48³⁰ 1 Chron 5¹⁶, otherwise Ps 68²⁰†.

81 (a) *Guilty, to be* (אשם)
Lev 4¹³ ²² ²⁷ 5²⁻⁵ ¹⁷ ¹⁹ 6⁴ Num 5⁶ *

(b) *Guilty, be* (*bring guilt,* אשמה)
Lev 4³ 6⁵ 7 22¹⁶*.

Guilt offering, see **118**ᶠ.

THE PRIESTLY LAW AND HISTORY BOOK, P

82 *Half* (מחצית)
Ex $30^{13\ 15\ 23}$ 38^{26} Lev 6^{20} Num $31^{29\ 42\ 47}$ Josh 21^{25} (1 Chron 6^{70}). Cp 1 Kings 16^9 Neh 8^3 1 Chron 6^{61}†. Otherwise חצי JEDP.

83 *Head* (or *poll, person*, גלגלת)
Ex 16^{16} 38^{26} Num 1^2 $^{18\ 20\ 22}$ 3^{47}*.

84 (a) *Heads of Fathers* (ראשי אבות)
Ex 6^{25} Num $1^7{}^3$ 31^{26} 32^{28} 36^1 Josh 14^1 19^{51} 21^{1}*. Afterwards only in Chron-Neh. Ct J 'heads of the people' Num 25^4, D 'heads of your tribes' Deut 1^{15} 5^{23} ᴰ57.

(b) *Heads of thousands of Israel*
Num 1^{16} 10^4 Josh $22^{21\ 30}$†.

(c) *Head* (*take the sum*, . . נשא את־ראש)
Ex 30^{12} Num 1^2 ^{49} 4^2 ^{22} 26^2 $31^{26\ 49}$†.

85 *Heave, to* (*offer, take up*, or *off*, ritually, הרים)
Ex 29^{27} 35^{24} Lev 2^9 4^8 $^{10\ 19}$ $6^{10\ 15}$ 22^{15} Num 15^{19} ^{20} 16^{37} $18^{19\ 24\ 26\ 28-30\ 32}$ $31^{28\ 52}$*. Ct ᴶᴱ176.

86 (a) *Holy, to be* (קדש vb, Qal)
Ex $29^{21\ 37}$ 30^{29} Lev $6^{18\ 27}$ Num 16^{37}.. Cp Deut 22^9*.

(b) *Sanctified, to be* (or *hallowed*, Niphal)
Ex 29^{43} Lev 10^3 22^{32} Num 20^{13}*.

(c) *Sanctify, to* (*hallow, keep holy*, Piel)
Gen 2^3 Ex 13^2 20^{11} 28^3 ^{41} 29^1 $^{27\ 33\ 36.\ 44}$ $30^{29.}$ 31^{13} $40^{9-11\ 13}$ Lev $8^{10-12\ 15\ 30}$ 16^{19} 20^8 $21^{8\ 15}$ ^{23} 22^9 $^{16\ 32}$ 25^{10} Num 6^{11} 7^1 Deut 32^{51}. Cp J Ex $19^{10\ 14\ 23}$ Josh 7^{13}, E Ex 20^8 ∥ Deut 5^{12}*.

(d) *Sanctify, to* (Hiphil)
Ex 28^{38} Lev 22^2. $27^{14-19\ 22\ 26}$ Num 3^{13} 8^{17} 20^{12} 27^{14} Josh 20^7. Cp Deut 15^{19}*.

(e) *Sanctify themselves* (Hithpa)
Lev 11^{44} 20^7. Cp J Ex 19^{22} Num 11^{18} Josh 3^5 7^{13}*.

87 (a) *Holy* (adj with verb 'to be,' היה קדוש)
Lev 11^{44}. 19^2 20^7 ^{26} 21^6 ^{8} Num 6^5 15^{40}, cp Deut 23^{14}. Ct 'a holy people' Deut 7^6 14^2 21 26^{19} 28^9*.

(b) *Holy place* (*in a*, במקום קדוש)
Ex 29^{31} Lev $6^{16\ 26}$. 7^6 10^{13} 16^{24} 24^9*.

88 (a) *Holiness* (in the sense of 'holy things,' 'holy place,' &c, הקדש and הקדשים)
Ex 26^{33} $28^{29\ 35\ 38}$ 31^{11} Lev 5^{15} 6^{30} 10^4 $^{10\ 18}$ 12^4 $16^{2.\ 16.\ 20\ 23\ 27}$ 19^8 21^{22} $22^{2-4.\ 6.\ 10\ 12\ 14-16}$ Num $4^{15.\ 20}$ 5^9. 8^{19} 18^8 ^{32} 28^7. Cp Deut 12^{26} 26^{13}*.

(b) *Minister in the holy place* (שרת בקדש)
Ex 28^{43} 29^{30} 35^{19} $39^{1\ 41}$ Num 4^{12} Cp Ezek 44^{27}†.

(c) *Holiness* (with the article in the sense of the 'sanctuary' or 'holy things' after a noun)

Charge of Num $3^{28\ 32}$ 18^5; *offering of* Ex 36^6 Num 18^{19}, *place of* Lev 10^{17} 14^{13}, *sanctuary of* Lev 16^{33}; *shekel of* Ex $30^{13\ 24}$ 38^{24-26} Lev 5^{15} 27^3 ^{25} Num $3^{47\ 50}$ 7^{13-86} (fourteen times) 18^{16}; *sockets of* Ex 38^{27}; *veil of* Lev 4^6, *vessels of* Num 3^{31} 18^3 31^6; *work of the service of* Ex $36^{1\ 3}$; *work of* Ex 36^4, 38^{24}; *service of* Num 7^9*.

(d) *Most holy* (*place* or *things*, קדש הק׳, קדש קדשים, קדשי הק׳) cp 90ᵃᵇ
Ex 26^{33}. 29^{37} 40^{10} Lev 2^3 ^{10} 21^{22} Num 4^4 ^{19} 18^9.*.

89 *Holiness* (as an epithet after nouns, קדש)
Holy anointing oil Ex $30^{25\ 31}$ 37^{29} Num 35^{25}; *convocation* Ex 12^{16} Lev 23^2. · (eleven) Num $28^{18\ 25.}$ $29^{1\ 7\ 12}$; *crown* Ex 29^6 39^{30} Lev 8^9, *garments* Ex $28^{2\ 4}$ 29^{29} 31^{10} cp $35^{19\ 21}$ $39^{1\ 41}$ 40^{13} Lev $16^{4\ 32}$; *name* Lev 20^3 22^2 ^{32}; *sabbath* Ex 16^{23}. Cp J Ex 3^5; E Ex 22^{31}; D Deut 26^{15} (33^2 reading doubtful); Song of Moses Ex 15^{13}*.

90 (a) *Holy, holiness, most holy* (*it is*, &c)
Ex $29^{33.\ 37}$ $30^{29\ 32\ (35)\ 36.}$ 31^{14} 35^2 40^9 Lev 6^{17} 25^{29} $7^{1\ 6}$ $10^{12\ 17}$ 14^{13} 19^{24} 21^6 24^9 25^{12} 27^9. ^{33} Num 6^{20} 18^9. ^{17}. Ct Josh 5^{15}* ∥ J Ex 3^5.

(b) *Holiness, holy, most holy, holy thing, to Yahweh or to his God*
Ex 28^{36} $30^{10\ 37}$ 31^{15} 39^{30} Lev (19^{24} cp ^{8}) 21^7 23^{20} $27^{14\ 21\ 23\ 28\ 30\ 32}$ Num 6^8 Josh 6^{19}*.

91 *Holy place* or *Sanctuary* (מקדש)
Ex 25^8 Lev 12^4 16^{33} 19^{30} 20^3 $21^{12\ 23}$ $26^{2\ 31}$ Num 3^{38} 10^{21} 18^1 19^{20}. Cp Song of Moses Ex 15^{17}, E Josh 24^{26}*, thirty times in Ezek.

92 (a) *Hosts* (of Israel, צבא) cp 16 18^1
Ex 6^{26} 7^4 $12^{17\ 41\ 51}$ Num $1^{3\ 52}$ $2^{3\ 9.\ 16\ 18\ 24.\ 32}$ $10^{14\ 18\ 22\ 25\ 28}$ 33^1 ct Deut 20^9* (cp sing of the tribes, twenty times) sing = 'war' Num $31^{5\ 21\ 32\ 36\ 43\ 53}$ 32^{27} cp Deut 24^5.

(b) *For the warfare* (or *service*, with *enter on, arm*, &c, לצבא)
Num $4^{3\ 30\ 35\ 39\ 43}$ $31^{3\ 4\ 6\ 27}$. cp Josh 22^{12} 33^*.

(c) *serve, to* (or *wait upon*, or *war*, צבא)
Ex 38^8 Num 4^{23} 8^{24} 31^7 ^{42}†.

93 *Hundred* (מאת for ordinary מאה)
Gen 5^3 $6^{18\ 25\ 28}$ 7^{24} 83^b $11^{10\ 25}$ 21^5 25^7 ^{17} 35^{28} 47^9 ^{28} Ex $6^{16\ 18\ 20}$ $38^{25\ 27abc}$ Num 2^9 $^{16\ 24\ 31}$ 33^{39}. So besides only Neh 5^{11} (probably corrupt), 2 Chron 25^9 Q'ri Est 1^4 (on Eccles 8^{12} cp Siegfried in *Hdkomm*)†, P uses מאה in such cases only twice Gen 17^{17} 23^1. Cp Driver *LOT*⁶ p 131.

94 (a) *I* (אני) Gen 6^{17} 9^9 ^{12} and onwards, about 130 times (Briggs, *Higher Criticism*² p 70)

(b) *And I, behold, I* (ואני, followed by הנה, cp ᴶᴱ133) Gen 6^{17} 9^9 Ex 14^{17} 31^6 Num 3^{12} 18^6 ^{8}. Cp Jer 1^{18} 40^{10}†. Ct אנכי ᴾ63 only in Gen 23^4

P 95 (a) *Incense* (קטרת) cp **72**
Ex 30¹ ⁸ ⁹ ²⁷ ³⁵ ³⁷ 31⁸ 37²⁵ 39³⁸ 40⁵ Lev 10¹ 16¹³ Num 7¹⁴·· (thirteen times) 16⁷ ¹⁷· ³⁵ ⁴⁰ ⁴⁶·*.   Ct קטרה Deut 33¹⁰.

(b) *Incense, sweet* (קטרת הסמים)
Ex 25⁶ 30⁷ ⁽³⁴⁾ 31¹¹ 35⁸ ¹⁵ ²⁸ 37²⁹ 39³³ 40²⁷ Lev 4⁷ 16¹² Num 4¹⁶*.

96 (a) *Inherit* (without an object, נחל Qal)
Num 18²⁰ 26⁵⁵ 32¹⁹ Josh 16⁴ 19⁹*.

(b) *Divide the inheritance, to* (Ḥ 'make inherit,' Piel) Num 34²⁹ Josh 13³² 14¹ 19⁵¹† (Hithpael) Lev 25⁴⁶ Num 32¹⁸ 33⁵⁴ 34¹³ cp Ezek 47¹³ Is 14²†. Ct Hiph ᴾ **65ᵃ**.

(c) *Inheritance, for an* (בנחלה)
Num 18²⁶ 26⁵³ 34² 36² Josh 19².
Cp Josh 13⁶· 23⁴ Judg 18¹ Ezek 45¹ 46¹⁶ 47¹⁴ ²²†.

97 (a) *Journeyed* (or *set forward*) *and encamped* (of the marches of Israel, ויסעו ויחנו)
Ex 13²⁰ 17¹ 19² Num 21¹⁰ ¹¹ᵃ 22¹ 33⁵⁻⁴⁸.
'Journey' Ex 14¹⁵ 16¹ 40³⁶. Num 2⁹·· 9¹⁷⁻²³ 10¹²⁻²⁸ 21⁴ᵃ Josh 9¹⁷.
Ct J Ex 12³⁷ Num 10³³ 11³⁵ 12¹⁶; E Num 20²²ᵃ 21¹². Deut 10⁶. Josh 3¹ᵇ; Deut 1¹⁹ 2¹.

(b) *Journeys* (always in P except Num 10² in pl)
Ex 17¹ 40³⁶ ³⁸ Num 10² ⁶ ¹² ²⁸ 33¹.
Ct Gen 13³ Deut 10¹¹†.

(c) *Journeys, journeyed according to their,* see **18**ᵏ.

98 *Jubile*
Lev 25¹⁰⁻⁵⁴ fourteen times, 27¹⁷· ²¹· ²³. Num 36⁴.
In meaning 'ram's horn' J Ex 19¹³, E Josh 6⁴⁻⁶ ⁸ 13†.

99 *Judgements* (שפטים)
Ex 6⁶ 7⁴ 12¹² Num 33⁴.
Cp 2 Chron 24²⁴ Prov 19²⁹ Ezek ten times †.

100 *Kill, to* (שחט)
Ex 12⁶ and onwards, forty-two times, ritually.
Ct J Ex 34²⁵ Num 11²², Rʲᵉ Num 14¹⁶, E Gen 22¹⁰ 37³¹*.

101 *Kin* (or *flesh*, שאר בשר, שאר)
Lev 18⁶ ¹²· ¹⁷ 20¹⁹ 21² 25⁴⁹ Num 27¹¹.
Cp E Ex 21¹⁰*.

Kind, see **18**ᵏ.

102 *Lay hands on, to* (סמך יד על)
Ex 29¹⁰ ¹⁵ ¹⁹ Lev 1⁴ 3² ⁸ ¹³ 4⁴ ¹⁵ ²⁴ ²⁹ ³³ 8¹⁴ ¹⁸ ²² 16²¹ 24¹⁴ Num 8¹⁰ ¹² 27¹⁸ ²³ Deut 34⁹.
Ct סמך in Gen 27³⁷ E*.

Left, see **56**ᶜ.

103 *Leprous* (*leper*, צרוע)
Lev 13⁴⁴· 14³ 22⁴ Num 5².
Ct Ḥ Ex 4⁶ J, Num 12¹⁰ E (also in Lev 14²)*.

104 *Light, the* (מאור)
Ex 25⁶ 27²⁰ 35⁸ ¹⁴ ²⁸ 39³⁷ Lev 24² Num 4⁹ ¹⁶.
Of the heavenly bodies, Gen 1¹⁴⁻¹⁶.
Cp Ezek 32⁸ Ps 74¹⁶ 90³ Prov 15³⁰†.

105 *Little, to be* (Hiph *diminish*, מעט)
Ex 12⁴ 16¹⁷. 30¹⁵ Lev 25¹⁶ᵃᵇ 26²² Num 26⁵⁴ 33⁵⁴ 35⁸. Cp J Num 11³²*.

106 *Lot* (גורל in various formulae chiefly connected with the distribution of the land)
Lev 16⁸⁻¹⁰ Num 26⁵⁵· 33⁵⁴ 34¹³ 36². Josh 14² 15¹ 17¹ 18¹¹ 19¹ ¹⁰ ¹⁷ ²⁴ ³² ⁴⁰ ⁵¹ 21⁴⁻⁶ ⁸ ¹⁰ ²⁰ ⁴⁰.
Ct J Josh 16¹ 17¹¹· ¹⁷, Rʲᵉ 18⁶ ⁸ ¹⁰*.

107 (a) *Male and (or) female* (זכר ונקבה)
Gen 1²⁷ 5² 6¹⁹ 7³ʳ ⁹ʳ ¹⁶ Lev 3¹⁶ 12⁷ 15³³; 'from male to female' Num 5³ cp **108**ᶜ.
Cp Deut 4¹⁶†.

(b) *Every male* (כל זכר)
Gen 17²³ 34²⁵ Lev 6¹⁸ ²⁹ 7⁶ Num 1² ²⁰ ²² 3¹⁵ ²² ²⁸ ³⁴ ³⁹ 18¹⁰ 26⁶² 31¹⁷ ¹⁷*.
Cp 'the males' pl J Ex 13¹² ¹⁵, Rᴾ Josh 5⁴ (?) 17².

(c) *Every male (shall be) circumcised*
Gen 17¹⁰ ¹² 34¹⁵ ²² ²⁴ Ex 12⁴⁸†.

(d) *Every female* (or *female* alone)
Lev 4²⁸ ³² 5⁶ 12⁵ 27⁴⁻⁷ Num 31¹⁵. Cp Jer 31²²†.

108 (a) *Man or woman* (איש או אשה)
Lev 13²⁹ ³⁸ 20²⁷ Num 5⁶ 6², E Ex 21²⁸·*.

(b) *Man and beast* (with prep ב, באדם ובבהמה)
Ex (8¹⁷· 9¹⁰) 13² 8¹⁷ 18¹⁵ 31¹¹ ²⁶* cp ב with other groups, **35**. Otherwise Num 31⁴⁷.

(c) *From man to beast* (both ... and מן followed by עד)
Gen 6⁷¹ 7²³ʳ Ex 12¹² Num 3¹³.
Cp E Ex 9²⁵¹, J Ex 11⁷*.

Meal offering, see **118**ʰ.

109 *Means suffice, his* (*wax rich, his hand can reach, according to ability,* השיג ידו)
Lev 5¹¹ 14²¹ ³⁰⁻³² 25²⁶ ⁴⁷ ⁴⁹ 27⁸ Num 6²¹.
Cp Ezek 46⁷†.

110 *Meat, for* (*food, to eat,* לאכלה)
Gen 1²⁹· 6²¹ 9³ Ex 16¹⁵ Lev 11³⁹ 25⁶.
Ct Gen 47²⁴. Elsewhere Jer 12⁹, ten times in Ezek†.

111 (a) *Meet* (of Yahweh with Israel, and more generally 'to be gathered,' נועד)
Ex 25²² 29⁴². 30⁶ ³⁶ Num 10³. 14³⁵ 16¹¹ 17⁴ 27³.
Ct J Josh 11⁵*.

(b) *Meeting, door of the tent of* (פתח אהל מועד)
Ex 29⁴—Josh 19⁵¹ forty-three times*.
Ct E Ex 33⁹. Num 12⁵ Deut 31¹⁵.

(c) *Appointed season* (ritually, pl only in P, מועדים)
Gen 1¹⁴ Lev 23² ⁴ ³⁷ ⁴⁴ Num 10¹⁰ 15³ 29³⁹*.
Ct sing JE Ex 13¹⁰ 23¹⁵ʳ 34¹⁸ʳ.

112 *Memorial* (אזכרה)
Lev 2² ⁹ ¹⁶ 5¹² 6¹⁵ 24⁷ Num 5²⁶†.

113 *Memorial* (זכרון)
Ex 12¹⁴ 13⁹ 28¹² ²⁹ 30¹⁶ 39⁷ Lev 23²⁴ Num 5¹⁵ ¹⁸ 10¹⁰ 16⁴⁰ 31⁵⁴ Josh 4⁷. Ct E Ex 17¹⁴.

Mercy-seat, see *Covering* **47**.

Minister in the priests' office, see **129**ᵃ.

THE PRIESTLY LAW AND HISTORY BOOK, P

114 (a) *Murmur, to* (לוּן Niph and Hiph)
Ex $16^{2\ 7\ 8}$ Num $14^{2\ 27\ 29\ 36}$ $16^{11\ 41}$ 17^5 Josh 9^{18}. Cp J Ex 15^{24} 17^{3*}.

(b) *Murmurings* (תְּלֻנּוֹת)
Ex $16^{7-9\ 12}$ Num 14^{27} $17^{5\ 10}$†.

115 (a) *Number, to* (פקד)
Ex 30^{12} 38^{21} Num $1^{3\ 19\ 44\ 49}$ $3^{15.\ 39.\ 42}$ $4^{23\ 29\ 34\ 37\ 41\ 45\ 49}$ 26^{63}.. In the sense of 'visit,' 'appoint,' 'muster,' frequent in **JEDP**, e.g. Gen 21^1 50^{24}. Deut 20^9 Josh 8^{10} Lev 18^{10} &c.

(b) *Numbered, they that were* (pass ptcp)
Ex 30^{12}—Num 26^{63} seventy-five times. 'Officers' Num $31^{14\ 48}$.
Cp 2 Kings 11^{15} 12^{11} 1 Chron 23^4 2 Chron 23^{14}†.

(c) *Numbered, to be* (Hothpael)
Num 1^{47} 2^{33} 26^{62} ct 1 Kings 20^{27}†.

116 *Number* (estimation, מִכְסָה)
Ex 12^4 Lev 27^{23} Num $31^{28\ 37-41}$†.

117 *Offer, to* (ℌ = *do*, cp occasional extension to other ceremonial observance)
Ex $29^{36\ 38}$. Lev 14^{19} 15^{15} 16^9 22^{23} Num 6^{16}. $15^{3\ 5\ 14}$ $28^{4\ 8\ 21\ 24}$.
Cp Deut 5^{15} 12^{27} 16^1 Judg 6^{19} 1 Kings 18^{23} Ezek 43^{25} $45^{17\ 22}$ 46^{12}.

118 (a) *Offer, to* (or *bring near, present*, הִקְרִיב). Ct ^{JE}**110**
Ex 28^1—Num 31^{50}, 146 times.
Ct Deut 1^{17} Josh 7^{16-18} 8^{23}. Intrans 'Draw near' J Gen 12^{11} Ex 14^{10*}. Cp Ezek 43^{22-24} $44^{15\ 27}$ 46^4.

(b) *Oblation* (or *offering*, קרבן)
Lev 1^2—Num 31^{50} seventy-eight times. Elsewhere only Ezek 20^{28} 40^{43}†.

(c) *Burnt offering* (עלה)
Ex $29^{18\ 25\ 42}$ 30^9 28 31^9 35^{16} 38^1 $40^{6\ 10\ 29ab}$ Lev sixty-two times, Num fifty-one times Josh $22^{23\ 26-29}$.
Cp JE Gen 8^{20} $22^{2.\ 6.\ 8\ 13}$ Ex 10^{25} 18^{12} 20^{24} 24^5 32^6 Num $23^{3\ 6\ 15\ 17}$ Deut 27^6, **D** Deut $12^{6\ 11\ 13.\ 27}$ Josh 8^{d31*}.

(d) *Drink offering* (נסך)
Ex 29^{40}. 30^9 Lev $23^{13\ 18\ 37}$ Num thirty-four times, J Gen 35^{14*}.

(e) *Fire, offering made by* (אשה)
Ex 29^{18}—Josh 13^{14r} sixty-three times. Cp Deut 18^{1}†.

(f) *Guilt offering* (or *guilt*, אשם)
Lev $5^{6.\ 15.\ 18.}$ 6^6 $7^{1.\ 5\ 7\ 37}$ $14^{12-14\ 17\ 21\ 24.\ 28}$ 19^{21}. Num 5^7. 6^{12} 18^9.
Ct J Gen 26^{10*}. Cp **81**.

(g) *Heave offering* (תרומה) cp **85**
Ex 25^2—Num 31^{52} forty times, cp Deut $12^{6\ 11\ 17*}$.

(h) *Meal offering* (מנחה)
Ex 29^{41}—Josh $22^{23\ 29}$, 101 times.
Ct JE Gen 4^3 $32^{13\ 18\ 20}$. 33^{10} $43^{11\ 15\ 25}$.*.

(i) *Peace offerings, sacrifices of*
Ex 29^{28} Lev $3^{1\ 3\ 6\ 9}$ $4^{10\ 26\ 31\ 35}$ 7^{11-37} 9^{18} 10^{14} 17^5 19^5 22^{21} 23^{19} Num 6^{17}. 7^{17-88} 10^{10} Josh 22^{23*}.
Cp 'peace offerings' simply Lev 6^{12} $7^{14\ 33}$ 9^4 22 Num 6^{14} 15^8 29^{39} Josh 22^{27}, E Ex 20^{24} 24^5 32^6 Deut 27^{7a} (Josh 8^{31}): so also Ezek 43^{27} $45^{15\ 17}$ 46^2 12.

(j) *Sin offering* (and *sin*, חטאת) cp **143**
Ex 29^{14}—Num 32^{23}, 126 times.
In sense of 'sin' used by **JED** Gen 4^7 18^{20} 31^{36} 50^{17} Ex 10^{17} $32^{30\ 32\ 34}$ 34^9 Num 12^{11} 16^{26b} Deut $9^{18\ 21\ 27}$ 19^{15} Josh 24^{19*}.

(k) *Thanksgiving* (תודה)
Lev $7^{12\ 15}$ 22^{29} (cp Josh 7^{19})*.

(l) *Wave offering* (תנופה) cp **175**
Ex $29^{24\ 26}$ 35^{22} $38^{24\ 29}$ Lev fourteen times, Num eight times*.

119 (a) *Old* (*was so many years*, ℌ *Son of five hundred years*, בן ... שנה) cp **169**^{b}
Gen 5^{32} 7^6 11^{10} 12^{4b} 16^{16} $17^{1\ 24}$ 21^5 $25^{20\ 26b}$ 26^{34} 37^{2a} 41^{46a} Ex 7^7 30^{14} 38^{26} Lev $27^{3\ 5-7}$ Num 1 and 4 twenty-nine times, 8^{24}. 14^{29} $26^{2\ 4}$ 32^{11} 33^{39} Deut 34^7.
Cp Gen 50^{26} Deut 31^2 Josh $14^{7\ 10}$ 24^{29*}.

(b) *Old* (*a year, of the first year*, בן שנה)
Ex 12^5 29^{38} Lev 9^3 12^6 14^{10} $23^{12\ 18}$. Num $6^{12\ 14}$ 7^{15-88} 15^{27} $28^{3\ 9\ 11\ 19\ 27}$ 29^{2-36*}.

(c) *Old, a month*, Lev 27^6 Num 3^{15-43} 18^{16} 26^{62*}.

120 (a) *Out of the camp* (or *city*, אל מחוץ למחנה לעיר)
Lev $4^{12\ 21}$ 6^{11} 10^4. $14^{3\ 40.\ 45\ 53}$ 16^{27} $24^{14\ 23}$ Num 5^3. 15^{35}. 19^3 31^{13}. Cp **D** Deut 23^{10*}.

(b) *Without the camp* (or *city*, מחוץ למחנה)
Ex 29^{14} Lev 8^{17} 9^{11} 13^{46} 14^8 (tent) 17^3 Num 19^9 31^{19} $35^{5\ 27}$ Josh 6^{23}.
Cp J Gen 19^{16} 24^{11}, **E** Ex 33^7 Num 12^{14}, **D** Deut 23^{12*}.

(c) *Without the veil* Ex 26^{35} 27^{21} 40^{22} Lev 24^3†.

121 *Over against* (נכח)
Ex 26^{35} 40^{24} Num 19^4 Josh 15^7 18^{17}.
Cp Ex 14^2. Ct לנכח J Gen 25^{21} 30^{38*}.

Peace offering, see **118**^{i}.

122 *Peoples* (*thy, his*, &c plural, in sense of kinsfolk)
In different formulae 'be cut off from his peoples' **50** (occasionally sing), 'be gathered to his peoples' **75**, 'among thy (his) peoples' P^{h} **208**.
Cp Ezek 18^{18} (perhaps Judg 5^{14} Hos 10^{14}, Driver *LOT*^{6} 133)†.

123 *Perfect* (or *without blemish*, תמים)
Gen 6^9 17^1, Ex 12^5—Num 29^{36} ritually (forty-three times). Ct JE Josh 10^{13} 'whole' 24^{14} 'in sincerity,' Deut 18^{13} 32^{4*}.

124 *Perpetual* (*alway, continually*, תמיד)
(a) generally, Ex 27^{20} $28^{29.\ 38}$ Lev 6^{13} 24^{2-4} Num 9^{16}. Cp Deut 11^{12*}.

(b) Of the shewbread, daily sacrifice, or incense
Ex 25^{30} $29^{38\ 42}$ 30^8 Lev 6^{20} 24^8 Num $4^{7\ 16}$ $28-29$ (seventeen times)†.

WORDS AND PHRASES

P 125 (a) *Plague* (נגף)
Ex 12^{13} 30^{12} Num 8^{19} 16^{46}. Josh 22^{17}. Ct Is 8^{14}†.

(b) *Plague* (מגפה)
Num 14^{37} 16$^{48-50}$ 25^8. ^{18} 26^1 31^{16}.
Ct R^{je} Ex 9^{14} pl*.

126 *Poor, be waxen* (מוך)
Lev 25^{25} ^{35} ^{39} ^{47} 27^8†.

127 (a) *Possession, to get* (vb אחז Niph). Ct ^{D}88
Gen 34^{10} 47^{27b} Num 32^{30} Josh 22^9 ^{19}.
Ct Gen 22^{13}*.

(b) *Possession* (אחזה). Ct ^{D}88^d
Gen 17^8 23$^{4\ 9\ 20}$ 36^{43} 47^{11} 48^4 49^{30} 50^{13} Lev
14^{34} 25$^{10\ 13\ 24.\ 27.\ 32-4\ 41\ 45.\ 27^{16}\ 21.\ 24\ 28}$
Num 27$^{4\ 7}$ 32^5 $^{22\ 29\ 32}$ 35$^{2\ 8\ 28}$ Deut 32^{49} Josh
21$^{12\ 41}$ 22$^{9\ 19}$. Cp Josh 22^4*.

128 *Pour, to* (or *cast*, יצק)
Ex 25^{12} 26^{37} 29^7 36^{36} 37^3 ^{13} 38$^{5\ 27}$ Lev 2$^{1\ 6}$ 8$^{12\ 15}$
9^9 14$^{15\ 26}$ 21^{10} (Hoph) Num 5^{15}.
Ct **E** Gen 28^{18}, **J** Gen 35^{14} Josh 7^{23} (Hiph)*.

Present, to, see **118**^{a}.

129 (a) *Priest's office, to minister in the* (כהן Piel)
Ex 28$^{1\ 3.\ 41}$ 29$^{1\ 44}$ 30^{30} 31^{10} 35^{19} 39^{41} 40$^{13\ 15}$
Lev 7^{35} 16^{32} Num 3^3. Cp Deut 10^6*.

(b) *Priesthood* (כהנה)
Ex 29^9 40^{15} Num 3^{10} 16^{10} 18$^{1\ 7}$ 25^{13} Josh 18^{7a}.

(c) *Minister, to* (שרת, often followed by 'in a holy
place'), of priests in the sanctuary, or of
Levites attending on priests
Ex 28$^{35\ 43}$ 29^{30} 30^{20} 35^{19} 39$^{1\ 26\ 41}$ Num 1^{50} 3$^{6\ 31}$
4$^{9\ 12\ 14}$ 8^{26} 16^9 18^2. Ct ^{JE}**109**, ^{D}**90**^{c}.

130 (a) *Priests, Aaron's sons the*
Lev 1$^{5\ 8\ 11}$ 2^2 3^2 13^2 Num 3^3 ('Aaron's sons the
anointed priests') 10^8 Josh 21^{19}*.

(b) *The sons of Aaron the priest*
Lev 1^7 Josh 21^4 ^{13}*.

(c) *The priests, the sons of Aaron*
Lev 21^1*.

(d) *Aaron's sons* (without 'priests')
Lev 3$^{5\ 8\ 13}$ 6$^{14\ 18}$ 7$^{10\ 33}$ (8$^{13\ 24}$ 9$^{9\ 12\ 18}$) Josh 21^{10}*.

(e) *The Priest*, as a designation for the order, frequent in **P**^{t} (*ante*, p 152) cp Lev 1^{5aN}, and in
P^h cp **209**.

131 *Prince* (or *ruler*, נשיא). Ct the 'elders' in **JED**,
and 'prince' ^{JE}**191**
Gen 17^{20} 23^6 25^{16} 34^2 Ex 16^{22} 34^{31} 35^{27} Lev 4^{22}
Num 1$^{16\ 44}$ 2 (twelve times) 3 (five times)
4$^{34\ 46}$ 7 (nineteen times) 10^4 13^2 16^2 17$^{2\ 6}$
25$^{14\ 18}$ 27^2 31^{13} 32^2 34$^{18\ 22-28}$ 36^1 Josh 9^{15c}.
$^{18.\ 21}$ 13^{21} 17^4 22$^{14\ 30\ 32}$. Ct Ex 22^{28}*.

132 (a) *Redeem* (גאל). Ct ^{D}**95**
Ex 6^6 Lev 25$^{25.\ 30\ 33\ 48.\ 54}$ 27$^{13\ 15\ 19.\ 27.\ 31\ 33}$.
Cp generally, **J** Gen 48^{16}, Song of Moses Ex 15^{13}*.

(b) *Avenger of blood* (ptcp גאל, or *kinsman*, or
avenger)
Lev 25^{25} Num 5^8 35$^{12\ 19\ 21\ 24\ 25\ 27}$ Josh 20$^{3\ 5\ 9}$.
Cp Deut 19^6 ^{12}*.

133 *Refuge, Cities of* (or *for*, ערי המקלט)
Num 35^6 $^{11-15\ 25-28\ 32}$ Josh 20^2. 21$^{13\ 21\ 27\ 32\ 38}$
1 Chron 6^{57} ^{67}†. Ct Deut 19^3...

134 *Remain over, to* (or *have over*, עדף)
Ex 16$^{18\ 23}$ 26^{12}. Lev 25^{27} Num 3$^{6\ 48}$ †.

135 *Remember my covenant* (of Deity)
Gen 9^{15}. Ex 2^{24} 6^5 Lev 26$^{42\ 45}$.
Cp Ezek 16^{60} Ps 105^8 106^{45} 111^5†.
With other objects Gen 8^1 19^{29} 30^{22a} Lev 26^{42}.
Ct $\mathfrak{H}$ Ex 32^{13} Deut 9^{27}*.

Right, see **56**^{d}.

136 (a) *Rule* (or *have dominion*, רדה)
Gen 1$^{26\ 28}$ Lev 26^{17} cp Num 24^{19}.

(b) *Rule with rigour*
Lev 25$^{43\ 46\ 53}$ (*rigour* only in Ex 1^{13}.)*.

137 (a) *Sabbath*
Ex 16$^{23\ 25.\ 29}$ 20^{11} 31$^{13-16}$ 35^2. Lev 16^{31} 19^3 ^{30}
23$^{3\ 11\ 15\ 32\ 38}$ 24^8 25$^{2\ 4\ 6\ 8}$ 26$^{2\ 34.\ 43}$ Num 15^{32}
28^9. Cp **E** Ex 20$^{8\ 10}$ || Deut 5$^{12\ 14}$..

(b) *Sabbath, to keep* (שבת, of sabbath rest)
Gen 2^2 Ex 16^{30} 31^{17} Lev 23^{32} 25^2 26^{34}.
Cp **J** Ex 34^{21}, **E** Ex 23^{12}*.

(c) (*Sabbath of*) *solemn rest* (שבתון)
Ex 16^{23} 31^{15} 35^2 Lev 16^{31} 23$^{3\ 24\ 32\ 39}$ 25^4.†.

Sacrifice, see **118**.
Sanctify, see **86**.
Sanctuary, see **91**.

138 *Self-same day, the* (or *this very day*, עצם היום הזה)
Gen 7^{13} 17$^{23\ 26}$ Ex 12$^{17\ 41\ 51}$ Lev 23$^{14\ 21\ 28-30}$
Deut 32^{48} Josh 5^{11} 10^{27r} Ezek 2^3 24^2 40^1†.

Separate, to, see *Divide* **53**.

139 *Separation* (or *impurity*, נדה)
Lev 12$^{2\ 5}$ 15$^{19.\ 24-26\ 33}$ 18^{19} 20^{21} Num 19$^{9\ 13\ 20\ 21}$
31^{23}. Cp Ezek 7^{19}. 18^6 22^{10} 36^{17} Zech 13^1
Lam 1^{17} 2 Chron 29^5 Ezr 9^{11}†.

140 (a) *Service* (the work of the Tent of Meeting, the
Dwelling, &c, עבדה)
Ex 27^{19} 30^{16} 35^{21} 36$^{1\ 3}$ 38^{21} 39$^{32\ 40\ 42}$ Num 3^{26}
31^{36} 4$^{4\ 19\ 24\ 26-28\ 32.\ 35\ 39\ 43\ 47\ 49}$ 7$^{5\ 7-9}$ 8^{24}. 18^4
$^{7\ 21\ 31}$. Cp Ex 1^{14} 2^{23b} 6^9 &c.

(b) *Service, to do the* (עבד את ע)
Num 3^7. 4$^{23\ 30\ 47}$ 7^5 8$^{11\ 19\ 22\ 26}$ 16^9 18^6 $^{21\ 23}$
Josh 22^{27}. Cp Ex 13^5*.

(c) *Servile work* (or *work of service*, מלאכת עבדה)
Lev 23^7. $^{21\ 25\ 35}$. Num 28$^{18\ 25}$. 29$^{1\ 12\ 35}$ cp
Ex 35^{24} 36$^{1\ 3\ 5}$*.

141 *Set, to* (i e make to stand, העמיד)
   Gen 47^7 Lev 14^{11} 16^7 ^{10} 27^8 ^{11} Num 3^6 5^{16} ^{18} ^{30}
   8^{13} 27^{19} ^{22}.
   Cp **E** Num 11^{24b}; differently **J** Ex 9^{16*}.

142 *Sign, be for a (token)*. Cp **27**
   Gen 1^{14} 9^{13} 17^{11} Ex 12^{13} 13^9 Num 16^{38} (17^{10}).
   Cp Ex 13^{16} Deut 28^{46} Is 19^{20} 55^{13} Ezek 20^{12} ^{20}†.

143 *Sin, to* (חטא)
   Not in **P** until Lev 4^2 and onwards, frequent in laws, but rare in narrative, e g Num 16^{22}.
   In **JE** common, Gen $20^{6\ 9}$ 39^9 40^1 42^{22} 43^9 44^{32} &c.

   (a) Piel, *to purify* (or *offer for sin*)
      Ex 29^{36} Lev 6^{26} 8^{15} 9^{15} $14^{49\ 52}$ Num 19^{19}.
      Ct **E** Gen 31^{39} 'bare the loss.' Cp Ezek 43^{20} ^{22}. 45^{18} Ps 51^7 2 Chron 29^{24}†.

   (b) Hithpael, *to purify oneself from sin*
      Num 8^{21} $19^{12\ 13\ 20}$ $31^{19.\ 23}$. Ct Job 41^{25}†.

   (c) *Sin, his, which he hath sinned*
      Lev $4^{3\ 23\ 28\ 35}$ $5^{6\ 10\ 13}$ 19^{22}. Cp Ezek 33^{16}†

   Sin offering, see **118**ʲ
   Slay, see *Kill* **100**.

144 *Sojourner* (or *stranger*, תושב)
   Gen 23^4 (cp Ps 39^{12} 1 Chron 29^{15}) Ex 12^{45}
   Lev 22^{10} $25^{6\ 23\ 35\ 40\ 45\ 47}$ Num 35^{15}.
   Cp 1 Kings 17^1 (𝔊 reads *of Tishbeh*)†.

145 (a) *Sojournings, land of* (ארץ מגרים)
      Gen 17^8 28^4 36^7 37^1 Ex 6^4, 'days of' Gen 47^9.
      Cp Ezek 20^{38} Ps 55^{16} 119^{54} Job 18^{19}†.

   (b) *Sojourneth, the stranger that* (הגר הגר) 'among' cp **22**
      Ex 12^{49} Lev 16^{29} $17^{(8)\ 10\ 12}$. 18^{26} $19^{(33)\ 34}$ 20^2
      $(25^{6\ 45})$ Num $(9^{14}$ $15^{14})$ $15^{15.\ 26\ 29}$ 19^{10} Josh 20^9*

   Solemn rest, see *Sabbath* **137**ᶜ.

146 (a) *Soul* (or *person, man, any*, נפש)
      Gen 12^5 17^{14} 36^6 $46^{15\ 18\ 22\ 25-27}$ Ex 1^5 $12^{4\ 15\ 19}$
      16^{16} Lev 2^1—Josh $20^{3\ 9}$ nearly 100 times.
      Cp Deut 10^{22} 24^7 Gen 14^{21}.

   (b) In the sense of *the dead*
      Lev 19^{28} $21^{1\ (11)}$ 22^4 Num 5^2 6^6 $9^{6.\ 10}$*

   South, see *East* **56**ᵇ.

147 *Spices* (סמים) cp **95**ᵇ
   Ex 25^6 $30^{7\ 34}$ 31^{11} $35^{8\ 15\ 28}$ 37^{29} 39^{38} 40^{27}
   Lev 4^7 16^{12} Num 4^{16}. Cp 2 Chron 2^4 13^{11}†.

148 *Sprinkle, to* (זרק)
   Ex $9^{8\ 10}$ $29^{16\ 20}$ Lev 1^5 ^{11} $3^{2\ 8\ 13}$ $7^{2\ 14}$ $8^{19\ 24}$ $9^{12\ 18}$
   17^6 Num 18^{17} $19^{13\ 20}$. Cp **E** Ex $24^{6\ 8}$*.

149 *Sprinkle, to* (הזה)
   Ex 29^{21} Lev $4^{6\ 17}$ 5^9 6^{27} $8^{11\ 30}$ 14^7 $16\ 27\ 51}$ $16^{14,\ 19}$
   Num 8^7 $19^{4\ 18\ 21}$*.

150 *Spy out the land, to* (תור i e to reconnoitre)
   Num $13^{2\ 16.\ 21b\ 25\ 32}$ $14^{6.\ 34\ 36\ 38}$ 15^{39} (metaph).
   Ct Num $10^{\circ 3}$ Deut 1^{33} in the sense to 'seek out' a place*

151 *Standard*
   Num 1^{52} $2^{2.\ 10\ 17.\ 25\ 31\ 34}$ $10^{14\ 18\ 22\ 25}$ cp Cant 2^4†.

152 *Stone, to* (רגם באבן)
   Lev $20^{2\ 27}$ $24^{14\ 16\ 23}$ Num 14^{10} 15^{35}..
   Cp Josh 7^{25} Deut 21^{21} (accidental substitution, Briggs *Higher Criticism*² 73)*. Ct סקל ᴶᴱ**216**.

153 (a) *Stranger* (זר)
      Ex 29^{33} $30^{9\ 33}$ Lev 10^1 $22^{10\ 12}$. Num 1^{51} 3^4 10 38
      16^{40} $18^{4\ 7}$ 26^{61}. Cp Deut 25^5 32^{16}*.

   (b) *Stranger that cometh nigh, the* (הזר הקרב)
      Num 1^{51} $3^{10\ 38}$ 18^7 ('come nigh' technically Num 17^{13} Ezek 40^{46} 45^4)†.

154 *Stranger* (or *alien, foreigner*, בן נכר)
   Gen $17^{12\ 27}$ Ex 12^{43} Lev 22^{25}*.

155 (a) *Substance* (or *goods*, רכוש)
      Gen 12^5 13^{6a} 31^{18b} 36^7 46^6 Num 16^{32b} 35^3
      Cp Gen $14^{11.\ 16\ 21}$ 15^{14} and Chron-Ezr Daniel fifteen times†.

   (b) *Get, to* (cognate vb, רכש)
      Gen 12^5 31^{18} 36^6 46^6†.

156 *Suburbs* (מגרש)
   Lev 25^{34} Num $35^{2-5\ 7}$ Josh 14^4 $21^{2.\ 8\ 11\ 13-39\ 41}$†.

157 (a) *Swarm, to* (or *creep, bring forth abundantly*, שרץ)
      Gen 1^{20} 7^{21} 8^{17} 9^7 Ex 1^7 Lev $11^{29\ 41-43\ 46}$
      Cp Ex 8^3 Ps 105^{30} Ezek 47^9†.

   (b) *Swarm, creeping things* (שרץ)
      Gen 1^{20} 7^{21} Lev 5^2 $11^{10\ 20.\ 23\ 29\ 31\ 41-44}$ 22^5.
      Cp Deut 14^{19}†.

158 *Sweet savour* (ריח ניחוח)
   Ex 29^{18}—Num 29^{13} thirty-eight times
   Cp Gen 8^{21} Ezek 6^{13} 16^{19} $20^{28\ 41}$†.

   Tabernacle, see *Dwelling* **54**ᵇ.

159 *Taken up, to be* (נעלה)ᵃ
   Ex $40^{36\ 37}$ Num $9^{17\ 21\ 22}$ 10^{11} (Num $16^{24\ 27}$)*.

160 (a) *Tenth part* (עשרון)
      Ex 29^{40} Lev $14^{10\ 21}$ $23^{13\ 17}$ 24^5 Num $15^{4\ 6\ 9}$
      28^9—29^{15} (twenty-four times)†.

   (b) *Tenth* (in various connexions, עשירי)
      Gen 8^5 Ex 16^{36} Lev 5^{11} 6^{20} 27^{32} Num 5^{15} 7^{66} 28^5.
      Cp Deut 23^2 *. In Jer Ezek Zech &c.

   (c) *Tenth day of the month, on the* (בעשור לחדש)
      Ex 12^3 Lev 16^{29} 23^{27} 25^9 Num 29^7 Josh 4^{19}.
      Cp 2 Kings 25^1 Jer $52^{4\ 12}$ Ezek 20^1 24^1 40^1†.

161 (a) *Testimony, the* (העדת)
      Ex 16^{34} $25^{16\ 21}$ 27^{21} $30^{6\ 36}$ 40^{20} Lev 16^{13}
      Num $17^{4\ 10}$*.

   (b) *Testimony, Ark of the*, ct ᴰ**19**
      Ex 25^{22} 26^{33} $30^{6\ 26}$ 31^7 39^{35} $40^{3\ 5\ 21}$ Num 4^5 7^{89}
      Josh 4^{16}*.

   (c) *Testimony, Dwelling of the*
      Ex 38^{21} Num $1^{50\ 53}$ 10^{11}*.

ᵃ Usually of the cloud on the Dwelling. Ct J's descriptions of Yahweh's descent ᴶᴱ**19**

P 161 (d) *Testimony, Tables of the*
Ex 31^{18a} 32^{15l} 34^{29x}. Ct Deut 5^{22} 9^{10} 10^1.

(e) *Testimony, Tent of the*
Num 9^{15} 17^7. 18^{2*}. 'Veil' Lev 24^3.

Thanksgiving, see **118**^{h}.

162 *Thou (you) and thy seed (your seed) after thee (you)* &c, or without 'thou and'
Gen 9^9 17^{7-10} 19 35^{12} 48^4 Ex 28^{43} Num 25^{13}.
Cp Deut 1^8 4^{37} 10^{15}. 'With' Gen 46^6 Num 18^{19}.

163 *Thousands of Israel*
Num 1^{16} 10^4 31^5 Josh 22^{14} 21 30. Cp **J** Num 10^{36*}.

164 (a) *Trespass, to commit a* (מעל מעל)
Lev 5^{15} 6^1 26^{40} Num 5^6 12 27 Deut 32^{51} Josh 7^1 22^{16} 20 $31*$.
Cp Ezek 14^{13} 15^8 17^{20} 18^{24} 20^{27} 39^{23} 26, elsewhere Chron-Ezr Prov 16^{10} Dan 9^7†.

(b) *Trespass* (noun, מעל)
Lev 5^{15} 6^1 26^{40} Num 5^6 12 27 31^{16} Josh 7^1 22^{16} 20 22 31.

165 (a) *Tribe* (מטה)
Ex 31^2 ^{6}—Josh 22^{14}, 162 times.
But cp שבט ^{P}**112** Gen 49^{28r} Ex 28^{21} 39^{14} Num 4^{18} 18^2 32^{33} 36^3 Josh 4^{8b} 13^{29} 33 21^{16l} 22^{9-11} 13 15 21.

(b) *Tribe of their fathers*
Num 1^{16} 47 13^2 26^{55} 33^{54} 36^4 .*.

166 *Uncircumcised* (ערל)
Gen 17^{14} Ex 6^{12} 30 12^{48} Lev 19^{23} 26^{41}, **R**^{d} Josh 5^{7*}.
Cp Gen 34^{14} ℌ.

167 (a) *Unclean, to be* (with derivatives, *to pronounce unclean, defile*, &c, טמא)
Gen 34^{13} 27 Lev 5^3—Num 35^{34}, 107 times.
Cp Deut 21^{23} 24^4 Ezek (thirty). In **JE** only Gen 34^5.

(b) *Unclean*, adj (טמא)
Lev 5^2—Josh 22^{19} sixty times.
Cp Deut 12^{15} 22 14^7. 10 19 15^{22} 26^{14*}.

(c) *Uncleanness* (טמאה)
Lev 5^3—Num 19^{13} twenty times*.

(d) *So that he is unclean thereby* (לטמאה־בה)
Lev 15^{32} 18^{20} 23 19^{31} 22^8 cp Ezek 22^3 44^{25}†.

168 *Unwittingly* (or *an error*, שגגה usually with ב)
Lev 4^2 22 27 5^{15} 18 22^{14} Num 15^{24-29} 35^{11} 15 Josh 20^3 9. Cp Eccles 5^5 10^{5}†.

169 (a) *Upward* (or *from above*, מלמעלה)
Gen 6^{16} 7^{20} Ex 25^{21} 26^{14} 36^{19} 39^{31} 40^{19}. Num 4^6 25 Josh 3^{13r} 16. This combination elsewhere only in 1 Kings 7^{11} 25 8^7 Jer 31^{37} Ezek 1^{11} 22 26 10^{19} 11^{22} 37^8 2 Chron 4^4 5^8†.
Ct ממעל Gen 22^9 Ex 20^4 Deut 4^{39} 5^8 Josh 2^{11}.

(b) *Upward, (twenty) years old and* (ומעלה)
Ex 30^{14} 38^{26} Lev 27^7 Num 1^3 $18-45$ $3-4$ (fourteen times) 8^{24} 14^{29} 26^2 4 62 32^{11*}.

(c) *Beneath* (מלמטה)
Ex 26^{24} 27^5 28^{27} 36^{29} 38^4 39^{20*}.
Cp Deut 28^{13} 43 Ezek 1^{27} 8^2 *al.* Ct Gen 49^{25} ℌ.

170 *Urim and Thummim*
Ex 28^{30} Lev 8^8 Num 27^{21}. Ct Deut 33^{8*}.

171 *Veil* (פרכת)
Ex 26^{31} 33 35 27^{21} 30^6 35^{12} 36^{35} 38^{27} 39^{34} 40^3 21. 26 Lev 4^6 17 16^2 12 15 21^{23} 24^3 Num 4^5 18^7.
Cp 2 Chron 3^{14}†.

172 *Vow, to make a special vow* (פלא נדר Pi and Hiph)
Lev 22^{21} 27^2 Num 6^2 15^3 8†.

173 *Wash clothes, to* (כבם)
Lev 11^{25} 28 40 13^6 34 $14^{8.47}$ 15^{5-8} 10 13 21 27 16^{26} 28 17^{15} Num 8^7 21 19^7. 10 19 21 31^{24}.
Cp Lev 6^{27} 13^{54-56} 58 15^{17} 17^{16}.
Ct **J** Gen 49^{11}; cp **E** Ex 19^{10} $14*$.

174 (a) *Wash, to, with water* (רחץ במים)
Ex 29^4 30^{20} 40^{12} Lev 1^9 13 8^6 21 14^8. 15^5... (twelve) 16^4 24 26 28 17^{15} 22^6 Num 19^7. 19.
Cp Deut 23^{11*}.

(b) *Wash, to* (alone)
Ex 29^{17} 30^{18} 19 21 40^{30-32} Lev 9^{14} 17^{16}.
Cp **J** Gen 18^4 19^2 24^{32} 43^{24} 31, **E** Ex 2^5, **D** Deut 21^{6*}.

175 *Wave, to* (הניף as a ritual term)
Ex 29^{24}—Num 8^{21} twenty-two times.
Ct Ex 20^{25} ('lift up') Deut 23^{25} 27^5 Josh 8^{31*}.

Wave offering, see **118**^{l}.

176 *With thee (him, thou and thy seed,* &c)
Gen 6^{18} 7^{7r} 18 8^{16} 18 9^8 28^4 46^6 7 Ex 28^1 41 29^{21} Lev 8^2 30 10^9 14 25^{41} 51 Num 18^1. 7 11 $19*$.

177 (a) *Work, to do* (עשה מלאכה)
Gen 2^2 Ex 12^{16} 31^{14} 15 35^2 29 35 36^{1-8} 39^{43} Lev 11^{32} 16^{29} 23^3 28 30. Num 4^3 29^7.
Ct Gen 39^{11} Ex 20^9. ‖ Deut 5^{13}. 16^{8*}.

(b) *Work* (or *service*, or *workmanship*, מלאכה)
Ex 31^8 5 35^{21} 24 31 33 38^{24} 40^{33} Lev 7^{24} 13^{48} 51.
Ct **J** Gen 33^{14} 'cattle,' **E** Ex 22^8 11 'goods'*.

Work of labour, see *Servile work* **140**^{b}.

178 (a) *Wrath* (in various phrases with the verb *to be*, היה קצף)
Num 1^{53} 18^5 Josh 9^{20} 22^{20} cp Num 16^{46}.
Ct 'in wrath' Deut 29^{28*}.

(b) *Wroth, to be* (קצף) ct ^{JE}**233**
Ex 16^{20} Lev 10^6 16 Num 16^{22} 31^{14} Josh 22^{18}.
Cp **E** Gen 40^2 41^{10}, **D** Deut 1^{34} 9^{19}, 9^7. 22 (Hiph)*.

179 (a) *I am Yahweh* (*I*, see **94**, אני יהוה) cp **203**
Ex 6^2 6 8 29 12^{12} Num 3^{13} 41 45.
With *your* (*their*) *God* Ex 29^{46} Lev 11^{44a}.

(b) *Know that I am Yahweh*
Ex 7^5 14^4 18, 'your God' Ex $16^{(6)}$ 12, 'which sanctify you' Ex 31^{13}; more than sixty times in Ezek. Cp **J** Ex 7^{17} 8^{22} 10^2, 1 Kings 20^{28}.

THE PRIESTLY LAW AND HISTORY BOOK, P   219

(c) *(Know that) I am Yahweh (your God)* or *(Who brought you out ... Egypt)*
Ex 6^7 29^{46} Lev 11^{45}.
Cp Deut 29^6.

180 (a) *Hand of Moses, command by the* (צוה ביד)
Ex 35^{29} Lev 8^{36} Num 4^{49} 15^{23} 36^{13} Josh 14^2 $21^{2.8}$*.

(b) *Hand of Moses, according to the commandment of Yahweh by the* (על פי יהוה ביד)
Num $4^{37.45}$ 9^{23} 10^{13} Josh 22^9*.

(c) *Hand of Moses, spake by the* (דבר יהוה ביד משה)
Ex 9^{35} Lev 10^{11} Num 16^{40} 27^{23} Josh 20^2.
Cp Lev 26^{46}*.

(d) *Hand of ..., by the*
Ex 38^{21} Num $4^{28.33}$ 7^8 33^1.

181 *The days of ... were* (summing up the lives of the patriarchs)
Gen $5^{4.8.11.14.17.20.23.27.31}$ 9^{29} 11^{32} 35^{28} 47^{28}*.

182 *The years of the life of ..* (used as a formula of age from Abraham to Amram)
Gen 23^1 25^7 17 47^8. 28 Ex $6^{16.18.20}$*.

183 (a) *Month and day* (mode of dating by the number of) cp *the tenth day*, **160**c
Gen 7^{11} $8^{4.13}$. Ex $12^{2.3.6.18}$ 16^1 19^1 $40^{2.17}$ Lev 16^{29} $23^{5.24.27.32.34.39.41}$ 25^9 Num 1^1 18 $9^{1.3.5.11}$ 10^{11} 20^1 28^{16}. $29^{1.7.12}$ $33^{3.38}$ Deut 1^3 Josh 4^{19} 5^{10}*.

(b) *Dates from the Exodus* (לצאת)
Ex 16^1 19^1 Num 1^1 9^1 33^{38} 1 Kings 6^1†.

184 *One ... another* (איש ... אחיו)
Gen 9^5 13^{11b} Ex 25^{20} 26^3 37^9 Lev 7^{10} $25^{14.46}$ 26^{37}; ct JE**188**, cp JE**112**.

185 (a) *Spake ... saying, and God* (Yahweh, Abraham &c) *spake unto* (occasionally, *with*) *Noah* (Moses &c) *saying* (וידבר ... לאמר)
Gen 8^{15} 17^3 $23^{3.8.13}$ $34^{8.20}$ Ex 6^{10}—Num 35^9 Deut 32^{48} Josh 20^1. 21^2 22^{15} 107 times.
Cp **JE** Gen 27^6 $39^{17.19}$ 42^{14} 50^4 Num 24^{12} Josh 9^{22} 17^{14}, **D** Deut 1^6 2^{17} 13^2 20^5 27^9.

(b) *Speak unto the children of Israel* (*Pharaoh*, &c) *saying* (דבר ... לאמר, or with slightly varying order, ואל ... לאמר, תדבר occasionally omitted)
Ex $6^{11.29}$—Josh 20^2 twenty-four times.

(c) *Speak and say* (דבר ואמרת)
Lev 1^2 15^2 17^2 18^2 19^2 (21^1 אמר וא׳) 22^{18} $23^{2.10}$ 25^2 27^2 Num 5^{12} 6^2 8^2 15^2 18 38 18^{26} 33^{51} 35^{10}*.

(d) *Said (spake) ... saying* (ויאמר ... לאמר)
Gen 9^8 34^4 47^5 Ex 7^8 12^1 31^{12} 35^4 36^5 Num 7^4 14^7 15^{37} 17^{12} 20^3 23 26^1 27^1 31^{25} 32^2 25 Josh 4^{15} 22^{24}.
JE Gen 21^{22} 27^{6ab} 31^{29} 39^{14} $42^{22.37}$ 43^3 Ex 5^{10} 15^1 32^{12} Num 14^{15} Josh 1^1 3^6 4^1 7^2 9^{11} 17^{17}, **D** Deut 1^9 2^2 9^4 13 Josh 1^{12} 4^{21} 22^8.

(e) *Speak with* (דבר את)
Gen $17^{3.22.23}$ 23^8 $34^{6.8}$ $35^{13.15}$ Ex 25^{22} 31^{18} $34^{29.32-35}$ Num 3^1 7^{89} Josh $22^{15.21}$.
Cp **J** Josh 17^{14}, **E** Gen 35^{14} 41^9 $42^{7.30}$ 45^{15}, Deut 5^{21}*.

Ct *speak with* (דבר עם) **JE** Gen $31^{24.29}$ Ex 19^9 20^{19ab} 33^9 Num 11^{17} 22^{19} Josh 24^{27}, **D** Deut 5^4 9^{10}, never in P.

186 *The border shall turn* (or *turned* נסב)
Num 34^4. Josh $15^{3.10}$ 16^6 18^{14} 19^{14} cp Jer 31^{39}†.

187 *The goings out shall be* (or *were*)
Num $34^{4.8.12}$ Josh $15^{4.7.11}$ 16^8 17^9 18, $18^{12.14.19}$ $19^{14.22.29.33}$. Cp **J** Josh 16^3*.

188 (a) *These are the ...* (in titles, summaries, &c) *burden* Num 4^{15}: *cities* Josh 20^9: *commandments* Lev 27^{34}: *commandments and judgements* Num 36^{13} (cp Ex 21^1 Deut 4^{45} 12^1 29^1): *days* Gen 25^7 cp 17^{9a}: *dukes* $36^{15-19.21.29.43}$: *families* cp **65** Gen 10^{32} Ex $6^{14.19.24}$ Num $3^{20.26f.}$.. (twelve times): *garments* Ex 28^4: *generations* Gen 2^{4a} cp **77**. *heads of their fathers' houses* Ex $6^{14.25}$ cp **84**. *inheritances* Josh 13^{22} 14^1 19^{51}: *journeys* Num 10^{28} 33^1: *kings* Gen 36^{31} (cp Josh $12^{1.7}$): *names* Gen $25^{13.16}$ $36^{10.40}$ 46^8 Ex 1^1 6^{16} Num 1^5 3^2. 18 $13^{4.16}$ 27^1 $34^{17.19}$ Josh 17^3: *the princes of the tribes* Num 7^2: *set feasts* Lev $23^{4.37}$: *sons of* Gen 10^{20} (cp 5) 31 25^{16} 35^{26} $36^{5.12-14.16-20.23-28}$ $46^{15.18.22.25}$ Num 3^{17} $26^{35-37.41}$ Josh 17^2: *statutes (and judgements and laws)* Lev 26^{46} Num 30^{16}: *the sum of* Ex 38^{21}: *waters* Num 27^{14}: *words* Ex 35^1 Deut 1^1 (cp Ex 19^6): *years* Gen 25^{17} cp **181**: *these are they that were (are) called* Num 1^{16}; *numbered* Num 1^{44} 2^{32} $4^{37.41.45}$ $26^{51.57.63}$: *over them that were numbered* Num 7^2: *that spake* Ex 6^{27}: *unclean* Lev 11^{31}: *they whom Yahweh commanded* Num 34^{29}.

(b) *This is (was, shall be) the ...* in similar formulae *anointing portion* Lev 7^{35}: *book* Gen 5^1: *border* Num $34^{6.9}$ Josh $15^{4.12}$ 18^{19}: *burnt offering* Num 28^{14}: *charge* Num 4^{31}: *my covenant* Gen 17^{10}: *dedication-gift* Num $7^{84.88}$: *Esau* Gen 36^{43}: *how thou shalt &c* Gen 6^{15}: *inheritance* Josh $13^{23.28}$ 15^{20} 16^8 $18^{20.28}$ $19^{8.16.23.31.39.48}$: *land* Num $34^{2.12}$.: *law* Lev $6^{9.11.25}$ $7^{1.11.37}$ 11^{46} 12^7 13^{59} $14^{2.32.54.57}$ 15^{32} Num 5^{29} $6^{13.21}$ 19^{14}: *living things* § Lev 11^2: *offering* Ex 25^3 Lev 6^{20} Num 7^{17-83} (twelve times): *offering made by fire* Num 28^3: *ordinance* Ex 12^{43} cp Lev 16^{34} 17^7: *quarter* Josh 18^{14}: *service* Num $4^{4.24.28.33}$: *statute of the law* Num 19^2 31^{21}: *suburbs* Num 35^5: *that which &c* Num 8^{24} 18^{11}: *thing which thou shalt do* Ex 29^1 cp 38: *thing which Yahweh hath commanded* Ex $16^{16.32}$ 35^4 Lev 8^5 9^6 17^2 Num 30^2 36^6: *token* Gen $9^{12.17}$: *unclean* Lev 11^{29}. *his uncleanness* Lev 15^3: *work of the candlestick* Num 8^4. Cp **E** Deut 33^1, **D** Deut 4^{44} 6^1 14^4 12 15^2 18^3 19^4 Josh 5^4 13^2.

WORDS AND PHRASES

P 188 (c) *This is (these are) . . . who (which) . . .* הוא וג׳
Gen 36^{24} Ex 6^{26}. 12^{42} $16^{15\ 23}$ Lev 10^3 Num 26^9.

(d) Note the peculiar Hebrew phrase אלה הם Gen 25^{16} Lev 23^2 Num $3^{20.\ 27\ 33}$ 1 Chron 1^{31} 8^6 12^{15} (also, differently, 1 Sam 4^8)†, cp Driver *Hebrew Tenses* § 201 3.

189 (a) [*Thus did Noah (Moses) &c . . .*] *so did he*
Gen 6^{22} Ex 7^6 $12^{28\ 50}$ (25^9) (27^8) $39^{32\ 43}$ 40^{16}
Lev 4^{20} Num 1^{54} 2^{34} 5^4 6^{21} $8^{20\ 22}$ 9^5 17^{11} 36^{10}.

(b) *And (Moses) did (so) as Yahweh commanded him*
Ex $7^{10\ 20}$ Lev 8^4 16^{34b} 24^{23} Num 20^{27} 27^{22} 31^{31}
Deut 34^9 cp Josh 14^5.

(c) *As Yahweh commanded Moses*
Ex (16^{34}) 39^1 $^{5\ 7\ 21\ 26\ 29\ 31}$ $40^{19\ 21\ 23\ 25\ 27\ 29\ 32}$
Lev 8^9 $^{13\ 17\ 21\ 29}$ 9^{10} Num 1^{19} 2^{33} 3^{51} 8^3 (9^5)
15^{36} 26^4 27^{11} 31^7 $^{41\ 47}$ 36^{10}. Cp Josh 11^{20}.
Cp similar formulae, '(according to) all that Yahweh commanded (him)' Ex 35^{10} 36^1 &c, 'as Yahweh commanded him' Num 3^{42} &c.

190 (a) *When (if) any one shall sin, vow &c* (נפש כי)
Lev 2^1 4^2 ^{27} 5^1 $^{(2)\ 4\ 15\ 17}$ 6^2 7^{21} $(27\ 17^{15}\ 22^6)$
Num 15^{27*}.

(b) *When any man* (אדם כי)
Lev 1^2 13^2 Num 19^{14*}.

(c) *When any man* (איש כי)
Lev $13^{29\ 38\ 40}$ $15^{16\ 19}$ 19^{20} 20^{27} $22^{14\ 21}$ $24^{17\ 19}$
$25^{26\ 29}$ 27^2 ^{14} Num 5^6 6^2 27^8 30^{2*}.

(d) *When any man* (איש איש כי)
Lev 15^2 24^{15} Num 5^{12} 9^{10}; cp איש . . . אשר Lev 17^3 $^{8\ 10\ 13}$ 20^2 ^{9} 22^{18}, otherwise איש איש
Ex 36^4 Lev 18^6 19^3 22^4 Num 1^4 $4^{-9\ 49*}$.
Cp Ezek 14^4 ^{7}.

191 *When ye be come to the land* (כי תבאו)
Ex 12^{25} Lev 14^{34} 19^{23} 23^{10} 25^2 Num 15^2 $(18)*$
cp Num 33^{51} 34^2.

P^h.

192 *Abomination*
Lev $18^{22\ 26.\ 29}$. 20^{13} cp ^p9 . Ezek (forty-three).

193 *Bear iniquity (or sin)* cp **23**
Lev 17^{16} 19^8 $20^{17\ 19}$. $22^{9\ 16}$ 24^{15} Ezek 14^{10} $44^{10\ 12}$.

194 *Blemish* (מום)
Lev 21^{17-23} $22^{20.\ 25}$ 24^{19}. Num 19^2 Deut 15^{21}
17^1 $(32^5)*$.

195 *Blood shall be upon him, his* (דמיו בו)
Lev 20^9 $^{11-16\ 16\ 27}$ cp Ezek 18^{13} $33^{4.\ }$†.

196 *Bread of God*
Lev 21^6 $^{8\ 17\ 21}$. 22^{25} cp Lev $3^{11\ 16}$ Num 28^2
cp 24 Ezek 44^7†.

197 (a) *Cut off, I will* (Hiph הכרית) cp **50**
Lev 17^{10} 20^3 ^{5}.

(b) *Cut off, be* (Niph נכרת)
Lev 17^4 $^{9\ 14}$ 18^{29} 20^{17}..

198 *Dead* (נפש = soul, person, &c) cp **146**
Lev 19^{28} 21^1 22^4 Num 5^2 cp $9^{6.\ 10}$, with מת Lev 21^{11} Num 6^{6*}

199 *Do . . and keep (observe) . . . (keep . . . and do . . . observe)* ct ^p82^b
Lev 18^4. ^{26} 19^{37} 20^8 ^{22} 22^{31}. 25^{18} 26^3.
Cp 'statutes and judgements' ^p**104**, keep my statutes Lev 18^4 ^{26} $19^{19\ 37}$.

200 (a) *Fear thy God, thou shalt* (ויראת מאלהיך) elsewhere in **D** with acc, or מפני Ex 9^{30})
Lev $19^{14\ 32}$ $25^{17\ 36\ 43*}$.

(b) *Fear (reverence) my sanctuary* (מקדשי תיראו)
Lev 19^{30} 26^{2}†.

201 *Heart* (לבב for לב) cp ^p**59**
Lev 19^{17} $26^{36\ 41}$ Num 15^{39}.

202 (a) *Holy, be* (of Israel, היה קדוש)
Lev 11^{44}. 19^2 20^7 ^{26} 21^6 Num 15^{40}† cp Lev 21^8 Num 6^5.

(b) *Sanctify yourselves* (התקדש) cp **86**^e
Lev 11^{44}. 20^7.
Cp **J** Ex 19^{22} Num 11^{18} Josh 3^5 7^{13*}.

203 (a) *I am Yahweh* (אני יהוה) cp **179**
Lev $18^{5.\ 21}$ $19^{12\ 14\ 16\ 18\ 28\ 30\ 32\ 37}$ 21^{12} $22^{2.\ 8\ 30.\ 33}$
$26^{2\ 45}$.

(b) *I am Yahweh your (their) God,* אני יהוה אלהיכם (occasionally followed by *which brought you out of the land of Egypt*)
Lev 18^2 $^{4\ 30}$ $19^{3.\ 10\ 25\ 31\ 34\ 36}$ 20^7 $^{(24)}$ 22^{32}. $23^{22\ 43}$
24^{22} $25^{17\ 38\ 55b}$ 26^1 $^{13\ 44}$ Num 10^{10} 15^{41ab}.
Cp Ex 29^{46} Lev 11^{44a*}.

(c) *I Yahweh (your God) am holy* (קדוש אני יהוה אלהיכם)
Lev 19^2 20^{26} 21^{8*}.

(d) *I (am) Yahweh which sanctify (hallow) you* (אני יהוה מקדשכם)
Lev 20^8 21^8 $^{15\ 23}$ 22^9 $^{16\ 32}$ Ex 31^{13}.
Cp Ezek 20^{12} 37^{28}†.

204 *Kin* (שאר) cp **101**
Lev $18^{12.\ 17}$ 20^{19} 21^2, שאר בשרו Lev 18^6.

205 *Lie with, to* (Qal and Hiph רבע הרביע)
Lev 18^{23} 19^{19} 20^{16}†.

206 *Neighbour* (עמית)
Lev 18^{20} $19^{11\ 15\ 17}$ 24^{19} $25^{14ab\ 15\ 17}$ cp Lev 6^{2ab} Zech 13^7†.

207 *Old* (ישן)
Lev 25^{22ab} 26^{10ab}. נושן 26^{10} cp 13^{11} Deut 4^{25*}.

208 *Peoples, among (from) thy (his)*, cp **122**
Lev 17^9 19^8 ^{16} 21^1 $^{4\ 14}$. 23^{29}.

209 *Priest, the (a)*, as a designation for the order, in contrast to 'the Sons of Aaron' **130**
Lev 17^5 19^{22n} 21^9 22^{10-14} $23^{10.\ 20}$. Cp **130**^c.

210 *Profane, to* (חלל) (a) *the name of thy God*
Lev 18^{21} 19^{12} 21^{6*}.

(b) *my holy name*
Lev 20^3 22^2 ^{32*}.
With ^{ab} cp Am 2^7 Ezek 20^9 $^{14\ 22\ 39}$ 36^{20-23} 39^7.

THE PRIESTLY LAW AND HISTORY BOOK, P

(c) *The holy thing, sanctuary*
Lev 19^8 $21^{12\ 23}$ 22^{15} cp Num 18^{32}.
Cp Ezek 7^{24} 22^{26} 23^{39} 24^{21} 25^3 28^{18} 44^{7*}.

(d) *Other objects*
Lev 19^{29} $21^{9\ 15}$ 22^9 (cp $21^{4\ 9}$) Ex 31^{14}
Ct Gen 49^4 Ex 20^{25} Deut 20^6 28^{30} P$_1^*$.

211 *Sabbaths, my, &c*
Lev $19^{3\ 30}$ 23^{38} $26^{2\ 34\ 43}$ Ex 31^{13}.
Cp Isa 56^4 Ezek $20^{12.\ 16\ 20.\ 24}$ 22^8 26 23^{38} 44^{24}†.

Sacrifice, to (זבח) cp ^{JE}**202**.

212 *Set the face against, to* (of Yahweh, נתן פנים ב ')
Lev 17^{10} $20^{3\ 6}$ (cp ^{5} שם) 26^{17}
Cp Ezek 14^8 15^7, with שם Jer 21^{10} 44^{11}†.

213 *Statutes and judgements* (or *judgements and statutes*) cp ^{D}**104**
Lev 18^4 ^{26} 19^{37} 20^{22} 25^{18} $26^{15\ 43}$ cp ^{46}.
Cp Ezek 5^6. $11^{12\ 20}$ $20^{11\ 13\ 16\ 18\ 21\ 24}$. 37^{24}.
Ct Jer 1^{16} 4^{12} (12^1 39^5 52^9).

214 *Turn, to* (idols &c, *have respect to,* פנה)
Lev $19^{4\ 31}$ 20^6 26^9.
Cp Deut $31^{18\ 20}$ 9^{27} Num 16^{15} Ezek 36^9.

215 *Uncover the nakedness, to* (לגלות ערוה)
Lev 18^{6-19} 20^{11-21}, cp Ex 20^{26} Ezek 16^{36} 22^{10} $23^{10\ 18\ 29}$†.
Ct Deut 22^{30} 27^{20} Hos 2^{10}.

216 *Vomit, to* (of the land vomiting its inhabitants)
Lev 18^{25} 28^{ab} 20^{22}†.

217 *Walk in the statutes of, to* (הלך בחקת) ct ^{D}**115**^{a}
Lev 18^3. 20^{23} 26^3.
Cp Jer $44^{10\ 23}$ Ezek 5^7 $11^{12\ 20}$ 18^9 ^{17} $20^{13\ 16\ 18\ 21}$ 33^{15} 36^{27} 1 Kings 3^3 6^{12} 8^{61} 2 Kings 17^8 ^{19}†

218 *What man soever* (with negative, *none,* איש)
cp **185**
Lev $17^{3\ 8\ 10\ 13}$ 18^6 $20^{2\ 9}$ $22^{4\ 18}$ 24^{15}.

219 *Whoring, to go a* (זנה after other gods, &c)
Lev 17^7 cp 19^{29} 20^5. Num 15^{39}
Cp J Ex 34^{15}, R^{d} Deut 31^{16*}.

220 *Wickedness* (זמה)
Lev 18^{17} 19^{29} 20^{14*} Hos 6^9 Ezek (fourteen) &c.

P^{h}

APPENDIX B

LAWS AND INSTITUTIONS

Introductory Note

The Hexateuch presents itself as a continuous work, but has been found on investigation to be highly composite. A large part of its contents is concerned with the Laws and Institutions of Israel; and this legislative material on the one hand furnishes assistance in the general task of analyzing the whole, and on the other contributes a number of problems peculiar to itself. This Appendix is intended both to confirm and illustrate the conclusions already reached in the General Introduction, and to throw fresh light on the internal relations of the Laws in the Hexateuchal Codes.

The argumentative process, by which such an analysis of the mass of legislation has been effected as to furnish a basis for the construction of the following Tables, may be made clear in a series of propositions.

(1) The laws and narratives differ widely in their representations of important national institutions, especially those connected with worship [a].

(2) Several collections or large groups of laws can be identified, by their peculiarities of style or expression, or by references to them in the context, as forming distinct codes [b].

(3) The differences of representation just mentioned (1) are not found to be internal to the several codes, but mark off one or more from the others as wholes [c].

(4) The codes are further distinguished by the proportion in which they deal with the various departments of the national life [d].

(5) The codes were in almost every case parts of larger documents before being incorporated into the growing Hexateuch, and were already more or less modified from their original form [e].

(6) For such a series of comparative summaries as is contained in ^{L}1–12 it is both safe and sufficient to follow the lines implied by the symbols J E D P^h P^t P^g P^s [e].

(7) In treating the codes separately, as in ^{L}13, there is sufficient internal evidence available to support much additional discrimination [f].

The object of the Tables may be further explained by an illustration. A geologist studying a country will not only need a good map to indicate the geographical features, but will require that map to be coloured to show the stratification. And conversely a geological map may serve as a useful guide to the geography even if the geological details are not all correct. Similarly, the critical student of so highly composite a work as the Hexateuch not only needs some brief conspectus or map of the whole as his guide, but requires that this shall show the literary stratification. And conversely such an analytical abstract or table of contents will be of service to the general student even where all the analytical details are not equally accurate. The Analysis and Synopsis in Appendix C may be compared to a small scale map of the stratification of the whole country; the Conspectus in ^{L}13 is like a series of large scale maps of particular districts; and the first eleven Tables serve as cross-sections showing the relative thickness and elevation of the several strata along different lines.

The arrangement of material follows as closely as may be the scheme of the text pages, and will be readily understood. Occasionally a supplemented passage like Lev 16 or 25 occurs under the head of P^s as well as P^g or P^h, and sometimes an assignment of a passage in the Tables follows the footnote rather than the text, as where a basis of P^t is recognized in a law printed in the text as P^s.

Tables 1 to 11 are the result of repeated gleanings, and are meant to be so far exhaustive that no ordinance or important narrative allusion has been omitted. Many ordinances, covering more than one subject, are referred to in different connexions. But it has not been possible to exhaust the minor allusions. No attempt has been made to preserve uniformity of scale in the various tables, and a large licence of expanded treatment has been freely taken wherever the analytical problems or the convenience of the student seemed to demand it.

An Explanatory Note on p 254 deals with ^{L}12–16.

[a] See references under ^{L}14a.   [b] See ^{L}14def, and cp the legal terms in the Word-lists.
[c] That is to say, the codes are first separated on grounds of *form*, and then their *contents* are found to be marked by the differences mentioned. The statement needs some qualification in respect to the separation of P^g from P^h and P^s, for the substantial differences discovered in passages distinguished by their form are used in some other places to effect the analysis where the formal grounds are inadequate for a conclusion.
[d] See ^{L}16a^N below.
[e] It may be convenient to give here the references to the pages of the General Introduction which treat specially of the codes :—J pp 101 109, E p 114, D pp 72–78 91–96, P^h pp 145· ·, P^t p 152, P^g pp 126–140, P^s pp 155· ·.
[f] The evidence for this is usually given in the notes to the Text in vol ii, but occasionally in minor points a further division is made in the Table on grounds easily perceptible.

LAWS AND INSTITUTIONS

1. The Family

	J	D	E	P^{ht}	P^g	P^s	L 1i
a Reverence for parents, cp **b**		$^E a$ Ex $20^{12\,N}$ b 22^{23} — Honour ^{a} parents, ^{b} judges and rulers. $^D c$ 5^{16}—Honour parents.		$^{Ph} d$ Lev 19^{1-3a} e ^{32}—^{d} Fear parents, ^{e} honour the aged.			
b Undutifulness		$^E a$ Ex 21^{15} b ^{17}—Death for ^{a} smiting, ^{b} cursing parents $^D c$ 21^{18-21} d 27^{16}—^{c} Stoning for rebellious son ; ^{d} curse on irreverence to parents.		$^{Ph} e$ 20^9—Death for cursing parents.			
c Teaching of children		$^D a$ 6^{6-9} b $^{20-25}$ c 11^{19-21} d 21^{18-21} e Ex 13^8 f $^{14\,N}$—Duty of teaching to children ^{abc} 'the statutes &c,' and about ^{e} mazzoth and ^{f} consecration of firstborn ; ^{d} teaching before punitive justice.					
d Primogeniture		$^D a$ 21^{15-17} b 25^6—^{a} Double portion for firstborn ; ^{b} Levirate law.					
e Restrictions on marriage	$^J a$ Gen 19^{30} b Num $25^{1b\cdot}$ —^{a} Incest of Lot's daughters not reprobated ; ^{b} judgement for unions with Moabitish women (cp Gen 24^3.). $^E c$ Gen 20^{12} d Num 12^1 —^{c} Marriage with a half-sister, and ^{d} with a Cushite not reprobated. $^D e$ 7^3 f 22^{30} g 27^{20} h ^{22}—Marriage f with father's wife, or ^{e} with a Canaanite, forbidden ; —^{g} with father's wife, or ^{h} with half-sister or mother-in-law cursed.		$^{Ph} i$ 18^{6-18} j 20^{11} k ^{14} l ^{17} m $^{19-21}$ n $21^{7\,13}$.—^{i} Marriage of near kin forbidden under seventeen heads ; ^{jklm} ten of these repeated, but in different order with penalties attached and interspersed with other matter ; ^{n} priests only to marry women of good character, the high priest only a virgin. $^{Pg} o$ Gen 28^{1-8} p Num 25^{6-9}—^{o} Jacob forbidden to marry a Canaanite ; ^{p} plague for unions with Midianitish women.			
f Levirate law		$^J a$ Gen 38^{1-11}—The custom illustrated by the story of Judah and his family. $^D b$ 25^{5-10}—The law laid down that a childless widow shall be taken to wife by her husband's brother, with provision for his refusal.					
g Female captives		$^D a$ 21^{10-14}—Rights of female captive, as wife or concubine.		$^{Ps} b$ Num 31^{15-18}—Virgins to be kept alive if taken in war.			
h Divorce		$^J a$ Gen 2^{18-25}—The ideal of marriage lifelong monogamy. $^E b$ Ex 21^{7-11}—A slave wife, when divorced, is free $^D c$ 24^{1-4}—Divorce unrestricted, effected by mere written notice from husband : irrevocable if another union has intervened.					
i Adultery		$^J a$ Gen 12^{14-19} b 26^{8-11} c 39^{7-12} — Condemned in the stories of ^{a} Abram and Pharaoh, ^{b} Isaac and Abimelech, ^{c} Joseph and Potiphar. $^E d$ Gen 20^{3-18} e Ex 20^{14} — Condemned ^{e} directly, ^{d} by the story of Abraham and Abimelech. $^D f$ 5^{18} g 22^{22-27}—^{f} condemned, ^{g} punishable by death of both, even if she be only betrothed, unless in that case she be overcome by force, cp jd **k**.		$^{Ph} h$ 18^{20} i 20^{10}—^{h} Condemned as defilement, ^{i} punishable by death of both. $^{Pt} j$ Num $5^{11-31\,N}$—A composite law dealing with cases of marital jealousy, one element providing a genuine ordeal.			

1e Without laying too much stress on the argument from silence, it seems natural to see in the increasing stringency of D and still more of P^h an evidence of a progressive strengthening of old custom into detailed law. No doubt the prohibitions in P^h had been frequently issued as oral *toroth* before being codified, but the crystallization in the code is the significant fact

h The existence of a custom of divorce is implied by E**b**, but in D custom has already hardened into law.

1 The following steps can be traced, ^{JE} bare prohibition, ^{D} provision for variety of cases, ^{Ph} reference to the principle of holiness, and ^{Pt} extension to jealousy and introduction of the sacrificial element.

224   *LAWS AND INSTITUTIONS*

	J	D	E	P^{ht}	P^g	P^s
^{L}**1** j Seduction	$^J a$ Gen 34^2	^{J}—Seduction of Dinah a *casus belli*. $^E b$ Ex 22^{16}—Seducer to pay dowry, and to marry the girl unless the father refuse $^D c 22^{28}$—Seducer must pay 50 shekels, and marry the girl without right of divorce.		$^{Ph} d$ Lev 19^{20}—Seducer of betrothed slave-girl punishable, but not with death, cp $1g$ $^{Ps} e$ Lev 19^{21}—A guilt offering prescribed in the last case		
k Slander		$^D 22^{13-21}$—A man slandering his newly-married wife fined 100 shekels, but she, if guilty before marriage, to be stoned.				
l Unnatural lusts		$^J a$ Gen 19^5—Conduct of the Sodomites reprobated $^E b$ Ex 22^{19}—Death for lying with a beast. $^D c 27^{21}$—Curse on lying with a beast, cp mb		$^{Ph} d 18^{19}$ $e\ 22$ $f 20^{13}$ $g\ 15$ $h\ 18$—Condemnation of ^{dh} lying with a separated woman, ^{ef} with mankind, or ^{ej} with a beast, ^{hfg} under pain of death		
m Prostitution		$^J a$ Gen 38^{14-26}—An accepted institution, but disgraceful if imitated by private persons. $^D b 23^{17}$—Harlots and sodomites forbidden, and their wages abominable as gifts to God.		$^{Ph} c 19^{29}$ $d 21^9$—^{c} Harlotry condemned, ^{d} in a priest's daughter on pain of death.		
n Indecent assault		$^D 25^{11}$—Punishable by loss of hand				
o Dress of the sexes		$^D 22^5$—Interchange an abomination.				

2. Persons and Animals

^{L}**2** a Strangers (גרים), cp $^L 4hgln$		$^E a$ Ex 20^{10} $b 22^{21-24N}$—Strangers may claim ^{a} sabbath rest, ^{b} freedom from oppression cp $^L 4ha$. $^D c 5^{14}$ $d 1^{16}$ $e 10^{18}$ $f 14^{21}$ $g\ 29$ $h 24^{14}$ $i 28^{43}$ $j 29^{10-12}$—Strangers (גרים) may claim ^{c} sabbath rest, ^{dh} justice, ^{e} love, ^{g} benevolence; ^{j} may share in the covenant; ^{i} one day may get the upper hand; foreigners $3fc$ exempted from the benefits of the year of release, and $3kb$ of the prohibition of usury		$^{Ph} k$ Lev 17^{8-16} $l 18^{25}$ $m 19^{33}$ $n 20^2$ $o 22^{18}$ $p\ 24$. $q 23^{22b}$ $r 24^{16}$ $s 25^{6\ 35}$ t^{47}—Strangers may claim ^{m} equal justice, ^{qs} benevolence, and ^{m} love; $^{klnop s}$ equal religious rights and obligations belong to them, ^{t} they must yield up Hebrew slave on redemption. $^{Pt} u$ Num 15^{29}—Strangers may claim equal justice.	$^{Pg} v$ Ex 12^{45}—A mere sojourner (*toshab*) is not to eat of the Passover, but the circumcised stranger (*ger*) may. Cp $^L 6me$	$^{Ps} w$ Num 9^{14} $x 15^{14-16}$ $y 35^{15}$—The ^{w} Passover and ^{x} other sacrificial laws apply equally to strangers; also ^{y} provision of asylum.
b Charity and benevolence		^{E} Cp $^L 3fb$. $^D a 15^{7-11}$—Generosity and benevolence enjoined Cp $^L 2aceg\ 3fde\ 1b$.		$^{Ph} b$ Lev 19^{17}—Hatred and wrongs prohibited and love enjoined Cp $^L 2aqs\ 31cd$ &c.		
c Hired servants, cp **4g**		$^D a 24^{14}$—Must be promptly paid, and not oppressed.		$^{Ph} b 19^{13b}$ $c 25^6$ $d 22^{10b}$—^{b} Must be promptly paid, and ^{c} should share in the produce of the sabbath year, but ^{d} may not eat holy food.	$^{Pg} e$ Ex 12^{45}—May not eat of the Passover.	
d Slaves		$^J a$ Gen 37^{27} b Josh 9^{22-27}—^{a} Servitude of Hebrews illustrated by the sale of Joseph, and ^{b} of aliens by enslavement of the Gibeonites. $^E c$ Ex 21^{2-11} $d\ 20$ $e\ 26$. $f 32^N$—^{c} A Hebrew male slave to be set free in the seventh year of servitude (without wife or child unless		$^P k$ Lev 19^{20} $l 22^{11}$ $m 25^{30-55\frac12}$—^{m} Hebrew slave to serve as an hired servant, without rigour of treatment, and to be redeemable; ^{l} may eat of holy food in a priest's family; ^{m} only foreigners to be slaves as heritable chattels; ^{k} seduction of betrothed slave girl not a capital offence		

1j ^{E} the first ordinance is ^{D} modified and further defined, ^{Ph} enlarged by treatment of a special case, and ^{Ps} related to the sacrificial system

k Cp the very different treatment of a similar case in $^{Pt} 1j$

l The fullness of prohibition in ^{Ph} suggests a time of national decadence when old moral sanctions have broken down

o It is worth noticing, as bearing on the individuality and unity of principle ascribed to D, that under every one of the above subdivisions relating to the Family and cognate subjects D has material to be recorded, and in five of them is alone

2a Strangers or settlers (*gerim*) are first ^{E} dependent persons, to be treated with mercy, kindness, and justice, and lastly ^{P} a large and important section of the community who by submission to the law may, as proselytes, become all but equal members of the Jewish Church. At ^{D} an intervening stage, while the emphasis is increased on mercy and kindness, the stranger is already admitted to instruction along with Hebrews Deut 31^{12}. Cp Addis *Hex* ii 243, Briggs *Hex* 85, Kuenen *Hib Lect* 182. Foreigners who do not settle down as citizens are, it will be observed, less favourably dealt with. Cp $^L 6cabc$, $^D 47$ 'foreigner' (נכרי), $^D 105$ 'stranger...,' $^P 144$ 'sojourner' (תושב), $^P 153$ 'stranger' (זר) i.e. non-Aaronite, $^P 154$ 'stranger' or 'alien,' 'foreigner' (בן נכר)

b The growth of the spirit of charity may be traced in the legislation from ^{E} its earliest shoots, to ^{D} its vigorous development, and ^{Ph} its ripe fruit, in the demand 'Thou shalt love thy neighbour as thyself.' Many of the headings in various ways afford illustration of this, cp $^L 2acd fgk$, $3fhik$, $4ghj$

cde The hired servant, joined to the religious community only by the 'cash nexus,' has the privileges neither of the stranger or settler auw nor of the slave dln

d On the successive modifications introduced into the law of slavery see IV § 2c 31, VIII 1 § 7 55, cp IX 1 § 2β § 3γ 75 78. Cp also $^J 41$ 'handmaid' (שפחה), $^E 99$ 'bondwoman' (אמה), $^{JE} 207^a$ 'servant,' $^D 75$.

	J	D	E	P^ht	P^g	P^s	
			his while free), or to be bound for life at his own discretion; rights of Hebrew concubine slaves defined, ^{d} a master only punished for a blow immediately fatal, but ^{e} freedom to follow loss of eye or tooth, ^{f} 50 shekels due as damages for a slave gored by an ox. ^{D} g 15^{12-18} h 16^{11} &c i 21^{10-14} j 23^{15N}—^{g} Hebrew slaves, male and female, to be set free in seventh year of servitude with liberal gifts, or bound for life at choice of slave; ^{h} share in family joys and feasts; ^{i} rights of foreign concubine slaves; ^{j} freedom for runaway slave.		^{Pg} n Ex 12^{43}—When circumcised may eat the Passover. ^{Ps} o Lev 25^{39-55}—Hebrew slave to serve till the jubile, but only as hired servant; redeemable at price varying with the distance of the jubile, and at the jubile to go out with his children.		^{L} 3b
e Battlements on houses		^{D} 22^8—Every roof to have a parapet for safety					
f Animals, cp 3cd, 6ab, 8b		^{D} 25^4—The ox to be unmuzzled while treading out the corn					
g Birds		^{D} 22^6—The dam not to be taken with young ones or eggs					
h Murder and Asylum	^{J} a Gen $4^{8-15\ 23}$—The cases of Cain and Lamech		^{E} b Ex 20^{13} c 21^{12-14} d 20 e 22^2—^{b} Murder prohibited ^{c} on pain of death, unless the slain be ^{d} a slave or ^{e} a night-robber; ^{c} asylum to be appointed for homicide, but a murderer to be dragged from the altar itself ^{D} f 5^{17} g 4^{41-43} h 19^{1-13} i 21^{1-9}—^{f} Murder prohibited ^{h} on pain of death; ^{h} asylum to be provided, three cities at once and three later, ^{g} three cities being named in a later passage as assigned by Moses; ^{i} form of inquest prescribed	^{Ph} j Lev $24^{17\ 21b}$—Two prohibitions of murder on pain of death.	^{Pg} k Gen 9^5—Murder a capital offence. ^{Ps} l Num 35^{9-34N} m Josh 20^{1-9}—l Six cities are to furnish asylum for cases of unintentional homicide, ^{m} and are named as assigned by Joshua.		
i Assault			^{E} a Ex 21^{18} b 22 c 26—^{a} Compensation for loss of time while recovering, and ^{b} for miscarriage; ^{c} slave losing eye or tooth by blow is free. ^{D} d 27^{24}—Curse on secret attack.	^{Ph} e Lev 24^{19}—Penalty ruled by *lex talionis*, cp 4e.			
j Kidnapping		^{D} b 24^7—Death for kidnapping Hebrew.	^{E} a Ex 21^{16}—Death for kidnapping.				
k Blind and deaf		^{D} a 27^{18}—Curse for misleading the blind.		^{Ph} b Lev 19^{14}—To curse deaf or make blind stumble forbidden.			

3. Property

	J	D	E	P^ht	P^g	P^s	
a Theft		^{D} c 5^{19}—Theft forbidden.	^{E} a Ex 20^{15} b 22^{1-4}—^{a} Theft forbidden, ^{b} fines and penalties for stealing cattle smiting night robber to death not murder. Cp ^{L}$3ea$.	^{Ph} d Lev 19^{11} e $13a$—^{de}Theft and fraud forbidden; ^{e} also withholding of wages. ^{Pt} f Lev 6^{1-7}—Theft atoned for by a guilt offering with restitution in full + $\frac{1}{5}$			^{L} 3
b Landmarks		^{D} a 19^{14} b 27^{17}—^{a} Landmark not to be removed ^{b} under pain of curse.					

2h On contrasts in the laws about the cities of refuge see VIII iii § 1η 66, and on modifications in D see IX 1 § 2γ 76 cp § 3γ 78 Cp ^{P}132 'avenger of blood,' ^{P}133 'city of refuge'

k The width of range found in D is again shown by its furnishing material under every heading We are reminded of the similar closeness of contact with common life manifested by the Prophets

3a The offences specified suggest a growing complexity of social life. To theft ^{P} fraud is added, and for ^{E} cattle-lifting ^{P} withholding of wages is substituted (cp 2ca^D and observe that the 'hired servant' does not appear in E). b ^{E} The penalty for theft of live animals is to pay double (cp ea), a much higher fine being exacted if the animal be sold or killed; damage from accident, and even negligence, is settled by mere restitution dab ea, but elsewhere ^{Ph} the loss is only to be made good dde, and yet again ^{Pt} the rule is restitution + $\frac{1}{5}$, with an added sacrificial element which seems altogether foreign to the earlier legislation af de ebc Cp ^{E}117 'steal'

b The warnings of the Prophets against laying field to field show that a tendency towards large properties with unscrupulousness in their acquisition was a growing danger in the eighth century.

LAWS AND INSTITUTIONS

	J	D	E	P^{ht}	P^s	P^r
^{L}**3 c** Straying cattle		^{E} a Ex 23^4—An enemy's straying ox or ass to be restored, his overburdened ass to be helped. ^{D} b 22$^{1-4}$—A brother's straying ox or sheep to be restored, or kept till claimed; fallen ox or ass to be helped.				
d Damage		^{E} a Ex 21$^{28-36}$ b 22^5—^{a} Penalties for ox goring persons or cattle, and for damage by unprotected pit, ^{b} also for trespassing cattle and for arson. ^{D} c 20^{19}—In besieging a city its fruit trees not to be cut down.		^{Ph} d Lev 24^{18} e ^{21a}—^{de} Any one killing a beast to make it good. ^{Pt} f Num 5$^{5-8}$—Injury to property atoned for by a guilt offering with restitution in full + $\frac{1}{5}$.		
e Trusts and lost property		^{E} a Ex 22$^{7-13}$—Various provisions in cases of damage to live stock and other property while in charge of another, with appeal to the sanctuary, double value to be paid by offender.		^{Pt} b Lev 6$^{1-7}$ c Num 5$^{5-8}$—^{b} Trespass against Yahweh by an offence in respect of a neighbour's property to be atoned for by a guilt offering with restitution in full + $\frac{1}{5}$; ^{c} if owner be dead or absent, payment to be made to the next of kin, or in his default to the priest		
f Loans		^{E} a Ex 22^{14}. b $^{25-27}$—^{a} Mortal or other injury to borrowed cattle to be made good, unless the owner be present, or the beast be hired ^{b} Exaction of debts from poor Hebrews forbidden, and a pledged garment to be restored at sundown. ^{D} c 15$^{1-6}$ d 24^6 e $^{10-13}$—^{c} Debts from Hebrews to be remitted at the end of every seven years, until poverty be extinct cp 9je, ^{d} millstones not to be pledged; ^{e} no right of entry to get pledge, nor power to detain a garment overnight				
g Primogeniture and inheritance	^{J} a Gen 25$^{31-34}$—Esau sells his birthright as firstborn.	^{D} b 21$^{15-17}$—The firstborn to have two shares, though his mother be hated.			^{Ps} c Num 27$^{1-11}$ d 36$^{1-12}$—^{c} Right of inheritance granted to daughters, or, in default of issue, to next of kin, ^{d} but the daughters only to marry within their own tribe. See 9k.	
h Redemption and restoration of land					See **9k** Jubile	
i Gleanings		^{D} a 23^{24}. b 24$^{19-22}$—A neighbour's grapes or corn may be plucked in passing, but not gathered in a vessel or reaped; ^{b} forgotten sheaves in harvest, and the after-gathering of olive trees and vines to be left for the poor.		^{Ph} c 19^9 d 23^{22}—^{cd} Corners, and gleanings of harvest fields, and fallen fruit and gleanings of vineyards to be left for the poor.		
j Coveting		^{E} a Ex 20^{17}—Coveting house (=household), wife, slave, cattle, or other property of a neighbour, forbidden. ^{D} b 5^{21}—Coveting wife, house (=building), field, slave, cattle, or other property of a neighbour, forbidden				
k Usury		^{E} a Ex 22^{25b}—Usury forbidden with a poor Hebrew. ^{D} b 23^{19}—Usury of all kinds forbidden with Hebrews, allowed with foreigners.		^{Ph} c 25$^{35-38}$—Usury of all kinds forbidden with a (Hebrew) brother.		
l Unlawful mixtures		^{D} a 22^{c-11}—Mixed seed in a vineyard, plowing with ox and ass, and wearing a fabric of wool and linen, forbidden.		^{Ph} b 19^{19b}—Breeding hybrid cattle, mixing seed in a field, and wearing a mixed fabric, forbidden.		

3c The passages are printed in full with a note on the modifications in D IX 1 § 2β 75

f ^{bde} These passages are printed in full side by side IX 1 § 2a 73.

g ^{cd} These ordinances, which on grounds of form are assigned to P^s, fit well an age when every one thought about his pedigree. They illustrate, by their isolation in the earlier tables, the almost total absorption of the later priestly canonists in matters relating to worship and ceremonial purity.

4. Judgement and Rule

		J	D	E	P^{ht}	P^g	P^s
							^{L}4i

a Judges appointed — ^{E} a Ex 18^{13-26} cp Num 16^{25} b Ex 24^{14}—^{b} Aaron and Hur made judicial representatives of Moses *pro tem*; ^{a} permanent judges appointed by Moses for minor causes on the advice of Jethro (referred to in the case of Dathan and Abiram).
^{D} c 1^{9-18} d 16^{18aN}—^{c} Judges appointed by Moses for minor causes, the people having the selection; ^{d} judges to be appointed in all towns.

b Supreme Court — ^{E} a Ex 22^8—Appeal to God, presumably at the sanctuary, in case of suspected theft.
^{D} b 17^{8-13N} c 19^{16-19} d 21^{1-9N}—^{c} In case of false witness or ^{b} any difficult case appeal to lie to the priests the Levites and to the judge or judges that shall be in those days in the divinely chosen place; ^{d} the local elders and judges, perhaps with the Levitical priests of the place (but see 21^{5N}), are to act as directed in a case of suspected murder.
^{Ps} e Num 35^{24-28}—The congregation to form the court for murder cases, to condemn the guilty, but to deliver to a city of refuge those whose act is short of murder, complete immunity being granted after the death of the high priest.

c Just judgement — ^{E} a Ex 23^2 b $^{6-8}$—^{ab} The poor to be fairly judged, a wrong sentence not to be given because popular, the innocent not to be condemned, bribes not to be taken.
^{D} c 16^{18b-20} d 24^{16} e 25^1 f 27^{25}—^{ce} Judgement to be just and impartial; ^{c} bribes not to be taken ^{f} under pain of curse; ^{d} none to suffer for another's crime
^{Ph} g Lev 19^{15} h ^{35}—^{g} The poor to be fairly judged, ^{gh} sentence to be just and impartial.

d Weights and measures — ^{D} a 25^{13-16}—Weights and measures not to vary, but to be perfect and just.
^{Ph} b Lev 19^{35-37}—Just balances, weights, ephah, and hin required.

e *Lex talionis* — ^{E} a Ex 21^{22b-25}—For assault to forfeit life, eye, tooth, hand, or foot, or to suffer burning, wound, or stripe, like for like
^{D} b 19^{21}—For assault to forfeit life, eye, tooth, hand, or foot, like for like.
^{Ph} c Lev 24^{19}—For a blemish caused, to suffer the like, as to forfeit eye or tooth, or to have limb broken.

f Witnesses — ^{E} a Ex 20^{16} b 23^1—^{ab} False witness forbidden, also ^{b} conspiracy for that purpose.
^{D} c 5^{20} d 17^6 e 19^{15-21}—^{c} False witness forbidden; ^{e} punishable with the penalty it would have brought on another, in ^{d} capital or indeed ^{e} any other cases two or three witnesses required; ^{d} the hands of the witnesses to be first upon a murderer in execution.
^{Ph} f Lev 19^{11b} g ^{16}—^{f} Perjury, false witness, ^{g} especially in a murder case, and tale-bearing forbidden.
^{Pt} h Lev 5^1—A witness withholding evidence after being adjured to speak must confess his fault and offer a sin offering
^{Ps} i Num 35^{30}—One witness insufficient in a murder case

g Justice to hired servants — ^{D} 24^{14} — Whether Hebrews or not, to be treated fairly, cp ^{L}2ca.
^{Ph} Cp ^{L}2cb

h Justice to the strangers and weak — ^{E} a Ex 23^{9N}—Oppression of strangers forbidden, cp ^{L}2ab.
^{D} b 24^{17} c 27^{19}—Injustice to the stranger, fatherless, and widow ^{b} forbidden, ^{c} under pain of curse, cp ^{L}2adeh.
^{Ph} d Lev 24^{22}—One law for strangers and homeborn, cp ^{L}2am.

i Justice to family of criminals — ^{D} 24^{16}—None to suffer for another's sin.

4a For a discussion of the Deuteronomic legislation on this head see X § 4γ 93, where the passages are printed in full; for E cp XII § 2ε 115. Cp ^{D}67 'judges,' ^{D}83 'officers'
b On modification by D see X § 1 (iii) 85, cp IX 1 § 2γ 76
d See XIII § 8δ 1 147, where the passages are printed side by side.
e The *lex talionis* is somewhat curtailed in scope in D, but generalized in P^h.
f P^h has here kept closely to the ancient type, but D is much elaborated
h For several passages printed side by side see IX 1 § 2a 74

228 LAWS AND INSTITUTIONS

		J	D	E	P^{ht}	P^g	P^s
^{L}**4** j	Forty stripes save one		$^D 25^{1-3}$—Flogging illegal beyond thirty nine stripes.				
	k The king	$^J a$ Gen 36^{31} $b\ 49^{10}$ c Num 24^{17}—Israelite kings ^{a} alluded to, and foretold by ^{b} Jacob and ^{c} Balaam. $^D d\ 17^{14-20}$—Not to be a foreigner; not to multiply horses, wives, or money; but to write out the law-book, read it, and keep its ordinances.					
	l Citizenship		$^D 23^{1-8}$—Mutilated persons disfranchised; bastards, Ammonites and Moabites excluded to the tenth generation, Edomites and Egyptians to the third only.				
	m Military service	^{JE} Cp Josh *passim*. $^D a\ 20^{1-20}$ $b\ 21^{10-14}$ $c\ 23^{9-14}$ $d\ 24^5$—^{a} The cities of the Canaanites and their populations to be destroyed; peace to be offered to foreign cities on condition of service; after a siege only adult males to be slain, other persons and property to be for spoil; ^{b} rights of female captives defined; ^{c} sanitary rules for the camp; ^{d} the owner of a new house or vineyard, and the newly betrothed or ^{d} married, to be exempt from service.		$^{Ph} e$ Num 10^9—In a war for freedom the blast of the trumpet is to be both a signal for commencement of hostilities and a sure appeal to Yahweh's protection.	$^{Ps} f$ Num 31^{1-54}—Typical case of war with Midian; elaborate provisions in case of victory; only unmarried women to be finally spared; the spoil to be distributed, with a share for the sanctuary.	
	n Foreign nations	$^E a$ Ex 17^{14-16}—Amalek to be blotted out. $^D b\ 25^{17-19}$—Amalek to be blotted out for his cowardly attack, cp $^L 41$.			$^{Ps} d$ Num 25^{16-18}—The Midianites to be vexed.	
	o General census at Sinai				$^{Pg} a$ Num $1^{1-46\frac{1}{2}N}$—A census ordered of all males of twenty years old and upwards, to be taken tribe by tribe under the oversight of a representative of each; (the census executed, total—603,550) $^{Ps} b$ Num 1^{1-46N} c Ex 30^{11-16N}—^{c} The census implied. ^{b} See ^{Pg}.	
	p Census of Levites.				$^{Pg} a$ Num 3^{14-39} $b\ 26^{57-62}$—^{a} A census ordered at Sinai of male Levites from a month old, and executed, total—22,000; ^{b} (in present form ^{Ps}, cp 26^{1N}) a second census ordered and executed in the plains of Moab, total—23,000 $^{Ps} c$ Num 4^{1-3} $d\ ^{21-23}$ $e\ ^{29}$ $f\ ^{34-49}$—^{cdef} A census of male Levites from thirty to fifty years old, total—8,580.	
	q Census of firstborn				^{Pg} Num 3^{40-51}—The Levites to be substituted for the firstborn, who number 22,273, the overplus to be redeemed at two shekels, payable to the priests.	
	r Places in camp				$^{Ps} a$ Num 2^{1-34} $b\ 10^{13-28}$—^{a} The twelve lay tribes to camp in four groups round the Levites and the Tent of Meeting; ^{b} the same order adopted on the march.	
	s Trumpets, use of	$^J a$ Ex 19^{13}—The priests to be summoned to meet Yahweh on Sinai by blast of ram's horn $^E b$ Ex $19^{16\ 19}$ Josh 6^{4-9}—The sound of a trumpet is heard on Horeb; the priests give with rams' horns the signal for the fall of Jericho.		$^{Ph} c$ Num $10^{9\ N}$—See me.	$^{Pg} d$ Num 10^{1-8}—Trumpets to be made of silver, and blown ('for the calling of the congregation, and for the journeying of the camps') by the priests alone.	

4k Cp X § 1 (i) 85 **l** Cp X § 5 95 **n** Cp XI § 3γ 104 for J, and XII § 3 115 for E
m The stories of Achan and Saul in reference to the spoil of enemies illustrate from the older sources the provisions of D P^s stands by itself. Cp $^D 77$ 'men of war,' $^P 16$ 'able to go forth to war,' $^P 92$ 'hosts (of Israel).'
o Cp Ex 12^{37N} J.—Under David a census is a criminal act. After the exile everybody thought much of his pedigree, and a census became a normal event, cp $^P 65$ 'family,' $^P 66$ 'fathers' house,' $^P 84$ 'heads of fathers,' and ct $^{Jh} 153$ for vaguer usage.

IDOLATRY AND SUPERSTITION

	J	D	E	P^{ht}	P^g	P^s	
t Census in plains of Moab				P^s Num 26^{1-51N}—A census to be taken of males of twenty years old and over, the families being named under their tribes, but no mention of tribal heads as superintendents, total—601,730, cf ^L40a.			^L5a
u Division of the land	^{J} a Josh $13^{1N\ 7a}$ $15^{14-19\ 63}$ $16^{1-3\ 10}$ 17^{11-18} 19^{47}—A series of passages imply that the land was allotted among the west Jordan tribes *before* it was conquered, and that they had varying success in subjugating their portions. ^{E} b Josh $19^{49\ N}$—An isolated fragment suggests that E had some account of the distribution of the land after gradual conquest. ^{Rje} c Josh 18^{2-10N}—The land is divided by lot, after complete subjugation, into seven portions after a survey by twenty-one representatives of the seven tribes involved (details are missing). Rd d Josh 12 $13^{2-14\S}$—A similar view is involved in these passages, which adopt the conception of ^{Rjec}.		P^s e Num 26^{52-56} $f33^{54}$ $g34^{1-29}$ h Josh $13-21\S$—^{ef} The land to be divided by lot among the tribes in proportion to population; ^{g} the boundaries of the land fixed; the division to take place under Eleazar and Joshua, with twelve tribal chiefs; ^{h} the conquered land is accordingly allotted with the utmost particularity.		
v Record and publication of law		^{D} a 17^{18} b 27^{2-48} c 31^{9-13N} d $24-26$ e Josh 8^{30-35}—^{c} 'This law' or ^{d} 'the words of this law' written by Moses 'in a book' and put in the custody of 'the Levites,' who are ^{d} to 'put it by the side of the ark of the covenant' and ^{c} in the seventh year, 'the year of release,' to read it publicly at the Feast of Booths; ^{b} Israel to write on Mount Ebal 'upon the stones all the words of this law'; ^{a} the king to make a private copy.				
w Moses' successor			^{E} a Deut 31^{14-23N}—Moses told by Yahweh he must die; Joshua called to the Tent of Meeting and charged as his successor. ^{D} b 3^{21-29} c 31^{1-8}—^{b} Moses forbidden to enter the land and told to appoint Joshua; ^{c} all Israel told and Joshua publicly charged.				

5. Idolatry and Superstition

	J	D	E	P^h			^{L}5
a Other gods	^{J} a Ex 34^{14-16} b Num 25^2—^{a} Worship of other gods, or alliances leading to it, forbidden; ^{b} the danger illustrated by the case of intercourse with Moab. ^{E} c Gen $31^{19\ 30\ 32}$ d 35^{2-4} e Ex 20^3 f 23^a g 22^{20} h 23^{13} i 24^a j ^{32} k Num 25^{3a} l Josh 24^2 $^{14-25}$—Israel forbidden ^{e} to have, ^{f} to make, ^{g} to honour by sacrifice, ^{h} to mention by name, ^{i} to worship, ^{j} to make a covenant with other gods. The danger illustrated ^{cd} by the usage of Jacob's wives, ^{k} by the case of Baal Peor, and ^{l} by the farewell address of Joshua, which recognizes such worship as pre-Abrahamic. ^{D} m 4^{19} n 5^7 o 6^4 p 14 q 8^{19} r 11^{16} s $26-28$ t 28^{13} u 31^{17}—The worship of other gods (often specified as the gods of the surrounding peoples) ^{o} inconsistent with the unity of Yahweh, and ^{np} forbidden ^{qst} under penalty of ruin and curse, and throughout regarded as the most grave danger of Israel. ^{m} The worship of heavenly bodies specified.			Ph Cp ^L5bjk.			^{L}5

4u Cp $^D88$ 'possess,' $^P127$ 'possession,' $^P106$ 'lot'
v Cp for Moses as writer II § 1 17. Cp also $^D120$.

5a See XII § 2a 112, cp § 5γ 119 for E's conception of ancient Hebrew idolatry, cp $^P23$ 85.

LAWS AND INSTITUTIONS

	J	D	E	P^ht	P^g	P^s
ᴸ**5** b Images	ᴶ *a* Ex 34¹⁷ cp ᴸ5*acd*—No molten gods to be made. ᴱ *b* Ex 20⁴ · *c* 23*b* *d* 32¹⁻²⁴§—It is forbidden *b* to make or worship any kind of image in view of the jealousy of Yahweh, or *c* to make gold or silver gods ; *d* the danger illustrated by the case of the golden calf, cp ᴸ5*acd* ᴰ *e* 5⁸ *f* 4¹⁵⁻²⁴ *g* 7²⁶ *h* 27¹⁵ *i* 31¹⁶⁻²¹—It is forbidden *e* to make or worship any image in view of the jealousy of Yahweh, or *gh* to bring an abomination into the house, under penalty of *f* ruin and *hi* curse.		ᴾʰ *j* Lev 19⁴ *h* 26¹—It is forbidden *j* molten gods or *k* idols, or *k* to rear up a graven image.		
c Blasphemy and false oaths	ᴱ *a* Ex 20⁷ *b* 22²⁸ᵃ—*a* None to 'take Yahweh's name for falsehood,' nor *b* to 'revile God.' ᴰ *c* 5¹¹—None to 'take Yahweh's name for falsehood.'		ᴾʰ *d* Lev 18²¹ᵇ *e* 19¹² *f* 22³² *g* 24¹⁵ᵇ⁻¹⁶ᵃ—An Israelite forbidden *e* to swear falsely, *def* to 'profane the name of his God,' *g* to 'curse his God,' or 'blaspheme the name of Yahweh'; *g* offender to 'bear his sin' or 'be put to death.' ᴾᵗ *h* Lev 5⁴ *i* 6¹⁻⁷—Any one *h* swearing rashly to bring a sin offering, or *i* swearing falsely to bring a guilt offering with restitution of any property concerned + ⅕. ᴾˢ *j* Lev 24¹⁰⁻¹⁶ *k* 23—*j* Case of 'blaspheming the Name'. penalty of death by stoning; *k* execution.		
d Canaanite peoples and their rites	ᴶ *a* Gen 24³ *b* Ex 34¹⁰ ᴺ—*a* Isaac not to have a Canaanite wife ; *b* (? ᴿᵈ) Israel not to 'make a covenant with the inhabitants . . . lest it be for a snare,' nor to marry their daughters. ᴱ *c* Ex 23³¹ᵇ⁻³³—Israel to 'make no covenant with' the Canaanites nor with their gods, but to 'drive them out' (? ᴿᵈ). ᴰ *d* 7¹⁻⁴ *e* 12²⁹⁻³¹ *f* 18⁹—Israel *d* not to 'make a covenant with the inhabitants . . . neither . . . make marriages with them,' but to 'smite' and 'devote' them ; *e* not to 'inquire after their gods,' or *f* learn to do after their abominations, cp 5*f*		ᴾʰ *g* Lev 18¹⁻⁵ *h* 24⁻³⁰ *i* 20²³—Israel *g* not to follow the 'doings' of Egypt or Canaan ; *h* not to 'do any of the abominations' or *i* 'walk in the customs of the nation . . . cast out before' them.		
e Idols &c to be destroyed	ᴶᵉ (or ᴿᵈ) *a* Ex 34¹³—Altars, pillars and Asherim to be destroyed. ᴱ *b* Ex 23²⁴ᴺ *c* 32¹⁻²⁴§—*c* The golden calf destroyed, *b* (ᴱˢ or ᴿᵈ) the gods of the nations to be overthrown and their pillars broken in pieces. ᴰ *d* 7⁵·²⁵ *e* 9¹²⁻²¹ *f* 12²—*df* Heathen altars, pillars and Asherim to be destroyed, and *d* graven images burnt with fire ; *e* the destruction of the golden calf related.		ᴾʰ *g* Lev 26³⁰ *h* Num 33⁵⁰⁻⁵⁶§—Figured stones, graven images, and high places to be destroyed, and the inhabitants of the land to be expelled.		
f Death to idolaters		ᴰ *a* 7² *b* 16 *c* 22⁻²⁴ *d* 17²⁻⁷ᴺ *e* 20¹⁶⁻¹⁸—*a* The seven idolatrous nations to be smitten and devoted ; *b* to be consumed without pity, *e* saving none alive, but *c* 'not quickly,' though their final destruction is decreed ; *d* stoning, at the mouth of two or three witnesses, for any who serve other gods, sun, moon, or host of heaven.				
g No Asherah or pillar, cp *eab de*	ᴶ *a* Gen 21³³ *b* 35¹⁴·²⁰ *c* Josh 4³⁻⁸§—*a* A tamarisk tree planted at Beersheba by Abraham ; *b* pillars erected by Jacob at Bethel and over Rachel's grave ; *c* twelve stones out of Jordan 'laid down' in 'the lodging place' after the crossing		ᴾʰ *k* Lev 26¹ᵇ—Pillars and figured stones forbidden.		

5*c* Cp ᴾʰ 210 'profane'
   d It is observable that this topic only occurs in codes which were in whole or part written down before the exile.
   e See X § 3β 1 91 for the connexion of D with the iconoclasm of the Josian reformation. The incident of the golden calf in E can alone be confidently assigned to JE, and even this would seem to be one of the later elements, if we may judge either from the silence of the historical books as to protests against idolatry from the earlier prophets, or from the advanced character of some of the context, cp Ex 32³⁰ᴺ But it is impossible to be certain There may have been contemporaneous but divergent tendencies at work which have found separate expression
   g The contrast is strongly marked between the implied approval of the stones in JE and the express prohibition of D, cp *h* See also X § 1 (vi) 1 85.

CLEAN AND UNCLEAN

		J	D	E	P^ht	P^g	P^s	
			ᴱ *d* Gen 28¹⁸ *e* 31⁴⁵⁻⁵⁴§ *f* Ex 24⁴ᵇ *g* Josh 4⁴ ²⁰ *h* 24²⁶ᵇ⁻²⁷ — Pillars erected ᵈᵉ by Jacob at Bethel and Galeed, *f* by Moses at Horeb, and by Joshua *g* at Gilgal and *h* Shechem. ᴰ *i* 12³ *j* 16²¹⁻ⁱ The Israelites ordered to 'destroy (the Canaanites') pillars' and to 'burn their Asherim with fire,' and *j* forbidden to 'plant an Asherah of any kind of tree beside the altar of Yahweh' or to 'set up a pillar, which Yahweh ... hateth.'					ᴸ **6a**
h	Seduction to idolatry		ᴰ *a* 13¹⁻¹⁸ *b* 18²⁰—ᵃᵇ A prophet, ᵃ dreamer, or private person seducing others to 'serve other gods,' to be ᵃᵇ put to death, ᵃ by stoning; ᵃ a city turning to idolatry to be destroyed utterly and never inhabited again.					
i	Molech worship		ᴰ *a* 18¹⁰ᵃ—None to 'make son or daughter pass through the fire.'		ᴾʰ *b* Lev 18²¹ᵃ *c* 20¹⁻⁵—ᵇᶜ None to 'give of his seed ... to Molech,' ᶜ on pain of death by stoning			
j	Divination	ᴶ *a* Num 22⁷··24¹ cp 23²³—Balaam a diviner, whose spells avail not against Israel. ᴱ *b* Ex 22¹⁸—Death to a sorceress.	ᴰ *c* 18¹⁰⁻¹⁴—All magic and like superstition forbidden, eight kinds named.		ᴾʰ *d* 19²⁶ᵇ *e* ³¹ *f* 20⁶ *g* ²⁷—ᵈ Enchantments and augury forbidden; ᵉ none to resort to 'them that have familiar spirits, nor unto the wizards,' *f* under pain of being 'cut off'; *g* death by stoning for practising witchcraft.			
k	Disfigurement in mourning		ᴰ *a* 14¹ᴺ—God's 'children' not to 'cut themselves' or 'make any baldness between the eyes for the dead.'		ᴾʰ *b* 19²⁷· *c* 21⁵—Neither ᶜ priests nor ᵇ others may cut hair, beard, or flesh in mourning.			

6. Clean and Unclean

		J	D	E	P^ht	P^g	P^s	
a	Food animals	ᴶ *a* Gen 7² c*t* 2¹⁶ 3⁷—The distinction of clean and unclean beasts recognized in the Flood story, but in and out of Eden previously a vegetable diet assumed	ᴰ *b* 12¹⁵ cp 15²² *c* 14³⁻²⁰ᴺ—ᵇ Flesh (of domestic animals) to be killed and eaten as freely as venison; ᶜ a list of clean beasts is given, with a general criterion, also rules as to unclean beasts, with stated instances; rules as to clean and unclean water-dwellers; all clean birds to be eaten, a list of the unclean following; winged creeping things to be unclean.		ᴾʰ *d* Lev 20²⁵—Separation to be made by the holy people between clean and unclean beasts, birds, and creeping things; cp *fg*. ᴾᵗ *e* 11¹⁻²³ᴺ *f* 41⁻⁴⁴ᵃ *g* ⁴⁶—*fg* Separation to be made by the holy people between clean and unclean; ᵉ general rules given for distinguishing clean and unclean beasts, with instances only of the latter; rules, redundantly given, as to clean and unclean water-dwellers, and a list of unclean birds, ᵉᶠ rules as to unclean creeping things, with ᵉ named clean exceptions. ᴾᵍ *h* Gen 1²⁹ *i* 9³—ʰ Only vegetable produce given for food, ⁱ the permission extended to 'every moving thing that liveth.' ᴾˢ *j* Lev 27¹¹—The distinction recognized in cases of vows.			ᴸ **6**

51 The silence of JE and P^gs is best explained by the supposition that this atrocious cult was confined to the closing century of the kingdom. The sacrifice of human beings to Yahweh seems in some early circles to have been approved, if we may argue from the stories of Abraham and Isaac, and Jephthah and his daughter, cp the slaying of the sons of Rizpah.

j There is no evidence that witchcraft ever was in any way grafted upon the religion of Yahweh, but the increased fullness and stringency of the prohibitions levelled against it in D and P^h agree with the protests of the prophets from Isaiah downwards Cp X § 1 (vi) 1 87

6 Under ᴸ111bc the attitude of JE towards ceremonial purity is illustrated. It might be conjectured that the old rule was mainly intended to secure that every one should be 'clean' when about to engage in any act of worship, while the later regulations required all to avoid uncleanness at all times, and to seek cleansing as often and as soon as one became unclean. This latter principle well suited a religion which for most of its adherents was deprived of the sacrificial elements on account of their exile in a land which might itself be unclean, but which could not prevent personal purity from asserting itself.—Cp ᴾʰ192 'abomination,' ᶠ42 'clean,' ᶠ167 'unclean', and for the subject-matter cp Drv-Wh *ad loc*, and on the ceremonial ordinances in D cp X § 5 1 95

a Probably the distinction of clean and unclean animals rested on immemorial practice, but the rules and lists cannot have been early. Cp further ᴸ13eg, and for D X § 5 1 95.

	J	D	E	P^ht	P^g	P^s
^L 6 b Uncleanness by touch		^D a 14^7-8 ^b 21^22—^a The carcases of unclean beasts not to be touched; ^b the land not to be defiled by the presence of the corpse of a criminal who had been hanged.		^Ph c Lev 21^1-4 11—The high priest not to defile himself for any dead person, and the other priests only for specified near relatives ^Pt d Lev 5^2 ^e 7^21 ^f 11^8 ^g 24-38 ^h 44b-45 ^i Num 19^14-22 ^j 22^4-7N ^k Num 6^6-12 —^c Uncleanness by touch a bar to sharing in a sacrificial feast; ^d if ignored through ignorance, to be purged by a sin offering; ^f the carcases of unclean beasts not to be touched; ^g rules given for defining such unclean beasts; ^h creeping things (when dead) not to be touched, ^g with list of such, and many details as to conveyance of contamination, cp ^L 6c f 9^d, ^j priests 'unclean by the dead' or otherwise to be purified at sundown after ablutions, but ^k a seven days' period with use of the 'water of separation' laid down as a general law	^Ps l Num 9^1-13 ^m 19^1-13—^l Supplementary Passover for those unclean by the dead; ^m preparation of water of separation from the ashes of the red heifer, and subsequent use.
c Unlawful eating		^D b 14^21a—The flesh of a beast dying of itself not to be eaten by a Hebrew, but may be given to 'a stranger,' or sold to 'a foreigner'	^E a Ex 22^31b—The flesh of a beast torn by wild animals not to be eaten, but cast to the dogs.	^Ph c Lev 17^15 N ^d 22^8—^c Any one, 'homeborn or stranger,' eating the flesh of a beast dying of itself to be unclean till purified by ablutions; if he omit these, 'he shall bear his iniquity'; ^d the same thing forbidden to a priest ^Pt e Lev 7^19 ^f 11^39—^f If a clean beast die, he who touches it is unclean till the even, he who eats or carries the carcase must also wash his clothes; ^e flesh that has touched an unclean thing shall not be eaten; and no one, while unclean, shall eat of peace-offerings on pain of being cut off.	
d Kid in dam's milk	^J a Ex 34^26b—Kid not to be seethed in its dam's milk	^D c 14^21b—Identical with a.	^E b Ex 23^19b—Identical with a.		
e Against eating blood or fat		^D a 12^16 ^b 12^23-25 ^c 15^23—^abc Blood not to be eaten but poured out, ^b 'for the blood is the life.'		^Ph d Lev 17^10-14 ^e 19^26a—^d Neither Israelite nor 'stranger' ^de to eat blood ^d of domestic or wild animal, but to pour it out and cover it with dust; penalty, to be 'cut off'; reason, 'for the life ... is the blood.' ^Pt f Lev 3^14-17 ^g 7^22-27—^fg No fat or blood to be eaten ^f for ever, ^g the fat 'of the beast of which men offer a fire offering,' the blood, 'whether of fowl or beast,' under pain of being 'cut off'; ^f 'all the fat is Yahweh's,' and so to be burned on the altar.	^Ps h Gen 9^4—Flesh not to be eaten 'with the life thereof, the blood thereof.'
f Purification after childbirth				^Pt Lev 12^1-8—After childbirth the mother to be unclean for seven days for a boy and fourteen for a girl, and to 'continue in the blood of her purifying' in all forty and eighty days respectively	

6b Uncleanness by touch is no doubt also recognized by antiquity, and is not in itself a chronological clue. But the elaboration of cases is hardly primitive, and in the two passages *j* on touching the dead there is a marked increase of stringency, the purification required for the priest in one P^hs being much less onerous than that laid down for all in the other P^t. On the ordinance of the red heifer see Gray, *Numbers* in *ICA*.—The same advance in elaboration is seen under c.

f g Cp P^139 'separation.'

CLEAN AND UNCLEAN   233

	J	D	E	P^{ht}	P^g	P^s
g Secretions		$^D a\ 23^{10}$—Involuntary uncleanness while in a war camp to be purged by ablution, readmission following at sundown.		$^{Ph} b$ Lev 22^4—A priest 'whose seed goeth from him' to be unclean till purified by ablutions. $^{Pt} c$ Lev 5^3 $d\ 15$—^{d} Detailed provisions for duration of uncleanness and process of purification in various cases of men and women, with rules for things and persons contaminated by touch; ^{c} a sin offering required where any one has unwittingly touched 'the uncleanness of man.'		$^L 6n$
h Leprosy in man		$^D a\ 24^8$—The priests the Levites to give teaching or 'torah' as God had commanded them, and the people to obey scrupulously, remembering Miriam.		$^{Pt} c$ Lev 13^{1-46N} $d\ 14^{1-8a}$ $e\ ^{54-57}$ $f\ 14^{8b-20N}$ $g\ ^{21-32}$—^{c} Elaborate directions to be followed by 'the priest' in discriminating between real and apparent cases of leprosy; if finally 'pronounced unclean,' the man is to live apart and proclaim himself, by word and appearance, unclean; if found not to be a leper, the priest is to 'pronounce him clean,' but in some cases $^{6\ 34}$ he is to 'wash his clothes and be clean'; ^{d} an archaic ritual is prescribed as needful before 'the leper' can be 'pronounced clean,' thorough-going ablutions being still necessary before he 'shall be clean'; ^{e} colophon; ^{f} detailed sacrificial ceremonies to be performed before the leper 'shall be clean,' preceded by a repetition of the ablutions; ^{g} alternative ritual for the poor.		
i Leprosy in a garment				^{Pt} Lev 13^{47-59}—Rules given for discrimination of 'leprosy' in a garment, which is to be burnt or washed as directed.		
j Leprosy in a house				^{Pt} Lev 14^{33-53N}—Rules given for discrimination of leprosy in a house; if condemned, it must be destroyed and its indwellers cleansed; if pronounced clean, the ceremonies of $^L 6h d$ must be applied.		
k Sanitary and general provisions		$^D a\ 23^{9-14N}$—Rules for personal cleanliness Cp burial of hanged criminal 21^{22}.		$^{Ph} b\ 22^{1-7}$—Priests not to eat the holy food while unclean from any cause. $^{Pt} c$ Lev 5^{2-6}—Involuntary contraction of any kind of uncleanness to be purged by a sin offering	$^{Pg} d$ Lev 10^{10N} e Num 18^{11}—^{d} Priests to discriminate between clean and unclean generally; ^{e} only to eat holy food when ceremonially 'clean'	
l Acceptable offerings	$^J a$ Gen 8^{20}—Clean and unclean animals distinguished, and the clean chosen by Noah for sacrifice. $^D b\ 15^{21}$ $c\ 17^1$—^{c} No blemished ox or sheep fit for sacrifice, ^{b} firstlings in particular may not be offered if deformed in any way, but may be eaten at home.			$^{Ph} d\ 22^{17-25}$ $e\ ^{26-28}$—^{d} Full specification of blemishes which disqualify an animal as a victim, for a vow or freewill offering; as a burnt or peace offering, from homeborn or foreigner, an animal must be a week old, and the dam and her young must not both be killed in one day.		
m Circumcision	$^J a$ Ex 4^{24-26} cp Josh 5^{2-9}—Strange story of the circumcision of Moses' son by Zipporah, cp the rite at Gilgal later			$^{Pt} b$ Lev 12^3—To take place on the eighth day.	$^{Pg} c$ Gen 17^{10-14} $d\ 21^4$ e Ex 12^{48}—^{c} Circumcision imposed on Abraham as a covenant-token, carried out on eighth day, extending to all homeborn and slaves, on pain of being 'cut off' for neglect; ^{e} 'strangers' to be circumcised before eating the passover.	
n Fruit trees				^{Ph} Lev 19^{23-25}—Trees newly planted to be counted 'as uncircumcised' for three years; in fourth year the fruit to be devoted to God, and in the fifth year eaten.		

---

61 See ^{L}13g.   m Cp ^{P}40 'circumcise.'

7. Sacrifices

	J D E	P^{ht} P^g P^s
^{L} 7 a Sacrifice in general, cp 10a	^{J} a Gen 4^3 b 15^9 c Ex 3^{18} &c d 10^{24} e 34^{25}— a Abel and b Abraham sacrifice, and ^{cd} sacrifice is the motive of the exodus, e 'Thou shalt not sacrifice the blood of thy sacrifice with leavened bread, neither shall the sacrifice of the feast of the passover be left unto the morning' ^{E} f Gen 31^{54} 46^{1b} g Ex 18^{12} h 20^{24b} i 23^{18}— f Jacob sacrifices, and g Jethro, h an altar is required for sacrifice; i 'Thou shalt not sacrifice the blood of my sacrifice with leavened bread, neither shall the fat of my feast remain all night unto the morning.' ^{D} j 12^{4-14} k $26-28$—jk All kinds of sacrifices to be brought to the central sanctuary, i e burnt offerings, vows, j sacrifices, tithes, heave offering, freewill offerings, firstlings, and k holy things; k the flesh and the blood of the 'burnt offerings' to be offered upon the altar, and the blood of the 'sacrifices' (= peace offering) to be poured out upon it, the offerer to eat the flesh, feasting joyfully before God with family and dependants.	^{Ph} l Lev 17^{1-7N} m ^{8}—l No more common slaying of animals for food to go on, much less the sacrificing of them 'in the open field' or to the satyrs after whom they go a-whoring, but ^{lm} all animals to be offered as burnt or peace offerings at the sanctuary on pain of being 'cut off.' ^{Pt} n Lev 7^{37}.—Colophon enumerating kinds of sacrifices treated in preceding code, i e burnt, meal, sin, guilt, and peace offerings ('and of the consecration' in ^{Ps}). ^{Pg} o Ex 29—Burnt, peace, sin, and meal offerings incidentally ordered and described in connexion with Aaron's consecration. ^{Ps} p Lev 8 q Num 28—The execution of the full ritual prescribed ^{o} is recorded; burnt, meal, drink, and oil offerings prescribed for every day in the calendar.
a Questions treated	^{JE} 'To whom?'—To Yahweh ^{D} 'Where?'—At the central sanctuary.	^{P} 'What?'—The ordained offering 'How?'—According to the prescribed ritual 'When?'—On the set day by the calendar 'By whom?'—By the Aaronic priesthood alone. But 'to whom' there is no question, nor 'where' except as to the exact point in the sanctuary, as 'at the door of the tent of meeting'
b Historical view	^{JE} $^{(P)}$ Sacrifice continuous and acceptable from Abel and Noah onwards.	^{Pg} Sacrifice never recorded before the erection of the sanctuary, the institution of the priesthood, and the giving of the Law; implicitly regarded as only legitimate under these conditions
c Common forms	Peace offerings, burnt offerings, (meal offerings cp Judg 6^{19-21}), oil (cp Hos $2^{5\,8}$ Mic 6^7), wine (cp Hos $2^{5\,9}$ 9^4), (shewbread cp 1 Sam 21^6)	Peace offerings, burnt offerings, meal offerings, oil, wine, shewbread.
d Peculiar elements	Wool Deut 18^4 (cp wool and flax Hos $2^{5\,9}$).	Sin, guilt, and incense offerings, and the use of salt.
e Predominant form	The peace offering far the most prominent, to 'eat and drink before Yahweh' = to sacrifice.	The burnt offering, with its accompanying meal offering, dominates the system of the Priestly Code.
f Relation to food	There are no clear directions about animal food in JE, but the permission of D to kill at home without sacrifice seems to show that it was never formerly partaken of except at a sacrificial meal.	^{Ph} seems to forbid slaughter except at the central sanctuary, but see Lev 17^{1N} ^{Pg} by the covenant of Noah sanctions it in advance. ^{Ps} regulates it Lev 7^{22-27}.
g Condition when offered	(The flesh boiled, cp Deut 14^{21} 16^{7N}, and the meal baked in cakes Judg 6^{19-21} 1 Sam 2^{13-16}, as for a feast given to a human guest.)	The flesh raw, and the meal preferably uncooked (see m below), as though to leave the materials as God had left them, and to avoid anthropomorphism
h Aspect emphasized	Burnt offerings being the exception, practically every sacrifice involved a sacrificial meal, so that the FEAST was an essential and outstanding part of the celebration, D suggesting that the poor should share in it. The blood may never be eaten, but is merely poured out.	No stress is laid on the feast, but throughout P, and increasingly in its later sections, importance is attached to the manipulation of the BLOOD, especially in connexion with the idea of propitiation.

7aa–k A good deal of material, properly belonging to the footnotes, has been inserted for convenience above, where a number of particulars, relating to all or several of the sacrifices, are collected in a summary comparative statement. It will be observed that the data of JE are occasionally supplemented from the historical books and prophets, the references being usually subjoined. A similar plan is pursued under ^{L} 9 a with the sacred seasons.

a See VIII i § 1 i 50 for a general comparison, cp XI § 2γ i 100 for J, XII § 2δ i 114 for E, and XIII § 4a i 131 for P. Various characteristic phrases may be referred to in this connexion, such as ^{E}110, ^{P}117, 118^{abegl} 'offer,' ^{JD}202 'sacrifice,' ^{Ph}196 'bread of (his) God,' ^{P}25 'atonement,' ^{P}158 'sweet savour.' See also the general comparative statement as to sacrifice inserted above in the main table under a, according to the preceding note.

SACRIFICES

	J D E	P^{ht} P^g P^s	
i Free or ordered	The manner of offering was no doubt regulated by usage which varied from place to place, but the choice of the victim, and of the time of offering (except as regards the three great feasts), was left to the offerer	Every detail is prescribed (cp *a* above), the predominant aim of the Priestly Code being to secure a uniform and stately round of sacrifices, cp ^{L}13g^i Num 28.^{N}	^{L}**7f**
j Personal or public	Individuals or families of their own motion offer sacrifice, and if they fail to furnish a victim there is no provision for any sacrifice at all at the feasts, or for any special occasion of joy, anxiety, or honour	Joint or representative sacrifices, independent of every special motive and of all spontaneity, are provided by law daily and at every sacred season, freewill or private offerings receding into the background, except in the case of the high priest, and where a sin or guilt offering is due	
b Burnt offering, cp **7d**	^{J} *a* Gen 8^{20c} *b* Ex 10^{25}—^{a} Noah 'took of every clean beast and of every clean fowl, and offered burnt offerings', ^{b} Moses required cattle from Pharaoh for burnt offerings. ^{E} *c* Gen 22$^{1-13}$ *d* Ex 18^{12} *e* 20^{24} cp 24^5 32^6 *f* Num 23$^{3\ 6\ 15\ 17}$ *g* Deut 27^{6b}—^{c} The immemorial usage is illustrated by the details of the sacrifice of Isaac, ^{d} at Horeb directions are given for an altar for burnt offerings, and instances occur in connexion with ^{d} Jethro's visit, ^{e} the sealing of the covenant and the making of the golden calf, and ^{f} the prophesying of Balaam; ^{g} burnt offerings are to be offered on the altar ordered at (Ebal). ^{D} *h* 12$^{6\ 11\ 13\ 27a}$—^{h} Burnt offerings named first among the list of offerings to be made at the central sanctuary.	^{Ph} *i* Lev 22$^{18-20}$—Conditions of acceptance for a burnt offering. ^{Pt} *j* Lev 1$^{1-13}$ *k*$^{14-17}$ *l* 6^{8-13N}—^{j} The offerer bringing a male calf, lamb, or kid to slay, flay, and dismember the victim, the priest to present the blood, and dash it around against the altar, to put fire (presumably fresh fire) upon the altar, to lay wood on it, and burn the whole, *k* the offerer bringing a bird, turtle dove, or young pigeon to leave all to the priest to do, i e to kill it and offer it as directed; *l* the burnt offering to be on the fire all night, and in the morning the priest to remove its ashes, while clothed in his linen vestments, then after changing them to carry the ashes unto a clean place; the fire to be perennial. ^{Pg} *m* Ex 29$^{15-18}$ *n* Lev 9$^{12-14\ 16}$—^{m} Orders for a burnt offering at Aaron's consecration, the ritual prescribed agreeing with ^{Pt} *l* above; ^{n} the burnt offering on the octave of the consecration follows the same ritual and is said to be 'according to the ordinance' ^{Ps} *o* Lev 7^8 *p* 8$^{18-21}$—^{p} The execution exactly follows the order ^{m}. ^{o} The skin is to be the officiating priest's perquisite.	
c Consumption, rule of	^{J} *a* Ex 34^{25b}—The sacrifice of the feast of the passover not to be left unto the morning. ^{E} *b* Ex 23^{18b}—The fat of God's feast not to remain until the morning. ^{D} *c* 16^4—The flesh of the sacrifice of the first day of the Passover-Mazzoth celebration not to remain until the morning	^{Ph} *d* Lev 19$^{5-8}$ *e* 22^{29}—^{d} An ordinary 'sacrifice of peace offerings' may be eaten the second day, but on the third any remnant must be burnt, on pain of the eater of it being cut off from his people. But ^{e} 'a sacrifice of thanksgiving' may only be eaten on the day of the sacrifice, none is to be left until the morning ^{Pt} *f* Lev 7$^{15-18}$—The provisions of ^{Ph} *de* are repeated with slight variations of terminology. ^{Pg} cp ^{L}7p*j*	
d Daily sacrifice		^{Ps} *a* Ex 29^{38-42N} *b* 30^7 *c* Num 28$^{3-8}$—^{ac}Aaron is to offer, both morning and evening, a lamb as a burnt offering with meal, oil, and wine offerings as appointed, ^{c} 'a perpetual incense before Yahweh' is to be burnt, morning and evening, upon the golden altar. (Lev 6$^{8-13}$ is by some referred to the daily sacrifice)	
e Empty-handedness forbidden	^{J} *a* Ex 34^{20c}—None to appear before Yahweh empty. ^{E} *b* Ex 23^{15N}—Identical with ^{a}, probably copied. ^{D} *c* Deut 16^{16}—Worshippers at the three pilgrimage-feasts not to appear before Yahweh empty.	^{Ph} *d* Lev 23$^{10b\ 17-20N}$—Israelites to present annually the wave-sheaf of firstfruits, and then at Pentecost two loaves and two lambs ^{Pg} *e* Lev 23§—On each of the 'set feasts of Yahweh' 'an offering made by fire' is to be offered ^{Ps} *f* Num 28—Burnt, meal, and drink offerings are prescribed for each day in the sacred calendar.	
f Fleece of wool	^{D} 18^4—The first shearing to be given to Levi, the sacred tribe.		

7b Cp ^{P}118^c.—*j* On the slaying of the victim see Lev 1^{14N}.   *d* See XVI § 10*a* 1 154, § 11*β* 1 156.

LAWS AND INSTITUTIONS

	J	D	E	P^ht	P^g	P^s
L **7** g Guilt offering				P^t a Lev 5^{14-16N} b $^{17-19}$ c 6^{1-7} d 7^{1-7} e Num 5^{5-8} f Lev 19^{21} —ac In cases where any withholding or misappropriating of property has taken place, whether a one of God's dues, or c a neighbour's rightful property, restitution with the addition of ¼ must be made a to the priest or c to the neighbour, and a guilt offering of a ram brought in order to atonement. e If the neighbour be dead or absent and have no kinsman as representative, restitution as above is due to the priest b If, possibly because of calamity, some unknown defect is suspected, the ram must be offered as a guilt offering, but no restitution can of course be made. After e confession has been made, d the victim is to be slain, its blood dashed against the altar, the fat, &c, burnt, and all the flesh given to the priests to be eaten in a holy place. f A guilt offering is required in the case of the seduction of a betrothed slave girl.	P^g g Num 18^9—Every guilt offering is most holy for Aaron and his sons, and is to be eaten by them alone.	
h Shewbread			^JE Cp 1 Sam 21^6 for antiquity of the shewbread.		P^g a Ex 25^{30} b Lev 24^{5-9}—a Shewbread ordered; b detailed provisions for its preparation and use.	
i Incense				P^t An accompaniment of the meal offering, see 7m.	P^g a Lev 10^{1-5} cp Num 16 b Lev 16^{12} c 24^7 —b Aaron to enter before the mercy-seat within the veil only with clouds of incense from a censer. a Nadab and Abihu destroyed for offering strange fire in their censers, also Korah and the two hundred and fifty princes for offering incense without authority, and atonement made in the ensuing plague by Aaron with a censer of incense; c incense an accompaniment of the shewbread.	P^s d Ex 30^{1-9} e $^{34-38}$—d A golden altar of incense to be made, and Aaron to burn incense upon it every morning and evening when dressing and lighting the lamps; no strange incense to be used; e the composition of the sacred incense prescribed, its imitation forbidden.
j Jealousy offering				P^t Num 5^{11-31N}—A composite ordinance requiring a specific offering and ritual in cases of marital jealousy.		
l Leprosy offerings				P^t a Lev 14^{2-7N} b $^{10-20}$ c $^{21-32}$ d $^{49-53}$—a For the cleansing of the leper a special ritual is prescribed, for which two living birds, cedar wood, scarlet, and hyssop are required; b to this a second series of ceremonies a week later is superadded, composed of familiar elements, three lambs, meal, and oil, used as in similar cases with an elaboration of detail; c provision is made for offerings of less cost for poorer people; d the first form of ritual is also prescribed for leprosy in a house.		
m Meal offering			^JE Cp n ab	P^t a Lev 2^{1-3} b $^{4-13}$ c $^{14-16}$ d 6^{14-18} e $^{19-23}$ f 7^9 g Num 15^{17-21N}—b Different forms of		

7g The difficulty of ascertaining the precise meaning of the rules for the guilt offering may be plausibly explained by the supposition that it had not had time to establish itself as an independent and precisely defined institution at the time when codification began. Some connexion with property can be traced in all cases but those of the leper Lev 14^{12} and the Nazirite Num 6^{12}.—Cp P118^f.

i Cp P72 'frankincense,' P95 'incense'

m The number and diversity of ordinances on the meal offering not only suggest that the usage of more than one place or period is represented, but that this kind of offering was a very popular one. Observe that *minha*, which in JE is generic,

SACRIFICES

	J	D	E	P^ht	P^g	P^s	L
m Meal offering (*continued*)				cooked meal offering recognized, cakes or wafers from the oven, or from the baking pan, or frying pan. On the other hand *a* m is required, presumably by a later ordinance, to be of fine flour uncooked. Further there is *c* a 'meal offering of firstfruits,' 'corn in the ear parched with fire, bruised corn of the fresh ear,' and *g* 'a cake for an heave offering of the first of the dough' *b* With the exception of this last and of certain cakes offered with the thank offering 7¹³, none of which are made to pass through the altar fire, *bd* no leaven allowed with a meal offering, *b* nor any honey, but *b* salt always to be used Frankincense ordered with 'the parched corn' and *ad* the uncooked meal offering of flour, and *abcde* oil with all the meal offerings of which part is burnt as a memorial. The priest to take *b* the memorial or *ad* his handful or *c* part of the bruised corn, and burn it on the altar with *acd* all the frankincense and *acd* part of the oil; *abd* the rest of the meal offerings to be for the priests, *f* those cooked in oven, baking pan, or frying pan being reserved for the priest offering them, but *c* the priests' own meal offerings to be wholly burnt, not eaten. *e* A morning and evening daily meal offering prescribed, of fine flour cooked with oil as directed Pg *h* Ex 29² ²³ ³² *i* Num 18⁹ —*h* A special meal offering, loaves, wafers, and cakes of fine wheaten flour cooked without leaven and placed in a basket, oil being used for the last two, prescribed for the day of Aaron's consecration; one of each to be 'waved' and then burnt as a memorial, and the rest eaten the same day, any remnants being burnt; *i* 'every meal offering' of the people, so far as '[reserved] from the fire,' to belong to the priesthood, and to be eaten 'as the most holy things' and shared by 'every male.'	Ps *j* Lev 8² ²⁶ ³¹ *k* Num 15¹⁻⁹ *l* Lev 10¹² *m* 7¹⁰ —*k* The 'basket of consecration' prepared and used as directed *h*, the ordinance *e* about the daily meal offering apparently being adapted to fit the same occasion; *k* every animal victim, offered as a burnt offering or a 'sacrifice' (i e peace offering) to be accompanied by its appropriate meal offering according to the scale prescribed; *l* Aaron and his surviving sons bidden to eat the meal offering as their due 'beside the altar' 'in a holy place.' *m* The restriction noticed above *f* removed by a later regulation, which provides that 'every meal offering, mingled with oil or dry, shall all the sons of Aaron have, one as well as another.'	**L 7n**
n No leaven	J *a* Ex 34²⁵—No leavened bread to be offered with the blood of Yahweh's sacrifice.		E *b* Ex 23¹⁸—No leavened bread to be offered with the blood of God's sacrifice.	Pt *c* Lev 2¹¹ *d* 6¹⁷ *e* 7¹¹⁻¹⁴ —*c* No leaven to be used with any meal offering, or fire offering of any kind, neither *d* shall the flour of a meal offering after the offering be baked with leaven for the priests' use. *e* Both unleavened cakes and wafers and leavened bread to be offered with a sacrifice of thanksgiving, but presumably without any part being burnt on the altar. Ps *f* Lev 10¹²—The priests' portion of the meal offering to be eaten without leaven.		

'offering,' becomes in P specific, 'meal offering,' see P118ʰ The story of Cain's 'offering' (⅏ 'present') at least proves the antiquity of this kind of gift to God, it is doubtful whether any disparagement of it is intended in the narrative —Cp P118ʰ.

238 LAWS AND INSTITUTIONS

	J	D	E	P^ht	P^g	P^s

^{L}**7 o** Oil in sacrifice
J a Gen 35^{14}—Jacob pours oil upon his votive pillar at Bethel.
E b Gen 28^{18}—‖ Ja

P^t Oil (^{L}7ma–e) as an accompaniment of the meal offering and ^{L}7lbc an element in the leprosy offerings.
P^s ^{L}7mh Prescribed proportion of oil in the meal offerings accompanying animal sacrifices.

p Peace offering
J See a, especially d, which specifies 'sacrifices' (i e peace offerings) 'and burnt offerings' as the offerings which Israel was to 'sacrifice' according to the demand of Ex 3^{18} &c (9).
E a Ex 20^{24} 24^5 32^6 Num 22^{40} b Deut 27^7— a Peace offerings ordered to be offered on the altar prescribed to be made, offered at the ratification of the covenant, part of the worship of the golden calf, and provided by Balak in honour of Balaam's arrival ; b peace offerings to be sacrificed on the altar ordered to be made (on Mount Ebal).
D c 12$^{6\ 11\ 27b}$ d 18^3—c Peace offerings among the offerings to be made only at the central sanctuary d The shoulder, the two cheeks, and the maw to constitute the priest's portion in a 'sacrifice' (i e peace offering).

P^h e 17$^{1-9}$ f 22$^{21-33}$—e No animal to be killed for food or as a sacrifice without offering it at the sanctuary for a sacrifice of peace offerings , f to be acceptable as a peace offering, an animal must be perfect according to the prescribed definition ; but of the three forms of peace offering, the freewill offering must be lowest, because f a lower standard of acceptance is prescribed for it, the thank offering highest, because to be consumed the same day as offered, cp ^{L}7t.
P^t g Lev 3$^{1-16}$ h 7$^{11-21}$—g The offerer to kill the victim (but see ^{L}7b^N), the priest to dash the blood against the altar, and to burn the fat with the prescribed portions included with it ; then h every person that is ceremonially clean may eat of the flesh, no doubt after the priest's portion, see ^{L}13g Lev 7^{31}, has been taken. Specific meal offerings are prescribed for a sacrifice of thanksgiving (see ^{L}7t), but not for a vow or a freewill offering (cp also ^{L}6ce 7cf 13gc)
P^g j Ex 29$^{29-34}$ k Lev 9$^{18-21}$—j A special form of peace offering, 'the ram of consecration,' ordered at Aaron's consecration ; the fat to be burnt ; and the priest's portion (here defined as 'the breast of the wave offering and the thigh of the heave offering') to be 'sanctified' ; the flesh to be seethed 'in a holy place,' eaten at the door of the Tent of Meeting by Aaron and his sons, and anything remaining till next day burnt. k A similar peace offering described as being brought by the people and offered on the octave of the consecration
P^s l Lev 7^{34}. m 8$^{22-32}$ n 10^{14}—ln The priests' due specified as above j ; m the offering of the ram of consecration described, the thigh being burnt, but the breast given to Moses.

r The red heifer
P^t Num 19^{1-22N}—A red heifer is to be burnt entire, that with its ashes a 'water of separation' may be prepared for use in purifying those unclean by the dead   This ordinance in its earlier portion seems to be much worked over, the reference to Eleazar being an indication of P^s.

s Sin offering
P^t a Lev 5^{1-6N} b 7^{-10N} c 11–13 d 6$^{24-29}$ e Num 15$^{22-31}$—a A sin offering, with confession of the offence, prescribed in cases of withholding evidence, swearing rashly, or unwittingly touching an unclean thing, or e if an unintentional failure to keep 'these commandments' (i e presumably of the ceremonial law) take place on the part of the congregation or of an individual   But e wilful transgression cannot be atoned for. In a the former series of cases a female

---

7p The contradictory statements ($^D d$ and $^P jln$) as to the priest's share point to a difference of date, unless we are to suppose that at the centralizing of the cultus varying usages were found side by side according to the varying praxis of the several sanctuaries, and that they are reflected severally in D and P. But if the arrangement in D had established itself firmly it could hardly have been upset by P —Cp ^{P}118^1.

s The notes on ab in vol ii refer to the peculiar phenomena of the sin and guilt offering laws, from which it is hard clearly to distinguish the two. In the history the allusions are even more

SACRIFICES 239

	J	D	E	P^{ht}	P^g	P^s	
s Sin offering (*continued*)				lamb or goat is required, with ^{b} a reduction for poverty to two turtle doves or young pigeons (one for a sin offering, the other for a burnt offering), or ^{c} to $\frac{1}{10}$ of an ephah of fine flour, ^{e} in the latter two cases a he-goat (in addition to a young bullock for a burnt offering) and a she-goat are respectively demanded. ^{d} The victim is to be killed 'where the burnt offering is killed,' 'the priest that offereth it for sin shall eat' the flesh 'in a holy place,' though it is added, either as explanation or correction, that 'every male among the priests shall eat thereof,' and the holiness of the blood and flesh is such as to affect garments and vessels. In ^{ade} the oldest ordinances nothing is prescribed as to the ceremonial of sacrifice, but ^{bc} the supplements are fuller.	^{Pg} f Ex 29^{11-14} g Lev $9^{8-11\ 15}$ h Num 18^9 — f A bullock ordered for a sin offering at Aaron's consecration, and the ceremonial prescribed Aaron and his sons to lay their hands on the victim's head, then Moses is to kill it at the door of the Tent of Meeting, and after some of the blood had been applied with the finger to the horns of the altar, the whole is to be poured out at its base; then the fat and the parts included with it to be burnt on the altar, but the flesh, skin, and dung to be burnt without the camp ^{g} On the octave of the consecration Aaron offers a calf as a sin offering after the same manner. ^{h} 'Every sin offering of the people' is to be eaten by the priests and by them alone	^{Ps} i Lev 8^{14} j 4^{1-35} k 6^{30} l 10^{16-20} N — i The sin offering ordered at Aaron's consecration f is described as being offered in the appointed manner, but the application of the blood to the altar is interpreted as being for its purification (cf ^{Pg} $^L7$ ^{g} a, and also ^{Ps} Ex 40^{10}, where the altar is to be 'sanctified' by unction with the anointing oil, and Num 7^1, where this is said to have been done) j Distinctive sin offerings required in cases of guilt unwittingly incurred by doing what was forbidden (again presumably by the ceremonial law), whether by 'the anointed priest,' 'the whole congregation of Israel,' 'a ruler,' or 'one of the common people'; the ceremonial practically as above f, but ordered in greater particularity, and in the first two cases the blood to be sprinkled seven times inside the Tent 'before the veil' and applied to 'the horns of the altar of sweet incense,' the rest being poured out 'at the base of the altar of burnt offering'; the bodies of the victims to be burned without the camp 'in a clean place, where the ashes are poured out.' k It is laid down as a rule that no sin offering whose blood as above (and cp Lev 16^{27}) is brought into the Tent is to be eaten, but burnt, l Eleazar and Ithamar, Aaron's surviving sons, are blamed for *not* having eaten a sin offering which was not covered by this rule	$^L7$s

puzzling (2 Kings 12^{16} gs money fines cp Am 2^8, 1 Sam 6 g 'jewels of gold') The absence of gs from Lev 1–3 suggests that they had not yet reached the same level of acceptance as bpm. It should be noticed that s has a positive consecrating power, restoring or dedicating the person to the worship and service of God, whereas g has rather a negative effect in making reparation and neutralizing guilt, cp also $^L7g^N$.—Cp ^P118j, $^P44$ 'confess.'

240 LAWS AND INSTITUTIONS

	J	D	E	P^ht	P^g	P^s

^{L}**7** t Sacrifice of thanksgiving

^{Ph} *a* Lev 22^{29}—'A sacrifice of thanksgiving' to be sacrificed 'so that it may be accepted,' i e presumably so as to satisfy the customary requirements of the oral priestly torah ; to be eaten only on the day of the sacrifice, and so connected with the peace offering, the only sort which furnished a feast for the offerer. See also ^{L}13f.

^{Pt} *b* Lev 7$^{15-18}$—The 'sacrifice of peace offerings for thanksgiving' expressly included under 'the law of the sacrifice of peace offerings' and distinguished from vows and freewill offerings which are the only other kinds specified The rule of consumption repeated, cp ^{L}7c.

w Wine offering

^{J} *a* Gen 35^{14}—Jacob pours out a drink offering upon his votive pillar.

^{Ps} *b* Ex 29^{40} *c* Lev 23^{13} *d* Num 15$^{1-16\aleph}$ *e* Num 28—Drink offerings prescribed *b* for the daily burnt offering, *c* for the offering of the day of the wave-sheaf, *d* for the occasional, and *e* for the prescribed sacrifices The scale is the same throughout, i e half a hin of wine for a bullock, one-third for a ram, and one-fourth for a lamb. Cp ^{L}13g; Num 28$^\aleph$.

y Yearly sin offering

^{Pg} *a* Lev 16$^{1-28\S}$—The germ of the developed law of the Day of Atonement is contained in the parts assigned to ^{Pg} in the text, vol ii (which see for details). It seems to be the original provision of ^{Pg} for the sanctifying of the altar, tent, and inner sanctuary, ct 7s1 above.

^{Ps} *b* Lev 16$^{1-34}$ *c* Ex 30^{10}—The ordinance, as successively supplemented, adds provisions for an atonement for Aaron and his house, for the repetition of the ceremony at the consecration of a high priest, and for its establishment as a yearly day of solemn observance *c* The altar of incense is to be used for atonement by the blood of the sin offering being annually applied to the horns of it by the high priest, this provision being possibly the result of interpreting 'the altar before Yahweh' Lev 16$^{12\ 18}$ as meaning this altar.

z The goat for Azazel

^{Pg} Lev 16$^{5-28}$—One of the original elements of the day of atonement, never elsewhere referred to, is the institution of the scapegoat, one of two chosen by lot, which is to be 'sent away for Azazel into the wilderness,' after Aaron had confessed over his head 'all the iniquities of the children of Israel, all their transgressions, even all their sins'

8. Sacred Dues

^{L}**8** a Firstborn

^{J} *a* Ex 13$^{11-16\aleph}$ *b* 34^{19}—^{ab} All firstborn males belong to Yahweh, and are to be redeemed, but the manner of redemption is undefined *a* The amplifier has connected this ordinance with the destruction of the Egyptian firstborn.

^{Pg} *d* Ex 13^1 *e* Num 18^{15}—*d* At the Exodus Moses is bidden to sanctify unto Yahweh all the firstborn, and *e* later it is laid down that this means that they are given to Aaron and his sons, and that in the case of the firstborn of man each must be redeemed.

7t Cp ^{P}118^k.
w Cp ^{P}118^d.
y z For another view see Enc Bibl under *Atonement, Azazel*.

On the date of introduction of the Annual Day of Atonement cp XIII § 11β 156
8a It might be conjectured that some provisions in JE have

SACRED DUES

241

	J	D	E	P^lit	P^g	P^s	L 8c
			ᴱ c Ex 22²⁹—The firstborn of Israel's sons to be given to God.	(See further 11 i k q)			

b Firstlings

ᴶ a Gen 4⁴ b Ex 13¹¹⁻¹⁶ᴺ c 34¹⁹—ᵃ Abel brings of the firstlings of his flock as an offering to Yahweh. ᵇᶜ Moses requires that 'all that openeth the womb,' male firstlings of beasts as well as firstborn of men, be reckoned as Yahweh's, and that the firstling of an ass be redeemed with a lamb, or its neck broken.

ᴱ d Ex 22³⁰—Firstlings of oxen and sheep to be given to God on the eighth day.

ᴰ e 15¹⁹⁻²² cp 14²³—Firstling males of the herd and flock to be 'sanctified unto Yahweh', the calf may not be worked nor the lamb sheared, but it is to be eaten in a sacrificial feast at the central sanctuary (it is implied, after being sacrificed as a peace offering), unless it have some blemish, when it is to be eaten at home without being sacrificed.

P^g f Ex 13¹ g Num 18¹⁵⁻¹⁸—f Firstlings included under same description as the firstborn of men, to be sanctified unto Yahweh, but ᵍ also expressly specified, and the rule laid down that the firstlings of a cow, a sheep, or a goat (i e clean animals available for sacrifice) may not be redeemed, and that their flesh after they have been sacrificed as peace offerings belongs to the priests; but the firstlings of unclean beasts must be redeemed from a month old, the price being settled 'according to thine (the priest's) estimation,' though the very next words state 'for the money of five shekels,' apparently a uniform price.

P^s h Lev 27²⁶—No one can, as of his own motion, sanctify a firstling as a gift to Yahweh, for it is his already; and if it be of an unclean beast he must redeem it according to the priest's estimation + ⅕, or let it be sold according to the priest's estimation.

c Firstfruits

ᴶ a Gen 4³ b Ex 34²⁶—ᵃ Cain brings 'of the fruit of the ground an offering unto Yahweh', ᵇ Moses commands Israel, 'The first of the firstfruits of thy ground thou shalt bring unto the house of Yahweh thy God.'

ᴱ c Ex 22²⁹ᵃ d 23¹⁹ᴺ—ᵈ The last command ᵇ is identically given, and ᶜ it is ordered, 'Thou shalt not delay to offer of the abundance of thy fruits and of thy liquors' (𝔊 'of thy fulness and thy tear')

ᴰ e 18⁴ᵃᴺ f 26¹⁻¹¹—ᵉ The firstfruits are part of the endowment of the priesthood; ᶠ they are to be brought in a basket, given to the priest with use of prescribed words, set down by him before the altar, and offered by the worshipper with other prescribed words, a rare instance of a rite thus fully furnished.

P^h g Lev 23¹⁰⁻²⁰—On 'the morrow after the sabbath,' whether the phrase refers to one of the days of Mazzoth, or to some other occasion, the sheaf of the firstfruits of the harvest which has been brought by the worshipper is to be waved before Yahweh, and none are to eat 'bread, nor parched corn, nor fresh ears' (i e of the new corn) until they have 'brought the oblation of their God.' Then after fifty days a 'new meal offering' is to be brought, 'two wave loaves of two tenth parts of fine flour, baken with leaven, for firstfruits unto Yahweh.' With these two yearling he-lambs are to be waved for a wave offering before Yahweh: 'they shall be holy unto Yahweh for the priest.'

P^t h Lev 2¹⁴⁻¹⁶ i Num 15¹⁷⁻²¹—h Directions given how to 'offer a meal offering of firstfruits unto Yahweh' (i e probably as a freewill offering), to be composed of 'corn in the ear parched with fire, bruised corn of the fresh ear, with oil and frankincense.' ⁱ The people when they come into the land are ordered, when they eat of the bread of the land, to offer up of the first of their dough a cake for an heave offering, as they heave the heave offering of their threshing-floor, this last being perhaps an allusion to the wave-sheaf.

P^g j Num 18¹²—'All the best of the oil, and all the best of the vintage, and of the corn, the firstfruits of them which they give unto Yahweh' and 'the first ripe fruits of all that is in their land, which they bring unto Yahweh' given to the priests.

---

been displaced as incongruous with later ordinances. Was the firstborn son bound to assist the head of the family in his priestly functions, and does the conception of P account for the discontinuance of any such lay priesthood? Were the 'young men' of Ex 24⁵ firstborn sons? Should the sacrifice of Isaac be used in illustration of the divine claim to the firstborn, Ishmael being neglected? At least it may be said that the later tradition failed to record the method by which in old times the firstborn sons were given to God or redeemed. Perhaps R found a clue in JE and expunged it. See also XII § 5δ (11) 119

8b ᴱ The offering of a firstling on the eighth day ᵈ ceasing to be practicable on the abolition of the local sanctuaries, ᴰ the provision is substituted that no profit may be made out of it before it is offered, cp IX 1 § 2β 75. In the later ordinances ᴾ the cases and conditions are as usual more fully treated

c Again an obviously ancient custom is embodied in different forms in successive periods. ᴶᴱ First the offering of all kinds of firstfruits at the local sanctuary is generally required; then ᴰ the ritual is defined and liturgically enriched; next P^ht a distinction appears between raw and cooked, and finally P^g this distinction establishes itself in the collateral terms *bikkurim* and *reshith*. Cp Bennett on 'Firstfruits' in Hastings' *DB*

R

242　　　　　　　　　　　　　　　LAWS AND INSTITUTIONS

	J	D	E	P^{ht}	P^g	P^s

^{L}8 d Tithes

E *a* Gen 28^{22N}—Jacob promises to God a tithe of all that he should give him, if he should be brought back home in peace and prosperity.
^{D} *b* 14$^{22-29}$　*c* 26$^{12-15}$—*b* The tithe of agricultural produce to be sold and the money spent on feasting at the central sanctuary, the local Levite being admitted to a share; but 'in the third year, which is the year of tithing,' to be given on the spot to the Levite, stranger, fatherless, and widow, with an appropriate prayer of dedication after a prescribed form.

^{Pg} *d* Num 18$^{21-24}$—'The tithes of the children of Israel, which they offer as an heave offering unto Yahweh,' to be 'given to the Levites.'
^{Ps} *e* Lev 27$^{30-33}$　*f* Gen 14^{20}—*e* 'All the tithe of the land, whether of the seed of the land or of the fruit of the tree, is Yahweh's,' but may be redeemed with the addition of a fifth. Also 'all the tithe of the herd or of the flock . . . shall be holy unto Yahweh,' and cannot be redeemed, and if one be changed for another, both shall be forfeited as holy. *f* Abraham is related to have paid tithes to Melchizedek of all the spoil of Sodom.

e Tithe of tithes

^{Pg} Num 18$^{25-32}$—The Levites are to treat the tithes as their income and to tithe them, giving the tenth as 'Yahweh's heave offering to Aaron the priest.'

f Vows

E *b* Cp Judg 11$^{30\ 34-40}$ (assigned to E), where Jephthah vows to offer up 'whosoever' should meet him 'as a burnt offering.' Cp *h e* and ct *fc*.
^{D} *a* 23^{21}.—A vow is a freewill offering promised beforehand with the mouth, and when once vowed is to be paid.

^{Pt} *b* Num 6$^{1-21}$—The vow of the Nazirite (see ^{L}11*p*).
^{Ps} *c* Lev 27$^{1-13}$　*d* Num 29^{39}　*e* Num 30^{1-16N}—*c* Where the subject of the vow is a living person, a scale of money equivalents is provided according to age and sex, and with power to the priest to reduce it for poverty: where it is a beast, it may not be redeemed if it is of a kind fit for sacrifice, and, if one be changed for another, both are forfeited; but if it be unclean, it may be redeemed at the priest's valuation + ⅕. *e* A vow once made by a man or woman must be fulfilled, but the father of a maiden or the husband of a married woman may annul her vows if he do so at once on hearing the utterance; the vow of a widow or divorced woman is however irrevocable. *d* The fixed offerings prescribed for ordinary and special days are to be independent of any vows offered in addition.

g Freewill offerings

^{D} *a* 16^{10}　*b* 12^5—*a* The feast of weeks to be kept, not with a prescribed tale of sacrifices, but with 'a tribute of a freewill offering' according to the measure of God's blessing. *b* Freewill offerings are among those which are only to be offered at the central sanctuary.

^{Ph} *c* Lev 22$^{19-24}$—A freewill offering may be a burnt offering or a peace offering, but the victim must satisfy the conditions prescribed ^{L}61*d*, which are less stringent in case of a freewill offering.
^{Pt} *d* Lev 7^{16}—One kind of peace offering is composed of vows and freewill offerings, and may be eaten on the second day.
^{Ps} *e* Num 29^{39}—Freewill offerings are to be in addition to, and independent of, the fixed order of periodical sacrifices.

h Sanctified and devoted things

^{D} *a* 7$^{25-27}$　*b* 13$^{12-18}$—*a* The graven images of the Canaanite gods, with the gold and silver on them, are devoted things and are to be burnt with fire and may not be taken into any one's possession; *b* an apostate and idolatrous city is to be treated similarly, its inhabitants and their cattle to be killed, and all the spoil burnt.

^{Pg} *c* Num 18^{14}—'Everything devoted in Israel shall be' the property of the priesthood.
^{Ps} *d* Lev 27$^{14-25}$　*e* ^{28}—*d* If a man sanctify a house, he may redeem it at the priest's valuation + ⅕; if he sanctify a field out of his patrimony, he may redeem it at the priest's true valuation if at and from the year of jubile, or with proportional abatement if from the year of jubile next following; but if he refuse to redeem it or sell it,

---

8d There are internal difficulties about the tithe in D, as to which see Driver ad loc, but nowhere is there a hint that it extended to anything but vegetable produce, the inclusion of cattle occurring only in P^s. If E's really connected tithes with Jacob (cp XII § 4 11*b*), he probably overlooked the fact that Jacob's wealth was to be in cattle, even as the need of corn later in Gen obviously implies an agricultural condition menaced by famine.

f The provisions of P^s (ct D) as to vows well illustrate the arrival of an era of defined praxis and written rubrics

g The freewill offering, which is in the foreground in D, has receded into the background for P^s.

h In D 'devote,' whatever its underlying meaning, involves destruction, as in the older usage, but in P^s the idea of 'devotion' is deemed adequately carried out in the case of things by consecrating them to the use of the priesthood. Cp ^{D}35

SACRED SEASONS

	J	D	E	P^ht	P^g	P^s	
i Poll tax						^Ps f Ex 30^11-16N.—As atonement money, to avert plague on account of the census, half a shekel is due from every person numbered over twenty years of age as a 'ransom for his soul,' and is to be spent for the service of the Tent of Meeting.	^L 9a

(preceding P^ht text: then no further power of redemption remains; if however the field be one bought and not inherited, the valuation shall merely cover the unexpired term till the year of jubile, when it must return to its owner; ^e but no devoted thing, whether person, animal, or inherited field, shall be redeemed, and no devoted person shall be ransomed, but put to death.)

9. Sacred Seasons

	J / E / D	P^h / P^g / P^s	
a Calendar	^J a Ex 34^18-25—Mazzoth (Unleavened-bread), Sabbath, Weeks, Ingathering, and Passover (but see ^25N) specified or alluded to, three annual appearances 'before the Lord Yahweh, the God of Israel,' being required. ^E b Ex 23^10-17—The Sabbatical Year, the Sabbath, and three specified obligatory feasts, Mazzoth, Harvest (= Weeks), and Ingathering. ^D c 16^1-17N—Three obligatory feasts specified, when all males are to appear before Yahweh at the Central Sanctuary, Passover and Mazzoth, Weeks, and Booths (= Ingathering).	^Ph d Lev 23^9-11 14-18a 19b. 39-43?—The Wavesheaf Festival (perhaps an element of Mazzoth), Pentecost (= Weeks), and Booths specified in the extant fragments of calendar. ^Pg e Lev 23^4-8N 21 23 33-38 44—The Passover, Mazzoth, Pentecost, Trumpets, and Booths specified, the list being amplified by adding the Sabbath and Day of Atonement, and also expanded by combination with ^Ph, the reference to Pentecost almost disappearing. The calendar closes as follows, ^37 'These are the set feasts of Yahweh, which ye shall proclaim to be holy convocations, to offer an offering made by fire unto Yahweh, a burnt offering, and a meal offering, a sacrifice, and drink offerings, each on its own day beside the sabbaths of Yahweh, and beside your gifts, and beside all your vows, and beside all your freewill offerings, which ye give unto Yahweh.' ^Ps f Num 28^N—Every day has its sacrifice to sanctify it, and in addition the Sabbath, New Moon, Passover, Mazzoth, Weeks, Trumpets, Day of Atonement, and Feast of the fifteenth of the seventh month (= Booths), have additional sacrifices specified as of obligation.	^L 9
a General comparison	^JE The sacred seasons are occasions when natural joy is organized in united festivals at the local sanctuaries, joyous sacrificial feasts being the most prominent elements in the celebration. ^D The same are centralized, becoming pilgrimages, and further organized, the leading feature still being to 'eat and drink before Yahweh.'	^Ph akin to ^JED. ^Pgs Marked mainly by prescribed public offerings, the element of feasting being lost, with the modified exception of the Passover.	
b Origin	^JE Agricultural, with the exception of the Passover in ^Js ^D Agricultural, with historical connexion beginning to be combined	^Ph Mainly agricultural still. ^Pgs Historical commemoration and religious ceremony as such tend to obscure agricultural connexion, even Pentecost was by the later Jews connected with the giving of the Law.	
c Number	^JE The Sabbath and three Feasts, the Passover being only mentioned in ^J and not related to Mazzoth. ^D The Sabbath and three pilgrimages, Passover and Mazzoth being united.	^Ph like ^JED. ^Pgs the number is successively increased in ^Pg and ^Ps, see a e f	
d Character	^JED All the celebrations are festal gatherings for thanksgiving to God and enjoyment of his gifts.	^Ph like ^JED. ^Pgs All are coloured throughout by the consciousness of sin, and need for expiation, culminating in the Day of Atonement.	

9a Again, as under ^L7a, a series of points, bearing on the whole subject, are given for convenience in the parallel columns above. See also VIII 1 § 5 53. For a general account of the variations in the calendar see VIII 1 § 5 iii § 2ζ 53 65, cp IX i § 3γ 78 on the rationale of the changes.

LAWS AND INSTITUTIONS

^{L}9a		J D E	P^{lt} P^g P^s
	e Date	$^{J\square}$ Settled by the seasons, Abib however being in one place apparently fixed as the month for Mazzoth ^{D} Mazzoth in Abib, Pentecost seven weeks from beginning of harvest, Booths at the end of the harvest.	^{Ph} Pentecost reckoned as seven weeks after the offering of the wave-sheaf on the 'morrow after the sabbath,' but Booths left unfixed. ^{Pgs} All fixed by the month and day, i e by the moon, the change being perhaps helped by Passover being a night feast and so requiring a full moon.
	f Duration	$^{J\square}$ Unspecified (the seven days of Mazzoth probably not belonging to the earliest tradition). ^{D} Fixed.	^{Ph} like ^{D} ^{Pgs} Booths extended from seven to eight days.
	b The Sabbath	$^J a$ Ex 34^{21}—'Six days thou shalt work ($\mathfrak{H}$ serve), but on the seventh day thou shalt keep-sabbath: in plowing time and in harvest thou shalt keep-sabbath.' $^E b$ Ex 20$^{8-10}$ c 23^{12}—^{c} 'Six days thou shalt do thy work ($\mathfrak{H}$ doing), and on the seventh day thou shalt keep-sabbath; that thine ox and thine ass may rest, and the son of thy handmaid be refreshed, and the stranger.' ^{b} 'Remember $^D d$ 5$^{12-15}$—'Observe ^{ED} the sabbath day to keep it holy Six days shalt thou labour ($\mathfrak{H}$ serve) and do all thy work ($\mathfrak{H}$ business): but the seventh day is a sabbath unto Yahweh thy God, in it thou shalt not do any work ($\mathfrak{H}$ business), thou, nor thy son, nor thy daughter, thy manservant, nor thy maidservant, ^{E} nor thy cattle, nor thy stranger that is within thy gates' ^{D} nor thine ox, nor thine ass, nor any of thy cattle, nor thy stranger that is within thy gates; that thy manservant and thy maidservant may rest as well as thou. And thou shalt remember that thou wast a servant in the land of Egypt, and Yahweh thy God brought thee out thence by a mighty hand and by a stretched out arm therefore Yahweh thy God commanded thee to keep the sabbath day'	$^{Ph} e$ Lev 19^{3b} f 19^{30a} g 26^{2a} h Ex 31^{12N}—^{efgh} 'Ye shall keep my sabbaths; ^{eg} I am Yahweh ^{e} your God, ^{h} which sanctify you' $^{Pg} i$ Gen 2^2 j Ex 20^{11} k Ex 35$^{1-3}$ m Lev 24^8—^{i} God hallows the seventh day as the sabbath in memory of his rest after the six days of Creation; ^{j} this motive is appended to the Fourth Commandment; ^{k} Moses commands, 'six days shall work ($\mathfrak{H}$ business) be done, but on the seventh day there shall be to you a sabbath of solemn rest to Yahweh: whosoever doeth any work therein shall be put to death. Ye shall kindle no fire throughout your habitations on the sabbath day'; ^{m} the shewbread is to be changed 'every sabbath.' $^{Ps} l$ Lev 23^3 n Ex 16$^{22-30}$ o Ex 31$^{14-17}$ p Num 28^9 q Num 15$^{32-36}$—^{l} Prefixed to the calendar ^{L}9ae is the ordinance, 'Six days shall work ($\mathfrak{H}$ business) be done: but on the seventh day is a sabbath of solemn rest, an holy convocation; ye shall do no manner of work: it is a sabbath unto Yahweh in all your dwellings'; ^{p} in addition to the daily morning and evening sacrifice an offering of twice the amount is ordered on the sabbath; ^{q} a man is stoned for gathering sticks on the sabbath; ^{n} the manna is given in double supply on the sixth day and withheld on the seventh in order to ensure that the seventh day shall be 'a solemn rest, a holy sabbath unto Yahweh.'
	c The New Moon		$^{Ph} a$ Num 10^{10}—Trumpets to be blown 'in the beginnings of your months' over the sacrifices $^{Ps} b$ Num 28$^{11-15}$—'In the beginnings of your months' sacrifices to be offered as prescribed.
	d The Passover	$^J a$ Ex 13^{21-27N} b 34^{25bN}—^{c} The Passover originally instituted as a domestic rite, a lamb to be killed and its blood applied by means of hyssop to the lintel and door-posts, and the family to keep indoors till	$^{Pg} d$ Ex 12$^{1-13}$ e 43^{-50} f Lev 23^5—^{d} The month of the Exodus to be the first month in the year, and on the tenth day a lamb to be chosen for each household (or for two households if of small numbers) 'without blemish,

9b The older authorities ^{JED} address themselves to masters of households and are principally concerned to secure rest from hard work, ^{D} the humane tendency being emphasized as time went on The sabbath was then a weekly festival, marked by joyous celebrations. The later ordinances ^{P} breathe a totally different spirit of stringency, and reflect a state of things in which the sabbath was almost the only outward observance of religion left to the exiles. Cp Addis ii 277^N, cp also ^{P}137 'the Sabbath.'

c The New Moon was an ancient festival, cp Isa 1^{13} 1 Sam 20$^{18-26}$, perhaps ignored ^{JED} at one time as having been abused by heathenish practices, and ^{P} then revived, and honoured after the analogy of other holy days

d The Passover is the only one of the four great feasts which could have been celebrated by Israel as a nomad people before the settlement in Canaan It is a plausible suggestion to connect the demand for leave to go into the wilderness to sacrifice with an ancient custom of sacrificing firstlings in the spring of the year, the smiting of the Egyptian firstborn being the penalty for refusal. In D the choice of the victim still extends to bullocks, but it is limited to sheep and goats by P, who also requires the victim to be 'roasted,' and forbids 'seething,' which D had required In JE the celebration is, of course, local as all were, in D it is centralized like the rest. Perhaps this was not found to answer In any case P does not centralize, but makes it a domestic rite, depriving it at the same time as far as possible of its sacrificial character, which however seems curiously to reappear in the expression used by P^s of the Passover, 'offer the oblation of Yahweh,' Num 9$^{7\ 13}$ cp 31^{50}† See further Addis (ii 241), who points out that whereas in JE the Exodus is occasioned by a demand to be allowed to keep the Passover, in P the Passover is instituted because of the Exodus, the mutual relations of event and rite being reversed Observe also that in JE Yahweh passes over the *threshold* for protection against 'the destroyer,' but in P he passes over the *house*, being himself the destroyer. See Trumbull, *Threshold Covenant*, 209 and context See also I § 2e § 5 13 54.

SACRED SEASONS 245

J	D	E	P^ht	P^g	P^s

morning, so that Yahweh might 'pass over the door' and so ward off 'the destroyer'; J^s adds that 'this service' is to be kept in the promised land; ^b the sacrifice not to be kept till morning, and so presumably to be eaten, but no directions survive in J as to the mode.

^D c 16^1-7—The Passover to be kept in the month Abib (the day not being specified), as being the month in which Yahweh had brought Israel out of Egypt by night; it is not a domestic rite, but the victim is to be sacrificed at the central sanctuary at even, and is to be 'of the flock and of the herd,' seethed and eaten without leaven, none of the flesh being left till the morning; and the ordinance closes thus, 'thou shalt turn in the morning and go unto thy tents.'

a male of the first year,' 'from the sheep or from the goats,' and to be killed on the fourteenth day 'between the two evenings,' its blood being put upon lintel and doorposts; the meal no leisurely festal banquet, but a hurried and frugal repast, the eaters all in travellers' dress; no flesh to be removed or left till morning and ^e no bone to be broken; circumcised strangers and slaves, but not sojourners or hired servants, to eat of it; ^f the rite included in the calendar.

^P^s g Num 9^1-14 h 28^16—h The Passover included in the final calendar with bare mention; ^g provision made for postponement in case of absence or temporary defilement, with penalty of being 'cut off' for total disregard.

e Unleavened bread (Mazzoth)

^J a Ex 13^3-10 b 34^18—^a The original form of the ordinance probably brief ('^4 This day ye go forth in the month Abib ^6 Seven days thou shalt eat unleavened bread (Mazzoth), and in the seventh day shall be a feast unto Yahweh. ^10 Thou shalt therefore keep this ordinance in its season from year to year'); trebly amplified by ^Rj, ^Rd, ^Rp, no substantial element being added, but the connexion with the Exodus being emphasized. ^b The Covenant-words contain a similar ordinance, 'The feast of unleavened bread shalt thou keep. Seven days thou shalt eat unleavened bread' (the clause following being probably editorial, 'as I commanded thee, at the time appointed in the month Abib: for in the month Abib thou camest out from Egypt').

^E c Ex 23^15N—The Covenant-book apparently contained already an ordinance identical with ^b, 'The feast of unleavened bread shalt thou keep,' and was expanded from ^J by adding the clauses following, 'seven days ... empty.'

^D d 16^3—'^3 Seven days shalt thou eat unleavened bread therewith [i e with the Passover, but the word may be an addition in this clause], even the bread of affliction, for thou camest forth out of the land of Egypt in haste: that thou mayest remember the day when thou camest forth out of the land of Egypt all the days of thy life. ^4 And there shall be no leaven seen with thee in all thy borders seven days' The rest may be an addition, '^8 Six days thou shalt eat unleavened bread: and on the seventh day shall be a solemn assembly to Yahweh thy God; thou shalt do no work therein.'

^Ph f Lev 23^9-14N—It is possible that the offering of the wave-sheaf of firstfruits 'on the morrow after the sabbath,' ^L8cg, was connected with Mazzoth (^12 specifying the offering required is ^Ps)

^P^g g Lev 23^6-8—'On the fifteenth day of the [first] month is the feast of unleavened bread unto Yahweh; seven days ye shall eat unleavened bread. In the first day ye shall have an holy convocation ye shall do no servile work. But ye shall offer a fire offering unto Yahweh seven days: in the seventh day is an holy convocation; ye shall do no servile work.'

^Ps h Ex 12^14-20 i Num 28^17-25N—h The provisions of ^Pg repeated in identical terms, but with amplifications defining the time, emphasizing the strictness with which the rest must be enforced, and enjoining the complete banishment of leaven from the house. ^i Sacrifices are prescribed to be offered.

f Weeks or Harvest (Pentecost)

^J a Ex 34^22—'Thou shalt observe the feast of weeks, even of the firstfruits of wheat harvest'

^E b Ex 23^16—'And [thou shalt keep] the feast of harvest, the firstfruits of thy labours, which thou sowest in the field.'

^D c 16^9-12—'^9 Seven weeks shalt thou number unto thee: from the time thou beginnest to put the sickle to the standing corn shalt thou begin to number seven weeks. ^10 And thou shalt keep the feast of weeks unto Yahweh thy God with a tribute of a freewill offering of thine hand, which thou

^Ph d Lev 23^15-20—'^15 And ye shall count unto you from the morrow after the sabbath ..., ^16 even unto the morrow after the seventh sabbath shall ye count fifty days; and ye shall offer a new meal offering unto Yahweh. ^17 Ye shall bring out of your habitations two wave loaves of two tenth parts of an ephah; they shall be of fine flour, they shall be baken with leaven, for firstfruits unto Yahweh. ^18a And ye shall present with the bread ^19b two he-lambs of the first year for a sacrifice of peace offerings. And the priest shall wave them with the

---

9f The relative fixing of the date is found in **D**, and a similar but not identical reckoning occurs in **P^h**, which, ambiguous though it is, seems to be adopted into **P^g** by **P^s** without any clearer definition. But the prescription of offering is quite new in **P**, **D** expressly requiring only a freewill offering.

	J	D	E	P^ht	P^g	P^s

^L 9f

| | | shalt give, according as Yahweh thy God blesseth thee.' ¹¹ The entire household, and the dependent and poor, are to share in the joy and feasting. ' ¹² And thou shalt remember that thou wast a bondman in Egypt.' | | bread of the firstfruits for a wave offering unto Yahweh. They shall be holy to Yahweh for the priest.' [¹⁸ᵇ⁻¹⁹ᵃ is an incorrect interpolation from Num 28, see Lev 23¹⁸ᴺ.]
^Pg e Lev 23²¹—The end only of ^Pg's paragraph on this feast is preserved in its due place in the calendar, providing that it should be a holy convocation, servile work being forbidden.
^Ps f Num 28²⁶⁻³¹—The specific ordering of sacrifices for this feast is thus introduced, 'in the day of the firstfruits, when ye offer a new meal offering unto Yahweh in your [feast of] weeks, ye shall have an holy convocation; ye shall do no servile work.' | |

g Trumpets

^Ph To be used on all New Moons and other feasts. Cp 4sa.
^Pg a Lev 23²³⁻²⁵—The Feast of Trumpets or New Year's Day to be kept with full stringency as a holy convocation, on the first day of the seventh month, and marked by 'a memorial of blowing of trumpets.'
^Ps b Num 29¹⁻⁶—The offerings of obligation specified, in addition to the Daily and New Moon sacrifices.

h Day of atonement

^Ps a Ex 30¹⁰   b Lev 16¹⁻³⁴ᴺ   c 23²⁶⁻³²ᴺ   d Num 29⁷⁻¹¹—ᵇ The solemn offering of a bullock and a ram as sin offerings for Aaron and his house and for Israel and the sanctuary, the sprinkling of their blood before the mercy-seat within the veil (7y), and the rite of the scapegoat for Azazel (7z) to be repeated upon a great day of humiliation and atonement in the seventh month on the tenth day. On this day all inhabitants and strangers to abstain from work and afflict their souls. ᶜ This day added to the calendar, with provisions of great stringency as to its due observance on pain of being 'cut off' or 'destroyed.' The time fixed as being from the evening of the ninth day to the next evening. ᵈ A costly burnt offering with its accompaniments, according to the analogy of other holy days and a single kid as a sin offering, prescribed in addition to 'the sin offering of atonement' and the daily sacrifice, and presumably in addition to the ᵇ two rams ordered as burnt offerings for Aaron and for the people. ᵃ On the same occasion it is provided, in the paragraph on the construction of the golden altar of incense, that 'Aaron shall make atonement upon the horns of it once in the year: with the blood of the sin offering of atonement once in the year shall he make atonement for it throughout your generations.'

i Ingathering or Booths

ᴶ a Ex 34²²ᵇ—The Covenant-words are brief, 'and [thou shalt observe] the feast of ingathering at the year's revolution'
ᴱ b Ex 23¹⁶—The Covenant-book is also short in its provision, 'and [thou shalt keep] the feast of ingathering at the close of the year, when thou gatherest in thy labours out of the field.'
ᴰ c 16¹³⁻¹⁵   d 31⁹⁻¹²—ᶜ 'Thou shalt keep the feast of booths seven days, after that thou hast gathered in from thy threshing-floor and from thy winepress.' The entire household, with the poor and dependent, are to

^Ph e Lev 23³⁹⁻⁴³ʳ—'When ye have gathered in the fruits of the land, ye shall keep the feast of Yahweh seven days And ye shall take you on the first day the fruit of goodly trees, branches of palm trees, and boughs of thick trees, and willows of the brook; and ye shall rejoice before Yahweh your God seven days. ... Ye shall dwell in booths seven days'
^Pg f Lev 23³⁴ᵇ⁻³⁶—'On the fifteenth day of this seventh month is the feast of booths for seven days unto Yahweh.' On the first and eighth days is to be an holy convocation, and a fire offering daily.

9g For a good note on New Year's Day and the reckoning of the months see Addis ii 241.

i Cp abef above, and see XIII § 4a 131 for a discussion of Solomon's celebration 1 Kings 8.

SACRED PLACES

	J	D	E	P^ht	P^s	P^s	
							^L10a

	share in the joyous festival, which is to take place at the central sanctuary. ^d Every seven years the feast is to be marked by the reading of 'this Law.'	^{Ps} g Num 29^{12–38}—Numerous and costly burnt offerings prescribed, with a separate requirement for each of the eight days; ^e the aim of the feast to recall the wilderness life.
j Sabbatical year	^E a Ex 23¹⁰ b 21^{2–7}—^a Every seventh year to be a fallow year, both for the corn land and for vineyards and oliveyards; the poor may eat, and 'the beast of the field' have what they leave. ^b A Hebrew slave shall serve six years and be free in the seventh, cp 2dc. ^D c 15^{1–6} d 15^{12–18}—^c 'At the end of every seven years' 'Yahweh's release' is to be 'proclaimed,' and all debts due to a creditor from 'his neighbour and his brother' are to be released, but 'of a foreigner' the debt may be exacted; cp 4va, where 'the year of release' is referred to. ^d A Hebrew slave may go free after serving a term of six years.	^{Ph} e Lev 25^{1–7} f ^{18–22} g 26^{34 43}—^e Every seventh year is to be kept with strictness as a fallow year, the crops being neither sown at the beginning nor reaped at the close, the vines not pruned and the grapes not gathered 'it shall be a year of solemn rest for the land' Yet it is said that 'the sabbath of the land shall be for good for you; for thee and for thy servant, and for thy maid and for thy hired servant, and for thy stranger that sojourn with thee; and for thy cattle, and for the beasts that are in thy land, shall all the increase thereof be for good.' f Any deficiency shall be made up by the exceptional fertility of the sixth year, which shall produce enough for three years, till the ninth year. Thus in the sixth year they are to sow and reap, in the seventh neither sow nor reap, in the eighth sow at the beginning and reap at the end in time to eat of the new produce in the ninth. g It is prophesied in the closing discourse that in the Exile 'the land shall enjoy her sabbaths.'
k Jubile year		^{Ph'} a Lev 25^{8–17 N} b ^{24–28}—^{ab} The fiftieth year to be marked by proclamation of 'liberty' for the land, which is then to return to the old ownership, but may be redeemed before. ^{Ps} c Lev 25^{8–17 23–26} d ^{29–34} e ^{40b–42} f ^{47–55}— c The fiftieth year to be a jubile year, in which land is to return to the old ownership, with redemption at proportionate price previously; ^d houses in walled cities to be sold outright without return and only redeemable in the first year after the sale; but ^e Levitical property excepted; ^e Hebrew slaves to be free at the jubile, but f may be redeemed earlier.

10. Sacred Places

a Sanctuary, Site of the	^J—No ordinance preserved on this point, but many sanctuaries lovingly recognized in the stories of the patriarchs For instances of pillars and altars erected see ^L5gabc 10dabcd, and for sacrifice, implying local sanctuaries, see ^L7aabcd. ^E a Gen 28²² b Ex 3¹ c Ex 20²⁴—^a God's house is to be at Bethel; in many places the patriarchs, &c, erect ^L5gdefgh pillars and ^L10defghjk altars; ^b Horeb is sacred as 'the	^{Ph} n Lev 17^{1–9} o 19^{30b} p 26^{2b} q 26³¹ r Ex 29⁴⁵—ⁿ Two ordinances provide that no animal shall be killed without being sacrificed, and that merely private sacrifice shall be abolished, 'to the end that the children of Israel may bring their sacrifices, which they sacrifice in the open field .. unto the priest, and sacrifice them for sacrifices of peace offerings unto Yahweh.' (These ordinances in their original application seem to	^L10

9j The variations are unusually many and substantial (1) ^E A seventh year fallow for the land and a seven years' term for slaves is required, nothing being stated or implied about any simultaneous reckoning of either period throughout the country (2) ^D A simultaneous remission of debts replaces the fallow year, the term of service remaining the same. (3) ^P A simultaneous seventh year fallow is ordered, remission of debts is dropped in favour of a general prohibition of usury, and emancipation at the fiftieth year is all that remains of the seven years' term of service. See for a general statement VIII 1 § 6 54.
 k See VIII 1 § 7 55.
10a The laws as to the site of the sanctuary present perhaps the clearest instance of the modifications introduced by time in the legislation. The stages are clearly marked from ^{JE} the earlier sanction of the primitive plurality of sacred places to ^D the urgent demand for centralization of worship, succeeded by ^P the quiet assumption of a single lawful sanctuary. The whole question is fully treated in the Introduction. For a general statement see VII § 4β 46, for further details cp VIII 1 § 1 50, for different conceptions of the divine presence as localized see VIII 11 § 2β 111 § 1 58 60, for modifications of JE and contrasts with P in D see IX 1 § 2γ 75, and more fully 11 §§ 1–3 79–82, cp X § 1 (v) 86, for the attitude of J cp XI § 2γ § 4a 100 104, and for E cp XII § 2δε 114. Cp also ^P87 'the place which Yahweh shall choose,' and ^P91 'holy place' or 'sanctuary.'

248 — LAWS AND INSTITUTIONS

ᴸ10a

| J | D | E | Pʰᵗ | Pᵍ | Pˢ |

J mount of God' on which Israel is to 'serve God' Ex 3¹², and presumably 'hold a feast' 5¹; ᵒ in every place where God records his name, or causes it to be remembered, there is a sanctuary to be marked by altar and sacrifice, and the usage described in Judg Sam Kings shows that these places are concurrently and not merely successively sacred.

D *d* 12²⁻¹²ᴺ   *e* 13–18   *f* 26   *g* 14²³⁻²⁶   *h* 15¹⁹   *i* 16¹⁻¹⁶   *j* 17⁸⁻¹⁰   *k* 18⁶⁻⁸   *l* 26²   *m* 31¹⁰⁻¹³—
def One central sanctuary, in 'the place which Yahweh shall choose to make his name to dwell there' ᴰ87, is alone recognized, and to it all kinds of offerings are to be brought; *g* there the tithes are to be eaten, *h* the firstlings sacrificed, and *l* the firstfruits offered; *i* thither all males are to repair for the Passover and other Great Feasts, *j* there is to be the court of appeal, and *m* the place of solemn publication of the law every seven years; and *k* in its services and endowments the country Levites shall have share at will.

Pʰᵗ fit a multiplicity of sanctuaries, within reach of all, they may then have been applied to the single sanctuary of the shrunk remnant of returning exiles, and were finally adapted to the camp form of legislation, the prohibition of slaughtering being understood as only meaning slaughtering for private and unauthorized sacrifice.) ᵒᵖ To 'keep (Yahweh's) sabbaths and reverence (his) sanctuary' is a pair of connected duties of high obligation. (The 'sanctuary' is not defined either as local or central.) *q* The discourse contains the divine threat, 'I will ... bring your sanctuaries unto desolation, and I will not smell the savour of your sweet odours'; and *r* the promise is preserved, 'I will dwell among the children of Israel.'

Pᵍ *s* Ex 25⁸   *t* 25²²   *u* 29⁴³—ˢ God says to Moses, 'Let them make me a sanctuary; that I may dwell among them. According to all that I shew thee, the pattern of the Dwelling, and the pattern of all the furniture thereof, even so shall ye make it'; *t* the mercy-seat above the ark is the actual point of meeting with the divine presence; or *u* it is said more generally of the whole sanctuary, 'there I will meet with the children of Israel, and the Tent shall be sanctified by my glory.' No other sanctuary is contemplated or alluded to For its central position in the camp see ᴸ4r.

Pˢ *v* Lev 17¹⁻⁹   *w* Josh 22¹⁻³⁴—*v* The expanded form of the opening ordinance in Pʰ requires all sacrifices to be brought to 'the door of the tent of meeting' cp Lev 1–7 as expanded, and *w* it is described how a crisis arose at the mere possibility of a second altar for sacrifice having been erected.

b Tent of Meeting

J No allusion has been preserved to a sacred tent, and Joshua speaks of the Gibeonites as destined to be 'bondmen ... for the house of (his) God' Josh 9²³.

E *a* Ex 33⁷⁻¹¹ᴺ   ᴱˢ *b* Num 11¹⁶⁻³⁰ᴱ   *c* 12⁴⁻¹⁰—Though no account of the construction of 'the tent of meeting' is preserved (but cp Ex 33⁷ᴺ), ᵃᵇᶜ its position 'without the camp,' *a* the usage of Moses in going into the Tent, ᵃᵇᶜ the habitual intercourse of Yahweh with Moses personally, *a* the descent of 'the pillar of cloud' or of Yahweh, *b* 'in the cloud' or *c* 'in a pillar of cloud,' and ᵃᵇ the habitual ministry of Joshua within the Tent are all described. The passage with analogous representations in Deut 31¹⁴ ᴺ is probably extracted from ᴱ.

Pᵍ *d* Ex 25⁸–27¹⁹—An elaborate and gorgeous movable sanctuary, called sometimes 'the tent of meeting' and sometimes 'the Dwelling' (see Ex 25¹ᴺ), ordered to be made, and minute directions given for its construction; its position is in the centre of the camp (implied in Num 10¹⁻⁸ and stated in Pˢ ᴸ4r); the place where Yahweh speaks with Moses is defined as 'from above the covering [or mercy-seat], from between the two cherubim which are upon the ark of the testimony' 25²² (cp Num 7⁸⁹); the cloud rests upon the Dwelling Num 10¹¹; and ᴸ11a*q* the exclusive right of access is reserved to the Levitical tribe. It is consecrated by the blood of the sin offering Lev 16¹⁶ ²⁰.

Pˢ *e* Lev 8 ⁰ᵇ⁻¹¹   *f* Num 9¹⁵⁻²³   *g* Ex 35⁴⁻⁴⁰—*g* The Dwelling and its appurtenances is duly constructed, and its erection is described; ᵉᵍ it is consecrated by being anointed with the anointing oil. *fg* The cloud filled the Dwelling at its erection, and 'covered it, and the appearance of fire by night,' the movement or rest of the cloud determining the journeying or abiding of the camp. [See Ex 25¹ᴺ.]

10b For a general statement of the relation between the codes on this point see IV § 2β 30, and for fuller details VIII 1 § 2 51, and for reference to Ezek and the historical books see XIII § 3δ 129; on the genesis of the Dwelling as it appears in **P** see Ex 25¹ᴺ, and for the use of the term in a non-technical sense cp Lev 15³¹ᵇᴺ 17⁴ᴺ 21²³ᴺ. Cp also ᴾ54 'dwell' and 'dwelling,' ᴾ60ᵇ 'establish the dwelling.'

SACRED PLACES

	J D E	P^ht	P^g	P^s	
c The Ark	^J a Num 10^33-36 b Josh 3^§ —^a The ark goes in the van of the hosts, and is advanced at the commencement and halted at the close of the march with an appropriate form of words; ^b it is borne by the priests, and is halted in the river at the passage of Jordan, as a pledge of the safety of the people, till all have passed over. ^E b Josh 3^E —The same representation is given by ^E of the part assigned to the ark in the passage of Jordan. ^D c 10^1-5 ^§ —An account is given, probably extracted from ^J, of the making of an ark of acacia wood by Moses in order to receive the second tables; the Levites are to bear it.		^Pg d Ex 25^10-22 —An account is given (see further ^L 12c) of the ordering and construction of an ark of acacia wood, of prescribed dimensions overlaid with gold, and furnished with a covering, into which 'the testimony' is to be put when it has been given to Moses. ^Ps d Num 3^31 e 4^4-15 —^de It is borne by the Kohathites, a Levitical clan, but ^e made ready for removal by the priests.	^L 10e
d Altar of sacrifice	^J a Gen 8^20a b 12^- c 13^18 d Josh 9^27 —Altars are built ^a by Noah after the Flood, and by Abraham ^b on Yahweh's appearing to him at Shechem after entering Canaan, and ^c 'by the oaks of Mamre,' where he settled after the departure of Lot; ^d the Gibeonites are given up for menial service about 'the altar of Yahweh.' ^E e Gen 22^9 f 33^20 g 35^1-7E h Ex 17^15 i 20^24-26 j 24^4a k Num 23^1-6 14-17 —^e Abraham builds an altar on Mount Moriah, lays the wood thereon, binds Isaac and places him upon the wood and raises the knife to slay his son. (It is doubtful how far this may be relied upon as indicating the procedure with an ordinary burnt offering.) Jacob builds an altar ^f at Shalem on the ground he had bought from the sons of Hamor, and ^g at Bethel by divine command on his return thither; Moses ^h builds an altar at Rephidim called Yahweh-Nissi in memory of the feud decreed between Israel and Amalek, and ^j another at the ratification of the covenant, ^i one of whose 'words' contained directions for the construction of altars which were to be of earth or of unhewn stone, and without steps for access. ^k Balaam builds altars for the sacrifices by which he sought oracles from God. ^D l 12^27 m 27^5-7 —^l In the great chapter on the unity of the sanctuary a single altar only is recognized, 'the altar of Yahweh (Israel's) God'; but ^m later, probably in a passage extracted from E, 'an altar' of unhewn stones is to be built for sacrifice.	^Pt n Lev 1^16 o 6^10-13 —^no 'Beside the altar' (^n on the east side) there is to be a place for the ashes, and ^o a perpetual fire is to be kept burning upon the altar (but see Lev 17^N) (Other allusions in ^Pt indicate the relation of the sacrifices to the altar in the prescribed ceremonial.)	^Pg p Ex 27^1-8 —Moses ordered to make an altar of acacia wood overlaid with brass, fitted for ease of transport with rings and staves, and duly furnished with vessels of brass. ^Ps q Num 7^1-88 r 16^36-40 s Josh 22^10-34 —^q The dedication of the altar accompanied by munificent gifts, elaborately described, from each of the tribal princes; ^r the brazen censers of the 250 princes to be beaten out into broad plates for a covering for the altar; ^s the Trans-jordanic tribes erect a great altar, but learning of the armed protest of the other tribes explain that it was not for sacrifice, but merely for witness to their share in the one legitimate altar and sanctuary.	
e Oil for lamps			^Pg a Lev 24^1-4 —'Pure olive oil beaten for the light' to be brought in by the people, and Aaron is to 'cause a lamp to burn continually,' ordering 'the lamps upon the pure candlestick' 'from evening to morning before Yahweh continually,' 'without the veil of the testimony, in the tent of meeting.' ^Ps b Ex 27^20 N c Num 8^1-4 —^b The last injunction ^a is practically reproduced; ^c when the lamps, seven in number, are lit they are to give light 'in front of the candlestick,' the making of which is described.	

10c For a summary account of the divergent representations as to the ark see IV § 2b 30, and for fuller details VIII 1 § 3 52, for references to the historical books see IX 11 § 1 79-82. Cp also ^D19 'ark of the covenant of Yahweh,' ^P161^b 'ark of the testimony.'

d For a comparative statement as to the number and nature of the altars ordered or permitted see VIII 1 § 1β 50, cp XIII § 3δ § 4a 129 131. Cp also ^JE137 'build an altar,' ^D16 'altar of Yahweh thy God,' ^L12dd 'altar of incense,' ea 'brazen altar.'

11. Sacred Persons: Clergy and Laity

J **D** **E** **P**ʰᵗ **P**ᵍ **P**ˢ

^{L}**11 a** Priesthood

J a Gen 41^{45a} Ex 2^{16} b Gen 47^{26} c 49^5 d Ex 19^{22}. e 32^{25-29N} cp 24^1 9 Josh 3—Interest is shown in the priesthood by the mention of ^{a} the marriages of Joseph and Moses into priestly families, and ^{b} the exemption from confiscation of the Egyptian priests' lands; d at the first theophany at Sinai there are already beside Aaron 'priests which come near unto Yahweh,' and ^{e} the devotion of the 'sons of Levi' to the cause of true religion is recorded for special blessing, though ^{c} Levi is grouped with Simeon for blame in Jacob's song; the priests bear the ark over Jordan.

^{E} f Deut 33^{8-11} g Ex 24^5—f The song of Moses ascribes priestly functions to Levi, the possession of Thummim and Urim, the duty of giving *torah*, and the right to offer incense and sacrifice; but ^{g} at the ratifying of the Horeb covenant 'young men' are the officiants. In Josh 3.§ the priests appear bearing the ark

^{D} h 10^8 i 18^{1-8N} j 26^3 k 27^{14} l 31^9—h The separation of 'the tribe of Levi' to bear the ark, minister, and bless recorded (perhaps on a basis of ^{E}); i 'the priests the Levites, [even] all the tribe of Levi,' including the local Levites, to receive equal endowment and enjoy common rights of ministry; j 'the priest that shall be in those days' to officiate at the presentation of firstfruits; k the Levites to pronounce the curses, and l be responsible, along with 'the elders' for the preservation and septennial reading of the law.

^{Ph} m Lev 21^1–22^{16N}—Detailed provisions laid down as to the stricter rules of ceremonial purity attaching to the clergy, who (in the present text, but cp 21^{17N}) are 'of the seed of Aaron the priest.' Their marriage relations regulated, and ministration forbidden in cases of bodily blemish Cp ^L6b b fb.

^{Pg} n Ex 29^{9b} o Num 18^{1-7N} p 25^{10-13} q Num 3^{5-10}—n The 'priesthood' assigned to Aaron and his sons for ever, and ^{p} confirmed to Phinehas and his seed; ^{o} they are to 'keep [their] priesthood' for all higher ministration, leaving menial attendance to the Levites; ^{q} Aaron and his sons to 'keep their priesthood,' and 'the tribe of Levi' to 'do the service of the Dwelling'

^{Ps} r Num 3^{1-4} s 4—Position and duties of the Aaronic priesthood and the Levitical clans differentiated.

b High-priesthood

J a Ex 4^{014} 24^1—Aaron given the office of being spokesman for Moses; with Nadab, Abihu and seventy elders he goes up on Sinai to see God and feast before him.

^{E}—Cp Deut 10^6 ^{E}, where Aaron's death at Moserah is recorded, and we are told that Eleazar his son 'ministered in the priest's office in his stead.'

^{Ph} b Lev 21^{10-15N}—A unique stringency of ceremonial requirement applies to him 'that is the high priest among his brethren, upon whose head the anointing oil is poured, and that is consecrated to put on the garments'

^{Pg} c Ex 28^{29} d Ex 29 Lev 9 e Num 20^{23-29} f 27^{21}—d Aaron to be consecrated with appropriate offerings, and a solemn observance of the octave of the consecration recorded; ^{c} he is to 'bear the names of the children of Israel in the breastplate of judgement,' and also 'the Urim and the Thummim'; ^{e} at his death he is succeeded by Eleazar his son; f before whom, as the custodian of the oracular Urim, Joshua is to stand

^{Ps} g Lev 8 h Num 35^{25-32}—g The consecration of Aaron with offerings as prescribed is duly recorded, and also his investiture with the breastplate in which were the Urim and Thummim; ^{h} the death of the High Priest to terminate the liability of a homicide to blood-revenge.

11a The remarkable development of the priesthood, and the traces in the legislation of its successive stages, are fully treated in the Introduction. For a general statement see VIII 1 § 3 53, for the peculiarities in D see IX 1 § 3a 76, for J cp XI § 2δ 101 *foot*, for E cp XII § 2δ∈ 114, for allusions in P^t cp Lev 1^{5aN}.

Cp also in the word-lists ^{E}109 ^{D}90 ^{Pt}129 ^{Ph}209 'minister,' 'priest,' &c, and ^{P}12 names and designations of the Aaronic priesthood.

b On the relations of the High Priest of the Priestly Code to Ezekiel and to the history see XIII § 3γ § 8∈ 128 149.

SACRED PERSONS

	J	D	E	P^{ht}	P^g	P^s
c The high-priestly dress				^{Ph} a Lev 21^{10N}—The sacred dress is one element in the description of the High Priest.	^{Pg} b Ex 28 c 29$^{4-6}$ d 29^{29}· e Lev 16$^{4-23}$ f Num 20$^{25-28}$—^{b} The sacred vestments both of Aaron and his sons are described in detail (see ^{L}12g below), ^{c} the investiture ordered, and ^{d} the transference to the son who should succeed; ^{f} the investiture of Eleazar being duly recorded subsequently; ^{e} the linen garments, coat, mitre, breeches, and girdle, without the gorgeous ephod, breastplate, or robe, to be worn on entering within the veil for solemn atonement and changed when the atonement is made.	^{Ps} g Ex 39$^{1-31}$ h 40^{13a} i Lev 8$^{6-9}$ j 16^{32}—^{g} The making of the garments is described, ^{h} the order for investiture repeated and ^{i} executed; ^{j} the successor of Aaron is to wear the same dress ^{e} on entering within the veil.	^{L}11f
d The high-priestly unction				^{Ph} a Lev 21$^{10\,12N}$—The High Priest is he 'upon whom the anointing oil is poured,' and 'the crown (or consecration) of the anointing oil of his God is upon him.'	^{Pg} b Ex 29^7—Moses to anoint Aaron only	^{Ps} c Lev 8^{12} d 16^{32} e 6$^{20-22}$ f Ex 40^{13b} g ^{15} h 28^{41N} i 29^{21} Lev 8^{30} j 7^{35} k 10^6—^{c} At the consecration of Aaron and his sons, only Aaron is anointed, and ^{de} the anointing is taken as connoting the high-priestly dignity; but ^{fgh} in later passages Aaron and his sons are ordered to be anointed alike, ^{i} the unction extending even to the garments of all, and ^{j} Aaron's sons are assumed to share in the anointing, ^{k} Eleazar and Ithamar being expressly described as having 'the anointing oil of Yahweh' upon them.
e The high-priestly atonement					^{Pg} Cp ^{L}7ya and Lev 16^{1N}.	^{Ps} a Lev 16$^{32-34}$ b Ex 30^{10}—^{ab} It is one of the principal duties of ^{b} Aaron and ^{a} his successors to make a solemn annual atonement ^{b} upon the horns of the altar of incense.
f The priests, their consecration and holiness			^{E} a Ex 20^{26}—A solitary ordinance is preserved, forbidding altar steps on grounds of decency (ct ^{g} below).	^{Ph} b Lev 21^{1-9N} c 16^{-24N} d 22^2 e 8^{-16} f 4^{-7}—^{b} The mourning for the dead and the marriage relations of the priests limited; ^{c} maimed or deformed members of priestly families disqualified for ministry, ^{d} none to minister while 'unclean'; ^{e} the privilege of eating the sacred food guarded; ^{f} the kinds of disqualifying uncleanness detailed (perhaps by ^{Pt})	^{Pg} g Ex 28$^{42\,N}$ h 29$^{1-37}$ i Lev 10^8—^{h} The sons of Aaron to be consecrated with Aaron; ^{g} on grounds of decency they are to wear linen breeches while ministering, and ^{i} while on duty they may not drink wine.	^{Ps} j Lev 8 k 10^6 l Ex 28^{41N} m 29^{21N} n 30^{19} o ^{30} p 40^{14} q Lev 8^{30} r Num 3^2—^{j} Their consecration is related, ^{klmopq} the unction extending to them as well as to Aaron (ct ^{L}11d^{abcde}); ^{n} ablution at the laver is required before ministration; ^{k} Eleazar and Ithamar forbidden to mourn the death of Nadab and Abihu.

11d The anointing of others than the High Priest is one of the marks of later supplements in P.

f Cp a and a^N, also ^{P}59 'fill the hand' or 'consecrate.'

252　　　　　　　　　　　　　*LAWS AND INSTITUTIONS*

	J	D	E	P^ht	P^s	P^s
^L**11** g The priestly dress				^Pt a Lev 6^10—The priest is to wear a linen garment and breeches when removing the ashes of the burnt offering from the altar, and then is to change his garment before taking the ashes outside the camp. ^Ps b Ex 28^4 40 42 c 29^8—^b Moses is ordered to make coats, girdles, and headtires for Aaron's sons, and ^c to clothe them with them; ^b linen breeches are also required. ^Ps d Ex 40^14 e Lev 8^13—Their investiture is ^d ordered and ^e executed.		
h Priests' duties other than sacrificial		^E a Ex 24^5 b Deut 33^11—(See under ^L11a/g) ^D c 17^9 12 d 18 e 19^17 f 20^2 g 21^5 h 24^8 i 31^9—^cef They exercise a concurrent jurisdiction with the civil judges; ^di they are the custodians of the law; ^f they are to rouse the courage of the army. Cp ^L6ha 11ahykl.		^Pt m Lev 10^10—They are to discriminate in cases of uncleanness, and to give *torah*. ^Ps j Lev 9^22 k Num 6^22-27 l 10^8N—^j Aaron blesses the people with uplifted hands; ^k the formula of benediction is recorded; ^l the priests are to blow with the trumpets. ^Ps n Num 4^5-15 o 16—^n When the Tent is moved on the march the priests are to cover over the sanctuary and all it contains before the Levites may bear any of the articles; ^o certain things are put under the special charge of Eleazar.		
i The Levites		^J a Ex 32^25-29N—The privileges of the Levites are foreshadowed in the praise given for their devotion in support of Moses at Sinai. ^E b Deut 33^8-11—Levi as a whole is called to the priesthood ^D c 10^8 d 17^9 e 18 f 27^14 g 31^9—'The priests the Levites' or 'the sons of Levi' discharge various responsible priestly functions (see 11ahkl hcdi).		^Ps i Num 3^5-10 j 12. k 45 l 17^1-11 m 18^2-7—^im The charge of the sanctuary entrusted to the Levites, who are given to Aaron and his sons solely for such subordinate ministries; ^j Yahweh claims the Levites instead of the firstborn, and ^k orders them and their cattle to be thus 'taken'; ^l the budding of Aaron's rod symbolizes the rightful sacerdotal supremacy of 'the house of Levi.' Cp also the censuses ^L4pab q. ^Ps n Num 1^48-54 o 2^17 p 3^23-26 29-32 35-38 q 41 46-48 r 4^4-20 s 24-28 t 31-33N u 8^5-22N v 23-26N w 16^1-50§—^q The Levites and their cattle to be 'taken' in place of the firstborn and firstlings, the odd two hundred and seventy-three firstborn being redeemed; ^o their place in the midst of the camp ^n 'round about the dwelling of the testimony'; their duties to be the charge of the Dwelling, and distributed among the three Levitical families, ^p once briefly with notes as to their position in camp and ^rst later in full detail; ^u an elaborate ceremonial of consecration ordered and its execution related; ^v their period of service to be from twenty-five to fifty years of age (cf ^L4pc, where service begins at thirty); ^w their pretensions to priestly rights rebuked in a modification of the Korah story.		
j The revenues of the clergy		^D a 12^18 16^11 14 b 12^19 c 14^25-29 d 18^1-8—^d The priestly tribe of Levi to receive the firstfruits of corn, wine, and oil, and the first of the fleece, and the shoulder, two cheeks, and maw of every ox or sheep sacrificed; a share to be given to 'the Levite' ^a at the sacrificial feasts, and ^c in the tithe festivities, and the tithe of the third year to be shared between the Levites and other dependent classes; ^b their support a moral charge on the community.		^Pt h Lev 2^3 10 i 6^16-18 26 29 j 7^6-9 k 31-33 l 10^12-15N m Num 5^9 n 6^19—^hijl What remains of every meal offering belongs to the priest; ^kl also the wave breast and the heave thigh of all peace offerings; ^i with all of the sin offering and ^j guilt offering not consumed on the altar; also ^m all special sacred gifts and ^n 'the sodden shoulder of the ram' brought by a Nazirite as his peace offering, with one cake and one wafer. ^Ps e Ex 29^27 f Lev 24^9 g Num 18^8-32—The priests are to have ^e the wave breast and heave thigh from all peace offerings, ^f the shewbread, ^g all special gifts, every meal		

11h Observe how under the Priestly Code, which provides written regulations very completely, the discretionary and judicial power of the priest almost disappear, he administers, not gives, *torah*.

i For the relation of Ezekiel to the distinction of priests and Levites see XIII § 3β 127.   See also refs to Introd under a.

j For a general statement and a comparison with the history see IX 1 § 3β 11 § 1β 77 80·, on the distinction between 'holy' and 'most holy' things cp Driv-Wh 64.

SACRED PERSONS

	J	D	E	P^ht	P^g	P^s

				P^s		

offering, sin offering, and guilt offering, the firstfruits ('all the best *or* the fat') of oil, vintage, corn, and fruits; everything devoted, all firstlings and the redemption price of firstborn males and unclean firstlings; while the Levites are to receive the tithe, though a tithe of that tithe is to be given to the priests

^Ps *o* Lev 7^{8 10}   *p* ^{34—36}—*o* The skin of the burnt offering, which in Ex 29^{14} Lev 8^{17} is burnt, is now made a perquisite of the officiating priest; *p* the wave breast and the heave thigh of the peace offering are 'the anointing portion' of Aaron and his sons, and *o* every meal offering belongs to 'all the sons of Aaron.'

k The property of the clergy

^D *a* 10^9 12^{12} 18^1   *b* ^{8}—*a* It is thrice stated that Levi has no portion or inheritance with his brethren, yet *b* a Levite may possess a 'patrimony.'

^{Pg} *c* Num 18^{20—24}—Neither Aaron, as representing the priests, nor the Levites are to have any inheritance in the land

^Ps *d* Lev 25^{32—34}   *e* Num 35^{1—8}   *f* Josh 21^{1—42}—*e* The Levites are to receive from the other tribes, in shares proportionate to the size of their inheritances, a total of forty-eight cities, including the six cities of refuge, each city carrying with it a suburban area of two thousand cubits square; *f* the distribution is duly made, and *d* it is provided that the surrounding fields may never be sold, and that the houses if sold must be restored at the jubile and may be redeemed at any time.

l Lay rights and duties

^J *a* Ex 34^{27}   *b* Gen 35^2 Num 11^{18} Josh 3^5—*a* The covenant includes the whole nation; *b* the need for ceremonial purification and change of garments as a preparation for worship is illustrated in the cases of Jacob and of Israel in the wilderness and at the Jordan.

^E *c* Ex 19^{3b—8}   *d* 10 14   *e* 24^{3—8}   *f* 22^{31a}   *g* Josh 24—*cef* The covenant is explicitly made, renewed, and confirmed with all the people; who *f* are to be 'holy men unto' God; *c* the whole people are to sanctify themselves to meet God at Horeb, and *e* 'young men' from among them offer the covenant sacrifice; *c* Israel is called to be 'a kingdom of priests and a holy nation.'

^D *h* 7^{6—8}   *i* 10^{12—16}   *j* 14^2   *k* 23^{1 N}   *l* 27^9   *m* 29^1   *n* 10—15   *o* 31^{9—13}—*m* The covenant made with all Israel, *n* even to the women, children, and dependants, and *o* all such are to be present at the septennial reading of the terms of the covenant; so that ^{hj} Israel is a holy and peculiar people, pledged to ^{il} obedience and *i* loving service; *k* illegitimate or mutilated persons excluded from 'the assembly of Yahweh.'

^{Pn} *p* Lev 18^{24—30}   *q* 19^{2b}   *r* 20^7   *s* ^{22—26}   *t* 22^{31—33} *v* Num 15^{37—41}—The Israelites are all called to be ^{qrstv} holy (cp ^P 202), ^{pstv} obedient, ^u Yahweh's servants, ^{ps} separate from the nations of the land, *v* as a mark of consecration there are to be 'fringes in the borders (or tassels in the corners) of their garments' with a blue cord worked in.

^{Pt} *w* Lev 1—3 5—7   *x* 11—15—*w* The privileges and obligations of sacrifice in all its five main forms rest upon the laity, who have also commonly an important share in the actual ministration; *x* the holiness of the people is promoted by an elaborate code of ceremonial purity binding on every member of the nation without distinction.

^{Pg} *y* Ex 25—28 and *z* Num 16^{1—50N§} 17^{1—11}— *y* Upon the laity lies the duty and privilege of providing by material gifts and skilled labour for the construction and maintenance of the sanctuary; *z* but so distinctly sacerdotal an element of ministry as the offering of incense is beyond their province, as is shown by the story of Korah and his company (see Num 16^{1bN}).

^{Ps} *a'* Lev 4   *b'* Num 7   *c'* 28—In the later strata of the Priestly Code *a'* discrimination is introduced in regard to the sin offering, *b'* the duty of liberality and *c'* the privilege of sacrifice lose something of spontaneity from the uniformity of gifts described and the rigid prescription of detail, in sacrifice.

m Lay dress

^D *a* 6^8   *b* 11^{18}   *c* Ex 13^9   *d* 16   *e* Deut 22^{12}— *abcd* Unless the expressions are to be taken figuratively, amulets upon the wrist and frontlets between the eyes are to be reminders of Yahweh's law; *e* there are to be 'fringes (or twisted threads) upon the four borders of' the Israelite's vesture.

^{Ph} *f* Num 15^{37—41}—There is to be 'fringe in the borders (or tassels in the corners) of' the Israelites' garments, with a blue cord worked in, as a memorial of their duty to Yahweh.

---

111 Cp for P XIII § 2δ 25   m *cd* R^d passages taken as D

LAWS AND INSTITUTIONS

	J	D	E	P^{ht}	P^s	P^s
^{L}**11** n Prophets	^{J} Num 22⁵ 24—Balaam is a diviner who is rapt by the spirit of God to utter the word of Yahweh.	^{D} d 13$^{1-5}$ e 18$^{15-22}$ f 34^{10}—^{e} The rise of prophets like Moses is anticipated, and the non-fulfilment of his prophecies disallows any prophet, but ^{d} even their fulfilment goes for nothing if he urge to apostasy, in which case he is to be slain; ^{f} Moses is as yet unrivalled as a prophet.	^{E} a Num 11$^{24b-30N}$ b 12^{5-9N} c 22⁵ 23—^{b} The office of the prophet is explicitly recognized, and the normal mode of communication is by vision and dream, Moses being more than a prophet; ^{b} a prophetic ecstasy seizes upon the seventy elders summoned by Moses to the Tent of Meeting, and also upon Eldad and Medad, who had stayed in the camp; Joshua protests, but Moses approves of the utmost extension of the prophetic enthusiasm; ^{c} Balaam is a prophet whom God instructs by dreams or meets with a message, and who must speak what Yahweh says and nothing else. (Cp ^{E}114 'prophet,' ^{E}101 'dream')			
p Nazirites					^{Ps} a Num 6^{1-12N} b 13–21—^{a} The Nazirite is one who has made a 'vow of separation' for a limited period the conditions of which are laid down; ^{b} the ceremonial for his re-entrance upon the unrestricted life of the community is duly prescribed	
q Foreign menials for the sanctuary	^{J} a Josh 9^{23}—The Gibeonites are condemned by Joshua to be 'bondmen for the house of (his) God.'				^{Ps} b Josh 9^{21} — 'The princes' make the Gibeonites 'hewers of wood and drawers of water unto all the congregation.'	

With ^{L}11 the series of Tables is concluded which presents, according to a uniform plan, though with variations in the scale of treatment, all the material in the Hexateuch bearing on Hebrew laws and institutions.

The Tables which follow are of a more miscellaneous kind. In ^{L}1–11 the subject-matter of the several documents is of necessity made to conform to a single systematic order of topics, which involves the complete neglect of the actual order of any one of the sources. But the Conspectus of Codes in ^{L}13 goes straight to the documents, and, behind the documents, to the incorporated codes, and displays them in such a way as to show up clearly in the case of each both its principles of arrangement and characteristics of structure, and also any intrusive elements of subsequent accretion.

In ^{L}12 we have a Table of a transitional sort, partly a subject division more minutely given, and partly a section of the conspectus (^{L}13ga) set out at length by a special method suitable to the peculiar phenomena of that section.

In ^{L}14, mainly on the basis of the facts presented in all the preceding Tables, the codes are concisely compared with one another both in respect of matter and form, and the chief conclusions reached with regard to them are summarized for clear apprehension and easy reference.

In ^{L}15 certain statistics of usage, relating to the form of the legislation, are collected and classified. The particulars are usually indicated in detail in ^{L}13.

Finally in ^{L}16 is given a Table of Contents, in a form which enables several interesting conclusions to be drawn from the relative length and frequency of the allusions to the various topics. An Alphabetical Index to the Tables is added.

11n. On references to prophecy in P cp X § 1 (ii) 85, and in E cp XII § 2βγ § 4 113 116 foot, cp also ^{E}114 'prophet' and 'prophesy.'

12. The Sanctuary in P

$\mathfrak{H}^1$	SUBJECT	$\mathfrak{H}^2$	$\mathfrak{G}^2$
	a Introductory		
a 25^{1-9}	a Appeal for gifts	35^{4-9}	a 35^{4-8}‡
	b The workmen and their work . .	$10-19$	$9-19$‡
	c Presentation of gifts	$20-29$	$20-29$
q 31^{1-11}	d Appointment of Bezalel . . .	$30-36^1$	$30-36^1$
	e Overplus of gifts	36^{2-7}	36^{2-7}
	b The Dwelling		
c 26^{1-14}	a The Curtains and coverings . . .	$8-19$	c 37^1‡
$15-30$	b The Boards	$20-34$	g 38^{18-21}‡
31.	c The Veil	35	d 37^3
e 36	d The Screen	37	5
	c The Most Holy Place		
b 25^{10-22}	The Ark and its covering . . .	37^{1-9}	f 38^{1-8}‡
	d The Holy Place		
$23-30$	a The Table and its vessels . . .	$10-16$	$9-12$‡
$31-40$	b The Candlestick or lamp-stand . .	$17-24$	$13-17$‡
h 27^{20}	c Oil for the lamps		
m 30^{1-5}	d The Altar of Incense	$25-28$	
$6-10$	e Its use		
p $22-33$	f Anointing oil	$29a$	l 38^{25a}
$34-38$	g Incense	$29b$	$25b$
	e The Outer Court		
f 27^{1-8}	a The Brazen Altar	38^{1-7}	h 38^{22-24}‡
o 30^{17-21}	b The Laver	8	j 38^{26}
g 27^{9-19}	c The Court itself	$9-20$	e 37^{7-18}
	f Summary of gifts	$21-31$	$19-21$
			l 39^{1-10}
	g Priestly garments		
1 28^{1-5}	a Holy garments for Aaron . . .	39^1	n 39^{13}‡
$6-12$	b The Ephod	$2-7$	b 36^{8-14}‡
$13-29$	c The Breastplate	$8-21$	$15-29$
30	d Urim and Thummim		
$31-35$	e The Robe	$22-26$	$30-34$
k 39	f Coat, mitre, girdle for A. . . }	$27-29$	$35-37$
$41-43$	g Coats, headtires, girdles, breeches }		
j $36-38$	h Plate on mitre	30	$38-40$
	h Summary of work		
	The things made and brought .	$32-43$	{m 39^{11}‡ / o 39^{7-23}‡}
	i Erection		
	a The order to erect, &c . . .	40^{1-15}	40^{1-13}‡
	b Brief statement of execution . .	16	14
	c Erection of the Dwelling . . .	$17-19$	$15-17$
d 26^{33-35}	d Placing of the furniture	$20-30$	$18-26$‡
	e The use of the laver	31	k 38^{27}
	f Erection of the court	33	p 40^{27}‡
l 29^{1-35}	*j Consecration of Aaron and his sons*	Lev 8	
36	*k Consecration of the altar*	Lev 8^{14}. cp Num 7	
	l Daily sacrifice		
$38-42$	The morning and evening burnt offering		
	m Poll tax for maintenance		
n 30^{11-16}	½ shekel atonement money . . .		

$\mathfrak{H}^1$ = Ex 25–31^{11} $\mathfrak{H}$ The sanctuary ordained.
$\mathfrak{H}^2$ = Ex 35–40 $\mathfrak{H}$ The sanctuary completed
$\mathfrak{G}^2$ = the $\mathfrak{G}$ of $\mathfrak{H}^2$.
‡ = 'in shorter form or differently expressed.'

12 In the columns under $\mathfrak{H}^1$ and $\mathfrak{G}^2$ the text order of paragraphs can be traced by means of the letters which are placed wherever a break in the order is occasioned by the arrangement adopted, which follows the logical order of $\mathfrak{H}^2$. In this way the priority of $\mathfrak{H}^1$ and of the original of $\mathfrak{G}^2$ is seen to be an almost inevitable conclusion, for the natural and systematic sequence of subjects in $\mathfrak{H}^2$ would hardly have been departed from if it had once established itself. Another table will be found under Ex 35^4 in which the order of $\mathfrak{H}^1$ is followed, and under $^L 13ga$ the contents of both are concisely given, in the actual text order of each. By the help of these tables the divergences may be readily traced.

It may be of interest to append for further comparison the items referred to in the two accounts of the duties of the Levites in Num 3 and 4, both in their present form ascribed to P^s. It will be observed that the order of the clans is different. That in 4 seems most natural, (1) the most sacred and precious objects, (2) the skin and canvas coverings, and (3) the framework. The second account is also much fuller

	Num 3		Num 4
25	*The Gershonites*	4	*The Kohathites*
	Dwelling	$5.$	Veil
	Ark		Ark, coverings, staves
	Tent and covering	7	Table, &c, coverings, staves
	Screen for Tent door		
26	Court hangings	$9.$	Candlestick, lamps, &c, coverings, frame
	Screen for Tent door		
	Cords	11	Golden altar, coverings, staves
	The Kohathites	12	Vessels of ministry, coverings, frame
31	Ark		
	Table	$13.$	Altar, &c, coverings, staves
	Candlestick		
	Altars		*Eleazar*
	Vessels		
	Screen (? = Veil)	(16	Oil for light
			Sweet incense
	The Merarites		Continual meal offering
	Boards of Dwelling		Anointing oil
	Bars		Charge of Dwelling &c)
	Pillars		
	Sockets	24	*The Gershonites*
	Instruments	25	Curtains of Dwelling
37	Pillars of court		Tent and coverings
	Sockets		Screen for Tent door
	Pins	26	Court hangings
	Cords		Screen for Court door
			Cords
			Instruments
			The Merarites
		31	Boards of Dwelling
			Bars
			Pillars
			Sockets
			Pillars of Court
			Sockets
			Pins
			Cords

^{L}13a

13. Conspectus of Codes

See ^{L}15 for explanation of Types of legal clauses as abbreviated below, e.g. *Thou*^{n} = 'Thou shalt not ...', and of introductory clauses, e.g. *And* .. = 'And Yahweh spake unto Moses, saying...'

a. *The Ten Words of the Covenant*—J

Exodus 34^{14-26}

14 '15.	1 Monolatry	*Thou*^{n}	$+^{23}$ "^{24}	Obligation to attend the feasts	*shall* pl
17	2 No 'molten gods' to be made	*Thou*^{n}	25^a	7 No leavened bread with a sacrifice	*Thou*^{n}
$18^{a/b}$	4 Feast of Mazzoth	*Thou*	25^b	8 Consumption of passover	*shall*^{n}
19—20^{ab}	5 Firstborn and firstlings	*thou* &	26^a	9 Firstfruits	*Thou*^{n}
$+^{20c}$	None to be empty handed	*shall*^{n} pl	26^b	10 Kid not to be seethed in dam's milk	*Thou*^{n}
21	3 The weekly sabbath	*Thou*			
22	6 Feasts of weeks (Pentecost) and of ingathering (Booths)	*Thou*			

b. *The Words of Yahweh, or the Book of the Covenant*—E

Exodus 20^{23-26} 23^{10-19}

20^{23-26} Worship		= 5	23^{10-19} 22^{29-31} Feasts and Sacrifices	23^{18} 22^{29-31} Sacred offerings	= 6
$23^{a\,\text{α}}$ Monolatry		*Ye*^{u}		23^{18a} No leavened bread with a sacrifice	*Thou*^{n}
23^b No gods of silver or gold		*Ye*^{n}	$4+6=10$	18^b Consumption of peace offering	*shall*^{n}
The altar of sacrifice			23^{10-17} A sacred calendar = 4	22^{29a} ($23^{19a\,\text{N}}$) Firstfruits	*Thou*^{n}
24 To be made of earth		*Thou*	10. The sabbatical fallow year *thou*	22^{29b} Firstborn of men	*Thou*
25 If of stone, then unhewn		*if thou*	12 '13 The weekly sabbath *Thou*	30 Firstlings	*thou*
26 To be provided with steps for decency		*thou*^{n}	14 Three feasts of obligation *Thou*	$+^{31}$ Improper food	*ye*^{n}
			$15^{a/b/c}$ 16 Mazzoth, Harvest, and Ingathering *Thou*	23^{19b} Seething of kid in dam's milk	*Thou*^{n}

c. *The Judgements*—E

Exodus 21^1-22^{28} 23^{1-9}

21^1 Heading			21^{12-17} Violence punishable by death	= 5(6)
21^{2-11} Hebrew slaves		$5+5=10$	12 Death for homicide *He that*	15 Smiting a parent *he that*
Case of a bondman		Case of a bondwoman ('*amah*)	13 Asylum for case of accident *whoso*	16 Kidnapping *he that*
2 Free in seventh year *When* *thou*		7 Bondmaid not to go free *when*	14 No asylum for murderer *when*	$+^{17}$ Cursing a parent *he that*
3^a Alone, if enslaved unmarried *If*		8 If espoused, may be redeemed, not sold *If*		
3^b With wife, if married already *If*		9 If given to a son, to be as a daughter *if*		
4 Alone, if married since *If*		10 Not to be deprived of rights *If*		
5. Option of remaining *if*		11 Otherwise to be set free *if*		

13a As observed on Ex $34^{10\,\text{N}}$ many different arrangements of J's 'Ten Words' have been proposed, as indeed the Decalogue itself is still divided differently by Churches which make it their moral compendium. The above is put forward as the simplest and most conservative. There are twelve ordinances in all (not thirteen, for in its original form it is likely that firstborn and firstlings were conjoined), and of these two have been omitted, 20^c 23, because (1) they are, like 25^b, different in form from the rest, and (2) they are also dependent in subject upon the others. But it is hard to be satisfied with the existing form or order as correctly representing the original. The only other legislation in J is of course the pair of passages, both much expanded, in Ex 12^{21-27} and 13^{3-16} on the Passover, Mazzoth, firstlings, and firstborn.

b The Covenant-book has been so much interfered with by editorial process that any suggestions for its reconstruction must necessarily be tentative. All that need be said as to analysis is said in the notes to the text. The re-united fragments, without very much forcing, yield a pentad and a decad of allied ordinances. Perhaps another pentad has dropped out. Dr. Briggs adds the miscellaneous ordinances given here as a sort of supplement to the Judgements proper, i.e. 22^{18-28} 23^{1-9}, and makes up three decads for what he calls the 'greater book of the covenant,' as compared with J's 'little book of the covenant,' as above, a (see *Higher Crit*, 189, 232).

c In the Judgements as supplemented there are seen to be fifteen groups in all, of five or less than five ordinances. The last four groups are clearly added, and the third, 21^{12-17}, by its form, proclaims itself not an original element, so that the Judgements in their original form are now represented by ten groups, alike in form and character, six of them perfect pentads, and the rest such as may well have been once arranged in the same way. There is no clue to the source of the added laws.

21^{17} This verse, though identical in form with ^{15}, hardly agrees in subject with its context. Could it have been added to assimilate with P^h, see below f Lev 19^3 and following group?

CONSPECTUS OF CODES 257

Ex 21$^{18-27}$ Injuries   3+4=7   Ex 22$^{7-17}$ Property—Breach of Trust   5+5=10 ^{L}**13e**

Personal	To slaves
18. Compensation for assault *when* men	20 Penalty for killing slave *when* m
(20. Misplaced, see next column)	21 Remitted if death be delayed *if*
22 Fine for causing miscarriage *when* men	26 Freedom for loss of eye *when* m
23 *Lex talionis* for further hurt *if*	27 Freedom for loss of tooth *if*

21$^{28-36}$ Cattle   5+3=8

Savage oxen	Damage to cattle
28 Ox goring any one to death *when*	33. Animal falling into a pit *when*
29 Death for negligent owner *if*	35 Ox killed by ox *when*
30 Alternative of ransom *if*	36 The ox known to be savage *whether*
31^N Case of son or daughter *whether*	
32 Thirty shekels fine for a slave *if*	

22$^{1-6}$ Property—Theft and Damage   5+3=8

Theft	Damage to crops
1 Fine for stealing animals *When* m	5a^N Damage *When*
3b Enslaved, if fine unpaid *If* m	5b ⓈSam Complete consumption *if*
4 Mitigation by restitution *If*	6 Arson *When*
2 A night-robber may be killed *If*	
3a Not after sunrise *If*	

22$^{7-17}$ Property—Breach of Trust

7 Property in trust stolen *When* m	14 Compensation for hurt to loan *when*
8. Trial, if thief not found *If*	15a Not if owner was in charge *if*
10. Animal dying by accident *When*	15b Or if hired *if*
12 Animal stolen *if*	16a Seducer to marry and endow girl *when*
13 Animal torn in pieces *if*	16b Or her father may exact dowry *if*

22$^{18-27}$ Various ordinances   (3)+(5)=(8)

18-20 Three capital offences	21-27 Kindness and humanity
18 No sorceress to live *Thou*^{n}	21a /b 23 /24 Equity towards strangers *thou*^{n}
19 Unnatural crime *He that*	+/22 *Kindness to widow and orphan* Ye^n
20 Sacrificing to other gods *He that*	25a Forbearance to borrowers *If thou*
	+25b *No usury* Ye^n
	26. Pledged garments *If thou*

22^{28} Reverence   =2

28a For God (M the judges) *Thou*^{n} | 28b for rulers *thou*

23$^{1-9}$ Administration of justice   5+5=10

1a False reports *Thou*^{n}	6 Injustice to the poor *Thou*^{n}
1b Conspiracy of witnesses ^{n} *thou*	7a Fraud ^{n} *thou*
2a Popular verdicts *Thou*^{n}	7b Condemning the innocent ^{n} *thou*
2b Popular testimony *thou*^{n}	8 Bribery *thou*
3 Favouring the poor *thou*^{n}	9a /b Justice to the stranger *thou*^{n} (ye)
+4 *Straying animals* When *thou*	
+5 *Overburdened ass* When *thou*	

d. The Decalogue—E D

Sins forbidden

E+R^d Ex 20	AGAINST PIETY	D Deut 5	E+R^d Ex 20	AGAINST MORALITY	D Deut 5
3 *Thou*^{n}	1 Apostasy	*Thou*^{n} 7	13 *Thou*^{n}	6 Murder	*Thou*^{n} 17
4a /b /5. *Thou*^{n}	2 Idolatry	*Thou*^{n} 8–10	14 *Thou*^{n}	7 Adultery	*thou*^{n} 18
7a /b *Thou*^{n}	3 Perjury	*Thou*^{n} 11	15 *Thou*^{n}	8 Theft	*thou*^{n} 19
8–10^r P11 [*Thou*^{n}]	4 Sabbath breaking	*Observe* +12–15	16 *Thou*^{n}	9 False witness	*thou*^{n} 20
12a /b [*Thou*^{n}]	5 Contempt of parents	*Honour* +16	17a /b *Thou*^{n}	10 Coveting	*thou*^{n} +21

e. The Statutes and Judgements, or the Book of the Law—D

(The Deuteronomic Code = Deut **12–26**)

12–18 26 THE MAIN THEOCRATIC INSTITUTIONS

D^g D^{gs}

Deut 12$^{2-27}$ Worship to be centralized

2 Destruction of high places	*Ye*
3 Destruction of idolatrous emblems	*ye* & =5
4–7 Centralization of worship	*Ye* & =5
8–12 *Centralization of worship*	*Ye*^{n} & =5
13 Centralization of worship	*thou* &
15 /16 Slaughtering allowed at home	*thou* &
17 Sacred food only for the sanctuary	*Thou* &
19 Levite to share	*thou*
+20 *Animal food freely allowed*	*When, thou*
+21 *May be killed at home*	*When, thou*
+23–25 *No blood to be eaten*	*thou* &
+26–27 *Sacred food only for the sanctuary*	*thou* &

12^{29}–13 Apostasy

+12$^{29-31}$ *Warning against apostasy and syncretism*   *When, thou*

13$^{1-5}$ Seduction to idolatry by a prophet   *When, thou & shall &*

6–11 Death by stoning for such seducers   *When, thou &*

12–18 Judgement on an apostate city   *When thou*

D^g D^{gs}

Deut 14$^{1-21}$ Ceremonial purity

1 /2 Restraint in mourning customs	*Ye*^{n} &
3 No abomination to be eaten	*Thou*^{n}
4–21 Clean and unclean m'eats	5+5=10
4. Clean beasts named	*ye*
6 Clean beasts described	*ye*
7. Unclean beasts described, with cases	*ye*^{n}
+8b *Carcases not to be touched*	*ye*^{n}
9 Clean water-dwellers	*ye* &
10 Unclean water-dwellers	
11 'All clean birds' allowed	*Ye*
12–18 Unclean birds named	*ye*^{n}
19 Winged creeping things unclean	*shall*^{n}
20 All clean winged things allowed	*ye*
21abcd Improper food	*Ye*^{n} *Thou* &
21e Seething a kid in its dam's milk	*Thou*^{n}

14$^{22-29}$ Tithes

| 22–27 Annual tithe | *Thou & when &* |
| 28. Triennial tithe | *Thou & shall &* |

15$^{1-18}$ Debtors and slaves

1–3 Release of debts in seventh year	1 3 *Thou* .. 2 *shall* =3
7–11 Treatment of Hebrew debtors	*When, thou*
12–18 Hebrew slaves	*When, thou &*

13d See Ex 20^{1N}. Dr Briggs' reconstructions of the fourth and fifth words are accepted, see $^{9N\ 12N}$.

e See Deut 12^{1N} for some remarks on the structure of **D**.

s

₁13e D⁵   D⁵⁵

Deut 15¹⁹⁻²³ Firstlings
¹⁹ To be sanctified, and eaten at the Sanctuary, *Thou & = 3*
²¹, ²³ⁿ If blemished, to be eaten at home *Thou & = 3*

16¹⁻¹⁷ A sacred Calendar
¹. Feast of the Passover *Thou &* | ⁹⁻¹² Feast of Weeks *Thou &*
+³. *Feast of Mazzoth combined* | ¹³⁻¹⁵ Feast of Booths *Thou &*
  with it *Thou &* | ¹⁶ᵃ Obligation of the three Pilgrimage Feasts *Shall pl*
⁵⁻⁷ The Passover (continued) *Thouⁿ* | ¹⁶ᵇ⁻¹⁷ All to offer according to means *Shallⁿ pl..shall*
+⁸ *Duration of Mazzoth* *Thou..shall..Thou*

16¹⁸⁻²⁰ Administration of Justice
¹⁸ᵃ Appointment of local judges *Thou*
¹⁸ᵇ Their duty of impartiality *shall pl*
¹⁹. Cautions to judges *Thou & = 4*

16²¹⁻17⁷ Offences against religion
²¹. No asherah or pillar *Thouⁿ & = 2*
17¹ No blemished animal to be sacrificed *Thouⁿ*
²⁻⁵ Death by stoning for apostasy *When found, thou*
⁶ Responsibility of witnesses *shall &*

17⁸⁻²⁰ Judgement and Rule
⁸⁻¹³ Central court of appeal *When, thou & . shall*
¹⁴ Choice of home-born king *When thou*
¹⁶ᵃ²⁰ Not to multiply horses, wives, money *shallⁿ = 3*
¹⁸ His duty to copy and read the law *shall &*

18 Priests and Prophets
¹ᵃᶜᴺ³ Dues of 'the priests the Levites' *shall pl &*
¹ᵇᵈ²⁴ Revenues of 'all the tribe of Levi' *shall..thou*
⁶⁻⁸ Provision for country Levites *when*
⁹⁻¹⁴ No divination or the like *When thou &*
¹⁵⁻²² Promise of a prophet *thou & (ye)*

19–25 MISCELLANEOUS LAWS

19 Administration of justice
¹⁻⁷ ¹⁰ Asylum for accidental homicide *When, thou .. whoso*
⁸. Provision for three more cities of refuge *if, thou*
¹¹⁻¹³ No murderer to escape death *when..elders shall..thou*
¹⁴ Neighbour's landmark *Thouⁿ*
¹⁵ Number of witnesses *Shallⁿ &*
¹⁶⁻²⁰ False witness *When*
²¹ Lex talionis *(thine eye) shall*

20 Warfare
¹ Duty of courage *When thou*
²⁻⁴ 'The priest' to encourage people *ye & shall*
⁵⁻⁹ 'The officers' to sift the warriors by applying a fourfold test, and to appoint captains *shall pl & = 5*
¹⁰⁻¹⁸ Sieges
¹⁰ Overtures of peace *When thou* | ¹³⁻¹⁵ Case of foreign cities *thou &*
¹¹ Reduction under tribute *if* | ¹⁶⁻¹⁸ Case of Canaanite cities *thouⁿ = 5*
¹² Laying siege *if*
¹⁹ Care of trees in a long siege *When thou &*

21¹⁻⁹ Administration of justice
¹⁻⁹ Inquest on one found dead ¹ *When found*
  ² ³ ⁴ ⁶ *elders shall* ⁷ *sha'l = 5*
⁵ Introduction of the Levitical priests *shall*

21¹⁰⁻¹⁴ Warfare
¹⁰⁻¹³ Marriage of a female captive *When thou & . shall*
¹⁴ To be set free if divorced *if thou*

D⁵   D⁵⁵

Deut 21¹⁵⁻²¹ The Family—Children
¹⁵⁻¹⁷ Rights of firstborn son *When*
¹⁸⁻²¹ Rebellious son *When*
21²². Body of a criminal hanged *When*

22¹⁻⁸ Kindness and humanity
¹⁻³ Lost cattle or other property ¹ *Thouⁿ*
  ² *if thou ³ᵃᵇᶜ thou = 5*
⁴ Fallen ass or ox *Thouⁿ*
(⁵ Probably should follow ⁸, see below)
⁶ Bird's nest *When, thou*
⁸ Parapet to house *When thou*

22⁵ ⁹⁻¹² Unnatural mixtures *= 5*
⁵ None to wear dress of the other sex *shallⁿ &*
⁹ Seed not to be mixed *Thouⁿ*
¹⁰ Ox and ass not to be joined at the plough *Thouⁿ*
¹¹ No mixing of wool and linen *Thouⁿ*
¹² Fringes on garments *Thou*

22¹³⁻³⁰ The Family—Purity
¹³⁻²¹ Doubt as to wife's virginity *Whenᵐ..if*
²²⁻³⁰ Purity towards woman *= 5*
²² Adultery *Whenᵐ* | ²³ Seduction *Whenᵐ*
²³. Seduction of betrothed girl | ³⁰ Marriage with stepmother *shallⁿ*
  When
²⁵⁻²⁷ Rape on betrothed girl *if*

23¹⁻¹⁴ The Nation—Purity
¹⁻⁸ Restrictions on citizenship ¹ ² ³ *shallⁿ ⁷ᵃᵇ Thou = 5*
⁹⁻¹⁴ Camp regulations ⁹ *When ¹² shall..thou = 3*

23¹⁵⁻²⁵ Miscellaneous
¹⁵ Kindness to escaped slave ¹⁵ ¹⁶ᵇ *Thouⁿ ¹⁶ᵃ shall = 3*
¹⁷ Purity—vice intolerable ¹⁷ᵃᵇ *Shallⁿ ¹⁸ Thouⁿ*
¹⁹ Kindness—No usury *Thouⁿ &*
²¹⁻²³ Keeping of vows *When thou*
²⁴ Regard for neighbour's grapes or corn ²⁴ *When thou = 2*

24¹⁻⁹ Miscellaneous
¹⁻⁴ Divorce *Whenᵐ &*
⁵ The year after marriage *Whenᵐ*
⁶ Millstones not lawful pledges *shallⁿ*
⁷ Kidnapping a capital offence *Whenᵐ*
⁸ Leprosy and priestly teaching *thou*

24¹⁰⁻²¹ Kindness and equity
¹⁰⁻¹³ Pledges *When..if = 2*
¹⁴ Hired servants *Thouⁿ*
¹⁶ Individual responsibility *shallⁿ*
¹⁷⁻²² Conduct towards dependants *= 5*
¹⁷ᵃ Justice to stranger and fatherless *Thouⁿ* | ¹⁹ᵃ Harvest gleanings *When thou*
¹⁷ᵇ The widow's garment *thouⁿ* | ²⁰ᵃ Olives ungathered *When thou*
+¹⁸ ¹⁹ᵇ ²⁰ᵇ ²¹ᵇ ²² Hortatory expansions | ²¹ᵃ Vineyard gleanings *When thou*

25 Miscellaneous
¹⁻³ Judicial use of bastinado ¹ *When* ² *if* ³ *shall*
⁴ Toiling ox unmuzzled *Thouⁿ*
⁵⁻¹⁰ Levirate marriage ⁵ *When* ⁷ *if*
¹¹ Immodest assault *When*
¹³⁻¹⁶ Weights and measures ¹³. *Thouⁿ = 2*
¹⁷⁻¹⁹ Amalek to be blotted out *thou*

26¹⁻¹⁵ Offering of firstfruits and tithe
  ¹ *when* ¹² *When*

27¹⁵⁻²⁶ The Solemn Curses *= 10(12)*
+¹⁵ *Idolatry* *the man who* | ²¹ Unnatural crime *he that*
¹⁶ Contempt of parent *he that* | ²² Incest (sister) *he that*
¹⁷ Removing landmark *he that* | ²³ Incest (mother-in-law) *he that*
¹⁸ Misleading the blind *he that* | ²⁴ Secret assault *he that*
¹⁹ Perverting justice *he that* | ²⁵ Murder for reward *he that*
²⁰ Incest (stepmother) *he that* | +²⁶ *Disobedience* *whoso*

ᴸ13e 27¹⁵⁻²⁶ This remarkable decad, though not part of the code, and now found in a later setting with new opening and closing 'statutes,' could not be omitted from the conspectus.

f. The Law of Holiness, or The Statutes of Yahweh—P^h

$L13f$

Lev 17^1–18^5   First Principles $5+5=10$

17^1–18^2 Slaughter and Sacrifice
(1. *And* . speak..A..sons. ch..say)
3,¹ °⁵–⁷¹ Lawful slaughtering
⁸ Lawful sacrifice *And to*   thou
¹⁰°¹¹. Blood of domestic animals
¹³°¹⁴ª ¹⁴ᵇ Blood of wild animals
³ ⁸ ¹⁰ ¹³ *Any man of the house of Israel* (⁸ ¹⁰ ¹³ add *or of the strangers that sojourn among them*) *who*
¹⁵ Eating carrion *every soul who*
(18^{1-2a} *And..speak. ch..say*)
²ᵇ Endorsement—'I am Yahweh'

18^{3-5} Wrong and Right Ways
³ᵃ Shun the doings of Egypt
³ᵇ Shun the doings of Canaan
³ᶜ Shun the religious customs of both   ³ᵃᵇᶜ *ye* ⁿ
⁴ᵃ Keep Yahweh's civil laws (judgements)
⁴ᵇ Keep Yahweh's religious laws (statutes)   ⁴ᵃᵇ *ye*
°⁴ᶜ–⁵ᵃ ⁵ᵇ Endorsement (expanded) 'I am Yahweh'

18^6–19^2 The family—Purity towards persons

18^{6-15} Those related through parents and children $5+5=10$

In the first degree	In the second degree
⁶ Any near kinswoman	¹¹ Stepsister
⁷ Mother	¹² Aunt on the father's side
⁸ Stepmother	¹³ Aunt on the mother's side
⁹ Own or half-sister	¹⁴ Uncle's wife
¹⁰ Granddaughter	¹⁵ Daughter-in-law
⁶ *Any man..ye*ⁿ ⁷⁻¹⁵ *Thou*ⁿ..	⁶⁻¹⁵ *uncover nakedness*

18^{16-23} Those more distantly connected or not at all

Those related through marriage	Other cases $5+5=10$
¹⁶ Brother's wife	²⁰ Neighbour's wife
¹⁷ᵃ Wife's daughter	²¹ Defilement for Molech
¹⁷ᵇ Wife's granddaughter	²² Mankind
¹⁸ Living wife's sister	²³ᵃ A beast
¹⁹ A woman in her separation	²³ᵇ A woman with a beast
all *Thou*ⁿ *uncover nakedness*	²⁰⁻²³ᵃ *Thou*ⁿ ²³ᵇ *shall*ⁿ

°²⁴⁻³⁰ᵃ ³⁰ᵇ 19^{1-2a} °²ᵇ Endorsement (much expanded) 'I am Yahweh' (*And..speak congr..ch..say*)

19^3 ³⁰ &c   Piety $5+4=9$

Worship	Reverence
⁴ᵃ ‖ 26¹ᵃ Apostasy *Ye*ⁿ	³ᵃ Reverence for parents
⁴ᵇ ‖ 26¹ᵇ Idolatry *Ye*ⁿ	*a man Ye*
[26¹ᶜ Erection of a figured stone *Ye*ⁿ]	[20⁹ᵃ °ᵇ Cursing parents *any man who*]
3ᵇ ‖ 30ᵃ ‖ 26²ᵃ Sabbath keeping *Ye*	[24¹⁵ᵇ Cursing God *any man when*]
[30ᵇ ‖ 26²ᵇ Reverence for the sanctuary *Ye*]	[24¹⁶ᵃ Blaspheming Yahweh *he that*]
3ᶜ ‖ 30ᶜ ‖ 26²ᶜ 'I am Yahweh'	

+19^{5-8} Acceptable offerings   See 22^{29}
+$19^{9.10}$ Gleanings.   See 23^{22}

19^{11} &c   Injuries $3+5=8$

[24¹⁷⁻²² Persons and animals]	19^{11} Property
24¹⁷ ‖ 21ᵇ Murder	11ᵃ Theft *Ye*ⁿ
a man when (he that)	[³⁵ Just weights and measures *Ye*ⁿ]
24¹⁸ ‖ 21ᵃ Killing a beast *he that*	11ᵇ Fraud *Ye*ⁿ
24¹⁹ Assault *a man when*	11ᶜ Lying *ye*ⁿ
	12ᵃ °ᵇ Perjury *ye*ⁿ
	12ᶜ Endorsement 'I am Yahweh'

Lev 19^{13-16}   Injustice $5+5=10$

In conduct	At law
13ᵃ Oppression *Thou*ⁿ	15ᵃ No unrighteousness *Ye*ⁿ
13ᵇ Exaction *thou*ⁿ	15ᵇ Justice to the poor *Thou*ⁿ
13ᶜ Withholding wages *shall* ᵗʰᵉᵉ	15ᶜ °ᵈ Impartiality *thou*ⁿ (thou)
14ᵃ Cursing the deaf *Thou*ⁿ	16ᵃ Slander *Thou*ⁿ
14ᵇ Endangering the blind *thou*ⁿ	16ᵇ Malicious witnessing *thou*ⁿ
14ᶜ ᵈ Endorsement 'I am Yahweh'	16ᶜ Endorsement 'I am Yahweh'

$19^{17. 32-34}$ Unkindness $5(6)+5(5)=(10)$

Towards equals	Towards dependants
17ᵃ Hatred *Thou*ⁿ	32ᵃ Saluting the hoary head
17ᵇ Reproof *Thou*ⁿ	*Thou*
17ᶜ Guilty (silence) *thou*ⁿ	32ᵇ Honouring the aged *thou*
18ᵃ Revenge *thou*ⁿ	[Ezek 22⁷ Wronging the widow
18ᵇ Grudging *thou*ⁿ	ib afflicting the fatherless]
18ᵈ Endorsement 'I am Yahweh'	°32ᶜ God to be feared 'I am Y'
	33ᵇ Wronging the stranger *ye*ⁿ
°19ᵃ Hortatory addition *Ye*	°34ᵇ Love to the stranger *thou*
	34ᶜ Endorsement 'I am Yahweh'

19^{19} &c $=4(5)$ Unlawful mixtures ‖ Deut $22^{5\ 9-12}=5$

[(missing) Dress of the sexes]	‖ Deut 22⁵
19ᵇ Hybrids *Thou*ⁿ	Cp Deut 22¹⁰ not to *plough* with ox and ass
19ᶜ Mixed seed *Thou*ⁿ	‖ Deut 22⁹ where 'vineyard' is narrower than 'field'
19ᵈ Dress of mixed materials *shall*ⁿ *thee*	‖ Deut 22¹¹
[Num 15³⁸ᵇ¹ Fringes *shall* pl Num 15³⁹⁻⁴¹ Endorsement (with hortatory expansion) 'I am Yahweh']	‖ Deut 22¹²

+19^{20} '²¹. Seduction of betrothed slave
     (²¹. *ritual supplement*) ᵃ *man when*
+19^{25-25} Fruit trees   See below, 25
19^{26a} Meat not to be eaten with the blood   *Ye*ⁿ

19^{26b-31}   Heathenish customs $5+3=8$

26ᵇ Enchantments *Ye*ⁿ	29ᵃ °ᵇ Religious prostitution
26ᶜ Augury *ye*ⁿ	ⁿ *thou*
27ᵃ ᵇ Cutting hair or beard	30ᵃᵇ (see above 19³)
*ye*ⁿ (thou ⁿ)	31ᵃ Necromancy ⁿ *ye*
28ᵃ Disfigurement in mourning *Ye*ⁿ	31ᵇ °ᶜ Witchcraft ⁿ *ye*
28ᵇ Tattooing *ye*ⁿ	31ᵈ Endorsement 'I am Yahweh'
28ᶜ Endorsement 'I am Yahweh'	

19^{32-34} Aged and stranger.   See above under 19^{17}
19^{35-36a} Weights and measures.   See above under 19^{11}.
19^{36b-37} Closing exhortation

20^{1-9}   Another version of various laws

(¹ *And*) ²ᵃ *And to*..thou
²ᵇᶜ °²ᵈ⁻⁵ Giving seed unto Molech   *any man who* ‖ 18²¹
⁶' Necromancy and witchcraft   *the soul who* ‖ 19³¹
⁷ Repetition of 'I am Yahweh' with hortatory additions
⁹ Cursing parents.   See above under 19³ᵃ

13f 17^1–18^2 P^h, in taking up an old pentad, has expanded the original largely, introducing into the first ordinance the reference to idolatrous worship ⁵⁻⁷, into the opening formula of the next three the reference to 'strangers' who first become prominent in D, and into the third and fourth the confirmatory reasoning ¹¹ ¹⁴ᵃ If the last be the real fifth of the pentad, it has been drastically revised by P^s according to the pattern of P^t in ¹¹⁻¹⁵ The original probably forbade absolutely the eating of carrion, but the compiler, while refusing leave even to the 'stranger' (ct D ^{L}6c), made ablution sufficient for absolution Paton's ingenious inclusion of 18^{2b} is adopted above as the concise form of the clauses, suggests that this is borrowed, and not composed, by P^h.

18^{3-5} P^h has added a pentad of a kind fitted to follow the first, and to lead up to the following legislation Paton points out that the order (1) judgements, (2) statutes (ct ⁵ &c), as well

19^3 A number of transpositions are made in connexion with this chapter For their justification see Paton, and cp $^L15f^N$

19^{20} is assigned to P^h in the text, but does not match the other precepts on sexual morality in 18 20, where we should expect to find it It might fitly replace Deut 22³⁰ as the close of the pentad on adultery and seduction Did a priestly editor of JEDP light upon the original pentad and extract this additional clause, change כי איש into איש כי, add ²¹ in the precise style of the ritualist, and place it in the margin, whence it has found its way hither? The formula ᵃ *man when* is more common in P^t than in P^h, and P^h uses *'amah* 25⁶ ⁴⁴, cp ᴱ99, ct *shiphcah* here, J41.

LAWS AND INSTITUTIONS

13f Lev 20^{10-24} Laws of Purity towards persons
(Second version) $= 10(12)$

10 Neighbour's wife	17 Own or half-sister
11 Stepmother	18 Woman having her sickness
12 Daughter-in-law	°19 Aunt by mother or father
13 Mankind	*thou* n
14 A woman and her mother	20 Uncle's wife
15 Man with beast	21 Deceased brother's wife
°16 Woman with beast	
woman who . , thou	

(Throughout, except $^{16\ 19}$, *a man who*)
22 Endorsement (much expanded) 'I am Yahweh'

20^{25}. Hortatory passage on Clean and Unclean,
'I Yahweh..' ‖ 11^{43}..

20^{27} Necromancer or wizard to be stoned
 man or woman when ‖ 19^{31}

21   Priestly holiness

21^{1-9} The Priesthood generally $5 + 2(3) = 7(8)$

(^{1a} *And .. said* speak .. priests s say)

Mourning for the Dead	Marriage
1b None to defile himself *Shall* n	7a Not a harlot *Shall* n
2. °4 Near kinsfolk excepted	7b Not a divorced wife *shall* n
shall n	+9 Priest's daughter a harlot
5a Shaving the head *Shall* n pl	8 Their holiness emphasized
5b Cutting the beard *shall* n pl	
5c Cutting the flesh *shall* n pl	
6 Their holiness emphasized	

21^{10-15} The High Priest $5 + 5 = 10$

Mourning for the dead	Marriage
10a °bc No dishevelled hair *shall* n	13 His wife to be a virgin *shall* n
10d No rending of clothes *shall* n	14a Not a widow *shall* n
11a No approach to a corpse	14b Not one divorced
shall n	14c Not a harlot
11b No exception to the rule	14d One of his own people *shall*
shall n	15 Endorsement (expanded) 'I
12a Not to absent himself *shall* n	am Yahweh'
12b Endorsement (expanded) 'I am Yahweh'	

21^{16-24} Disqualification for ministry
(^{16} *And* .. speak .. A)
17 None with a blemish to draw near to offer the bread of
  his God   *a man who*
18 °21, Twelve kinds of blemish specified *a man who*
22a /b He may eat the bread of his God   *shall*
23a,l He may not come to the altar
23b 'I am Yahweh...'
(^{l24} *Fragment of a title*)

22   Holy things—gifts and offerings
°$^{1-3a'}$ Title by R^p (*and* .. speak .. A .. s .. say), now combined with
   mutilated hortatory introduction of P^h
$3b-16$ Disqualification for the Holy Food $5(6) + 5(6) = 10(12)$

Temporary	Permanent
3b' Uncleanness of any kind	10'a b No sojourner or hireling
man who	*shall* n
4a Leprosy or an issue *man who*	11 A bought slave may eat *when*
4b Uncleanness by touch *he that*	One home-born may eat *shall*
5 Other cases of the same	12 Not priest's married daughter
man who	13 Widowed daughter may *when*
6. Purification *soul who*	+14 Accidental eating
+8 Eating carrion *shall* n ‖ 11^{39}	*a man when*
Endorsement (expanded) 'I am Yahweh...'	15. Endorsement (expanded) 'I am Yahweh...'

Lev 22^{17-25} Conditions of acceptance $2 + 5 = 7$

The Burnt offering	The Peace offering
($^{17-18a}$ *And* speak..A..s ch..say)	21 Sound animal of herd or flock
18b-19 A male of the beeves,	*a man when*
sheep, or goats and un-	22 Blemishes to disqualify *ye* n
blemished *any man who*	23 Misshapen animal to serve
20 None with a blemish *all who*	for freewill offering, not
	vow *thou*
	24 Other disqualifications *thou*
	25 Such not accepted even
	from an alien *ye* n

$^{26-33}$ & 19^{5-8} Times of offering $5 + 5 = 10$

Young animal and Thank offering	The Peace offering
(^{26} *And* .. saying)	19^5 To be acceptable *when* ye
27 Acceptable from eighth day	6a Two days for eating *shall*
when	6b The rest burnt *shall*
28 Not to be killed with its dam	7 Abominable on third day *if*
ye n	8 Eater to bear .. iniquity *shall*
29 Thank offering to be accept-	22^{31} Endorsement (expanded)
able *when* ye	'I am Yahweh'
30a To be eaten same day *shall*	
30b None left till morning *ye* n	
30c Endorsement 'I am Yahweh'	

23§   Sacred Days
($^{9-10a}$ *And*   speak .. ch)
$10b-12$ 14^l Festival of the Wave-sheaf of Firstfruits
                       when ye ... land
$15-18$, $19b-20$ Pentecost or Harvest Festival
                       ye
22a Gleanings to be left
22b Endorsement 'I am Yahweh'
$39-42^l$ 'The Feast of Yahweh,' kept in booths   *ye*
$+24^{15b-22}$ Irreverence and injuries. See under 19^3 above

$[19^{23-25}]$ 25^{1-22}§ Sacred Years
(25^{1-2a} *And ... in mount Sinai* .. speak .. ch .. say)

       Fourth and Seventh Years $4 + 4 = 8$

For fruit trees	For field and vineyard
[19^{23a} Young trees uncircum-	25^{2b} Sabbath year
cised *When* ye .. land	*When* ye .. land
23b Three years without eating	3-4a In the seventh year *Thou*
fruit *shall*	4b-5 No agricultural work *thou* n
24 Holy to Yahweh in the	6 Produce to be shared *shall*
fourth year *shall*	19-22 Concluding assurances
25a May be eaten in the fifth *ye*	
25b Endorsement 'I am Yahweh']	

           Fiftieth Year $4 + 1 = 5$

Year of liberty	Influence on land purchase
25^{8a} Forty-nine years to be	14 Equity in buying land
reckoned *thou*	*when* ye .. thy
9a 10a Fiftieth a year of liberty	
thou	
10c Resumption of land-owner-	
ship *ye*	
11b 12b To be kept as a fallow	
year *ye* n	
17°a b Endorsement (expanded)	
'I am Yahweh'	

25^{25-55}§   Hebrew Poor Law $5 + 4 = 9$

Debt	Slavery
25 Land redeemable by kins-	39 Hebrew sold to Hebrew, no
man *When*	slave *when*
26,' (Or by himself) *a man when*	40 To be as a wage earner *shall*
28^l (Or restored at year of	$47-48^l$ Hebrew sold to stranger
liberty) *if*	redeemable *when*
35 Poor brother to be relieved	53 To be as a wage earner
when	55 Endorsement (expanded) 'I
36. No usury n *thou*	am Yahweh'
38 Endorsement 'I am Yahweh'	
&c	

$+26^1$. Worship. See 19^3. above

g. Analysis and Conspectus of Priestly Laws—Ex 25 to Num 36

L13gb

i = 'introduced by editorial formula, And ...'

$$P^t_g{}^h_s \quad \text{Exodus } 25_{1-27_{19}}{}_{20.} \; 28_{1-25} \; {}^c26-28 \; 29-40 \; {}^{42}_{41} \; 29_{1-20} {}_{21} {}^{22-37}_{38-42} \; {}^{45}_{43.} \; 30 \; 31_{1-}{}_{11} \; {}^{12a-14a}_{14b-17} \; {}_{18a} \; | \; 35_{1-3}{}_{4-} \; 40_{38}$$

$$P^t_g{}^h_s \quad \text{Leviticus } 1^{1v-13r} \; {}^c14-17 \; 2^{1-3} \; {}^c4-16 \; 3^{1-17r} \; 4_{1-35} \; 5^{1-6}$$

EXODUS

$P^t \quad P^g \quad P^s$

a. Ex **12** The Passover and Mazzoth
   ¹ The year to begin in spring henceforth
     ³⁻¹³ The Passover   [And .. M and A .. Egypt
     ¹⁴⁻²⁰ Mazzoth instituted
     ⁴³⁻⁵⁰ Persons who may eat Passover   And .. M and A

13¹. Firstborn and firstlings   And ..

$P^g \quad\quad\quad\quad\quad\quad\quad\quad\quad\quad P^s$

25–31¹¹ Sanctuary and   **35⁴–40** Sanctuary
    Priesthood ordered   Prepared
25¹⁻⁹ Gifts asked   And ..   35⁴⁻²⁹ Gifts and aid
10–40 Ark, Table, Candlestick   30–36⁷ Bezalel, gifts
26¹⁻³² Curtains, Boards, Veil   8–36 Curtains, Boards, Veil
33–35 Arrangement of furniture   37 The Screen
36. The Screen   37¹⁻²⁴ Ark, Table, Candle-
27¹⁻⁸ The Altar   stick
9–19 The Court   25–28 Altar of Incense
20. *Oil for light*   29 Anointing oil, incense
28¹⁻³⁵ Aaron's Ephod, Breast-   38¹⁻⁷ Altar of Burnt
    plate, Urim and Thummim,   offering
    Robe   8 The Laver
36–38 Plate on Mitre   9–20 The Court
39 Coat, Mitre, Girdle   21–31 Summary of gifts
40–43 Coats for sons of Aaron &c   39¹⁻²⁶ Aaron's Ephod,
29¹⁻³⁷ Consecration of priests   Breastplate, Robe
    and altar   27–29 Rest of dress of Aaron
      38–41 The Daily Sacrifice   and sons
    30¹⁻¹⁰ Altar of Incense,   30. Plate on Mitre
      and its use   32–43 Summary of entire
      11–16 Poll tax   And ..   work
      17–21 The Laver   And .   40¹⁻¹⁹ Erection ordered
      22–38 Anointing oil and   and effected   And .
        incense   20–33 Furniture arranged
      31¹⁻¹¹ Bezalel &c engaged   34–38 Cloud and glory

$P^h \quad P^g \quad P^s$

The Sabbath

31¹²⁻¹⁴ᵃʳ Yahweh's Sabbaths to be kept
    (And ... speak ch)
    ¹⁴ᵇ⁻¹⁷ The command further expanded

35¹ An introduction (misplaced)
    ² The Sabbath to be kept strictly; no
      fire lighting

LEVITICUS

The Laws of Sacrifice—1–7

$P^t \quad P^g \quad P^s$

b. Lev **1–6⁷** A Manual for Worshippers
(¹⁻²ᵃ Heading, fixing the Tent of Meeting as the scene
    of revelation)
1²ᵇ Oblations to be from the herd or flock
                           a man (*adam*) when
1³⁻¹⁷ The Burnt Offering
    ³ᵇ⁻⁹ Victim from the herd   *If*
    ¹⁰⁻¹³ Victim from the flock   *if*
  + ¹⁴⁻¹⁷ Victims doves or pigeons   *if*

2 The Meal Offering
    ¹⁻³ Of fine flour   soul *when*
  + ⁴⁻¹⁶ Other kinds   = (5)
    ⁴ Cakes or wafers from the oven   *when* thou
    ⁵. From the baking pan   *if* thy
    ⁷ ⁄⁸ From the frying pan   *if* thy
    ⁄⁹ Priest to burn a memorial   *shall*
    ⁄¹⁰ The rest to go to Aaron and sons   *shall*
    ¹¹ No leaven or honey in fire offering   *shall*ⁿ
    13a (13b Pʰ) Salt with all   *thou*
    14 15 Parched corn as firstfruits   *if* thou

3 The Sacrifice of Peace Offerings
    ¹⁻⁵ Victim from the herd   *if* = 5
    ⁶ Victim from the flock   *if*
    ⁷⁻¹¹ a lamb, ¹²⁻¹⁶ a goat   *if* = 5 *if* = 5
  + ¹⁷ No fat or blood to be eaten   Ye, ᵐ

4–5¹³ The Sin Offering
    4¹⁻²ᵃ And .. speak .. ch
    ²ᵇ Persons sinning unwittingly   soul *when*
    ³⁻¹² The anointed priest (bullock)   *If*
    ¹³⁻²¹ The congregation (bullock)   *if*
    ²²⁻²⁶ A ruler (he-goat)   *who*
    ²⁷⁻³¹ One of the people (she-goat)   *if*
  + ³²⁻³⁵ 'If he bring a ewe lamb' ..   *if*
5¹⁻⁶ Four cases and conclusion   = 5
    ¹ Suppressing evidence   soul *when*

13ga The conspectus of the Priestly legislation would have been incomplete without an outline of Ex 25–40, containing the core of Pᵍ. The limits of Pᵍ in its original shape are better seen here than in either of the other tables L12 (where the order of Ex 35 is taken) or Ex 35⁴ᴺ (where the parts assigned to Pˢ are not indicated)

b 1²ᵇ is perfectly general, and might include burnt and peace offerings Moreover it opens with 'and when a man ..,' which is followed by ³ 'If his oblation be a burnt offering,' and then by 3¹ 'And if his oblation be a sacrifice of peace offerings' It is likely then that 3 once followed 1 And as, according to Num 15¹⁻⁶, neither burnt offering nor peace offering may be offered without a meal offering, an editor may have followed up the burnt offering by its needful accompaniment. But the fact that nothing is said in 1–3 of this requirement may perhaps indicate that Num 15¹⁻⁶ represents a later stage of ritual

2⁴⁻¹⁶ is only 'supplementary' in the literary sense, and is probably as a whole older than 1–3, cp L7mabc. The older parts seem to be ⁴⁻⁷ on the three kinds, ¹³ on salt (with the doublet in ᵇ from Pʰ), ¹⁴ on firstfruits, and ¹¹· against leaven But they may have been separately written (cp 'ye' in ¹¹·), though it is curious that those in 2nd person sing 'thou' 'thy' make up a pentad The rest is mere repetition

3 The section on the peace offering seems somewhat more primitive than 1–2³, perhaps because it was the most frequent kind of offering. It easily falls into three pentads, if ⁶ be neglected.

LAWS AND INSTITUTIONS

^{L}**13**gb

P^t_g ^h_s Leviticus 5 $^{\circ7-16}$ 17-19 6 $^{\circ1-7}$ 8i-18r $^{\circ}$19i-23r 24-29 7 $^{1-7}$ $^{\circ}9$ 11-21 $^{\circ}22i$-27 $^{\circ}28i$-33 37 8
                                                                                                30   8 10 $'$34 35 38   1-10a $'$10b-11 12-29

P^t_g ^h_s 8   9i-10$_5$ $^{10}_8$ $^t_{t'}$ 11 $^{1i-8}_{9-23}$ $^{\circ}24$-31 $'$32-37 39   45b-47   12 $^{1i-7}$ $^{\circ}8$ 13 $^{1i-46a}$ $'^b$ 47-59
              $'$30 31-36 $'$6-7 12-15 $'$16-20 $_s$ 41-44a

P^t P^g P^s		
Lev **5**^{4} Rash swearing		or soul *when*
^{2} Unclean from a carcase		or soul *who*
^{3} Unclean from a man		or *when*
^{5} To confess and bring ewe lamb or kid		*when*
+$^{7-10}$ *Or two doves or pigeons*		*if*
+$^{11-13}$ *Or a portion of fine flour*		*if*

5^{14}–**6**^{7} The Guilt Offering
(^{14} *And* ..)
$^{15-16}$ For trespass in holy things .... soul *when*
+ $^{17-19}$ *For unknown sins* .... if soul *when*
(**6**^{1} *And* ..)
$^{2-7}$ For trespass against a neighbour ..... soul *when*

c. **6**^{8}–**7**^{38} A MANUAL FOR PRIESTS
(**6**$^{8-9a}$ *And* .. command A .. s)

6^{9b-13} The Burnt Offering
Ritual; the perpetual fire .... *This* .. law

6$^{14-18}$ The Meal Offering
Ritual; consumption by priests alone ..... *this* .. law
(^{19} *And* .)
+ $^{20-23}$ *The priest's meal offering* ...... *this* obl
($^{24-25a}$ *And* . speak . A .. s)

6^{25b-29} The Sin Offering
Ritual; consumption by priests alone ..... *This* .. law
^{30} Not to be eaten if blood enter Holy Place ..... *shall*^{n}

7$^{1-7}$ The Guilt Offering
Ritual; consumption by priests alone ..... *this* .. law
^{8} Priest to have skin of the burnt offering ..... *shall*
+ ^{9} *Priest to have cooked meal offerings* ..... *shall*
^{10} Meal offerings of flour to be shared ..... *shall*

7$^{11-35}$ The Sacrifice of Peace Offerings ..... *This* .. law
$^{12-15}$ Thank offering—with cakes, wafers, and flour, to be eaten on the day ..... *If*
$^{16-18}$ Vow or freewill offering—two days for eating *if*
^{19} || ^{21} Provisions against uncleanness
($^{22-23a}$ *And* . speak . ch)
+ $^{23b-27}$ *No fat or blood* .... = 5
^{23b} Fat (ox, sheep, goat) not to be eaten ..... *Ye*^{n}
^{24} Fat of animal found dead .... *shall*
^{25} Eater of fat of clean beast doomed ..... *he that*
^{26} Blood (fowl, beast) not to be eaten ..... *ye*^{n}
^{27} Eater of blood doomed .... soul *who*
($^{28-29a}$ *And* . speak .. ch)
+ $^{29b-35}$ *The priest's portion*
^{29b} Offerer to bring his oblation portion ..... *He that*
^{30} Fat and breast for wave offering ..... *shall*
^{31} Priest to burn fat and keep breast ..... *shall*
+ ^{32} *Right thigh a heave offering for the priest who offers the blood and fat*
^{34} Wave breast and heave thigh both due ..... ye ('I')
+ ^{35} *The anointing portion of priests* ..... *This*
^{37} $'^{38}$ Colophon Burnt, Meal, Sin, Guilt, (Consecration,) and Peace offerings (ordered in Mount Sinai) ..... *This* .. law

P^t P^g P^s	
d. Lev **8–10** THE CONSECRATION OF THE PRIESTHOOD	

P^g | P^s
(Ex **29**) || **8** Aaron and his sons consecrated
$^{1-3}$ || $^{1-5}$ Preparations .... *And* ..
$^{4-6}$ || $^{6-9}$ Ablutions, investiture of Aaron
^{7} || ^{10a} **12** Aaron anointed
— || + ^{10b} **11** *Dwelling, altar, laver, anointed*
^{8}. || ^{13} Investiture of Aaron's sons
$^{10-14}$ || $^{14-17}$ Bullock for sin offering
$^{15-18}$ || $^{18-21}$ Ram for burnt offering
$^{19, 22-26}$ || $^{22-29}$ Ram of consecration offered
^{21} || + ^{30} *Oil and blood on Aaron, his sons, and dress*
$^{31-34}$ || ^{31}. Feast on the ram of consecration
$^{35-37}$ || $^{33-36}$ Seven days of consecration

Lev **9** The octave of the consecration
$^{1-24}$ Inaugural sacrifices (^{L}**7**sbpm); fire from heaven

10 Death of Nadab and Abihu, with sequels
$^{1-5}$ Consumed by fire from heaven for sacrilege
^{6} Aaron and sons not to mourn them
^{8} Priests on duty not to drink wine ..... *And* .. *A*
^{10} Priestly duty as to clean and unclean ..... *ye*
^{11} Duty of instruction .... *ye*
$^{12-15}$ Priest's dues, meal and peace offerings
+ $^{16-20}$ Blame for not eating sin offering

e. **11–16** LAWS ON CEREMONIAL PURITY

11 Eating and Touching Animals
($^{1-2a}$ *And* .. *M* and *A* saying unto them, speak .. ch)
$^{2b-8}$ Clean and unclean land quadrupeds ..... ye &
+ $^{9-23}$ *Food that is abomination* .... ye & shall
+ $^{24-40}$ *Uncleanness by touch, cleansing* ... ye & shall
+ ^{41} *(continuation of* $^{9-23}$) .... ye ^{n}
+ $^{43-44a}$ *Conclusion from* ^{Ph} .... ye ^{n}
$^{44b-45}$ Another conclusion from ^{Ph}
^{46} Colophon .... *This* .. law

12 Purification after childbirth
($^{1-2a}$ *And* . speak .. ch) | ^{5a} Unclean fourteen days for
^{2b} Unclean seven days for son | daughter ..... *if*
^{When} | ^{5b} Separation sixty-six days
^{3} Circumcision on eighth day | ..... *shall*
..... *shall* | $^{6-7a}$ Offerings for cleansing *shall*
^{4} Separation thirty-three days | ^{7b} Colophon .. *This* .. law
..... *shall* & | + ^{8} *Case of poverty* ..... *if*

13. Leprosy
13 Detection and discrimination; rules
(^{1} *And* . *M* and *A*) | ^{38}. A harmless kind
$^{2-8}$ In the skin ..... adam *when* | man or woman *when*
$^{9-17}$ Later stages ..... *when* | $^{40-44}$ Leprosy in the head
$^{18-23}$ Distinguished from boils | man *when*
..... *when* | ^{45}. Behaviour of leper .. *whoso*
$^{24-28}$ And from burns .... *when* | + $^{47-59}$ *Leprosy in clothing, with*
$^{29-37}$ And from baldness | *separate colophon*
man or woman *when* | .. *This* .. law .. *when* ..

13gd 8–10 After the great interpolation of the Laws of Sacrifice *bc*, the thread is picked up from Ex 40 as if nothing intervened (see 8^{1N}), though 8^2 so quietly assumes the directions of Ex 29 as familiar that we have another reason for thinking that, when Lev 8 was written, the place of Ex 35–40 was occupied by a much shorter account, perhaps only occupying a few lines

11 Paton (*Holiness Code* p 42) arranges a decad out of this chapter combined with Deut 14 But the materials have undergone too much handling to follow him with confidence, though it is extremely probable that the original source in P^h was a decad. Its elements may be reconstructed thus —
1. General (cp Deut 14^3).   6 Clean birds (cp Deut 14^{11}).
2. Clean land quadrupeds $^{2b-3}$ 7 Unclean birds $^{13-19}$.
3. Unclean land quadrupeds $^{4b-7}$. 8 Insects forbidden ^{20}.
4. Clean water-dwellers ^{9}.   9 Exceptions $^{21-23}$.
5. Unclean water-dwellers ^{10}.   10. Wingless vermin ^{41}.

CONSPECTUS OF CODES

$P^{t'}_g{}^s$ Leviticus 14 $^{1i-8a}$ $'^b$ $^{9-20}$ $^c{}^{21-32}$ $'^{33-53}$ ^{54} ^{55a} $'^b$ ^{56} 15 $^{1i-33a}$ $'^b$ 16 $^{2-28b}$ $'^1$ ^{h} $^{29-31}$ $^{32-33}$ $'^{34a}$ ^{34b} $^{h'}$ 17 $^{1i-14r}$ 15. 18 $^{1i-30}$ ^{L}**13g**g

$P^{h'}_g{}^s$ 19 $^{1i-20}$ $^{23-37}$ 21. 20 $^{1i-3}$ $^{6-27}$ 4. 21 $^{1i-15}$ $^{16i-23r}$ 24 22 $^{1i-16}$ $^{17i-25}$ $^{26i-33}$ 23 $^{1i-2a}$ $^{4-10a}$ $^{2b-3}$ $'^{13}$ $^{10b-12}$ ^{14r} $^{15-17}$ $^{18-20r}$ 21 ^{22} $^{23-25}$ $^{26-32}$ $^{33-38}$

$P^{h'}_g{}^s$ 23 $^{39-43r}$ 44 24 $^{1-9}$ $^{10-15a}$ $^{15b-22r}$ 23 25 $^{2b-7}$ $^{1-2a}$ ^{8a} ^{9a} ^{10a} ^{c} ^{11b} ^{12b} ^{14} $^{17-22}$ 24 ^{8b} ^{9b} ^{10b} ^{11a} ^{12a} ^{13} ^{15}. 23 $^{26-31}$ $'^{32-34}$ $^{35-40a}$ $^{40b-42}$ 43 $^{44-46}$ 47 $^{48-52}$ 53 $^{54-55a}$ ^{55b}

$P^t_g{}^s$ 26 ^{1} $^{2-45}$ ^{46} 27 $^{1-34}$ Numbers 1 $^{1-16}$ $^{17-19a}$ $^{20-53}$ ^{19b} ^{54}

P^t P^g P^s

Lev 14 Cleansing from leprosy
(^{1} *And* ..)   +^{32} *Colophon to same* This .. ^{law}
$^{2-8a}$ $'^b$ Special rites   *This* ^{law} (^{33} *And .. M and A* ..)
+$^{9-20}$ Ordinary sacrifices   +$^{34-53}$ Leprous house   *When* ^{ye}
+$^{21-31}$ Case of poverty   *if*
14^{54-57N} Colophon to 13$^{1-46}$ (expanded) .. *This* .. ^{law}

15 Secretions
(^{1} *And .. M and A* .. ^{speak} .. ^{ch})
$^{2-18}$ Of men ^{2} any man *when* ^{13} *when* ^{16} man *when*
$^{19-30}$ Of women ^{19} ^{25} woman *when* ^{28} *if*
+^{31} Exhortation to priests (? older fragment) ^{ye}
$^{32-33a}$ $'^b$ Colophon   *This* .. ^{law}

16 The Day of Atonement
^{1} ^{3} ^{6} ^{11} ^{14} For Aaron and his house   *And* .. ^{after} ..
$^{2-28§}$ ^{34b} For people and sanctuary   *And* .. ^{speak} .. ^{A}
+$^{29-31}$ ^{34a} *Annual fast day*   *statute for ever*
+^{32} Repetition by each high priest

P^h P^g P^s

f. **17-27** HOLINESS CODE (SEE **f** ABOVE), WITH ADDITIONS

17-22 Main portion of Holiness Code

23 Sacred Calendar (much expanded)
$^{1-2a}$ Heading *And* .. ^{speak} .. ^{ch} .. $^{and\;say}$
$^{2b-3}$ The Sabbath
^{4} Introduction
$^{5-8}$ Passover and Mazzoth
($^{9-10a}$ *And* .. ^{speak} .. ^{ch} .. $^{and\;say}$)
$^{10b-14r}$ Wave sheaf festival   *When* ^{ye}
$^{15-20}$ Harvest Festival (Weeks) ^{ye}
^{21} Feast of Weeks (fragment)   .. ^{ye} ^{n}
^{22} Gleanings
($^{23-24a}$ *And* .. ^{speak} .. ^{ch} ..)
$^{24b-25}$ Feast of Trumpets   .. ^{ye} ^{n}
$^{26-32}$ Day of Atonement   *And* .. (^{29}. *soul who*)
($^{33-34a}$ *And* .. ^{speak} .. ^{ch})
$^{34b-36}$ Feast of Booths   .. ^{ye} ^{n}
^{37} Colophon   *These* ..
$^{39-42}$ Feast of Booths   *when* ^{ye}

24 Lamps; shewbread; blasphemy
$^{1-4}$ Oil and lamps   *And* .. ^{command} ^{ch}
$^{5-9}$ Regulations for the shewbread
$^{10-14}$ Stoning for blasphemy, story
(^{15a} *And thou* ^{speak} .. ^{ch})
$^{15b-22}$ Blasphemy, murder, assault (see **f**)
^{23} The blasphemer stoned

P^h P^g P^s

Lev 25 Sacred Years
($^{1-2a}$ *And* .. *Sinai* .. ^{speak} .. ^{ch} .. $^{and\;say}$)
$^{2b-7}$ The Sabbatical fallow year   *when* ^{ye}
$^{8-17§}$ **24** Fiftieth year, of liberty
  $^{8-17}$ **23** Fiftieth year, of jubile
$^{18-22}$ Sabbatical year, exhortation
$^{25-55§}$ Hebrew Poor Law
  $^{25-28}$ Redemption of land
  $^{29-31}$ House property   *man when*
  +$^{32-34}$ Levitical land and houses
  $^{39-55a}$ Hebrew slaves

26 Concluding discourse

27 On Vows and Consecrated Gifts
$^{1-2a}$ *And* .. ^{speak} .. ^{ch} .. $^{and\;say}$
$^{2b-13}$ Vows of persons and animals   = 10
$^{2b-3}$ A male from twenty to sixty years   *man when* ^{7} Over sixty years   *if*
      ^{8} Reduction for poverty   *if*
^{4} A female of same age   *if* ^{9} A clean beast   *if*
^{5} Between five and twenty-five years   *if* ^{10} Exchange forbidden   *if*
      ^{11}. An unclean beast   *if*
^{6} Between one month and five years   *if* ^{13} Redemption price   *if*
$^{14-25}$ Consecrated gifts   = 10
^{14} A house   *man when* ^{19} Redemption price   *if*
^{15} Its redemption price   *if* ^{20}. If sold, irredeemable   *if*
^{16} A field, valuation   *if* ^{22}. A purchased field   *if*
^{17} From the jubile   *if* ^{24} Restoration at jubile   *Shall*
^{18} After the jubile   *if* ^{25} The standard shekel   *shall*
$^{26-33}$ Firstlings, devoted things, tithes   5 + 5 = 10
^{26} Clean firstlings *only* . *shall* ^{n} ^{30} Tithe of produce   [*shall*]
^{27a} Redemption of unclean firstlings   *if* ^{31} Redemption price   *if*
      ^{32} Tithe of cattle   *shall*
^{27b} Option of sale   *if* ^{33a} Exchange forbidden   .. *if*
^{28} Devoted things *only* .. *shall* ^{n} ^{33b} No redemption   *shall* ^{n}
^{29} Devoted persons   *shall* ^{n}

P^t P^g P^s

NUMBERS

g. **Num 1-10^{11}** The Camp at Sinai

1. THE TWELVE LAY TRIBES

1 First Census at Sinai
^{1} Heading, giving place and date
^{2} Adult males to be numbered by Moses
$^{4-16}$ Tribal representatives to assist
  $^{17-19a}$ Moses and Aaron take the census
^{19b} Moses takes the census
  $^{20-46}$ Census returns for the twelve lay tribes
  +^{47} Omission of Levi
  +$^{48-53}$ Duties and position of the Levites   *And* ..
^{54} Compliance of the people

13g*f* 27 The analysis here offered supports the suggestion that an older original is the basis of this series of ordinances.

LAWS AND INSTITUTIONS

^{L}**13**$_{gg}$ $\mathrm{P}^t_g{}^h_s$ Numbers 2$_{1-34}$ 3$_{1-4}$ $^{5-22}_{23-26}$ $^{27}_{29-32}$ $^{33}_{35-38}$ $^{39}_{40-43}$ $^{44}_{46-51}$ 4$_{1-15}$ '$_{16-19}$ $_{21-49}$ 5$_{1-4}$ $^{\circ 5\iota-8}$ ^{9} $^{11\iota-31^N}$ 6$^{1\iota-21}_{22-27}$ 7$^{89}_{1-88}$

$\mathrm{P}^t_g{}^h_s$ 8$_{1-10}$ '$_{11}$ $_{12-15a}$ '$_{15b-26}$ 9$_{1-23}$ 10$_{1-8}$ $^{11}_{13-28}$ $_{34}$ 15$^{1\iota-16}_{32-36}$ $^{17\iota-31}$ $^{37\iota-41}$ 17$_{1-18_{32}}$

P^t P^g P^s | | P^t P^g P^s |
---|---|---|---

Num 2 Order of tribes in Camp and on March
^{1} *And . . M and A*
^{2} General directions
$^{3-9}$ East camp
^{3} Judah *shall*
^{4} Total 74,600 *were*
^{5} Issachar *shall*
$+^6$ Total 54,400 *were*
^{7} Zebulun *shall*
$+^8$ Total 57,400 *were*
$+^{9a}$ Grand total 186,400 *were*
^{9b} These to march first *shall*
$^{10-16}$ South camp
^{10} Reuben *shall*
$+^{11}$ Total 46,500 *were*
^{12} Simeon *shall*
$+^{13}$ Total 59,300 *were*
^{14} Gad *shall*
$+^{15}$ Total 45,650 *were*
$+^{16a}$ Grand total 151,450 *were*
^{16b} These to march second *shall*

^{17} Levites round tent in centre *shall*
$^{18-24}$ West camp
^{18} Ephraim *shall*
$+^{19}$ Total 40,500 *were*
^{20} Manasseh *shall*
$+^{21}$ Total 32,200 *were*
^{22} Benjamin *shall*
$+^{23}$ Total 35,400 *were*
$+^{24a}$ Grand total 108,100 *were*
^{24b} These to march third *shall*
$^{25-31}$ North camp
^{25} Dan *shall*
$+^{26}$ Total 62,700 *were*
^{27} Asher *shall*
$+^{28}$ Total 41,500 *were*
^{29} Naphtali *shall*
$+^{30}$ Total 53,400 *were*
$+^{31a}$ Grand total 157,600 *were*
^{31b} These to march last *shall*

3. THE LEVITES
3^{1-13} Their appointment and office
$^{1-4}$ Aaron's sons and their fate
$^{5-10}$ The Levites to do the service of the Dwelling *And ..*
$^{11-13}$ The Levites instead of the firstborn *And ..*
3^{14-39} Census of all males, (positions, princes, duties)
^{14}. All Levite males to be numbered *and* Sinai .. *thou*
$^{16-20}$ Numbered by families *were*
^{21}. Gershonites, total 7,500 *were*
$+^{23-26}$ Placed on west, duties *shall*
^{27} Kohathites, total 8,600 *were*
$+^{29-31}$ Placed on south, duties *shall*
$+'^{32}$ Eleazar to have supreme charge *shall*
^{33} Merarites, total 6,200 *were*
$+^{35}$. Placed on north, duties *shall*
$+^{38}$ M and A and sons on east *shall*
^{39} Grand total 22,000 *were*

3^{40-51} Levites for firstborn; census of latter
$^{40-43}$ Census of firstborn, 22,273 ; Levites instead *And ..*
^{44} Levites instead of firstborn *And .*
$^{46-51}$ Redemption of surplus firstborn

4 Census of adult males
^{1} *And ... M and A ..*
^{2}. Kohathites to be numbered (thirty to fifty years)
$+^{4-15}$ Their duties in full *shall*
$+^{16}$ Eleazar's special charge *shall*
$+^{17}$ And . M and A ..
$+^{18-20}$ Priests to guard Kohathites from risk of sacrilege *ye*
$(+^{21}$ And .. $)$
^{22}. Gershonites to be numbered *thou*
$+^{24-28}$ Duties under Ithamar *shall .. ye*
^{29}. Merarites to be numbered *thou*
$+^{31-33}$ Duties under Ithamar *shall . ye*
$^{28-49}$ Census taken, total 8,580 *were*

5–6^{21} Group of laws
$^{1-4}$ Lepers excluded from Camp *And .. command ch*
$(5^{-6a}$ *And .. speak .. ch*)
$^{6b-8}$ Guilt offering, special case man or woman *When*
^{9} Heave offerings given to priest *shall*
$^{11-.1}$ Marital jealousy (composite) *This law*
A^{12} any man *when* B^{29} Whoso $(\mathrm{T}$ *when*)

Num 6$^{1-21}$ The law of the Nazirite
$(^{1-2a}$ *And .. speak .. ch .. say*)
$^{2b-8}$ His separation defined man or woman *When*
$+^{9-12}$ Involuntary defilement *when*
$+^{13-20}$ Ritual at close of separation *This .. law*
$^{21a/b}$ Colophon (expanded) *This .. law*

6^{22-27} Priestly benediction *And ..*

7^{1-88} The Dedication of the Altar
^{1} Dwelling, altar, &c, anointed and dedicated
$^{2-9}$ Waggons and oxen given
$^{10-88}$ Silver and gold dishes, &c, and twenty-one victims from each tribe

7^{89} Divine voice from the Mercy-seat

8. Group of priestly laws
$^{1-4}$ The sacred lamps *And .. speak .. A . say*
$^{5-15a}$ '^{11} Moses to sanctify the Levites *And ..*
$+^{15b-22}$ Aaron to 'wave' them
$+^{23-26}$ Levites begin work at twenty-five instead of thirty

9^{1-5} The Second Passover
$^{6-8}$ Case of men unclean
$^{9-14}$ Postponement for a month *And . ch any man when*
$^{15-23}$ The Cloud and the Dwelling

10$^{1-10}$ Use of Trumpets
P^h $^{1-8}$ Signal for meeting or march *And ..*
^{9} For alarm in war *when ye*
^{10} On Festivals over sacrifices, 'I am Yahweh' *ye*

P^t
$h.$ **15** Group of laws
$(^{1-2a}$ *And . speak .. ch .. say*)
$^{2b-16}$ Law of drink offerings, &c
$^{2b-3}$ Any offering of herd or flock
 When *ye .. land .. shall*
^{4}. Meal, wine, and oil for lamb *thou*
^{6}. Meal, wine, and oil for ram *thou*
$^{8-10}$ Meal, wine, and oil for bullock *when thou*
^{11}. Summary for bullock, ram, lamb, kid *shall . ye*
$^{13-16}$ Home-born and stranger alike *ye &*
$(^{17-18a}$ And . speak .. ch .. say)
$^{18b-21}$ Dough offerings *ye*
$^{22-31}$ The sin offering *when*

P^h 15^{32-36} Sabbath-breaker stoned
$(15^{37-38a}$ *And .. speak .. ch .. say*)
$^{38b-41}$ Fringes on garments, 'I am Yahweh' (they) .. *you*

16 Incident of Korah and his company
$^{1-50\S}$ Laity against the priesthood
$^{8-40\S}$ Levites against the priesthood

17 Aaron's rod that budded

18 Priests and Levites: duties and dues
$^{1-7}$ Respective duties and mutual relations *And Yahweh said unto A*
$^{8-19}$ Revenues of priests *= 10*
^{8} All heave offerings for the priests
 and .. A (om saying) .. all
^{9} Meal, sin, and guilt offerings *This . all*
^{10} These priests only may eat *all*
^{11a} Heave and wave offerings *all*
^{11b} These all clean inhabitants may eat *all*
^{12} Firstfruits· corn, wine, oil *all*
^{13} First ripe fruits *all*
^{14} Devoted things *all*
$^{15-18}$ Firstlings or their value *all*
^{19} Bound by 'covenant of salt' *all*

CONSPECTUS OF CODES

^L13gi

^h_g P^t_s Numbers 19 $^{14-22}_{1-13}$ 25 $^{6-15}_{16\cdot\cdot}$ 26 $_{1-}$ 27 $_{14}^{15-23}$ 28 $_{1-}$ 31 $_{54}$ 33 $^{50t-53\ 55\cdot}_{54}$

P^t P^g P^s
$^{20-32}$ Revenues of the Levites
^{20} Aaron to have no share in the land
                          And Yahweh said unto A
$^{21-24}$ The tithe goes to the Levites
(^{25} And ..)
$^{26-32}$ That tithe tithed for the priests   When

19 Uncleanness by the dead
    ^{1} And . M and A ..
    $^{2-10}$ Red heifer: ashes for water of separation
                    This is the statute of the law ..
    ^{11} Use obligatory   He that &
    $^{13-22}$ Use described: case of death in a tent
               This ... law   man who

i. **25** $^{6-18}$ The Plague because of Midianite women
    $^{6-9}$ Man slain by Phinehas with a woman
    $^{10-15}$ Priesthood sealed to Phinehas   And ..
    $^{16-18}$ Midianites to be vexed   And ..

26 Census in Plains of Moab, and sequels
  $^{1-51}$ Lay tribes counted

^{1} Heading (peculiar)	$^{20-22}$ Judah	76,500	
And .. M and Eleazar	$^{23-25}$ Issachar	64,300	
$^{2-4}$ Introduction (in altered state)	^{26} Zebulun	60,500	
	$+^{28}$ Joseph's sons		
5^{1-7} Reuben 43,730	$^{29-34}$ (? ^{33}) Manasseh	52,700	
$+^{8-10}$ *Descent of Dathan and Abiram*	$^{35-37}$ Ephraim	32,500	
	$^{38-41}$ (? ^{40}) Benjamin	45,600	
$+^{11}$ *Survival of Korah's sons*	^{42} Dan	64,400	
$^{12-14}$ Simeon 22,200	$^{44-47}$ (? ^{46}) Asher	53,400	
$^{15-18}$ Gad 40,500	$^{48-50}$ Naphtali	45,400	
$+^{19}$ *Judah's sons who died*	^{51} Grand total	601,730	

  $^{52-56}$ Division of the land by lot among these   And ..
  $^{57-62}$ Census of Levites
    ^{57} The three Levitical Clans
    $+^{58a}$ *Subordinate families*
    $+^{58b-61}$ Families of M and A
    ^{62} Total   23,000

P^t P^g P^s
^{27} $^{1-11}$ Zelophehad's daughters: law of inheritance ^{8} man *when* ^{9} ^{10} ^{11} *if*
$^{12-14}$ Moses to die (|| Deut 32^{48} ..)
$^{15-23}$ Joshua to succeed Moses

28. Calendar of sacred seasons: offerings prescribed
$^{1-2a}$ And . command .. ch .. say
^{2b} Periodical oblations required
$^{3-8}$ Daily sacrifice (d), morning and evening $b^lm^1o\tfrac{1}{4}w\tfrac{1}{4}$
^{9}. Sabbath $2b^lm^2ow + d$
$^{11-15}$ New moon $2b^bm^3ow\tfrac{1}{2} + b^rm^2ow\tfrac{1}{3} + 7b^lm^1ow\tfrac{1}{4} + s^g + d$
^{16} The Passover
$^{17-25}$ Mazzoth   as new moon daily (om w)
$^{26-31}$ Pentecost   as new moon (om w)
29^{1-6} Trumpets $b^bm^3o + b^rm^2o + 7b^lm^1o + s^g +$ (new moon) $+ d$
$^{7-11}$ Day of atonement   as trumpets $+ y$
$^{12-16}$ Booths, first day $13b^bm^3o + 2b^rm^2o + 14b^lm^1o + d$
$^{17-34}$ Second to seventh days
    the same, but one bullock less per day (and add w)
$^{35-38}$ Eighth day $b^bmow + b^rmow + 7b^lmow + s^g + d$
^{39} Colophon

30 On vows of men and women $5 + 5 = 10$
(^{1} Heading peculiar, see ^{1N}) ^{9} Vow of a widow or divorced woman inviolable   *shall*
^{2} A man's vow inviolable   man *When* ^{10}. Wife's vow confirmed if her husband was silent   *if*
^{3}. Maiden's vow confirmed by father's silence   woman *when* ^{12}. Dissolved if he disapproved   *if*
^{5} Dissolved by his disapproval   *if*
                   ^{14} Continued silence implies approval   *if*
^{6} Confirmed by betrothed husband's silence   *if* ^{15} Responsible for subsequent breach   *if*
^{8} Dissolved by his disapproval   *if* $+^{16}$ *Colophon*   These ..

31 War with Midian: regulations   And ..

P^h **33** ^{50}–^{36} The Land: Conquest and Possession
(^{50} And ..... in the plains of Moab ..)
^{51} Expulsion of people, destruction of idols *When* ye
^{54} Division of the land by lot
^{53} Danger in not expelling them   *i*

13gi 28. It has been thought well to give the full particulars of the prescribed offerings at the point where they are treated most systematically. The abbreviations will be readily followed, many being used above under $^L7$.

b burnt offering.   m meal offering   s sin offering
b bullock $m^{1, 2, 3}$ = one or more tenths of an ephah   t turtledove
c bull calf   o oil offering   w = wine or drink offering.
d daily sacrifice. $o\tfrac{1}{4}$ = a quarter of a hin $w\tfrac{1}{4}$ = one quarter of a hin.
g guilt offering.   p peace offering   y yearly wine or drink offering
^{g} he-goat.   P pigeon.
$^{g'}$ female goat.   r ram.   z goat for Azazel
l he-lamb
l ewe lamb.

The chief particulars of a similar kind are collected for comparison.
Ex 29^{1-35} P^g (|| Lev 8 P^s) Consecration day
                  $s^b + b^r + p^r + m^{\text{bread, cakes, wafers}}$
^{36}. P^g Seven days following s^b
^{38}. P^s Daily Sacrifice, morning and evening $b^lm^1o\tfrac{1}{4}w\tfrac{1}{4}$
Lev 4 P^s s^b, s^b, s^g, $s^{g'}$ (or s^l)
5^{1-13} P^t s^l or $^{g'}$ (or s^t or $p + b^t$ or p) (or m^1)
5^{14-67} P^t (three times), cp 19^{21} g^r
^{9} P^g Eighth day of consecration, for Aaron
       $s^c + b^r$, for people, $s^g + b^c + b^l + p^{ox} + p^r + mo$

^{12} P^t Childbirth $b^l + s^t$ or p (or b^t or $p + s^t$ or p, cp $15^{14\ 29}$
23^{12} P^t Wave sheaf b^l ($m^2w\tfrac{1}{4}$)
$^{17-20l}$ P^h $2p^l + m^2$ loaves ($+ 7b^lmw + b^bmw + 2b^rmw$)
Num 6 P^t Vow broken s^t or $p + b^t$ or $p + g^l$
Vow ended $s^l + b^l + p^r + m^{\text{loaves, cakes, wafers}} (+ mw)$
^{15} P^t m and w prescribed in right proportions for victims as b or p
^{22} E Balak $7b^b + 7b^r$

It will be observed that the drink offering w is only mentioned outside Num 15 in passages assigned on independent grounds to P^s. On closely comparing the allusions in 15 and 28· it becomes doubtful if in either of these passages the allusions to w are original. If they are interpolated the confusion of persons in 15 (see ^{1N}) and the sporadic allusions to w in 28· would be accounted for. It is possible that 28 has been also supplemented by adding the numerous clauses providing that the special offerings shall be cumulative, not in place of the daily sacrifice or other appointed offering

30 The structure is closely parallel to other parts of P^t and the language in the body of the ordinance not decisively different, so that the chap is here placed under P^t, though its editor is clearly later than the editor of the rest of P^t, and hence in the text all is printed under P^s.

^{L}**13**gi $\mathrm{P^t_g \atop s}{}^h$ Numbers $34_{1-}36_{13}$

$\mathrm{P^h\ P^g\ P^s}$		$\mathrm{P^t\ P^g\ P^s}$	
34^{1-15} Boundaries of the land beyond Jordan		$10^{b-15)}$ Asylum for homicide	
And . . . . command . . ch . . say	*When ye*		*When ye*
$16-19$ Tribal representatives for division		16 Iron instrument used	*if*
And .		17 A stone thrown	*if*
		18 The weapon of wood	*if*
$\mathrm{P^t}$ 35^{1-8} Forty-eight Levitical cities		$+ {}^{19}$ *Avenger of blood to slay murderer*	
And . . . . Moab . .		$20.$ Hatred or enmity	*if*
$^{9-34}$ Six cities of refuge: regulations	$=10$	$22-25)$ Accidental cases	*if*
$^{9-10a}$ *And . . speak . . . ch . . say*		36^{1-12} Marriage of heiresses	
		^{13} Late colophon	*These . .*

$26-29)$ No safety outside asylum		*if*
30 Witnesses in murder case		*he that*
31 No ransom for murderer		*ye* n
32 No ransom for homicide leaving asylum		*ye* n
$33.$ Hortatory conclusion		

14. The Codes compared

a b &c in the body of this table refer to the sections of ^{L}13 above.

^{L}**14** **a Religious and social Institutions**

The comparison of the codes in respect of these cannot be conveniently summarized here. A general sketch, embracing the most important points, is given in *Introd* pp 49–56. See also special summaries under ^{L}7a 'sacrifice,' ^{L}9a 'calendar', cp ^{L}10abd 'site of sanctuary' 'tent of meeting' 'altar' ^{L}11aj 'priesthood' 'endowments,' ^{L}2ad 'strangers' 'slaves.'

b Relation to contemporary religion

J D E	$\mathrm{P^{ht}}$ $\mathrm{P^g}$ $\mathrm{P^s}$
J The ten Words of the Covenant **a** enshrine the leading principles of the cultus of the day, as derived from Moses, and closely connected with the common life of the people, the one anxiety being to keep the worship pure. **E** The Covenant Book **b** and the Judgements **c** similarly accept and endorse the best features of the religious and moral life already present, but warn against corruption and syncretism in worship. **D** The demand for unity of worship and destruction not only of idolatrous emblems but of all local sanctuaries constitutes this code **e** a programme of reform, not to say religious revolution.	$\mathrm{P^h}$ The Holiness code f, whose main source seems to take the standpoint of **JE**, yet on the whole as a compilation adopts the position of **D**, and indeed assumes it as accepted. It seeks to guard the heritage of the past, not to modify the positive institutions of the present. $\mathrm{P^t}$ By the codifying of the sacrificial praxis and ceremonial usage a silent revolution was inaugurated by $\mathrm{P^t}$, which, when completed, substituted the letter of the law as interpreted by the scribes for the living torah of the priests. $\mathrm{P^g}$ The enlargement and definite dating of the calendar, the sharp distinction between priests and Levites, and the regulations for their support, render $\mathrm{P^g}$ unmistakably the programme of a reform party. $\mathrm{P^s}$ In the supplements we can trace the culminating influence of the successful school of priestly editors whose first formulated code was $\mathrm{P^g}$, but whose work was continued for generations, marked by enrichment of ritual, elaboration of detail, increased redundancy of style, and a desire to supplement and complete the existing laws.

c Leading motives and characteristic features cp ^{L}15c

(J) **E** The Israelites bound by a peculiar tie to one another and to Yahweh, a jealous and righteous God, his sanctuaries easily accessible for worship, appeal, or asylum; a high ethical spirit pervading the moral code. **D** Most of the religious institutions and many social laws modified by the centralizing of worship, religion, based on love between Yahweh and Israel, shedding a warm and kindly glow upon moral duties.

$\mathrm{P^h}$ Watchword a holy people, worshipping a holy God, in a holy land. $\mathrm{P^t}$ Personal religion elaborated on the sides of sacrifice and ceremonial purity, priests for the benefit of the people. $\mathrm{P^g}$ The organization of public worship, in which priestly functions bulk largely, the people mainly coming in as providing the means for the celebration of the prescribed rites and the maintenance of the ministering priesthood. $\mathrm{P^s}$ As $\mathrm{P^g}$, only more so, the claims of the higher clergy, and the expiatory side of worship becoming more prominent.

d Structure of codes; relation to context

J The short code **a**, engraved by (Moses) on the 'tables of stones,' relates to worship, and is now introduced by a hortatory passage. Its separate character is explicitly recognized in the context. **E** The Covenant Book **b**, as first embodied by **E** in his narrative, opens with a law on the place of sacrifice, consists of laws about worship, and is closed by a discourse. It has been dislocated by the insertion of the Judgements, and the Decalogue **d** is introduced as the beginning and basis of Divine law. The 'words of Yahweh' are explicitly recognized as forming the 'Book of the Covenant'

$\mathrm{P^h}$ The Holiness Code opens with a law of sacrifice, contains laws about offerings, feasts, and the priesthood, and closes with a discourse. It now includes also a series of laws, roughly parallel to the Decalogue and the Judgements in Lev 18–20. They may or may not have been originally incorporated by the compiler, but their dislocated condition would be better explained, if $\mathrm{P^h}$, like **E** and **D**, be supposed to have been supplemented by the original compiler, or by one of the same school. No allusion to it as a body of laws occurs in the context, but a suitable colophon ends the code.

35^{9-34} The style and structure of the ordinances in this section bear traces of the schools of $\mathrm{P^h}$ and $\mathrm{P^t}$. But they have been more drastically re-written by their editor than the bulk of $\mathrm{P^h}$ or $\mathrm{P^t}$.

THE CODES COMPARED

	J D E	P^{ht} P^g P^s
		^{pt} The Priestly teachings do not constitute a general code, but include several collections, apparently independent in origin. They relate exclusively to sacrifice and ceremonial purity, contain no hortatory sections, and are never referred to as a whole in the context. They are only called a code in a loose sense for convenience
	in the narrative of the making of the covenant Ex 24^3, a reference to 'the Judgements' being interpolated ^{3}.	
	^{D} The Deuteronomic Code, as it may be supposed to have been found by Hilkiah, opens with a law about the place of sacrifice, contains laws about offerings, feasts, and the chief theocratic institutions, and closes with a discourse, see Synopsis, below. It has been enlarged by the incorporation of a series of miscellaneous laws, corresponding to E's Judgements. And the Decalogue has been introduced as the law written by God on the tables, and as the basis of the covenant. The Code is abundantly referred to in the added context of narrative and discourse.	^{pg} The Priestly groundwork of Law and History presents both inextricably mingled together, ordinances being introduced in connexion with the events that occasioned them
		^{ps} The Priestly supplements are of course only in the most extended sense a code at all. The code is really P^g as enlarged by P^s, and the additions, except where mere expansions, obstruct and obscure the original lines of the structure.
e Structure of constituent groups (see ^{L}15f)	^{J} The covenant words a are directly stated to have formed a decad, though it is doubtful if the members of it can be recovered	^{Ph} Except where, as in Lev 23 25, P^h is much interpolated and expanded, the presence of pentads or decads, some of them very perfect, can be readily detected. Indeed it is reasonable to suppose that all the laws were once thus grouped, and a good deal can be done to suggest the original structure where it is now broken
	^{E} The three codes in E, b c d, all witness to the presence of groups of five or ten laws, or clauses of laws, on kindred subjects. It may be conjectured that originally they were wholly made up of such pentads and decads	
	^{D} Here also e are found occasional evidences of groups of five, but as a rule the literary structure is of a looser and more irregular type.	^{pt} Occasionally the pentad structure shows through, but as a rule considerations of subject determine the structure
		^{pg} The groups in P^g follow the appropriate incidents, and all are cast in the same mould, diffuse and repetitious
		^{ps} A new kind of group is formed by a story, of the nature of a midrash, and a law founded on it (e g Lev 24$^{10-16}$ 23 Num 15$^{32-36}$)
f Structure of clauses (see ^{L}15a-e)	^{J} All 'Words' in a.	^{Ph} 'Words,' 'Commandments,' 'Statutes'^{b} and 'Judgements'^{bc}
	^{E} b d, all 'Words', c, mostly 'Judgements'^{ac}, but supplemented by a few 'Statutes'^{a} and 'Commandments'	^{pt} Mostly 'Judgements'^{bc} and 'Laws', also 'Words,' 'Commandments' and 'Statutes'^{b}.
	^{D} 'Words,' 'Judgements'^{ac} and 'Statutes'^{a} supplemented by 'Commandments.'	^{pg} 'Words' and 'Commandments,' but of a totally different type from the earlier.
		^{ps} Heterogeneous in structure, but mostly as P^g.
g Original sources, oral or written	^{JE} The facts described under the last two heads make it highly probable that the originals in J and E were pentads of concise uniform ordinances on related subjects, strung together in this fashion for easy recollection, and preserved by oral repetition, or possibly in some cases by being engraved on wood, stone, or metal	^{Ph} Nowhere do the original, presumably oral, sources obtrude themselves more plainly than in Lev 19. And the structure both of groups and clauses throughout again favours an oral stage in the formation of the whole code
	^{D} As it is clear that D knew and used JE, so he must have had laws in written form before him, but he may well have also utilized decisions and ordinances preserved only by hearsay	^{pt} While resting, no doubt, in part on oral priestly directions, probably many of these teachings are notes of things seen as done, rather than of words heard as said; they are rubrics, defining older usages for the sake of security, and then modifying them for the sake of present use.
		^{pgs} For these, the latest strata, we have no reason to postulate any sources other than the documents traced elsewhere, though existing no doubt in a fuller state
h The editorial process	^{JE} Not only have the first compilers in introducing the codes often added to or altered them, but the laws have received far more attention from later editors than the narratives, J^s E^s R^{je} and R^d being detected again and again. Still, though two of the 'words' of the Decalogue even have lost their original form, for the most part the editors have only added little expansions or explanations or hortatory passages and have left the ordinances unmutilated	^{Ph} It is the compiler and later editors who have expanded the endorsement, 'I am Yahweh,' added the hortatory passages and discourse, and elaborated the chapters on worship 17 21-23 (cp also 25). Many of the peculiar phrases and much of the characteristic tone are due to the compiler
	^{D} The method followed by the Deuteronomic school was to rewrite nearly every ordinance they touched, so that only here and there can the original form of words be made out with confidence. The insertions of D^s in the code may however be plausibly identified with the plural passages ('ye'), though it has not been found possible to draw any similar inference from the conflicting phenomena of the discourses and narratives in D.	^{pt} Here the editor's work has been to piece together the existing collections of earlier codifiers and to enrich them with such duplicates and supplements as he could obtain. The later harmonist who united P^t to P^g introduced in a sparing fashion allusions to the 'Tent of Meeting,' 'Aaron and his sons' &c
		^{pg} Here editor and author are one, and the process is one of re-writing the history and laws of the past with an eye on the present and its needs. Probably the attempt had been made before, but few traces are left of it (cp Ex 25^{1N}).
		^{ps} The groundwork was not long left alone, and was not only embroidered and filled out by overlayings and insertions, but in many places was replaced by more exuberantly diffuse passages, cp Ex 35-40 Lev 8 &c.

	J D E	P^{ht} P^g P^s
^{L}14 i Persons addressed (cp ^{L}15d)	^{JE} The laws are indefinitely addressed to the Israelite whoever he might be, but were probably framed first, if not also written down later, for the use of the priests, elders, and judges who were to impart the knowledge of them to the people, and to administer them as occasion required ^{D} Deuteronomy is addressed to the nation, and is intended to catch the national ear, it is a people's book, the first 'Bible.'	^{Ph} What was said of JE would apply to the source of P^h, but the complete code was no doubt meant for the nation, though Lev 21 refers only to the priest-hood ^{Pt} Commonly impersonal, but sometimes addressed to the worshipper, written for the priests, either merely for their own guidance, or for them to impart to the laity, rarely as Lev 15^{31} addressed to the priests ^{Pg} Mainly addressed to Moses, for him to pass on to Aaron in the case of the numerous ordinances taken up with the affairs of the priesthood, or to the children of Israel, who are regarded almost exclusively as a worshipping congregation ^{Ps} More variety of address, but the principle as in P^g.
j The date implied	^{JE} If the codes had been preserved without any setting, they would have been seen at once to fit the time of the monarchy. As it is, they are ascribed to Moses at Sinai ^{D} The situation implied throughout is the eve of the conquest, though in the code we often forget the implied presupposition amid the minute provisions for life in the land *ex hypothesi* unknown.	^{Ph} The compiler attributes the code to the Sinaitic sojourn, and expressly anticipates the future, but the ordinances themselves hardly ever, even in their present form, suggest anything but legislation for the existing situation. ^{Pt} No date implied ^{Pgs} The Mosaic date is not only stated, but continually suggested by the systematic use of typical forms, Tent or Dwelling for Temple, Aaron for high priest, the camp for the city or land, and so forth
k Origin and authorship	^{J} Derived from the *torah* of the priests at the sanctuaries ^{E} b, as J, d, see Ex 20^{1N}, c, derived from the decisions of the old and wise among the judges and elders sitting for judgement in the gate, or from the king giving counsel to his nobles ^{D} Derived from E and sources similar to those used by E and including many fresh ordinances, but moulded anew by a prophetic school, including probably members of priestly families (cp Jeremiah), under the influence of the eighth-century prophets.	^{Ph} Derived from a genuinely priestly section of the priesthood (cp Ezekiel), working on old models (perhaps once included in J), and representing the loftiest levels of priestly teaching ^{Pt} Derived from a school of priestly ritualists, and embodying both the rules laid down by the older priests for the younger members of the order to follow in their ordinary ministrations, and the directions given as to ceremonial by priests to the individual lay worshippers. ^{Pg} Designed perhaps on the basis of an earlier draft, by a statesman priest or priestly scribe, on the basis of previous records read in the light of present convictions ^{Ps} Derived from successive generations of imitators of P^g.
l Approximate dates of origin or compilation	^{JE} The close resemblances postulate a substantial body of accepted custom, developed during the settled days of the undivided monarchy, and seem to many to suggest a considerable Mosaic nucleus The differences, in the documents J and E generally, require a date after the Disruption for the origin of the legislation in written form. The compilation of the codes can hardly be earlier than the eighth century, in view of their polemic against idolatry. The editorial additions stretch into the seventh century (cp pp 107 109 119..). ^{D} The code, early in the reign of Josiah, the ritual and other supplements, indefinitely later (cp p 96..).	^{Ph} The original groups, of varied ages, some very early; the compilation of the code in the last years of the Judean monarchy, the completion of the final discourse, and its re-editing (cp the handling of Jeremiah's prophecies), in the early years of the exile, the ritualistic revision, later still ^{Pt} The occasional traces of pentads, the resemblances with P^h, and the apparently traditional character of much of the ceremonial, suggest a pre-exilic date for the first drafts, but the number of supplements, which seem to have been suggested by the actual provisions failing to work satisfactorily in practice, perhaps indicates that the process went on till P^h and P^t were incorporated in the new law-book adopted and introduced by Ezra, which set the seal of authority on a new style of ritual legislation, and first gave wide publicity to P^h and P^t ^{Pg} Some time in the fifth century, not long before 458 B C, and possibly later still (cp pp 136..). ^{Ps} From the fifth to the third century B C (pp 154.. 179).

15. Statistics of usage

^{L}15 a—e. **Types of Hebrew Law.**—Dr Briggs *Higher Crit* ^{2} 242-257 (cp 'Arts' in *New Heb Lex*) classifies in a useful way the principal types of ordinance. His contention is further, that the various names used for the several laws were not always practically synonymous with one another (cp Ps 119), but had also earlier specific meanings, each connoting a distinct variety. The case for this view might be considerably strengthened, but it must always be largely matter for conjecture. The connotation of the 'words' and 'judgements' is best made out. But the series is used, as Dr Briggs gives it, for convenience sake The abbreviated forms mark the usage under ^{L}13 above. When the clause begins with 'and' or any other connecting particle, the initial capital is not used in 13, e g *thou*, not *Thou*.

STATISTICS OF USAGE

Totals of Legal Clauses

	J	E	D	P^h	P^t	P^s
	17	92	179	170	139	52

a. Words

		J	E	D	P^h	P^t	P^s
a	*Thou* = 'Thou shalt ...'		8	11	35	9	3
b	*Thou*^n = 'Thou shalt not ...'		5	19	22	36	
c	^n*Thou* = '... not thou' (imper)			3		2	
	Total	13	33	57	47	3	

b. Commandments

		J	E	D	P^h	P^t	P^s
a	*Ye* = 'Ye shall ..'				9	11	14
b	*Ye*^n = 'Ye shall not ...'			5	6	24	13	2
c	^n*Ye* = '... ye not' (imper)					2		
	Total		5	15	37	27	2

c. Statutes

a Earlier forms—חקים

		J	E	D	P^h	P^t	P^s
a	*He that* = 'He that ...' (participle)			6	10	4	7	
b	*Shall* = '... shall ...' (3rd pers)	1		28	13	17	5
c	*Shall*^n = '... shall not ...' (3rd pers)	2	1	14	16	3	5
	Total	3	7	52	33	27	10

b Later forms—חקות

		J	E	D	P^h	P^t	P^s
d	^man *Who* = איש אשר				1	16	3
e	^any man *Who* = איש איש אשר					7	
f	^woman *Who* = אשה אשר					1	1
g	^soul *Who* = נפש אשר					3	3	1
h	*Whoso* = אשר				1	2	1	3
	Total			1	3	28	10	1

d Judgements

a Main clauses—earlier forms

		J	E	D	P^h	P^t	P^s
a	*When*^m = 'When a man .'		4	6			
b	*When*^men = 'When men ...'		2				
c	*When*^thou = 'When thou ..'		1	11		2	
d	*When*, thou = 'when ..., thou (shalt)'			11			
e	*When*^ye = 'when ye .'				8	1	2
f	*When* = 'when (an ox)...'		10	14		7	11
g	*Whether* = או		2				
	Total		19	42	15	14	2

b Main clauses—Later forms

		J	E	D	P^h	P^t	P^s
h	^man *When* = איש כי				6	2	6
i	^any man *When* = איש איש כי				1	2	1
j	^man (adam) *When* = אדם כי				8	1	
k	^soul *When* = נפש כי					9	
l	^man or woman *When* = איש או אשה כי					4	
m	^woman *When* = אשה כי					1	1
n	... *When* = כי ...				1	1	
	Total				1	10	20	8

c Subordinate clauses

		J	E	D	P^h	P^t	P^s
o	*If* ^thou = (אם) 'If thou ...'	1	3	2		1	
p	*If* = (אם) 'If ...'		24	7	8	31	36
	Total	1	27	9	9	32	36

e. Laws

Torah applied to single ordinances

		J	E	D	P^h	P^t	P^s
a	*This ... law* = 'This is the law of .. ' (introd)					10	
b	*... this law* = 'This is the law of ' (concl)					6	
c	*This . statute* = 'This is the statute...'					1	1
	Total					17	1

f Pentads (see footnote)

Groups of five ordinances or clauses

		J	E	D	P^h	P^t	P^s
a	Uniform and complete (P^g 2)	1	10	5	12	1	5
b	Complete but not uniform	1	4	7	12	5	5
c	Uniform but incomplete		4	4	1		
d	Otherwise doubtful		2	9	9		
	Total	2	20	25	34	6	10

g. Introductory Clauses in P

		P^h	P^t	P^g	P^s
a	*And ...* = 'And Yahweh spake unto Moses, saying'	2	4	12	18
b	*And ... speak ...* A (. .^s) = add 'Speak unto Aaron (and to his sons), saying'	4	1	2	1
c	*And ... speak...* ch = add 'Speak unto the children of Israel, saying'	8	11	4	4
d	*And ... command* = add 'Command ..'		1	1	4
e	*And .. (M and)* A = '*And* spake unto (Moses and) Aaron'		1	4	5
f	*And .. said* = 'And Yahweh said unto (Moses)'	..		4	1
	Total	14	18	27	33
	Number occurring at a junction with another source	4	12	9	7

---

a The 'word' is the earliest type, and after P^h this form was practically dropped, for the 2nd pers sing ordinances in P^g and P^s are addressed, not generally, but to Aaron or some other individual, and so have no claim to be included Some of the 'words' in P^h are probably imitative and not ancient

b The 'commandments' are distinctly later, perhaps after D^g, for the plural clauses in E and D generally are for other reasons taken as interpolated. Very many of those in P^h look as if they were simply 'words' with the plural substituted

c^a Statutes of the first type ^a are found in all the sources, but much most numerously in D P^h P^t, representing the middle period of legislation, after JE and before P^g The few in JE are most naturally regarded as inserted or altered.

c^b The other types are practically confined to P^t and the later sections of P^h outside Lev 18

d The extensive employment of the first type ^a of 'Judgements' in E and D confirms the correctness of the note of time, 'earlier.' The preference shown by P^h for the 2nd pers pl is seen here again under e, and may point to a radical difference in the ultimate source. Did P^h draw mainly from the decisions, directly expressed, of the priests at the sanctuaries, and E and D from the more impersonal dicta of the secular judges, sitting in the gate? The entire absence of the second series of forms ^b from JED renders it highly probable that they are indeed 'later.' The subordinate clauses ^c of course fit either type of main clause

e This usage is of course one of the distinguishing marks of P^t, though the earliest sections of all (cp ^L13gbc) do not use this formula. The progression, from the living *torah* (= 'instruction'), in process of utterance by priest, prophet, and judge, to the written *torah* (= 'code') of D, is not more marked than from the wider application to a code to its restriction to a single ordinance, not the 'law of Yahweh' or the 'law of Moses,' but the 'law of leprosy.'

f In this little table decads have been reckoned as two pentads The elements of a group are considered 'uniform' when all are taken from one or other of the classes abcd above. Some groups are counted 'complete' which have one or two intruded clauses beyond five. E and P^h have preserved the pentad form best, almost all the ordinances preserved by either finding a place in one or other pentad. A large proportion in each case seem to be preserved approximately in their original form. In D it is far more precarious to attempt the reconstruction of pentads, and a mass of ordinances gives now no indication of being based on pentads The groups separated in P^t are almost as indefinite as in D, but the ten identified in P^s occur in three chapters only (Lev 27 Num 30 35), and are so sharply marked as to confirm the suggestion that in each case they rest upon an earlier basis, which was more probably P^h than P^t.

g The particulars collected as to the use of introductory clauses do not give much help in distinguishing between P^g and P^s, or between the editors of P^h and P^t. But certain broad results appear The preference of P^g and P^s for the direct forms of address *aef* arises from the fact that Moses and Aaron are in the centre of the foreground in the view of these writers, while the circumlocutions in the types *bc* preferred by P^h and P^t were only rendered necessary when the editor had to fit into the Mosaic scheme ordinances which originally had little or no literary relation to Moses and the wilderness. The large number of cases also, especially in P^h and P^t, in which the clause is prefixed where a junction has been effected with a section of another document or other foreign element suggests that where these clauses come in the body of these codes there may have been a dislocation This agrees very well with the view taken in this work of the structure of these two codes, both of which show independent signs of having been disorganized and reconstructed in the process of incorporation into the main body of P.

16. Contents and Index

^{L}16

a. Contents of Tables 1-15

1-11 Tables uniformly arranged under subject headings, with comparative statistics of occurrence of topics.

See footnote for explanation of figures

		Topics		J	E	D	P^h	P^t	P^g	P^s	Totals
1	1	The Family	a–o (15)	10	11	25	19	1	2	2	70
	2	Persons and Animals	a–k (11)	3	15	30	30	—	4	3	85
	3	Property	a–l (12)	1	10	14	8	4	—	2	39
	4	Judgement and Rule	a–w (24)	10	16	33	11	1	5	15	91
	5	Idolatry and Superstition	a–k (11)	13	22	33	22	1	—	2	93
11	6	Clean and Unclean	a–n (15)	7	2	14	12	24	7	4	70
	7	Sacrifices	(a–z) (21)	12	19	10	9	37	18	27	132
	8	Sacred Dues	a–1 (8)	7	5	11	2	3	8	9	45
	9	Sacred Seasons	a–k (11)	7	8	9	15	—	11	21	71
	10	Sacred Places	a–e (5)	6	14	13	5	2	7	11	58
	11	Sacred Persons	a–q (18)	16	15	41	16	12	35	52	187
	(Topics 151)	Gross totals of references		92	137	233	149	85	97	148	941
		Amount of material in inches of printed matter		12	36	140	70	130	130	310	828
		Average length of quotation		$\frac{1}{8}$	$\frac{1}{4}$	$\frac{3}{5}$	$\frac{1}{2}$	$1\frac{1}{2}$	$1\frac{1}{3}$	2	$\frac{7}{8}$

a Explanations

(1) *Definition of documents for the purpose of this table* The references counted, as explained in the introductory note, cover both allusions in narrative passages and legislative ordinances proper, and extend over the whole of the documents as separated in vol 11

(2) *Mode of reckoning* The gross totals of passages quoted are taken throughout, without deduction for the fact, affecting all documents, that the same ordinance may bear on several topics and so be referred to under several heads The length of the ordinances in P^g and P^s secures to them a preponderance of gain on this score, which is balanced by the larger number of allusions from the narratives of JE and the enveloping discourses of D, compared with those from the more colourless, purely historical parts of P^g

(3) *Stricter definition of codes for the estimates of length* All the legislative material in Ex—Deut has for this purpose been included, with the secondary expansions or additions in JED, and the concluding discourses in E D P^h (i e Ex 23$^{20-33}$ Deut 28 Lev 26) All mere narrative is omitted, but this rule has in the case of P^g and P^s only been held to exclude narratives combined with JE (as the incidents of the spies and of Korah Num 12 16), and in addition Num 32 , all other P narratives in Ex—Num being considered as constituent parts of the legislative corpus, and as not admitting of severance into so much law and so much history (The measurement into inches follows the text in vol 11, allowance being made for passages in smaller type)

Remarks

(1) *Total length of codes* The small amount of material in J and E, the virtual equality of D P^t and P^g as to size, and the disproportionate mass of P^s are made clear

(2) *Average length of ordinances* (The estimate is of course only approximate, because one ordinance may mean several references, but the comparison following is only weakened by the disregard of this consideration, cp Explanation (2) above) The average length for all the documents taken together is $\frac{7}{8}$ in. Now ordinarily, in striking an average, the separate totals cluster closely about the central point, but here the difference is startling between the first four and the last three The highest of the first four code averages is more than $\frac{1}{4}$ in lower than the final average, and the lowest of the last three is nearly $\frac{1}{2}$ in above it To put it another way, the steps of increase are, from J to E $\frac{1}{8}$ in, E to P^h $\frac{1}{4}$ in, P^h to D $\frac{1}{10}$ in, then a gap of more than $\frac{3}{4}$ in, followed by smaller increases, P^g to P^t $\frac{1}{6}$ in, P^t to P^s $\frac{1}{2}$ in Or, once again, the average length in the four earlier codes is $\frac{1}{3}$ in and of the three later ones $1\frac{1}{4}$ in It is obvious how strongly this conclusion reinforces the suggestion ^{L}14g that the former rest mainly on oral sources, concise by necessity, and that the latter are based on written memoranda, where they are not literary re-constructions or compositions. The higher average length in D compared with P^h also confirms the view, suggested by the study of the structure of these codes, that D has been much more re-written than P^h, where the first compiler has been content mainly to copy.

(3) *Proportion of topics.* The Tables may be divided into two classes, (i) the first five relating to social morality and the avoidance of heathenism, (ii) the last six being wholly concerned with the positive institutions of the religion of Yahweh Now under ^{L}1-5 the four earlier documents J E D P^h have together 326 references, but the other three P^t P^g P^s only 42 (or 29 if we deduct those under ^{L}4 on the numberings which have no parallel elsewhere), giving a proportion of 8 to 1 (or 11 to 1 with the deduction) Yet the former have considerably less than half the bulk of matter to draw from, 258 *in* compared with 570 *in* On the other hand, in the second class the four earlier are practically equal in number of allusions to the three later So that, if J E D P^h on the whole have all but double the number of allusions obtained from P^t P^g P^s (611 to 330) in less than half the space, this is entirely accounted for by the singular silence of the later codes on the matters of social morality and avoidance of heathenism

(4) *General and special treatment of institutions* The greater equality in number between the two contrasted groups J E D P^h and the rest in ^{L}6-11 is of course coincident with an extraordinary difference in treatment, general injunction or allusion being usual in the former, elaborate prescription of minute details in the latter.

12-15 Miscellaneous Tables

12 The Dwelling, commonly called the Tabernacle, in P

13 Conspectus of Codes

    i Codified before the Exile
- a *The Ten Words of the Covenant*—J (Ex 34^{14-26}).
- b *The Words of Yahweh*, or *the Book of the Covenant*—E (Ex 20^{23-26} 23^{10-19}).
- c *The Judgements*—E (Ex 21^{1}-22^{28} 23^{1-9}).
- d *The Ten Words* of God, commonly called the Decalogue—ED (Ex 20^{3-17}, Deut 5^{7-21}).
- e *The Book of the Law* or the Deuteronomic Code—D (Deut 12-26).

    ii Edited after the fall of Jerusalem, perhaps codified before
- f *The Judgements and Statutes* of Yahweh, or the Holiness Legislation—P^h (Lev 17-26).

    iii Codified edited and written in or after the Exile
- g The Priestly legislation proper (Ex 25 to Num 36^b), comprising *The Law of* worship and ceremonial purity—P^t, *The Commandments* of Yahweh in Sinai and Moab—P^g, and a mass of supplements—P^s.

14 The Codes compared
- a Religious and social institutions.
- b Relation to contemporary religion
- c Leading motives and characteristic features.
- d Structure of Codes; relation to context
- e Structure of constituent groups.
- f Structure of clauses.
- g Original sources, oral or written
- h The editorial process
- i Persons addressed.
- j The date implied.
- k Origin and authorship.
- l Approximate dates of origin or compilation.

15 Statistics of usage
- a-e Types of legal clauses
- f Pentads, clear and doubtful cases.
- g Types of introductory clauses

b. *Alphabetical Index to Tables of Laws and Institutions*

Adultery 1 i
Altar of sacrifice 10 d, brazen 12 e a, golden 12 d d
Animals, kindness 2 f, lost or hurt 3 c d, eaten or touched 6 a b, firstlings 8 b
Ark 10 c
Asherah 5 g
Assault 2 i, indecent 1 n
Atonement, Day of 7 y, 9 h

Battlements or houses 2 e
Benevolence 2 b
Birds 2 g
Blasphemy 5 c
Blind and deaf 2 k
Blood, eating 5 e
Booths, Feast of 9 i
Burnt offering 7 b

Calendar, with special tabular comparison 9 a
Camp order 4 r
Canaanite rites 5 d
Census 4 o p q t
Characteristics of codes 14 c
Charity 2 b
Childbirth 6 f
Children, teaching 1 c
Circumcision 6 m
Cities of refuge 4 l
Clean and unclean 6
Clergy 11
Codes, conspectus 13, comparison 14, statistics 15
'Commandments' 15 b
Court of appeal 4 b
Coveting 3 j
Criminal responsible 4 i

Daily sacrifice 7 a
Date of codes, implied 14 j, actual l
Destruction of idols 5 e
Divination 5 l
Divorce 1 h
Dress of sexes 10
Drink offering 7 w
Dwelling 10 b, 12 b

Eating 6 a c
Editorial process 14 h

Empty-handedness forbidden 7 e

Family 1
Fat, eating 6 e
Feasts 9
Firstborn 8 a, as heir 1 d, 3 g
Firstfruits 8 c
Firstlings 8 b
Fleece of wool 7 f
Flogging 4 j
Food animals 6 a
Foreign menials 11 q
Foreign nations 4 n
Freewill offerings 8 g
Fruit trees 6 n

Gleanings 3 l
Gods, other 5 a
Guilt offering 7 g

Harvest, Feast of 9 f
High priest 11 b, dress 11 c, 12 g, unction 11 d, atonement e
Hired servants 2 c, 4 g

Idolatry 5, image-worship a, destruction of images e, death for idolatry f, seduction to h
Incense 7 i
Ingathering, Feast of 9 i
Institutions, religious and social 14 a
Issues 6 g

Jealousy offering 7 l
Jubile year 9 k
Judgement and Rule 4
'Judgements' 15 d
Judges appointed 4 a
Just judgement 4 c

Kid in dam's milk 6 d
Kidnapping 2 j
King 4 k

Laity, rights and duties 11 l, dress m
Land 9 k, division of 4 u
Landmarks 3 b

Laver 12 e a i e
'Laws' 15 e
Leaven 7 k
Leprosy, in man 6 h; in garment i, in house j, offering 7 l
Levirate law 1 f
Levites 11 i, revenues j, property l
Lex talionis 4 e
Loans 3 f
Lost property 3 e

Marriage, restrictions on 1 e; adultery i, divorce h
Mazzoth, Feast of 9 e
Meal offering 7 m
Mercy-seat or covering 12 c
Military service 4 m
Mixtures, unlawful 3 l
Molech worship 5 h
Mourning, disfigurement in 5 k
Murder and asylum 2 h

Nazirites 11 p
New moon 9 c

Offerings 7, acceptableness 6 l; consumption of 7 c
Oil, anointing 12 d f, for lamps 10 e, in sacrifice 7 o

Parents, reverence for 1 a b
Passover 9 d
Peace offering 7 p
Pentads 13, 14 e, 15 f
Persons addressed in codes 14 i
Pillars 5 g
Poll tax 8 i
Priesthood 11 a
Priests, consecration and holiness 11 f, dress 11 q, 12 g g, duties 11 h, property k, revenues j
Prophets 11 n
Prostitution 1 m

Record of law 4 v
Red heifer 7 r
Religion, relation of codes to contemporary 14 b

Sacred places 1 o
Sacrifice 7, in general a; summary comparison a a-k
Sanctified gifts 8 h
Sanctuary in P 12
Sanctuary, site of 10 a
Sanitary arrangements 6 k
Scapegoat 7 z
Seasons, sacred 9
Secretions 6 g
Seduction 1 j
Sexes, relations of 1 e-p, dress o
Shewbread 7 h
Sin offering 7 s
Slander 1 k
Slaves 2 d, female concubines 1 g
Sources of codes, oral or written 14 g
'Statutes' a b 15 c
Strangers 2 a
Structure of codes 14 d, of groups of laws e, of clauses f
Successor of Moses 4 w
Superstition 5

Tent of Meeting 10 b 12 b
Thanksgiving, sacrifice of 7 t
Theft 5 a
Tithe 8 d, of tithe 8 e
Touch, uncleanness by
Trumpets, feast of 9 g; use of 4 s
Trusts 3 e
Types of legal clauses 15 a-e, of introductory clauses g

Uncleanness 6
Unleavened Bread, Feast of 9 e
Usury 3 k

Vice, unnatural 11
Vows 8 f

War 4 m
Weeks, Feast of 9 f
Weights and measures 4 d
Wine offering 7 w
Witchcraft 5 l
Witnesses 4 f
'Words' 15 a

APPENDIX C
ANALYSIS AND SYNOPSIS

For some remarks on the purpose and use of these pages see foot of pp 278-79.

Analysis

r Traces of editorial revision.
° Supplements from writers of the same school.
′ In J or E lines—R^{je}, in P line—R^p.
″ In J or E lines—R^d.

J^g J^s	Genesis 1		2	4b-9 10-14	15-25	3	1-21 23 22 24	4	1 2b 2a 8-16a	16b-24 25.	5	29	6	1-4 5-8	7	1-5 7-10 r	12	16b		
P		1-31		1-4a								1-28 30-32		9-22		6		11 13-16a		
J^g J^s	7	17b	22 r	8	6a 2b-3a	6b-12 13b	20-22	9	18a′b 19	20-27	10	1b 8-19 21 24-30	11		28-30						
P	17a 18-21	24		1-2a	3b-5	13a 14-19		1-17		28		1a 2-7 20 22	31.		10-27 31.						
J^g J^s	12	1-4a 6-8 °9 5 4b	10-20	13	°1 2 5 °3	6b-11a	12a-13	18 14-17	14	J E 15	3 6 7a ′b 1 r 5	8-11 ′12-15	17-18a ′b 16	″19-21	16	1b-2 1a 3					
P					6a		11b-12a			°1-24 P											
J E	16	4-8 11-14 ″9.		17		18	1-16 °17-19 20-22a °22b-33a 33b		19	1-28 30-38		20	′18 1-17	21	1a 2a 6 8-27	7	28-30 33 31 34				
P				15			1-27			29					1b 2b-5						

Synopsis

J	E	P

GENESIS

§ 1. Early History of Mankind

J	E	P
2^{4b}-3 Creation and fall.	. . . .	1-2^{4a} *Tol^{e}dhoth* of the heavens and the earth : creation.
4 5^{29} Early history of mankind.	. . . .	5$^{1-28\ 30-32}$ *Tol^{e}dhoth* of Adam : early history of mankind.
6$^{1-4}$ Sons of God and daughters of men		
6$^{5-8}$ Corruption of the earth, and flood.	. . . .	6$^{9-8}$ *Tol^{e}dhoth* of Noah : corruption of the earth, and flood.
		9$^{1-17}$ Noachic law and covenant
9^{18}-10^5 Noah and the dispersion.		9^{28}-10^5 Death of Noah . *tol^{e}dhoth* of the sons of Noah : the dispersion.
11$^{1-9}$ The tower of Babel.		

§ 2. Abraham

J	E	P
11$^{28-30}$ Abram's family.	. . . .	11$^{10-27}$ *Tol^{e}dhoth* of Shem : *tol^{e}dhoth* of Terah · lineage of Abram.
12$^{1-4a\ 6-9}$ Migration of Abram and promise of the land.		11^{31} 12$^{5\ 4b}$ Migration of Terah and Abram.
12^{10}-13^1 Abram in Egypt		
13$^{2-18}$ Separation of Abram and Lot.	.	13$^{6a\ 11b\ 12a}$ Separation of Abram and Lot.
	14 Invasion of Chedorlaomer and his allies.	
15^8 Promise of seed and covenant-gift of the land.	15$^{1\ 5}$ Promise of seed.	
16$^{1b\ 2}$ Barrenness of Sarai.	16 Return in the fourth generation.	16$^{1a\ 3}$ Barrenness of Sarai.
16$^{4-14}$ Expulsion of Hagar, promise of Ishmael.	(‖ 21$^{8-21}$.)	16^{15}. Birth of Ishmael.
18$^{1-15}$ Promise of a son to Sarah.		17 Revelation of El Shaddai · promise of the land and of a son : ordinance of circumcision.
18$^{16-33}$ Intercession for Sodom.		
19$^{1-28}$ Overthrow of Sodom and Gomorrah : Lot escapes	. . . .	19^{29} Overthrow of Sodom and Gomorrah : Lot escapes.
19$^{30-38}$ Origin of Moab and Ammon.		
	20 Abraham at Gerar (cp 12$^{10-20}$ 26$^{6-11}$)	
21$^{1a\ 2a\ 7}$ Birth of Isaac.	21^6 Reference to Isaac's name.	21$^{1b\ 2b-5}$ Birth and circumcision of Isaac.
(‖ 16$^{4-14}$.)	21$^{8-21}$ Expulsion of Hagar and Ishmael.	
21$^{28-30\ 33}$ Abimelech and Abraham : Beer-sheba.	21$^{22-27\ 31\ 34}$ Abimelech and Abraham : Beer-sheba.	

GENESIS 1–35

J	22 1-18	'15-18 20'ab-24 °14 19	23	24 1-67	25 °1-4 5 11b '6		18a °b 'c 21-25a 26a 28 25b 27 29-34	26 1-3a 6-14 16 'b-5 '15 '18
E								
P			1-20		7-11a 12-17	19.	26b	

J	26 19-33	27 1a 2 4b 5b-7a 1b 4a 5a	15 7b-14 16-18a	18b-20 21-23	24-27 29ac 30ac 28 29b 30b 31a	31b-34 35-41a	41b-42 43b 45a 43a 44 45b	28 10 13-16 11 17
E									
P	'34.						'46		1-9

J	28 19a'b 20-21a 22a'b	21b	29 2-14 1 15-23 25 27-28a	26 30	31-35	3b-16 30 1-3a 17-20	22c-28a 24. 27 29-31a 22b 23b 26 28	34-38a 39-40ac 31b-33 38b
E								
P			24	28b-29		'21 22a		

J	30 41-43 40b	31 1'3 '10 2 4-9 11-12a	'12b 17-18a 13-16	25 27 19-24 26 28-30	31 43 46 48 50a'b 32-42 45 47 '49 51-55r	32 3-7a 1. '7b-12 18a	13b-22a 28b 28a 22b 23c	
E								....
P				18b				

J	32 24-29 31-32a'b 30	33 1-17 18a 18c-20	34	2b-3a c 5 7 11 19 26 29b-31	35 1-4 6b-8	14
E						
P			18b	'1-2a '3b '4 '6 '8-10 '12-18 '20-25 27-29a	'5 6a 9-12a 'b 13a 'b 15	

J	E	P
22²⁰⁻²⁴ Family of Nahor	22¹⁻¹⁹ The sacrifice of Isaac, averted.	
		23 Death of Sarah: cave of Machpelah purchased.
24 A wife for Isaac		
25¹⁻⁶ ¹¹ᵇ Children of Keturah and of the concubines.		
		25⁷⁻¹¹ᵃ Death and burial of Abraham.
25¹⁸ Descendants of Abraham between Havilah and Shur.		25¹²⁻¹⁷ Tol*e*dhoth of Ishmael
	§ 3. Isaac	
		25¹⁹ Tol*e*dhoth of Isaac: his age at marriage
25²¹⁻²⁸§ Rebekah's children.	25²⁵ᵇ ²⁷ Rebekah's children 25²⁹⁻³⁴ Esau sells his birthright. (‖ 20 21²⁵⁻³²§)	25²⁶ᵇ Isaac's age at his children's birth.
26¹⁻³³ Isaac at Gerar.		26³⁴ Esau's wives.
27§ Isaac blesses Jacob, who flees to Laban.	27§ Isaac blesses Jacob, who flees to Laban.	28¹⁻⁵ Isaac blesses Jacob and sends him to Laban. 28⁶⁻⁹ Esau takes additional wives. (‖ 35⁹⁻¹³ ¹⁵.)
28¹⁰⁻²¹§ Revelation of Yahweh at Bethel.	28¹¹⁻²²§ Revelation of Elohim's angels at Bethel	
29²⁻¹⁴ Jacob received by Laban	29¹ Jacob journeys to the East.	
29 ²⁶· Marriages with Leah and Rachel.	29¹⁵⁻³⁰§ Marriages with Leah and Rachel	29 ²⁴ ·²⁸ Marriages with Leah and Rachel: Zilpah and Bilhah.
29³¹⁻³⁵ The children of Leah	30¹⁻³ᵃ Rachel envies Leah.	
30³ᵇ⁻¹³§ Jacob's children by the concubines.	30⁶ ⁸§ Jacob's children by the concubines.	
30¹⁴⁻¹⁵ Leah and the mandrakes.	30¹⁷⁻²⁰ Children of Leah	30¹⁷ Leah bears Dinah: ²²ᵃ God remembers Rachel.
30²²⁻²⁴§ Rachel bears Joseph	30²²ᵇ ²³ᵇ Rachel bears Joseph.	
30²⁵ Jacob proposes to depart.	30²⁶ Jacob proposes to depart.	
30²⁷⁻⁴³§ Jacob's wages and wealth.	30²⁸⁻⁴⁰ᵇ§ Jacob's wages	
31¹ Motives for return.	31²⁻¹⁶ Motives for return.	
31¹⁷ ¹⁸ᵃ Jacob's departure.	31¹⁹⁻²¹ Jacob's flight.	31¹⁸ᵇ Jacob's migration.
31²⁵⁻⁵⁰§ Laban's pursuit: the heap	31²²⁻⁵⁵§ Laban's pursuit: the pillar and the heap	
	32¹ God's host at Mahanaim	
32³⁻²¹§ The present for Esau.		
32²²ᵃ ²³ᵇ Jacob sends his wives and children across the Jabbok	32¹³ᵃ ²²ᵇ ²³ᵃᶜ Jacob crosses the Jabbok with his wives and children.	
32²⁴⁻³²§ The wrestling at Penuel.	32³⁰ Peniel	
33¹⁻¹⁶ Jacob meets Esau, who then returns to Seir.		
33¹⁷ Jacob builds a house at Succoth.	33¹⁸ᵃᶜ Jacob comes to Shalem.	33¹⁸ᵇ Jacob comes to Shechem.
	33¹⁹ Purchase of ground and erection of altar.	
34§ The seduction of Dinah, and war with the Shechemites.	[? An E story beneath P*s*.]	34§ The wooing of Dinah, and war with the Shechemites.
	35¹⁻⁵ The strange gods buried by Shechem.	
35¹⁴ The pillar (at Bethel).	35⁶ᵇ⁻⁷ The altar at Bethel.	35⁶ᵃ ⁹⁻¹³ ¹⁵ Revelation of El Shaddai at Luz (Bethel) ct 28¹⁰⁻²² and cp 17¹.
	35⁸ Death of Deborah	

ANALYSIS AND SYNOPSIS

Gen J	35 16–22a			32–39	37	2b 2d–4 5–11	12–13a 13b–14a	14b '15–17a 17b–18a 19	18b 21 22–25a	25b–27 28b 28a
E			36							
P		22b–29	1a 'b–5a 5b–8 '9–28 29 '31	40–43	1–2a c					

J	37	32a	33b 35	38 1–30	39 1–4a 4c–5 6b 7b–23	40 (1 3 5 15) r	41 14b 31 34 35b 36b 41–45a	46b
E	28c–31	32b–33a 34 36			4b 6a c 7a	1–23	1–30 32 35a c 36a 37–40	47.
P								45b–46a

J	41 49	56a 57	42 2 4·7a c	27–28a	38	43 1–13 15–34	44 1–34	45 1a	2b 4–5a c	9–11 13
E	50–55 56b		1 3 6 8 9a 7b 9b–26	29–35 28b 36	14			1b–2a 3	5b d–8 12 15–18
P									

J	45 19'a b–21a	28	46 1a r	28–34	47 1–4 6b 12–27a	29–31	48 1–2a 2b	9b–10a 13–19
E	21b r–27		2–4 1b 5a 'b		5–6a 7–11		8–9a 10b–12 20–22
P			6 '8–27		27b–28		3–6 '7

J

35¹⁶⁻²⁰ Birth of Benjamin: death of Rachel.
35²¹ ²²ᵃ Reuben and Bilhah.

36³¹⁻³⁹ The kings of Edom.

37²ᵇ⁻³⁵§ Jacob's partiality to Joseph (gift of the coat) excites his brothers' hatred: they sell him to Ishmaelites.
38 Judah and Tamar.
39§ Joseph, bought from the Ishmaelites by an Egyptian, is tempted by his wife, and imprisoned.
40¹⁵ Joseph protests his innocence.
41¹⁴ᵇ Joseph is brought out from the dungeon.
41³¹⁻³⁶ Measures against the famine.
41⁴¹⁻⁴⁵ᵃ ⁴⁶ᵇ Pharaoh appoints Joseph over Egypt: his marriage.
41⁴⁹ Corn laid up as the sand of the sea.
41⁵⁶ᵃ ⁵⁷ The famine outside Egypt.
42§ Joseph's brothers go to buy corn, and are recognized... on the journey back one of them finds his money in his sack's mouth.
43¹⁻¹³ ¹⁵⁻³⁴ The brothers' second journey, with Benjamin.
44 The cup in Benjamin's sack.
45§ Joseph makes himself known, and sends his brothers to fetch Jacob to live in the land of Goshen.
46¹ᵃ Israel's journey.

46²⁸⁻⁴⁷¹²§ Arrival of Israel with flocks and herds in Goshen: Pharaoh sanctions their settlement there.

47¹³⁻²⁶ Joseph's famine-administration.
47²⁷ᵃ ²⁹⁻³¹ Israel in Goshen: his approaching death.
48²ᵇ⁻¹⁹§ Israel blesses Joseph's two sons.

E

§ 4. Esau

§ 5. Jacob-Israel

37⁵⁻³⁶§ Joseph's dreams excite his brothers' envy: they throw him into a pit, and he is kidnapped by Midianites, who sell him to Potiphar, Pharaoh's chief executioner.

39⁴ᵇ ⁶ᵃᶜ ⁷ᵃ Joseph serves his master.

40 Joseph interprets the dreams of the chief cupbearer and chief baker in the house of the chief executioner.
41¹⁻²⁸ Pharaoh's dreams are interpreted by Joseph.
41²⁸⁻³⁶§ Measures against the famine.
41³⁷⁻⁴⁰ Pharaoh appoints Joseph over his house.
41⁴⁷ The food of the good years stored in the cities.
41⁵⁰⁻⁵² Birth of Manasseh and Ephraim.
41⁵³⁻⁵⁶ᵇ§ The famine begins in Egypt.
42§ Joseph's ten brothers go to buy corn, are recognized, and required to bring Benjamin: Simeon is bound: on their return their money is found in their sacks.
43¹⁴ [The brothers go again with Benjamin] Jacob's prayer for Simeon and Benjamin.

45§ Joseph makes himself known: Pharaoh instructs him to invite Jacob to settle in Egypt.
46²⁻⁴ ¹ᵇ ⁵ Vision at Beer-sheba: Jacob starts for Egypt.

48¹⁻²²§ Jacob blesses Joseph's two sons.

P

35²²ᵇ⁻²⁶ The sons of Jacob.

35²⁷⁻²⁹ Death and burial of Isaac.

36¹⁻³⁰ ⁴⁰⁻⁴³ Tolᵉdhoth of Esau, migration, and descendants.

37¹ ²ᵃ ᶜ Jacob in Canaan: tolᵉdhoth of Jacob.

41⁴⁵ᵇ ⁴⁶ᵃ Pharaoh appoints Joseph over Egypt: his age.

46⁶⁻²⁷ Migration of Jacob and his descendants to Egypt.
47⁵⁻¹¹ Arrival and settlement in the land of Rameses.

47²⁷ᵇ ²⁸ Prosperity of Jacob in Egypt: his age.

48³⁻⁷ Jacob adopts Joseph's two sons into El Shaddai's blessing at Luz.

GENESIS 35 — EXODUS 12

J	**49** 1b-24a 27		**50** 1-11 14 18 21 24		Exodus **1**	6 8-12 14a 20b 22		**2** 11-23a	
E	'24b-26	33b	15-17 19. 22 25.			7 15-20a 21		1-10	
P	1a '18 28'a b-33a c		12			1-5 13 14b		23b-25	
J	**3** 2-4a 5 7-9a '14 16-18	**4** 1-12 °13-16 19-20a '21-23 24-26 29-31	**5** 3-23	**6** 1	**7** 14 16-17a 18
E	1 4b 6 9b-13 15 '19 21.	17. 20b 27	1 4		15 17b
P				2-12 '13-30 1-13	19-20a
J	**7** 21a 24.	**8** 1-4 8-15a 20-32	**9** 1-7 13 °14-16 17 23b 24b 25b-29a °b °30 33	**10** 1a '1b-2 3r-11
E	20b 23		8-12 '19-21 22-23a 24a 25a 31 35r	
P	21b-22	5-7 15b-19		
J	**10** 13b 14b-15a 15c-19 24-29	**11** 4-8	**12** 21a °21b-23 °25-27a 27b 29-34 37-39
E	12-13a 14a 15b 20-23	1-3	'35.
P		'9	1-13 '14-20 24 28 '40-42 43-50 '51

J	E	P
49 1b-27 Jacob declares what shall befall his sons. 33b prepares for death.	. . . . .	49 1a 28-33a c Jacob blesses his sons, gives them a charge, and dies.
50 1-14§ The burial of Jacob.		50 12 The burial of Jacob.
50 18-24§ Joseph comforts his brothers, and announces a divine visitation.	50 15-26§ Joseph allays his brothers' fears, announces a divine visitation, and dies.	

EXODUS

§ 6. Israel in Egypt

J	E	P
		1 1-5 The Israelites in Egypt.
1 6 Death of Joseph.		
1 8-12 14a Oppression of the children of Israel by the Egyptians		1 7 Their increase.
1 20b 22 Pharaoh charges the people to throw the male children into the river.	1 15-21§ Pharaoh commands the midwives to kill the male children	1 13 14b And oppression by the Egyptians
	2 1-10 Moses rescued from the bulrushes.	
2 11-22 Moses kills an Egyptian and flees to Midian. marries Zipporah.		
2 23a Death of the king of Egypt.		2 23b-25 God hears the cry of the children of Israel.
3 2-18 The commission to Moses at the burning bush.	3 1-22§ The commission to Moses. the revelation of the name Yahweh.	(∥ 6 2-9.)
4 1-9 Signs for convincing the Israelites.		
4 10-12 Yahweh will be with Moses' mouth.		
4 13-16 Aaron shall be his spokesman.		
	4 17. 20b The gift of the rod. Farewell to Jethro.	
4 19-23§ Moses directed to return.		
4 24-26 'A bridegroom of blood.'		
4 29-31 The people believe.	4 27 Aaron goes to meet Moses.	
5 3 Permission asked to go three days' journey to sacrifice.	5 1 Permission asked to go and hold a feast in the wilderness.	
5 5-23 Increased tasks. (∥ 3§.)	5 4 People sent to their burdens. (∥ 3§.)	
		6 2-9 Revelation of Yahweh and commission of Moses.
		6 10-7 7 Instructions to Moses and Aaron (Genealogies).
		7 8-13 Rod and Serpents.
7 14-25§ Nile water smitten.	7 15-20§ Water turned into blood.	7 19-22 Water turned into blood.
8§ Frogs and Flies.		8 5-19§ Frogs and Lice.
9 1-17 Murrain on cattle.		9 8-12 Boils on men.
9 13-35§ Hail and Thunder.	9 22-35§ Thunder, Hail and Fire.	
10 1-29§ Locusts.	10 12-20§ Locusts.	
	10 21-23 27 Darkness.	
11 4-8 Death of Firstborn announced.	11 1-3 One plague more announced.	
L 12 21-27 The Passover.	. . . . .	L 12 1-28§ 43-50 Passover and Mazzoth.
12 29-34 Death of Firstborn.		

§ 7. The March to Sinai—
Ex 12 37-18

J	E	P
12 37 March to Succoth.	. . . . .	12 40 51 March out.

ANALYSIS AND SYNOPSIS

Ex
J	13	3a ⁰5 6 ⁰7 10–13		21	14	5.	10a 11–14		19b 20b 21b	24a 25	27b 28b 30	15	1
E		″3b	″9	″14–16 17–19		7 9a	10b	15a 16a	19a 20a	24b	′31		′2–18
P		1.			20	1–4 8 9b*r*		15b 16b–18	21a 21c–23	26–27a 28a ′29			

J	15		22–25a	27	16	4		17	8 2b 7a c	18	′2–4 7 9–11	19
E		20.		25b ′26					1b–2a 4–6 7b 8–16		1*r* 5 8 12–27	
P		′19				1–3 ′5 6 ′8 9–14a 15 ′a b–21 ′22–30 31–35 36			1a				2a 1

J	19		′3b–6	11b–13	18 20–22 24	20	″2 ″4b–6 ″7b ″9. ″12b ″17b	21	22	′21b–22 ′24	
E		2b–3a	7–11a	14–17 19	′23		13–4a 7a 8 12a 13–17a 18–26	1–36	1–21a	23 25–31	
P							11				

J	23		′13	′15b ′17 ′19	′23–25a	′27	′31b–33	24	1 9–11		25	31		32	7–14
E		1–9a ′b	10–12	14–15a 16	18 20–22	25b–26 28–31a			3–8 12a ′b 13–15a	18b			18b		1–6
P										15b–18a	1–		18a		

J	32	15a	25–29	33	1 3–4a ′b ⁰12–23	34	1*r*–5 ⁰6–9 10a ⁰10b–13 14 ⁰15. 17–18a ′b 19–23 25–28
E		16–24	′30–34 35		″2 ′5 6–11		″24 29–33 ′34.
P		′15b					

J	35	40
E		
P	1–	38

J	E	P
ᴸ13³⁻¹⁶ Mazzoth, Firstborn, Firstlings.	. . . .	ᴸ13¹. Firstborn and Firstlings.
13²¹ Yahweh leads the march.	13¹⁷ · March to Red Sea: Joseph's bones.	13²⁰ March from Succoth.
14§ Pursuit; the Pillar; crossing; Destruction of Egyptians.	14§ Pursuit; Angel of God; Egyptians discomfited.	14§ Pursuit; crossing; Egyptians overwhelmed.
15¹ Song of Moses (²⁻¹⁸ added).	15²⁰ Song of Miriam.	
15²²⁻²⁷§ Shur, Marah, Elim.	15²⁵. Proving (at Massah).	
(‖ Num 11§.)	16⁴ Proving by bread from heaven.	16§ Elim, Sin, manna and quails.
17³⁻⁷§ No water at Massah.	17¹ᵇ⁻⁷§ No water at Meribah.	17¹ Rephidim.
	17⁸⁻¹⁶ Fight with Amalek.	
18⁷⁻¹¹§ Visit of Moses' father-in-law.	18¹⁻¹²§ Visit of Jethro.	
	18¹³⁻²⁷ Appointment of Judges.	

(In the notes to vol ii will be found reasons for thinking that 16–18, in whole or part, belongs to a later stage in the history.)

§ 8. Israel at Sinai—Ex 19-Num 10¹⁰

J	E	P
	19²⁶ Israel before the mount.	19¹⁻²ᵃ Arrival at Sinai.
19¹¹ᵇ⁻²⁵§ People to keep away, priests to draw near, Theophany.	19³⁻¹⁹§ Moses goes up, message, people to be hallowed, Theophany.	
	ᴸ20¹⁻¹⁷ The Decalogue (‖ Deut 5⁶⁻²¹, cp ᴸ13d).	
	20¹⁸⁻²¹ People fear, Moses approaches.	
(‖ 34¹⁰⁻²⁶.)	ᴸ20²²⁻23¹⁹ Words and Judgements combined (ᴸ13bc).	
	23²⁰⁻³³ Concluding discourse.	
24¹ ⁹ Moses, Aaron, and seventy elders go up, see God, and feast.	24³⁻⁸ Moses binds people by a covenant; sacrificial feast.	
	24¹²⁻¹⁸§ Moses goes up to receive the Tables and remains forty days.	24¹⁵ᵇ⁻¹⁸ᵇ Moses goes up; the cloud and glory.
		ᴸ25–31 Instructions as to Sanctuary and Priesthood (ᴸ12).
(‖ 34²⁷.)	31¹⁸ᵇ Gift of tables of stone.	31¹⁸ᵃ Gift of tables of the testimony.
32²⁵⁻²⁹ Revolt, loyalty of Levites.	32¹⁻³⁵§ The Golden Calf, breaking of tables, Intercession of Moses.	
33¹⁻⁴ Instructions to depart, mourning.	33⁶ People strip off ornaments.	
33¹²⁻²³ Moses' colloquy with Yahweh.	33⁷⁻¹¹ Tent of Meeting, Moses' colloquies with Yahweh.	
34¹⁻⁹ Tables hewn, Theophany.		
ᴸ34¹⁰⁻²⁶ Ten words of Yahweh (ᴸ13a).	(‖ 20²²⁻23¹⁹.)	
34²⁷ Covenant, Tables engraved.	(‖ 31¹⁸.)	(‖ 31¹⁸.)
		34²⁹⁻³⁵ Moses descends, his face shines.
		35–40 Sanctuary prepared and erected (ᴸ12).

EXODUS 13—NUMBERS 36

J/E	Leviticus 1	27	Numbers 1	10	29-33	25.	11 1-3	4-10a	10b-12 13 15	18-24a	30-35	12 16 1-15
P		1-	34		1-	28 34			14 16.	°24b-30		

J	13	17b	18b 19	22	27a 28 30.		14 1c 3	8 9b '11-24	31	41-45	15	16 1d
E		17c-18a c	20-21a 23.	26b 27b 29 33r		1b 4	25	39b-40			1c
P	1-17a		21b 25-26a		32	1a 2 5-7 9a 10	26-30 32-39a		1-41	1a b

J	16	13-14a 15		27c-31	33a		17 20	3a	5	8b	19. 21b
E	2a	12	14b	25 26b 27	32a 33b 34			1b			14-18 21a 22a
P	2b-7 '8-11		'16. 18-24 26a 27a	'32b	'33c 35 '36-40 41-50	1-	1a 2 3b-4 6-8a c-13			22b-29

J	21 1-3	16-20	24b-25	32	3b-5a c-7	11 17.	22-34 35r 36a	37b 39	'22.
E		4b-9 11b-15	21-24a	'26 27-31 '33-35	22 2-3a	5b 8-10 12-16 19-21	36b-37a 38 40.	23 1-21 24-26
P	4a 10				1			

J	23 28	24 1-25	25 1b-2 3b-4	26	36			
E	27 '29.		1a 3a 5					
P			6-18	1-	13			

LEVITICUS
(For a full Analysis and Conspectus of the legislation of P see ^{L}13g, the sections of which are referred to by italic letters.)

P^h	P^i	P^g	P^s
1-7§ Sacrifice bc.		9 Consecration of priesthood, sequels d.	4 The sin offering b.
11-15 Clean and Unclean e.		16$^{2-28§}$ Aaron to atone for the people e.	8 Consecration of priesthood d.
17-26§ Holiness Code f.		23§ Calendar of sacred days f.	16 Annual Day of Atonement e.
			25 Sacred Years f.
			27 Vows f.
5-6^{21} Various laws g.		1§ 3§ The camp; numberings g.	1-4 The camp; numberings and arrangements g.
			7-9 Altar; Levites; Passover; cloud g.
10^9 Use of trumpets g.		6$^{22-27}$ Priestly benediction g.	
		10$^{1-8}$ Use of trumpets g.	

§ 9. Israel in the Wilderness—Num 10^{10}-21

J	E	P
10$^{29-36§}$ March from Yahweh's mount.	. . . .	10$^{11-28\ 34}$ March from Sinai.
11$^{4-35}$ Manna and Quails, Kibroth-hattaavah, Hazeroth.	11$^{1-3}$ Taberah incident. (‖ Ex 16^4.)	(‖ Ex 16.)
	11$^{24-30}$ The seventy elders.	
	12$^{1-15}$ Aaron, Miriam and Moses.	
12^{16} Hazeroth to Paran.		
13§ Spies and their report.	13§ Spies and their report.	13§ Twelve spies and their report.
14 People weep, and are all excluded, but Caleb and family, and the little ones; advance, defeat at Hormah.	14 People mourn and rebel, are turned back to wilderness, attempt to advance.	14 People murmur, all excluded but Caleb and Joshua.
		^{L}15 Various laws (^{L}13gh).
16§ Revolt of On.	16§ Revolt of Dathan and Abiram.	16§ Korah and his company.
		17 Aaron's rod that budded.
		^{L}18 Priestly revenue; defilement (^{L}13gh).
20$^{4-8§}$ Water from the rock.	20^1 Kadesh; Miriam's death. (‖ Ex 17^1..)	20^1 Wilderness of Zin.
20^{19} · Way by Edom barred.	20^{13-22a} Way by Edom barred, departure from Kadesh.	20$^{2-13§}$ Water from the rock.
		20^{22b} Arrival at Hor; death of Aaron.
21$^{1-3}$ Canaanites beaten; Hormah.	21$^{4-9}$ Fiery serpents.	21^4 Hor left.
21$^{16-32}$ '33-35 Itinerary, conquest of the Amorites (and Bashan).	21^{11b-31} Itinerary; conquest of Sihon and Amorites.	21^{10} Itinerary.

§ 10. Israel in the Plains of Moab—Num 22-Deut 34

J	E	P
22-24§ Balak and Balaam.	22-23§ Balak and Balaam.	22^1 Camp in plains of Moab.
25$^{1-4§}$ Moabite women.	25$^{1-5§}$ Shittim; Baal-Peor.	25$^{6-18}$ Midianite woman; Phinehas.
		^{L}26-27^{11} Census; inheritance (^{L}13gi).
		27$^{12-23}$ Moses' successor.
		^{L}28-31 Offerings; vows; war (^{L}13gi).
		32$^{1-38}$ The Trans-Jordan tribes.
32$^{39-42}$ Manasseh in Gilead.		33 Itinerary; the future.
		^{L}34 Canaan and its distribution.
		^{L}35 Forty-eight Levitical cities to give
		^{L}36 Rights of heiresses. [asylum.

ANALYSIS AND SYNOPSIS

D^g D^s JEP	**Deuteronomy** $1_{1a}\ ^a1b-2\ \ 4-7a\ 'b7\ 8-30\ '31-33\ 34-36\ '37\ -39r-45\ '46\ 2_{1-6}\ '7\ 8-10\ '10-12\ 13\cdot\ '15\ 16-19\ '20-23\ 24-37$ P 3	
D^g D^s JEP	$3_{1-7}\ '8-11\ 12-13a\ '13b\quad 16\ '17\ 18-29\ 4_{1-4}\ 5-40\quad ^{45-49}_{'44}\ 5_{1-4}\ '5\ 6-33\ 6_{1-3}\ 4-25\ 7_{1-26}\ 8_{1-20}\ 9_{1-17}_{18-20}\ 21_{22-25}\ 26-29$ Rp 14. Rp 41-43	
D^g D^s JEP	$10_{1-5}\ ^{10-22}_{8\cdot}\ 11_{1-32}\ 12_{1-7}\ ^a8-12\ ^{13-15}_{'16}\ 17-19\ ^o20-27\ 28-32\ 13_{1-18}\ 14_{1\ '2}^B\ _{4-21a}^{21b-29}\ 15_{4-6}^{1-3\ 7-23}\ 16_{1\cdot\ ^o3\cdot\ 5-7}$ E 6.	
D^g D^s JEP	$16_8^{9-22}\ 17_{2-7}^1\ ^{8-16a}_{'16b}\ ^{17}_{18}\ ^{20}_{\cdot}\ 18_{1-22}\ 19_{8\cdot}^{1-7\ 10-21}\ 20_{2b-4}^{1-2a\ 5-20}\ 21_5^{o1-4\ o6-9\ 10-23}\ 22_{1-30}\ 23_{1-12\ 15-25}$	
D^g D^s JEP	$24^{1-7\ o8\cdot\ 10-15\ o16\ 17-22}\ 25_{1-16}\ ^o17-19\ 26_{1-19}\ 27_{1-4}\ \ ^o7b-8\ 9\ ^o11-13\ '14-26\ 28^{1-25a}_{25b-26}\ ^{27-34}_{35}\ ^{38-40\ 43-46}_{'36\cdot}\ _{41\cdot}$ E 5-7a	
D^g D^s JEP	$28_{47-57}\ '58-68\ 29_{1-28}\ '29\ 30_{'7}^{1-6\ 8-10}\ _{11-20}\ 31_{1-6}\ '7\cdot\ ^{9-13}_{'16-22}\ _{24-29}\ '30\ 32_{1-43\ 44-47}^J\ _E\ 33_{1-2a}\ '2b-5$ E 14. E 23 P 48-52	
J E P	$33_{6-25}\ '26-29\ 34\ _{1a\ 1c}^{1dr\ 4}\ _{5b\ 7-9}^{''2\cdot 5a\ 6r\ ''10-12}$	

D^g	D^s	J	E	P
	DEUTERONOMY			
4^{45-49} Introduction to the original code.	$1-4^4$ Historical Introduction enriched by archaeological notes and other supplements.			$^P1^3$ The fortieth year the eleventh month.
$+ 5^1-6^4$ $+ 6^{4-25}\ 8$ $+ 7$ $+ 9-11^§$ Opening homilies.	4^{5-40} (see below).			
			$^E10^6$ Death of Aaron, appointment of Eleazar	
$12-18^§$ Code of religious laws connected with the law of the central sanctuary or otherwise needing special enforcement				
$+ 19-25$ Groups of miscellaneous laws. 26 Continuation of 12-18.				
	$+ 27^§$ Memorial stones, blessings and curses.		$^E27^{5-7a}$ Altar for sacrifice to be built (on Ebal).	
$28^§$ 30^{1-10} } Closing discourse, with blessings and curses.	27^9 4^{5-40} 30^{11-20} 32^{45-47} } Closing discourse.			
	$+ 29$ Another closing discourse			
	$+ 31^{1-8}$ Farewell of Moses and charge to Joshua.		$^E31^{14\ 23}$ Charge to Joshua.	
	$+ 31^{16-22}$ Introduction to Song			
31^{9-13} Writing of the law and provision for periodical reading.	31^{24-29} The law written in a book and placed in the ark.			
	$+ 32^{1-44}$ Song of Moses.		$33^§$ Blessing of Moses.	
			$^P32^{48-52}$ $34^{1-9§}$ } Moses sees the land and dies.	
			$^J34^{1-4§}$ Moses sees the land but enters not.	
			$^E34^5$ Moses dies and is buried.	

REMARKS ON THE ANALYSIS AND SYNOPSIS

The above pages reproduce the text in miniature by two different methods concurrently

The SYNOPSIS is intended both to give the best possible representation of the contents of each document short of printing it separately in full, and to provide on the same page the means of comparing it with the contents of the parallel documents. The text order of each document has been followed precisely, but where parallel narratives occur at different points in the several sources, cross-references are inserted. No attempt has been made to indicate all the dislocations or transpositions of order mentioned or adopted in the notes to the text The evidence is here graphically presented both of the surprising extent to which parallelism can be traced, and at the same time of the occurrence of large blocks of material which are not analyzed but wholly assigned to one or other source If the analysis were the effect of a subjective theory, so many exceptions would not be left

The ANALYSIS gives the full details of the distribution effected

DEUTERONOMY 1—JOSHUA 24

J		2–3a c	4b–5a	6 8–9a	12 13b–14	17 18ar c	19–21	1a cr	5 9–10a	11r	13r
E	Joshua 1¹		3b 4a	5b 7	13a	15.	18b	22–24a	1b 2. 6		12 14
Dˢ	³⁻⁶ ᶜ⁷. 9	2¹						24b	3 4b 7	10b	
Pˢ	10–11a 11b–18		9b–11						4a 8		15

J	17a	3br 6–7a	8br	10b–11	18r	2	9	13–15	2. 7a	10–12a	14 r	16b–17a–b	20a c
E	3	4 1b–8a 4			20	5			6 1 4–6 7b–9	12b–13 16a			20b
Dˢ	17b	1a	9–10a	12r 14	21–24	1 4 ᶜ5 6–8							18
Pˢ		7b–8a		13 15–17 19			10–12						'19

J	21	25	2–26r	1ar	2b–8a 9–11	14–17 19–23r	25	29	4. 6b–7	11b–14 15b	16b d	22b–23 26 r
E	6 22–24r	7	8 1b–2a	8b	12 '13	18	24r 26	27. 30–35	9 3 6a 8–9a	11a	15a 16ac	22a
Dˢ		27							1.			24.
Pˢ		'1							9b–10	15c	17–21	

J	1ar c 2.	5b–6a c	7a	9	10b 12r–14	16–24r 26.	1 4–9		1 7	13	
E	10 1b 4–5a	6b d		10a 11			11 2	10–23	12 1–24	13 2–6 8–12 14r	
Dˢ		7b–8		15	25	28–43					
Pˢ										15–21a '21b–22 23–32 '33	

J		14–19 63	1–3	10	11–18			47
E	14 6–15	15	16	17 1a '1b–2 3. '5. 7 '8 9.	18 '2–6r '8–10a	19
Dˢ	1–5	1–12 '13	20–62	4–8 '9	1 '7 '10b 11–28	1–46 48–51
Pˢ						

J							1–12r 14–30r 32.
E	20	21	22 1–6 ᶜ7a ''b–8	23 1–16	24 13 31
Dˢ		43–45			
Pˢ	1–3 '4 5r–9	1–10 '11 12–42	'9–34		

J	E	Dˢ	P

JOSHUA

§ 11. The Conquest of Canaan

J	E	Dˢ	P
	1¹. ¹⁰. Preparations for crossing the Jordan	1²⁻⁹ Joshua exhorted.	
		1¹²⁻¹⁸ The Trans-jordanic tribes to help.	
2§ Spies sent to Jericho.	2§ Two spies sent to Jericho.		
3 § Passage of Jordan.	3§ Passage of Jordan.	3 § Passage of Jordan.	3.§ Passage of Jordan.
5². ⁹ Circumcising at Gilgal.		5⁴⁻⁸ The circumcising.	5¹⁰. . At Gilgal, Passover.
5¹²⁻¹⁵ Captain of Yahweh's host			
6§ Taking of Jericho.	6§ Taking of Jericho.		
7²⁻²⁶ Defeat at Ai, Achan.			7¹ Achan's trespass.
8§ Taking of Ai.	8§ Taking of Ai.		
		8³⁰⁻³⁵ Altar on Ebal	
9§ The Gibeonite envoys.	9§ The Gibeonite envoys.		9¹⁶ ¹⁷⁻²¹ The Gibeonite envoys.
10¹⁻²⁷§ Battle of Beth-horon.	10¹⁻¹¹§ Battle of Beth-horon.	10²⁸⁻⁴³ Southern conquests.	
11¹ ⁴⁻⁹ Battle of Merom.		11² ¹⁰⁻¹⁵ Northern conquests.	
		11¹⁶⁻²³ Survey of Joshua's victories.	
		12¹⁻²⁴ Lists of conquered kings.	

§ 12. The Division of the Land

J	E	Dˢ	P
13¹ ⁷ᵃ ¹³ Joshua to divide the land.		13²⁻⁶ ⁸⁻¹² The Trans-jordanic tribes ¹⁴ Levi.	13¹⁵⁻³² The Trans-jordanic tribes ³³§ Levi.
			14¹⁻⁵ The 9½ tribes.
		14⁶⁻¹⁵ Caleb.	
15¹⁴⁻¹⁹ ⁶³ Caleb, Jebus.			15¹⁻¹² ²⁰⁻⁶¹ Judah.
16§ Joseph.			16 § Joseph
			18¹ Assembly at Shiloh.
	Rʲᵉ 18²⁻¹⁰ Seven tribes.		18¹¹⁻19⁵¹ Seven lots.
19⁴⁷ Dan.			20¹⁻⁹ Cities of refuge.
			21¹⁻⁴² Levitical cities.
		22¹⁻⁸ Return of Trans-jordanic tribes.	22⁹⁻³⁴ Return of Trans-jordanic tribes, altar.
	24 Joshua's farewell.	23 Joshua's farewell.	

in the text, chapter by chapter, and verse by verse[a]. It provides, in a manner appealing very readily to the eye, a representation of the material as highly composite. By reference to the Synopsis below, the subjects of the sections are readily identified. It is hoped that this condensed Analysis will be of great service in tracing references quickly from the word-lists, from the margin of the text, or from the concordance.

The codes are only mentioned in the Synopsis as wholes, or by their main sections, as their details would have obscured the impression of the narrative sequence. But they are given very completely in the Conspectus of Codes (ᴸ13 above), where also a full Analysis of the Laws in P is given concurrently. The analysis of the codes in JED has been included sufficiently in this appendix.

---

[a] Where a passage narrating an incident is composite the reference in the Synopsis is usually to the whole passage, the sign §referring the reader for details to the Analysis or to the full Text.

www.ingramcontent.com/pod-product-compliance
Lightning Source LLC
Chambersburg PA
CBHW081840230426
43669CB00018B/2763